"Dr. Lloyd-Jones's preaching was based on deep reading and scholarship, yet it was accessible to everyone. It was close, instructive Bible exposition, yet it stirred the affections and changed the heart. It was highly effective at a city-center in a secularizing society, but it has had broad, worldwide appeal. The Doctor's preaching ministry is, I believe, unique in the English-speaking world during the last hundred years."

Timothy Keller, Redeemer Presbyterian Church, New York

"Martyn Lloyd-Jones was one of the titanic figures of twentieth-century Christianity. What now sets him apart is the fact that his writings, sermons, and other messages are even more influential now, more than two decades after his death, than when he engaged such a massive ministry at Westminster Chapel and beyond. Why? I think the answer is simple: his profound commitment to biblical exposition and the great skill with which he preached and taught the Word of God. In an age when so many preachers seem so unsure of what preaching is, in Lloyd-Jones we find a minister who leaves no doubt."

R. Albert Mohler Jr., President, The Southern Baptist Theological Seminary

"Martyn Lloyd-Jones was one of God's special gifts to the church in the twentieth century."

Mark Dever, Capitol Hill Baptist Church, Washington, DC

"Martyn Lloyd-Jones was without question the finest biblical expositor of the twentieth century. In fact, when the final chapter of church history is written, I believe he will stand as one of the greatest preachers of all time. His style of biblical exposition was meticulously thorough and yet full of energy. 'Logic on fire' was his famous description of preaching, and he had an amazing gift for blending passion and precision in copious measures. He influenced countless preachers (myself included), and he stood steadfastly against the superficial, entertainment-oriented approach to preaching that seemed to dominate the evangelical world then as it does now. Lloyd-Jones still desperately needs to be heard today."

John MacArthur, Grace Community Church, Sun Valley, California

"I regarded Martyn Lloyd-Jones with admiration and affection during the years that we were both preaching in London, so I am delighted that his unique ministry is to be more widely available in the United States."

John Stott, Rector Emeritus, All Souls Church, London

"The preaching and subsequent writing of Martyn Lloyd-Jones have been and continue to be a huge source of inspiration in my own life and ministry."

Alistair Begg, Parkside Church, Cleveland, Ohio

"Martyn Lloyd-Jones was one of the great preachers of a previous generation who rooted his message in God's Word. For those wondering how the Word applies to life or seeking textually rooted preaching, his ministry provides a solid model. His books and messages are worth pondering. His messages encourage us to faithfulness. That is commendation enough."

> **Darrell L. Bock,** Research Professor of New Testament Studies,
> Dallas Theological Seminary

"From my student days onwards Dr. Martyn Lloyd-Jones was a preacher whom I loved to hear for the sheer quality of his biblical expositions and his stance for evangelical Christianity. It is good to know that efforts are being made to introduce him to a new generation."

> **I. Howard Marshall,** Emeritus Professor, University of Aberdeen

"Martyn Lloyd-Jones was one of the twentieth century's finest gospel preachers—clear, warm, intelligent, Christ-centered."

> **Cornelius Plantinga,** President, Calvin Theological Seminary

"Martyn Lloyd-Jones was one of the great expository preachers of the Bible in his era. His expositions over many months on Romans are in fact the stuff of legend. Few preachers have ever better exhibited what it takes and what it means to do one's exegetical homework before preaching and then bring that information to light and to life in life-changing sermons. May they provide the necessary spur and antidote to those preachers who now think that the art of preaching involves dumbing everything down and over-simplifying things. As Martyn knew, it's not a matter of boiling down the gospel, rather it's a matter of boiling up the people, teasing their minds into active thought and engagement with the gospel."

> **Ben Witherington III,** Amos Professor of New Testament Interpretation
> for Doctoral Studies, Asbury Theological Seminary; Doctoral Faculty,
> St. Andrews University

STUDIES IN JOHN 17

The
ASSURANCE
of
OUR
SALVATION

Exploring *the* Depth
of Jesus' Prayer *for* His Own

MARTYN LLOYD-JONES

:: CROSSWAY®

WHEATON, ILLINOIS

First printing, one volume 2000

Printed in the United States of America

Trade Paperback ISBN: 978-1-4335-4051-6
ePub ISBN: 978-1-4335-5199-4
PDF ISBN: 978-1-4335-5197-0
Mobipocket ISBN: 978-1-4335-5198-7

Library of Congress Cataloging-in-Publication Data
Lloyd-Jones, David Martyn.
   The assurance of our salvation : exploring the depth of Jesus' prayer
for His own : studies in John 17 / Martyn Lloyd-Jones.
      p.   cm.
   Originally published separately in four vols, 1988-89.
   ISBN 13: 978-1-58134-140-9 (alk. paper)
   ISBN 10: 1-58134-140-7
   1. Bible. N.T. John XVII—Sermons. 2. Sermons, English. I. Title.
BS2615.4.L53   2000
252'.058—dc21   99-045041

Crossway is a publishing ministry of Good News Publishers.

V P   27   26   25   24   23   22   21
14   13   12   11   10   9   8   7   6   5

CONTENTS

PART ONE

SAVED *in* ETERNITY

Preface

The sermons in this book form the first part of a series on John 17 which Dr Lloyd-Jones delivered on Sunday mornings in Westminster Chapel between 1952 and 1953. (Subsequent volumes will be published over the next few years.) These particular sermons were preached between April and July 1952, a period when Dr James Packer felt that he was 'on a plateau of supreme excellence'. Many others would endorse that view today, which is why these sermons have now been published.

CHRISTOPHER CATHERWOOD
Editor

I

The Lord's Own Prayer

John 17:1

It is customary for us to refer to the prayer which we find recorded in the Sermon on the Mount and in Luke 11 as the Lord's Prayer; but in reality, of course, that was the prayer which he gave as a kind of model to his disciples and to others, whereas here we have what can truly be called our Lord's own prayer, for here we find him praying his own personal prayer to the Father. The circumstances in which he came to do so are familiar to all of us. 'These words spake Jesus', are a reference to the great and mighty discourse which is recorded in chapters 14, 15 and 16 of this gospel. Then, having spoken those words about the Holy Spirit who is to be given to the believers, about what he could do in them, and all the results of his coming, our Lord lifted up his eyes to heaven and began to pray.

A quaint preacher in the seventeenth century said what is, I believe, the eternal truth about this prayer: 'It is the greatest prayer that was ever offered on earth and it followed the greatest sermon that was ever preached on earth'. In a sense nothing can be added to that. Here you have this sermon in those three chapters, then, immediately at the close of the sermon, our Lord offers up this prayer. It is one of the richest and most sublime statements to be found anywhere, even in the Scriptures themselves. And there is a sense in which one preaches it with fear and trembling, lest one may in any way detract from its greatness and from its value. There have been those in the past who have felt that here we are dealing with something which is so sacred, because it is the very opening into our Lord's own heart, that the only right thing to do with this prayer is to read it. There was a great man living in Germany in the seventeenth century called Stein (the leader in many ways of the great Pietist Movement which was practised by the Moravian Brethren and others) who said he dared not preach on John 17, and there have been many others who have agreed with him.

Yet it seems to me that that is a mistake, for I would argue that our Lord would never have uttered this prayer audibly unless he had intended that we should hear it and that we should be able to study it and, above all, that we should be able to grasp its teaching. He did not merely pray to God, he prayed *audibly* to God, and the disciples heard him. Thus the prayer was preserved, and it seems to me that in this we have a wonderful illustration of the kindness of our Lord in allowing his disciples to hear this prayer and in arranging that it should be recorded in this way.

And, of course, as you look through the history of the church you will find that this prayer has been used of the Spirit in a very exceptional way to sustain people and to support them as they face difficulties in life, and especially when their time has come to die. The most notable example, perhaps, is that of John Knox, that great leader in the Protestant Reformation in Scotland, and mighty man of God. It is said that during the last days of his life, realizing that he was about to die, he asked his wife to read John 17 to him, and it was actually as she was reading this wonderful chapter that he passed from time to eternity. This is in no way surprising when you come to realize the wealth that there is here for us.

I am calling attention to it now because I am more and more convinced that half our troubles are due to the fact that we fail to realize what exactly is offered in the Scriptures. All our anxieties and troubles, all our uncertainties and hesitations, and so much of our unhappiness in our spiritual lives, is to be traced simply to the fact that we do not realize what is provided for us. The apostle Peter, in his second epistle, does not hesitate to say that 'all things that pertain to life and godliness' are given to us (2 Pet 1:3). And the claim that is made constantly in these New Testament epistles is that there is no conceivable condition which we can ever know, there is no state of the soul which we can ever enter on, that has not already been prepared for. There is teaching concerning it, and God's people are meant to be people who are always rejoicing in the Lord. We are meant to know the fullness and the triumph, we are meant to experience a glory even here on earth.

But the question that arises is this: why are we not all, therefore, glorying and rejoicing in this great salvation? Why is it that so often we are apologetic and give the impression of being defeated? Why are we often so fearful of the world and of the future, concerned about God's cause and about the church? Why do we frequently, in this morbid concern, resort frantically to things that are often unworthy? Now I suggest that the explanation of all these things is our failure to realize what is provided for us, our failure, if you prefer it, to realize our position in Christ, and to enter into our heritage. We are, of course, entirely without excuse because, as I have been reminding you, it is all here for us. If we had nothing but John 17 we would surely have more than enough to sustain us, because here our Lord has given us an insight into our whole position, and into everything that is of importance and of value to us while we are in this world of time. We can do nothing better, therefore, than to look at this prayer, and to consider what he has to say.

Here is the position. He was about to leave the disciples, he knew how troubled they were, because they had already shown it, and he had started his sermon by saying, 'Let not

your heart be troubled.' They were troubled because he had
just been telling them that he was about to go from them,
and that had come as a shattering piece of information. Here
they were, they had been following him for three years, they
had listened to his teaching, they had observed his miracles,
they had come to rely upon him, and he had given them
certain powers. If there was a problem or difficulty they
turned to him at once and put their questions; he was always
ready to answer, and he was very patient. And now, after
these wonderful three years and after all this intimacy and
rich fellowship, he tells them that he is about to leave them.
They are utterly crestfallen and dumbfounded, and he, looking at them, can see it. He reads their minds and understands
their spirits, and so he begins by saying, 'Let not your heart
be troubled, ye believe in God, believe also in me.' Then he
proceeds to unfold for them this wonderful doctrine, this, to
them, amazing idea that it was expedient for them that he
should go away, that they were going to be in a better, not a
worse, position as a result of his going, because he was going
to prepare a place for them. Not only that, he was going to
send them another Comforter who would be *in* them and he
would come and dwell in them by the Holy Spirit—that
extraordinary doctrine of the indwelling Christ, of the abid-
ing of the Father and the Son in the very life of the believer.
And he goes on to work out and explain that blessed and
wonderful doctrine.

But he does not stop at that. He now prays for them, in
order that they may know that when he has left them here on
earth, when he has gone to be with the Father, he is still
going to go on praying for them. He says in verse 11, 'And
now, I am no more in the world, but these are in the world
and I come to thee. Holy Father, keep through thine own
name those whom thou hast given me . . .' He not only tells
them in doctrine and teaching, he wants them here to see that
he is committing them to the Father, so that they may know
that they are never left to themselves, but that in all circum-

stances and conditions he will still be looking after them. He will be their great Intercessor, indeed the Father himself is concerned about them. That is his object and purpose in praying this prayer audibly, that they may come to know, while he is still with them, the concern that he has about them, and will continue to have even though he is going to be out of their sight.

That is the essence of this prayer and what I want to do now is to take a general view of the prayer. Later I hope to consider it more in detail, and to expound and unfold its rich, its glorious and priceless teaching. Let me ask some questions before we go any further. How often have you read this chapter? What has been the value of this chapter to you hitherto? How often have you explored its riches? How often have you turned to it in distress? Do you understand John Knox's feeling when he wanted it to be read to him? It does seem to me that many of us are guilty of putting this great prayer as it were on one side in a kind of mock humility. Our greatest danger—indeed I feel it is my greatest danger—is to read the Scriptures too generally instead of looking into them, listening to every phrase, taking hold of every utterance, asking questions concerning every statement. Every one of these statements has a profound and rich meaning if we but take the trouble to look for them.

Let us, then, begin to do that together. Let us take a general view of this prayer, and discover some of the obvious lessons which are here on the very surface. The first thing which I think we must learn is how to pray. It is, after all, a model prayer, not in the sense that the so called Lord's Prayer is a model prayer, but in the sense that this is the way in which our Lord himself prayed, and it is an example, or an illustration in practice. We can always be quite certain that the right way to pray is the way in which he prayed. His whole life, in a sense, was a life of prayer. Though he was the Son of God, he spent so much of his time praying, and this is his way of praying.

Now we all need instruction on this matter. We some-times think that prayer is simple, but it is not. The great saints of all the centuries are agreed in saying that one of the most difficult things of all is to learn how to pray. If any Christian has been feeling cast down because he or she has found prayer difficult, they must not be discouraged, be-cause it is the common experience of the saints. The person I am worried about is the one who has no difficulty about prayer, there is certainly something wrong about him. Prayer is the highest achievement of the saint. It does not just mean 'saying a prayer'—incidentally, what a horrible phrase that is—people talk about 'saying a prayer', but that is a very different thing from praying. It is a comparatively easy thing to say or read a prayer, but the main thing is to pray, and here we find our Lord praying.

You will see that there is a great logical sequence in the various petitions; our Lord does not merely utter a number of petitions at random, there is a definite arrangement, there is a very precise order, so that we have to realize that in prayer we must exercise a certain amount of discipline. The first thing always in prayer is to recollect ourselves—the act of recollection—a pausing to meditate and consider what exactly we are about to do. We begin to realize the Person whom we are going to address, and that leads to a certain inevitable consequence which will emerge as we analyse this great prayer.

John 17, therefore, is a wonderful illustration of the way in which we should pray. But at the same time it at once leads us into an understanding of who this person is who begins to pray. There is no chapter, perhaps, which gives us a greater insight into the person of our blessed Lord himself than this very prayer which we are considering together. He addresses his Father: 'Glorify thy Son, that thy Son also may glorify thee'; he talks about the glory which he had with the Father before the foundation of the world. We are at once reminded that we are in the presence of no mere man, we are in the presence of the Son of God—the God-Man—the One who shared the glory of the Father before the foundation of the world, from all eternity, and as we go on with our consideration of this prayer we shall be led into some of the richest and profoundest doctrines concerning the person and the work of our Lord and Saviour Jesus Christ.

Now I have often emphasized the point that there is nothing which is so marvellous about Scripture as the way in which it varies its presentation of the truth. There is a great objective, dogmatic pronouncement of the truth concerning the person and work of the Lord Jesus Christ, but sometimes you will find that doctrine most perfectly taught in illustration and in practice, in the things which he says about himself, or in the things which he assumes, and as we consider this prayer we come face to face with this rich doctrine concerning this blessed person. Oh, if we could but lay a firm hold upon it and realize again that the Son of God came down into this world of time—we are facing here the whole mystery and glory of the incarnation, of the virgin birth, the humiliation of the Son of God. But the astounding thing is that this person who is praying to the Father, was equal to the Father. He assumed human nature, he came in the flesh, he lived as man in the likeness of sinful flesh, and here he is himself praying. Indeed, we read elsewhere of him crying out, with strong crying and tears, unto his Father. It is a marvellous, wonderful thing to contemplate, that God has come down in the flesh in order to rescue and redeem us, and opens his heart here to show us his wonderful concern for us, and his amazing love with respect to us; and as we go on we shall enter into this rich doctrine concerning his person.

And in a very specific manner we find here, in his approach, the whole reason why he came into the world. He tells us that he had a certain task laid upon him, he came to do it, and, still more glorious, he has done it. But as we listen to him praying, we have, if we have never seen it before, an insight into his reason for doing it—we begin to

see the plan of salvation. Now here again is something which
we modern Christians have ceased to remember, and what a
loss it is to us. Our fathers, in the great days of evangelism,
used to speak about the 'plan of salvation', 'the scheme of salvation'. We hear very little about that today. We are so
subjective, we are so interested in particular benefits, far too
infrequently do we stand back and view the whole grand
sweep of the plan of salvation. But you find it all here, you
will find it as he speaks of that glory in eternity before the
foundation of the world. You will see him leading us on step
by step and then going back into that glory. You cannot
listen to this prayer, or read it, without starting in glory and
without ending in glory, and without, in the meantime, having come right down to the very depths of the degradation
and shame of the cross and then to the rising again. It is all
here: the great plan with regard to us; this great purpose of
God with respect to certain people whom he has given to his
Son as the special object of salvation, and all that is to be
done for them in order to bring them to that ultimate consummation.

I know nothing which is more encouraging and more
exhilarating than that. There is no greater ground of security
in this world of time than to feel that you are a part of the
grand plan and purpose of God. None of these things are
accidental, none of them are fortuitous. It does not matter
what may happen in the future, nothing can disturb this
plan. My friend, if you are a Christian, do you know that
you were the object of God's interest and concern before the
foundation of the world? All these things have been worked
out in eternity, before time, so we must always remember
that nothing can happen in time which will make the
slightest difference. That is the argument which we find so
constantly in the Scriptures. We must never be tired of quoting those great words: 'For I am persuaded, that neither
death, nor life, nor angels, nor principalities, nor powers,
nor things present, nor things to come, nor height, nor

depth, nor any other creature, shall be able to separate us from the love of God, which is in Christ Jesus our Lord' (Rom 8: 38-39). And if you have ever been in any doubt about that, read this prayer and see the security as he outlines it here.

And then we come on to look at what he has done for us. 'I have finished the work which thou gavest me to do,' he says, and as we go on from that we see that he has done certain things for us which none other could ever do for us and which we can never do for ourselves. He has been telling his disciples about it in the earlier chapters, and here he sums it up. What he has done for us is that he has satisfied the law and all its demands. It is amazing to me how people can look at and preach about Christ, his life and death and never mention the law. But unless the law of God is satisfied, there is no salvation. The law is opposed to us; it stands there and demands a perfect, absolute obedience and it threatens us with death if we fail in any one respect. If Christ has not fulfilled the law, we are yet in our sins, we are undone, we are damned and we are lost; but he has finished the work, the books have been cleared, the law has been satisfied, there is therefore no condemnation to them that are in Christ Jesus. Do you know that? Are you rejoicing in it? Are you ready to take your stand with Toplady and say:

> The terrors of law and of God
> With me can have nothing to do,
> My Saviour's obedience and blood
> Hide all my transgressions from view.

What a wonderful thing it is that here, just before he actually goes to the cross, he anticipates it all. He knows what he is going to do, and there is no uncertainty about it. He says, 'I have finished the work which thou gavest me to do.' It is already done, it is complete. We preach, therefore, a completed salvation. There is nothing left for us to do but to receive it; there is nothing that we must add to it; there is no good work or any merit that we must provide: it is all in Christ and in Christ alone. And we have a wonderful view of that as we go through this prayer.

The next thing, therefore, is a realization of some of the things that are possible for us even in this world and life. I would remind you again that because of this blessed doctrine we should be rejoicing. All the fruits of the Spirit should be manifest in our lives—a joy and peace, longsuffering, gentleness, goodness, meekness, temperance and faith, all these things should be present possessions. The Christian man, according to this doctrine, is not hoping to be saved, he is not constantly dwelling in mysteries, sometimes better, sometimes worse; no, he is a man who rejoices in Christ Jesus—listen to Paul: 'Rejoice in the Lord always: and again I say, rejoice' (Phil 4:4). But are we rejoicing? Do we realize the possibility of rejoicing? If we only grasp what this prayer is saying, and understand this teaching, we shall be able to smile in the face of the world and in the face of hell. He means us to be rejoicing, to know this fullness that God has provided for us in him, and, I say, shame on us, Christian brothers and sisters, unless we are partaking of it, participating in it, and rejoicing in it altogether!

Here, in his prayer, the Lord allows us to see something of this wonderful possibility, and then, as I have already hinted, he shows us the source of security and strength in this world. Can you imagine anything that is more comforting than this, that the Lord Jesus Christ has prayed for you: 'Neither pray I for these alone, but for them also which shall believe on me through their word'? Do you realize that when he was praying this prayer the Lord Jesus Christ was praying for *you?* Now, if we are Christians, we all like to have people praying for us. There are many people in the Christian life today because somebody prayed for them, a saintly father or mother, perhaps, who prayed throughout the years of disappointment, and went on praying. And God heard the prayer and they have become Christians. Is there anything that gives greater consolation than to know that people are praying for you? I know of nothing that is a greater encouragement to me, in my work and in my ministry, than to know that people are praying for me. They are going to God who is the source of all power and asking him to fill me with power.

So, then, if you believe in the prayer of a saintly person, how much more should you believe in the prayer of the Son of God for you. Here he lets us know that he prayed for us and he goes on praying for us, and, most wonderful of all, what he does is to put us into the hands of God. He says: 'Holy Father, keep through thine own name those whom thou hast given me, that they may be one, as we are. While I was with them in the world, I kept them in thy name: those that thou gavest me I have kept . . . and now come I to thee' (verses 11-13). 'Father,' he says in effect, 'I hand them back to you, you keep them.' If only we could somehow take hold of this wonderful truth, that the Lord Jesus Christ, himself, has put us into the safe keeping of God and that we are therefore in God's safe keeping! Our Lord was never tired of expounding this doctrine. In the Sermon on the Mount, for instance, what he keeps on saying, in effect, is, 'Foolish people, if only you realized that God is your Father, if only you realized his concern for you, if only you took to heart the lesson of the birds and the flowers! Look at his concern for them—how much greater is his concern about you, oh you of little faith.' And here, in his last prayer, he hands us over to the Father's care and says, 'Father, keep them.' Oh, it is a wonderfully consoling and comforting thought, to know that God the Father is looking upon us, and caring for us, and keeping us at this present time.

And finally we are going to learn from this prayer what is our relationship to this world, and our business in it. We have not only been saved for our own sakes, we have been saved in order that we may pass on this good news to others. 'As thou hast sent me into the world, even so have I also sent them'—he was leaving them in the world with a message, he was sending them to do something, as God had sent him before.

So there we have hurriedly looked at some of the things that stand out on the very surface of this prayer. You will find there are certain natural divisions: from verses 1–5 our Lord prays mostly for himself and about himself; then from verses 6–19 he prays for the disciples in particular, those who are around and about him; and from verses 20–26 he prays for the church universal at all times and in all places. There is the logical division to which I have just referred. He starts with adoration and worship, his prayer for himself, then prays for the disciples and then for those who are going to believe through the demonstration of the disciples. In other words, it is a great prayer that covers the whole of the Christian era and the entire course of the Christian church. Therefore, as we study it, we must observe it very carefully, and especially the way our Lord approaches his Father.

There are certain things about which we should always be certain, things about which Christ was certain. First: 'Father,' he says. He is not in doubt about him. He addresses God as Father six times—he knows the relationship, he was one with the Father from all eternity. God is his Father in the sense that he is the Father in the blessed Trinity of Father, Son and Holy Ghost. God is also his Father in the sense that Jesus has now become man and so is looking to God as his Father. Again, God is now his Father because he, the Son, is the representative of the many brethren whom he has come to save and for whom he has come to die. As he is the first born of many, many brethren, so God is his Father in that sense, in the relationship of the children to God their heavenly Father.

But notice that he not only addresses him as 'Father'. In verse 11 he addresses him as 'holy Father'. How vital it is to remember that—that God is holy. He is our Father who is in heaven, so his name must be hallowed. We must always approach him with reverence and godly fear for our God is a consuming fire. Though our Lord was one with the Father, though nothing had ever come between them, though he never needed to ask for forgiveness of his own sins because he had never sinned, he still addressed God as holy Father. How often do we forget that even our blessed Lord addressed him as holy Father?

Lastly, he addresses him as 'righteous Father'—'O righteous Father,' he says in verse 25, 'the world hath not known thee: but I have known thee, and these have known that thou hast sent me.' This is a wonderful thought and when he says this, he is referring to the character of God, to the faithfulness of God. In other words, our Lord is saying, in effect, 'I know that what you have promised, you will perform. You have made certain promises to me concerning these people for whom I have done this work, and I know that you will never fail in any one respect with regard to all those promises. You are a righteous Father.'

If we remember nothing else from this study, God grant that we should learn just that, that when we pray in Jesus Christ's name, we are praying to *our Father*. Yes, he is the great, almighty, eternal God, but he has become our Father in Christ. He is a holy Father, nothing unworthy must be mentioned in his presence; we must not present unworthy desires, nor selfish thoughts before our holy Father. But, thank God, he is a righteous Father, faithful and just, and if we truly confess he forgives us all our sins and cleanses us from all unrighteousness. As you come before him, conscious of your sins and maybe doubtful and hesitant, remember this, he is righteous, he has promised forgiveness in Christ. Remember his righteousness and remember that every promise that he has ever given, he will most certainly and most surely fulfil.

Oh, how we should thank God that our Lord offered this prayer audibly, and how we should thank God that it has been recorded! Let us look into these things. Let us meditate upon them. I know of no wealthier place than this. Let us enter into it. Let us receive of these riches, that we may realize that while we live in this world of time there are certain things that are absolutes surrounding and encompassing us, and that we are in the hands of One who has said, 'I will never leave thee, nor forsake thee' (Heb 13:5).

2

Why Pray?

John 17:1

I should like to look once more at John 17 in a more or less general sense, not so much from the standpoint from which we have just seen it, but rather as this chapter and this prayer have some lessons to teach us about the whole subject of prayer itself. I sometimes think that there is no subject, perhaps, in connection with the Christian life, which causes so many people such perplexity as this one, I think we all understand very well the feelings of the disciples when they turned to our Lord on one occasion and said, 'Lord, teach us to pray,' because, for some peculiar reason, prayer does tend to be a problem to people. I think any pastor of souls will agree with me when I say that this question of prayer is one that is very frequently brought to his notice. Anyone who takes the Christian life at all seriously is probably concerned about his or her prayer life, and very great difficulties and perplexities often surround this question.

Now obviously in the space of one sermon I cannot hope to deal with all the problems, indeed, I am not proposing to go into it in detail—that would require a whole series of sermons on the subject of prayer as such. I am simply concerned to gather certain general lessons which seem to me at any rate to be taught us on the very surface of the prayer of our Lord which is recorded in this particular chapter. In order to concentrate attention on this, let me put it to you in this form. I think there are two main difficulties that tend to present themselves to people as they contemplate this whole question of prayer, and these perplexities are generally due to two extreme positions which have been taken up by Christian people in the past and are still taken up by some today.

First of all there is the extreme position of those who seem to have no difficulty in prayer, the people who give the impression that there is nothing so easy or so simple. They are very fond of using the phrase 'prayer changes things', and give us the impression that whatever their problem, the answer comes and all is well. They are sure that nobody should be in trouble about these matters, that prayer is the most natural thing in the world, involving no effort, no difficulty at all; they just do it so easily and talk so glibly about it.

That, I think, is a position which does raise problems and queries in the minds of many other Christian people, who find it very difficult to reconcile that with some of the plain teaching of Scripture. Those friends who find prayer so easy seem to forget all the conditions that are attached to these promises and to these great offers. There are many souls who, having listened to such teaching and having tried honestly and genuinely to put it into practice, have found that it does not work out like that with them. As a consequence, being disappointed, they begin to question the goodness of God. They question all the teaching of the Scriptures with regard to the Fatherhood of God and with regard to the whole question of prayer. This perplexity arises from exaggerations on the part of that particular school which I have just described.

But, on the other hand, there is another position which is taken up by some and which again leads to all sorts of difficulties and perplexities. It is the position of those who more or less deny the value and the point of prayer at all. Their argument is that God knows everything and that everything that happens, happens as the result of God's will, and therefore, surely, there is no point in praying. God is omniscient, they say. He knows everything; he is the sovereign Lord of the universe; nothing does happen or can happen outside his will or control. And so they question the purpose of prayer. This is the position which is sometimes described as determinism. It is an attitude which regards life and everything that happens in this world as being part of a rigid and closed process, and clearly, if that is true, there is no point in prayer. Furthermore, there are many people who have so exaggerated the doctrine of the sovereignty of God, or have drawn such wrong deductions from it, that they have rendered those who listen to their arguments and teaching almost incapable of praying with any sense of confidence and assurance.

There, then, are the main positions. I have chosen these two simply because they are the two extremes, but many others are to be found between them. The question, therefore, arises as to how we approach all this. How do we try to arrive at the true position with regard to prayer, in the light of these two extreme positions that lead us to so many problems and perplexities? Well, I would lay it down as a principle at this point—and it is applicable not only to this question of prayer but to many other problems as well—that the one thing we have to do in a situation like this is to avoid becoming slaves to our own theories and ideas and to our own understanding of the truth. In avoiding that danger we should go to the Scriptures, and look at the Bible's plain and obvious teaching with as dispassionate and open a mind as we are capable of. We should do that, I say, not only with regard to this problem of prayer, but with regard to any other problem that may arise in our spiritual experience. There are certain doctrines taught in Scripture quite clearly, but then we come up against something that we cannot quite fit into our doctrinal pattern, and the danger at that point is to stand on our own doctrine and to try to explain away the Scripture. If ever we find a point that seems to conflict with our clear grasp of doctrine, it seems to me that, for the time being, the essence of wisdom is to leave our doctrine where it is. It is not that we deny it, we just leave it for the moment, we come back to Scripture and we note what Scripture has to say everywhere about this particular matter. Then having done that, we again attempt to relate this obvious and clear teaching of Scripture with the doctrine of which we are equally sure.

Now that is the kind of thing which we must do with this whole question of prayer, and fortunately there is a great wealth of material in the Bible at our disposal. I am merely going to select certain points of which we can be absolutely sure, things which are beyond doubt and peradventure. I do not pretend I can solve every problem with regard to prayer; there are certain ultimate difficulties here, as there are with many other points touching our relationship to God, which perhaps we will never fully understand in this life and world. But it is our bounden duty to go as far as we can and to understand the teaching as far as that is possible.

The first obvious point is that a very prominent place is given in the Scriptures to prayer. According to Scripture, prayer is an important and essential element in the godly life. Indeed, the Scriptures actively teach us to pray, both by precept, and by example. We are exhorted to pray, our Lord himself exhorted people to do so. He said that men should always pray and not faint. He taught his disciples how to pray, and he urged them not to give up. You also find the same thing in the epistles: 'Keep steadfast in prayer' is their argument, always encouraging us to pray. Now whatever your view may be of the sovereignty of God and of man's relationship to him, you have to reckon with this obvious, plain teaching of the Scriptures, so that prayer must be a very prominent part of the life of any godly person in this world.

Furthermore, it is not only by precept that we are taught

to pray. We are taught by example also. If you read the Old Testament you will find that the patriarchs talked with God and spoke to him—that is prayer. Look at the psalms, most of them are prayers. Consider, for instance, Psalm 74; that is typical of the psalmists and of how these men prayed to God. Then you find prayers in the prophetic books, indeed you have them everywhere in the Old Testament. You also find the apostles praying, but above all, as we see in this great chapter, our Lord himself prayed, and all these facts urge us to pray. We see, then, that the Bible teaches us to pray, it urges us to pray, in a sense it pleads with us to pray.

But I can draw a second deduction, which is also very plainly taught in the Scriptures: the more saintly, the more godly a person, the more time he spends in prayer. Take any example you like in the Scriptures and you will find it absolutely invariable. Now if you and I had argued on general principles, we might have come to the opposite conclusion. We might have considered a man very saintly because his will was conforming to the will of God, and because he meditated about these things and because his supreme desire was to live to the glory of God. Well, you might say, such a man would have much less need of prayer than anybody else, but it is not the case. Look at the most outstanding godly men and women, how often they spent much more time in prayer than anybody else. They did not just passively wait for God's will to be done, no, they, more than anybody else, went, rather, and talked to God. And as you proceed to read the history of the church throughout the centuries, you will find exactly the same thing. Whether he belongs to the Roman Catholic Church or the Protestant Church, it is always the hallmark of a saint that he is a great man of prayer. John Wesley used to say that he had a very poor opinion of a Christian who did not spend at least four hours in prayer every day, and that is but a typical statement of God's outstanding people in the church throughout the centuries.

But, and this of course brings us directly to John 17, the

most striking and important thing of all is the fact that prayer played such a prominent part in the life or our Lord himself. Now I wonder whether we have ever stopped to contemplate that? Of course we all know that he prayed. We say that we have read our gospels and have known that since we were children. But I am not talking about an intellectual awareness of the fact, I am asking whether we have ever understood that fact, and meditated upon it, because the more you stop to think about it, the more you see that one of the most astounding things in Scripture is the fact that the Lord Jesus Christ ever prayed at all. The fact is, however, that he did pray, and not merely that he prayed, but that he prayed constantly; indeed you find that he prayed for very long periods. On one occasion he spent the whole night in prayer—the Son of God praying right through the night! We are constantly told that he rose a great while before dawn and went up into a mountain somewhere to pray.

Now his disciples always noticed that he was praying, and that was, in a sense, one of the things which prompted them to ask him, 'Lord, teach us to pray.' They felt that he was doing something which they did not quite understand; they wondered what the reason was for the delight and pleasure which he took in the act of prayer, and why it meant so much to him. They could not say they felt like that. But they knew that there was no one like him. They saw something in his face and demeanour, they saw his miracles and they said, Ah, there is something in that prayer life, oh that we might have that!

They noticed especially the fact that he always prayed a great deal, and in an exceptional way, in times of crisis and in times of great importance. You remember it was before he chose his twelve disciples that he spent the whole night in prayer. This was a very important and a very vital decision to take, so he spent the whole night in prayer to God before he selected these men. There was another occasion when he prayed like this, we read about it in John 6. He had just fed the five thousand and some of the people were so deeply impressed that they decided that he was the Messiah, and that they must take him up to Jerusalem and crown him king. But when our Lord saw that they were going to take him by force and make him a king, he went up into a mountain, himself alone, and there he communed with God, and prayed to him. It was one of the critical moments in his life and experience. Here was a great temptation—he had already met it in the wilderness—to bring in his kingdom in a kind of human political sense, and the temptation was so strong that he went away alone to pray with God.

You find him doing it, too, at the grave of Lazarus. This again was a momentous, tremendous occasion—he was going to raise the dead—and so he prayed to God and thanked God that he knew that God had heard his voice and always heard it. Then you remember how he prayed just as he was going up to face the cross—you find it recorded in John 12:27-28—and, too, you see him praying in the Garden of Gethsemane, praying to the Father in an agony that produced blood-stained sweat. Then here we have this great high priestly prayer, in his last hours with his disciples before he goes to finish the work upon the cross, and here he prays audibly in their presence.

What, then, does all this teach us? We might very well spend much time in deducing certain things about the person of our Lord. We will not do that now, but at least we must note that it tells us a great deal about him. If ever you are in trouble about the incarnation this one prayer of our Lord's prayer life in general ought at once to put you at rest and keep you at rest. He is truly man. It is not a case of God in a kind of phantom body, it is not a theophany, it is the incarnation, the Word made flesh and dwelling among us. He is truly God, yes, but he is truly man. Here you begin to understand what Paul was talking about in Philippians 2, when he says, 'He emptied himself' (see the Revised Version). What Paul meant is that while he was here on earth our Lord did not make use of his powers as God. And because he lived as a man, prayer was essential to him—even he could not go on without prayer. In other words, it teaches us what he said so often himself, that he was entirely dependent upon his Father. He said, 'The words that I speak unto you I speak not of myself: but the Father that dwelleth in me, he doeth the works' (Jn 14:10).

That is the astounding thing about our Lord's life. Here he is, very Son of God and perfect man, and yet he does nothing of himself, he gets all his orders, as it were, from God. God gives him the words to speak, God tells him what to do, and gives him the power to do it—that is why he prayed before calling his disciples. He looked to God for light and guidance, perfect man but in utter dependence upon his Father. As God, there was no need for him to pray. As God, he was co-equal with God, he was omniscient and all powerful, but here on earth we see him in his true character, the mediator, God-Man. And as we watch him in prayer we see him there as the appointed mediator, the One who has been sent by God to do certain work and to complete it here on earth for us. Therefore, to look at our Lord praying is perhaps one of the most wonderful doors of entry into the great mystery of his blessed person. I repeat, if there is anyone in trouble about the person of Christ, about the God-Man, oh, just watch him praying, and you have to include that in your doctrine of his person. So many think of him as God only, with a kind of clothing of flesh. That is wrong, because if he were God only, there would be no need for prayer. No, we must insist upon man also—God-Man.

But next I want also to draw certain more general deductions about prayer itself, and I think we can draw them very definitely from the points I have established. Watch those patriarchs, watch King David, watch the prophets, all praying, and the more saintly they were the more they prayed. Watch the apostles praying, and above all, watch the Son of God praying. What, then, is prayer? What is the explanation of all this? I suggest that we must inevitably come to the conclusion that prayer, to the Christian, to God's man, is something natural and almost instinctive; prayer is something which is expressive of the relationship between the child and the Father. Now I think that is a very important argument. You show me a man who does not pray very much and I will tell you the real problem of that man. It is that he does not know God, he does not know God as his Father. That is the trouble. The problem is not that he is not a moral man, or that he is not a good man. He can be highly moral, he may be very faithful in Christian church work, there may be nothing he is not prepared to do, but if he does not pray, I tell you that the essence of that man's trouble is that he does not know God as his Father. For those who know God best are the ones who speak to him most of all.

There is no need to prove a thing like this—the little child always speaks to his Father. Have you not often noticed how the child of some great man talks to him freely, while another man going into his presence is nervous. Not so the child; the child speaks freely, because he knows the relationship and so he speaks to his father. And that is why the most saintly people are the ones who pray most; that is why the Lord Jesus Christ prayed more than anybody else, because he knew God in a way nobody else knew him. That, then, is the way to approach this question of prayer. The whole trouble with people who get into difficulties over prayer is that they start at the end instead of at the beginning. You do not start with the desire for answers, you start with adoration, and it is because we forget this all important matter that we tend to get into such perplexities. To pray is the obvious, natural thing for a child to do and there is nothing that expresses more eloquently or more cogently the whole relationship of man to God as prayer. That is the first thing. So, then, I think that the saints and, supremely, our Lord himself, prayed to God, primarily, not to ask for things but to assure their own hearts and to maintain their contact with

God and to make certain of their contact and communion with him.

Our whole idea of prayer is false. We think of prayer only as guidance and requests. Now if you were to put that into practice in human relationships you would regard it as insulting. No, the thing the saint wants to know above everything else is that all is well between his soul and the Father. There is nothing the saint delights in more than to know God as his Father. He likes to maintain the contact and communion, to assure his heart before God and in the presence of God. The saint is in this difficult world, there are temptations from the outside and the whole world is against us, and the saint is tried—sometimes he almost despairs. So he goes to God immediately, not to ask this or that but just to make certain that all is well there, that the contact is unbroken and perfect, that he can assure his heart and know that all is well.

That is what our Lord is doing here in John 17, and that is the thing which stands out most frequently in this prayer. Our Lord is assuring his own human heart in the presence of his Father. We saw earlier how he did that when he was raising Lazarus from the dead; indeed he puts it in words for us: 'Then they took away the stone . . . And Jesus lifted up his eyes, and said, 'Father'—he is praying—'I thank thee that thou hast heard me'—always he is assured in his heart—'And I knew that thou hearest me always: but because of the people . . .' (Jn 11:41-42). He just turns to God. He knows all is well, but, he is assuring his heart in the presence of God.

Let me put it like this: the saints always prayed to God, and our Lord supremely did so, because they believed in God's power, because they believed in God's ability to help, and, above all, because they believed in God's willingness and readiness to help. That is tremendously important. They, of everybody, knew the power of God, yes, but the world and its trials tend to shake our confidence in him and there is no better way of reminding ourselves of the power and the greatness of God, his ability and his readiness to help, than to go and talk to him; that is why the saints always fly to prayer. 'The name of the Lord is a strong tower: the righteous runneth into it, and is safe' (Prov 18:10). In other words, the saint rushes to God in prayer and reminds himself of these things.

Prayer, in many ways, is the supreme expression of our faith in God and our faith and confidence in the promises of God. There is nothing that a man ever does which so proclaims his faith as when he gets down on his knees and looks to God and talks to God. It is a tremendous confession of faith. I mean by this that he is not just running with his requests and petitions, but if he really waits upon God, if he really looks to God, he is there saying, 'Yes, I believe it all, I believe that you are a rewarder of them that diligently seek you, I believe you are the Creator of all things and all things are in your hands. I know there is nothing outside of your control. I come to you because you are in all this and I find peace and rest and quiet in your holy presence and I am praying to you because you are what you are.' That is the whole approach to prayer that you find in the teaching of Scripture.

And finally I can put it in this way, that the saints and our Lord clearly prayed to God in order that they might discover his will. They were much more concerned about discovering his will than having their own way and will. 'Ah,' they said, 'the one thing that matters at this juncture is that we may know what God's will is', so they went into his presence. If you read the marvellous prayers of the saints, as in Daniel 9, for instance, you will learn a great deal about how to pray. The prophet did not quite understand what God was doing. The whole thing was perplexing to him and he went to God and talked to God about it. He said various things to God of which he was certain and then he said, in effect, 'I do not quite understand this, but I want to do your gracious will and you understand what you are doing.'

Jeremiah did exactly the same thing. God told him to go

and buy a particular field. Jeremiah's first reaction was that it was impossible because God was also telling him that the Children of Israel were going to be carried into captivity. If this was going to happen, what was the point of buying a field? Then he reminded himself of the great character of God, and having done that he said, in effect, 'Enlighten my perplexity, let me see what you are doing, explain your holy will to me.'

We have now reached the point where we can draw certain general conclusions, and here they are. Whatever else I do not understand about prayer, I think I now understand this: that God has chosen to do his work in this world in that way, through praying people. He need not have done so, he could have done it without them, but it is perfectly clear that God has ordained and decreed to do his work in this world through men and women, like you and me, and through our prayers. He calls us to pray. He urges us to do so and then he answers our prayers—even though he could have done without our prayers at all.

'Ah,' says someone, 'that is what I want to know—why does he do it?'

My dear friends, who can answer such a question? I cannot, but I thank God that he does it in that way. I do not know why he elected to do it, but I know he does it. That is his way and I accept it. And I am grateful for this reason: it is in this way that God reveals himself to us. Read about prayer in the Scriptures and especially watch these people praying, even our Lord himself, and I think you will find that as the result of prayer all these people come to know God better than they would have ever known him apart from this. It is in this way that God shows himself, and reveals his Father-heart to us. For example, there is this difficult circumstance with which I am faced. I do not know what to do. I tend to become unhappy and miserable. But then I go to God and wait upon him and he begins to show himself and his purpose to me; he reveals himself to me. If you have not learnt

more of God through prayer there is something wrong with
your spiritual life. It is there that he teaches us things and in
this way draws out our faith. So, then, since this is one of
God's ways of revealing himself to mankind and bringing his
purposes to pass, the whole problem and question of God's
omnipotence is removed. You should never be perplexed by
it. God has chosen to do these things in this way, so his
omniscience should never arise as a problem. And in the
same way I can say that it in no way affects the sovereignty
of God. It is one of God's ways of displaying his
sovereignty. There is no conflict between the sovereignty of
God and prayer, for it is the sovereign God who has chosen
to do his work in this world through praying men and
women. Far from being contradictory, they work together.

And, finally, we can draw some wonderful practical conclusions from this teaching and especially from this chapter.
The supreme object of prayer should be to glorify and mag-
nify God and that is why we must always start by worshipping him. The model prayer does that: 'Our Father which
art in heaven, Hallowed be thy name. Thy kingdom come
. . .' Not, 'Give me this little request . . .' No, you start by
worshipping. It is the personal relationship; you pray because you like the person, because you want to show your
respect to the person, because you delight to be in the
presence of the person—that is the essence of prayer.

Then another thing we can draw as a practical deduction—
and I am grateful for it—is that God delights to be told things
he knows already. I am addressing certain intellectuals who
are very fond of making fun of people who in their prayers
tell God certain things. You will have heard the criticism.
But to tell God what he knows is an essential part of prayer.
Read the Bible and you will find John, for example, telling
God things he knew already. The writers of the psalms did
the same thing—why? It is because God is a Father. God is
not a machine, if I may say it with reverence. He is our
Father, and as a Father he delights to be told these things by

his children. He means us to tell him, so do not be afraid to tell God things he knows already. Do not say, 'God is omniscient and, because God knows everything, I must just wait silently in his presence.' No, tell him these things, he likes to hear, he wants to be in communion with you, he delights in fellowship with you.

The next thing I would say is that our object in prayer should never be to change God's heart or will. There is never any need to do that, for if you think you need to change God's heart you are insulting him. God's will is always perfect, and he is a loving Father. Rather, come to him to discover his will, to see that it is right and to rejoice in it—that is the object of prayer. But that does not mean that you do not take your requests to him. Again, as your Father, he is there waiting for you to do that and willing for you to do that; he is there ready to listen to our requests and petitions. So tell him all about them. Do what these men did and what our Lord did in the Garden of Gethsemane—'If it be possible . . . nevertheless not as I will, but as thou wilt.' Make your requests known, tell him your desires but always immediately say, 'I am so small and finite, I do not understand. This is what I would like, but if it is not your will, well I do not ask, I am content with your will, whatever it may be'—an attitude of utter resignation. If you have started your prayer rightly, if you have started by glorifying God and saying, 'Hallowed be thy name, thy kingdom come on earth, thy will be done,' and so on, you have already been saying, 'God, my supreme desire is that your will be done in me as in the whole world.' Therefore you are very ready, when you bring your requests, to say, 'If it be your will.' I cannot understand the approach to prayer which says you should not add 'If it be your will.' I have the authority of the Son of God, the Lord Jesus Christ himself for saying that we must always say, 'If it be your will.' It is *God's* will that has to be done, so make your requests and desires known but always submit utterly and absolutely to the will of God.

And the last point I make is this, that pleas and arguments and requests are perfectly legitimate in prayer. Have you noticed these men of God praying? They knew God was omniscient, yes, so they not only made their requests known to him but also pleaded with him. And what I like above everything else is the way they argued with him. Moses, for example, did so. On one occasion he came down from the Mount and found the people rebellious, and when he found God threatening to disown them and leave them to their own devices, Moses said to God, You cannot do this. Look too at the man in Psalm 74, who says, in effect, 'Lord why do you allow men to do these things?' I believe God as Father delights in listening to such pleas and reasonings and arguments. This flabby generation of Christians seems to have forgotten what our fathers used to delight in when they talked about 'pleading the promises'. They did not regard that as offensive. They had no sort of mock humility but they felt they were entitled, according to this teaching, to go to God as the psalmist did and remind him of his own promises. They said, 'Lord, I do not understand, I know it is my imperfection, but I am certain of these promises. Lord, help me to see how the promises are to be related to these perplexities.'

So it is perfectly right to plead with God; our Lord pleaded with him. In this great prayer he argued with God by bringing these requests. He reminded him of his own promises, and of his own character. I believe God delights in this as Father, and as we do these things in this way our hearts will be reassured before him and, oftentimes, we shall be amazed and astonished at the answers that we receive. Whatever happens, prayer will always bring us nearer and closer to God if we pray in the right and the true way.

So, then, we have looked together at this great prayer and at some of the great lessons that are obvious on the very surface; God grant that we may learn them and implement them. My dear friends, think before you pray. Go into the presence of God realizing that he is in heaven and that you are upon the earth. Look at these great examples, and above all look at your blessed Lord himself. Remember that he suffered against himself the contradiction of sinners, that he resisted unto blood striving against sin and that he prayed with cries of agony and with sweat and was heard because of his reverence and godly fear, though he was indeed the only begotten Son of God.

3

The Glory of God in the Plan of Salvation

John 17:1

So far, in considering this great prayer, we have been looking at the matter in general. We can now proceed to look at
the actual subjects which our Lord dealt with in his prayer,
the thoughts that were uppermost in his mind as thus he
prayed to his heavenly Father. Let me remind you that the
prayer can be divided into three main sections: the first is
from verses 1–5, in which our Lord prays for himself; then in
verses 5–19 we have his prayer for his immediate disciples,
those who were around and about him; and from there on he
prays for the church universal.

In the first section, where our Lord prays for himself, we
find that the essence of his petition is that the Father may
glorify him, in order that he also may glorify the Father:
'Father the hour is come; glorify thy Son, that thy Son also
may glorify thee.' In other words, his main concern at this
point is that he may glorify God. That is the supreme thing,
but, you notice, he tells us why that is so, and he does this in
terms of God's great purpose in the matter of our salvation.
The whole idea here expressed is that our Lord is anxious
that God's glory may be manifested, and manifested especially in the salvation of men.

As a result, in these five verses we have one of the most
marvellous displays of the whole gospel of salvation and of

the plan of salvation which is to be found anywhere in the Scriptures. There is nothing which is more characteristic of the Scriptures than the way in which here and there they give us a kind of complete synopsis, or compendium, of doctrine and theology. In this prayer in particular, our Lord opens our eyes and instructs us with regard to some of the vitals and fundamentals of our faith. And as one can well anticipate, in view of the fact that it is our Lord himself speaking and praying, there is no more glorious statement of the gospel than you find in these five verses.

Why is it, do you think, that we hear so little today about the plan of salvation, the scheme, the whole object and purpose of it? I use the phrase that was so frequently used by our fathers but which, for some reason, is so infrequently used today. Our fathers delighted in looking at and contemplating, or, if I may use the words of Isaac Watts, *surveying*, the plan of salvation. I have no hesitation in saying that most of our troubles as Christian people, and the whole state of the church today, is to be explained very largely by our failure to consider the plan of salvation as a whole.

The trouble with us is, as I am never tired of pointing out, that we are so utterly subjective. That is the essence of the trouble with this modern generation to which you and I belong. Now I am not talking about people outside the church, but about ourselves, who are inside the church. It may be that we have all been influenced by the climate of thought and by this morbid interest in psychology and in analysing ourselves, but whatever it is, we have become self-centred and that is the curse of this generation. We are always looking at ourselves, at how things affect us and at what we want for ourselves. Now there are many possible explanations for that, which need not claim our attention now, but the fact of the matter is that we are slaves to our own habits and states and desires, and to our own likes and dislikes, and the result is that we approach everything from the standpoint of what it means to *us*. And the tragic thing is that we tend to approach the gospel of Jesus Christ in that particular way, with the result that we fail to realize the truth either about ourselves or about this wonderful salvation which we have, because we particularize on points. We look solely on what the gospel has to say 'to me', how the gospel can 'help me', and we fail, therefore, to hear what the gospel has to say about us, and we fail also to realize the scope and the greatness and the vastness of the gospel itself.

The writer of the epistle to the Hebrews described the gospel as 'so great a salvation'. My suggestion is that we seem to be missing this greatness at the present time and that this is simply because, instead of looking at it as it is, and as it is displayed here, we look at ourselves and what it has to give us. The gospel is presented purely in this personal manner and we forget the greatness which we discover when we look at God's plan of salvation as a whole, and when we allow the gospel to put it before our wondering gaze. You will find in many of our hymns that this idea of the greatness is most forcibly and magnificently expressed.

Charles Wesley says, "'Tis mercy all, immense and free,' and yet so often the impression is given that the gospel is something subjective and small, something which just does this or that. Thank God it does these things, too, for me, but it is not only that. If you are subjective in your approach you will often find yourself feeling unhappy; if you think of the gospel as something coming to you, or happening in your life, immediately you will be upset and you will have nothing to fall back on. The tragedy of the subjective approach is that it is essentially so selfish that eventually it fails us.

But if we take this objective approach to start with and then come on to the subjective we shall gain everything; we shall start on such a vast plan and scheme that we shall be taken up into it, and when anything goes wrong with us, we will relate it to the whole. So to avoid that danger of the subjective, we must study the great subject which we have in these five verses. Not that we must study it for that reason only. It is our duty to study it and I want to impress that upon us all. We claim that we are so busy that we have not the time to read. We know our forefathers used to read the doctrines, but we have not got the time. We want it all in a nutshell, and we want to go through the whole gospel of John in one address. We want a bird's eye view of the whole Bible, and the result is that we miss the doctrine. But here it is displayed, and because God has displayed it to us here, it is our duty to study it, in order that we may find some of the great possibilities that lie open to us. It is a tragedy that we tend to live as paupers in the spiritual realm, when God means us to be princes. But, above all, we study this in order that we may assert a confidence and a certainty and a stead-fastness in our Christian lives.

Now you will find, if you analyse these five verses, that the main things they display to our wondering gaze are these. First, they show us something of the origin and the plan of salvation; they then direct our attention to the One by whom the plan has been carried out, and this leads us into a consideration of the things that he has done, and eventually shows us the purpose and object of it all. There it is, then, the whole purpose and plan of salvation. And now, of course, we must start with the first thing. That sounds a trite, almost ridiculous remark, and, yet, as I have been trying to show, it is essential that we should start at the beginning. Strangely enough, the Christian gospel—let me say this with rev-erence, lest I be misunderstood—the Christian gospel does not start even with the Lord Jesus Christ, it starts with God the Father. The Bible starts with God the Father always, everywhere, and we must do the same, because that is the order in the blessed Trinity: God the Father, God the Son, God the Holy Spirit. You find that very thing emphasized and impressed here, for the statement is that salvation is entirely of God; this is the first thing we must always say when we begin to consider this question of salvation. Sal-vation is entirely of God, it is the gift of God: 'As thou hast

given him power over all flesh, that he should give eternal
life to as many as thou hast given him'—it is all there.

Let us therefore remind ourselves before we go any further
that the gospel announces, at the very beginning, that man is
absolutely helpless in the matter of his salvation, he can do
nothing at all about it. The gospel is not a scheme or pro-
posal to enable men to save themselves, nor is it a pro-
gramme which God has outlined, an example of which has
been given in the person of the Son of God, telling us how
we can raise ourselves and lift ourselves into heaven. No, it
starts by telling us that we cannot do it, we are all dead in
trespasses and sins, we are utterly helpless, we are quite
powerless, and while we were yet without strength Christ
died for the ungodly. It was while man was in a state of
complete bondage to sin and Satan and hell that God did
something. Now that is the very essence of this message. It is
impressed upon us here at the beginning, indeed, we find
that our Lord goes on repeating it. The gospel is just the
good news which tells us what God has done about us men,
and about our salvation. I trust that no one still thinks of
salvation as something that he or she has to arrive at for
himself or herself. I hope nobody will think that church
attendance, for instance, is going to gain them their salvation
before God. That is a complete fallacy, for this message starts
by saying that it is entirely and utterly of God, and comes
solely from him.

'The wages of sin is death'—that is something that you
and I have—'but the gift of God is eternal life through Jesus
Christ our Lord' (Rom 6:23). That is how Paul says it, but
our Lord says it here in the same way: 'As thou hast given
him power over all flesh, that he should give eternal life to as
many as thou hast given him.' This gospel of John has been
saying it from the very beginning, it was the whole essence
of the word to Nicodemus; you have to be *received*, then you
have to be born again—it is all of God. 'God so loved the
world, that he gave his only begotten Son . . .' The quota-

tions are endless. But we must emphasize this at the very
beginning. It is only as we begin to realize this that we can
grasp something of the essential greatness of this salvation,
that the great, almighty, eternal God should have done anything at all about it. But the message is that he has, and in the
way that we are now going to consider.

It is, then, because of all that, that our Lord in his prayer
here at the crucial moment, is concerned above everything
else about glorifying God. 'Father,' he says, 'glorify thy Son,
that thy Son also may glorify thee.' Now his main concern is
not simply that *he* should be glorified. He is only concerned
about that because of this greater thing: he is so anxious to
glorify the Father that he wants the Father to glorify him, he
wants the Father to glorify himself. This is, of course, one of
the most stupendous things we can ever contemplate. Our
Lord's one great desire throughout his life here on earth was
to glorify his Father. He keeps on saying it. He has not come
to do his own will, but the will of his Father who has sent
him. He speaks the Father's words, he does the Father's
works, and his one concern is that he may never fail him,
that he may never falter in the great task that has been allotted to him. He lives entirely and exclusively to glorify his
Father. He has not come to show himself, or to glorify
himself. 'He humbled himself,' wrote the apostle Paul and
that is the whole meaning of that term, for, in his abasing
himself, he put himself as the Son in the Eternal Trinity, he
glorified the Father; that was the whole purpose of his
coming, and everything he has done was designed for that
one and only supreme object—the glory of the Father, and,
here, he prays for it.

But I cannot say a thing like that, of course, without deducing and adding that the whole purpose of your salvation
and mine is that *we* should glorify the Father. Oh, that we
might grasp this! I know that we are all guilty at this point—
and I am as guilty as anybody else—of tending to think of
God and the whole Christian salvation as something to solve

our problems. People come and talk to me, and it is generally put in that way: 'What will salvation do for me?' they ask. And the answer that is given so often in our evangelism is, 'Believe the gospel, and it will do some marvellous things for you.' I say, thank God that that is true, but, my dear friends, we should not put that first. The ultimate aim and object of our salvation is that we may glorify God. The essence of sin is that we do not glorify God—let us be quite clear about this; the essence of sin does not lie in the particular acts or actions of which you and I and others may be guilty. Now that is where we go wrong. We think of sin in terms of particular sins and that is why respectable people do not think they are sinners. They utterly fail to realize that the essence of sin is not to glorify God, and anybody who does not glorify God is guilty of sin of the foulest kind. Even though you may never have got drunk, though you may never be guilty of adultery, if you live for yourself and your own glory you are as desperate a sinner as those other people whom you regard as sinners. That was put very plainly by the prophet Daniel to King Belshazzar in Daniel 5, when he pointed out to him that the essence of sin was not that he put wine in the holy cups of God and drank out of them with his wives and concubines, but that he had not humbled himself before the Lord, he had exalted himself and not given God the glory.

We can put this principle very briefly in this way. The first question in the shorter Catechism of the Westminster Confession is, 'What is the chief end of man?' and the answer is, 'The chief end of man is to glorify God and to enjoy him for ever.' So that I assert that the essence of salvation is to bring us into the state in which we *do* glorify God. It does not matter what is happening, or what goes wrong for us, we are meant to glorify him and live thus to his glory. It is the object of salvation from which, therefore, I deduce this final principle, that the ultimate proof of the fact that we are Christians is that we desire to do that. The final proof of our salvation is not that we are happy whereas formerly we were unhappy. Christian Science or the cults can do that, and so can psychotherapy. These can take the miserable, and those who are worried and anxious, and can give them treatment so that they find that all their problems vanish and they are perfectly happy and contented; they have merely been able to forget their troubles and have undergone some change in their life. If that alone is the test of salvation, well then, I have nothing to say to the cults or to psychology.

But that is not the essential proof of salvation. The essential proof is that the supreme object and ambition of the Christian's life now is to live to the glory of God. If we say that when a man is saved he becomes a partaker of the divine nature, that he is born again, and that Christ dwells in him, then it follows that a Christian is a man who becomes progressively more and more like the Lord Jesus Christ. And when I look at him this is what I find: I find that he was a man of sorrows and acquainted with grief. He had great and terrible temptations pressing upon him, but I find that in all circumstances, and in all places, he had but one great desire and that was to live to the glory of God. Christianity is not something light and superficial that just does certain things to you, and gives you certain pleasant feelings. It is something that brings you into a relationship with God. You begin to fix your gaze on him, and to be awed by his holiness. You approach him with reverence and godly fear, you do not drop lightly into his presence. No, you address him, as his Son did, as Father, holy Father, righteous Father, and over and above what may happen, and over and above your feelings of salvation, is this deep desire to live to his glory, to display it, to give yourself to it—the glory of God.

I want to take it a step further, in this way—the chief end of salvation is, as I say, that God may be glorified and that his glory may be displayed and acknowledged. The result of that is that it is the gospel of salvation that really reveals to us the *glory* of God. Our Lord puts that in the form of a petition. Here he is, just before the cross, the crucial moment is at hand. He knows something about the agony and the sweat of Gethsemane, and his one desire is this: Father, enable me to go on, give me strength to bear, give me all I need to do this, in order that your great glory in this matter of salvation can be revealed and made manifest. I have come to do that, enable me to do it that your name may be glorified. That is his petition, that is his plea.

How, then, does the gospel of Jesus Christ thus manifest the glory of God in a way that nothing else does? Again I would remind you that that is his chief purpose. Even before he is concerned about saving us, he is concerned about revealing the glory of God. Have you realized that, or have you always thought of salvation only as something that is meant to save men? It does do that, of course, but before that, it is meant to display the glory of God. It does so first of all by revealing the character of God. The gospel of Jesus Christ displays, in a way that nothing else does, the *holiness and the righteousness* of God; the whole plan and scheme of salvation proclaims the fact that God cannot ignore sin. God cannot say, 'Well, I will pretend I have not seen it; yes, they have sinned and gone astray and rebelled against me, but I am a loving Father, I do not see things like that, it is all right, I will have them back.' No, the gospel plan of salvation tells us that God—I say it with reverence—cannot do that. The holiness and the righteousness of his eternal being and character mean that he cannot ignore sin. Sin is a reality, a problem (I say it again with reverence), even to God. It is something he sees and has got to deal with, and so he displays the glory of his being in his holiness and righteousness.

But thank God he does not stop at that, for the next thing he does is to reveal his *benignity*, his *mercy* and his *compassion*. You start with sin and the holiness of God, but if you leave it at that, if that were all, there would be very little difficulty about knowing what God would have done. He would simply have blotted out man from the world. He could have done it so easily—he could have consigned all the world, and all its designs, to perdition and eternal torment, and he would have been utterly justified in doing so. But the gospel tells us that he has not done so, he has done the opposite—why?—it is because of his benignity, because of his mercy, which means his pity, for us, his sorrow for us, because of his compassion.

We shall be seeing later on how our Lord displayed all this in his own personal life. How often do the evangelists tell us that he looked upon and had compassion upon some poor suffering person? It is because he was like his Father; the glory of God's character is thus revealed in the gospel. He does not destroy our world, but rather he does something else—and this leads me to his wisdom. Paul was very fond of emphasizing this when he addressed the clever philosophers at Corinth and others, too. Christ, he says, is the power of God, and the wisdom of God, and nowhere is the wisdom of God so gloriously and magnificently displayed as in this Christian gospel. Let me explain this. Here is man in sin, there is God in the heavens. God must recognize this and yet because of his character he does not blot us out. He is going to do something about it because of his mercy and compassion. How is he going to do it? The answer is the plan of salvation, this way that God employed, in his amazing wisdom. He sent his Son, and the Son came through the whole miracle of the virgin birth; he took human nature unto himself and lived as a man—the wisdom:

> Oh loving wisdom of our God!
> When all was sin and shame,
> A second Adam to the fight
> And to the rescue came.
>
> *J. H. Newman*

I am simply noting these things in passing. Have you ever stood in amazement as you have contemplated the loving *wisdom* of our Lord as displayed and revealed in the plan of

salvation? Oh, we must go back to these things! We must
come and look at the plan, its whole conception and the
carrying out of it, and behold the perfection of the plan,
contemplate, dwell upon it, meditate upon it, forget everything else for a while and give ourselves to this.

But not only that, I want to emphasize the way in which
the gospel displays the great *love* of God. You notice I draw a
distinction between the benignity, the mercy and compassion, and the love of God. I feel we must do that, for,
after all, the love of God is displayed in particular in this
matter of salvation, in his actual sending of the Son, his
sparing him, if I may so put it, from the courts of heaven.
My dear friends, God is no philosophic concept! God is a
person and, as a person, God is, and God loves, and the
essence of the life of the blessed Trinity is the love of the
Father to the Son and the Spirit, and the love of the Son to
the Father and the Spirit, and the love of the Spirit to the
Father and the Son. We cannot conceive of that perfect unity,
that perfect bliss, that absolute love, and yet it is all found in
salvation. 'God so loved the world that he gave . . .'—yes,
and I put it negatively, too, as Paul puts it in writing to the
Romans: 'He that spared not his own Son.' It is there, you
see, the love of God, in that he sent the Son of his love, the
only begotten Son, into this cruel, sinful world; allowed him
to live life in that way as a man, and allowed him to suffer
'such contradiction of sinners against himself'. And he placed
your sins and mine upon him on the cross in such a way that
at that moment Father and Son were separated, and the Son
cried out, 'My God, my God, why hast thou forsaken me?'
When I believe that that is possible within the Father-heart of
God, then I cannot believe the doctrine of the impassivity of
God. I say that God in his love suffered in his Son, and it is
there I see the marvellous love of God displayed. And this
great gospel manifests, too, the glory of God in revealing his
character in this way.

But we should see also the way in which this plan of

salvation reveals the *justice* of God. God, because he is righteous and holy cannot, even in his love, do anything that is unjust. God, says Paul in Romans 3, must find a way of salvation which enables him at one and the same time to be just, and the justifier of the ungodly. If God forgave sin without still ministering his own justice, he would no longer be God. The marvel of this plan is that God, in putting our sins on Christ and dealing with them and punishing them there, can forgive us, and still be just. He has punished sin, he has not forgotten or ignored it. What happens in salvation is not that God says, Ah, they have sinned, I ought to punish them, but after all that would be rather hard. No, he does it through the Son, in the way I have outlined, and he is just. So the plan of salvation displays to us the glory of God's being by showing us the justice and absolute rightness of his holy character.

And, finally, it displays to us, again in a way that nothing else does, the *power* of God. The power of God was manifested in the incarnation when he prepared a body for his Son and worked the miracle of the virgin birth—what a marvellous power! But not only that. I rather prefer to think of it like this: it is as we look at God in Christ and all that he did in him through this plan of salvation, that we see his complete power to master everything that is opposed to himself, everything that is opposed to the best interests of man and everything that is opposed to the best interests of this world.

For the fact is that the whole problem has arisen in this way. One of the brightest of the angelic beings that were created by God, rebelled against God, and raised himself up against him. That is the origin of Satan. He is a power, a person, an angel of great might. He is as great as this: that he deluded a man and conquered him, thereby making himself the god of this world, and the 'prince of the power of the air' (Eph 2:2). There has never been a man in this world who has been able to stand up to beat him in fight and in combat. The power of the devil is something that we seriously underestimate, for he is such a power that he does not feel ashamed to pit himself against God himself. He verily believed he had overturned all the work of salvation when the Son of God went to the cross.

But, says Paul in Colossians 2, it is there he made his greatest blunder, for by the cross God, 'spoiled principalities and powers, he made a shew of them openly, triumphing over them in it' (verse 15). Christ met Satan face to face in single combat and routed him; at the cross he fulfilled the promise given to man at the beginning, when Adam was told that the seed of the woman should bruise the serpent's head—it was in the plan of salvation. Ultimately, therefore, the power of God is a great power to rout Satan and all his cohorts, and it assures us that finally he will be cast into the lake of fire and every evil will be destroyed and burnt out of existence.

We see thus, at the very beginning of this prayer, that the primary object of this great and wondrous gospel is to display the glory of God. 'Father, the hour is come; glorify thy Son, that thy Son also may glorify thee.' How much time do we spend in contemplating this glory, in looking at it? Oh, let us study it! Let us forget ourselves and our moods and states and feelings and desires, and just stand back for a moment and meditate upon it. Let us contemplate the plan and the scheme of salvation and feel ourselves lost in wonder, love and praise.

4

Our Security in God

John 17:1–5

In our study of this great chapter we have been concentrating in particular upon the great doctrine of salvation as it is revealed and displayed to us in these five verses. So far we have seen that the entire glory for salvation must go to God, and we have been looking at this truth in general. We have seen how the plan of salvation manifests God's great character, his holiness, his mercy, his wisdom, his love, his justice and his power. We have just noted these things, but we know that as we go on and follow what we are told here, and particularize a little more, we shall see the glory of God in a still more wonderful manner. Now I trust that no one is doubtful as to the importance of this consideration. I hope there is no one who is thinking, 'All this would be fine if one had leisure and nothing else to do. It is quite all right to be considering the glory of God and meditating upon it, but speaking for myself, I find life very difficult and trying. I am hard pressed. All my energies have to go to making a living. I have problems in my own life. I have sickness in the family. I am literally hemmed in by difficulties of all kinds and forms. What has all this to do with me?'

So often men in their ignorance and folly have taken up that position. They have regarded this wonderful doctrine of the glory of God as something theoretical and remote. But, my dear friends, there is no greater fallacy than that! The very fact that our Lord offered this prayer proves in and of itself how completely foolish that is. Why did he offer that prayer, and especially why did he offer it audibly? There is only one answer to that question: he was concerned about these disciples. He had to leave them. He was no longer going to be with them in the flesh, and he reminded his Father, in this prayer, of what he had done for them while he was with them. But now, he continues, 'I am no more in the world, but these are in the world, and I come to thee' (verse 11), and he makes known what his desire is for them. His desire for them is that they may come into such a knowledge of their relationship to God that in spite of the fact that he is going to leave them, and in spite of the fact that the world is going to hate and persecute them, they will not be shaken.

There was never anything more practical than this, because the only ultimate strength and hope and consolation that the Christian gospel offers to anybody in this world is just that of understanding the plan of salvation and knowing our relationship to God. And there is no question about this in practice. I have certainly observed during many years in the Christian ministry and as a pastor that, generally speaking, most of the problems and difficulties which people have are due to the fact that they have not taken a firm hold of this great doctrine. As we have seen, it is subjectivity that accounts for our troubles, because we only look to ourselves. But once a man sees himself as part of this great plan, most of his problems are solved almost automatically. So that is why we are going on to consider some of the detailed aspects of the plan of salvation as it is revealed in these five verses in particular.

Having said that the plan of salvation reveals the character of God, I want to put to you, as my next proposition, that salvation is something which has been entirely planned by God, and that this is something which is suggested here on the very surface: 'Thou hast given him power over all flesh, that he should give eternal life . . . . I have finished the work which thou gavest me to do.' That is the first thing, therefore, that we have to take hold of. Salvation, if we may so put it, is entirely the idea of God; it emanates from and has its source and origin in God the Father. Now this is a staggering thought! So often you and I feel we have to placate God because of sin, sin in us, sin in our mind and whole outlook and thought, and sin in the world. We tend to think of God as being opposed and antagonistic to us, and therefore we are always thinking of him as someone we have to appease and placate. We regard God as Someone who is unwilling to be kind and gracious to us and to love us. We think of him as Someone in the far distance in his eternal glory and absolute righteousness who is not well disposed towards us. We feel we have to put forward these great efforts in order to get him to look upon us with favour.

That is a complete fallacy. Salvation has all originated in the mind of God—it is God's own purpose. I go so far as to say that even the Lord Jesus Christ does not have to placate God. Sometimes our hymns can be rather dangerous, and there are certain of them that would lead us to the conclusion that the Son of God has to plead with the Father to have mercy and pity upon us. But that is a gross misunderstanding of the term 'Advocate', it is something that is absolutely foreign to biblical teaching. Rather, the Bible teaches that 'God was in Christ, reconciling the world unto himself, not imputing their trespasses unto them' (2 Cor 5:19); 'God so loved the world, that *he gave* his only begotten Son . . .' (Jn 3:16). It is all from God. So this idea that the Lord Jesus Christ is at great pains to persuade God the Father to forgive and accept us is utterly unscriptural and entirely false; the source and origin of salvation is the great and eternal heart of God.

But we go from that to this further point. It is not only God's idea, we see here that it has been perfectly planned from the very beginning to the very end. Here we come to something that is the source of the deepest assurance and consolation that any Christian person can ever know in this world of time. What could be more comforting and reassuring than the fact that there is nothing contingent about this salvation, nothing accidental, nothing that needs modification? It is a perfect plan. God has planned it from eternity, before the foundation of the world, it is eternally in the mind of God. There is nothing, therefore, that is accidental about this. It never needs to be modified, or changed or altered in any respect. Here again is a point at which so many have gone astray. There are those who believe and even teach— you will find it in the case of a certain well-known Bible— that God sent his Son into this world to found and establish a kingdom, but because the Jews rejected him, God had to modify his plan; he had to introduce this way of salvation and so the church was brought into being and ultimately, at some future time, the kingdom will be introduced. They believe that it was all a modification of God's original plan. But that, I say, is a theory without the slightest vestige of a basis in Scripture. Scripture, rather, teaches that this plan was worked out before the foundation of the world, before a single man was ever born. And we find this here in these words. 'Father, the hour is come.' What hour? The hour that God had determined. You see that the whole purpose is to be found in that one word—'the hour'. We shall return to this, so for the moment I merely note it in passing, in order to deduce from it this great truth that the plan of God is absolutely complete, and was complete, even before the world was created.

But let us just glance at this time element in order that we may have it firmly in our minds. The plan was there, but it has been revealed in parts, and the great emphasis in the Bible is that everything is always, absolutely on time, with never a second or a moment's delay. Every item has been fixed, everything happens at its appropriate moment. The promise at the beginning was given at the right moment, the flood came at a particular point, and warning was given to mankind: 'My spirit shall not always strive with man' (Gen 6:3). He is still doing the same now, but there is an end, there is a limit to it. A time is coming when God will judge the world, and he fixes a time when it is to happen. The call of Abraham was not something accidental, it was done at a precise moment. It was to Abraham that the statement was made that certain things should not happen until the iniquity of the Amorites should be completed. The going down to Egypt was not accidental, it was prophesied, and Abraham was told exactly how long they would be there—430 years— before it ever happened. All these things were perfectly planned because God has his time, God has his exact moment.

But let us come to Moses, to whom the promise was given just at the time when it was necessary, and, again, the promise was given to David in his day. You certainly find this argument employed in the writings of the prophets. They foretell these things with a minuteness and an exactness which to the natural man is quite astonishing, but when we realize that it was God who laid down that great plan in eternity—that everything was determined and everything planned so that things should happen in order for this great design—there is no difficulty at all about it. To anybody who realizes this, it is rather what you would expect, and it is exactly what you find in the Scriptures. And then, of course, there is the well-known verse in Paul's epistle to the Galatians: 'When the fullness of the time was come, God sent forth his Son, made of a woman, made under the law . . .' (Gal 4:4).

Now people often ask the question—'Why didn't Christ come earlier? Why did he come at that particular point?' Well, though we cannot answer this question in detail, we can say that there are many reasons why that was the right time. God had given his law to his own people. Men always want to claim that they can save themselves, so God gave them time to see and understand that they cannot do so. He gave them a perfect law and said, If you keep that you will be saved; you will be righteous in my sight. He allowed them to try to do that for at least fourteen centuries, but they failed completely. And he also allowed the great succession of Greek philosophers to come and put their thoughts before man. Men said, 'Give us the right idea and we will carry it out.' They tried to, but they failed. The same thing happened with the Romans and their legal system—all that had been tried and failed before God's hour arrived, the hour that had been planned in eternity.

I commend this to you as a fascinating study, apart from the wonderful spiritual truth. As you read through the Old Testament try to put yourself in the position of that anicent race and you will often feel that God had forgotten his own people and his plan of salvation. But every time you begin to think that, and feel that the enemy was triumphant all along the line, God does something again, and you will find that it is not only the exact moment but also the exact thing for the exact moment. It is always the case—and there is nothing that is so comforting as this thought—'The Lord reigneth; let the earth rejoice'; 'The Lord reigneth; let the people tremble' (Ps 97:1;99:1). We must get hold of this truth that the whole plan is already made in the mind of God. It is because of this that the Son of God can turn to his Father at this particular point and say, 'Father, the hour is come', the hour that we originally agreed about is at hand. He had been preparing his disciples for it, as we see, both in John 12 and even earlier than that at the wedding in Cana, when he said, 'Mine hour is not yet come.' The time was all determined, and planned.

But we do not stop at that—thank God for this—for the end is likewise planned and certain. There are many Christian people today who are asking questions. Why does God allow the church to languish? Why does he allow certain things to happen in the church? Why does he allow this liberal criticism of the Bible that has been going on for a hundred years? Why doesn't he put a stop to all this? Well, that is not God's way, but there is one thing about which we can be certain, and that is that God reigns; and those who may be perplexed about the state of the church here or any-where else under the sun need not trouble and worry and vex their righteous souls. God reigns! God is still seated there in the heavens and he looks upon the citizens of the earth as grasshoppers. What he has determined is going to be carried out; the hour and the end of history and the world is deter-mined. God knows it, but nobody else knows the hour, says Christ, no, no man, not even the Son, but the Father only and he knows it. And if you are not comforted and en-couraged by that, well I doubt whether you are a Christian at all. The consolation of the glorious biblical affirmations—that neither death nor life nor anything else can separate us from the love of God—rests upon the fact that everything is purposed and planned in the mind of God who sees the end from the beginning and whose power is such that no one can withstand it. He can even take up a man like Pharaoh and use him like clay to bring his own great purpose to pass.

So let us now, with reverence, look into this plan in a little more detail. I like to take a glimpse into it and I am going to do something now that some of you may regard as strange and odd. I am going to ask you to come with me and look into the Council that was held in eternity, the great Council that was held between the Father and the Son and the Holy Spirit. What was it all about? It was about this very question of salvation, and what happened there was that the Son, the second Person in the blessed Trinity was given an assign-ment; he was appointed the heir of all things. See him re-minding his Father of that eternal Council here: 'As thou has given him [the Son] power over all flesh, that he should give eternal life to as many as thou hast given him . . .' Let us look into these things with wondering gaze, with amaze-ment and astonishment and remember, as we are doing it, that we are really in a sense still thinking about ourselves, because that Council was held with respect to us.

So the first thing we see here is that contemplating what was going to happen to man and to the world, seeing the entry of sin and the fall, this eternal Council decided what should be done about it. And the first great decision was that this matter should be handed over specifically to the Son. It is the purpose of God, says Paul in Ephesians 1:10, that all things should be wound up in Christ, 'that in the dispensation of the fullness of times'—you see the time element again —'he [the Father] might gather together in one all things in Christ, both which are in heaven, and which are on earth; even in him.' In other words, the Lord Jesus Christ, in that Council, was appointed as the head of mankind. He was made responsible for the world, a kind of head and representative of all the earth and its peoples. He himself told us this at the end after he had risen, when he said to the disciples: 'All power is given unto me in heaven and in earth' (Mt 28:18).

Now this is one of those crucial principles which we must never fail to understand, one which throws great light upon many an obscure incident in the Old Testament which otherwise cannot be understood. Take, for instance, those appearances to men of the so-called 'Angel of the Lord'. There can be no question at all but that these are the appearances of the Lord Jesus Christ—what are called the 'theophanies'. He was interested in the world even then; it had all been given to him; that was why the world came to be created, it was in him and through him and by him. He is the One in eternity who is deputed to do this particular task. And the record, in a sense, is the record of our Lord carrying out this great task that had thus been given to him. That is the explanation, too, of John's vision in Revelation 5. John is perplexed that no one is big enough or strong enough to open the books—the books of history—then suddenly he sees the Lion of the tribe of Judah stepping forward and the whole of heaven seems to applaud. At last there is One who is big enough and strong enough to take complete charge of history and to break the seals and to open the books. He is the Lord of history, yes, it has already been given to him, and it belongs to him.

So, then, we must look at it like this, that everything with respect to this world and to man has been handed over to the Lord Jesus Christ. He has been given this authority, this power over all flesh. He rules and reigns and controls everything that is in the world—the sun, the moon and the stars, the rivers and the streams—that is why he can hold back or send the rain and the thunder storms. He can produce an earthquake. He is controlling everything, for everything has been put into his hands. He is the Governor of the earth. He is in charge of the kingdom and he will remain in charge right on to the end when, according to Paul in 1 Corinthians 15, he will finally finish the work, and hand the kingdom back to his Father.

But I must not stop at that. God had not only, in that eternal Council, handed over the world and its powers to the Son, he has also given him a people. I wonder how often you have stopped to consider the second verse of this chapter of John, and how often you have battled with its tremendous doctrine? I wonder what you have made of it. 'As thou hast given him power over all flesh, that he should give eternal life to as many as thou hast given him.' Does he say, 'As thou hast given him power over all flesh, that he should give eternal life to all flesh'? No—'that he should give eternal life to *as many as thou hast given him*'. The universal and the particular are both here in one verse. This is indeed high doctrine, so high that no human can understand it, but so high and glorious, that every man who has the mind of Christ in himself, bows before it in humble reverence, in amazement and in astonishment.

Scriptural teaching is that while God has given to his Son power over all flesh, without any limits whatsoever, he has in particular given him a special people who are to enjoy the blessings of Christian salvation and eternal life. He has to give eternal life to as many as God the Father has given him, but what I am emphasizing here is that it is God the Father who has given him these people. He gave him these particular people who are coming into the church and into eternal life, from the very beginning to the very end. All of them were given to the Son, there in that eternal Council. It is God who chooses them, and, according to John 6, it is God who draws them to him, for unless, Jesus says, God does draw them to him, they will never come. 'All that the Father giveth me shall come to me; and him that cometh to me I will in no wise cast out . . . And this is the will of him that sent me, that every one which seeth the Son, and believeth on him, may have everlasting life: and I will raise him up at the last day' (Jn 6:37,40).

This is something that you find running right through these Scriptures. God, from before the creation of the world, had chosen these people. He gives these particular people to his Son, and he says, I give them to you for you to save them for me. 'Those whom thou hast given unto him'—that was another decision of this great and eternal Council.

But, you see, it is even more particular than that, for God the Father prescribes the particular work the Son has to do in order to save these people. The Lord says, 'I have glorified thee on the earth: I have finished the work which thou gavest me to do.' I propose to come back to this again and to look at it in more detail, but all I am emphasizing at this point is that the work of saving these individuals was given by the Father to the Son. Thus we find our Lord constantly saying that he does nothing of himself. He says in effect, 'I am simply doing the work which the Father has shown me and given me to do.' It all comes from God the Father, who then sends the Son into the world to do it—to give the Father back the glory that the Son had with him before he ever sent him. But it was God the Father who sent him, for 'God so loved the world that he gave his only begotten Son'—his Son, with power to save. And the purpose of it all, I would remind you again, was that you and I might become the children of God; that we might have this eternal life which is to know God, the only true and living God, and Jesus Christ whom he has sent into the world in order to bring us to this blessed knowledge.

My dear friends, are we not guilty of neglecting this glorious doctrine of the glory of God and the plan of salvation in eternity? Evangelical Christians, how often have *you* meditated about these things? Do you not think that we have been guilty of judging particular aspects of salvation instead of regarding this glorious plan? This is why we are so superficial and why we are so shaken in our faith when adversity comes to try us. Our faith is not sufficiently broadly based—we must go back into eternity.

Let me summarize the message by putting it like this— what I deduce from this doctrine is that the eternal God knows us and is interested in us and has a plan for us. If that is not enough for you, then I despair! The astounding thing I find here is that the eternal and absolute God knows me, that he thought of me before the foundation of the world, not only before I was born, but before he even made the world; that this eternal, absolute Being is interested in me, even me, as an individual and as a person, and that I was in his mind when he conceived this amazing plan that includes the incarnation and the cross, and the resurrection and the ascension, and the reign of his Son at his side that is going on now. What a staggering, yes, but what a glorious thought!

The next thing I deduce is that there is therefore nothing uncertain about my acceptance with God, nor about my forgiveness, nor about my sonship. When I realize that I have been brought into God's plan I know that nothing can frustrate this. Now there are many people who talk about the Protestant Reformation, and the influence it had upon the world. You find that certain statesmen do this. They say you cannot explain the history of England apart from the

Protestant Reformation. Neither, they say, can you explain the United States of America apart from these things, because they all had their origin in that Reformation. But how little do these people really see what it all means and what it really represents, which is that these great truths are absolute and certain. Do you know why the Pilgrim Fathers made that attempt, and succeeded in crossing the Atlantic? What was it that enabled men to do things like that, and to do things which were even more hazardous? It was that they believed in what is called the 'Doctrine of the Perseverance of the Saints', it was because they had seen themselves in the plan of God which cannot be broken and which cannot fail. It is as absolute as God, himself; he knows the end as well as the beginning. 'Neither shall any man,' said Christ, 'pluck them out of my hand.' It is unthinkable.

So the next deduction is: if God has done all this for us in Christ, and especially in his death, we can be certain that he will carry on with the work until it is completed. That is Paul's argument: 'He that spared not his own Son, but delivered him up for us all, how shall he not with him also freely give us all things?' (Rom 8:32). 'If, when we were enemies, we were reconciled to God by the death of his Son, much more, being reconciled, we shall be saved by his life' (Rom 5:10). Let me put it like this: God, who is sufficiently concerned about me to send his Son to die on the cross of Calvary for me, is not going to let me down when any difficulty or temptation faces me. My dear friends, there is *nothing* for you to fear! You belong to One of whom we are told that all power has been given to him over all flesh. You are in the hands of the Lord Jesus Christ if you but knew and realised it, and he controls everything. He controls every human being, all the affairs of nature, he is even controlling the devil himself. All power is given unto him, thrones, dominions, principalities and powers are subject unto him, so you need never fear! You and I have but to realize that we are in those mighty hands, that that strong arm is engaged

on our behalf, that all flesh   under his power, and that all
authority in heaven and on earth has been given to him.

Therefore, when you are troubled and perplexed and har-
rassed, and when all things seem to be against you and you
despair, when you pray to him, before you say a word, just
remind yourself of his authority and of his power: 'As thou
hast given him power over all flesh . . .' He that has formed
you has a power like that, and therefore, being in his safe
keeping, why should you fear man or beast or the powers of
nature or of hell? Simply trust in him, he has so loved you
that he has died for you, and his power on your behalf is
indisputable.

5

The Lord Jesus Christ, the Lord of Glory

John 17:1–5

We have been considering the way in which we see in these five verses the particular glory of the Father being revealed in salvation, and now we take a step forward and come on to consider the way in which our salvation has actually been produced. We have looked at it in the eternal Council and as God planned it, and as he set aside and separated his Son for the work. We now look at something of the detail of the way in which this was planned and conceived and was put into practice, so that we are looking especially at the glory of God in salvation as it is revealed in the person of the Son. And again, the same thing will strike us, namely, this emphasis upon the *glory*. It all has to do with the glory of the eternal Godhead. We have seen the glory of the Father, and we are now looking at the glory of the Son, and here again in an extraordinary manner we have before us this wondrous panorama, as it were, of the whole movement of salvation with regard to the Son himself.

Now this is something which is staggering not only to the mind but even to the imagination. The whole sweep of salvation is unfolded here and displayed before us from glory back to glory and it is all in the compass of these few verses. So we approach a subject like this with a sense of awe and wonder and adoration.

And as we do so, shall we not honestly admit that perhaps one of the greatest lacks in our modern Christianity—and here I speak not only of the church in general, but also, if we are to be quite honest, even of many of us who claim to be evangelical—that perhaps the greatest lack in our worship and practice of the Christian faith is the absence of a sense of wonder, a sense of adoration and a sense of worship. I have no doubt at all that this is very largely to be explained by the fact that we are so subjective. I have said this ever since we started considering this chapter, and I propose to go on saying it, because it seems to me to be one of the great lessons which we do need to learn especially at this present time. We are all too interested in our own moods and states and conditions; we are all too psychological and introspective, and too concerned, therefore, about the benefits that the Christian gospel and salvation have to give to us. And the result of this is that we miss something of these great glories of the gospel as it is unfolded in the New Testament itself. This comes out very clearly if we listen to one another; have you not noticed how there is a tendency to be talking about ourselves? We are always telling people what has happened to us. 'Testimony' today generally means what we have experienced, or what has happened to us. How rarely do we speak about him!

Now there is the lack and the need. If you read the lives of the saints who have gone before us in this world, you will find that they spent most of their time in talking together about Jesus Christ. Their testimony was a testimony to him, and to his praise. Their emphasis was upon him. They spoke about this wonderful Christ and the glory of his person, whereas we always tend to talk about ourselves, the things that we have found, the happiness that we have discovered, or some experience that we have had. And I think if we are honest we will find that the emphasis is always more or less centred upon self.

We have deviated very far indeed from what was so true

of the saints of the centuries. Take, too, your hymn books and read the great hymns, especially, perhaps, the hymns that were written before the middle of the last century. (The subjective element seems to have come in just about then.) Start with Isaac Watts and come down the great succession and you will find they have this glorious objectivity. They rejoiced in their experiences, yes, but the note you find outstanding in their hymns is always their praise of the Lord, their glorying in *him*. With Isaac Watts they surveyed the wondrous cross on which the Prince of glory died. That is the predominant thought. They always spent their time in worship and adoration and in the glorification of him.

It seems to me that this is the note that we must recapture, and that there is no real hope for revival and true awakening until we come back to this. And the way to do that is to study the Scriptures, to spend our time in reading and meditating upon them and then in humbling ourselves in worship and in adoration before such a marvellous truth. Now I am saying this not merely in a theoretical manner for I am anxious to be extremely practical. No, I advocate this because, apart from anything else, the real cure for most of our subjective ills is ultimately to be so enraptured by the beauty and the glory of Christ that we will forget ourselves and will not have time to think about ourselves at all. Now that is a good bit of psychology. The trouble with our generation, and let us not be too hard on ourselves, is that we are living in a very difficult age. We have had to face problems which mankind has scarcely ever had to face in such an acute form, and such an age always tends to produce morbidity, a concern about oneself. We are living such a ridiculous type of life that our nerves are tired and frayed, and as a result we are all of us concerned about self, and the great problem is how to get away from it. The high road to that is to be so absorbed by someone else, something outside oneself, which is so glorious and wonderful that, without knowing it, we forget all about ourselves. This can happen as you look at some marvellous scenery, or fall in love and forget yourself; well, multiply that by infinity and look into the face of Jesus Christ and catch something of his glory, and I assure you that most of the 'mumps and measles of the soul' will automatically be cured, and you will find yourself in a healthy condition, mentally, spiritually and even psychologically.

But even more important than that is the fact that God has caused these Scriptures to be written in order that we may know something about this great salvation, 'so great salvation', as the New Testament describes it in Hebrews 2. I wonder whether we modern Christians realize the greatness of this Christian salvation as we ought, because if we do not, the way to do so is to learn something about the greatness of the glory of the person of our Lord and Saviour Jesus Christ. That is the way to measure the greatness of the salvation, not just by something that happens to us. Let us deliver ourselves from that! For if we are going to measure our salvation by what has happened to us, I suggest that finally we have no answer at all to give to the Christian Scientists, nor to the psychologists. If you make it subjective, you are still in the past. No, the way to measure the greatness of this salvation is to look at the greatness of the person and his glory and to realize something of what he has done.

Now this is the very thing that is shown to us in these verses. Look at the movement, beginning at verse 5: 'And now, O Father,' he says at the end of his earthly life, 'glorify thou me with thine own self with the glory which I had with thee before the world was.' That is the starting point. You just try to consider and contemplate this amazing and glorious person before he ever came to earth. You do not start with the babe in Bethlehem, that was not the beginning of his life. He *came* into this world, he was not born into it in the way that everybody else has been born into it. He came from the glory. He entered into this world from another world, and what he himself says here is precisely what is said everywhere else in Scripture, that he came out of the eternal, everlasting glory of the Godhead. He also says here that he shared that essential glory of the eternal God from all eternity —'Glorify thou me now with thine own self with the glory which I had with thee before the world was.'

Once again we must admit that we are trying to look at something which transcends the reason and the grasp of our finite minds. But it is the teaching of the Scriptures—the eternal triune God, the Father, Son and Holy Spirit, yet but one God, and this Son of God, the Second Person in the Trinity is sharing in all the fullness of that glory. As the author of the epistle to the Hebrews puts it, 'Who being the brightness of his glory, and the express image of his person' —that is the description of the Lord Jesus Christ. He is the effulgence of the glory of the Father, the express image of his person. Paul, in Philippians 2, expresses the same truth when he says, 'Who, being in the form of God, thought it not robbery to be equal with God.' He is, to use an old phrase, self-substantial, co-equal, co-eternal with the Father. He is the eternal Son in the eternal bosom of the Father, one with God, the Second Person in the blessed, holy Trinity. 'In the beginning was the Word, and the Word was with God, and the Word was God'—that is it. He shared in full the ineffable, indescribable glory of the eternal Godhead. That is the way you start thinking about the Lord Jesus Christ.

So, then, the next step, obviously, is this: he prays that God the Father will glorify him again with that glory which he had with him before the world was, the implication being that something has happened to that glory. And that is precisely the teaching of the New Testament. In order to become man he laid aside this eternal glory which he had with the Father in heaven. Let us be careful here, and let us be quite sure that we know exactly what we are saying. I am not saying that he laid aside his deity, because he did not. What he did lay aside was the glory of his deity. He did not cease to be God, but he ceased to manifest the glory of God.

Perhaps the best way of understanding this is to consider what happened on the Mount of Transfiguration when he was transfigured before Peter and James and John. A kind of radiance came upon him, surpassing anything that had ever been seen before by those disciples. Now contrast that with what he normally appeared to be. Or again, take the case of Saul of Tarsus going down to Damascus. He suddenly saw a light in the heavens brighter than the shining of the sun itself, and he saw it came from a face, that of this glorified Jesus of Nazareth (Acts 9). Now you see exactly what is described here.

Again, contrast that glory with what we are told about him when he was here on earth: 'There is no beauty that we should desire him . . . a man of sorrows, and acquainted with grief' (Is 53:2–3). People would look at him and say, Who is this fellow? 'Is not this the carpenter, the son of Mary?' (Mk 6:3). He had laid aside the glory, he had not laid aside anything of his essential being or person or of his essential deity. But neither had he held on to it, he had not clutched at the manifestation of his glory, he had laid that aside as one would a cloak and had come in the likeness of man. Indeed, I must go much further than this, because this is the wonder of it all. He decided that his glory should be veiled by flesh. Think of it like this: the glory is there still shining in all its power, but a veil of flesh has come over it so that mankind cannot see it. Take an Old Testament illustration. In the wilderness Moses went on to the Mount and spoke with God, and when he came down his face was shining. The people saw the glory and it was so bright that he had to put a veil over his face; the glory was still there but it was hidden from them. Something like that happened to our Lord. Yes, but he not only came as man, nor is it only true to say that his glory was veiled by flesh. It is not true to say simply that the eternal Son of God was made flesh. We are told that he was made 'in the likeness of sinful flesh' (Rom 8:3). Indeed, he not only came into this world as a man, he took on him the 'form of a servant' (Phil 2:7). It would have been a wonderful and astounding thing if this eternal King and Prince of glory had come on earth and lived in a palace as a human king with all the pomp and glory of an earthly kingship—but not at all! He was born as a babe in very poor circumstances. Mary and Joseph did not have the money to offer the usual offering. They could only offer two turtle doves when he was born. He worked as a carpenter and he had to earn his living. He did not have a home he could claim for himself, or a place to lay down his head. He took upon himself the form of a servant and was dismissed and derided by the so-called great ones of this world of time; he stooped as low as that from the height of the glory from which he had come. Thus here on earth, in a sense, he had not that glory and he asked his Father to restore that glory to him.

There is no better way of saying all this than to put it in the words of Charles Wesley's hymn—and how foolish we are to think that such hymns were only meant for special seasons of the year!

> Veiled in flesh the Godhead see!
> Hail, the Incarnate Deity.

or again:

> Mild, He lays His glory by;
> Born, that man no more may die.

Look at these paradoxes, these tremendous contrasts, but it is all the simple and literal truth. He thus mildly lays aside his glory and comes right down to earth, takes on human nature, lives as man in the likeness of sinful flesh and in the form of a servant. In these things we behold the amazing descent from the glory.

The next thing we are told is that we must look at his work here on earth, which really is that of glorifying the Father. He did this in many ways. He says here, 'I have glorified thee on the earth,' and in doing that, of course, he, in a sense, manifested his own glory, veiled in flesh. He revealed and declared the Father by just being what he was. He said on one occasion, 'He that hath seen me hath seen the Father' (Jn 14:9); look at him and you see something of the glorious God, the Father himself. You see the eye of compassion, the understanding, the readiness to help and to bless.

If only we could see the Father, said Philip on one occasion: 'Lord, shew us the Father, and it sufficeth us.'

And the Lord turned to him and said, 'Have I been so long time with you, and yet hast thou not known me, Philip? he that hath seen me hath seen the Father . . .' (Jn 14:8–9). In other words, he manifested the Father and the glory of the Father in his life and all his activities and in being what he was.

But then he also does the same thing, of course, in his teaching. There was never such teaching concerning God the Father as fell from the lips of our blessed Lord and Saviour Jesus Christ. Man's ideas of God are always incomplete and imperfect, even the Old Testament revelation was not enough. As the author of the epistle to the Hebrews puts it, God has revealed this truth concerning himself in parts here and there—'in time past unto the Fathers by the prophets'— but now he has revealed it in his Son, perfect, final, full and complete. It is all there in this wonderful person, the blessed Lord and Saviour Jesus Christ—and in all his teaching and all his references concerning the Father we find all this revealed.

But then he did it in a still more striking way by doing the work which the Father had sent him to do—'I have finished the work which thou gavest me to do'—and what was the work? First and foremost, he kept the law himself. God had given his law to mankind and he had told them to keep it, in order to glorify him. The whole spirit of the law is that we should glorify God; it is not merely to keep a number of rules and regulations, doing this and not doing that. The real object of the law is that mankind might be taught and shown how to glorify God. But mankind had failed, and so the first thing the Son was sent to do was to honour and keep the law, and thus to glorify God, and he did it perfectly. It was an essential part of his work.

Not only that, he came in order that he might be a perfect High Priest to represent those redeemed people whom God the Father had given to him. In Hebrews 5 we are told a very remarkable thing about our blessed Lord in that respect. We are told that 'learned he obedience by the things which he suffered'. The Lord Jesus Christ, the Lord of glory, had to be taught certain things before he could become a perfect High Priest and to represent us in the presence of God. He came into this world in order to be the Captain of our salvation, our Leader, and he had to be prepared for that work and to go through this process. He had to be tempted in all points even as we are in order that he might succour us when we are tempted and be a sympathetic and understanding High Priest. He came down from the realms of glory and sub-mitted himself to all that, and as he was doing it, he was not only showing something of his own glory, he was showing us the glory of the Father who had ever planned such a way of salvation.

What an amazing and astounding thing this is! Oh, my friends, as we read these gospels we must always be remind-ing ourselves of that. Look at it in detail, look at the life of our Lord Jesus Christ and remember that this is the Lord of glory. Remember that this is the One who is the brightness of the Father's glory, the express image of his person. But look at him in the manger, or upon the Mount, suffering hunger and thirst; the Lord of glory, mildly laying by his glory and thus living life in this world as a man, being pre-pared to be the Captain of our salvation.

But now we come to one of the most remarkable things of all. In the first verse we read, 'Father, the hour is come; glorify thy Son, that thy Son also may glorify thee.' Is this the same petition as that in verse 5: 'And now, O Father, glorify thou me with thine own self with the glory which I had with thee before the world was'?

I suggest to you that it is not the same thing, and that the two petitions do not have reference to precisely the same matter. I think that the petition in verse 1 means that the hour is come, he is about to die, about to face the greatest crisis of all. Oh, it was a mighty thing, transcending thought and imagination, for him to leave that glory, to be born as a babe and to take unto himself human nature. It was a tremendous thing for the eternal Son of God to be lying in the womb of a woman. All his trials and difficulties are something that we will never grasp and never understand in this world. And deeper and greater and beyond it all was this trial that he was now about to endure, the cross and all that it meant. So here, living life as a man, he prays to the Father, 'Father, glorify thy Son', by which he means, Strengthen me, enable me to show and to give proof of the fact that I am your Son. Again, in Hebrews 5, we are told that he prayed with crying and strong tears unto God to hold him and strengthen him, and we are also told there that he was heard because of his reverence and godly fear, and his beautiful piety.

And this means that he realized what he was about to do. He realized that the moment was coming when the weight of the world's sins were to be put upon him, when he was to bear the staggering load of the guilt of the whole of mankind, that the Father had placed upon him, and it was an overwhelming thought. Would his human nature, as it were, crack and break under it? Could he stand this load, could he stand the thought of losing sight of his Father's face as he was made sin for man, and as he bore the sin and punishment of man? Father, he says, strengthen me, hold me, prove to the world that I am your Son, glorify your Son in this world. That is the meaning of the petition in the first verse, and the prayer was answered. Oh yes, he came from the highest heaven of glory, and, as I have reminded you, was born as man, made flesh, made in the likeness of sinful flesh. He took on him the form of a servant. He endured the contradiction of sinners against himself. And, as Paul says in Philippians 2, he became obedient unto death, even the death of the cross. He was crucified and nailed upon a tree, there is no deeper death than that—

> From the highest realms of glory
> To the Cross of deepest woe.

He asked that the Father would enable and strengthen him and his Father heard his prayer. He was glorified, he was strengthened and he was enabled, so that at the end he was able to say, 'It is finished.' He had borne it all; it had not crushed him; the body had not cracked under it. The work was done, he had accomplished everything: 'Father,' he said, 'into thy hands I commend my spirit.'

Then, secondly, comes the petition in verse 5. The Lord is still looking to what is before him, and this is his prayer. Having completed all the work, having done everything which the Father had appointed him to do, he asks, as it were: Has not the time now arrived when I can come back to you, exactly where I was before? I have done the work. 'Father, glorify thou me with thine own self with the glory which I had with thee before the world was.' But the astonishing thing for us to remember at this point is that he goes back as God-Man! In eternity he was God the Son, pure deity, and he shared the glory, but now he goes back as God-Man. And as God-Man, and our representative, the glory which he momentarily laid aside at the request of the Father is restored to him, and thus as God-Man and Mediator he again shares this ineffable glory of the eternal God.

And so this prayer, too, was answered. It began to be answered at the resurrection, the event which finally convinced even the disciples that he was the Son of God. They did not quite understand it before, but, as Paul puts it in

writing to the Romans, our Lord was, 'declared to be the
Son of God with power, according to the spirit of holiness,
by the resurrection from the dead' (Rom 1:4). Who is this
who has conquered death and the grave? He must be, he is,
the Son of God. Consider the appearances after the resurrection. You find the disciples in Jerusalem behind locked doors
because they were afraid of the Jews, and suddenly he came
in without the door being opened. They thought it was a
ghost. But he showed that he was not by asking them to give
him something to eat. So they gave him 'a piece of a broiled
fish and of an honeycomb'. 'You see who I am,' he says in
effect, 'I have flesh and bones, and I can eat'—the glorious
person of this risen Lord.

Then perhaps still more strikingly we see it in the
ascension. Many of us do not observe Ascension Day, do
we? We are a little inconsistent in this; we observe
Christmas, Good Friday, and Easter Sunday! We observe
Whit Sunday, but we do not observe Ascension Day, and it
is a very essential part in all this movement of God's plan.
His disciples were with him on the Mount and while he was
speaking, he was lifted up and he ascended into heaven. His
glory was manifested in a most amazing manner there. And
then he manifested it still more by sending the gift of his
Holy Spirit on the Day of Pentecost. It is a proof that he is
the Son of God, the Messiah, this glorious being. And there
he is now, sitting at the right hand of God in the glory,
reigning until all his enemies shall be made his footstool.

And so I have tried to hold before you something of the
glory which is depicted in these five verses, from the glory,
down to the depths of the cross and to Hades, and back again
via the ascension to that ineffable glory once more, and he
now takes human nature with him. But why has he done all
this? I can imagine someone saying, 'My dear Sir, this is all
very well, you know. If we were living in a leisurely world
and had no business and no cares and no worries and trials
perhaps we could take all these remarks objectively. But we

want something that will help us now, here and now in the immediate present, have you not something to say to us?'

I hope nobody feels like that after what we have just been considering? I have just been reminding you of what the eternal Son of God has done for you, that you might be saved from the wrath of God and from hell, and from sin, and from yourself. He has done it that you might become a son of God, that you might begin to enjoy 'a joy unspeakable and full of glory', and that you might receive the Holy Spirit with all his power and might. That is what it is all about. If you feel that all I have been saying is something theoretical and remote, it is because you do not understand, because you are not related to it, and because you do not realize it has all been done for you. That is the greatness of the glory; he has done all this for us.

> From the highest realms of glory,
> To the Cross of deepest woe,
> All to ransom guilty captives
> Flow my praise, for ever flow.

And then I turn to him and say—

> Go, return, Immortal Saviour,
> Leave Thy footstool, take Thy throne,
> Thence return and reign for ever,
> Be the Kingdom all Thine own.

That is the true reaction to the things we have been considering together. He did it all to ransom guilty captives, and if you realize that he has done that for you, you will agree with Robert Robinson when he wrote these words: 'Is your praise flowing? Do you praise the Lord Jesus Christ? Do you praise him to other people; do you talk to them about him?' People talk today about those whom they like and admire. I read of them praising actors and actresses and all sorts of politicians and people; you see it in the newspapers, and you have to listen to them when you are trying to read in a railway compartment. But do we praise the Lord Jesus Christ? If we do not it is because we do not realize what he has done for us. Again, I would agree with Robert Robinson when he says—'Break my tongue, such guilty silence.'

Oh, my dear friends, if you do not realize the glory of these things, hasten to God and confess it. Ask him so to give you his Holy Spirit that your eyes will be opened to these precious, glorious truths. The Holy Spirit was sent in order to make these things real to us. If we but realized these things then we would inevitably be praising with the whole of our being, and our whole life would be to his praise. The Holy Spirit will enable us to realize these glorious things. He will so imprint and impress them upon mind and heart and understanding that they will be real to us, so real that finally we shall be able to join Paul in saying, 'To me to live is Christ.'

6

Antidote to Introspection

John 17:1–5

We have been looking together in some detail at the first five verses in this chapter because we have suggested that in them we have a wonderful display of the scheme of salvation. I also suggested that it was good for us to be looking at this, because it is undoubtedly the most important thing that anybody can ever grasp in this life and world. The one message which the gospel of Jesus Christ has to give to the world outside the church is the message concerning the way of salvation. But we must never forget that it is also always the central message which is needed by the church herself, because we have considered together the fact that, even having believed the gospel, we often find ourselves spending our Christian life in what may be called 'shallows and miseries'. We often seem to be living a life which is full of problems and perplexities, without much happiness and joy, a life, as it were, of struggling, of barely succeeding and barely avoiding defeat. The main explanation of that, when it is true, is that in one way or another we have ceased to look at and to realize the truth about this great plan of salvation as it is unfolded in the Bible.

There can be no doubt at all but that one of the besetting temptations and sins of the average Christian is the tendency to be looking in a wrong way at oneself. Now it is true that

the Bible is full of exhortations to us to examine ourselves
and to prove ourselves, yes, but there is all the difference in
the world between doing that in the right way, and becoming introspective. You are introspective when you spend the
whole of your time looking at yourself, looking inward, and
being concerned only and supremely about yourself. The
antidote to that, I suggest, is that we look again at the plan of
salvation as it is unfolded in the Bible. And here, in this
chapter, in the brief compass of these first five verses, we
find it clearly summarized. There are many additional
reasons why we should always be doing this. One all important one for us to remember here is that it is only as we
remind ourselves of this plan, both in its various parts and as
a whole, that we shall not only be able to counteract certain
doubts that may arise in our own minds, but, still more
important, we shall also be able to answer those who attack
our position and attack the Christian faith from the outside.

Now it is no final answer to one of the most subtle attacks
upon the Christian faith today simply to say that we have
experienced certain things, or that we are in a certain position
now. Many people take up that argument and they often
imagine that it is a cogent one. They turn to the world and
say, 'You can say what you like about the Bible, you can
criticize the Christian faith as much as you like, but you
cannot make any difference to me because I am happy. The
gospel has done this and that for me and as a result I am quite
immune to all your criticisms.' I know what such friends
mean when they say something like that, but it seems to me
that it is not only putting the Christian position at the very
lowest, but there is also a sense in which it does not begin to
meet the attack made upon the faith. For the fact is, of
course, that if we are going to base our position solely upon
what we feel, and what we are at this moment, then we have
nothing to say to the attack thus made upon the Christian
faith, especially by psychology.

There are many today who would explain all our faith in

terms of psychology. They claim it as a very clever and subtle form of self-persuasion, just a way of shifting your difficulties on to another plane. 'It is good psychology,' they say, 'and anything that makes a man happier is a good thing, in and of itself; Christians may use all these great terms, but actually it is nothing but a bit of psychology. As you know, there are many false teachings, such as Christian Science, which are quite unjustifiable, but which can make people very happy.'

So, then, if we base our position entirely upon experience, we will convince nobody. The answer to the good psychology argument is that we are dealing with certain historical events and facts which we must never allow ourselves to forget. Indeed, I am prepared to go as far as to say that whatever I may feel at this moment, though I may feel that I am in a state of darkness and blackness, and am utterly discouraged, my position is still safe and I am secure because of these things that have been done in history outside of me and before I was ever born. Thank God I do not base my position on how I feel. Feelings are treacherous, they come and go, and what little control we have upon them! We have all had the following experience, have we not? We wake up one morning and find ourselves full of peace and joy and happiness, and all seems to go well. We have a marvellous day, we read our Bibles, we have freedom in prayer, and all is well, so we look forward to the next day being still more wonderful. But, strangely enough, we find that when we wake up the next morning we are lifeless and dull. If you are going to base your whole position upon experience and feelings, you are going to be a very unhappy person and your Christian life is going to be very unstable. But the answer is, I repeat, this marvellous plan of salvation. I must, of course, know that I am related to it—that is essential—but what I am arguing for is that if you want to enjoy these blessings and if you want to live this Christian life truly, you do so by looking at these things, by resting upon them and by saying, if you like, in the words of a hymn:

> My hope is built on nothing less
> Than Jesus' Blood and Righteousness,
> I dare not trust my sweetest frame,
> But wholly lean on Jesus' Name.
> On Christ the solid rock I stand,
> All other ground is sinking sand.
>
> *Edward Mote*

That, then, is what we are doing by looking together at the plan and scheme as it is here unfolded. So far we have seen something like this. We have seen that the great object and intent of the plan of salvation is the glory of God, and if we do not see that first and foremost, then there is something wrong with our whole conception of salvation. If we look at salvation only in terms of ourselves or of something that happens to us, and do not see in it primarily the glory of the almighty God, then our view of salvation is grossly inadequate, indeed, it may even be a false one. It is the glory and the wonder of the triune God which our Lord emphasized and he is our supreme authority.

Now we have been looking at the plan in its different parts. We have seen that it originates with the Father. He planned and purposed it, and set it into operation in the eternal Council. Then we have seen how the work was divided, the Son was sent, a commission was given to him, and he accomplished the work to the glory of God the Father. And he himself, as we were considering in our last study, was glorified in the resurrection and the ascension, but the final manifestation of the glory of the Son was that which was given on the Day of Pentecost when the Holy Spirit was sent down upon the infant church gathered together at Jerusalem. That is the final proof of the fact that Jesus of Nazareth is the only begotten Son of God. The Scripture talks about the 'promise of the Father': the Father had promised the Children of Israel in the old dispensation that he would send his Spirit. He keeps on saying that he is going to make a new covenant with them, that the day is coming when he will take out their stony heart, give them a heart of flesh, and pour out his Spirit upon them. That is the thing to which they were looking forward, and, in a sense, the work of the Messiah, the Deliverer, the Saviour, was to send this promise of the Father. And that is the very thing that happened on the Day of Pentecost when the Lord Jesus Christ sent the Holy Spirit.

Now the Scripture uses two terms. In one place it tells us that the Lord Jesus Christ sent the Holy Spirit, and in another place it tells us that God the Father sent the Spirit after listening to the prayer of his Son, but it is the same thing, since the Spirit proceeds from the Father and from the Son. What I particularly want to emphasize at this point, however, is that this teaching is included even in these five verses that we are looking at in John 17: 'These words spake Jesus . . .' and then he began to pray. 'These words' refers to the words that are recorded in chapters 14, 15 and 16 of this particular gospel, which are all to do with this promise of the coming of the Holy Spirit. Our Lord began to speak about this in chapter 14. He found that the disciples were crestfallen because he had said that he was going to leave them, so he told them, 'I will pray the Father, and he shall give you another Comforter, that he may abide with you for ever; even the Spirit of truth; whom the world cannot receive, because it seeth him not, neither knoweth him: but ye know him; for he dwelleth with you, and shall be in you' (Jn 14:16–17). And he proceeded to teach them about the coming of the Holy Spirit.

So here, you see, in John 17:1, the coming of the Holy Spirit is introduced as a part of this great and vital plan of salvation, and it is, of course, one of the most wonderful aspects of all. There, in the Council in eternity, as we have already seen, God the Father, God the Son and God the Holy Spirit spoke together and planned the salvation of man; the

Father reiterated the great scheme, and the Son accepted the decision that he should be the one to carry out the plan; and then it was equally decided that the Holy Spirit should complete what the Son had done for mankind. This is what is sometimes called the 'economy of the Trinity', the division of the work between the three Persons, and it is something that appears very clearly right through the Scriptures. It appears, for example, in the very beginning, in Genesis, where we are shown how the creation itself was the work of the Trinity—'In the beginning God . . .' Then we are told that 'the Spirit moved . . .'; everything was made through the Word, but in a sense the agency was still the Spirit.

However, what I am anxious to look at now is the way in which this verse brings out the point. The Father sends the Son, and the great business of the Son is to glorify the Father. He says, 'I have glorified thee on the earth; I have finished the work which thou gavest me to do.' For there is a sense in which the Lord Jesus Christ never glorified himself. That is why he laid aside his glory, and why he was not born in a king's palace but in a stable. That, too, is why he took upon himself the form of a servant; it was all to glorify the Father. All his life as a man was in a sense lived just in this way, in order that all the glory and power might be of God the Father.

But here we are told another wonderful thing. After he went back to heaven, he sent upon the church the Holy Spirit, and the business and the work of the Holy Spirit is to glorify the Son. Now this is a marvellous statement. We do not see the Holy Spirit, he is invisible, and, in a sense, that is because his work is to glorify the Son. Indeed, we read about the Holy Spirit in John 16:14 the same thing that we read elsewhere about the Son. Our Lord says that the Holy Spirit does not speak of himself, but, 'He shall glorify me: for he shall receive of mine, and shall shew it unto you.' We are told precisely the same thing about the Son in relation to the Father. Therefore, the great controlling thought we must hold in our minds is that the chief work of the Holy Spirit is to glorify the Lord Jesus Christ.

In a sense, the final glorification of the Lord Jesus Christ was the coming of the Holy Spirit. We are told in John's gospel that the Holy Spirit was not yet come because Jesus was not yet glorified. We see this in the great promise our Lord made one day in the Temple when he said, 'If any man thirst, let him come unto me, and drink. He that believeth on me, as the scripture hath said, out of his belly shall flow rivers of living water' (Jn 7:37–38). And John expounds that: 'This spake he of the Spirit, which they that believe on him should receive: for the Holy Ghost was not yet given; because that Jesus was not yet glorified.' So the Holy Spirit could not be given until Christ had finished the work the Father had given him to do, until he had died and risen again, until he had ascended and taken his seat at the right hand of God. God then said, in effect, 'I give you the promise, you send it upon the people.'

Now this is something that can be worked out in many different ways. I want to do it here in a more or less objective manner, but the subjective part is important in this way: If you claim that you have received the Holy Spirit in his fullness, then the best test of that is whether or not you are glorifying the Lord Jesus Christ. There is a danger that again we put such emphasis upon the Spirit himself that we do so at the expense of the Son. There are some people who are always talking about phenomena in the Christian life. They like talking about the gifts of the Spirit and boasting that they possess one or other of them: 'Do you speak in tongues? Have you got the gift of healing?' Their talk always seems to be about these things. Well, thank God, the Holy Spirit does give these gifts, but let us never forget that his main function is to glorify the Son, so that if our life is not always pointing to the Lord Jesus Christ and glorifying him, we had better be careful. There are other spirits, and these other spirits are very powerful, and can give wonderful gifts. Satan can counterfeit most of the gifts of the Holy Spirit. For example, there are spirits who can heal. There are strong phenomena in this world in which we live, and the test of the gifts of the Spirit is this: do they testify to the fact that Jesus is God in the flesh? Do they glorify the Son of God? As that is the supreme work of the Holy Spirit, so every spirit must be tested by that particular test.

How, then, does the Holy Spirit glorify Christ? It seems to me that the best way to look at this is to divide it into three main headings. First of all, he reveals the Lord Jesus Christ and his person. Paul in his letter to the Corinthians talks about the Lord of glory. Paul writes: 'But we speak the wisdom of God in a mystery . . . which none of the princes of this world knew: for had they known it, they would not have crucified the Lord of glory' (1 Cor 2:7–8). But we, he says, have received the Spirit, and 'the Spirit searcheth all things, even the deep things of God'. Do you see what that means? When the Lord Jesus Christ was here as man, the Pharisees and the doctors of the law did not recognize him —it was they who incited the people to cry out, 'Away with him, crucify him.' The Greeks did not know him either, nor did the great philosophers, they all rejected him. They said it was nonsense and impossible that a carpenter like that should be the Son of God. And the reason why they did not know him was they had not received the Holy Spirit. Paul says in 1 Corinthians 12:3, 'No man can say that Jesus is the Lord, but by the Holy Ghost.'

Have you not often been perplexed by the fact that many able men in this modern world of ours do not believe in the deity of Jesus Christ? They say that he was only a man. They praise him, and say he is the greatest man, or teacher the world has ever known, but they do not see in him the Son of God. We should never be unhappy about that. To recognize the Lord Jesus Christ is not a matter of intellect, because the greatest brain can never come to see it and believe it. It is a spiritual truth and something which is spiritually discerned.

The Bible tells us that it was not surprising that these people did not believe on the Lord Jesus Christ as the Son of God. It was because they were blind, because their understanding had not been enlightened by the Holy Spirit and, in a sense, their unbelief proves the truth of the gospel. Thank God that it is not a matter of intellect, because if the recognition of the person of the Lord Jesus Christ were a matter of intellect and ability, then the way of salvation would not be a fair one. People with brains would have a great advantage over everybody else, and those who were ignorant and had not much intellectual power, would not be able to understand and grasp the truth. Consequently, they would not be saved and it would be a salvation for certain special intellectual people only.

But thank God it is not that at all! In this matter of the recognition of the Lord Jesus Christ we are all exactly on a level, we are all in the same position. The greatest brain is never big enough to understand and to grasp it, but the Holy Spirit can enable the most ignorant and the most unintelligent to understand. A person without any educational advantages can accept the great salvation because it is the work of the Holy Spirit. The Holy Spirit alone can reveal the person of Christ, but he *can* do it and he can do it to anybody and to everybody.

Furthermore, the Holy Spirit not only reveals the person, he also reveals the work. The preaching of Christ, says Paul, is a stumbling block to the Jews, and foolishness to the Greeks (1 Cor 1:23). These so-called wise men frequently stumble at the cross especially. You see, the preaching of the first disciples was not only that Jesus of Nazareth is the Son of God, but that he came into the world in order to deal with the problem of sin. They taught that the meaning of his death upon the cross was not merely that he was arrested by the Romans at the instigation of the Pharisees, and put to death by crucifixion. No, they taught also that God had made him to be sin for us—it was a great transaction between the Father and the Son. To the philosophers, this was nonsense. They did not understand because they did not receive the Holy Spirit. 'But we,' says Paul again to the Corinthians, 'have received, not the spirit of the world, but the Spirit which is of God; that we might know the things that are freely given to us of God' (1 Cor 2:12).

I want to ask a simple and plain question here: have you understood this matter of the atonement? Are you clear about the work of Christ? Do you see and know that the Lord Jesus Christ has taken your sins upon himself and has died for them on the tree: Is that real to you? Does that make sense to you, or are you stumbling at it? If you are in difficulty, it is because you have not been enlightened by the Holy Spirit, and, believe me, the only way you can come to know, is not to try to understand it intellectually, but to ask God to enlighten you by the Spirit and to enable you to see and understand and receive this truth as he unfolds and displays the work of Christ. If you read the sermon, delivered by Peter on the Day of Pentecost you will find him doing that very thing.

Then the Holy Spirit not only reveals the person and work of Christ, he also reveals the teaching of Christ. Our Lord said to these disciples before he left them, 'I have yet many things to say unto you, but ye cannot bear them now. Howbeit when he, the Spirit of truth, is come, he will guide you into all truth' (Jn 16:12–13). He will remind you of the things I have said and which you cannot grasp now and he will make them plain to you.

So if you are in trouble about the understanding of this gospel, ask God to give you his Spirit in all his fullness, and you will begin to understand. The fatal thing in these matters is to bring your natural intellect to bear upon them: 'The natural man receiveth not the things of the Spirit of God . . . neither can he know them, because they are spiritually discerned' (1 Cor 2:14).

Read 1 Corinthians 2 again, and understand that these

things are in a different realm, they belong to a different order, and the only way to understand the teaching of the New Testament about Christ's personal work and his teaching is to have the eyes of your understanding enlightened by the Holy Spirit. Therefore, if you are in trouble, do not waste your time trying to read books of philosophy about these matters, do not try to grasp them with the natural intellect, for it is impossible. We are dealing with miracles. We are in the realm of the supernatural and the spiritual, and the only hope for us is that the Holy Spirit will come with that unction, with his eye salve, to anoint our eyes so that they will be opened to the blessed truth.

But the Holy Spirit not only reveals Christ, he also *applies* his word, which is to convict us of sin. I have sometimes met people who have said to me, 'I do not understand this teaching about sin, I do not feel I am a sinner.' Well, if you do not feel you are a sinner, it is simply because you do not know yourself, and you do not know yourself because the Holy Spirit has not convicted you. Some of the best people who have ever trodden this earth have been those who have been most conscious of their sinfulness. I cannot imagine a worse state for anybody to be in than for him or her to say they do not feel they are sinners. The Holy Spirit convicts and convinces of sin, and if he has not done it for you, as you value your own soul, ask him to do it. Christ came to die for sinners, not for the righteous, and the first work of the Spirit is to convict of sin, of righteousness and of judgement. We come to Christ for salvation after the Spirit has convinced us of sin, because the Lord Jesus Christ is the answer to our need.

The Holy Spirit then gives us assurance of our acceptance and of our forgiveness. He is a seal given to us to show that we belong to God. He testifies with our spirits that we are the children of God. No Christian has a right to be uncertain about his or her salvation; the Holy Spirit has been given in order that we might be certain for, 'The Spirit itself beareth

witness with our spirit, that we are the children of God'
(Rom 8:16). If any Christian who is reading this is uncertain,
or is lacking in assurance and in happiness, let me urge this
upon you—ask for the gift of the Spirit in his fullness, ask for
this blessed assurance, tell God you long for it, do not give
yourself rest or peace, and, in a sense, do not give God rest
or peace until you have it. You are meant to have it, therefore pray that the Spirit will lead you to it and, if you are
genuine and sincere, you will have it. You may have been
praying for months, or even years, but go on, I say, keep his
commandments, live the life he has marked out for you, but
above all ask that the Spirit may give this witness within
you. He was sent to do that and thus he links us to Christ. It
is beyond understanding; it is the mystical union between the
believer and Christ. As our Lord said in John 15, we are
bound to Christ as the branches to the vine; his life is in us
and it is a part of this blessed work of the Spirit. Then he
goes on to work in us, sanctifying and perfecting us—'Work
out your own salvation,' says Paul in Philippians 2, 'with
fear and trembling. For it is God which worketh in you both
to will and to do of his good pleasure.' He even helps us in
our prayers: 'We know not what we should pray for as we
ought: but the Spirit itself maketh intercession for us with
groanings which cannot be uttered' (Rom 8:26). He then
goes on to produce the fruit of the Spirit in us: 'love, joy,
peace, longsuffering, gentleness, goodness, faith, meekness,
temperance' (Gal 5:22–23).

These are the things which are the work of the Spirit and
they can be summarized like this: he is sent to make the Lord
Jesus Christ real to us. So do not waste your time in trying to
picture the Lord Jesus Christ. Do not go and look at portraits
of him which are wholly imaginary. There is a sense, I believe, in which nobody should ever try to paint him—it is
wrong. I do not like these paintings of Christ, they are the
efforts of the natural mind. No, if you want a photograph of
the Lord Jesus Christ, the Holy Spirit will give it to you in

the inner man. Christ said himself, in John 14: 'He that hath my commandments, and keepeth them, he it is that loveth me: and he that loveth me shall be loved of my Father, and I will love him, and will manifest myself to him.' That is the work of the Spirit, to make Christ living, to make us certain he is there, so that when we speak to him, and he to us, the Spirit makes him real, he is formed in us. Indeed, the Spirit takes the place of the Lord Jesus Christ with us. Christ has said, 'I will not leave you comfortless.' I am going away and you are beginning to be unhappy, but I will not leave you orphans. I will send another Comforter, the Holy Spirit. He will be with you, and he will always be with you so that you will always know what you should do. He will work in you, and you will know that you are walking with him. The Christian life is fellowship with the Father and the Son Jesus Christ, through the Holy Spirit.

And, finally, what he does is to enable us, to give us his wonderful power in order that we may witness to the Lord Jesus Christ. Have you ever thought of that? Have you ever thought about how the Christian church came into being, or how she has persisted throughout the centuries?

Have you ever thought of how that handful of ignorant men, fishermen and ordinary people, were able to turn that ancient world upside down? Have you ever wondered how it happened? There is only one answer, and that is that the power of the Holy Spirit came upon them on the Day of Pentecost. They were not able to reason or argue, it was not their eloquence or persuasive power. No, it was the mighty power of the Holy Spirit upon them!

And Paul writes the same thing about himself. He tells the Corinthians that when he preached the gospel to them at Corinth he deliberately eschewed the methods and manners of the Greek philosophers, 'For,' he says, 'I determined not to know anything among you, save Jesus Christ, and him crucified . . . and my speech and my preaching was not with enticing words of man's wisdom'—he would have nothing to do with these intellectual things—'but in demonstration of the Spirit and of power,' so that the glory might be to God and not to man (1 Cor 2:2,4).

The Holy Spirit gives this power, and, thank God, he not only gave it to the first apostles, he has also given it to quite unknown people, throughout the centuries. He has enabled some simple people just to speak the right word at the right moment. John Bunyan tells us in his autobiography, *Grace Abounding*, that one of the greatest blessings and helps he ever had was one afternoon listening to three ignorant women who were doing some knitting together in the sunshine, outside a house, and talking about the Lord Jesus Christ. He got more from them than from anybody else. And you find that that is what happens. God gives this power to the simplest, humblest Christian to testify to the Lord Jesus Christ, of what he has done and the difference he has made to human life. That is how the Holy Spirit glorifies the Son. When he works in us, what he does is to make us glorify the Lord Jesus Christ. The man in whom the Spirit dwells does not talk about himself; whether he is a preacher or whatever he may be, you do not come away talking about him.

You and I have the inestimable privilege of being men and women who in this life and in our daily work and vocation can be glorifying the Lord Jesus Christ. Oh, God grant that we all may be filled with this Spirit, the Holy Spirit, of God, that we may 'know him, and the power of his resurrection, and the fellowship of his sufferings, being made conformable unto his death'; that we may know what he has done for us; that we may know we are the children of God and joint heirs with Christ; that we may have glimpses of the glory that awaits us and that we may find our lives transformed and filled with his power, so that we may say with Paul, 'I live; yet not I, but Christ liveth in me.'

7

It Is Finished

John 17:1–5

Having considered in general the particular glory of the Father, the Son and the Holy Spirit, we come now to the place where we must look a little more closely at one of the detailed statements which are made here in these five verses. We shall be considering especially the statement in the fourth verse, where our Lord, speaking to his Father, says, 'I have glorified thee on the earth: I have finished the work which thou gavest me to do.' The two parts of that statement, of course, are complementary. He had glorified his Father on the earth by finishing the work which the Father had given him to do. He came in order to glorify the Father, and all he did accorded with this, so we can concentrate in particular on the second statement, 'I have finished the work which thou gavest me to do.' Let us therefore, look at this work about which he speaks.

It is of course one of the best ways of considering the Christian salvation; it is a glorious statement of what it all is, and of what it all involved and what it all cost. It is the way in which the Scripture constantly urges us to think about these things. Again, let me point out in passing that there is nothing that is so calculated to help us as to have a correct and large objective view of the way of salvation. It is always true that the direct road to peace, and joy and happiness, is never to start with, and concentrate upon, yourself. It is, as we have seen, to look, instead, at this great way of salvation, this amazing plan; and the people who are always at peace in this life and world are those who, to use the phrase of the hymn writer, are 'lost in wonder, love and praise'. The happiest people the world has ever known have always been those who have had the glorious view of salvation, and who have seen that they are 'in him'—that is the great New Testament phrase, 'in Christ'—and that they are lost in him. And so they live as more than conquerors in this world and are immune to most of the things that are finally responsible for all our unhappinesses and our miseries.

So, then, we are going to look at salvation in terms of this comprehensive statement, 'I have finished the work which thou gavest me to do.' Let us try to approach it in this way. The first thing we must notice is that this work which was given him to do is obviously something definite and special and concrete. There is nothing vague and indefinite about the New Testament teaching concerning Christian salvation. It is exactly, if one may use such a term, like someone who has been briefed to do a particular work. Now this word 'briefed' has become extended in its meaning in the last few years. We used to think of it in terms of barristers, but we became familiar with it during the war when men in the Air Force were 'briefed' to do a particular thing. The work is as definite, as concrete and as circumscribed as that; and that is the first thought which we must always hold very clearly in our minds with regard to this Christian salvation.

It is not a bad thing, therefore, as we begin to think about it, to test ourselves. If someone came to me and asked me what Christian salvation is, would I be able to give an *exact* definition? According to this term, I should be. It is not some general inference, or vague impression, nor is it one of those things about which you can make a number of statements, and yet never quite describe it. No, it is a definite and parti-cular work, and there are, of course, many definite state-

ments with regard to what it is in the Scriptures themselves.
The work that was given our Lord to do was that of saving
mankind. You remember his own words: 'The Son of man
is come'—why?—because he has been given a particular
assignment from the Father—'to seek and to save that which
was lost' (Lk 19:10).

Then look at the way in which the apostle Paul puts it in
Galatians 4: 'When the fullness of the time was come, God
sent forth his Son, made of a woman, made under the law,
to redeem them that were under the law'—that is the particular task for which he was briefed. Or, if you like it in a more
general form, we can look at it like this: the work that our
Lord was given to do was the work of restoring men to
fellowship and communion with God. That is exactly why
he came; he came all the way from heaven to earth, and did
everything he did, in order that men and women like ourselves, who were out of relationship with God, might be
restored to that relationship. He came to bring together man
and God. He says here, 'I have finished the work which thou
gavest me to do,' and in these words he says he has given
eternal life to as many as God has given him. The work is as
definite as that: to reconcile men to God, to bring God and
man into this particular relationship and fellowship with one
another that had been lost and destroyed.

That leads me then to a second statement, which I put in
this form: what was it that made this work necessary? If it
had not been necessary the eternal Council would never have
been held, God the Father would never have sent forth his
Son into the world, and the Son would never have endured
and suffered all that he did. So we see that there was some
special and peculiar reason why this work was necessary. I
emphasize this because I find there are so many people who
never seem to have seen the necessity of this work. They say,
'I have always believed in God, and in the love of God.' But
the whole of this work which Christ came to do is to them
absolutely unnecessary. You ask them what they hope for

and they say that they hope they will get to heaven. If you ask them how they are going to do so, they reply, 'Well, I have always believed in God,' and they talk about this and that, but they never mention the Lord Jesus Christ and his work at all. His work is unnecessary as far as they are concerned.

Yet, obviously, by definition, this is a work which was absolutely essential. The Son was sent, and given this assignment, because without this work man and God cannot be reconciled. And so here, you see, we are plunged immediately into the profundities of Christian theology. What made this work necessary was the problem raised by sin. You do not begin to understand the work that was given to the Lord Jesus Christ unless you are perfectly clear about the problem of sin. Of course, we now begin to understand why it is that there is so little said today about the plan of salvation, and why men and women think so infrequently about this magnificent scheme. It is because they do not like the doctrine of sin and dismiss it lightly, yet that, according to the Bible, is what made all this work necessary.

Have you ever wondered why the ceremonial regulations were given to the Children of Israel? I mean the ceremonial regulations about the burnt offerings and the sin offerings and the trespass offerings—all that long list of things that had to be done: the killing of animals, the shedding of blood and the presenting of it in the Temple. The reason for it all is the problem of sin and what made this work of Christ so essential was sin, and man's condition in sin.

But that was not the only thing that made it necessary. There is something else which made it still more necessary and that is none other than the holy character of God himself. I have to put sin first because unless I do so we cannot see the problem that was, in a sense, raised even in the heart of the Eternal himself. For before God and man could be reconciled, something had got to be done both from the standpoint of God and of man. The problem from the

Godward side I can put in this way—I use the terms used by the apostle Paul in Romans 3—how could God at one and the same time remain just and yet be the justifier of the ungodly? How could God remain holy, and unchangeable, and eternal, and righteous, true and just, and yet forgive sin and forgive the transgressions of man?

Let me put it in a simpler way. God, being God, cannot just forgive sin. Now the common idea about God, the one that we have instinctively, is that when we admit that we have sinned, all that is necessary is that we should come to God, say we are very sorry, and God will forgive us. But according to the Bible that is impossible, and I do not hesitate to use that word. As a preacher of the Christian gospel, I am compelled to say this and I say it with reverence: God, because he is God, cannot just forgive sin like that.

If you want me to prove what I am saying, this is how I do it. If God could have forgiven sin just by saying, 'I forgive', he would have done so, and Christ would never have been sent into this world. The work that was given to him to do, this work, this assignment, this task, was given to the Lord Jesus Christ because, I say again, without it, God cannot forgive sin. He must not only justify the ungodly, he must remain just. The way of salvation must be consistent with the character of God. He cannot deny himself, he cannot change himself, he is unchangeable. 'God is light, and in him is no darkness at all'; (1 Jn 1:5); he is 'the Father of lights, with whom is no variableness, neither shadow of turning' (Jas 1:17). He is eternally, everlastingly, the same, and he is absolutely righteous and holy and just. He cannot remain that and simply forgive sin and no more.

So you see this work of Christ was absolutely essential and I think we can see why it is that many people's ideas of salvation are so terribly wrong. They really do not see the necessity for Christ himself and his work; they say, 'God is love and because he is love, he will forgive me.' My friend, he cannot, because he *is* God! The work of Christ was essential because of the character of God, and it was essential because of man in sin; something had to be done to render man fit for God. So there are two mighty reasons why this work was essential.

Let us go on to another problem. The work was something that Christ himself had to do, and he can therefore speak of it as being done. 'I have finished the work which thou gavest me to do.' Now I want to put that in the form of a negative like this. The Lord Jesus Christ did not come into this world to tell us what *we* have to do. He came himself to do something for us which we could never do for ourselves. These negatives are all so essential, because there are people who believe in the deity of the Lord Jesus Christ, but if you ask them what he came into this world to do, their answer will be that he came to tell us what we must do ourselves. Or they talk about good works and say that if we do this or that we will make ourselves Christian and make ourselves right with God. No! Our Lord says here, '*I* have finished the work which thou gavest *me* to do.'

I am sometimes afraid that we are all guilty of missing the wood because of the trees, and sometimes the people who are most guilty are those who delight to call themselves Bible students. They go through the gospels with their analyses and look at the Lord's teaching, but they are so taken up with the details that they never see the whole grand plan itself. The truth which we have to take hold of is that which is emphasized here, and the best way to understand it is to consider what it was that he did, and, too, what he was doing beforehand. He came to do certain things himself, and we are saved by what Christ has done for us, and not by what he tells us to do. The work of salvation is his work and his doing, and he came specifically to do it, and here, in these words, he looks ahead, as it were, to the death on the cross, as well as back to what he has already done. Under the shadow of the cross, he reviews the whole work, and he is able to say, 'I have finished the work which thou gavest me to do.' I have completed it. On the cross he said it again in the words, 'It is finished.' It is his work and not yours and mine. So a very good way of testing whether we have a right or wrong way of looking at salvation is to ask ourselves whether we see Christian salvation as something which is exclusively and entirely the work of the Lord Jesus Christ. We are his workmanship; it is all of God in Christ. He has completed the work, and we simply have to receive his salvation as a free gift.

That leads me to what is, of course, the most important thing of all, which is to look in detail at something of this work which he has done. Here again I want to emphasize that the work which Christ came to do was not simply to give us incomparable teaching about God, and about the love and the fatherhood of God. How often has that been put forward as the sole business of Christ in this world? He did that, of course, but that is not the specific purpose for which he came. That had already been revealed in the Old Testament. In the Old Testament you have some of the most glorious statements of the character and love of God, and of the fatherhood of God; you will find statements there that are in no sense inferior to the statements of the New Testament. God's ancient people had been taught about him in his love, and in his fatherhood, and in his holy character; they knew them, in a sense, and Christ did not come only to tell us those things.

Or look at it like this. Whatever else Christ came to do, we must realize that it was something that necessitated the incarnation, the life, the death and the resurrection of the Son of God. So when I come to face this question of what this work was, I must be certain that my answer defines it in a way that makes the incarnation an absolute necessity, the death on the cross an absolute necessity, and the resurrection an absolute necessity. The teaching concerning the love and character and fatherhood of God, therefore, has to make the fact of these great truths inevitable.

But the same thing is true with regard to our teaching about his death upon the cross, we must so define the work, and all these events, as to make them absolute necessities. And the way to approach them is to understand that the problem was about how God and man could be reconciled. It was not merely that man might know certain things about God. Something had to be done to bring them into fellowship and communion with one another. If we remember that *that* is the controlling thought, I think we will begin to see exactly what the work was which the Lord was sent to do. He is the One who was sent in order to bring that to pass; he is the One who has come as the Messiah; he has come to seek and to save, to be the Mediator, between God and man.

'The work', in other words, is that he was appointed as man's representative. Man at the beginning had a representative called Adam. He was the entire human race in himself, and acted as its representative, so that when he sinned, we all sinned. What is the answer to this? It is that we need someone to represent us with God, someone who alone can lift us up again, someone who can set us free, and present and introduce us to God. That is the task and nothing less than that. What was necessary was a representative of mankind, or, to use the phrase in Hebrews 2, we need 'a captain of our salvation', a leader, someone who can speak for us. A new originator of a new race, corresponding to Adam, was essential, and it was in order to do this that the Son of God came into this world, and the special task that was given to him involved this.

First of all, of course, it involved the incarnation. A new humanity is necessary, a new man, if you like, who can stand before God on our behalf, and the Son of God came in order to start this new humanity. That is why he ever came into the world, that is why the miracle of the virgin birth ever took place, and that is why you have the mystery and the marvel of the God-Man—two natures in the one person. That is why, as Hebrews 2 puts it, he held out a helping hand

and took on himself the seed of Abraham. He took humanity into his deity: that is the whole meaning of the incarnation, that is precisely what happened at Bethlehem. So the point I am emphasizing is that his task was not merely to tell us about God and his love. He could have done that in the form of a theophany—he could have made one of those appearances to mankind, and given certain revelations about God and his love. But that is not enough: he has to represent man, and he became man, hence the incaration. Before he can represent us as High Priest he has to become one of us, so he takes unto himself human nature.

But it means even more than that, for having been born as man, in the likeness of sinful flesh, he then went to John the Baptist and asked John to baptize him. John stood back in amazement and said, 'I have need to be baptized of thee, and comest thou to me?'

No, said Christ, 'Suffer it to be so now: for thus it becometh us to fulfil all righteousness.'

What was happening there at that baptism? It is, again, one of those essential steps in this great work that he came to do. Being born a man was not enough in and of itself, he had to do this as well. He was absolutely sinless, why then did he need to be baptized? He was baptized because he identified himself with us in our sin. He was taking the responsibility for us and our sins, and taking our sinfulness upon himself.

Or you can look at it in another way: it was at his baptism that the Holy Spirit came upon him in the form of a dove, which means that not only was he being given strength, he was being anointed for his task. He was being set aside in a very special way as the Messiah, the Anointed One who was to deliver the people for whom he had come. Therefore, he had his ordination, the oil of the Spirit was poured upon him, and he was announced as the Messiah. So the baptism was essential; it was part of the work which he came to do, which was not only to take on our nature but to identify himself with us in sin.

Then we can go on and watch him and see his life of perfect, spotless obedience. Once again, he did not live a perfect life simply in order to show that he was the Son of God. No, something much more profound, and much more vital for you and for me, had to take place. It was that in living that perfect life of obedience to the law he was not only honouring the law as our head and representative, but also as the captain of our salvation, as the first born among many brethren. He was honouring the law for you and for me and for all who believe in him; he was not only gaining positive righteousness for himself, he was gaining it for us. He was keeping God's law for us and it was part of the work he came to do.

Is it not true to say that far too often we tend, as we read the gospel, to admire his perfect life and say, 'Yes, he is undoubtedly God as well as man', and then to stop at that? But we should always look at him and see him honouring God's law and keeping it perfectly, and we should see that he was doing it as your representative and mine. He was doing it for us: he came to do that, not merely to teach about God and the forgiveness and love of God. He had to honour God's law before God could forgive us, and he did that.

But not only that, we behold him conquering Satan. In Hebrews 2, which is a great commentary upon this very verse we are considering together, we are told that he came into the world that 'through death he might destroy him that had the power of death, that is, the devil; and deliver them who through fear of death were all their lifetime subject to bondage' (Heb 2:14–15). John in his first epistle says that Jesus came into the world to destroy the works of the devil. In other words, mankind in sin had become subject to Satan, and before we could be saved, and before we could be truly reconciled to God, Satan had to be conquered. We had to be emancipated and delivered out of the dominion of Satan and transferred to the kingdom of God, and it is only Christ who could do that. All who came before him and who tried to be emancipated from the thraldom of Satan, had been defeated and overcome by the devil. So before we could be redeemed the devil had to be conquered. Our Lord had to do it, and he had to do it as a man, before our freedom could take place—and he has done it.

And then, of course, he was confronted by the final task, which was to deliver us from the guilt of sin, and that is the whole meaning of his death upon the cross. There I see him allowing sin to be punished in his body and giving himself as a sin offering, for without the shedding of blood, there is no remission of sin (see Hebrews 9:22). That is true of God. God, because he is what he is, cannot forgive us sinners without the shedding of blood. Before God could forgive sin, it had to be punished, and by Christ's death upon the cross your sins and mine have been dealt with. They have been punished, their guilt has been expiated—there on the cross he was made sin for us, 'God was in Christ reconciling the world unto himself' (2 Cor 5:19). So Christ has come to do this—this work of presenting himself as a man without spot and without blemish, and it could not have been done without his coming into this world and without his doing all he did. And so, by doing this, he has conquered death as well. He has taken the sting out of it because 'the sting of death is sin; and the strength of sin is the law. But thanks be to God, which giveth us the victory through our Lord Jesus Christ' (1 Cor 15:56–57).

I merely put these headings before you. I plead with you to consider them one by one at your leisure. That was the work which he came to do. He came in order to honour God's law perfectly by keeping it, by living it. He came to satisfy it by bearing the punishment he pronounced upon sin and guilt and evil. He has done that, and thus the law is satisfied. Yes, but as I have reminded you, we need to be delivered from the power of the devil, we need death and the grave to be conquered, and he has done it all. And beyond all

that, we need a new nature, because we need not only forgiveness of sins, but to be made fit to have communion and
fellowship with God. We need to have a nature that can
stand the sight of God, for 'God is light and in him is no
darkness at all'. And Christ has come and given us himself,
his own nature, the eternal life of which he speaks in this
very prayer that we are considering together.

So here, looking at it all, he can say, 'I have finished the
work which thou gavest me to do.' He has done everything
that is necessary for man to be reconciled to God. Have you
realized, my friends, that this work is finished? Have you
realized that it is finished as far as you are concerned? Do you
still think that you have to make yourself a Christian? You
are asked whether you are a Christian, and you reply that
you are hoping to be, but that you need to do this, that and
that other . . . No! Christ says, 'I have finished the work
which thou gavest me to do.' The work has been done, and
what proves whether we are truly Christians or not is the
fact that we know and realize that the work has been done,
and that we rest, and rest only, upon the finished work of
our blessed Lord and Saviour Jesus Christ. If we see it all in
him and the work done and completed in him, it means we
are Christian; if in any sense we are uncertain or doubtful, or
think we have to do something ourselves, it means we are
not. The beginning of Christianity is the acceptance of this
statement: 'I have finished the work which thou gavest me to
do.' The way for you to know God, and to be reconciled to
him, is wide open in the Lord Jesus Christ, and his perfect
work on your behalf. If you have never entered in before,
enter in now, rest upon the finished work of the Lord Jesus
Christ and begin to rejoice, immediately, in your great salvation.

8

The Hour Is Come

John 17:1

I want in particular now to look at the phrase, 'the hour is come'. My whole case is that if we fail or falter in the Christian life, either in thought or in action, if we are unhappy or defeated, if in any way we are failing to function in this world as a Christian should, and as the Christian life is portrayed so plainly in the New Testament, then such failure is ultimately due to the fact that our view of our position as Christian people in Christ Jesus is in some way or another defective.

There is no question but that the New Testament has the answer to all the problems and difficulties of the Christian life, and its object is to bring us back to the truth itself and to give us a still clearer view of it. So we are not doing something theoretical. There is nothing more fatal than the kind of dichotomy that some people seem to recognize between belief and life, faith and practice, for these are indissolubly mixed. The most practical people, who pride themselves on being so, the people who say they are not very interested in doctrine, but who believe in *doing* things, are the very people who will, sooner or later, find themselves in grave trouble. It is fatal only to recognize one or the other—the two things must be taken together. So we have spent some time in looking at this plan of salvation as it is unfolded here.

But now we must look at this phrase, 'Father, the hour is come', for the great doctrine concerning 'this hour' is again something that is of vital importance to us. In a sense, the whole of salvation is seen as we look at our Lord facing this hour, and the very essence of the truth is emphasized by the doctrine that is here outlined. As he points out so often, he came from heaven, and did all that we were considering earlier in order to come to this hour, for this hour was essential to the completion of that work which the Father had given him to do. There can be no doubt but that this hour is the focus and climax, at one and the same time, of everything that our Lord came to do. It is the crucial, climactic point in the whole of that mighty work that we have been looking at in general.

The best way, it seems to me, of approaching the teaching and doctrine concerning 'this hour' is that we should remind ourselves of some of the statements which our Lord himself made with respect to it. For instance, we are told that on the occasion of the marriage in Cana of Galilee, when his mother asked him to do something about the shortage of wine, he turned to her and said, 'Woman, what have I to do with thee? mine hour is not yet come' (Jn 2:4). He is already speaking of it. Again, he had to say the same thing to his brethren who upbraided him for not going to the feast at Jerusalem. He said, 'My time is not yet come' (Jn 7:6), and that phrase has a special meaning to it. Then we are told on another occasion that his enemies sought to take him, but that, 'No man laid hands on him, because his hour was not yet come' (Jn 7:30). Later on we read again that no man laid hands on him for his hour was not yet come (Jn 8:20).

Then take the statement in John 12:23, 'And Jesus answered them, saying, The hour is come, that the Son of man should be glorified.' And, just after that, hear him saying, 'Now is my soul troubled; and what shall I say? Father, save me from this hour: but for this cause came I unto this hour.' Then there is the reference in the thirteenth chapter to

the same thing: 'When Jesus knew that his hour was come
. . .' and again, later, he says, 'Behold the hour cometh, yea,
is now come, that ye shall be scattered, every man to his
own, and shall leave me alone.' Then we have the statement
here, 'Father, the hour is come. . .' and there is also another
very interesting and important statement in Luke 22:53,
where we read that he turned to the authorities that were
against him and hated him and said, '. . .but this is your
hour, and the power of darkness.'

Now in order to interpret this verse in John 17 aright, we
must bear all this in mind, and as we do so, I think there are
certain things which can be said quite plainly. The first is that
this 'hour' is obviously a predetermined hour. You notice
that all those statements regarding it have something very
special, and definite to say. When he says, 'Mine hour is not
yet come', he is, in effect, telling them, 'My time is not yet
come; your time is always here, but there is a special time as
far as I am concerned. You want me to come and declare
myself; no, you do not understand it, the time for that has
not yet come.' In other words, you find our Lord always
looking forward to this hour. Indeed this theme of expec-
tation is to be found running right through the whole of
Scripture.

This whole problem of time is a particularly important
and fascinating one; there are some who would say that in
many ways it is the biggest and most important point in the
whole of theology, and the question of how to relate time, as
we know it, to eternity and timelessness causes a great deal
of confusion. Now if you are a philosopher, it can be a
profound problem, yet, if we take the Scripture as it is, I
think it becomes comparatively plain and clear. God has
brought the time process into being, and, having done so, he
has appointed that certain things should take place at a certain
time. It is not that God is bound by time, but that he has
ordered that things should happen in the realm of time, and
thus you find in the Old Testament and in the New that God

has appointed minutes.

Take the flood as an illustration. God had said, 'My Spirit shall not always strive with man' (Gen 6:3). He had focussed upon a determined point; he was able to call Noah to start building the ark 120 years before the flood came. He knew when the flood was coming—all these things are plain and open unto the eye of God. And so it was that 'when the fullness of the time was come'—when the hour had come— 'God sent forth his Son, made of a woman, made under the law, to redeem them that were under the law' (Gal 4:3–4).

This, surely, is a thought that liberates us at once from most of the thraldom of life in this world. You look at life today, and at history, and at the whole course of the world, and if you look at it with the human eye alone, you will find it very difficult to see any meaning in it. But the moment we begin to look at it in the light of this doctrine of 'the hour', though we may not understand it fully with all its details, we can at once be certain that the Lord still reigns and that life in this world is not out of hand. As we read this biblical history and see the clashing of the nations, with the people opposed to God, and apparently out of control, we find that at a given point God does redeem the world in spite of man. When God's time arrives God comes in and the whole world has to conform again to his plan and purpose.

So the great consolation for us is that though we see the Christian church and Christianity derided and apparently counting for so little in this modern world; and though we may see on the surface that the enemy opposed to the church is triumphant all along the line, and that God's people are languishing, we nevertheless know for certain, beyond any doubt whatsoever, that God's hand is still upon the situation, and that in a moment he can arise and confound all his enemies. 'He that sitteth in the heavens shall laugh' (Ps 2:4), as he sees these pigmies exalting themselves, for he knows that at a word he can destroy them, and they will perish out of sight.

But in particular for our purpose as we consider the plan of salvation, the important thing is that all the things that happened to him did not take our Lord by surprise. That has been the fatal view of our Lord, his person and his work, ever since the advent of the so called higher criticism movement. They represent our Lord as a human teacher who had his plan of teaching the people, his own nation, and converting them to his point of view, and then sending them out to spread this wonderful teaching. But, suddenly, these people tell us, after three years the whole thing came crashing to the ground. He never anticipated this rejection, they say, he never thought they had it in their hearts to do such a thing. That is the picture that is painted, and we are left feeling very sorry for this 'pale Galilean', this incomparable teacher, this Galilean peasant, born before his time with his exalted idealism, and so on, who saw it all brought to nothing, and broke his heart at the failure of it all, so that he died of a broken heart upon the cross.

What a travesty of this glorious gospel! My friend, he came from heaven, he laid aside his glory, as we were considering earlier, in order to come to 'this hour'. He knew it from the beginning. He came to die, specifically to die. We have seen that, apart from that death on the cross, he cannot deliver me; that apart from the death on the cross, I say it again with reverence, even God cannot forgive man. The cross is absolutely essential, the cross was planned before the world was ever created. So the hour that produced the cross is the central, pivotal point, of history and God always knew about it, the Lord came for that hour. So we must never think of this hour as taking him by surprise, it was an hour that was appointed and determined, it was the crisis of the world itself.

But let us go on to the second point, that this hour is the crucial hour of history. There is no question about that. It was the most momentous hour since the beginning of the world, it is indeed the turning point which determines everything—it is the greatest event, the most—yes, let me use the word again—climactic event that has ever taken place in this world. Everything leads up to that hour, everything eventuates from that hour. That is the hour to which the whole of prophecy is looking forward, and to which the whole of the church, and her doctrine and history look back. It is the central, focal, point which determines and controls everything. It was the point on which everything that God had planned depended, and if there were failure at this point everything would fail. Hence our Lord's prayer to his Father, 'the hour is come glorify thy Son, that thy Son may glorify thee'.

If the Son had failed at this particular point, everything else would have been useless. His teaching would have been of no value whatsoever, because, though we might have tried to live it, and carry it out, yet we would have lacked the strength and the power. He would have been giving us a law even more impossible than the law given through Moses, and thereby he would have condemned us and left us under a still greater condemnation. It is the most vital hour of all, for, I say again, if he cannot bear the punishment of our sins, then he does not save us. But having borne the punishment, he *does* save us, so it is what happened in that hour that really holds, within itself, the entirety of our salvation.

There are people who would sometimes preach a gospel apart from this. You ask them what the gospel is, and they reply that the gospel is the Lord Jesus Christ somehow or other giving new life to men, lifting men out of their failure and giving them new life. And they sometimes present that without mentioning the cross. But, my friends, before you and I need a new life, we need forgiveness. Something has to be done about the past before we face the future. You cannot suddenly decide that you are going to live a better life, you have to deal with the problem of your past and your sin. It is this hour that deals with that, for there is no re-generation, no new life, except for those who are forgiven and justified in the sight of God. This, then, is a crucial hour.

But I must say something about what I would call the drama of the hour. There is a kind of mystery about this hour. It is very interesting as one reads the gospels to keep one's eye on the references to it. We have been looking at our Lord coming up to this hour, but he is not the only one who is preparing for it. The forces on the other side are also interested in this same hour and you can watch the plan developing from their side as well as from his side. That is where the statement in Luke 22 comes in—'this is your hour'. You cannot read the story of our Lord's experiences without seeing this tremendous fight, and I am emphasizing it here because nothing is so sad to me as the failure of many people to realize the conflict that is going on in this world. We are ready to fight against certain evil tendencies, but over and above the fight against the sin that is within us, there is this cosmic fight against sin.

There is a sense in which the Bible is nothing but a great drama in which you find depicted the mighty conflict between God and the powers of hell. The background to the Bible is something that happened before human history began—the great question of the devil and the origin of the devil and of evil. We do not know everything about it—it has not pleased God to reveal everything—but he has revealed this much, that quite apart from our history there was a kind of cosmic fall. As we have seen, one of the greatest of God's angelic beings rebelled against him. He is the devil, called Satan, and his one object is to defeat God. And what is unfolded in this great drama in the Bible is the attempt of the devil to destroy God's works, and to defeat God. God made his world perfect—Paradise—but the devil came in and started a fight. He persuaded man that an injustice had been done against him, and the whole of humanity, and the whole universe.

And the fight continues. Read your Bible with that in view and you will find it will be a transformed book; you will see the failure in God's own people, quite apart from the others, and it is all because the devil tried to turn them against God. You find it even when the Son of God comes into this world. The devil tried to destroy him at the beginning, the moment he was born. He took hold of King Herod and persuaded him to try to destroy this Child, this Messiah, the Saviour. Keep your eye on the malignity of the scribes and Pharisees, and the doctors of the law and the violent hatred that was manifested by them because they saw in him the representative of God. You remember how the devil said the thing explicitly on one occasion, 'I know thee who thou art; the Holy One of God' (Lk 4:34). They realized that they were fighting for their lives. The devil tempted him in the wilderness; the devil was fighting for his life and the whole of his forces were being marshalled for this ultimate clash when the two forces came together. And the clash takes place at this tremendous hour, when the Son of God is going to give his life a ransom for many. So we have to look at this hour from both these angles.

What, then, does our Lord mean exactly when he says in the Garden of Gethsemane, 'This is your hour, and the power of darkness'? It seems to me that the only possible explanation must be that this hour would never have come to pass were it not for the power of darkness. What makes this hour and all that it involves necessary and essential? It is again the problem of sin and of evil, the problem of Satan and of hell. It is the kind of hour that the devil has staged and brought into being, for, in one sense, he has manipulated it, though in a much higher sense he has not. I think that this is the way to look at it—it is the work of the devil that makes the hour essential from God's standpoint; it is because of what Satan has produced by sin and evil that God has to do this in order to overcome it.

So it is, in a sense, their hour, and it is there that we really see the essence of evil and of sin. It is such a terrible thing that nothing less than this could deal with it. It is not a question of

God's love and forgiveness, it is evil that has to be dealt with in this radical way. The devil has produced such a situation that this hour alone can deal with it.

So this hour can be described as 'their hour', and the hour of the glorification of the Son at the same time, and that is why he prays that his Father may glorify him. It is in going through this hour, that has been produced by Satan and hell, that our Lord really is glorified. It is there we know for certain that he is the Son of God. No one had ever before had to meet Satan and conquer him, no one had been able to destroy the power that Satan had over death—that is the way the author of the epistle to the Hebrews puts it: 'That through death he might destroy him that had the power of death' (2:14) and thus he sets the children free, and Christ has done it through this, his glorification. The death and the resurrection is the proof that he is the Son of God.

But let us, if we can, try for a moment, with reverence, to look at it in this way. What did this hour mean to our Lord himself? Well, he has given us an indication. Consider the statement in John 12:27, 'Now is my soul troubled; and what shall I say? Father, save me from this hour'—then he answers himself and says—'but for this cause came I unto this hour.' There I think is the right approach to any consideration of what this hour meant to him. He knew it was coming, he had known that all along, and now here he was actually facing it. But although his soul was troubled, he did not ask God, his Father, to save him from this hour. No, that was impossible, he could not do that, for 'this hour' was his reason for coming to the world.

'Well,' says someone, 'if he always knew about this hour, if he had come from heaven in order to come to this hour, if he knew for certain, as he did, that beyond that hour he was going to rise again from the grave and go to the glory'— indeed, every time our Lord spoke to his disciples about his coming death, he always went on to speak of the resurrection. He knew he was going to rise again, and go to the glory. The author of the epistle to the Hebrews reminds us of that when he says. 'who for the joy that was set before him endured the cross'—'so then,' the questioner continues, 'if all that is true why does he say, "now is my soul troubled"? How could he know the glory that is coming, and the triumph of the resurrection? How could he know he had come to this climactic hour which was going to make salvation possible and yet say, "Now is my soul troubled," and, "Father, save me from this hour"? What was the cause of the trouble?'

There are those who think this is quite a simple problem. They say it was nothing but his physical shrinking from death; he knew about the glory of the resurrection, but the thought of physical suffering troubled him and he shrank from it as a man. In his body, in his flesh, he shrank from the thought of this physical dissolution. But to me that very thought is insulting. It is not only insulting to our Lord as a man, it is such a tragic failure to understand what happened there. No, that is no explanation, for if you accept it, then you make our Lord a lesser person than the martyrs. The martyrs faced death without a fear because they believed the gospel of the resurrection. Their knowledge of it was nothing by contrast with our Lord's knowledge, but it was enough to enable them to go boldly to the stake without a quiver or a fear. And so that supposition makes our Lord less than his own followers and inferior to some of his own martyrs. No, such an explanation is impossible. It is a tragic blindness that makes us try to view these things from the standpoint of human reasoning, instead of in terms of biblical doctrine.

What, then, did he shrink from? What was it that troubled his holy, righteous soul? It was the fact that he knew what was going to happen in that hour. He knew that the full, total wrath of God against sin was to be manifested and poured out against him—*that* was what he shrank from. If physical suffering holds no terrors to a courageous man who may not even be a Christian, it is still less to a Christian saint or martyr, and to the Son of God, it is nothing at all. There was only one thing that the Son of God shrank from, and that was to be separated from the face of his Father; he shrank from anything that could interrupt that love that had existed between them from all eternity. The one thing the Son of God shrank from was to look into his Father's face and see there that holy wrath against sin, and he knew that that was what he would have to experience in that hour. His soul was to be made an offering for sin, he himself was to be made sin, so that at that hour God was going to look at him, and he was not going to see the Son in whom he was well pleased, but this horrible, foul, ugly thing.

And that is why the Son says, in effect, 'Now is my soul troubled—what shall I say? Shall I ask him to save me from this hour? No, because if I do, I shall not save man from all that wrath of God which shall be poured out upon me. I have come for that hour, it is the purpose of my coming into this world. God cannot be just and the justifier of the ungodly unless I bear it, so I will bear it.' 'That hour'—his hour—what an hour!

The one thing, therefore, that made him speak like this was his certain clear knowledge of what was involved in this one moment, as it were, and it was the thing that broke his heart. It was the thing that killed him. In a sense, our Lord did not die of crucifixion, but because the wrath of God against sin was so poured out upon him. We are told that the soldiers, when they came, were amazed that he was dead already. Crucifixion was a slow process of death, the man who was crucified took a long time to die, but here was one who died quickly, and they were amazed. And the cause of it was a ruptured heart. So that is why his soul was troubled. It was the thought of losing the face of his Father, the thing that made him cry out on the cross. 'My God, my God, why hast thou forsaken me?' He really saw sin, and he was made sin, and all God's holy wrath against him was poured on him. He bore it all and that is what the hour meant to him.

But I want to say a final word on the results of the hour, which are put very plainly by Jesus in John 12:31. What an hour this is! Do you not begin to see that it is the most momentous hour of all time? We talk about those pivotal points of history, but they are all nothing when you look at this. 'Now is the judgement of this world'—the whole world, in the sense that it is the hour in which the world was really revealed for what it is. It was there that sin was revealed. There, shown plainly and clearly once and for ever, is the whole state of mankind apart from God. I do not know whether we realize this as we ought; sin is something so fiendish and so foul that it led to that terrible hour. So the next time the devil tempts you, remember that you will not merely be doing something which you should not be doing. No, you will be putting yourself into the realm of sin, opposed to God. But not only does the cross reveal sin for what it is, at one and the same time it pronounces doom on the whole world and everything that belongs to that realm. The cross of Jesus Christ makes this great proclamation. Unless I believe in him, unless I believe that his death at that hour is the only thing that reconciles me to God, I remain under the wrath of God. If I do not see that the wrath of God against my sin has been borne there by the Son of God, then the alternative is that I must live to experience the wrath of God: that is the essence of the Christian gospel. I either believe that my sins have been punished in the body of the Son of God or else they will be punished in me. It is the judgement of the world.

The world apart from him is under the wrath of God, it is doomed, it is damned and he alone can save it in that way. There was no other way, for God would never have allowed his Son to endure all that if there had been another way. It is the only way, so it is the judgement of the world. And we, all of us, either believe that the Lord Jesus Christ saved us in that hour, or else we remain in our sins, we belong to the world that is going to be condemned and finally judged. The gospel tells us that he will come back again and that this time he will return to judge. The one question that will face everybody is this: do you belong to him or do you not? The books will be opened; the names of the people who believe in Christ are in one book, the book of the Lamb of God, and if you belong to his book you are saved. But the world is damned and destroyed and cast into a lake of fire—the judgement of this world. But the judgement was pronounced at the cross. Though the *nature* has been postponed and is still being postponed, judgement has been pronounced, so that anyone who dies without believing on the Lord Jesus Christ belongs to the world and that has already had judgement pronounced upon it.

Likewise, the prince of this world shall be cast out. The devil has already been defeated, for Christ defeated him on the cross. The devil was working up to this hour, and when the Lord died he thought he had defeated him at last, but he did not realize the truth of the resurrection. Christ rose again and by so doing he has destroyed principalities and powers and triumphed over them by his own cross, which they thought was their masterpiece. The very death which they thought was his defeat turns out to be the greatest victory of all and by it they are finally doomed. The devil is still very active in this world, but he is already defeated. In a sense he is already cast out, and has no authority at all. Christ's people, all who belong to Christ, all that the Father has given him, are going to be drawn to him. The devil is already defeated, and is going to be cast into that lake of fire and will be destroyed eternally.

What an hour! Oh, that the Holy Spirit would open our eyes to see and to know something of these things! We are talking about historical events, this hour belongs to time, it belongs to history. It is not an idea, it is not some wonderful theory that men have woven out of their imagination. These things have literally happened, so I am left with this fact that the Son of God has been in this world, and has passed through that hour for my sins. If I believe that, I know that that hour is the one which has saved me from everlasting destruction, but if I do not believe, I am left condemned. Our Lord puts it again in John 12: 'I came not to judge the world . . . the word that I have spoken, the same will judge. . .' (verses 47,48). Though he did not come to judge, yet he is giving his judgement. We cannot escape, the devil is judged by this hour, the world is judged by this hour.

Oh, may God grant us to see sin for what it really is! We cannot be indifferent to these things, for if we believe them our way of life is going to be determined. If I believe all this, how can I be indifferent to sin? No, the One who has done this for me deserves my life, my soul, my all. He must be my Lord and my Master. I say again that failure in the Christian life is the failure really to see the meaning of this hour, to see the meaning of sin, the failure to realize what he suffered for you, the failure to realize the consequences of not believing in him. May God give us grace, therefore, to meditate upon this hour, this astounding, crucial, climactic hour in which the essence of our salvation was worked out and achieved by the Son of God in his terrible agony and suffering upon the cross.

9

'That He Should Give Eternal Life to as Many as Thou Hast Given Him'

John 17:2

No one, I think, reading the New Testament, can fail to see that it is the most lyrical document. The great note that runs right through it all, in spite of the tragic things that it has to record, is the note of victory, and rejoicing. You find it in the gospels, and in the Acts of the Apostles, and you find it in the epistles. Our Lord himself, right under the shadow of the cross, spent a good deal of his time showing his followers how, in spite of the things that are about to happen to him, they could nevertheless be full of rejoicing. He has a joy to give them, he tells them, that no man can ever take from them. Temporarily, they will be cast down because of his crucifixion, but soon they are going to receive that joy which the world cannot understand and can never take away, and certainly the Acts of the Apostles is one of the most exhilarating books that has ever been written. In spite of everything those first Christians stood out, dominating the whole world, full of joy and rejoicing, and the great appeal in all the epistles in that those Christians to whom they were written, should rejoice. That is the great characteristic note of the New Testament, and the same thing has been true of all the great hymns of the church throughout the centuries.

> Children of the heavenly King,
> As ye journey sweetly sing,

says John Cennick, and as these men have contemplated their salvation in every century and every country it has been something that has always led them to 'wonder, love and praise'. The note of praise is dominant and characteristic, and, therefore, this is what we, who claim to be Christian, should be experiencing. A miserable Christian is, in a sense, a contradiction in terms. A Christian is one who is meant to be rejoicing, full of a sense of wonder, of praise and of adoration as he contemplates this great salvation. Furthermore, he rejoices in spite of his circumstances, for the gospel of Jesus Christ, thank God, not only offers to make us happy when all is going well with us, its great aim is that we should be able to rejoice even in tribulation and in the worst circumstances. That is its plan, and this is something that we all ought to be experiencing. But, it we are honest and frank, I think that many of us would have to admit that that is not our condition, and I am suggesting in these studies that the real explanation of that is our failure to grasp and understand the greatness of this Christian salvation.

Now, so far, we have been concentrating on it from the godward side, and we have been trying to see salvation as conceived in the mind of the eternal God, planned before the foundation of the world, and the work divided up between the Father, Son and Holy Spirit. And I would say again that if, as the result of doing all that, we are still unmoved, we are still not amazed and astounded, if we still do not feel that this is the most precious and wonderful thing in the world and that everything else in comparison with this pales into utter insignificance, then, as I understand my New Testament, it is high time we examined ourselves very seriously and discovered whether we are Christian at all. If a man can contemplate this salvation as thus looked at from the standpoint of God himself without feeling its greatness, then I do not understand such a person. Surely if one really sees these things even dimly and vaguely, it must revolutionize one's mind and it must be the dominating factor in the whole of our existence.

But now we must move on to a further aspect of the subject. I feel there is a second explanation of our failure to be rejoicing as we ought to be as Christians, and that is our failure really to grasp this salvation from *our* side, not only from God's side, but also from our own. This is surely something that should fill us with a sense of astonishment. If we read our New Testament and consider what the gospel of Jesus Christ really offers us, and then look at ourselves and our life and experience, we are confronted by this tremendous gulf. So we go on to ask the obvious question—why do we rob ourselves like this? We have all this wealth and riches offered us, why are we so poor?

Now I suggest to you that this is really the problem that confronts us all. In a worldly sense, if we were offered great wealth and riches, we would need no encouragement to take hold of them and possess them. But here we are offered the greatest riches of all, the fullness of God, the treasures of grace and wisdom that God has placed for us in the Lord Jesus Christ, the fullness that the New Testament speaks of, that is available for us, and yet we continue in a state of penury and poverty. We are half-hearted and ill at ease and shuffling along, instead of availing ourselves of these greatest of all riches. Why is it? That is the great question. Why do Christian people need these encouragements and exhortations?

And the answer is, according to the Bible, that it is all due to sin. We have a mighty enemy and adversary of our souls, one whose supreme object is not only to rob God of his glory, but to rob God's people of the things that God has provided for them. And, of course, as he robs us of the blessings, he is most effectively robbing God of his glory also, because, as far as this world is concerned, God's greatest glory is his people. God expresses his praise and glory most of all in his people, so if God's people are apologetic, hesitant, unhappy and uncertain, God is being robbed of his glory. Therefore the devil concentrates on that. The teaching of Scripture is that he is ever busy in trying to stand between us and a full realization of what God has intended for us in the Lord Jesus Christ.

He fights, he thwarts us, he dulls our faculties, he holds us down and he binds us to earth. So, as I see it, the great function of Christian preaching is not only to warn us of these things, but also, positively, to present before us the greatness of our salvation. For if once we see it from God's side and from our side, then we will be able to resist the devil and he will flee from us. We will be able to resist him stead-fastly and fully, and all his suggestions and all he tends to do to us personally in the physical sense. The ultimate way of conquering the devil is really to lay hold of this life that is offered us in the New Testament gospel, and that is the thing to which we are referring here.

According to this statement of our Lord here in his prayer to his Father, one of the objects which he had in view, in doing all the things that we have been looking at in so much detail, was that you and I might have eternal life. The plan in eternity, the laying aside of the glory, the incarnation, the birth in Bethlehem, all he endured for thirty-three years, all his preaching all his miracles, his death upon the cross, his resurrection, the ascension, the sending of the Holy Spirit— one of the great objectives for which all that was designed was that you and I might have eternal life. Here he is at the end, and he prays the Father, 'The hour is come; glorify thy Son, that thy Son also may glorify thee: as thou hast given him power over all flesh, that he should give eternal life to as many as thou hast given him.'

What then is this eternal life of which he speaks? Anyone who reads the New Testament must know at once that it is one of the central themes of the New Testament itself, and especially of this gospel of John. It is the theme above all else which is emphasized by John, not only in this gospel but also in his epistles. Take that well-known verse, John 3:16, 'For

God so loved the world, that he gave his only begotten Son'—why?—'that whosoever believeth in him should not perish'—that is the negative, and here is the positive—'but have everlasting life.' That is it! Again we read of the Lord saying, 'I am come. . .' Why did he come from God? Why did he leave the courts of heaven? Why did he humble himself? Why was he made in the likeness of sinful flesh? The answer is 'that they might have life, and that they might have it more abundantly' (Jn 10:10), And in John 6 you will find that he repeats it frequently: it is the great emphasis.

Paul, too, puts the same point when he says, 'The wages of sin is death; but the gift of God is eternal life through Jesus Christ our Lord' (Rom 6:23). Thus, you see, it is the great central message of the New Testament. Paul is constantly dealing with it: 'Reckon ye also yourselves to be dead indeed unto sin, but alive unto God through Jesus Christ our Lord' (Rom 6:11). This therefore is surely something which we must look at a little more closely, though I can only introduce the subject, because it is, as I have shown you, the great central theme of the New Testament, and obviously no man can even attempt to deal with it fully in just one discourse. I am going to show you certain things which are laid down here concerning the matter, before we go on to attempt to define it in detail.

The first principle that I would lay down is that the essence and the end of salvation is that we should have eternal life. What is a Christian? What is Christianity? The definition of the New Testament is that a Christian is a man who possesses eternal life. Perhaps the best way of emphasizing that is to consider how it is that we hold such a low view of Christianity and the Christian life. What is the average person's conception of a Christian and what makes one a Christian?

There are many strange answers to that question. Some people seem to think of it in terms of country. They still speak about Christian countries and non-Christian countries, as if the whole country could be Christian. Then others think of it in terms of being christened when you were a child, or even baptized when you were an adult. Others think of it in terms of church membership, some action which is taken, some formality, a name on a register showing that you belong to a society or an institution, and they say that makes you a Christian. Others think of it as living a good life, following Christ and his teaching, trying to apply it personally, and getting other people to do the same, imitating his example, emulating the perfect specimen which he has provided for us. I am going up the scale, and that last, I think, is the highest, the best definition of a Christian that man by his own unaided understanding can ever arrive at.

But according to the New Testament, all that does not even begin to make one a Christian, and the world is very often quick to detect the hollowness of the claims in such people who call themselves Christian. I was reading of a distinction which I think was common among many Chinese people in past years. They called all the ordinary foreigners Christians, but others they called 'Jesus people'. What they meant was that they regarded everybody who went to China from the West as Christians, because they came from so-called Christian countries, and most of them claimed that they were Christian. But the Chinese saw that they were often drunkards, and immoral and so on, and they felt that if that was Christianity then they did not want it. But then they found that there were other people who came from the same countries who also called themselves Christians. But these lived a pure, holy kind of life, they seemed to be out to help people, and were altogether different, and the Chinese began to call them 'Jesus people', because they seemed to be like the Lord Jesus Christ himself.

Now that is the way to make the distinction, so I want to go one step further and suggest that to be a Christian (and to know the very essence of Christian salvation), it is not even enough just to believe in the forgiveness of sins. The people I

have been describing may not even have talked about forgiveness of sins, that was not the distinguishing feature.
Because a man talks about forgiveness of sins in the Lord
Jesus Christ, he is not of necessity a Christian, or at any rate
his definition of a Christian is very imcomplete. The essence
and the end of Christian salvation is the possession of eternal
life: 'As thou hast given him power over all flesh'—Why?—
that their sins might be forgiven? No—'that he should give
eternal life to as many as thou hast given him.' That is
what makes the difference, we must never stop short of that.

It is perhaps important that we should hurriedly glance at
the relationship between these two matters. I feel that many
go astray, and that many heresies have crept into the church
at this point, because of the failure to see this. There is indeed
a direct relationship between the forgiveness of sins and eternal life. Perhaps the best way to put it is that we must never
think of the possession of eternal life as something in and of
itself, as something that is directly possible. We must never
think of the possession of eternal life unless we have first of
all considered the forgiveness of sins. I know of many people
today who say they are not interested in the terms justification and sanctification. But you ignore them at your peril,
because the New Testament teaches us that justification and
forgiveness are an absolute essential before you can receive
eternal life. If you try to forget that this love of God first of
all came by the way of forgiveness and justification, you will
find that you are indulging in a false mysticism, and that you
are deluding yourself and doing something that has often led
people into the greatest misery and unhappiness. So while
Christian salvation does not end at forgiveness, it does start
there; there is no short cut to eternal life except via grace,
repentance, justification, and acceptance in the sight of God.
Eternal life is not the same as justification, it is based upon it.
Justification is the preliminary cleansing of the ground.

Let me illustrate this. Take any of the buildings that were
damaged during the war. There they were, crumbling and

ruined, bits of wall standing here and there. Now before a new building could be put up on that site, the ruins had to be cleared away, the remaining walls pulled down, the rubbish taken away, and the site cleared. It is exactly like that in the Christian life, in this spiritual experience. You cannot possess eternal life from God, until the ruins caused by sin have been dealt with, and these can only be dealt with by the death of the Lord Jesus Christ upon the cross. We need to be reconciled to God before we can receive life from God. We must be justified from our sin and guilt in the sight of God before he will give us this blessing. It is in this way that we establish the relationship between the two. If you begin by seeking this life from God without forgiveness, that is the false way of mysticism. But on the other hand, you must not stop at justification, it is the basis on which we are entitled to ask God for this divine life, which is the essence of Christianity. John Wesley, for example, found his favourite definition of Christianity in the title of a book that was written in the sixteenth century by a Scotsman called Henry Scougal: *The life of God in the soul of man*. That is it, the possession of the life of God in one's own soul. That is the essence and the end of salvation.

But we must proceed to lay down a second proposition, which is that by nature we all lack this life and are entirely without it. You notice how our Lord puts it here: 'that he should give eternal life to as many as thou hast given him'. The obvious implication there is that apart from this gift we are all without this life, and here again is something that is absolutely basic and vital to the whole of the New Testament position. We can see this, for example, in Ephesians 2:1–3: 'And you hath he quickened, who were dead in trespasses and sins; wherein in time past ye walked according to the course of this world, according to the prince of the power of the air, the spirit that now worketh in the children of disobedience: among whom also we all had our conversation in times past in the lusts of our flesh, fulfilling the desires of the flesh and of the mind; and were by nature the children of wrath, even as others.'

That is the condition and the position of the whole of mankind, until we receive this gift from the Lord Jesus Christ.

Now the question that obviously arises at once is this: how did mankind ever come into such a condition? It is important that we should realize that that is the truth about us, for if we do not realize it, then we are utterly dead in trespasses and sins, and the gospel has nothing to say to us, except to convict us of that fact. So the question is, how did man ever get into such a state? And the answer is to be found in Genesis 3—a vitally important and essential chapter. I find there are so many Christian people today who seem to think you can be fully a Christian and shed the first chapters of Genesis. 'There is no need to believe in all that,' they say, 'because scientific knowledge has made it quite impossible.'

But let us see whether that is a tenable position or not. It seems to me that the biblical doctrine all hangs together, and that we will never see the true greatness of Christian salvation until we fully see and realize the nature of man. According to Scripture, the trouble with man by nature is not that he is incomplete but that he is dead. Now evolutionism tells us that man is just evolving out of the animal stage; he obviously has still a great deal of the bestial in him, but he is advancing up to perfection. The trouble is that he has not climbed high enough yet. But if that is true, then I have to cut out a great deal of my Bible, I have to eschew a great deal of that talk about being 'the children of wrath', for the Bible tells me that I am not only incomplete and inadequate, I am positively evil, I am under the wrath of God, I am subject to perdition because of something that is true of me. That is the meaning of the wrath of God. And that is not just Paul's teaching. The Lord Jesus Christ said, 'He that believeth on the Son of God hath everlasting life: and he that believeth not the Son shall not see life; but the wrath of God abideth on him' (Jn 3:36). No one taught this doctrine more clearly than our Lord himself, and that is why he said, 'I am come that they might have life.'

All this, therefore can only be explained truly in terms of what we are told in Genesis. God made man and made him perfect, and then, we are told, God breathed into man the breath of life and he became a living soul. God thus breathed into man something of his own life, and in that state and condition man was a living soul enjoying the life of God and in correspondence with him. But God, you remember, told man that if he wanted to maintain that life he must be obedient. He could eat of all the trees of the garden, except the particular tree of the knowledge of good and evil. But man disobeyed, even though God had warned him what would have to happen. God had said, 'But of the tree of the knowledge of good and evil, thou shalt not eat of it: for in the day that thou eatest thereof, thou shalt surely die' (Gen 2:17); and, remember, death does not only mean physical death, it means, still more, spiritual death, falling out of relationship with God, and out of correspondence with him.

And the account goes on to tell us what happened. Man disobeyed and though hitherto he had delighted in hearing the voice of God in the Garden, the moment he disobeyed, the link was broken and the voice of God frightened him. But God did not stop at that, he threw man out of the Garden and placed cherubim and a flaming sword to prevent man from going back to that perfect life. Left in his own strength and power, man is condemned to a spiritual death. He loses the voice of God, and the possession of life eternal. From there on man is a creature without a knowledge of God. He lives in ignorance, indeed he becomes an enemy of God. He is, the Bible teaches, dead to spiritual things. He does not enjoy or see any point in prayer; doctrine is mere theory to him, not in any way relevant to his life; and, the Bible tells us, he is now of his father the devil, manifesting in his nature and life the characteristics of the devil, the worst of which is enmity against God, and a hatred of him.

Now it seems to me that this doctrine of the fall which I have been putting to you, is an essential part of the biblical doctrine of salvation. Man has lost this eternal life, which is why he is under the curse and wrath of God, and needs to be given this gift of life. This is not something that I have deduced from the Scriptures, you will find it stated explicitly in I Corinthians 15: 'For as in Adam all die, even so in Christ shall all be made alive', and you will find it also in Romans 5. So I suggest to you that the work of the Lord Jesus Christ— the work of which he says here, 'I have finished the work which thou gavest me to do'—cannot be truly understood until we understand this doctrine of the fall. We do not need some human knowledge telling us that we just have to be raised up and so drawn up a little bit higher. No! We need to be delivered from the wrath of God. It is because of the fall that man is dead in trespasses and sins; he is spiritually dead and that is why he is in that condition.

Let me go on to my next proposition, which is that eternal life is a gift from God. That is made very plain by our Lord's words: 'that he should give eternal life to as many as thou hast given him', and I think that this follows very logically from what I have just been saying. There is, indeed a perfect logic and wholeness in scriptural doctrine, and if you trip up over one part, then the whole of the doctrine is going to be involved. Man, though spiritually dead decided to live the life of God, but he could never produce or generate that life for himself. It is impossible, he was not allowed to do so— there was that flaming sword to bar his way back to that life from which he was dismissed. It cannot be done, no man can ever make himself a Christian, for no man can ever produce the Christian life within himself.

Not only that, it is something that we never arrive at, it is something that we never merit. It does not matter what good you may do, you will never win eternal life. You may have spent the whole of your life in doing good works, but I say that you have no more right to eternal life than the most dissolute vagrant in the world today. You say you believe in attending a place of worship and doing good, but I say that if you are trusting to these things you are condemning yourself. All our righteousness is but as 'filthy rags', our greatest virtues are ugly and foul in the sight of God, because they are all tainted by sin. 'The gift of God is eternal life through Jesus Christ our Lord' (Rom 6:23): we are saved by grace 'through faith; and that not of yourselves: it is the gift of God' (Eph 2:8). The whole message of the New Testament is the message of the grace of God, the gift to undeserving sinners, and we only have eternal life when we receive it as a gift.

There is one further point, which is that there is only one person who can give us the gift and that is the One who is praying: 'As thou hast given him power over all flesh, that he should give eternal life to as many as thou hast given him.' It is Christ alone who can give us this eternal life. Once more we see the terrible danger of mysticism, or at any rate of the mysticism which does not make Christ central. There are many people in the world who are anxious to possess this life of God. You will find them writing about it, and one of the most remarkable examples of this has been Aldous Huxley, who used to be a complete sceptic, but who came to believe that nothing can save the world but mysticism, and who became a Buddhist for that reason. Such men believe that there is this eternal life of God to be had, that what we need is that life of God in ourselves and that our trouble is that we have not got it. They are using the same definition as Henry Scougal, but notice the difference: these people think that they can get this life of God in themselves without mentioning the Lord Jesus Christ at all. You get it, they say, by contemplation of the Absolute, by increasingly sinking into the eternal and being lost in him, because as you do so, you are receiving life from him.

I do not want to sound unsympathetic. I think it is a good thing that men and women are beginning to see that man alone is insufficient. It is all right as far as it goes, but the vital question is, how do you see it? It is possible to talk about sinking into the heart of the Eternal, but it takes many forms and assumes many guises. There are those who tell you that you can know God and begin to share his life immediately just as you are. They say that the moment you begin to feel your need of God all you have to do is to turn to God and he will begin to speak to you. They do not mention the Lord Jesus Christ at all.

But, my friends, it is he and he alone who can give eternal life. He claims it here and Scripture says it everywhere: 'As thou hast given him power over all flesh that he should give eternal life. . .' There is no one else who can give eternal life to man except the Lord Jesus Christ. If it were possible in any other way, why did he ever come to earth? Why did he work as a carpenter? Why did he endure all he endured? Why the death on the cross? Why the agony and the shame and the blood-stained sweat? There is no other way—the whole plan of salvation centres on him. He alone is the giver of eternal life, and we seek life from God in any other way at our greatest and gravest peril. I am not denying that you may have had experiences, but it is my business to proclaim that whatever happiness you may find, whatever release and freedom, whatever guidance, whatever magic, whatever miraculous things may seem to be happening to you, unless you obtain them directly and only through the Son of God, the Lord Jesus Christ, it is not life from God, and you are the victim of a terrible delusion. One day you will awaken to find that that is a fact; it is he and he alone who is the giver and the transmitter of the life of God to the souls of men.

10

The Only True God

John 17:2–3

We have been seeing together that the ultimate purpose of our salvation is that we might have the gift of eternal life; and we have seen that that is the grand object and the final explanation of everything that was planned by the blessed Trinity. So this is obviously the most important thing we can ever consider together, and we began our consideration of it by realizing that it is something which, as we are by nature as the result of sin, we all lack, because we are 'dead in trespasses and sins' (Eph 2:1). And furthermore we saw that it is something which we have to receive as a gift because however wonderful our morality and conduct may be, they will never rise to the level of the eternal life.

The difference between being a Christian and not being a Christian is not one of degree, it is one of essence and quality, so that the most unworthy Christian is in a better position that the best man outside Christianity. Perhaps the best way of understanding all this is to think of it in terms of relationship. It is a question of blood, if you like; the humblest and the most unworthy member of the royal family is in a more advantageous position from the standpoint of social arrangements in most countries than the greatest and most able person outside that family. A man outside the royal family may be much more cultured, may be a finer specimen of humanity in every respect, yet on all state occasions and great occasions, he has to follow after the humblest and the least worthy member of the royal family. How do you assess his position? You do not assess it in terms of ability and achievement, you assess it in terms of blood relationship. Now that is precisely what the New Testament says about the Christian. He is one who had become a partaker of the divine nature; he is in an entirely new relationship; he has a new nature and quality; a new order of life has entered into him.

Furthermore, we found that it is our Lord alone who can give it to us, and that is what he is emphasizing here. He asks God to glorify him because, he says, in effect, 'If you do not glorify me by enabling me to do this last bit of work which I have to do, if you do not enable me to be a Sin-Bearer of the whole guilt and sin of the world, then the whole of mankind will remain dead in trespasses and sins.' He pleads with and urges his Father to glorify him so that he can give eternal life. So any attempt, as we have seen, to arrive at God, and have communion and fellowship with him, except in and through Christ and all his work, is a snare and delusion.

We now come on to deal with some practical questions. We saw that by definition a Christian is one who has eternal life, so what is this life, and how can one obtain it? I want to take that second question first because it seems to me to be the one that is dealt with first of all in these verses that we are considering. Verse 3 says, 'And this is life eternal, that they might know thee the only true God, and Jesus Christ, whom thou hast sent.' What does that mean exactly? Is it a definition of what is meant by eternal life, or is it a description of the way in which eternal life is to be obtained? Those are the two possible explanations and expositions.

I suppose that in an ultimate sense it is right to say that both are true, and yet I find myself, on the whole, agreeing with those who think that it is probably a description of the way in which etrnal life is to be obtained. Now John has his own style of writing and you will find he always puts things in this particular way. Let me give you an illustration of this same thing from John 3:19 where he says, 'And this is the condemnation, that light is come into the world, and men loved darkness rather than light. . .' Notice what an exact parallel that is with this statement: 'And this is life eternal, that they might know thee the only true God, and Jesus Christ, whom thou hast sent.' It is the same form of expression so that John 3:19 is probably a safe guide to follow in the interpretation of this verse.

Let me explain. When John says, 'this is the condemnation', he is not giving us a definition of the condemnation; rather he is telling us the cause of it, which is 'that light is come into the world, and men loved darkness rather than light'. Surely, therefore, this verse can be interpreted in the same way. This is the thing that causes, or leads to life eternal —'that they might know thee the only true God, and Jesus Christ, whom thou hast sent'. I can give you further examples and illustrations of the same thing. John says in his first epistle, 'This is the true God and eternal life' (1 Jn 5:20) by which he means, 'This is the true God, and the cause of eternal life'—referring again to the Lord Jesus Christ. So we have here primarily an account of the way, or the means, by which eternal life is to be obtained. Or, if you prefer it, we have here a description of the origin of eternal life rather than a definition of its essence. Yet, as I have said, it is very difficult to separate these two things from each other: that which gives me eternal life is the eternal life itself, for as I receive and enjoy the means of obtaining eternal life, I am obtaining it at the same time. However, we should hold these things as separate ideas in our mind.

Let us look therefore at the mechanism by which eternal life comes to us. As we do so, God grant that we all may realize that this is not only our greatest need, but also the most wonderful privilege that can ever come to us men and women. By giving us his eternal life God is saying that we can have the right and the authority to become sons of God, that we may indeed and in truth become partakers of the divine nature, and that we may have, here, at this moment, a true reminder in our earthly course of this relationship to God that is going to make us heirs of God and joint heirs with Christ. God has given us his nature, and not even death and the grave can rob us of our heritage. It not only means a transformed life while we are still here in this world, it is a guarantee of such great things.

How, then, are we to get eternal life? Well, the essential thing we are told here is that it is ultimately a question of knowing God, and that is of course the great question that is held before us everywhere in the Bible. God is Someone who is to be known by us, and there is no possibility of eternal life apart from this knowledge of him. John says this in his first epistle. He has become an old man and is at the point of death, and he tells the people to whom he is writing that he wants them to be happy, and to be sharing the same joy that fills his heart. There is a joy possible in this life, he says. Your joy can be full in this world, and it is a joy that is based upon fellowship with God. We have a wonderful fellowship to share, and truly 'our fellowship is with the Father, and with his Son Jesus Christ' (1 Jn 1:3). You notice how these New Testament writers repeat themselves, and they do this because they are always talking about this wonderful fact; a man who knows anything about this intimate fellowship with God cannot stop speaking about it. We can all speak about the things that interest us, we go on talking about them, and here is the greatest thing of all, eternal life, knowing God and having fellowship with him—it is no wonder that they keep repeating themselves!

How then do we know God? The Lord Jesus Christ divides it up into two main headings, and I merely want to consider them briefly now. He says, 'This is eternal life, that they might know thee the only true God', and he puts it like this because he is issuing a warning, or, if you like, he is stating this truth in the form of a contrast. He is emphasizing that we must be absolutely certain that the God in whom we believe, the God whom we claim to know, is the only true God. Now by using these words 'only' and 'true' he is clearly presenting God to our consideration as over and against something else, and it is obvious that he is warning against idols and false gods.

You find a great deal about that in the New Testament. John, again, ends his first epistle with these words, 'Little children, keep yourselves from idols.' That is the last word of this old man as he writes his farewell letter to the infant churches. He starts by saying that nothing matters but that we have fellowship with God the Father and with his Son Jesus Christ; he then goes on to warn them against certain heresies, and he sums it all up by saying, 'Keep yourselves from idols.' And the warning is as necessary today as it was in the first century. We must be absolutely certain that the God we worship is the only true and living God. Paul, also, in writing to the Thessalonians reminds them of how, when he first preached the gospel to them, they 'turned from idols to serve the living and true God' (1 Thess 1:9)—that is it. Again, the account in Acts 17 of Paul's visit to Athens tells us how that cultured city was full of temples to the various gods. The people of Athens were too 'religious' in a sense, worshipping all these gods, Mercury, Jupiter, Mars and then, lest any should be left out, there was a curious temple 'To the unknown God'. And yet the whole time they were ignorant of God himself. 'Whom, therefore,' says Paul, 'ye ignorantly worship, him declare I unto you' (Acts 17:23). That is the great business of the Bible, to hold before us the only true and living God.

And, let me repeat, this is as essential today as it was in the first century. It is not, perhaps, that we worship those old pagan deities, but we have a tendency today to worship philosophic abstractions in the same way as they did. You find people today writing in very learned terms about the

Absolute or the Ultimate, or the Source of all being, or the life in the universe. God, to so many people, is nothing but a sheer abstraction, nothing but a philosophical concept, and when they speak of God it is of some kind of philosophical 'X': God is to so many some great force or energy. The Bible is constantly warning us against all that, and, as in the words of our Lord here to his Father, the Bible is always calling us to realize that there is only one true God.

Then there are certain things we must know about him before we can possibly have fellowship with him, and before we can receive life from him. First, obviously, we must believe he is a person. That is a very difficult concept, and yet it is vital and essential. God says, 'I AM that I AM'; God is God, and God, therefore, is a person. The author of Hebrews puts it like this in a very important passage in his epistle. He is talking about the life of faith, and about the secret of men like Moses and others who went through the world as great heroes, mastering their circumstances, and standing out above all the average men in this life—what, he asks, was their secret? And the answer he gives is that their secret was faith, and their relationship to God. Yes, but if you want to be in that full relationship to God, there is one absolute condition—'He that cometh to God must believe that he is, and that he is a rewarder of them that diligently seek him' (Heb 11:6).

You see, when you come to God, you must not come in the wrong way. There was a poem which was very popular and often quoted some years ago, which ran:

> Out of the night that covers me,
> Black as the pit from pole to pole,
> I thank whatever gods there be
> For my unconquerable soul.
>
> *W. E. Henley*

Rubbish! That is the very kind of nonsense against which the Bible warns us. If you come to God and really want to know and please him, you do not come in this mood of 'whatever gods there be'. No, 'He that cometh to God must believe that he is, and that he is a rewarder of them that diligently seek him.' That is inevitably our starting point. God is a living God, not a concept or abstraction or term in a philosophical category. If you want a perfect exposition of that, you should read the accounts which are given in the Old Testament of some of the false gods that people worshipped. I commend to your study Isaiah 46, where the prophet mocks at the false god Baal that the foolish children of Israel had been worshipping. They had to carry him from one place to another because he could not walk! Why worship such a god when you have a God who will carry you? asks Isaiah. Or what about the description of false gods in Psalm 115? 'Eyes have they, but they see not: they have ears, but they hear not: noses have they, but they smell not . . . they that make them are like unto them' (verses 6–8).

There you have one of the most glorious bits of sarcasm in the whole of Scripture.

And the verse which we are considering here is urging us to start by a preliminary realization of this same tremendous truth—that he is the living God, he is the Creator. In all our preoccupation with God the Saviour, we must never forget God the Creator. God is our Saviour but he is also the Lord of the universe. He is the One who said, 'Let there be light: and there was light.' He has brought everything into being. He is in the heavens and everything is at his feet. So we must remember that we start with the Lord of the universe, the Creator, the Instigator of everything that is.

And then we must come on to a consideration of his character. 'God is light,' says John in his first epistle, 'and in him is no darkness at all' (1 Jn 1:5). Before you drop on your knees next time and begin to speak to God, before you seek him and his face and this life he has come to give, never fail to remind yourself of these things. Try to remember his greatness and his majesty and his might, and then go on to remember that he is life, that he is holy, that he is righteous, that he is just, and that he is of such a pure countenance that he cannot even look upon evil. Remember that you are speaking to the Judge of the whole world. All these things are emphasized by this little phrase 'the only true God'. He is not like those false gods, those abstractions. You are going into the presence of the eternal God, a living God, One who is, who always has been, the Great I AM from eternity to eternity. That is the essential starting point and, I repeat, until we have that clear in our minds and in our understanding our prayer to God is probably nothing but a mere crying out to him in desperation. God, if I may so put it, has taken the trouble to reveal himself to us—that is the whole point of the Old Testament—so we have no right to go to God in ignorance, we must make use of the knowledge he has given us. He says that he is a jealous God, emphasizing his personal quality, and that he will not allow us to have any other gods beside him: 'Thou shalt worship the Lord thy God, and him only shalt thou serve' (Lk 4:8). We must, therefore, take the trouble to get hold of this knowledge and information. We must really wrestle with this revelation and then, in the light of that, come to God believing that he is. It is not that we understand his absolute qualities, but we realize that we are speaking to One who has called himself, Father, and who wants us to come to him in that way.

But we do not stop at that. 'He that cometh to God must believe that he is', yes, but he must also believe that 'he is a rewarder of them that deligently seek him' (Heb 11:6)—which is put here in John 17 in this way: 'And this is life eternal, that they might know thee the only true God, and Jesus Christ, whom thou hast sent.' This is obviously crucial, and in its essence it means that we must not only know him as the only true God, we must also know him as the God of our salvation, because unless we know him in this second sense, we will never obtain eternal life from him. I can put it like this. We have seen that our Lord's first warning is against the false gods, a warning to the Gentiles, and this second warning is a warning to the Jews, to people who only think of God in terms of the Old Testament, and who still go to God as if the New Testament had never been given to us. They come to God only in terms of law and have never come into the relationship of grace, and because of that, they are going to rob themselves of the greatest and the chief blessing of salvation.

That is the glory of our Bible, we have the Old and New Testaments, and may I emphasize again the vital importance of taking *both*. It is quite wrong to take the Old Testament alone, and there is a sense in which it is almost equally wrong to take the New Testament alone. It was the Holy Spirit that guided the early church to interpret the two together. We must remember that God is the Creator, and also the Saviour; and, too, we must remember that he is not only the Saviour he is the sole Creator—we worship a blessed triune God.

But here the emphasis is upon God as life, God not only as he is in and of himself, but in his relationship to the world and especially in his relationship to man. We must realize as we approach God that his ultimate, gracious purpose with regard to man has been revealed to us, and it is a purpose of love and mercy, and of kindness and compassion. And, as we have seen, this is something that is only known fully and finally in and through the Lord Jesus Christ. That is why this statement must be put like this, 'This is life eternal that they may know thee the only true God, and Jesus Christ, whom thou hast sent.' This truth is an absolute necessity. That is why our Lord said, 'I am the way, the truth, and the life: no man cometh unto the Father but by me' (Jn 14:6). He is the way to God, he is the truth about God, and apart from the life he gives us, we will never share or know the life of God. So there is no knowledge of God apart from him, through him comes this ultimate true and saving knowledge, the saving relationship.

Of course, every word in this statement has supreme significance. You notice what this verse tells us about the Lord Jesus Christ—'That they might know thee the only true God, *and* Jesus Christ. . .' At once we are told there that he is equal with God, for immediately this man, Christ Jesus, is put into the same category as the only true and living God. Here is One who is on the face of this earth but who can be bracketed with God the Father. Some foolish people, such as the Unitarians, have often tried to use this phrase in order to prove their particular theory. They say that there is only one God and that Jesus Christ was not God, and they try to prove is by saying that Christ himself, while he was in the world, said that there is only one true God. But they stop at that point and forget this vital thing, that the One who says those words, 'the only true God, and Jesus Christ. . .', immediately puts himself into the same position as God. Here is One who is co-equal with God and co-eternal with God. Here is One who is God himself, God the Son, ever eternally in the bosom of the Father—'and Jesus Christ. . .' Thus we are fully entitled to make this statement that God is not only eternal and true but cannot be fully and finally known except in and through One who thus adds himself, as it were, to him.

Then here is the name, *Jesus*, which reminds us of the truth of the incarnation that this eternal Son of God was made man—the man Jesus. But the man Jesus is One who is God and who is co-equal with him and whom, therefore, you think of in terms of God and with God—'and Jesus'.

But he is also Jesus *Christ*, and 'the Christ' means the Messiah, the One who has been anointed to do this special work of bringing men to God and of giving God's life to man. You see how all this mighty doctrine is put here as it were in a nutshell for us—'and Jesus Christ'. It is all there—the ultimate object is to know this only true God; yes, and the way to know him is to know Jesus Christ.

Our Lord goes on to say, 'O righteous Father, the world

hath not known thee: but I have known thee, these [disciples] have known that thou hast sent me' (verse 25). And because they know that thou hast sent me, they know the Father and they have eternal life.

So we must realize that Jesus Christ gives us the revelation of God as no one else can give it. 'No man hath seen God at any time; the only begotten Son, which is in the bosom of the Father, he hath declared him' (Jn 1:18). He has manifested and revealed him, he has taught us about him. Yes, but you see he has gone further, as we have already seen. He has not only declared him, he has also taken out of the way the things that prevented our being in communion with him, he has removed the barrier of sin. If he had not done that, the knowledge and the revelation would avail us nothing.

But I just want to take one final step before we end this study. So far we have found that the knowledge of God is based upon these statements. It is based first upon the Old Testament revelation of God, the God who has differentiated himself from all the pagan gods and idols, the only true God who has revealed himself in the Ten Commandments and the moral law and the prophets. We then go on to the revelation of the Lord Jesus Christ and all that he has revealed, which makes him say, 'He that hath seen me hath seen the Father' (Jn 14:9). We have seen that he also removes the barrier of sin, the thing that comes between us and God and blinds our eyes and minds to the vision of God.

But he even goes a step beyond that. The Lord Jesus Christ gives us eternal life in a still deeper way. He gives us eternal life not only by giving us a knowledge about God, but by giving us the very life of God himself. This, says John, is the true God, the eternal life. We have seen, too, how Paul puts it: 'As in Adam all die, even so in Christ shall all be made alive' (1 Cor 15:22). Of course, this is a profound doctrine. We have all fallen because we are all 'in Adam'. Adam was the first man, the father of the human race, and the entire human race and the whole of humanity was in him. The result was that when Adam fell the whole race of man fell. He was not only the representative, we were in him, in his line, and death has come upon us all because we are in Adam, and because of what we have inherited from him.

Now over and against that, the New Testament puts the Lord Jesus Christ, and its amazing doctrine is that every true Christian is related to Christ, as every natural man was related to Adam. In other words, it means that if we are Christian, if we believe in the Lord Jesus Christ, we are incorporated into him, we become part of him, we share his life, and we are born of him. We are in him in exactly the same way as we were in Adam. This is the special work of the Holy Spirit. It is he who quickens us and brings about our regeneration. It is he who unites us to Christ and makes us a part of the life of Christ, and it is in that way, by sharing the life of Christ himself, that we receive the gift of eternal life. That is why he is so absolutely vital and essential. It is not something outside him, he gives us eternal life by giving us himself, and by this mystic union with Christ, by this relationship to him, we become participators of his own life. We are partakers of the divine nature, we have fellowship with God and the life of God enters into our souls.

So this is eternal life, this is the means of eternal life, 'that they might know thee the only true God, and Jesus Christ, whom thou hast sent.'

If we know this Christ, if we believe on him, we have eternal life, we have already become the sons of God.

11

A New Principle

John 17:2–3

In the light of our two preceding studies, the question which each one of us should be asking before we go any furher is this: do I possess eternal life? Have I received the gift of eternal life? It is the most momentous question we can ever ask ourselves in this life, because our eternal destiny depends upon our answer to it. That is the message of the Bible everywhere, from beginning to end. It emphasizes a Day of Judgement when certain great books will be opened, and unless our names are written in the Lamb's book of life— which means that we are possessors of eternal life—we go to destruction, to damnation and to eternal punishment. Clearly, therefore, this is the most important matter of all, and not only from the standpoint of our eternal destiny. Of course, we have to put that first, because it is the most serious matter, but it is also important from the standpoint of our life in this world, and the enjoyment and the success of that life, in the highest sense.

So, then, we have found that this life becomes possible to us only in and through a knowledge of God in the Lord Jesus Christ, and we have seen, too, that he enables us to know God by imparting himself to us, through the Holy Spirit. By entering into us and giving us life, he enables us to know God, and that is the point at which we start, when we discover the way to this life, the way in which it is obtained.

It is necessary, perhaps, that I should emphasize this word 'know'—'that they might *know* thee'—in order to bring out clearly that that does not mean merely an intellectual awareness. This word 'know' is a strong and powerful word. It does not just mean that you are acquainted with or aware of something; it does not even mean an intellectual acceptance of a number of propositions; it is much deeper than that. When God spoke to the Children of Israel through the prophet Amos, he said, 'You only have I known of all the families of the earth' (Amos 3:2). Obviously that does not mean that God was not aware of the existence of other nations; this word 'know' is a word which means 'you only have I known in an intimate way', you are the only people, in a sense, in whom I have been particularly interested. That is how this word is constantly used in Scripture and that is its meaning here. The knowledge of God about which our Lord speaks here means an actual living realization of him, not just believing in the being and existence of God, but knowing him as One who is living and dwelling in us. It is a living knowledge, and we must be careful that we do not attach a meaning to this word which falls short of that exalted conception.

Having said that, we now go forward to consider exactly what that means. We have seen the way in which we obtain eternal life. If a man really does not know God in Christ in that intimate sense, he has not got it. But what is this life which is claimed in that way? The first thing which we must emphasize is that it is a quality of life. Eternal life must be conceived of in terms of quality rather than mere quantity, or duration. That does not mean that the element of length and duration does not enter in, because it does. But over and above that, is this question of the quality—the thing that is always emphasized in the Scriptures. Our Lord puts it like this: 'I am come that they might have life, and that they might have it *more abundantly*' (Jn 10:10). So we see that, according to Scripture, what is offered to us is a type and kind of life which is available to us at this present time and which will go on right through the remainder of our lives in this world, and, still more important, beyond death and the grave and into eternity. That is really what is meant by eternal life.

Now both these aspects need to be emphasized. The astounding thing, in other words, is that the Christian is one who can receive here in this world, now in the present, something of the very life of glory itself. The apostle Paul speaks of that in Romans 8:23, where he refers to himself as one of those who have received the 'firstfruits', or, as he says, who have received a kind of foretaste. You see what is in his mind?

It is like the first gleanings of the crop. You go out into your garden and you pick the first raspberries, the full crop will soon come, but here is a preliminary instalment. You have the first fruits, the foretaste; you do not have it all, but you have a handful of what you are going to receive in an ultimate, complete fullness. And that is the way in which the Christian comes into eternal life, and it is surely one of the most remarkable and astounding things we can ever realize, that here on earth we can begin to experience something of the life of heaven, something of the life of glory.

Now the time element comes in like this. Though we receive the life itself here in this world, because we are in the flesh, and because of the imperfection that sin has introduced into every part of our being, there is a kind of limit. The apostle Paul makes this plain in writing to the Corinthians, 'For now,' he says, 'we see through a glass, darkly. . .' (1 Cor 13:12). Some people say it should be translated, 'we see in a sort of riddle', but that does not matter, both show that we do see after a fashion. But then note the difference: 'For now we see through a glass, darkly; but *then face to face.*' There is a certain amount of distortion in what we see at the present time we are seeing the real thing but 'darkly'. Then

we shall see it even as it is, '. . .then shall I know even as also
I am known.' 'Now,' Paul says again, 'I know in part'; it is
the difference, says the apostle, between the knowledge of a
child and the knowledge of a grown up person. The child
has, in a sense, a real knowledge, but it is an elementary and
an imperfect one. 'When I was a child, I spake as a child, I
understood as a child, I thought as a child: but when I became a man, I put away childish things' (1 Cor 12:11). That
is exactly the difference, says Paul, between eternal life in
this world and eternal life as we shall enjoy it in the
glory. The life is the same, only here it is partial, and imperfect 'as in a glass darkly'. But thank God that this is what is
offered to us even in this life and world. We can begin the life
of glory here on earth: 'Celestial fruits on earthly ground
may grow,' says the hymn writer, and that is the thing that
our Lord would have us realize constantly as Christian
people.

Very well, let us hold these two elements in our minds.
It is a quality of life, and that quality is the life of heaven, the
life of glory itself. We start it here, we can have it now and it
will continue, it will grow, it will increase, and ultimately it
will blossom out into that life of perfection when we shall see
with an utterly open face and 'know even as also we are
known' by him. I think that this is one of the most thrilling
things a man can ever learn in this life, so I summarize it by
putting it like this: It is possible for us as Christian people, to
receive here and now something of that life which the Lord
Jesus Christ himself enjoyed. He enjoyed this eternal life
while he was here on earth, and what he offers and what he
gives, he tells us, is something of that life—'that he should
give eternal life to as many as thou hast given him'.

So, then, having described it in general, let us try to
understand it a little more personally and see what exactly is
true of this life. Let me give you some of the New Testament
definitions of it. We are told that as a result of having this life
we become sons of God, or children of God—'For ye are all

the children of God,' says the apostle Paul in Galatians 3:26. Another phrase, used by John in his first epistle, is that we are 'born of God' (1 Jn 5:1) and in John 3:8 we read that we are 'born of the Spirit'. The apostle Peter describes it by saying that we become 'partakers of the divine nature' (2 Pet 1:4)—an astounding statement. In another place he tells us that we are 'begotten again' (1 Pet 1:3), we are regenerated. Now all those terms, and others too, are used in the New Testament in order to give us some conception and under-standing of the quality and nature of eternal life. And it was in order to give us this marvellous life that the Lord Jesus Christ came into the world. That is why he went to the cross, that is why he was buried and rose again, it was that you and I might become sons of God, children of God, born of God, partakers of the divine nature, that we might be regenerated, and made anew, and receive a new life. But, I must hasten to add, it is very important that we should not misconstrue any of these great, exalted terms.

Not one of them means that you and I become divine. We do not cease to be human. We are not turned into gods. We must never put such a meaning to those great terms. It does not mean that the divine essence, as it were, is infused into us. I put it in this negative form because some of the mystics have crossed the line and have taught—indeed you will find it very often in Roman Catholic teaching—that the divine nature is infused into us. That is something which is in the background of their doctrine of transubstantiation. Now there is no such teaching in the Bible and it savours of the monastic, and of Greek philosophy; we must be careful not to interpret those terms as meaning that we actually become divine. We are still human, though we are partakers of the divine nature.

I would even go beyond that. When you and I are in heaven and in glory, when our very bodies shall have been glorified and every vestige of sin shall have been purged out of us, when we shall see him face to face and be like him,

even then we shall still be men. The Lord Jesus is God-Man.
We never become God-men. We still remain man, but glorified man, perfect man. We are not transfigured or transformed into God.

This is obviously a very high and difficult doctrine to
understand, and I suppose that we are not meant to understand it fully in this life and world. The safe way of expressing it is to say that what happens to us when we receive
eternal life is that something entirely new comes into us and
into our life and experience. The Scripture says we become
new men, a new creation. The New Testament refers to a
new man and an old man, and we are told to put off the old
and to put on the new man. A new principle of life comes
into us which produces a profound change in us, and gives
us, therefore, a new quality of life and being. This new
principle produces in us a new nature, a new outlook, so
much so that having received it, we are able to say with
Paul—and he knows exactly what he means when he says
it—'If any man be in Christ, he is a new creature'—a new
creation —'old things are passed away; behold, all things are
become new' (2 Cor 5:17). It is all because of this principle
that enters into our lives.

I am tempted to say a word at this point about the
relationship of this new principle to the natural qualities and
faculties of man, because people are often in trouble and
difficulty about that. They wonder what happens when a
man receives this new life, what happens when he is born
again. Is he given an entirely new faculty or a new set of
faculties? The answer, of course, is, no. What he receives is a
new principle that affects all his faculties. Let me explain
what I mean. This new principle is something apart from
our faculties but it affects all of them. It is, as it were, something that comes in and enlivens them and enables us to use
them in an entirely different manner. Now that is very important for this reason: the Christian life, the receiving of this
eternal life, is absolutely independent of our natural faculties,

and qualities—and let us thank God for that fact. We all differ, for example, we all differ intellectually some are born with a greater ability to understand, with better brains, than others; some are able to read and understand what they read better than others. There is an endless variety and variation in people by nature, from the standpoint of propensities and abilities. The glory of this eternal life is that it can come into the life of any kind of person, and it really does not depend in any sense upon their individual qualities and faculties. The result is that a person who is unintelligent can receive this principle of new life quite as much as the most intelligent person in the world. And, furthermore, he can be as spiritual as that intelligent person. It is a principle apart from the natural faculties.

But of course it is at the same time a principle that can use the natural faculties. That is why when God wants a great teacher of the Christian gospel, he chooses a man like the apostle Paul. Yes, but Paul was no more a Christian than the most ignorant person in the church at Corinth. It is the *principle* that matters—we must not merely consider this in terms of understanding and ability, it is something much more wonderful and glorious than that. And that is why Paul was able to say in 1 Corinthians 1:21: 'For after that in the wisdom of God the world by wisdom knew not God, it pleased God by the foolishness of preaching to save them that believe.' God, he says, takes the ignorant and by means of them he confounds the wise, and he takes the weak and confounds the mighty—because of this new principle which he introduces. What, then, is the effect of the introduction of this principle? This life eternal, about which we are speaking, is, as I have said, something which affects the entire man. But it is especially interesting to observe the way in which it affects a man's understanding and apprehension of spiritual things. And the way to look at that is to contrast the natural, unregenerate man, who is not a Christian, with the man who is a Christian. According to Scripture, the natural man

is spiritually dead. May I be so bold as to put it like this: if
there is anybody to whom these things about which I am
speaking are really utterly meaningless, then, as I understand
Scripture, it means that such a person is spiritually dead and
has not received eternal life, because, as Paul puts it, 'The
natural man receiveth not the things of the Spirit of God: for
they are foolishness unto him' (1 Cor 2:14). They are meaningless to him, they are like a foreign language, and he is
bored by them.

Paul works this out in great detail in 1 Corinthians 2. He
says that we, as Christians, have not received 'the spirit of
the world, but the spirit which is of God', and we will never
know them until we receive the Spirit. 'Eye hath not seen,'
he says, 'nor ear heard, neither have entered into the heart of
man, the things which God hath prepared for them that love
him' (verse 9). And these things about which Paul is speaking do not refer to heaven, but to things here on earth.
However, Paul goes on, we understand because 'the Spirit
searcheth all things, yea, the deep things of God' (verse 10).
Now that, I think, is something wonderful and glorious.
The princes of this world do not understand these things,
and let us remember that when he is talking of princes, he is
not only referring to people who are crowned kings, he is
including the philosophers, he is talking about the Greeks
who sought and worshipped wisdom. When Paul says that
the princes of this world do not know the Lord Jesus Christ,
he means they do not understand or grasp the truth because
they are spiritually dead. Living in terms of their natural
powers and faculties, they come to these spiritual things with
their natural intellect and they see nothing in them. And he
goes on to say that they never will see anything in them until
they have received the light of the Spirit. But, he says, 'he
that is spiritual judgeth'—which means he understands, he
can evaluate all things—'yet he himself is judged of no man'
(verse 15). The Christian is an enigma to the non-Christian,
the Christian does not really understand himself! He has an

understanding and an insight which the other man does not have.

Then there is the wonderful statement at the end of the chapter, 'For who hath known the mind of the Lord, that he may instruct him?' And Paul gives this amazing answer—'But we have the mind of Christ.' He does not mean by this that we have the perfect knowledge that Christ has. He means that we have the spiritual understanding of Christ himself. He has given it to us, and we have received it as a gift from him. It is one of the aspects of eternal life—the mind of Christ. And this means that the new man, the man who has received this gift of eternal life, has an interest in spiritual things. The other man has not got this, but the new man has, and he begins to look at himself in a new way. He realizes that he is not merely an animal sent into this world to eat and drink and sleep and make money. No! He realizes that he is a spiritual being. He knows within himself that there is something which lifts him up beyond the whole universe, that he is meant for God and that he has God's Spirit within him. He did not know that before, but he knows it now. He has an entirely new view of death as well as of life and he faces his life in this world in an entirely new way.

My dear friends, if you want to know whether you have eternal life, that is a simple way of deciding it. When you think about yourself do you stop merely at the point at which the man of the world stops, or do you remind yourself every day of your life that you have a soul, a spirit; that what really matters is not this brief span of life in this world, but that destiny for which we are meant, that life that is awaiting us with God, that glory to which we are going? The Christian views himself with a spiritual mind and he faces God in an entirely different way.

The Christian also has an entirely different view of the world in which he lives, it is a spiritual view. What is your view of the world at this moment? Are you troubled or grieved about it? Are you hurt by it? Paul says of the Christian that 'we that are in this tabernacle do groan, being burdened' (2 Cor 5:4). Or again, even we 'which have received the firstfruits of the Spirit, even we ourselves groan within ourselves, waiting for the adoption, to wit, the redemption of our body' (Rom 8:23). Does the world trouble you? You see, if you have received eternal life you become like the Lord Jesus Christ. In this world he was a man of sorrows and acquainted with grief because he saw what sin had done to his Father's great and glorious world, because he saw men and women in the shackles of sin and dupes in the service of Satan. It grieved him at heart and the man who is spiritually minded knows something of that view of this life and world, and of the men and women who are in it.

In other words, spiritual things become real to the man who receives eternal life. These things are not theoretical to him, they are not merely philosophical or academic. He does not feel that they are something he has to force himself to take up. They are the centre of his life, the most vital things of all to him. Do we have to force ourselves to think about these things? Do we have to say, 'It is Sunday again and I suppose I had better do so and so?' Or do we delight in it, wishing, in a way, that we could spend every day looking into these things? Do we hunger and thirst after righteousness? Are these to us the most vital, momentous, central things? They are to the spiritual man, and they must be, because of what has happened to him. The principle of the life of Christ has come into him and he becomes like Christ.

And the last thing I would say about him is that he has an understanding of spiritual things which he never had before. John, in his first epistle, warns those first Christians against certain dangers and heresies. There is, he says, a sense in which he need not keep on reminding them, because they 'have an unction from the Holy One' (1 Jn 2:20). It is true of the Christian: he has a spiritual understanding of spiritual things, he knows the truth about the Lord Jesus Christ. There are people who are always arguing about the person of Christ. They are always in trouble and want to understand this, that and the other. But the spiritual man is not like that. I do not mean that he can necessarily explain everything to you. Look at those Corinthian Christians, the people of whom Paul said that they had 'the mind of Christ'. They were not great philosophers, for, he says, 'not many mighty . . . are called'. And yet you know they could see the Lord Jesus Christ in a way that the princes of this world could not. The Christian is the man who does not understand intellectually, he understands spiritually; he knows because of this principle of life that is come into him—life recognizes life.

The knowledge which is given to the Christian is almost an instinctive knowledge. I think the best analogy is this. It is comparable to the knowledge which a man has who is in love with a woman. It is not possible for him to sit down and write out a philosophical account of his love, he cannot explain it rationally: he knows it, but here his reason ceases. The great love which reason and knowledge do not understand—that is it. We know, because we have love and love recognizes love, and love attracts love. The little lamb cannot give you a rational reason why it should pick out one sheep as its mother but it knows that sheep is his mother. The Christian's knowledge of his Lord is something like that, he *knows* and he knows the way of salvation. People say, 'I cannot understand why one man had to die on the cross for all,' but the Christian does understand. He cannot fully understand the doctrine of the atonement, but he is not in any trouble over the fact that the sins of the world were laid upon the innocent body of the Son of God. He has the mind of Christ and an understanding of these things by means of this unction of the Holy Spirit. Spiritual truths are not strange to him, they are life, they are everything. He delights in them, he lives by them and his one desire is to know more and more. Have you received 'eternal life'? It is a gift, he gives it, he has done everything so that you may have it. You find that the things that used to interest you now carry no meaning to you, and these other things become the only things that matter.

> Perish every fond ambition,
> All I've sought, and hoped, and known;
> Yet how rich is my condition—
> God and heaven are still my own!
>
> *Henry Francis Lyte*

The moment a man receives this life he becomes a kind of stranger in this world. They are pilgrims, strangers, sojourners, men who have their eyes set and fixed upon 'the glory that remains', though living still in this world of sin and shame.

God grant that we all may know that we have eternal life. If you know that you have not, confess it to God and ask him to give it to you by his Spirit. If you have it, dwell upon it that you may grow in grace and in the knowledge of God, and be changed from glory into glory even as you look at it and contemplate it.

12

Filled with Life Anew

John 17:2–3

As we have been considering the eternal life which we receive through our Lord Jesus Christ, we have seen that it is something that we cannot analyse too carefully or too closely. The danger is always that we stop short at certain points such as forgiveness and assurance without realizing that we are really called to share this life of God. Christianity, we reminded ourselves, in the terms of the definition of the Scotsman, Henry Scougal, is 'The life of God in the soul of man'. So the object of all our endeavours, of all our worship, of our prayers and of our Bible reading, indeed, of everything we do, should be to experience what is expressed in that old hymn.

> Breathe on me, Breath of God,
> Fill me with life anew,
> That I may love what Thou dost love,
> And do what Thou wouldst do.
>
> *Edwin Hatch*

and nothing less than that. And here we are reminded of this glorious objective towards which we should all be striving and which should be the supreme desire of our lives.

We have been looking at only one aspect of the radical manner in which eternal life manifests itself in our life and living, namely, the ways in which it affects our thought, our outlook and our attitude—the difference, if you like, that it makes to us in an intellectual sense. We must now go on to consider certain other manifestations of this glorious and wondrous life which God gives to us through our Lord and Saviour Jesus Christ. He is sent from heaven to earth, to the cross and the grave, to the resurrection and the ascension, in order that he might give eternal life to those whom God has already given him. There is a sense in which the best way of looking at it is to say that those who have this eternal life begin to live the kind of life that the Lord Jesus Christ himself lived; that is perhaps the most accurate definition of it. We are meant to be living the kind of life that he lived, for, let us never forget, while he never ceased to be God, he became truly man as well. He is God and man, He is perfect man as well as perfect God, and what he says here is that he has come in order to give the type of life which he lived to those whom God has given him. So, then, as we come to examine the kind of life which we live, we who possess this eternal life, the best way of doing so is to look at the life of our Lord himself, and to see that the principles which characterized his life should be the very principles that animate and characterize our own.

Again, I have selected certain principles. The obvious one —and we touched on this in our last study—is that the man who has received the gift of eternal life knows God. It is not only that he knows things about God, it is not even that he believes certain things concerning God, it is beyond that, he *knows* God. You cannot read the gospels and their accounts of the life of our Lord without seeing that this was clearly the fundamental and the basic thing in his life here on earth as man. He knew God. He keeps on saying it—'I thank thee, O Father, Lord of heaven and earth, because thou hast hid these things from the wise and prudent, and hast revealed them unto babes. Even so, Father: for so it seemed good in thy sight' (Mt 11:25,26). He says, 'Neither knoweth any man the

Father, save the Son. . .' (Mt 11:27). God was not some stranger in the far distance; no, he knew him with an intimacy and frankness which enabled him always to come into his presence. He seemed to be longing to be there at all times. And all that is something which is offered to the Christian. He is meant to know God, by which I mean that God becomes real to him. God is not merely an intellectual concept to the man who has eternal life, he becomes an actuality and a reality. He really does know God and he knows what it is to realize the presence of God.

Now on the one hand this is a high and difficult subject and one about which people can often go astray; and yet on the other hand we must be very careful not to stop short of the fullness which the Scripture thus offers. There are two types of knowledge of God which we must always hold. There is, first of all, the knowledge of faith, the knowledge that is common to most people who are at all religious. It means a belief in God, a fulfilment of what the author of the epistle to the Hebrews says in chapter eleven, verse 6, 'He that cometh to God must believe that he is, and that he is a rewarder of them that diligently seek him.' That is what I call the knowledge of faith.

But something beyond that is offered to the Christian. There is a kind of spiritual knowledge which is more direct and more immediate, and which you will find often described in the psalms, under the Old Testament dispensation, and also in the New Testament. You remember the knowledge of God that came to Moses when God put him in the cleft of the rock so that Moses could have a glimpse of him as be passed by. God revealed his glory to Moses and when he came down from the Mount his face was shining with the reflection of this divine glory. You find the apostle John having a similar experience on the Isle of Patmos. It is just as clear in the epistles; the apostle Paul knew what it was to be taken up into the third heaven, and there to experience things unseen and indescribable. He was a man, and yet he had that amazing experience.

And it is not merely confined to the people of whom we read in the Bible. It is something which has been experienced on innumerable occasions by those of God's people who have realized the possibility of this, and have sought it as the most precious thing they could have in this life and in this world. One of the great Puritans, John Flavel, was taking a journey and suddenly, as he travelled along, God revealed himself to him. He did not have a vision, or see anything with the external eye, he just knew he was in the presence of the glory of God. He was so overwhelmed by it that he did not know how long he was there; he said that he 'utterly lost sight and sense of the world and all the concerns thereof'. He was, as it were, just enjoying the presence of the glory of God.

Those who have read the autobiography of Jonathan Edwards will know that he had a similar experience of just finding himself in the presence of the glory of God. Again, there was no vision but just this sense, this consciousness, of the reality and nearness, and the holiness and the majesty, of the glory of God.

You can read of the same thing in the the life of D. L. Moody, Moody was actually walking along Wall Street, New York, of all the streets in the world, when, suddenly, he had a similar experience. God, as it were, revealed and manifested himself to him in an immediate way; he had believed in him before, he had been used by him, he was a great Christian man, but here was something new, this consciousness of the immediate presence of God, the glory of God. It was such a marvellous thing that he turned into an hotel, and asked for a room for himself. He wanted to be alone and the glory became so tremendous that he asked God to withhold his hand lest it might crush him—the surpassing glory of it all.[1] I give these illustrations to impress the point that the possession of eternal life, which is life from God, leads to such a knowledge of God if we but realized it and cultivated it and developed it. And I do not hesitate to say that this is something which goes beyond the reaches of faith based upon knowledge. Genuine faith, established upon the full doctrine of the Bible, leads us to a knowledge of God which is more immediate and more direct, what the Puritans called a spiritual knowledge of God, over and above the knowledge of faith.

And that of course leads in turn to a fellowship with God. See this in 1 John 1. The old apostle realizes that he is coming to the end of his life, and as he writes to the young Christians in the churches, he tells them what he desires for them. It is that they might have fellowship with him, but, he says, not merely that they might have fellowship with him, because 'truly our fellowship is with the Father, and with his Son Jesus Christ'. I want you to know that, says John. I want you to know that in spite of things that may happen to you in this world, you can be enjoying active fellowship with God. You are meant to be walking with God now, and you are never meant to feel that you are alone. You are meant to know for certain that God and Christ are with you, and that your life is to be a walk and a pilgrimage in the presence of God the Father and God the Son, by the Holy Spirit which is in you. That fellowship is meant to be unbroken. Should you fall into sin, you will break the fellowship, and you will be so conscious of sin that you will be aware you have been left alone. But, says John, I want to assure you that if you realize what you have done, and if you confess and acknowledge it, and go back to God, the blood of Jesus Christ is still efficacious. Your sin will be wiped out, you will be renewed, and you will continue in this holy walk in life in the presence of God.

Christian people, that is the thing to which we are called, that is the kind of life we are meant to be living. That is eternal life—to be walking with God, to be sharing his life, and to be having fellowship with him; not feeling that God is a stranger far away from us, whom we try to find when we are in trouble, but realizing that we are always with him, always in his presence, conscious of his presence, and walking together in fellowship with him in the light. That is the Christian life, to be always with God, not just during our special times of prayer. Our whole life is to be lived in the conscious presence of God.

And that, in turn, leads to the next thing, which is that knowing him in this way we come especially to know his life. When the apostle Paul prayed for the Ephesian church, he prayed that they might know the love of Christ, the height, the depth, the length, the breadth of that love 'which passeth knowledge', that they might join together with all the saints in knowing this. You know, my friends, I feel increasingly that this is our greatest lack; it is the greatest need of the modern church and the modern Christian. What we do not realize—and it accounts for most of our errors and deficiencies—is the amazing love of God. Oh, if we but knew this love! If we but knew and understood something of the whole mystery of the incarnation and the atonement, this astounding love of his towards the world, in spite of its sin! But the man who has eternal life begins to know and to realize this. It becomes attractive to him, and that is why he is able to smile at cruel foes. He can know and say with the apostle Paul that nothing can separate him from the love of God.

So, then, the man who has eternal life is the man who knows God, the man who enters into an increasing awareness of the character and nature of God. Here again I would ask a question: as we look back across our lives and review them, can we say that we are coming to an increasingly greater knowledge of God? Do we feel that we understand the whole nature of God more than we did before? Is God becoming more and more real, and are we increasingly aware of his astounding, amazing love?

Let us now come on to the second big principle, which is that having eternal life means that we not only know God in that way, but we begin to become increasingly aware of our relationship to God. This is something that the apostles emphasized without ceasing. The man who has eternal life, says Paul, is the man who has the spirit of adoption, who now really knows God as his Father, and I suppose it is in a sense the distinguishing feature of Christianity. The Jews of old believed in God in a general sense, in God as Creator, in God as the Maker of the world, but, surely, the special thing that our Lord introduced was this sure and certain knowledge and assurance of God as Father. 'Ye have received,' says Paul, 'the spirit of adoption, whereby we cry, Abba Father' (Rom 8:15). Now that is inevitable, of course, from äll we have been saying; it is the inevitable outcome of our knowledge of God. We begin to realize the truth about ourselves in our relationship to God, and I know of nothing which will enable us to know more certainly whether or not we have received this gift of eternal life than our answer to a simple question: when we think of God and when we come into his presence, what is our thought, what is our idea of God? Do we realize and know for certain that he is our Father? When we say, 'Our Father which art in heaven' do we really mean that?

Our Lord described this in the Sermon on the Mount. He was anticipating there what was to be true of the Christian and he says, You should not worry about food and clothing, 'for your heavenly Father knoweth that ye have need of all these things' (Mt 6:32). We are coming to our Father, and as we come to him we should realize that he is our Father. Indeed, we should not only believe that, we should have a consciousness of it, the spirit of adoption which makes us cry, Abba Father—this intimate relationship. The Christian begins to realize that God is indeed his Father, that the hairs of his head are all numbered, and that his relationship to God is not something mechanical, it is experiential. That, of course, leads to a sense of dependence upon God, and the consciousness that, as time passes, we are in his hands. And that, further, means that we begin to look to him for strength, and for power, and for everything.

Oh, what fools we are! I make no apology for using such a phrase. How foolish we are as Christian people in failing to realize that in this relationship to God our every need can be supplied and our every want satisfied. The life that was lived by the Lord Jesus Christ here on earth, he himself tells us repeatedly, was a life that was lived in constant dependence upon his Father. He says, 'The words that I speak unto you I speak not of myself: but the Father that dwelleth in me, he doeth the works' (Jn 14:10). But it is only as we realize this that we begin to understand why our Lord ever prayed. So many people cannot understand why the Son of God prayed while he was here on earth. The answer is that his life as a man was dependent upon God. He looked to God for the works he was to do and received power to perform them by receiving the Holy Spirit. He was constantly being filled with the Holy Spirit that was given to him without measure, and it was in this strength and power that he offered up himself. It was through the Spirit that he offered himself up to God, and he was 'declared to be the Son of God with power, according to the spirit of holiness, by the resurrection from the dead' (Rom 1:4).

This is surely one of the most staggering things that man can ever learn in this world, but it is an essential part of knowing God. And thus you find, as you read the lives of the saints throughout the ages, that they have always been people who have spent much of their time in prayer. They realized that they were supposed to live this life as Christ lived it in dependence upon God, so they did not rely upon their own strength and ability. They sought his mind and will, they sought the fullness of the Spirit, they sought the power which God alone could give and they drew from God and lived their life of victory and triumph.

But I want to emphasize another suggestive aspect of this great life, which is that the man who has eternal life not only knows God and his relationship to him, he delights in God, and his supreme desire is to know God better. Here again I take you back to the psalms. Do you remember what David felt like when he came again to the house of God? He tells us, 'As the hart panteth after the water brooks so . . . my soul thirsteth for God, for the living God' (Ps 42:1–2). Now that inevitably happens if we possess eternal life; like always attracts like. The characteristic of love is that it desires to be in the presence of the object of its love, and the receiving of eternal life leads to that attitude with respect to God. And thus you find, as you read your Scriptures about these holy men of God and as you read the lives of all the saints, that their greatest desire was to know God better. They were always seeking his presence, and an ever greater realization of it. It was this that led them to examine themselves every day and to discover how they lived. It was this which made that saintly man John Fletcher ask himself a series of questions when he went to bed every night. These questions were all destined to establish this point: had he been walking with God as he should have been? Had this walk been neglected in his life? Had there been any break in the fellowship? Had sin come in and spoilt and tarnished it? This is something that is universally true of all the saints, whatever the century, whatever the nation to which they belong; they have set before them, above everything else, a realization of the presence of God, and they have done so because they have delighted in him. To spend time in reading the Bible and in meditation is no burden to those who have eternal life. They delight in it, it is their greatest joy, because knowing God as they know him, they enjoy him. The first question of the shorter Catechism is: 'What is the chief end of man?' The answer is, 'The chief end of man is to glorify God and to enjoy him for ever.' And you cannot read the Bible honestly without seeing that those who are described in the Old Testament knew and enjoyed God and enjoyed living their life with him. Our Lord's chief delight was to be talking to his Father, to be communing with him. He enjoyed God and we are meant to enjoy God. Oh, God should not be a taskmaster to the man who has eternal life, to the man who is a true Christian! God should be the supreme object of his joy and his delight and of his pleasure.

My friends, if we but knew God in his holy, loving, character, if we but knew his love, we would want to spend our whole life in his presence and with him. That is the thing to which these men were looking forward. 'That I may know him,' says Paul; he is forgetting the things that are behind and he is looking forward to this unmixed enjoyment of God in heaven. That is the reality of heaven, to be basking in the love and glory of God. The man who receives eternal life begins to awaken to these things. I do not want to discourage anybody. I am describing this life in its fullness, but I am obviously suggesting, as I do so, that if we are utter strangers to this and know nothing about it, even in the most elementary form, then it is time we asked ourselves whether we have received eternal life. Am I a Christian at all? Do I know anything about these things? Have I ever had a passing second in my life in which I have known something of God and realized his presence and known something of his astounding love? The man who has this life is the man who loves God. You see, God does not stop at asking us to believe in him. 'The first and great commandment,' says our Lord, is, 'Thou shalt love the Lord thy God. . .' Faith is insufficient, we are meant to go on to love God and to love him with the whole of our being.

But obviously I must come to the next principle, which is that the man who has eternal life loves to do the will of God. That is the logical sequence. The man who loves is the man who is anxious to please the object of his love. There is no better test of love than that, and unless you desire to please someone whom you claim to love, then I assure you, you do not love that person. Love always wants to be pleasing and to give itself, and anyone who loves God wants to do the

will of God. If you look at Christ, you see that the whole of
his life, his one object, was to do the will of his Father. He
did not care what it was; even in the Garden of Gethsemane
when he faced the one thing he did not want, even there he
said, 'Nevertheless not my will, but thine, be done' (Lk
22:42). He says, I do not want to drink this cup, but if it is
doing thy will, I will do even that—that is love at its maximum and its best, and it is true of all who have his life. The
chief end of the true Christian is the glory of God, therefore
he spends his time in seeking to know the will of God and in
doing it. He strives to do it and he loves to do it. He is
controlled by this one idea. Having learnt what God has
done for him and what God is to him, having realized something of this love of God, he says, 'Love so amazing, so
divine, demands my soul, my life, my all.' And man, therefore, who has eternal life, has this as the supreme object and
desire of his life, to do the will of God.

And this brings me to my last word. The ultimate manifestation of the possession of eternal life is that it produces
certain results in our lives. Fortunately for us they have all
been set out in a very brief compass by the apostle Paul in
Galatians 5, verses 22 and 23, where he talks of the fruit of
the Spirit. A man once said a very profound thing when he
described these verses as 'The shortest biography of Christ
that has ever been written.' He was absolutely right. That is
the perfect description of the life of the Lord Jesus Christ;
those were its characteristics—'love, joy, peace, longsuffering, gentleness, goodness, faith [or faithfulness], meekness,
temperance', and anyone who has received this gift of eternal life from him is one who in turn begins to manifest that
sort of life; that is the kind of person he becomes. 'The
kingdom of God,' says Paul to the Romans, 'is not meat and
drink; but righteousness, and peace, and joy in the Holy
Ghost' (Rom 14:17). 'The carnal mind is enmity against
God' (Rom 8:7); 'to be carnally minded is death; but to be
spiritually minded is life and peace' (Rom 8:6). So that as we

examine ourselves at this moment, we must again ask ourselves this vital question: can Christ fulfill in me the object of his coming and dying? He says he has done it all to give eternal life. Have I received eternal life? And a very good way of testing it is to ask further: is the fruit of the Spirit manifesting itself in me? Because Christ is the eternal life and the Spirit produces its fruit in us.

Do you know this life of God in your own life? Have you this joy in the Holy Ghost, something that makes you independent of circumstances? Do you know a great peace in your heart, peace within, peace with other people, something that, whatever happens, leaves you unruffled. Are you longsuffering? He was longsuffering when he suffered the contradiction of sinners against himself. Are we gentle; are we good; are we patient with people or do we lose our tempers with them? Are we constantly manifesting our irritability and touchiness, or do we manifest longsuffering, gentleness and goodness, faithfulness, meekness, humility and temperance—or self-control? Is there a discipline in our lives? There is a control and balance in living the life of Christ. See these things and remember that he offered them to us. And I put these questions not only that we may know these things here and now, but that we may *enjoy* them. We can receive the gift of eternal life in this life and in this world, but if we die without receiving it, we cannot possibly enjoy the life of God in eternity. This is but a preparation, it is a foretaste. We are not given the full possession of the great estate, but we are given the seal, the earnest, the title deeds, so that I know I am going to get it all, because of what I receive now. And if I have not received the title deeds and the earnest of the inheritance here, it just means that I will never receive the full inheritance there.

Have you received eternal life, my friends? The most momentous challenge you have ever faced is the Lord Jesus Christ who died on the cross and who rose again to give you this gift. Do you find something of this life in you? If you do, well pledge yourself from this moment to live for it, to receive more of it, that it may grow and develop. But if you feel you have never received this life, hasten away quietly somewhere into the presence of God and tell him you see clearly that you have never had it; acknowledge and confess your sin to him, and give up relying upon yourself and your own goodness.

This is the test of a Christian, not to be better than anybody else, not to be a church member, not simply to hold certain views, nor to pride yourself in some strict morality. No, this is the test of Christianity and nothing less, and if you realize that you do not have it, confess it to God, confess all your self-righteousness, acknowledge it all. Cast yourself upon God's offer of salvation freely in Christ who has died for you, and ask him to give you this gift of eternal life, this gift of life divine which is life indeed. And once you have it, you will begin to manifest these things and you will begin to live for God and his glory and to enjoy him. Religion will no longer be a task, it will be your chiefest delight. I end as I began, and ask you to pray:

> Breathe on me, Breath of God,
> Fill me with life anew,
> That I may love what Thou dost love,
> And do what Thou would'st do.

[1] For a fuller treatment of these experiences, readers might be interested to read M. Lloyd-Jones, *Joy Unspeakable* (Kingsway, 1984).

13

Safe in His Eternal Kingdom

John 17:1–5

Perhaps it is as well, at this point, to remind ourselves of the fact that when our blessed Lord and Saviour offered this prayer to his Father, he did so audibly. It was a prayer addressed to God, but it was meant to be overheard by the disciples. And the whole character of the prayer, not only in this first section, which we have been considering, but the entire prayer as recorded in the whole chapter, drives us to the same conclusion—that our Lord had one great object in thus praying this prayer audibly, and that was that these disciples and followers of his might know for certain the security of their position. The whole tenor of the prayer is that our Lord is handing over these disciples to God the Father, and praying to him to look after them, as it were, and he does so audibly in order that they might know that. But in so doing, he enters into certain details, and it is as we look at these details, as we have been doing, that we really grasp all the great and high doctrine, and come to the conclusion that our position is safe and secure.

In other words, we have been engaged in an analysis of these verses, in order that we all might really find ourselves experiencing what Augustus Toplady expresses in his well-known hymn, that position in which a man is confident and assured, certain that nothing can ever separate him from the love of God:

> Things future, nor things that are now,
> Nor all things below or above,
> Can make Him His purpose forego,
> Or sever my soul from His love.

That is the great doctrine that is announced here in these verses—the security of the believer. Our Lord was coming to the end of his earthly life. He was leaving the world and going back to God to share that eternal glory in all its fullness, and our Lord's great concern was that these followers of his—and through them all who would believe because of their preaching and all Christians in all ages everywhere—should know for certain the security of their position. And we find it, as a result, one of the greatest themes in all the New Testament epistles. In a sense, that is why every one of these epistles was written, in order that all Christians might *know*, and the writers exhort them to live a certain type of life because of this. Christians are not exhorted to do certain things in order that they ultimately might arrive in heaven. Rather, they are told to live this kind of life because they are destined for it, and it is because of this that sin is so unthinkable, and so incompatible.

John summarizes that in his first epistle when he says, 'Every man that hath this hope in him purifieth himself' (1 Jn 3:3), so the great thing is to know that we have this hope. You find it again, for example, in Hebrews 6, where the author exhorts the Hebrew Christians to continue to give diligence to good works, 'to the full assurance of hope unto the end' (verse 11)—it is the same thought. He wants them to know that they have an anchor within the veil, 'Whither,' he says, 'the forerunner is for us entered' (verse 20). That is the way to live the Christian life. The Christian was never meant to go through this world haltingly and uncertainly, wondering whether he is a Christian, hoping that sometime or other before death something may suddenly happen to him. No, he should start in this position and he should walk steadfastly and assuredly in the diretion of his eternal hope. That, I say, is the purpose of this great prayer and it comes out especially in the gréat and high doctrine we have looked at together in these first five verses. Indeed, it has been our object and endeavour, as we have been considering them, to bring out that aspect of the truth, in order that we all might enjoy 'the full assurance of hope right unto the end'.

Now we have been doing it in a detailed manner, and what I want to do here is to try to sum it all up and to take one of those synoptic views of the whole, so that we may see ourselves as we are in God's great plan and purpose. We have outlined that as it is taught here and we have seen certain things about it. We have seen that it is not something contingent or fortuitous, it is something that has been planned, and the names of God's people have been written in the Lamb's book of life from before the foundation of the world. That is the starting point and we have looked at it as it is unfolded and as it has been enacted and brought to pass in this world. In other words, our salvation is dependent upon God's eternal purpose, carried out in history, so that we are not saved by ideas or by theories, but by certain things that have been done and enacted once and for ever. Our salvation must always be thought of in those terms and categories. It belongs to history and it is as definitely historical as the fact that Julius Caesar invaded Britain in 55 BC. It is all dependent on certain events, things that have actually taken place. So, having gone into these things in detail, I want now to gather up the grounds for our belief in the security of the Christian believer, and to put it in the form of a number of principles.

First, we are told that the Christian is one who has been chosen by God and has been given by God to his Son, our Lord and Saviour Jesus Christ: 'As thou hast given him power over all flesh, that he should give eternal life to as many as thou hast given him.' Now that is a vital statement. I wonder whether you have ever noticed that our Lord repeats it seven times in this one chapter. I do not want you to become interested merely statistically—that is not the point—but I do want you to see the importance of this statement. There it is in the second verse: 'that he should give eternal life to as many as thou hast given him'. Then in verse 6, he says, 'I have manifested thy name unto the men which thou gavest me out of the world', and again 'thine they were, and thou gavest them me'—so he says it twice in that sixth verse. Then we find it again in the ninth verse: 'I pray for them'—notice this—'I pray not for the world, but for them which thou hast given me; for they are thine.' He does not pray for the world, he prays only for those who belong to God and whom God has given to him—there is the great division. Then we find it in verse 11: 'And now,' he says, 'I am no more in the world, but these are in the world, and I come to thee. Holy Father, keep through thine own name those whom thou hast given me, that they may be one, as we are.' It is the same reference. And again in the next verse: 'While I was with them in the world, I kept them in thy name: those that thou gavest me I have kept, and none of them is lost, but the son of perdition.' And finally we are given it for the last time in verse 24: 'Father, I will that they also, whom thou hast given me, be with me where I am; that they may behold my glory, which thou hast given me: for thou lovedst me before the foundation of the world.'

Now the plain teaching of these scriptures is obviously that God the Father has given a certain people to God the Son, and the Son has come into this world specifically to give eternal life to those people and to nobody else.

'Ah,' you say, 'but I do not understand that sort of doctrine!'

But I am simply explaining to you the statement of the Scriptures. If there is any other conceivable explanation of these statements I shall be interested to hear what it is. This is not my theory, or that of any other man. Our Lord says it seven times in this one chapter, and it is a statement you find repeatedly running through the Scriptures, namely that God his Father has given him, as it were, a mass of people, that he should give eternal life 'to as many as thou hast given me'. So that the business of the Son is to give eternal life to each one of those people. That is what our Lord himself says in this great high priestly prayer under the very shadow of the cross.

But when I say something like this, people immediately begin to ask questions. They say, 'I do not understand the love of God that can do this for some and not for others.'

My dear friends, I do not understand it, neither does anybody else understand it. Our business is to come to Scripture and to believe it. I do not pretend to understand the eternal mind of God and how it works. I am not meant to do that. This is the trouble with the philosophers. They say that they do not understand how God can to this or that, they want to explain the mind of the almighty God with their pigmy minds and it cannot be done. And that is why the philosophers find it so difficult to become Christians. All I know is that the blessed Son of God, standing in this world, says, 'I pray not for the world'; he prays only for those whom God has given him. He does not even say that he has chosen them, he says that God the Father has chosen them and given him these people. And as I understand this doctrine, it is that when the Son came from heaven, he came with a great commission from the Father. It was that he should do certain things in this world in order that he could give eternal life to those people whom God had set apart unto himself and whom he had given to the Son as his inheritance.

If you trace that doctrine through the Scriptures, you will find it in the Old Testament quite as plainly as in the New; you will find it everywhere. Your salvation and mine was something that was known to God, and our names written in the Lamb's book of life, before the creation of the world. You do not understand it, neither do I, but, thank God, we are not saved by our understanding, but by our acceptance of the truth. Indeed, it is quite unscriptural for men and women to put their intellectual difficulties before the plain statement of Scripture, and I think we need to reconsider this matter. It is not a bit surprising that we find it difficult to equate certain scriptural statements with our conception of the love of God. But the apostle Paul in his letter to the Corinthians, says that 'It pleased God by the foolishness of preaching to save them that believe' (1 Cor 1:21), but the wise, those people who trust to their own understanding are confused—'to the Greeks foolishness'.

My dear friends, the way to start considering these matters is just to remind yourself of what you are. Measure your mind, which you have set up as the ultimate court of appeal and authority, how big is it? What do we really understand with our minds? Do we understand ourselves, do we understand life, do we understand the whole mystery and marvel of creation? Do we understand 'the meanest flower that blows', electricity, or something as small as an atom? Of course we do not! And yet we put up our little minds against the mind of God. Our minds are too small, their scope is too limited. But that is not the whole truth about us. Not only are our faculties limited to start with, we are, furthermore, sinful creatures. We see nothing straight and everything is influenced by that fact. Our mind is naturally at enmity with God and all our understanding is defective, tarnished and soiled by sin.

That is why the Christian position is that henceforth I cease to put anything in terms of 'my mind and my understanding'. And I come as a little child to the Bible, realizing that it will not be open to me except my mind be enlightened by the Holy Spirit—so I do not trust to my mind. Faith means that we voluntarily and deliberately open ourselves up to the revelation of the Bible and that when we do not understand things we say, 'I do not understand, but I am content not to understand. I believe the word of God and I rest myself and my whole position entirely upon it.' That is the faith position. The moment that you begin to bring in your mind and natural arguments and say that you cannot see or understand something, you are turning from the revelation and are reverting back to the sinful position of putting your mind up as the supreme court of appeal. In Romans 8 we are told that 'whom he did foreknow, he also did predestinate to be conformed to the image of his Son . . . and whom he called, them he also justified: and whom he justified, them he also glorified' (verses 29–30). He has done it; the Christian is already glorified as he is justified in the sight of God, though still on earth. He may be 'accounted as sheep for the slaughter' (verse 36), but he is glorified. God does not do things in a piecemeal manner, he does everything as a whole, and he knows his people. 'The foundation of God standeth sure, having this seal. The Lord knoweth them that are his' (2 Tim 2:19). God has known his people from the very beginning, and he has separated them unto himself. Paul prays for the Ephesians that the eyes of their understanding may be enlightened, that they may know 'what is the hope of his calling and what the riches of the glory of his inheritance in the saints' (1:18). It is the same doctrine; we find it everywhere in the Bible.

So, this is the first basis and ground of our security and our assurance. My assurance rests upon the fact that, if I am a Christian at all, I am a Christian because God has chosen me unto salvation and separated me; he has taken me out of it all, and has given me to his Son that the Son might give me eternal life. What a blessed basis on which to live! What an astounding fact! Oh, the unutterable folly of men and women who try by philosophy to understand the inscrutable, the eternal, and reject such a doctrine! Some people believe that you can receive eternal life from the blessed Son of God and then lose it, then regain it, and then lose it again, and go on thus uncertainly in this world until you come to die. My friends, it is an insult to God! It is an insult to God's glorious plan of redemption, it is an insult to God's eternal

way of doing things—'that he should give eternal life to as
many as thou hast given him'. What a conception, that God
has given me to Christ, that Christ might save me and might
give me eternal life.

That is the first ground, but let us come to another. The
second basis of security and assurance, according to our
Lord, is that every hindrance and obstacle to our receiving
this gift of eternal life has been removed by the blessed work
of the Lord himself. 'I have glorified thee on the earth: I have
finished the work which thou gavest me to do.' Many things
have had to be done before I could receive the gift of eternal
life. As a natural man I wondered how I could get it. Now
we have already considered what it is. You remember that
eternal life really means that we are sharers of the life of God
and are in communion with him. Is it not obvious, therefore,
that a great many things have to happen before we can come
into that condition? So, thank God, my second ground for
assurance is that it has all been done. There is nothing that
has been left undone. He has dealt with the problem of my
guilt, by removing it. He has reconciled me to God, the law
of God has been satisfied—'Who shall lay any thing to the
charge of God's elect?' (Rom 8:33). I can ask, and without
any qualification: 'Is there anybody anywhere who can bring
any charge against me as a child of God?' There is none, for,
'It is God that justifieth' (Rom 8:33). He himself has done it
for, 'It is Christ that died, yea rather, that is risen again, who
is even at the right hand of God' (verse 34).

Christian people, *this* is the position we are meant to occupy. Let me quote another hymn of Augustus Toplady:

> The terrors of law and of God
> With me can have nothing to do.
> My Saviour's obedience and blood,
> Hide all my transgressions from view.

That is not boasting for I am not relying upon myself, but
upon him—'My Saviour's obedience and blood, hide all my

transgressions from view', and unless you can say that, there is something defective about your faith. Far from being boastful, that is the thing that humbles a man, the thing that makes him strive after holiness, because it is true. Or take again that line.

> Of covenant mercy I sing.

Now that is what our Lord is saying here. He tells his Father that all which was necessary has been done, the guilt removed, the law satisfied, the Father reconciled, the new nature given, the Holy Spirit given, and the work going on until ultimately this child of God will find himself faultless and blameless without spot or blemish, perfect in the presence of God. Our security is that the work has been done, every hindrance, every obstacle, every barrier has been removed, because Christ has done it all, He said, 'I go to prepare a place for you' (Jn 14:2), and he has done what he promised, so that the ultimate outcome is, as Toplady says—

> More happy but not more secure,
> The glorified spirits in heaven.

What a statement to make! According to Augustus Toplady, on the basis of these things, the glorified spirits in heaven are not more secure than we are here on earth, because our security is in Christ. Of course, they are happier than we are, they are in a land where there is no sin, no shame, no sorrow, no sighing; more happy—yes—but they are not more secure.

And I will tell you why this is so. To be a Christian, you see, does not just mean that I believe on the Lord Jesus Christ and have my sins forgiven. It also means that I am in Christ, I am in him and he is in me. I am a part of him; I have died with him; I have risen with him. He is my life and I am in him. So, being in him, I am as secure as those who are with him in heaven, and it is because he has dealt with every barrier and hindrance and obstacle to our receiving this blessed life.

Then the third ground and basis of my security and assurance is the very character and nature of the life itself. I need not dilate on this, because we have already spent some time in considering it. But to make this statement complete, I must just refer to it in passing. You remember that the nature of the life is that we really do become 'partakers of the divine nature', that we are born of God, that we are his children and that we are sharers in the life of God himself. Now I argue that because of that, it is something which cannot come and go. It cannot change. It is something which is stable and everlasting. It is, indeed, *eternal* life, and we saw as we analysed it that 'eternal' implies duration. We are all destined either for eternal life or for a life of condemnation and destruction, and they both go on for ever. Eternal life is the life of God, and because of that, it is everlasting, so it is eternal life in that sense.

I find it quite extraordinary that anybody calling himself a Christian can believe that he can receive this gift of the life of God, and then, because of sin, lose it and then accept it again and then lose it once more. You cannot go on being born and dying! No, if you receive the life of God, then God himself gives you this gift through his Son, and the very quality, the nature and character of the life means that it is imperishable. Our Lord has already said this in the gospel of John, 'Neither shall any man pluck them out of my hand' (Jn 10:28)—it is impossible. Or again, the apostle Paul says, 'Neither death, nor life, nor angels, nor principalities, nor powers, nor things present, nor things to come, nor height, nor depth, nor any other creature, shall be able to separate us from the love of God, which is in Christ Jesus our Lord' (Rom 8:38–39). Furthermore, this is especially true because he himself has given us this life. So we are in this new relationship, we belong to the family of God, we are separated out of the world, we are separated unto God, we are a part of his plan and purpose, and we belong to him. That is why Paul can say with such confidence that 'the sufferings of this present time are not worthy to be compared with the glory which shall be revealed in us' (Rom 8:18). We are saved by hope, hope which is sure and certain, because it is based upon the character, indeed upon the life, of God himself. Therefore, if we know that we have eternal life, it should encourage us, and strengthen us. It should enable us to know that because God has given us that gift, it is indeed, as God himself has said, an *eternal* life.

'Well, then,' says someone, 'because I am saved, it means that I can blaspheme and do anything I like.' But the man who knows that he has eternal life, never reasons like that— 'Every man that hath his hope in him purifieth himself, even as he is pure' (1 Jn 3:3). The man who knows that he has eternal life, and that he is going on to face God in heaven, is the man above everybody else who is going to be striving after holiness. That has always been the case, it is the argument of the Scriptures, and that is how God's people have argued throughout the centuries. Did you know that foreign mission work was started originally by people who believed things like this? The greatest motive of the missionary enterprise has always been that they have known that God is the means as well as the end. They have believed that God has called them to propagate the gospel, and because of that they have sacrificed everything, even their lives, and gone and preached. The man who is most ready to sacrifice his life for the gospel is the man who knows that even death cannot separate him from the love of God and that he has the life of God in him. This is why the men who believe these truths have always been the greatest workers in the kingdom of God. It has been their certain knowledge that they are the children of God and possessors of eternal life.

My next basis is one of the most precious of all. We must work out the argument based upon the fact that our Lord has suffered so much and so many things, in order that all this might be possible for us. This is his statement, 'I have glorified thee on the earth: I have finished the work which thou gavest me to do.' He was referring to his coming from heaven, to the fact that he had laid aside the signs of his glory. He did not clutch at his power or exhalt it. Though he was in equality with God, he humbled himself and decided to live as man. He relied entirely upon God and the gift of the Holy Spirit which he received. He humbled himself. He endured the contradiction of sinners, and he sweated blood in the Garden of Gethsemane. He staggered beneath the weight of the cruel cross, the nails were hammered into his hands and feet, he suffered intolerable thirst, and he died. He has done all that, so then—this is the argument—'If, when we were enemies, we were reconciled to God by the death of his Son, much more, being reconciled, shall we be saved by his life' (Rom 5:10); 'He that spared not his own Son, but delivered him up for us all, how shall he not with him also freely give us all things?' (Rom 8:32).

This logic is quite inevitable and I work it out like this: Christ has borne and suffered all that for me in order that he might give me the gift of eternal life. So, in the light of that, is it still feasible to believe that he should do all that for me and my salvation and then suddenly leave me and let me perish? It is impossible! 'If, when we were enemies, we were reconciled to God by the death of his Son, much more, being reconciled, shall we be saved'—and saved to the very end—'by his life' (Rom 5:10). What a wonderful powerful argument this is! I believe that is why he prayed aloud in the presence of these men, 'I have glorified thee on the earth: I have finished the work which thou gavest me to do.' I have done all this for them, and if I have done all this for them, I will never leave them to perish or sink now.

We must understand that argument and employ it. The Son of God has done the greatest thing for us and he will never fail us. If he suffered even to the cross, there, glorified in heaven, 'He ever liveth to make intercession for them' (Heb 7:25). This is the logic, according to the author of the epistle to the Hebrews. 'He saves to the uttermost. . .' (verse

25), to the very end. He will never fail, for his blood, his cross, is a guarantee of that. If he had come to do the work while here on earth, how much more will he do it now in heaven, in his glorified state. So as we use that argument we find it a great and grand basis of security and assurance.

But the last basis on which I stand, is the one which he puts in these words: 'As thou hast given him power over all flesh, that he should give eternal life to as many as thou hast given him.' It is a literal statement of fact. God the Father has given to the Son, the Lord Jesus Christ, power over all flesh, over everything—there is nothing that is not placed under him. That is Scripture again. You realize what that means. The universe, the cosmos, every star in its orbit, the sun and moon, every power, every atom with its magnetic force and power, all are under his power. Everything in nature and creation, man and all his powers, his devices, his machinations, everything that he is capable of doing, it is all under the power of God, under the power of Christ.

It goes even beyond that. The future is in his hands. There is a picture in Revelation of the book that was sealed up, and we are told that no one was found who was big enough or strong enough to open the book of the course of history, until suddenly there appeared the Lion of Judah. He prevailed because he was strong enough and mighty enough to open the book. All this simply means that the whole of future history is in the hands of the Lord Jesus Christ. You may be worried about the international situation, you need not be, nor about any earthly force or power, because the whole of history is in his hands. Of course, we do not understand it all. He permits many things that we do not understand, but the fact that he permits it means that it is still in his power. There is nothing out of hand.

I want to go one step further and say that the devil is under his power. The devil is under the control of Christ, because he has absolute power and even the devil is subject to it. Christ has conquered, and what the devil does is under the sufferance of God, for God's inscrutable reason and purpose. We are so clever with our philosophies that we say, 'Now why did God do that? Why didn't he decide to make us perfect? Why is Satan allowed to do this?' And we go on asking our questions. But the faith position is that you and I just humble ourselves as little children, and bow to the fact that God has so ordered and ordained it. He has determined the times, but there is a very definite limit to the time. God knows the day on which the Lord Jesus Christ will come back into this world. Men, and nations, and powers, and all that is opposed to God, will be taken by him and cast into the lake of perdition, and he will give the final proof that all flesh has been subjected to him and to his almighty power.

But the argument here is that all power has been given to him over all flesh in order that he might give eternal life. So Christ has done all that I have described in order to give to me the gift of eternal life. In this life and world the flesh is within me, and it drags me down. There are lusts and passions and desires in me. There is no such thing as a perfect human being in this world, even though he may be a Christian. Things are here trying to drag me down and to rob me of eternal life. Against me are the world and the devil, who even tempted the blessed Son of God. How can I stand against all this? There is only one way: he is able to control it all. The guarantee that you and I can arrive in heaven and in glory is that he does control it all and that we are saved in spite of the world and the flesh and the devil. This is because the 'power that worketh in us' is the power of God, the power that brought Christ from the dead, and it enables us to go through and beyond it all.

Paul puts it in as extreme a form as this. There are, he says, certain preachers who are building upon a foundation of wood and hay and stubble. And at the end, when the testing comes, all their works will be burnt and destroyed, so that there will be nothing left. It will all be burnt up because it was so shoddy and useless. Yet, he says, they themselves will be saved 'so as by fire' (1 Cor 3:12–15). And what has saved them? It is this power of the Lord over all flesh. He suffers us to be tried and tempted, but he will never suffer us to be lost. No man, nothing, can pluck us out of his hand. He exercises the power, and he will continue to do so, so that neither man, nor history, nor the devil, nor hell, nor anything at all can ever separate us from him. So in the words of the hymn we can say—

> From Him who loves me now so well
> What power my soul can sever?
> Shall life or death, shall earth or hell?
> No, I am His for ever.
>
> *James Grindlay Small*

My dear friend, if you are relying upon your love for him or upon your grasp or hold of him, I am sorry for you. I pity you, because my only reliance is upon him. The gift he gives us is eternal life—it is himself. So the end and the consummation of all this is that we must trust, and trust alone, to the faithfulness of Christ. He has done everything for you and he will hold you and save you to the end, and will present you faultless before the presence of God's glory with exceeding joy. Oh, how we should thank him that he offered this prayer audibly, that we might know where we stand, and know that we are surrounded by his love, and saved eternally, safe in his eternal kingdom.

PART TWO

SAFE IN
the WORLD

1

Our Lord Prays for His Followers: His Reasons and Requests

I have manifested thy name unto the men which thou gavest me out of the world: thine they were, and thou gavest them me; and they have kept thy word. Now they have known that all things whatsoever thou hast given me are of thee. For I have given unto them the words which thou gavest me; and they have received them, and have known surely that I came out from thee, and they have believed that thou didst send me. I pray for them: I pray not for the world, but for them which thou hast given me; for they are thine. And all mine are thine, and thine are mine; and I am glorified in them. And now I am no more in the world, but these are in the world, and I come to thee. Holy Father, keep through thine own name those whom thou hast given me, that they may be one, as we are. While I was with them in the world, I kept them in thy name: those that thou gavest me I have kept, and none of them is lost, but the son of perdition; that the scripture might be fulfilled. And now come I to thee; and these things I speak in the world, that they might have my joy fulfilled in themselves. I have given them thy word; and the world hath hated them, because they are not of the world, even as I am not of the world. I pray not that thou shouldest take them out of the world, but that thou shouldest keep them from the evil. They are not of the world, even as I am not of the world. Sanctify them through thy truth: thy word is truth. As thou hast sent me into the world, even so have I also sent them into the world. And for their sakes I sanctify myself, that they also might be sanctified through the truth (John 17 vv. 6–19).

In the first part of our study of John 17, we finished at the end of verse 5.[1] We have seen how this great high-priestly prayer of our Lord can be divided up naturally into three main sections: in the first, verses 1–5, he prays for himself; then from verses 6–19 we have his prayer for his immediate followers, and, finally, from verse 20 to the end we have his prayer for those who would believe on him through his disciples – 'Neither pray I for these alone, but for them also which shall believe on me through their word.'

We have already considered the first section, in which our Lord prayed for himself. It is a great, comprehensive prayer in which we saw outlined and displayed, in a sense, the whole realm of Christian doctrine, as our Lord pleads with his Father that he might grant him grace to go on with the work which he had given him to do, and that he might not fail or falter as he came to the supreme test and crisis, namely, the laying down of his life as a ransom for many.

So now we come to this second section which starts at verse 6 and goes on to the end of verse 19. There has been much debate as to whether in this section our Lord was praying for the apostles only or whether he was praying for all who had believed on him up to that point. It is a question which cannot be finally decided. Those who believe he was praying only for the apostles, the innermost circle, always quote verse 12, in which he says, 'While I was with them in the world, I kept them in thy name: those that thou gavest me I have kept, and none of them is lost, but the son of perdition; that the scripture might be fulfilled.' That seems to indicate that he was talking about the twelve, and saying that he had kept all but one, Judas, who would fail and deny him, according to the scriptural prophecy to be found in the Old Testament. But most of the remaining statements would indicate, I think, a wider circle: those to whom he had manifested his name, all those who had been given to him. He had not only been given the apostles, he had been given all believers: 'Now they have known that all things

[1] *Saved in Eternity* (Crossway Books, 1988)

whatsoever thou hast given me are of thee' (v. 7) and this is something which is true, of course, of every believer. So, in the last analysis, we cannot settle this question any more than we can settle many other questions which are of no final importance. We cannot be dogmatic about it, and this does not matter, because even if the statement is confined to the apostles, it is obviously something that is true also of all who are believers in the Lord Jesus Christ. Indeed, that is confirmed by verse 20, where he says, 'Neither pray I for these alone, but for them also which shall believe on me through their word.' And he goes on, in a sense, to offer the same petition for future believers as he has offered at this point for those who have already believed.

That, then, is just a mechanical, preliminary point. The great matter before us is to observe the terms of the prayer, and it divides itself up very naturally. There are two great things here: our Lord prays for his followers, and he says why he does so. Some would put it as strongly as to say that he pleads for them; he does not merely make requests, he produces arguments and makes statements. In other words, he is giving reasons for praying for them. This is a point which we must surely observe, for it is of great value to us. It reminds us again that God's omniscience is no reason for our not telling him things which he already knows. You must often have found yourself facing a particular difficulty or situation. You feel that because God knows everything, there is no point in telling him anything about it. God knows our need, he knows all about us before we get on our knees to pray, so why then do we need to tell him anything? And the quite obvious conclusion to that thought is that there is no need to pray at all: if God knows all about us, why not let things take their course and all will be well.

Now the answer to that is what we find in this prayer. Our Lord knew, in a way we can never know, about God's omniscience, his perfect and complete knowledge, and yet he told his Father certain things about those disciples, things which God knew already. He prayed about them and repeated them, and, of course, that is characteristic of Bible prayers everywhere, not only the prayers of our Lord but also those of the apostles and of the saints of the Old Testament. This is something which is wonderful the moment you begin to contemplate it. God after all desires us to think of him as our Father. It is a kind of anthropomorphism; it is God stooping to our weakness. The human parent enjoys listening to the child saying things and telling him things which he knows already; he does not resent them, nor does he regard them as a waste of time. He derives great pleasure from them, and we are to learn from this that our heavenly Father delights to see us coming to him, and stating our requests, and giving our reasons. There is an example of prayer in the Old Testament, where that good man, Hezekiah, even takes a letter and spreads it out before God, as if God did not know all about it, and as if to say, 'Here it is, I come to you with this letter and I ask you to take charge of it and to do something about it' (2 Kings 19:14).

So as we come into the presence of God with our requests and our petitions, let us never fear to bring the details, for nothing is too small for God's loving care and attention. He is interested in us as a father is in a child, everything about us is of the greatest interest to him. Read again the Sermon on the Mount and you will find that our Lord says that in an extended form in Matthew 6 where he uses the argument about God clothing the lilies and caring about the birds of the air. Nothing, he says, happens to them apart from God, so how much more is he interested in you and me, and in everything that happens to us, and everything that is connected with the minutest detail of our lives. 'In *nothing* be anxious,' writes the apostle Paul. It does not matter what it is (he uses the most all-inclusive word he could have chosen). 'In nothing be anxious; but in everything' – there it is again! – 'by prayer and supplication with thanksgiving let your requests be made known unto God' (Phil 4:6, RV). Our Lord prays for his people and he adduces the reasons why he prays. Let us ever, as we come to God in prayer, remember his great and glorious example and do the same ourselves.

So I should like first to look at this section, from verse 6 to verse 19, as a whole. There are many ways in which one can approach a passage of Scripture such as this. One way is just to take it verse by verse, verse 6, verse 7, verse 8, and so on, right through. This is a legitimate way of approaching the Scriptures, but it seems to me that a better way, especially with a section like this, is first to look at it as a whole and to extract from it the great principles, and then, having them firmly in our minds, to come back to the details. I have often compared this with the analysis of a great piece of music, which is divided up into movements, each of which may again be sub-divided. It is a great thing to listen to the whole. It is a great thing, too, to listen to these separate big parts and to analyse them. It is much better to do that than to go along thoughtlessly from movement to movement, section to section, and note to note, as it were. So with a passage of Scripture, having got hold of the big principles of the essential teaching, you are able to understand the details in a way that you would not be able to do if you had not started in that manner.

With this section, therefore, I propose to adopt the method we used with verses 1–5. We saw that there were great doctrines enunciated in that first section and we shall find exactly the same thing here. It seems to me that the fundamental division of this passage can again be put in this form: firstly, *why* our Lord prays for his followers, and secondly *what* he prays for them. It is as simple as that. Now if we take the chapter and just read it through, without trying to get at the principles, then there are certain statements here which seem to be rather difficult and almost confusing. But we must realize that there are only these two big things dealt with here: our Lord puts first the reasons why he prays for these people, and then he gives the requests afterwards. Therefore, as we start reading at verse 6 we find a positive statement – 'I have manifested thy name unto the men which thou gavest me out of the world: thine they were, and thou gavest them me; and they have kept thy word.' He makes a categorical statement like that in his prayer because it is only after he has adduced certain reasons that he brings the petition. Of course you find that the two things are really intermingled but for the sake of clarity of thought they ought to be kept separately in our minds as we look at any particular detailed statement.

Let us, then, summarize the first section. Why does our Lord pray for these people at all? Here he is facing his own death, the greatest and the most terrible moment in his life is at hand, and yet he pauses to pray for them. Why does he do it? The answer is all here. He does it first and foremost because of his great concern for the glory of God. While he is on earth, the glory of God is, in a sense, in his hands. He has come to glorify his Father and that is the one thing he wants to do above everything else. And now as he is going to leave these people, over and above his own concern about dying is his concern about the glory of God: it is the one thing that matters.

Secondly, he prays for them because of who and what they are. They are the people to whom he has manifested the name of God; the people who have been given to him; the people to whom he has given the word: people who believe certain things. That is the definition of a Christian and they, and they alone, are the people for whom he has prayed.

Then he prays for them because of their task, because of their calling. He is going and he is leaving them in the world to do something; they have work to do, exactly as he had been given work to do. You see the logic of it all? God sent him, he sends them, and he prays for them especially in the light of their calling and their task – the work of evangelizing. There are other people who are going to believe on him through their word, and so they must be enabled to do this work.

He also prays for them because of their circumstances, the circumstances in which they were placed in the world. He says that they are going to have trouble in the world: 'I have given them thy word; and the world hath hated them, because they are not of the world, even as I am not of the world' (v. 14). There is an antagonism to the Christian in this world – the Bible constantly tells us that the world hates a Christian as it hated his Lord. The apostle Paul reminds Timothy of this. Timothy is frightened because he is being persecuted. He cannot understand it, but Paul tells him that 'all that live godly in Christ Jesus shall suffer persecution' (2 Tim 3:12). Our Lord says the same thing in John 15: 'The servant is not greater than his lord. If they have persecuted me, they will also persecute you' (v. 20), and again: 'If they have called the master of the house Beelzebub, how much more shall they call them of his household?' (Mt 10:25).

That is the argument here. He is thinking of these people in this gainsaying, contradictory world, and because he knows what they are going to endure, he prays for them. He knows the persecution which follows inevitably, in some shape or form, whenever anybody becomes a Christian. It does not always mean that we will be thrown into prison or a concentration camp, or molested in a physical sense, but as certainly as we become like the Lord Jesus Christ we will have to suffer for it – 'We must through much tribulation enter the kingdom of God' (Acts 14:22). Persecution can be very subtle – a mere glance from one person to another, the faintest suspicion of a smile or a curl of the lip, some little indignity thrust upon you – it manifests itself in a thousand and one ways. The astounding thing is that though we are told to be prepared for it, so often when we receive it, we are taken by surprise and wonder why it happens. Do not expect, my friend, that the whole world will rejoice if you become a Christian. You will probably receive enmity and hatred and persecution from certain people. It happened in the case of our blessed Lord, and his followers must always be ready to meet it.

But the last reason he seems to adduce here for praying for these people is that he is anxious that his own joy may be fulfilled in them. We must not stop at what I have just been saying. Our Lord was a man of sorrows and acquainted with grief, he was condemned and crucified on a cross, yet the author of the epistle to the Hebrews says, 'Who *for the joy that was set before him* endured the cross, despising the shame...' (Heb 12:2). There was a fundamental joy deeper than all the suffering, deeper than all he endured by way of the contradiction of sinners against himself, and he was anxious that his followers might know this. He wanted them to experience his own peace, his own inimitable joy. This is possible for any Christian, in spite of all I have said, and in spite of the world in which we live. So if we are not experiencing this joy as something deeper than all these other experiences, then, to that extent, we are failing in our discipleship.

Then, secondly, let me summarize *what* he prays for them. The primary object of his prayer is not so much that they may be one with one another, as that they may be kept in true unity with him, with God the Father, and therefore with each other. That is the nature of the communion. Obviously this has to be worked out in greater detail, and never perhaps was this more necessary than today. This is a chapter which has been much misquoted and misinterpreted, so we must be clear as to what exactly this prayer for unity among believers really is; our Lord does pray for them in that context, and he goes on repeating it.

The next thing he prays for them is that they may be kept from the evil one – the devil, the god of this world, the prince of the power of the air – and the evil that is in the world as the result of his activities and efforts. Our Lord does not pray that they may be taken out of the world – we sometimes wish we could pray that, the idea of monasticism is somewhere down in the depths of all of us. We want to retire out of the world and arrive in some magic circle where nothing can disturb us. There is a longing in the suffering, persecuted Christian to get out of the world. But our Lord does not pray that they may be taken out of the world in any sense, nor that they may be taken out of it by death, but rather that in it they may be kept from the evil. Your business and mine as Christian people is to be in the midst of this world and its affairs, and still remain true and loyal to God, and be kept from the evil. 'Pure religion and undefiled before God and the Father is this,' says James, not to retire out of every vocation in life, but rather, 'To visit the fatherless and widows in their affliction, and to keep himself unspotted from the world' (Jas 1:27). What a glorious but tremendous task it is! And of course it is much more difficult than segregating yourself and going away to live in seclusion and isolation. The task of the Christian is to be right in the midst of this world and its affairs in order that he may do this work of evangelism, spreading the gospel and the kingdom of God, while the whole time, keeping himself unspotted from the world. Christ prays that his followers may be kept unspotted, that they may not be harmed and tarnished and polluted by the evil world in which they find themselves. It is a glorious task.

And his last petition is that they may be sanctified, that they may be set apart for this great work which he has given them to do: 'As thou hast sent me into the world, even so have I also sent them into the world. And for their sakes I sanctify myself, that they also might be sanctified through the truth' (v. 19). He sanctifies himself and he wants them to be sanctified in the same way. That throws an interesting light on the meaning of sanctification. If you just extract the word 'sanctify', what our Lord is praying here is that these Christians may have some additional blessing of sanctification. But you can see at once, when you take it in its context, that it again means that he is still concerned about this great and grand objective which he always has in the forefront of his mind and of his heart.

There, then, is a general analysis of his prayer for these people. Why does he pray for them? Well, we have seen the answer. What does he pray for them? Once again we have seen that the requests and petitions arise naturally and inevitably from a consideration of who these people are, the circumstances in which they are placed and the task which they have been given to do. And the only further point I would make here is one which is surely of the greatest possible value, something which comes with comfort and with consolation and encouragement, namely, what we see here in this section about the Lord himself. Here he is praying for his followers, not only for those immediately of his own time but for all who are going to believe in him throughout the centuries, and therefore for us. Let us look at him as he thus prays; let us look at certain things which stand out very clearly about his person. Notice his claims. He says, for instance, 'They ... have known surely that I came out from thee' (v. 8). Here is, apparently, one who is just a man. He is to be taken by cruel people in apparent helplessness and weakness and is to be crucified on a cross, yet he speaks of himself as one who has come out from God. Here is another great assertion of his unique deity: he is proclaiming that he is the eternal Son of

God come from heaven to earth to dwell among men. He repeats it by saying, 'Thou didst send me.' He is not one who has just been born like everybody else, he has been sent by God into this world.

Then in verse 10 he does not hesitate to say a thing like this: 'I am glorified in them' – a tremendous assertion that he is not only man, he is the Son of God, verily God himself, and that as he is the glory of the Father, so the disciples are to be his glory. He has glorified the Father, and he is glorified in them by what they are going to be, and what they are going to do. You notice our calling, you notice that we, as Christians, have the privilege of being men and women in him – that through us the Lord Jesus Christ himself is glorified. It is our conception of the Christian that is wrong. I feel more and more that most of our troubles arise from that fact. We must start by contemplating again what a Christian is, how the New Testament describes him, the place in which he is put, the dignity it ascribes to him – the glory, this special relationship to the Lord and to the Father.

And then he says in his prayer, 'That they may be one, even as we are.' He is one with God. He does not hesitate to assert it and to claim it: 'I and my Father are one' (Jn 10:30). He, a carpenter, one who had not passed through the schools, is one with God, God in flesh on the face of the earth – it is stupendous. In other words, to sum it all up, he has been sent by God into the world for this specific task. He said it in verse 4 when he prayed for himself: 'I have glorified thee on the earth: I have finished the work which thou gavest me to do.' There is the most exalted claim that a person in the flesh has ever made, but at the same time, observe his humility. He, who is the Son of God, does not hesitate to say so and to assert it, but notice the way in which he describes his coming into the world. He has been sent into it by God. Did he come to speak of himself and manifest himself and his own glory? No, he says, 'I have manifested thy name unto the men which thou gavest me out of the world.' That is something which should humble and humiliate us to the very dust as we read these gospels and look at this person who is none other than the only begotten Son of God. Observe his self-abasement;

he does not call attention to himself, he is all along manifesting the glory of his Father. It is God's name, the Father's name, that he is concerned about, and here he reminds his Father of that: 'I have manifested thy name ...'

And then we see how he describes the Christians as his Father's people: 'I have manifested thy name unto the men which thou gavest me out of the world.' He does not say, 'I am going to pray to you about my converts', or 'I am coming to you about the people who believe because of my preaching', or 'because of my miracles', or 'because of what I have done'. No, his view of his people is that they are the Father's people, the Father's children, and they believe on him because they have been given to him by God for that purpose. Was there ever such humility, such self-abasement and self-effacement? He is God, very God, and yet everything belongs to the Father, and the praise and the glory are ascribed to him.

Then you notice that in the eighth verse he goes so far as to say, 'I have given unto them the words which thou gavest me', and we find him constantly repeating that right through the gospel records. It is one of the most amazing things of all, that here we have the Son of God teaching the people, and yet he always emphasizes that nothing he says is of himself. This means that he never uses his own thoughts or words. The Father has given him certain words to speak, and he speaks them.

There is something terrifying about this. If that is true of the preaching of the only begotten Son of God, how much more should it be true of our preaching. The business of a man standing in a pulpit is not to speak his own words but to be biblical. He must expound this word because it is God's word, and he must speak the word that he is enabled to speak by the Holy Spirit. Our Lord was in utter subjection to the Father and everything he did and said was that which was given to him by the Father. So I would beg you again to meditate upon this. Consider this picture and examine yourself in the light of it – see the utter humility of our Lord, his self-abasement, his self-effacement and his complete dependence upon his Father.

Then the other thing, as I have already mentioned, is his supreme concern about the glory of God, which comes out everywhere. In both the first and the second sections this is his one petition: 'Father ... glorify thy Son' – why? – 'that thy Son also may glorify thee.' That is the reason – not himself, but that he may go on to glorify the Father to the end. And here he prays the same thing for these disciples. He says that this is really the only motive for making disciples at all, it is the only reason for preaching the gospel. Let us not misunderstand one another about this, but, I repeat, over and above our concern for the souls of men and their salvation should be our concern for the glory of God. What we should emphasize to men and women outside Christ and sinners in the world today is not, primarily, the fact that they are sinners, and unhappy because they are sinners, but the fact that their sin is an assault upon God and is detracting from his glory. Our concern about the glory of God should come even before our concern for the state and the condition of the sinner. It was true of our Lord, and it is he who sends us out.

But let me end on this note. Observe his care for his followers. He reminds his Father that he kept them while he was in the world. How easy it is to read the gospels without seeing that all the while he is watching them, and keeping them, and shielding them against the enemy. But now he is going out of the world and here he is praying to his Father to keep them. He pleads with him to look after them and commits them to his care. They are his Father's but they have been given to him and he gives them back – 'keep them from the evil' (v. 15). If we but realized the concern of our Saviour for us as we are tried and tempted and beset by sin and Satan, it would revolutionize our whole attitude towards everything.

And, last of all, we should note his loving attitude towards them. Some astounding things are said here. Indeed we would almost be right to query them when we read what he says of these disciples: 'I have manifested thy name unto the men which thou gavest me out of the world' – then notice – 'thine they were, and thou gavest them me; and they have kept thy word.'

How can he say that? As we read the gospels and look at these disciples, we see them quarrelling with one another, we see their jealousy of one another and their desire for pre-eminence over one another, and finally we read how at the end they all forsook him and fled. Yet what he said about them was, 'they have kept thy word'. He did not criticize them, he prayed for them. I thank God for this above everything else. 'If thou, Lord, shouldest mark iniquities, O Lord, who shall stand? But there is forgiveness with thee, that thou mayest be feared' (Ps 130:3–4). We have such a High Priest, sympathetic and understanding, loving, seeing what is true of us, committing us to God in terms like that, not mentioning the deficiencies, the weaknesses, the faults and the failures, but saying, 'they have kept thy word'. And because of that he commends us to God the Father and beseeches his loving protection around and about us.

Well, we have simply entered into the portals. These are but preliminary considerations on our way into this magnificent edifice in which we shall be reminded, as I have been trying to show you, of our Lord's own view of the Christian, what he is, his task, his business in the world, his destiny, and the glory which belongs to him.

May God bless these thoughts to our minds and to our hearts, and, above everything, let us ever think of him, our faithful High Priest, our Representative, our Advocate, our Intercessor, who, in heaven and in glory at this moment, has the same character as he had when he prayed on earth for his followers.

2

Not of the World

I pray for them: I pray not for the world, but for them which thou hast given me; for they are thine (v. 9).

We have seen that before our Lord makes specific requests for his people, he first gives his reasons for praying for them. So in this verse he starts off with a definition and description of the people for whom he is praying, and, therefore, of the Christian. This, then, is his first reason for praying for them and it is this which we must now consider together. The more I try to live this Christian life and the more I read the New Testament, the more convinced I am that the trouble with most of us is that we have never truly realized what it is to be a Christian. It is our whole conception of what a Christian is, and of what the Christian life is meant to be, that is so defective, and that is why we miss so many blessings. That is why, too, we are often so troubled and perplexed and bewildered and why we react as we do to so many of the things that happen to us in this life and in this world. If only we understood what the Christian really is and the position in which he is placed, if only we realized the privilege and the possibilities of that position, and, above everything, the glorious destiny of everyone who is truly a Christian, then our entire outlook would be completely changed. It would be revolutionized, or, as Paul puts it in writing to the Romans, our whole outlook would be transformed by the renewing of our minds (Rom 12:2).

The New Testament is literally full of this teaching; there is a sense in which it can be said quite truly that starting with Acts and going right through to the end of Revelation, there is only one theme, and that is the theme of what a Christian is. Why were these New Testament epistles written? It is clear that they were not written merely because the men who wrote them rather liked writing letters! No, there was a reason for every letter, there is a kind of urgency behind every one of them, because the men who wrote the letters were pastors who were concerned about the souls of the people to whom they were writing. The early Christians were in this difficult world, in which you and I still have to live, they were surrounded by very many problems, and all these letters were written in order to help them to live as Christians in such a world. You can sum up the argument of every letter by putting it like this: what all the writers are saying, in effect, is, 'If you only realized who and what you are, you would have gone eighty per cent of the way to being a complete victor over everything that assails you.' Read the introductions, listen to these writers in their salutations; they remind the people of who they are and of what God has done in Christ, and therefore of all the possibilities which are theirs.

That is the whole case, and surely there is nothing that we need more at the present time than just this reminder. That is the way, and the *only* way, according to the New Testament, in which we can live in a world like this, and, furthermore, that is not only the case of the New Testament, it is substantiated and proved in the long history of the Christian church. Read the stories and accounts of every period of revival and reawakening, when the Holy Spirit has been present in power and in might. At such times men and women have known these things as they should be known, and they have been able to rise above all their circumstances. Indeed, you cannot understand the history of the church throughout the centuries apart from this. Think of every revival and period of reformation, all the great history, the stories of the martyrs and confessors, and all that stands out so gloriously in church history – how do you explain it? There is only one explanation: those people knew what it was to be a

Christian. Their view of this was the New Testament view of the Christian and the result was that they could defy tyrants without any fear, they could look into the face of death and say, 'It is well.' They knew who they were, and where they were going. They were not afraid of men, of death, or even of hell, because they knew their position in the Lord Jesus Christ, and the result was that these people triumphed.

We are reminded of this when we read that great eleventh chapter of the Epistle to the Hebrews – indeed it is the whole case of the New Testament, and once we accept this view, then like Abraham, and Moses and all the rest, we can go on 'as seeing him who is invisible' (Heb 11:27). We can go out not knowing where we are going, but quite happily, because we know that he is with us. And in his prayer here our Lord seems to me to start at that very point. He knows that the supreme thing for the disciples, in this world, is that they should be certain of these great centralities. Perhaps I should pause and ask a question at this point. How do you and I react to the things that happen to us in this life, and in this world with all its uncertainty? Now I argue that what determines that, finally, is our view of ourselves as Christians.

We must, therefore, consider what our Lord has to say about the Christian. Our method, you remember, of approaching this paragraph is first of all to extract the doctrine, then, having done that, to go back to the details in the light of that doctrine. Here, then, is the essential doctrine – the character of the Christian – and the first thing I notice is a negative. He says in the first phrase, 'I have manifested thy name unto the men which thou gavest me *out of the world.*' Now that is the theme, that is the first thing he says about the Christian. Need I apologize again for starting with a negative? If I understand the times in which you and I are living, I think that the greatest need is for negatives. People do not like them, they so easily condemn us, but whether we like it or not, the first thing that is true of the Christian is that he is not of this world, and does not belong to it. Now you notice that in this one section he repeats that four times. Verse 6: 'I have manifested thy name unto the men which thou gavest me out of the world'; verse 9: 'I pray for them: I pray not for the world, but for them which thou hast given me'; again, verse 14: 'I have given them thy word; and the world hath hated them, because they are not of the world, even as I am not of the world'; and then verse 16: 'They are not of the world even as I am not of the world'. Our Lord goes on repeating that phrase because he wants to impress it upon us. The first thing that is true about the Christian is that he does not belong to this world.

This is, obviously, a very big point. I chose to quote verse 9 as my particular text here because it seems to put it more pointedly than any of the others. Our Lord says that he prays for them only. He does not pray for the world; there is only one prayer that he offers for the world, and there is only one prayer that we should offer for the world, and that is that it may be saved. But here he is praying and interceding for all who belong to him. He is praying as the mediator, offering a particular prayer as the representative of his own people, and that is where the practical urgency comes in. In this frightening and uncertain world in which we find ourselves, surely, if we are Christian at all, we must feel that the biggest and the most important thing for us to know is whether or not the Lord Jesus Christ is praying and interceding for us.

In the light of this, it is vital that we should ask ourselves the question: am I of the world or am I not? That is the fundamental distinction which runs right through the Bible from beginning to end. Again I refer you to Hebrews 11, and you find the same thing, also, right through the Old Testament. There are only two groups of people in the world today – those who are of the world and those who belong to Christ. In the last analysis there is no other division or distinction that has the slightest importance or relevance. That is why most of us are defeated by life in this world – we recognize other distinctions that are quite unimportant. But when we all come to die, does it make the slightest difference as to which political party we belong to? Does it matter whether we are rich or poor, learned or otherwise? Does it matter what our social status is? It is all utterly irrelevant, it does not matter. As the old English proverb says,

'Death is the grand leveller.'

How foolish we are, how superficial we are, to bother ourselves, as we do, with these other distinctions. I know that, in a sense, they have their place, but what I am saying here is that they are not fundamental things. There is only one fundamental distinction and that is whether we belong to the world or to Christ. That is the only thing that matters on our death-bed, the other things will not be of the slightest value to us, they will be utterly insignificant.

The Christian, then, is one who has been separated from the world. 'Ah!' says someone, 'There you are, you Christians, putting yourselves into a separate compartment and category.' That is quite right – I do not resent that charge at all. I deliberately assert that I am not of the world, I am not in the same category as those who belong to it and I thank God for that. It is not something to be ashamed of, but something to glory in. What a tragedy it is that Christian people seem to be ashamed of this and are ever trying to conform to the world. We should desire to be entirely different, to be not of the world as he was not of it. We are meant to be marked men and women, different in every respect. This, therefore, is what we must consider together in order to make quite certain that we can rest in the quiet confidence and assurance that the Lord Jesus Christ is concerned about us and that he is interceding on our behalf. He says, you remember, 'Neither pray I for these alone, but for them also which shall believe on me through their word' – and that is you and me.

Scripture is full of this doctrine. We have seen Paul's appeal to the Romans: 'Be not conformed to this world: but be ye transformed by the renewing of your mind' (Rom 12:2). James says the same thing: 'Know ye not that the friendship of the world is enmity with God? whosoever therefore will be a friend of the world is the enemy of God' (Jas 4:4). Could anything be plainer or clearer than that? Then let me remind you of those forcible words in 1 John 2:15–17: 'Love not the world, neither the things that are in the world. If any man love the world, the love of the Father is not in him. For all that is in the world, the lust of the flesh, and the lust of the eyes, and the pride of life, is not of the Father, but is of the world. And the world passeth away, and the lust thereof: but he that doeth the will of God abideth for ever.' This is a momentous statement. And we find John saying exactly the same thing in chapter 5 of that same epistle: 'We know we are of God, and the whole world lieth in wickedness', or 'in the evil one' (v. 19).

Obviously, therefore, the practical question for us is to know for certain that we are 'not of the world', and there are many ways in which that question may be answered. Certain specific distinctions are given, and I want just to call your attention to these basic points. Take, for instance, how Paul puts it in Ephesians 2:1–3, 'You hath he quickened, who were dead in trespasses and sins; wherein in time past ye walked according to the course of this world, according to the prince of the power of the air, the spirit that now worketh in the children of disobedience. Among whom also we all had our conversation in times past in the lusts of our flesh, fulfilling the desires of the flesh and of the mind; and were by nature the children of wrath, even as others.' That is a most comprehensive definition of what it means to belong to the world, and so, too, is the statement quoted above from 1 John 2.

So let us face the question in the light of these definitions. To be of the world can be summed up like this – it is life, thought of and lived, apart from God. In other words, what decides definitely and specifically whether you and I are of the world or not is not so much what we may do in particular as our fundamental attitude. It is an attitude towards everything, towards God, towards ourselves, and towards life in this world; in the last analysis, to be of the world is to view all these things apart from God. So let us get rid of the idea that worldliness just means going to the theatre or the cinema; do not think that if you do this or that you are therefore a worldly person. It is not that, for there are many people who never do any of these things but who, according to the Scriptures, are thoroughly worldly-minded. Indeed – and this is a terrible thing – as I understand this definition, you can even subscribe to the Christian faith in an orthodox manner and still be of the world. If anybody disputes this, let me give you my authority at once. The word uttered by our Lord to those people who at the last day shall say, Lord, Lord, haven't we done this, that and the other in your name? is, Depart from me, I never knew you – you do not belong, you never have belonged to me (Mt 25:31–46). To belong to the world is a fundamental attitude, and, as I am going to show you, we betray ourselves and our attitude by what we are in general, and by the way in which that is manifested in various respects.

To be of the world – and this is repeated by the apostles – means that we are governed by the mind and the outlook and the way of this world in which we live. Paul says in Ephesians 2:2 that we are governed by 'the prince of the power of the air, the spirit that now worketh in the children of disobedience'. In 2 Corinthians 4:4 he talks about the 'god of this world' and it is the essence of biblical teaching that this world and its ways are under the dominion of Satan. According to this teaching, everybody who is of the world is governed and guided and dominated and controlled by that outlook which is opposed to God. Consequently, every man who is not a Christian and who talks so much about his free will is the greatest dupe of all. He is so much a slave of Satan that he does not know it; he is so blind that he cannot even begin to think about it. It is a domination, which holds us in its grip, and of course we all know about it from experience. The greatest tyranny which we have to meet in this life is that of the worldly outlook. It insinuates itself into our thinking everywhere, and we get it immediately we are born. We belong to a particular family and have certain ideas before we are very old; we turn to our newspapers and they are always suggesting things, as do the books we read. Indeed, everything seems to be suggesting a way of life to us, and we absorb it unconsciously – it is a domination, it is 'the god of this world'. And the first thing that happens to a man when he is convicted of sin and begins to repent is that he realizes the thraldom of the world and its way.

But let me divide it up into detail in order that we may think it through at our leisure. The world tends to control our thought, our outlook, and our mentality. The fact of the matter is that the whole thinking of the world conforms to a pattern. Oh, I know all about the different schools of thought, but in the end they all conform to a pattern, and they all have something in common. But surely, says someone, there is nothing in common between the communist and the man who is extreme on the other side? I say that there is; they are both very much interested in material things and material welfare and they are both probably controlled by this. There is a fundamental, common platform and they only differ in detail. One man says, 'I ought to have this', and the other man says, 'No, I ought to have it' and they quarrel with each other, but there is really no quarrel in their thought and outlook – 'One touch of nature makes the whole world kin.'

The fundamental philosophy common to all is that all this thinking is entirely confined to this world. It is on that level and never rises above it. It has no revelation, it does not believe in such a thing – and indeed that is another way of dividing everybody in the world today. The Christian's fundamental thinking is controlled by the Bible, by revelation from above. Philosophy – what man thinks, what man has discovered – that is the characteristic of the world, and it is at that point that you see the utter folly of all the other divisions, because worldly thinking is all on the human level, and it never contains anything from above. It is an outlook which never thinks of anything beyond this world, and this is true in all the different realms and departments. There is a hatred of the thought of death in the world today. I do not care which group of society people may come from, or what kind of person they are. They all hate it because they are living entirely for this life and for this world, and they are not prepared to consider anything beyond it. That is characteristic of the worldly outlook.

But I can sum it all up by saying that the man who belongs to the world is completely dead to spiritual things. The classic statement of this is again made by the apostle Paul. These things, he says, are spiritual, and 'the natural man receiveth not the things of the Spirit of God: for they are foolishness unto him: neither can he know them, because they are spiritually discerned' (1 Cor 2:14). 'You hath he quickened,' he says in another passage, 'who were dead in trespasses and sins' (Eph 2:1) – dead to everything that is of the Spirit and of the soul and of eternity. These things make no impact upon those who are in the world. They do not see anything in them and they cannot understand people wasting their time on these things, which they find so dull. These poor people are just confessing that they are spiritually dead in trespasses and in sins and their souls are in a state of death.

But obviously this also manifests itself in the desires and pleasures, and the ambitions of such people. The general description is 'the lust of the flesh, and the lust of the eyes and the pride of life' (1 Jn 2:16), and that is a perfect analysis. In some people it seems to be a delight in the things that belong to the animal, to nature, to pure carnality. Life is full of it today, and men and women are only living to the flesh. They must always be reading about it, so the newspapers and the periodicals are full of it. That is life, they say – it is astounding, but how true it is – the lust of the flesh.

Then the lust of the eye. This is a little more refined, not quite so gross, but it is the same thing. It is a concern about personal appearance. Think of the space that is given to this, too, in the press; think of the appalling amount of time and thought and money which people give merely to how they look, or to the figure they cut. They even study and practise the very way they walk – a living soul and spirit, made in the image of God! – but that is the world.

And then the pride of life, which is even more subtle than the lust of the eye. The things we boast of, the things about which we are so proud: our birth, our family, our background, our forebears, the school we went to, the university in which we studied – are not these the things that are the pride of life? We preen and pride ourselves on something that we are, and that somebody else is not. But it is all entirely of the flesh and the animal. These things are utterly irrelevant before God but they are the things that the world likes – the pride of life, intellectual pride. These are the things that are characteristic of the world, this is where it derives its pleasure, this is its ambition. It is exalted by these things, it lives for them, it talks about them. These are the things which are supreme in people's lives, this is their whole outlook, and, I ask a solemn question, can it be said that those of us who are in the realm of the church are free from such things? Let every man examine himself.

And, finally, the world shows itself in conduct, the conduct which corresponds with the outlook and the desire. The result is that people who are in the world live only for such things and on such a level. Let me put it quite plainly, for I want to show how universal this is. It is in all of us until the grace of God comes into our life and shows what it is, and makes us heed it, and delivers us out of it. It is a terrible thing to think that there are many people around us who are living this sort of life. They are not guilty of the things I have just been mentioning but they are just living life for themselves and their families. Think of many quite ordinary people, quite respectable people. They are not concerned about these subtle forms of sin which I have been enumerating, but the tragedy about them is that they are just living for their own little family circle. They never think of God and they never praise him. There are many thousands of such families living within the confines of life and time on earth, never rising above it all.

All that, then, is the negative, it is 'of the world'. That, says our Lord, is the kind of life which such people lead and they are not the ones I am praying for here.

But now let us look at the positive. The Christian is not like that, the Christian is like Christ himself: 'I have manifested thy name unto the men which thou gavest me out of the world: thine they were, and thou gavest them me, and they have kept thy word.' And again in verse 16: 'They are not of the world, even as I am not of the world.' Do I want to know for certain whether I am a Christian? Well, am I like those who are of the world? If I am not, I can take comfort, but I must be positive also. I must be like the Lord Jesus Christ. He says his people are like him. Is he the centre of my life? Is my relationship to God the controlling thing in my life? I am not saying I am perfect, but, as I understand this teaching, I do say that I cannot be a

Christian unless I can say quite honestly that the basis of my life is in God and that he is at the centre. However much I may fail from time to time in practice, I am centred on God. This means, therefore, that in terms of the revelation of the Bible, I, like those people in Hebrews 11, view all things in this life and world according to that outlook. My governing thought is that I am a pilgrim and a stranger in this world, going on to God, so that of necessity I spend my time in thinking of my soul and of my destiny. I do not get annoyed when somebody faces me with the fact of death, because I remind myself of it day by day; I realize that this is the one thing I have to start with and that I am a fool if I do not. The Christian always holds that before him, his whole life is lived under God and he realizes the nature of life in this world. He is controlling his life so that he does not foolishly spend most of his time and energy in trying to forget that it must come to an end. He deliberately keeps that before him.

And from that, of course, follows this desire to know God and his love in Christ; a desire to be more like Christ; a desire to be holy; a desire to spend more and more time in fellowship with God and with Christ, that we may conform more and more to his image; a desire to be well pleasing in God's sight. Let me put it as strongly as I can. When a man is like Christ he hates the world – the outlook, not the people – the mentality, the type of life. He realizes it is subtle, in that it is trying to keep him from God, whatever form it may take. He realizes, too, that these things are damnable, and against God. They take a pride in something that belongs to a fallen world, and he hates it as Christ hated it. He turns his back upon it, so he prays a great deal to be delivered from it. He separates himself as much as he can to meditate upon heavenly things and he lives his life in the fear of God.

That is what the Bible tells us is meant by not being of the world even as Christ was not of the world (v. 16). Oh my beloved friends, let me plead with you to face this, to face it every day and never to forget it. The consequences are so vital. If you and I are of the world it means that Christ is not praying for us, but if we do belong to him we are not of the world. Remember that God is your Father and that he will not let anything happen to you that will harm you. That does not mean that no distressing event will befall you, but that when it does, in the amazing will and purpose of God, even that is going to be a good thing, and you will understand it in glory. What a wonderful thing it is to go through life knowing that your life is in the hands of God, knowing that your Father is thus concerned about you and that your blessed Mediator who prayed for you on earth is still interceding for you in heaven.

To be 'not of the world' means that we are children of God, though once we were 'children of wrath'. Let us make no mistake about this. If you and I go out of this life belonging to the world, and of the world, we have nothing to look forward to but wrath. I do not know if you can tell me of a sadder statement in Scripture than John 17:9: 'I pray not for the world.' Those who are of the world are under the wrath of God until they come out of that position, until they believe in Christ and until they are saved and reconciled to God. He does not pray for them, they are just left, and it is an appalling thing to think that people who go out like that go to nothing but the wrath of God. Oh the folly of being of the world! For, as John tells us, the world passes away and the lust thereof. Is it not astounding that everybody does not realize that? Let us pay heed to the warning of things that happen. The world is passing away. Your pride in your appearance, in your life and position, all you have and what you are, my friend, is decaying and rotting even as you are boasting of it. And a day will come when it will be useless and your naked soul will be there alone. 'The world passeth away, and the lust thereof: but he that doeth the will of God abideth for ever' (1 Jn 2:17).

I trust that as the result of this examination we are all able to say quietly and to the glory of God, 'I am not of the world, I belong to God in Jesus Christ and I am safe in his holy, heavenly keeping. Come what may, I can say that "neither death, nor life, nor angels, nor principalities, nor powers, nor things present, nor things to come, nor height, nor depth, nor any other creature, shall be able to separate us from the love of God, which is in Christ Jesus our Lord".'

3

God's People

I have manifested thy name unto the men which thou gavest me out of the world: thine they were, and thou gavest them me; and they have kept thy word (v.6).

In our last study we saw that nothing is more important and reassuring in a world like this than to be sure that the Lord Jesus Christ is praying for us and interceding on our behalf. But now we must go on to the next step. We have seen that Christians are people who are not of the world. There is a great division in mankind: there are those who belong to the world and those who do not. The second group have been placed in a special position. They have been segregated from everybody else, and the great question that arises at once is what has happened to them and why? Why should they be the special object of our Lord's solicitude and care? Why this fundamental division in mankind? What is it about Christian people that puts them into a separate position?

That is one of the most profound and fundamental questions that a human being can ever consider. The fact is beyond dispute, as we saw in our last study, but let me put it still more directly. As we think of the great mass of people in the world today who are leading worldly lives, what is it that makes us different? Why are we not like them? In saying that, I am not speaking like a Pharisee, for as I have already pointed out, a Christian must know that he is different. If he does not know that, then he is not a Christian at all, because the term itself describes certain people. It is not that the Christian says in a superior way, 'I thank God that I am not like that other man.' We shall see, however, that we do use those same words, not as the Pharisee used them but in a very different manner.

Why, then, are Christian people not of the world? It is because *they are God's people*. 'I have manifested thy name' – to whom? – 'unto the men which thou gavest me out of the world: thine they were, and thou gavest them me.' That is the answer. That is the first, and indeed the ultimate explanation, the one which includes all the others. We hope later to show how exactly this was done, and how we are put into that position, but the fundamental answer to the question is that we are there and that we are what we are because we are God's people.

Here we come again to one of those foundational doctrines of the Bible and of the Christian faith and it is one of the most glorious of all the doctrines. It is a point which is constantly neglected in our day, and we neglect it to the great impoverishment of our souls and Christian experience. This is something which is central to the whole biblical view of life, and especially of salvation. The importance of the doctrine can be seen at a glance in this very chapter. Whenever our Lord repeats a thing we can be quite sure that he regards it as absolutely vital. We are familiar with the fact that whenever he introduces a statement by saying, 'Verily, verily' we ought to pay unusual attention to it, so, if he repeats a statement frequently in a short space, we can be equally certain that it is something which we should lay hold of very firmly. Now you notice how he repeats it in this particular section. Here it is in verse 6, but again we have it in verse 9: 'I pray for them: I pray not for the world, but for them which thou hast given me; for they are thine.' In verse 10 he says, 'All mine are thine, and thine are mine; and I am glorified in them', and then again in verse 11: 'And now I am no more in the world, but these are in the world, and I come to thee. Holy Father, keep through thine own name those whom thou hast given me, that they may be one, as we are one.' Finally, in verse 12 he says, 'While I was with them in the world, I kept them in thy name: those that thou gavest me I have kept, and none of them is lost, but the son of perdition; that the scripture might be fulfilled.'

So we have this statement five times in this passage, and we have already met it in verse 2 of the first section: 'As thou hast given him power over all flesh, that he should give eternal life to as many as thou hast given him.' And we will find it again in the last section, in verse 24: 'Father, I will that they also, whom thou hast given me, be with me where I am; that they may behold my glory, which thou hast given me.' Thus, in the space of these twenty-six verses, our Lord makes that particular statement seven times. In this short prayer he seven times describes the people for whom he is praying, his followers, as those who have been given to him by God.

Nothing, then, ought to establish in our minds the all-importance of this doctrine and teaching more than that, but you will also find that it is something which is taught everywhere in the New Testament. We find it in John 6:37 where our Lord says, 'All that the Father giveth me shall come to me; and him that cometh to me I will in no wise cast out'; and again in verse 39 where he says that he will keep all that the Father has given to him and that he will raise them up at the last day. It is exactly the same principle: the ones who will come to him are the ones whom the Father has given him. And further on in chapter 6, in verse 44, we read, 'No man cometh to me' – he puts it in a slightly different way – 'except the Father ... draw him.' This teaching is given in a very remarkable manner in that sixth chapter of John's gospel, but indeed, as I said, it is a doctrine which is taught everywhere throughout the New Testament.

It is found, for instance, throughout that mighty first chapter of the Epistle to the Ephesians, but especially in Paul's prayer for the church at Ephesus. He prays that the eyes of their understanding may be enlightened. He wants them to grasp this truth with their minds and with their understanding because it is so vital. He prays that they may know what is the hope of their calling and then, secondly, what is 'the riches of the glory of his inheritance' – God's inheritance – 'in the saints', which just means this very matter that we are looking at together. I want you to know, he says, and to see yourselves, as God's inheritance. I want you to grasp this great idea of God's special segregated people. It is his prayer, above everything else, that these people might know this.

Consider, too, what he wrote to Timothy. Timothy was very troubled and worried about certain things that were happening in some of the churches for which he was responsible, and Paul, in effect, says, 'Timothy, you need not be troubled, "The Lord knoweth them that are his."' He knows his own people and that means that he not only knows them but he looks after them, he keeps his eye upon them. Then in Hebrews 2:13 these words are applied to our Lord: 'Behold I and the children which God hath given me.' That is how the Lord Jesus Christ refers to Christians and to the members of his church. Peter also writes on the same theme in his epistle: 'Ye are a chosen generation, a royal priesthood, an holy nation, a peculiar people' (1 Pet 2:9), which means, a people for God's special interest and possession. I could go on and give you other quotations from the New Testament, but look them up for yourselves, and you will find that it is a doctrine which keeps on appearing everywhere.

Of course you have it equally strikingly in the Old Testament. Nothing perhaps is more true of the Old Testament than to say that it is, in a sense, just an elaboration of this idea of God's people, God's peculiar interest in his own people, the Children of Israel, and his dealings with them. All the nations of the world belong to God, but these are his special people, the people of his choice. For instance, those words which I have just quoted from Peter's epistle were first of all applied in Exodus 19 to the Children of Israel, just before the giving of the Law when God reminded them that they were his own special people. Indeed, I do not hesitate to assert that we do not understand the Bible in a radical sense unless we grasp this doctrine of God's people. Paul sums it up in Romans 11 by talking about the 'fulness of the Gentiles': '... until the fulness of the Gentiles be come in. And so all Israel shall be saved' (vv 25–26) that is, God's people, Israel, and all God's special people throughout the ages.

This teaching, therefore, is vital and because of that, because of its prominence in the Scriptures, quite apart from the consolation it gives to us, we must look at it a little more closely. What does it mean? I would suggest to you that it means something like this: God has chosen and marked out and separated a people for himself. There is no question about that. We have seen that it is the biblical teaching from beginning to end. God has put these people there on one side, on their own, in a special position of privilege and of blessing. 'Thine they were, and thou gavest them me.' It is ultimately the action of God himself.

Take the argument in Ephesians 1, in which such mighty terms are used. Let me plead with you, when you read a great chapter like that, to forget prejudice and not be so foolish that you stop at certain words in a way which raises the old arguments and enters at once into some ridiculous attempt to understand the mind of the eternal God. It is tragic that we should rob ourselves of these great doctrines and their benefits, and indeed that we should insult God himself and his gracious purpose, by taking up our little positions. Let us read a wonderful chapter like this and just listen to what it says. It tells us that God has done this before the foundation of the world, that before you and I were ever born, before the world was ever created, we were then known to God. He himself has determined these things. When you pause to think about it, it is one of the most staggering things that can ever come to a man's mind and comprehension, that though man sinned and rebelled, and as a result brought chaos into the universe, this almighty God who made the world and created everything in it, should nevertheless be concerned in this way and should separate certain people unto himself.

Secondly, he has done this solely and entirely of his own grace and love and not because of anything that he saw or found or ever will find in us. He has done this moved by nothing but his own glorious, ineffable nature and character. Oh, I do not understand it, I do not understand it from any aspect, and it is when we begin to try to understand these things that we always get into trouble. Many questions are thrown up at us; for example, 'Why did he only choose certain people and not others?' Or, to put it the other way round, 'If my brothers were not cho-

sen, why did he ever choose me?' I do not understand it either
way, and one is as baffling as the other. But let us leave our
pigmy understanding to the realm of time and earth, and let us
look at the glorious statement, which is that in spite of the fact
that we are all born in sin and 'shapen in iniquity' (Ps 51:5), in
spite of the fact that we are all by nature the children of wrath,
though we all by nature hate God and deliberately disobey him
and follow our own desires and our own lusts and self-will, and
glory in ourselves rather than in him, in spite of the arrogance
and pride and rebellion of all men, in spite of all these things, this
almighty God has looked upon certain people and has placed his
mark upon them. And not only that. He has done something to
them and about them, and has taken them from that evil world
into which they were born and has set them aside as his own special people.

Then we come to the next step, which is that he desires us as
his own particular possession and portion, and ultimately as
those who are to share his glory. Look again at Paul's prayer for
the Ephesian church in Ephesians 1. It is that they may know
what is 'the hope of his calling, and what the riches of the glory
of his inheritance in the saints'. To talk about God's inheritance
in the saints, the God who made everything and to whom all
things belong, and by whom all things are, to talk in this way is
the most amazing and daring piece of anthropomorphism that
Paul ever produced, and yet he has to put it like that in order to
give them an understanding of it. What he means is that these
are the people in whom God delights and this is what God is
going to enjoy.

Let me give an illustration in order to make this point clear – I
think we are entitled to do so in terms of the apostle's language.
Take a child who has many toys and dolls, all of which he likes.
Yes, but there is one particular favourite, the doll which is
always with him and sleeps with him . The child is fond of them
all but that one is something special. And it is the same with us.
We all have certain possessions which we prefer to others, there
is always something especially dear and of concern and interest
to us. That is the idea – that the great Lord of the universe has a

special object of interest and affection in his own people, in those whom he has taken and, as Paul puts it in writing to the Galatians, separated out of this evil world and put into a special category and compartment. That is the whole message of the Bible – God preparing for himself a people who are going to be his joy and rejoicing throughout eternity. So that is the beginning of the great truth. A Christian is one who is not of the world because God has chosen him – it all starts with the heart of the Eternal himself.

But let me take it a step further. God who had thus separated and marked a people for himself, then gave them to Christ: 'I have manifested thy name unto the men which thou gavest me out of the world'; 'As thou hast given him power over all flesh, that he should give eternal life to as many as thou hast given him.' It is always that. This is not merely a manifestation of our Lord's astounding humility, it is a literal, actual fact. Let us look at it like this. As we saw in our study of the first section of this prayer, a covenant was made between the Father and the Son; that is what the Bible tells us, and that is why I thank God for it – that we can enter into such glorious depths and swim in such oceans of mighty thought. This covenant was to the effect that the Father handed over these people whom he had chosen for himself before the foundation of the world. He handed them to the Son in order that the Son might make of them a people fit for God's special possession and enjoyment. So when the Son left heaven to come on earth, to be born as a babe in Bethlehem and to do all that he did, he was coming to carry out that plan. He came because God had handed these people to him and the Father had said, in effect, 'These people cannot be my people as they are. I have chosen them but they are not yet fit and I cannot truly enjoy them until they are. So I give them to you. Go and save them, go and redeem them, go and sanctify them and make them a people that I can enjoy and in whom I shall have my great joy and pleasure.'

So the Lord Jesus Christ came from heaven to earth in order to do that. That is the whole meaning of the incarnation, of his suffering, and of his being subjected to temptation. It is the whole meaning of his agony in the Garden, his death upon the cross, his resurrection and of everything else that he did. It has all been done for these people of God. The design is to prepare them for the Father in order to make them fit and meet for him. So as we look at the accounts in the gospels and see all that happened to our blessed Lord, we just realize that all that was done for us, for these people amongst whom we find ourselves, as the result of God's grace. Our Lord is described as the Mediator of the New Covenant; God made a covenant with him. Our Lord took those whom God had given him and he prepared them for God because they are God's peculiar possession.

And the end will be this, according to 1 Corinthians 15:24–25: 'Then cometh the end, when he shall have delivered up the kingdom to God, even the Father; when he shall have put down all rule and all authority and power. For he must reign, till he hath put all enemies under his feet.' When the last enemy shall have been destroyed, when every vestige of sin and evil shall be removed and purged out of the whole cosmos, when the contract has been finally completed, our Lord will have perfected the people and he will hand them back. The kingdom will be handed back to the Father and God shall be all and in all. That is what this teaching about God's people really means, and that is what it involves.

Let me, finally, draw certain simple, obvious conclusions from this high and exalted doctrine. As I look at these things and meditate upon them, my first conclusion is that our normal, ordinary view of salvation is hopelessly and ridiculously inadequate. Our trouble is that we always start with ourselves instead of starting with God. Instead of going to the Bible and looking at its revelation and discovering there what salvation means, I start with myself and certain things that I want and desire, certain benefits that I always want to enjoy in this life and in this world. I want forgiveness of sins; I want peace of conscience and of mind; I want enjoyment and happiness; I want to be delivered from certain sins; I want guidance; I want this and that; and my whole conception of salvation is reduced to that level.

Do not misunderstand me, the Christian salvation does those

things and contains them all, but how pathetic it is that we should start in that way and only look at that. How sad that we should not look at it in this other way and start with God – before the foundation of the world – and see this great and gracious purpose, and view ourselves as a people brought into it. We do not start with ourselves, but with God and the amazing fact that he should have brought us in and made us to be like this. To me the most wonderful thing of all is not that my sins have been forgiven, nor that I may enjoy certain experiences and blessings as a Christian. The thing that should astound me now and that will astound me to all eternity, especially when I get to heaven and glory and really begin to see it truly, is that I am a child of God, one of God's people.

The psalmist had some insight into this when he said in that graphic phrase of his, 'I had rather be a doorkeeper in the house of my God, than to dwell in the tents of wickedness' (Ps 84:10). He preferred to be in the vestibule, in the portal, of the house of God than to dwell in the greatest palace of the ungodly – it is the relationship that matters. I would sooner be a slave in God's house than be a dictator in the world. Moses chose 'rather to suffer affliction with the people of God, than to enjoy the pleasures of sin for a season' (Heb 11:25). He did so because he was interested in the recompense of the reward, and he did not take a short view. Moses said to himself, in effect, 'This is the overwhelming thing: that I am one of God's people. I do not care what I am now, even though I am only a shepherd away on the far side of a mountain with just a little flock. This is better, because I am God's, than to be accounted great as the son of Pharaoh's daughter.' Once more, it is the relationship that matters, and it seems to me that the tragedy is that we do not know enough about this relationship. Let us forget our particular blessings and enjoyments and realize that we are children of God, we are among God's people, the people whom he knew before the foundation of the world.

The second conclusion that I would draw is that we are very guilty of misunderstanding the work of Jesus Christ. I have two points here. Does it come as a surprise to anybody that, accord-

ing to this doctrine, it is no part of the work of the Lord Jesus
Christ to make us God's people? Have we not always thought
that that was his work – that he suffered for us and made us the
people of God? But he did not; we were the people of God first
and it was God who gave us to him. If that comes as a surprise to
us, it is because we read our Bible with prejudiced eyes instead
of looking at what it really says. 'Thine they were, and thou
gavest them me.'

My second point is equally important. This is that it is no part
of the work of the Lord Jesus Christ to secure God's love for us.
I am very fond of our hymns, but I always try to remember that
they are not divinely inspired, indeed some of them are tragically wrong and misleading. So many of them give the impression that our Lord is having to plead with his Father on our
behalf, that God, as it were, is opposed to us, that our Lord has
to engage his love for us and secure it for us. This doctrine
shows us that it is not a part of the purpose of the Lord Jesus
Christ to do that. It is because God loved us that he ever gave us
to Christ. Christ has died for us not to secure the love of God for
us, but because God has marked out his people before the foundation of the world. He hands them to the Son and says, Go and
save them, they are mine, I leave them to you, make them fit for
me. For, 'God so loved the world, that he gave his only begotten Son' (Jn 3:16); 'God was in Christ, reconciling the world
unto himself' (2 Cor 5:19) – not himself to the world. Oh how
foolish we are and what an injustice we do to the name of our
God and to his glorious love and grace! How frequently,
because we neglect this fundamental doctrine, do we go wrong
in our doctrine of the work of the Lord Jesus Christ!

But there are other conclusions which we can draw. Think, in
the light of all that I have been saying, of the place we occupy in
the interest and love of the Father and the Son. I confess that I am
almost overwhelmed when I think of this. I so often spend my
time, as I am sure many of you do, wondering why it is that I do
not experience more of the love of God; why God does not, as it
were, love me more and do things for me. What a terrible thing
that is! The trouble is that I do not realize his love to me, that is

my difficulty. People often come and say, 'I feel my love for God is so small' – quite right, I say the same thing myself:

> Lord it is my chief complaint,
> That my love is weak and faint.
> *W. Cowper*

That is true, but the best cure is not to try to do things within yourself and work up some love from the depths of your being. The way to love God is to begin to know God's love to you, and this doctrine is the high road to that love. Before time, before the creation of the world, he set his eye upon you, he set his affection upon you, you were marked, you were already put among his people. And all that has been done, all the person and the work of Christ, all this manifestation of his ineffable love, was done because of God's love to you. Therefore, realize his interest in you. The God who has loved you to the extent of sending his only begotten Son to endure and to suffer all that for you, loves you with a love which you will never understand, a love which passes knowledge. If we but knew God's love to us, it would revolutionize our lives.

And then the next conclusion is this: what sort of people ought we to be in the light of all this? Again, we are too troubled about the details of this question of holiness and sanctification – what method must I adopt? What must I do? We have been given lectures and addresses on the mechanism of obtaining this gift or that particular something. I do not see it like that in Scripture. There, I see it put like this – realize who you are. 'Ye shall be holy' – why? – 'for I am holy' (Lev 11:44). You are God's child, and one of his people. The way of holiness is to realize who you are, and always to remember it and the honour of the family, the honour of your Father, the honour of God. 'Every man that hath this hope in him purifieth himself, even as he is pure' (1 Jn 3:3). That is the argument and if you and I but realized our relationship to God now, and the presence of God with us always, it would very soon solve the problem of holiness and sanctification for us. We would not have to be waiting for particular experiences, we would realize that we are one with God and that we are in that relationship, and because of that, everything else is unthinkable.

And ultimately there is our wonderful security. Our Lord says in John 10:28, 'I give unto them eternal life; and they shall never perish, neither shall any man pluck them out of my hand' – we will come to that later. And here he is saying, I have kept them and now that I am going out of the world I hand them back, as it were, to you. Oh the eternal security of all who are God's people and who are known unto him before the foundation of the world!

Beloved friends, let us meditate upon these things; let us not start with self and its little needs, but let us rather lift up our minds and our hearts and contemplate this glorious plan of God into which we have been brought, which we can enjoy, and which is preparing us for that everlasting and eternal glory. Let us pray for ourselves what Paul prayed for the church at Ephesus, that the eyes of our understanding may be opened and that we may know the riches of the glory of his inheritance in us.

4

The Name of God

I have manifested thy name unto the men which thou gavest me out of the world: thine they were, and thou gavest them me; and they have kept thy word. Now they have known that all things what-soever thou hast given me are of thee. For I have given unto them the words which thou gavest me; and they have received them, and have known surely that I came out from thee, and they have believed that thou didst send me (vv. 6–8).

We saw in our last study that God separated us unto himself, and that having done that, he gave us to his Son, who came and worked out redemption for us, to fit us in a full sense to become God's people. The next step, therefore, that we must be concerned about is this: if I am a Christian at all, it is because God has looked upon me and set his mark upon me before I was ever born, before the world was created, but I still want to know how that becomes actual and how it literally becomes operative in me, in my life and in my experience. And that question is answered in these three verses that we are looking at now. To put it another way, what proof have we that this has taken place in us? How do we know that we are Christians? What exactly has happened to us to take us from the world into which we were born? We are all born the children of wrath and enemies of God. We are all born belonging to the world and subject to the prince of the power of the air, 'the spirit that now worketh in the children of disobedience'. We were all there once, says

Paul, and it is true of all of us. So, then, we ask, what has brought us here? And the answer is in the teaching of these three verses. In these verses we are told what it is that makes one a Christian, we are told exactly how it is that one becomes a Christian. There is a most extraordinary definition of the Christian here; everything that is vital will be found in these verses and therefore we must look at them carefully together.

You notice first that the key to understanding the whole passage is that it all depends upon the Lord Jesus Christ himself, he is absolutely central and vital to this matter. Verses 6–8 are all about him and he says the same thing again towards the end of the prayer, in these words: 'O righteous Father, the world hath not known thee: but I have known thee, and these have known that thou hast sent me.' So once more we see that he is at the centre. He himself constantly repeats this, and, too, it is something that is emphasized everywhere in the Scriptures.

Let me put it another way: there is no real knowledge of God except that which comes through the Lord Jesus Christ; as he said, 'I am the way, the truth and the life: no man cometh unto the Father, but by me' (Jn 14:6). No man can really know God without having life eternal. But what is life eternal? He has already told us: 'This is life eternal, that they might know thee the only true God, and Jesus Christ, whom thou hast sent.' We should observe how our Lord goes on repeating this. He puts himself, as it were, in the centre, and says that he is essential; he emphasizes it, and the reason for this is that mankind always thinks that it can arrive at a knowledge of God apart from him. Let me repeat once more that never was this emphasis more essential than it is at this present moment. Constantly and increasingly we find people teaching and saying that God can be known and that certain blessings can be obtained from him, but they never even refer to the name of the Lord Jesus Christ. They hold that you can get some important blessing, like healing, but Christ is not even mentioned. It comes, they claim, from God immediately and directly. But according to the teaching of the Bible there is no true and real knowledge of God except in and through Christ. That is the essential principle of Christianity, it is the meaning of the very term.

How, therefore, does our Lord bring us this knowledge? How does he let us know that we are God's people and that these various and glorious blessings which God is offering his people will become our portion and lot in this world? He answers this question immediately at the beginning of verse 6: 'I have manifested thy name unto the men which thou gavest me out of the world.' Now this is very important. Why does he put it in that way, instead of simply saying, 'I have manifested thee', or, 'I have manifested certain truths to them'? Why does he put it in terms of manifesting the name of God?

The answer is that this is the form in which the Bible habitually puts this particular teaching. In Scripture the name always stands for the character; it stands for the perfection of the person, and for his attributes; it represents what a person really is. The name is that which truly reveals the person and it is the connotation of everything that the person is in essence. Of course we are familiar with that usage of the term. We say about a doctor, for example, that he has 'a very good name'. We mean by this that he has the reputation of being a very good doctor, but we do not put it like that. We say that he has a very good name, and that expression stands for all the propensities and powers, all the skill and all the understanding, that this man happens to have.

Let me remind you of some of the ways in which this word is thus used in the Scriptures. Take, for instance, the story in Genesis 32:22–32 of Jacob at Penuel. It was a momentous night for him. He knew he had to meet his brother Esau the next day and he wondered what was going to happen. It was the most critical moment that Jacob had ever passed through. Having sent forward his goods and possessions and, last of all, his wives and children, Jacob was left alone, and it was then that a man came and began to struggle with him. Jacob realized that this was no ordinary encounter but that it was something divine and supernatural, so as he went on struggling with the man, he summed up all the knowledge that he had and said to him, 'What is thy name?' – I want to possess you, as it were. He knew that the name would tell him everything.

Then, again, the wise man, Solomon, says in one of his proverbs, 'The name of the Lord is a strong tower: the righteous runneth into it, and is safe' (Prov 18:10). In this world with its problems and difficulties and perplexities, there is only one place of safety says this man; it is the name of the Lord. It is like a strong tower and when I am besieged and attacked I run into that tower, and I am surrounded by the name of the Lord, which means everything that God really is, everything that is represented by the name.

Again, we find it in a still more specific form when God appeared to Moses and gave him his great commission and promise. He said to him, 'I appeared unto Abraham, unto Isaac, and unto Jacob, by the name of God Almighty, but by my name Jehovah was I not known to them' (Exod 6:3). In effect, God came to Moses and said, 'I am going to start something new. I am going to do something fresh. There is going to be a great turn-about in the history of my people. From this moment I am going to give you a great assurance, and before anything happens at all, I am going to give you a new name and I want you to realize what is meant by this name.'

We also have a definition of it in Exodus 34: 'The Lord descended in the cloud, and stood with him there, and proclaimed the name of the Lord' (v. 5) and then in verses 6–7 he began to tell Moses certain extraordinary and remarkable things about himself.

So when our Lord here turns to the Father and says, 'I have manifested thy name ...' what he is saying, in effect, is this: 'You sent me into the world in order to manifest and declare your name, and I have done it.' He has done that which was prophesied of him in Psalm 22:22: 'I will declare thy name unto my brethren: in the midst of the congregation will I praise thee.'

Now I want to put this in a very practical form. I wonder whether we have come to realize that the greatest need of everyone in this world is to know the name of God, because, when we know his name, we really know God himself, and are coming into an intimate knowledge of him. The final trouble with all of us is our ignorance of God. We talk about God, we say we pray to him, but the question asked everywhere in the Bible is: do you *know* him? Has he revealed his name to you? Do you know him in the sense that his name is to you a strong tower, and that whatever happens in this world you are absolutely safe because you run into that tower? Have you found the name of the Lord a shield, a protection, a hiding place when everything else has failed, when the world and its wisdom and science and knowledge can do nothing for you, and when your nearest and dearest are standing by looking helplessly on? Do you view things differently because the name of the Lord is there, and because inside the strong tower you are calm and quiet and serene, and full of joy and happiness? Does the name of the Lord protect you against everything? It is meant to do that.

As you read the lives of the saints in the Old Testament, you will find that this was always their lot and their experience. They were always safe and happy: 'When my father and my mother forsake me, then the Lord will take me up' (Ps 27:10). He never fails, but alas, the tragedy with us is that we do not know the Lord in this way. We often feel that he is against us or that he is unjust or unfair to us. People often suggest that he is cruel and unkind. The simple trouble with all such people is that they do not know him, for if they had known him – known his name – they would never harbour such thoughts concerning him. Such people are, of course, entirely without excuse, because God has revealed himself and his name to us. Indeed, even before his Son ever came into this world, God had revealed and manifested his name to the Children of Israel, so that we are altogether without excuse.

Let me, then, remind you of some of the names that God has given and has revealed about himself, and concerning himself even as we find them in the Old Testament. The first term for God that we find appears in a family of names: 'El, 'Elohim, 'El Shaddai, 'El Elyon – the strong and the mighty One. And this is the first thing we always need to know about God. We need to realize his might and strength and power. We talk so glibly about him, we argue and discuss these matters about God and we say what we think he ought to do. But we should remember that we are speaking about the Almighty, the Strong One. There is no limit to his power, he is the Creator, the Originator, of everything, the one who sustains everything – without him nothing can continue to exist at all. The first name of God is a name of strength, of absolute power, of almightiness.

But of course the name to which we must give particular attention is the special name which he revealed to Moses. This name was known before, but now it was given as a name representing certain things – the great name *Jehovah*. When God gave the promise of deliverance to Moses, he said, I am giving you my special name, Jehovah – that is, the self-existent one, the self-subsistant one, he that *is* – 'I am that I am' (Ex 3:14). God tells us that about himself, that he always was – there is no beginning to God. But it is agreed by all that in that self-same name, Jehovah, there is a further suggestion. It is a name that at one and the same time tells us that God is the self-existent one from eternity to eternity and yet at the same time he also becomes something – he becomes known.

In other words, the name Jehovah suggests a continuous and increasing revelation of God; or perhaps a better definition is that Jehovah is the self-existent one who reveals himself; he does not change in himself, but reveals himself increasingly to his people in their needs. He does not change, he is self-existent – I am that I am – but there is an extra dimension in the sense that he is manifesting and revealing himself. What a wonderful and precious promise that was when it first came to Moses. Can you imagine its effect upon him? But we must remember that we are not only thinking of Moses but also of ourselves. What God has said about himself to Moses he says to us – he is the self-existent one who is ready to reveal himself to us. We can see that if this were not true of God, if God did not reveal himself, we would know nothing about him, and we could not worship him. But he is the self-existent one who reveals himself.

But the most astounding thing about this name of God is the fact that it includes all the promises. We can put it like this. This is definitely the name of God in his relationship to man and it is particularly the name of God in the matter of redemption, which is why it is so germane to what we are discussing at the present time. There is God in his heaven in eternity and in the glory of all his qualities and perfection. And here is man on the ground. There is not only an awful difference in might and power, but there is a further terrible difference. God is holy and God is light; man is in shame and unworthiness. How can the two ever come together? The answer is that God is Jehovah – it is the name that comes to man in his sin and shame.

This is perfectly illustrated in the call of Moses. God's people, the Children of Israel, are in the captivity of Egypt. They are under cruel bondage, and are absolutely helpless. They are small in number, and they are in the hands of the mighty king, Pharaoh. How can they get out and be saved? And this is the astounding thing. We are told that God goes to a man who has been living as a shepherd for forty years, knowing himself to be a stranger in a strange land. Then God appears to him in the burning bush and he says, I am Jehovah, I am going to do something about those people, I am going to rescue them and redeem them.

It is God in the name of Redeemer, a name which includes everything connected with our redemption. He is the self-existent one who does not turn his back upon us, but looks upon us, and comes to us. He does something about us for he is Jehovah, the redeeming God. Keep your eye on that as you read the Old Testament Scriptures. This name always stands for God in his relationship to man in redemption. In other words, it is always when God is making a covenant with man that he uses it. He says to Moses, I am going to make a covenant with them, and this is the name in which I make it.

Yes, but more than that, he has condescended to break up even that name and in a sense to break it up by adding to it – if we have nothing else but this left in our minds as a result of this study we shall be the wealthiest people in the world. If only we realized what God has told us about himself in his relationship to us! Do you feel that I am being academic? If so, I am failing lamentably. What I am trying to say is that what God has revealed about himself, he has revealed *to us* – this is his relationship to us, if we but knew it. In all the names he has told us certain things about himself. Here is one great name – Jehovah-jireh. You will find it in the story of Abraham going up into that mountain to sacrifice his only son Isaac. He was on the point of striking his son when suddenly God stopped him and said, 'Do not strike him, I have another offering.' And Abraham found a ram in the thicket. The Lord had provided the offering and the sacrifice, so he gave that name, 'The Lord Will Provide'. And so, whenever you go into the presence of God, whatever your need may be, however disturbed you may be, whatever form the need may be taking, remind yourself that you are praying to Jehovah-jireh, the Lord who has promised to provide. He will be with you for he says, 'I will not fail thee, nor forsake thee' (Josh 1:5).

And then he gave another name at a time when a certain disease had broken out among the Children of Israel as they were marching from Egypt to Canaan. The whole situation seemed hopeless, but God healed them in a miraculous manner and, having done so, he gave them a name concerning himself: 'The Lord that healeth thee' (Ex 15:26). As the psalmist said, 'Bless the Lord, O my soul ... who healeth all thy diseases' (Ps 103:2–3), and by this he means that it is always in the power of God to do this. That is not to say he will always do it, but that he can and does do so when he chooses. When Paul had the thorn in the flesh, he turned to God and asked him to remove it. But it was not removed because it was not God's will in that particular case. God can heal and, in an ultimate sense, of course, he does heal all our diseases, because the ultimate disease is sin itself. It is a great promise of ultimate redemption and it does hold in embryo this further promise that is given, that the Lord Jesus Christ shall even take these bodies of ours and change them: 'Shall change our vile body' – the body of our humiliation – 'that it may be fashioned like unto his glorious body' (Phil 3:21) according to his mighty power.

There is another name which God is given: Jehovah-nissi, the Lord our Banner (Ex 17:15). That is the name he revealed to the

Children of Israel after a great victory, a victory won not by their own strength, nor by their own military prowess, but because God enabled them to obtain the victory – the Lord our Banner. And you and I have enemies to meet in this world – sin and temptation. The world is full of these subtle enemies and behind them all is the devil himself with all his power. Do you know what it is to be attacked by him? Do you know, for example, what it is to have blasphemous thoughts insinuated into your minds? The saints of God have had to experience that. The devil hurls the fiery dart, says Paul, and who are we to meet such a foe? We are small and weak and helpless, but, thank God, we know one whose name is Jehovah-nissi, the Lord our Banner, who can help us smite every foe and rout and conquer every enemy.

But then let me give you another: Jehovah-shalom – The Lord is Peace. This was the name that God gave to Gideon who was fearful and unhappy but God told him that he was Jehovah-shalom (Judg 6:24), and this is one of the most precious promises. It does not matter what kind of turmoil you are in, or how heart-sore you may be. If you are beside yourself and cannot understand why things are happening to you, go to him. He has promised to give you peace. Remember, too, that noble statement in Hebrews 13:20, that marvellous blessing and benediction, '...the God of peace that brought again from the dead our Lord Jesus' – Jehovah-shalom, The Lord is Peace, he makes peace with his people.

And then, thank God, there is that precious word which you find in the twenty-third psalm, 'the Lord is my shepherd' – Jehovah-ro'eh and, because of that, 'I shall not want'. Can you say that? Do you know God like that? He has revealed himself in that way, he is your shepherd and you need never want in an ultimate sense. 'The Lord is my shepherd, I shall not want.'

Then there is The Lord Our Righteousness, the name given to Jeremiah in Jeremiah 23:6: Jehovah-tsidkenu, The Lord Our Righteousness. And lastly, Jehovah-shammah, The Lord is There (Ezek 48:35). He is always present. You cannot in a sense be out of his presence because he is always there and especially in times of trouble.

I have, thus, just held these names before you, and my object in so doing is that we may remind ourselves that such is the God whom we worship and whom we adore, eternal, absolute and self-existent, but who nevertheless deigns to reveal himself to man, and those are some of the ways in which he has done so. You would have thought that this would have been enough and more than enough; you would have thought that mankind, hearing these names and having such a revelation of God through them, would have clutched at them and held on to them and that all would have been well. But such was not the case. Mankind, in spite of all this, still did not really know God and then – and this is the message of the ages, the particular message of the church – then, when man had not grasped it, this God who '... spake in time past unto the fathers by the prophets, hath in these last days spoken unto us by his son ...' who is '... the express image of his person' (Heb 1:1–3). Yes, our Lord puts it all here in these words, 'I have manifested thy name unto the men which thou gavest me out of the world' (v.6), and 'he that hath seen me hath seen the Father' (Jn 14:9).

We must leave it at that now. The Lord Jesus Christ has manifested his Father, and has manifested these names in a way that transcends everything that I have been saying. Go back to the Old Testament, look at those names, study them, read them – we are meant to do so, for they are absolutely true today. What Christ has done, in a sense, is to let the floodlight in, to open them out, and to enable us to grasp them, because he has done it in his person. Study them, and remember that what God has said is this: he is 'The Lord, The Lord God, merciful and gracious, longsuffering, and abundant in goodness and truth, keeping mercy for thousands, forgiving iniquity and transgression and sin and that will by no means clear the guilty' (Ex 34:6–7). Remember that his name is ultimately Love, that he has loved us with an everlasting love and knowing him thus, we can appropriate unto ourselves all the gracious promises. He will provide, he will heal, he will lead, he will enable us to conquer, but above all, and thank his great and holy name for this, he will never leave us nor forsake us, he will always be with us.

5

The Name of God Revealed

*I have manifested thy name unto the men which thou gavest me out
of the world: thine they were, and thou gavest them me; and they
have kept thy word. Now they have known that all things whatsoever thou hast given me are of thee. For I have given unto them
the words which thou gavest me; and they have received them, and
have known surely that I came out from thee, and they have
believed that thou didst send me (vv. 6–8).*

At this point in our study of our Lord's prayer, let me remind
you, we are concentrating in detail upon the definition which
we have in these three verses of what it really means to be a
Christian. Here is a description of the people for whom Christ
prays and for whom alone he prays. The first thing he says
about them is that they are God's people, marked out by God,
chosen of God: 'Thine they were, and thou gavest them me.'
And then we are interested in discovering how it is that they
come into this relationship. It is originally an action of God, but
how does it become actual in us? How are we to know that this
is really true of us in particular?

The first thing our Lord tells us is that he has manifested the
name of God to these people and they have understood it. There
are two main ways, it seems to me, of looking at these three
verses. You can look at them from the standpoint of what Christ
has done, or from the standpoint of what the Christian believer
has done – there are obviously two ultimates. Our Lord says

that he has done certain things to these people and they in turn
have accepted and have known assuredly these things that he has
spoken clearly. The two things must go together to make a
Christian. This message is proclaimed to the world and yet
there are many in the world who have not believed it and are not
interested in it. So the two things are essential and it is indeed
very important that we should bear both these aspects in mind
as we are considering this matter.

In these verses, our Lord confirms once more – and he repeats
this throughout the prayer – that his supreme object in coming
into the world was to manifest and to glorify the name of God.
That must always be the starting point in any consideration of
the Christian gospel or of salvation. I have been at pains to
remind you more than once that for about the last fifty years this
is surely the note that has been most seriously lacking in much
of our thinking as evangelical people. Far too often we start with
ourselves and end with ourselves, and with the Lord Jesus
Christ. How little have we emphasized the glory and the
majesty of God who is the source and fount of it all! Surely that
is why so often in our religious Christian life there is so little
reverence, so little awe. Our whole view is short of it, it is much
too subjective. We do not start with this grand conception of the
holiness of God. But that is where our Lord starts. The first
thing he says when he begins to pray is, 'I have manifested thy
name unto the men which thou gavest me out of the world,'
because ultimately that is the end and object of salvation. Or, to
use a technical term, it is the *summum bonum* of salvation.

In the Sermon on the Mount, our Lord puts it in these words,
'Blessed are the pure in heart: for they shall see God' (Mt 5:8) –
that is the goal. It is our first great need and without it we can
do nothing. To think that the Christian salvation ends with forgiveness or with some subjective hope of peace and joy – invalu-
able as these are – is to fall hopelessly short of the end and the
design of salvation, which is that we might know God: 'This is
life eternal, that they might know thee the only true God, and
Jesus Christ, whom thou hast sent' (v. 3). This, therefore, is the
greatest need of all, that we may know God, or, as our Lord puts

it here, that we might know the name of God, a term which we
have already considered from the Old Testament standpoint.

Now this is the greatest need because it is at this point that we
are all guilty of the greatest ignorance. We talk about God, we
argue about God, we express our opinions and we pray, yes,
but the question is, do we *know* God, is God living to us, is he
real to us? Is our prayer, therefore, vital? Is it a living communion and is a real transaction taking place? We all know, and we
must admit it with shame, that it is the easiest thing in the world
to be on our knees saying a prayer. We may do it for a long time,
and yet not for a moment realize the presence of God. If you
read the lives of the saints, you will find that they all emphasized
this point, that the first and the most vital thing of all is always
to realize the presence of God. George Müller, for example, in
giving advice to a number of ministers, put that point first. He
emphasized this important point that before you begin to speak
at all in your prayer, you must realize the being and the presence
and the reality of God.

Indeed, all the experts – if one may use such a term in such a
connection – in the devotional life and in the soul's relationship
to God have always emphasized that. They have said that we
must take trouble about it, we must not go on to petition until
we have 'recollected'. We must rid ourselves of hurry and
excitement and of a desire for particular things, and we must
restrain ourselves from rushing to petitions for the things we
want at this particular time. Before we come to anything like
that, we must realize where we are and what we are doing. We
must realize in whose presence we are and to whom we are
speaking, and we must remind ourselves of our relationship to
him – this knowledge of God without which prayer is not real
prayer. Real prayer is communion with God, it is fellowship
with him, it is a conversation with God, and obviously, therefore, we must start by this active realization that we are in his
presence.

Nothing, then, is more essential than that we should know
the name of God. It is a terrible and a tragic thing to realize that
we can be religious for a very long time and yet never really

know him, not know him as he is, not know the name of God. Indeed, we have seen that it is quite inexcusable. God took pains under the old dispensation to manifest himself, according to his name, the name which he split up, the name to which he added adjectives, in order that he might reveal himself in his great character to the people and that they might know him.

But, because of sin, and because of man's inability and man's incapacity, the Old Testament revelation was not enough. So the amazing and astounding thing with which we are confronted in the New Testament is that God has now given a revelation of himself in a way that is clear and unmistakable. That is the argument of the first verses of the epistle to the Hebrews: 'God, who at sundry times and in divers manners spake in time past unto the fathers by the prophets, hath in these last days spoken unto us by his Son.' That is the New Testament gospel, that is the very essence of it all. But you notice that the emphasis is still the same. It is God who speaks, it is God's action, it is something initiated by God himself and what the Son did was to bring us into this knowledge of himself which is the ultimate object of salvation.

Now our Lord, therefore, having done his work, is at the point of going back to the Father, and he sums it all up by saying, 'I have manifested thy name unto the men whom thou gavest me out of the world.' I have done the work, he says, and so the question is, how did he do it and how did these men know that he had done it? How did they realize what he was doing? And that is what our Lord himself explains to us here. He divides it up, and puts it in different ways: 'I have manifested thy name unto the men which thou gavest me out of the world: thine they were, and thou gavest them me; and they have kept thy word. Now they have known' – they have come to know this, though they did not know it before, that is the emphasis – 'that all things whatsoever thou hast given me are of thee' – that is part of the manifestation of the name of the Father – 'for I have given unto them the words which thou gavest me; and they have received them, and have known surely that I came out from thee, and they have believed that thou didst send me.'

Thus in these various ways our Lord has manifested the name of the Father unto these people for whom he now prays.

The thing, therefore, for us to do is to consider this, and here we are looking at the very heart and centre of the gospel. Let us forget everything, if we can, for the time being. Let us forget about our personal needs and problems and all our desires and everything else. No, that is not an unkind thing to say, it is the kindest thing of all. For the teaching of Scripture is that our particular and individual personal problems will only, ultimately, be resolved as we come to know the Lord Jesus Christ, so that the most direct way to tackle them is to come to 'consider him'. If we spend our time with our problems without knowing him, we will be left with our problems, and that is why the great invitation of the epistle to the Hebrews, to a people who were in trouble is, 'Consider him' (Heb 12:3). We must not look at immediate things only, we must look at him, and as we do so and see him as he really is, as our Saviour and Mediator and Lord, all these problems will be dealt with.

Now you notice that our Lord says here that he has *manifested* the name of God unto the men whom God had given him out of the world. He does not say merely that he told them about it, he goes beyond that, he says, 'I have manifested ...' – there has been a revelation, there has been an expounding of the name. That which was concealing it has been taken away and there has been an unveiling or an unfolding – that is the meaning of the word 'manifest'. Our Lord has made the name appear, and he has put it obviously before them. This is a very rich and comprehensive term, and our Lord undoubtedly uses it deliberately so that these men who are listening to him as he prays to God might realize the variegated and manifold character of this manifestation of the name of God which he has given.

So how does the Lord Jesus Christ manifest the name of God and, especially, how does he do so in a way that is superior to the Old Testament revelation? We have been through the names, and we have seen there the wealth of the manifestation through them. Yes but here is something more. Here, as the author of the letter to the Hebrews argues, is the pre-eminence of Christ. The Old Testament was a true revelation but it was only in part and in pieces; now, in Christ, it has come in all its fullness and glory.

Here, then, our Lord's first answer is that because he is the Son of God, he has manifested the name of God in a way that nothing and no one else could ever have done. He puts that like this: 'They have received them, and have known surely that I came out from thee.' These, he says, are thy people; these are true Christians because they know that I have come out from thee. That is just another way of saying that these people have known that he is, in a unique and absolute sense, the Son of God. That is always the first thing about a Christian. There is no such thing as being a Christian unless we are perfectly clear about the person of the Lord Jesus Christ. He is, according to this revelation, the Son of God, and he is this full and final manifestation of the name of God. And because he is the Son of God, the effulgence of his nature and of his glory, the fullness of God himself – as Paul says, 'in him dwelleth all the fullness of the Godhead bodily' (Col 2:9) – it is because of this that his manifestation and revelation of the name of God is altogether superior to everything else. He is God himself in the person of his Son. 'They have known surely that I came out from thee.' 'They shall call his name Emmanuel, which being interpreted is, God with us' (Mt 1:23). It is the difference between God telling us certain things about himself and God dwelling among us in the person of the Son.

This clearly, therefore, must be a unique revelation and that is the reason why our Lord was able to say to the disciples, 'He that hath seen me hath seen the Father' (Jn 14:9) – you look at me and you see him because the Son is like the Father and partakes of the Father's nature. He is not merely saying things about the Father, he is the representative of the Father in the way that a son represents his father. A servant may be able to say everything that is right about his lord and master, he may know him well and intimately, but he can never represent him in the way that the son can. The son is a manifestation of the father by being what he is. Thus our Lord himself, while here on earth, represented and manifested the name of God in a way that is incomparable and greater than all others, because he is the Son of God. We see this in John 4, in the account of our Lord's conversation with the woman of Samaria. He had been talking about worshipping God in spirit and in truth, and on hearing his words, the woman said, 'We know that Messias cometh, which is called Christ: when he is come he will tell us all things ...' Then our Lord looked at her and said, 'I that speak unto thee am he' – Look at me, and, in a sense, you see God. And that is what he constantly repeated in many different ways.

This is a thought that is staggering in its immensity. The apostle Paul, in 2 Corinthians 1:3, says, 'Blessed be God, even the Father of our Lord Jesus Christ.' Why does he put it like that – why does he not simply say, 'Blessed be God'? Why does he describe him as 'the Father of our Lord Jesus Christ'? I once heard an old preacher give an excellent definition of this. He said, 'You may describe God as Father and it is a great term; and if you go to people and tell them that God has revealed himself as Father, you may think it conveys a very definite meaning and impression. But,' he would say, 'you have to be careful. You must not think of the term "father", or "fatherhood", as an abstract term which has no particular associations. Different people listening to the word "father" have different conceptions and ideas. You cannot assume that to say "God is Father" is going to convey a good impression to everyone, because you may be saying it to someone whose idea of "father" is of someone who is constantly under the influence of drink, someone who is blaspheming and cursing, smashing up the home, turning out his wife and children – a hateful person, a hateful term, a hateful thought. That is inevitably that poor person's idea of father because it is the only kind of father he has ever known. So,' went on the old preacher, 'that is why Paul says, "Blessed be the God and Father of our Lord Jesus Christ." As long as you remember that he is the Father of our Lord Jesus Christ, then you will never have a wrong conception of the fatherhood of God.'

In other words, we look at the Son and see what he was, and

we realize that the Father is like that. The Lord Jesus Christ is, in a sense, the Father himself appearing before us. He is not the Father, but he is the brightness, the effulgence of his glory and the express image of his person. That is the first way in which our Lord manifests the name of God. 'They have known surely that I came out from thee', and that is always one thing you know about the Christian. He knows that the Lord Jesus Christ is the only begotten Son of God, he believes in the miracle of the incarnation. He knows that Jesus was not mere man, not merely a great teacher, he is God come in the flesh: 'The Word was made flesh, and dwelt among us' (Jn 1:14). That is the belief of the Christian, he knows that, and without that there is no knowledge of God, there is no salvation.

But you notice that our Lord puts it in another form also, and how important it is that we should watch every phrase. He seems on the surface to be repeating himself, but that is not so: 'They have known surely that I came out from thee, and they have believed that thou didst send me.' Is that the same thing? Clearly, it is not. This is something different. There is a very important distinction here. The first tells us that he comes, he is the Son, the manifestation of the Father, but when he says, 'They believe that thou hast sent me', there is a further revelation of the name of God, a revelation of the peculiar, special, love of God. Yes, we start by saying that Jesus of Nazareth is the only begotten Son of God, but then we ask ourselves the question: what is he doing in this world? What is the purpose, and the object of it all?

And there is only one answer – 'God so loved the world that he gave his only begotten Son' (Jn 3:16); 'Herein is love, not that we loved God, but that he loved us, and sent his Son to be the propitiation for our sins' (1 Jn 4:10). The New Testament is full of this truth, and by emphasizing it, our Lord was revealing and manifesting the love of God in its most perfect form: 'I have manifested thy name unto the men which thou gavest me.'

How, then, did he manifest the name of God as love? He did so when he told them that he was in the world because God had sent him. It was the Father who had initiated and called him to do this. God made a covenant with him, and the fact of his coming into the world is a manifestation of the eternal heart of God as the heart of love. God had manifested his love many times in the Old Testament. You cannot read the stories there without clearly seeing his love towards those recalcitrant, rebellious Children of Israel. All that was amazing and glorious but it is nothing, I speak with reverence, when you put it into the light of this: 'He spared not his own Son', but sent him from glory into this world of sin and shame, into this rebellious, unworthy world of man. God sent his own Son, made of a woman, made under the law, because he so loved the world – we read all these great biblical statements and in that knowledge we know the love of God in a way we can never know it otherwise.

But then he also manifested the name of God by his very life and character and deportment. Read the gospels with this in mind. Look at the figure of Jesus of Nazareth and remember that you are there seeing a manifestation of the character and being and person of God. Observe his holiness, his spotless holiness, tried and tempted 'in all points like as we are, yet without sin' (Heb 4:15), walking through the mud and mire of this world yet keeping himself absolutely unspotted from it. No one could point a finger at him, no one could charge him with any fault; they tried to but he was sinless, he was absolutely perfect. The holiness of God was manifested in the perfect life and walk of his Son.

But not only that, observe, too, his hatred of sin and especially of hypocrisy. Read carefully his words spoken to the Pharisees and Scribes, see the righteous anger and indignation that fills his heart as he observes the twisting and the contortion of these hypocrites. Read the woes that he pronounced upon them, as recorded in Matthew 23. That is nothing but a manifestation of God's utter abhorrence and detestation of sin and of evil. Our God is a holy God. Yes, with all the intensity of his holy nature he hates sin and all that belongs to it. Look at the life of our Lord and you will see that he drives people out of the Temple because they are making the Father's house a house of merchandise; he pronounces his woes upon these men, and there, again, he reveals the name of God.

But thank God there is something else. We see, at the same time, his compassion, his longsuffering, his mercy, and his kindness. He was called 'the friend of publicans and sinners' and he gives again a manifestation of God by being what he was. By his character and his life he was ever revealing a great truth about God: how that, at one and the same time, God hates sin but is full of compassion towards the sinner.

And then our Lord reveals his Father not only by his life, but also by his teaching. Go through the gospels and you will find his explicit teaching about God and about his character and nature and being. And then he does the same thing by his works. Every miracle he performed was a manifestation and demonstration of the power of God, and each one, almost invariably, had the same effect upon these people. They were frightened when they saw the miracles but they glorified God, saying, 'We never saw it on this fashion' (Mk 2:12). Another time they said, 'This is the finger of God' (Lk 11:20), and indeed it was, for the works manifested the name of God. The name of God was powerful in his miracles and mighty deeds.

But, finally in these verses, we must notice the most interesting statement of all – that in verse 7. It is surely one of the most fascinating aspects of our Lord's revelation and manifestation of the name of his Father. These people, he says, 'have known that all things whatsoever thou hast given me are of thee', which surely means that our Lord is saying, in effect, 'I have shown these people and at last I have convinced them, and they have come to see that my entire ministry in this world is something that you have given me.'

With that key in your mind, go again through the four gospels, observing those extraordinary and beautiful statements of our Lord and you will find it most revealing. Here is the Son of God on earth and he says, 'The words that I speak unto you I speak not of myself' (Jn 14:10) and again, 'The word which ye hear is not mine, but the Father's which sent me' (Jn 14:24). Again, he says, 'The Father that dwelleth in me, he doeth the works' (Jn 14:10). And he is reminding us in these verses of this very thing: 'I have given unto them the words which thou gavest me.' He is here teaching that his entire ministry is something which has been given to him by God the Father. We have already considered the fact that the people have been given to him – 'Thine they were, and thou gavest them me.' Now in a sense it is not the Lord who is gathering the flock together, it is God, and he has given them to the Son. He says in verse 2 that God has 'given him power over all flesh': and he also says, 'All power is given unto me in heaven and in earth' (Mt 28:18). God has given it to him, he has given him the words to speak, he has given him the works to do, but above everything else he has given him the mediatorial office which he has come to occupy.

And finally there are those striking words of his in John 6 where he says, 'for him hath God the Father sealed' (v. 27). God has anointed him and set him apart. The disciples understood it, for in a few minutes Peter was saying they were not going to leave him for they were assured that, 'Thou art that Christ, the Son of the living God', the anointed one, the sealed one, the separated one. And that is the tremendous fact which is before us in this chapter, that all our blessed Lord came to do and all that he did, was but the carrying out of a ministry that had been given him of the Father. I am not sure but that this is not the ultimate way in which he reveals the name of the Father to us. We look at him, at his person, his life, his work, and his death upon the cross. We see it all. Yes, but do we see that it is all a ministry that is given to him of the Father? What love there must be, therefore, in the Father for him to have given the Son this wonderful office. The Son does nothing of himself. It was God the Father who determined it all. It was given to the Son to carry out, and the height of the revelation lies in that realization that it is all because God is who he is and what he is. You look at Christ, therefore, in the light of his person and work and you see there what God is. We now understand the name of God. The Old Testament terms are all suddenly illuminated, the God who is our shepherd, the God who is righteousness and justice, the God who is all powerful, the God who is peace, the God who is health – we see it all in this one person. We see all these attributes and characteristics of the almighty God in the ineffable person, portrayed and manifested before our eyes. In looking at Christ we see God, and we know God as our Father and the Father of the Lord Jesus Christ.

May God in his infinite grace grant us the enlightening of his Holy Spirit that we may so dwell upon these things, so grasp them and so realize them, that each of us shall be able to say honestly and truly, 'I do know God and I have come to know him, the only true and living God, through Jesus whom he has sent.'

6

The Christian and the Truth of God

I have manifested thy name unto the men which thou gavest me out of the world: thine they were, and thou gavest them me; and they have kept thy word. Now they have known that all things what- soever thou hast given me are of thee. For I have given unto them the words which thou gavest me; and they have received them, and have known surely that I came out from thee, and they have believed that thou didst send me (vv. 6–8).

We have seen that the teaching of the Bible is that finally nothing really matters in this world apart from the certain and sure knowledge that the Lord Jesus Christ is concerned about us at this moment and interceding on our behalf, and that God him- self is concerned about us and caring for us. There are many other things with which we have to deal. We are citizens of earthly kingdoms, we live our life in the world like everybody else, and yet we know that all these things about which we are rightly and legitimately concerned are things that are passing and transient. We know that in addition to this life that we live and share with others, there is a unique, personal life of our own with which we shall finally be left. When all earthly scenes pass away and the kingdoms of this world and all their pomp and glory are as a mere nothing, we ourselves will still be there in a state of consciousness, taking that final journey. Surely the thing that matters, therefore, is that we should be prepared for that and should so understand this truth that we are enabled to live in the present and in the future, whatever may come to meet us, without being surprised, without being alarmed, without being baffled. But above all, there is nothing more important than that we should know for certain that we are the objects of God's special care and interest, and it is because this section deals with that in such a glorious and perfect manner, that we are concerned about studying it together.

Now our Lord has been telling us in these verses that the first characteristic of the people for whom he is praying is that he has revealed the name of God to them. Having in that way told us what he has done for them, he also indicates what is true of these people themselves in the light of that knowledge. There are always these two aspects: he has revealed the truth, yes, but although he has revealed it to certain persons, it has in a sense also been revealed generally to the whole world, and some people are Christians and some are not. What exactly makes the difference? Well the answer is that there is a difference in the response that is made to the revelation which has been given, and we must now consider what it is that our Lord tells us about the response which is made by those who belong to him, those who are truly Christian. In other words, when we look at what exactly it is to be a Christian, we can see here another great distinction, and I make no apology for dealing further with this subject. It seems to me that of all the words which are misunderstood in this modern world, there is none which is so misunderstood as this word 'Christian'. Some think of it purely in terms of a particular attitude towards war, others think of it in terms of a general friendliness, some vague emotion or feeling that one has on certain occasions. There are very many different views and there is indeed even a kind of paganism that often passes under the name of Christianity. This is truly appalling to contemplate, especially as one thinks of it all in the light of the Old and the New Testaments. It is vital, therefore, that we should be clear about these things, because we finally have no excuse: the revelation has been given, and we shall have to face it and give an account of what we have done with respect to it.

There is nothing, I repeat, which is more important for each one of us than to know for certain whether we are Christian or not. It is not only a matter of being able to face death, it is also a matter of being able to face life. According to the Scriptures, there is no real life apart from that which is given by the Lord Jesus Christ; everything else, apart from him, is mere existence. Though worldly success may be attached to our life and though it may lead to certain great things, ultimately it is utterly empty if it is without Christ. It does not satisfy the total personality, it leaves a great void, and there is a hunger and a thirst which nothing can satisfy save this life of God which comes to us through our Lord and Saviour Jesus Christ. That is why it is vital for us to know that we have this life. So here our Lord gives us one of his great distinctions.

These disciples, as we see very clearly from the records, were far from being perfect. They were guilty of many blunders and mistakes, they did many things which they should not have done, and they failed in a very pathetic manner right at the end when our Lord was facing the cross. Yet you notice that our Lord says certain things about them here. In spite of all their weakness and imperfection there is something about these people that differentiates them from everybody else, and it is this something that really makes them Christian. I suggest to you, therefore, that we have in these verses what we may call a kind of irreducible minimum of that which is essential for us before we have the right to apply the term Christian to ourselves.

There are certain things which are obvious on the very surface. Firstly, the thing that makes a man a Christian is something that is clearly defined and stated. People who have the idea that to be a Christian is something you cannot actually define are thereby proclaiming that they are not Christians. It is not a loose or indefinite term, it is perfectly clear and specific. The Scriptures themselves tell us to examine and prove ourselves whether we are in the faith or not, and, obviously, if we are exhorted to do that, then there must be some means by which we can do so. That is provided for us in the statement we are looking at now. It is one of the most clearly defined designations that you can ever consider.

Secondly, it is important to notice the way in which our Lord defines a Christian – it is not primarily a matter of experience. He does not talk about those people in terms of their having had a certain experience. They have had one but that is not what he puts first, that is not what he emphasizes and stresses. Neither, you observe, does he describe it in terms of some feelings which they have had. They certainly have had feelings – the Christian is aware of feelings – but that is not the way in which our Lord defines it. Neither does he put it in terms of their having taken a certain decision, or having arrived at some determination to live a better life or to do this or that. He does not define this basic demand, which is essential to being in the truly Christian position, in any one of those ways. Rather, he describes it as an attitude towards truth and especially towards the truth concerning himself.

That is, therefore, the first thing that we must emphasize: the basic, central thing about the Christian is that he is in a given relationship to the truth concerning our Lord and Saviour Jesus Christ. Now this is really one of the foundation truths and principles. Truth is obviously something that comes primarily to the mind and to the intellect, but it does not stop there, it ultimately affects the heart and the will. The Bible itself calls this particular message the truth, and clearly, therefore, it is something that comes to the whole person, to his mind and intellect, to his understanding, to his reason and to his ability to comprehend, and that is the way in which our Lord puts it here. The first thing he says about the Christian is that, 'they have kept thy word', and by using that expression 'thy word', he is describing the message, the truth, this presentation of doctrine. It comes to a man and it makes it possible for him to be a Christian.

The importance of that, of course, arises in this way: just to have a good feeling inside you does not make you a Christian. You can have that without being a Christian. Indeed, you can do a lot of good, you can hold very high and noble views and ideals and still not be a Christian, and there are many such people in the world today. They are not interested in God, nor do they believe in him; they are not interested in Christianity at all, but they are very good people. They spend much of their time trying to get rid of war and making this world a better place to live in and many other good things. I am not criticizing them. I am simply saying they are not Christians, because to have good feelings and sentiments and ideas and ambitions is not enough. The essential thing is to be definitely related to this message, to this word – 'they have kept thy word'. Our Lord then goes on to say, 'I have given unto them the words which thou gavest me.' This, therefore, is something that must come in the first position. The Christian is in a given relationship to this 'word'. This is the whole of the Christian revelation; it is the word of the gospel, the word of salvation; it is God's message to mankind. So the first thing we have to do is to ask ourselves, 'What is my relationship to that word?'

But what is this word, this message to which we are referring? Well, our Lord has analysed it into its component parts and divided it up for us, so that we shall be in no difficulty whatsoever with regard to our attitude in respect to it. He starts by telling us that the first essential message in that word which he has brought to us, is that he himself has come from God. He says, 'They ... have known surely that I came out from thee.' That is just another way of saying that the first thing that is true about the Christian is that he is clear about the person of the Lord Jesus Christ; he believes, he knows, that Jesus of Nazareth is the only begotten Son of God. That is our Lord's own definition of it (and we have already seen that this is a central theme in this prayer). A man, therefore, who is not clear about the person of the Lord is not a Christian. My first concern is not what sort of life he is living. If he regards Jesus of Nazareth as only a man, he is not a Christian. The Christian believes in the incarnation, he believes that almost two thousand years ago the Son of God came into this world and entered into time, 'The Word was made flesh, and dwelt among us.' He does not say that that is irrelevant, or that he believes in the Christian dogma but that the great thing for him is how to get rid of this or that international problem. The Christian cannot speak like that because to the Christian the most momentous fact in the whole of history is the incarnation of the Son of God. It towers in importance over and above the conquest of Julius Caesar; it is altogether more important than all the world wars put together. These things have their significance, but when you put them in the light of the incarnation even they pale into nothing. This is the most vital thing in life and history.

The Christian is, of course, interested in those other things, but only in the light of this central fact, this momentous thing which took place when the eternal Son of God was born as a babe in a stable in Bethlehem and put in swaddling clothes there in a manger. That is the first thing in this word, that Christ speaks about. It is the word about himself, that he has come forth from God. He is not a man like other men, for he was not born in a natural manner. It was a virgin birth, a miraculous birth, the unique event of all history, the great watershed of time determining the whole of human existence. Are we quite certain about the person of the Lord Jesus Christ? Do we know for certain that he is the only begotten Son of God? Do we accept this record concerning him? Do we believe it, because, let me repeat, if we do not, we are not Christian, it is the first, absolute, essential.

Then he goes on to emphasize the second thing which is, 'they believed also that thou didst send me'. Now that is a different thought from the one which we have been considering and our Lord separates them for a reason. Did you notice how he links up these various thoughts and concepts with the word 'and'? There is a distinction, the word covers them all but these are the component parts. The Christian, having believed that Jesus of Nazareth is the only begotten Son of God, also believes that God has sent him and commissioned him to come into this world. We have already seen this from the standpoint of our Lord himself and his work, and how marvellous this is! And this again differentiates between the Christian and the non-Christian in this world. Everybody who is not a Christian looks at the problems of mankind and of the whole world just along the human level – what can be done about it? What arrangements can be made? What can be done at the next conference? What party are you going to put into office in order that these problems may be solved? They are looking at the problems from that level only and they are trusting to the ingenuity of man somehow to deal with the situation. But the Christian does not look at it like that; the Christian knows that God is interested in this world, and that he has done something about it, in that he has intervened in the history of mankind.

In other words, to the Christian there are two types of history, whereas to the non-Christian there is only one, and that is human history – what men do and arrange. But to the Christian there is another type of history, also, which is what God has been doing. You will find these two types of history in the Bible. Sometimes they have no connection with one another, then they come nearer, until they coincide. They coincide at the incarnation when eternity came into time and God was made flesh. But the great principle to hold on to is that God has sent his Son into this world, 'God so loved the world, that he gave his only begotten Son.' We are not left with mere man, we are not just left with the world as it is. In addition to human history, there is this other dimension, and as you look at the whole course of history in the light of this event of God sending his Son, it gives you an entirely new view of the world of time, of the future, and of all things. It does not leave us on the horizontal level, but enables us to see a new possibility. The Christian believes that Christ came into the world because God sent him there.

But, thirdly, perhaps this is best put in terms of the statement in the seventh verse: 'Now they have known that all things whatsoever thou hast given me are of thee', which is just another way of stating that there is a great plan of salvation, and that the Christian is a man who knows something about this plan. The Christian is not someone who has a feeling in a meeting and then goes to the penitent form or to the decision room without knowing why he has done so. The apostle Peter says that as Christians we should be ready at all times to give a reason for the hope that is in us (1 Pet 3:15). The Christian, therefore, is not merely a man who says, 'I feel wonderful, I have marvellous new life, and I am filled with hope.' For if someone else asks him what his hope is based upon, or someone says, 'Why do you feel like this? What has given you this feeling?' and he cannot answer that question, he is not a Christian.

As I understand my New Testament, the Christian is able, however falteringly, to give a reason for the hope that is in him, because he knows the plan of salvation. He knows that God has appointed his Son to be the Saviour. These disciples for whom Christ was praying, and whom he described in this manner, were very imperfect and full of faults. But there was one thing they knew, and that was that he was the Messiah, the Saviour. On one occasion, when our Lord asked his disciples if they also were going to leave him, Peter replied, 'To whom shall we go? thou hast the words of eternal life. And we believe and are sure that thou art that Christ, the Son of the living God' (Jn 6:68–69). With all their faults and imperfections they knew that God had sent him to be the Saviour of the world, and that his words were not those of a mere man, but the words of eternal life. The Christian is the man who has come to see and to know that God sent his Son into this world to bear the sins of many, that he has come to give his life a ransom for many. There is only one way of knowing God and knowing that your sins can be forgiven. It can only be because the Son of God came into this world and took them upon himself. He bore their punishment – that is what the Christian knows.

And he knows likewise that Christ is the bread of life, that he gives him new life, new power, and a new understanding. He lives on Christ, who, himself, has told him that he must eat the flesh and drink the blood of the Son of Man. This means that he depends upon Christ and draws his life from him. He is in that intimate relationship with Christ. The Christian knows that and believes it, says our Lord. That is the word which the Christian believes – the whole plan of salvation.

If that, then, is the truth which the Christian is to believe, what is his peculiar relationship to that truth, for that, after all, is our basic definition of a Christian? Again, our Lord has answered the question in these three verses. What a perfect analysis this is of faith, what an incomparable analysis of the relationship of the Christian to truth. This is a great and profound subject. I merely note it to you, for your own meditation, but each word and each step is vital. The whole is there, of course, but our Lord breaks it up for us into these component parts.

Let me just give you the headings. What is the relationship of the Christian to this message, to this word of God that has come into the world? The first thing we are told about the Christian is that he is *one who receives*: 'I have given unto them the words which thou gavest me; and they have received them.' Our Lord was drawing a contrast here between the disciples and those who rejected the word, those who always criticized and ridiculed it, or who were always arguing about it – read the gospels and you will see what I mean. Our Lord there often uttered many gracious words, but the Pharisees' response was to look at one another and say, Who is this man who is teaching in this way? He is only a carpenter's son, the son of Joseph and Mary. He has no learning. He has not even been to the schools. And so they argued with him and tried to trap him. That is the opposite of receiving the word, because to receive it means to appropriate it in your heart.

There is a great illustration of this in Acts 17. We read there of certain people who lived in a place called Berea and who, when they heard the word, were ready to listen to it and went to the Scriptures to confirm it. That is the attitude of receiving, and obviously this is the first thing that is true about the Christian, the thing that differentiates him from the non-Christian. He accepts the word. He is not like others who are always trying to find holes in the argument, or to discover a contradiction in it, or who, if they hear that someone, some dignitary perhaps, has cast doubts upon the faith, are ready to believe him and to question the truth. No, Christians receive and accept. Often there may be things about the truth that they do not understand, but they believe that this is the Son of God, they listen to him, they receive his word, and give it a real place in their heart. They are open to it.

Then the next thing is '*they have believed*'. There is a difference between receiving and believing. Believing is, I would say, a step forward. It means that not only is there an openness to the word and a general state of receptivity, but, beyond that, it has been literally taken hold of – which is much more specifically faith. Belief, then, appropriates the word, it grasps it and says, 'I believe it. I am not only open to receive it, I listen, and I accept it. I commit myself to it because I know it is right.' 'They have believed,' says our Lord, 'that thou didst send me.' That was even used as a confession in the early church, like the confession of Peter at Caesarea Philippi. People were saying that our Lord was John the Baptist, Elijah, Jeremiah or one of the prophets, so he asked his disciples, 'Whom say ye that I am?' And Peter's answer was, 'Thou art the Christ, the Son of the living God' (Mt 16:13–17) – we believe that.

Then the next term he uses is the term 'know'. 'Now *they have known* that all things whatsoever thou hast given me are of thee.' He says, 'They have received them [the words], and *have known surely* that I came out from thee.' This again is obviously another stage forward. There is a sense, of course, in which faith and knowledge cannot be separated. The relationship between them is a great question for discussion and in one sense they cannot be separated. There is always a kind of certainty about faith, not a certainty that you can prove scientifically, but an absolute certainty – 'faith is the substance of things hoped for' (Heb 11:1). Paul uses the great word 'I am persuaded' – I am sure – and there is, therefore, this kind of sequence in the attitude of the Christian towards truth. He receives it, he believes it and then he comes to know it. From believing he gets assurance, and he is as certain of the truth as he is of anything in existence, if not more so. It is very difficult to put these things into words but one of the greatest blessings of being in the Christian position is that one is really assured about these things. It is not an assurance that you can generate for yourself, but one that is always produced by the Holy Spirit. It is his peculiar work to do that, and to the man who wants to believe he will give the knowledge. Then he will give the assurance and so we advance from reception, to belief, to knowledge and to assurance.

And that brings me to my last point, a wonderful description of faith which our Lord puts first because it includes all the others: 'they have *kept* thy word.' What does it mean? In the first place, it means an intent watching, an observing of the whole revelation. You cannot keep a thing unless you have your eye on it, as it were, and therefore a good definition of the Christian is that he is a man who has always kept his eye on the truth. In every realm and department of life this is the thing that really controls him. He does not merely think of it and try to concentrate on it, and then forget it – not at all! His eye is always on the truth. The revelation is to him the great thing in life and he keeps it ever before him. It is a fundamental attitude which is always true of the Christian, always looking at the whole truth and meditating upon it – the word carries the meaning of watching. 'They have kept thy word.'

There were many who seemed to have received it but who did not keep it, as we see in John 6. These people were following our Lord in crowds because they had seen his miracle of the feeding of the five thousand. They thought it was wonderful and they had never seen anything like it before; our Lord had become 'the latest craze'. Having seen the miracle, they crowded after him and then he began to preach to them. But when he began to tell them that they must eat his flesh and drink his blood and live on him, they stood back and said, 'This is an hard saying; who can hear it?' And they went back and walked no more with him – they had not kept his word. But his disciples were different and, as we saw earlier, it was then that Peter made his great statement – 'To whom shall we go? ...' There is no one to go to, says Peter. We cannot always understand you, you are an enigma, but we will not leave you. They had kept the word, they held on to it through thick and thin. They did not allow others and their difficulties to loose their hold of him; they did not allow the devil to shake their belief, nor did they allow the detraction of the world to keep them away. They put the word in their heart, as the psalmist said, 'Thy word have I hid in mine heart, that I might not sin against thee' (Ps 119:11). Those people were guarding it, watching it, so that nothing should succeed in an attempt to take it from them.

And the last meaning of this word – you will find this rendering in other translations – is that they *obeyed* God's word, because finally you do not really keep the word of God unless you obey it. It is a word that cannot be kept only in your intellect; it has to be put in your heart and in your will also. The man who keeps the word of God is the man whose whole personality is keeping it, the man who is meditating and rejoicing in it, whose heart warms to it, and so he obeys it.

I sum it all up, therefore, by putting it like this: ultimately the Christian is a man who realizes that in this life and world nothing really matters but this truth of God, this truth about the Lord Jesus Christ. He knows that Christ is the Saviour of his soul, the Saviour of the world, the one who has been, the one who has gone, the one who will come again. He is the one who will come on the clouds of heaven as King of kings and Lord of lords and rout his every enemy and rid the world of sin and evil and introduce that blessed, glorious state in which there shall be 'new heavens and a new earth, wherein dwelleth righteousness' (2 Pet 3:13). That is the Christian, the man whose life is dominated and controlled by that truth, who keeps himself in every realm by that word, which comes to his mind, moves his heart and exercises his will. He lives by the truth of God as it is to be found only in our blessed Lord and Saviour Jesus Christ.

My beloved friends, are you keeping this word? Are you safeguarding it, holding on to it, practising and living it? That is the one thing that matters. And if you have kept this word – well, then, blessed be his name, you can be certain that he will keep you.

7

Christ Glorified in Us

And I am glorified in them (v. 10).

As we consider these words it will be well for us also to bear in mind verse 18 which reads: 'As thou hast sent me into the world, even so have I also sent them into the world.'

In dividing up this section which runs from verses 6–19, we indicated, you remember, that there are two main divisions. Our Lord is here praying for his own immediate followers. First of all he gives the reasons why he prays for them, and then he brings his specific petitions to his Father's notice. At the moment we are dealing with the reasons which he adduces for praying for his own, and for a number of studies we have been considering the first reason, which is given in verses 6–8. He prays for these people because they are who and what they are, and we have worked that out in detail.

We come now to our Lord's second reason for praying for them. He prays for them because of what they are meant to do, because of their calling and their task; and that is stated here in this phrase at the end of verse 10. Having described them, having enumerated the things that characterize them, he now reminds his followers of their function and their business in this world of time, and he puts that in the remarkable phrase which we are now considering. He says that as his Father had sent him into the world, even so he has sent them into the world (v. 18). God, we have seen, in sending the Son, had a specific object in view, that the Son should do certain things, and the greatest of them all was to glorify his Father. Now here our Lord says that he has sent, and does send, his people into the world, in exactly the same way as God had sent him, and the great task and function of his people is to glorify him.

Now our Lord said many things about those of us who are Christians, but I am sure you will agree that this particular statement is one of the most amazing – indeed staggering – of all, and it is one which is obviously full of real significance for us. Observe, for instance, the sequence in which this statement comes, and the context in which we find it in this chapter. Our Lord himself, he tells us here in this prayer, glorifies his Father. There in the heavens is the Father, God in his ultimate being and essence, and the Son of God has come into the world to glorify him. That is the first step.

Then the next step is that the Holy Spirit has been sent in order that he may glorify the Son. We are shown this abundantly in the chapters leading up to this seventeenth chapter, which you remember starts like this: 'These words spake Jesus, and lifted up his eyes to heaven, and said...' and then follows the prayer. The phrase 'these words' refers to chapters 14, 15 and 16, in which you have that great teaching about the Holy Spirit, his person and his work. It can all be summed up like this: he does not speak of himself or about himself. The peculiar function and purpose of the Holy Spirit is to reveal, to manifest and therefore to glorify the Son.

But you notice that it does not stop at that. The next step is this phrase that we are looking at here. The result of the coming of the Holy Spirit and his entering into the believer, and into the believer's life, is that the believer also glorifies the Son. 'I am glorified in them,' he says, and he sends them to do this specific work. Thus at once we find here that those of us who are Christians are brought into this very sequence – the sequence which contains the blessed Holy Trinity. Everything is for the glory of God. The Son has come, he speaks, he lives, he dies, he does everything to that end. The Spirit glorifies the Son and we, as the result of the operation of the Spirit, also glorify him. It is, indeed, a staggering thought and conception.

Again, you can look at it from the standpoint of the Lord Jesus Christ himself being glorified. You remember that at the beginning of the prayer we found that he asked that his Father would glorify him.[1] 'Father,' he says, 'the hour is come; glorify thy Son, that thy Son also may glorify thee.' The teaching is, therefore, that the Father does glorify the Son. The Son is the centre, the Father glorifies him from heaven, and, as we have said, the Holy Spirit also glorifies him. He has been sent to do so, and we read in those early chapters of Acts how Peter in his preaching explains clearly that that is the work of the Holy Spirit. We find it put still more specifically in chapter 5, where the apostle says, 'We are his witnesses of these things; and so is also the Holy Ghost, whom God hath given to them that obey him' (Acts 5:32). So here we see the Son in the centre with the light and the radiance of the Father upon him to glorify him; then we see the light of the Holy Spirit, too, focussed upon him, revealing him in his glory and in all his splendour. But the remarkable, almost incredible, thing is that you and I also are called to do exactly the same thing: to glorify the Son.

Here is something that really does come to us in a most amazing way, that the one who is glorified by the almighty Father in heaven, and by the blessed Holy Spirit with all his power, should also be glorified by us, and through us. Our Lord says this quite specifically, and it is something which is taught concerning the Christian right through the New Testament. Take, for instance, the way in which the apostle Peter puts it in his first epistle where he makes precisely this same point: 'But ye are a chosen generation, a royal priesthood, an holy nation, a peculiar people' – why? – 'that ye should show forth the praises' – the virtues, the excellencies – 'of him who hath called you out of darkness into his marvellous light' (1 Pet 2:9). That is Peter's description of the Christian, that is what we are here for. Our business is to manifest, to make a display of, the glories and the power of our Lord Jesus Christ.

[1] See *Saved in Eternity* (Kingsway Publications 1988).

And the apostle Paul in Ephesians 3:10 says very much the same thing: 'To the intent that now unto the principalities and powers in heavenly places might be known by the church the manifold wisdom of God' – it is by means of, or through, the church, that these principalities and powers are really going to be given a view and an insight into God's wisdom. In a sense it seems ridiculous that these bright angelic spirits who are constantly in God's presence, could be helped in any way by the church, but it is through the church that they come to know this manifold, many-sided wisdom of God. That is the teaching, and therefore it brings us, at once, face to face with one of the most remarkable definitions of the Christian that is to be found even in the realm of Scripture itself.

Now we must pause for a moment at this point, just so that we may consider the privilege of being a Christian. Let us look at the fact that you and I are put into a position in which Christ can be glorified in us – for that is precisely what we are told. But how sadly lacking we are in this realization of our privilege. Everybody is interested in privileges; the newspapers are full of it. People are fighting for them, they will spend fortunes in order to get a certain privilege and position, or to hold on to one. But is there anything that the world has ever known which is in any way comparable to this? All the pomp and greatness and ceremony of the world just vanish into utter insignificance by the side of what is said here about any and every Christian: namely that to us is given this astounding privilege of glorifying the Lord Jesus Christ, that he, the Son of God, the effulgence and brightness of the Father's face, should be glorified in us.

Or think of it for a moment from the standpoint of our responsibility as Christians. Whether we are fully aware of it or not, the fact is that the Lord says here that he is glorified in his people. Anybody, therefore, who professes and claims the name of Christian is in this sense a custodian of the name, the glories and the virtues of the Lord Jesus Christ, and through him of God himself. That is the responsibility of a Christian. An ambassador from any country is always conscious of the fact that he has a tremendous responsibility because he is the representative by whom his country is going to be judged. And to us is given the privilege and the responsibility of being the representatives of the Son of God in this world. We stand for him, people judge him by what they see in us, and they are perfectly entitled to do so because we are the ones through whom and in whom he is glorified. Do we, I wonder, always realize this?

But then let us also look at it like this: there is surely nothing, it seems to me, that so helps us to rise to the height of our great calling as the realization of this very thing. As I have said before, our main trouble as Christians is that we do not realize the truth about our position. Our further trouble is that we do not realize who and what we are, what we are meant to be, and what we are meant to do. Now the way in which the New Testament teaches sanctification and holiness is just to hold these things before us constantly, and it seems to me that the 'holiness' teaching which concentrates on the experiences which one receives is completely false. The New Testament comes and says, do you realize who you are? Do you realize that Christ is glorified in you? Do you realize that you are his representative here on earth and that all this responsibility and privilege is yours?

Then, having told us that, the Bible puts certain questions to us. It says, in view of this can you possibly continue being slack as a Christian? Can you be negligent in your Christian duties? Can you take these things lightly and loosely, scarcely ever giving them a thought? The man who is representing his family or his nation among other people is very careful to remind himself of that fact; he is always careful to remind himself, daily, of the responsibility that is upon him and of the consequences of his possible failure. I wonder how often we stop and just say to ourselves, 'Now because I am a Christian I am going to be a representative of Jesus Christ. Christ is going to be glorified in me; that is my business. I cannot afford to be slack, or to take these things for granted, nor can I afford to give my time and energy and my spare time to things which I know are of no ultimate value.' Surely if we realized this it would immediately correct any tendency to indolence or slackness in our Christian lives.

Or look at it in this way. We are told here by the Lord himself, 'I am glorified in them' – they are the people who are expressing my glories, my excellencies and my virtues. But let us look at them, miserable, uncertain about themselves and their position, afraid, perhaps, that certain of their friends or their superiors should know that they are Christians at all, apologizing almost for it – is that not the picture which we far too often present, without enthusiasm, without zeal? We see other people getting excited even about such things as football matches, shouting for their side, wearing colours so that everybody may know which side they support. We see people boasting about all kinds of things in this life and world. Yet when we come to our Christianity and Christian profession, oh, how often we lack enthusiasm and energy, and pride in being what we are. Instead of proclaiming it to the whole world, we conceal it or are uncertain about it and even present the aspect of being defeated, and so on. If this is true of us, then surely there is only one explanation for it and that is that we do not realize that Christ is glorified in us. We have never realized the truth about ourselves, nor the privilege and the responsibility of our exalted position. We have never realized truly that we are the children of God and joint heirs with Christ – the children of the heavenly King. But the moment we do realize this, it becomes a corrective to us.

In the same way, that is surely how to conquer sin, and to overcome temptation and evil. If only we would remind ourselves in the moment of temptation that we are the representatives of Christ, and that it is through us that his glories are to be manifested. Is there anything that is so likely to make us withstand and avoid temptation as the realization of this wonderful thing? *That* is how the New Testament calls us to behave, that is what we are to be, worthy of our calling – 'Be ye holy; for I am holy,' says God himself (1 Pet 1:16). This therefore is the thing to which we are called. Christ sends us into the world in order that we may glorify him. Again I ask my question – are we doing that? Is he being glorified in us? Do people think well and highly of him because they know us and because of the way in which we represent him? I am not surprised that he prayed for his disciples – God knows we need his prayers. He knows the task to which he is sending his people and he knows his people. So he prays to his Father for us, and I thank God that he is interceding on my behalf at the right hand of God's glory at this moment.

How does the Christian glorify Christ? How is it possible for us, evil creatures as we are, to add in any way a kind of glory or lustre to his name? The answer is given very freely here in this chapter and indeed everywhere in the New Testament. Our Lord has already been dealing with one way in which we glorify him: we do so by believing in him. He says here about these people that they have glorified him already because they recognized who he was. The world in general did not, nor did the Pharisees, who called him 'this fellow', 'the carpenter', and 'the son of Joseph and Mary'. The apostle Paul tells us that the princes of this world did not recognize the Lord of glory, for if they had, they would not have crucified him (1 Cor 2:8). Because he was born in humiliation, because he came in a particular way, the great and noble and the mighty of the world did not recognize him. Therefore they did not glorify him, or worship him, nor did they praise him. It was his own people who recognized that he was the Son of God. And you and I, by believing in the Lord Jesus Christ, glorify him. To recognize him as the incarnate Son of God, to believe that he has come into this world in the flesh and has lived amongst us in the likeness of sinful flesh – that, in and of itself, is to glorify him.

But we go beyond that. It means that we recognize also why he came and what he has done in this world. To glorify Christ, says the apostle Paul in 1 Corinthians, is to recognize in him the wisdom and the power of God. To the Jews, he says, he is a stumbling block, and to the Greeks he is foolishness, but 'unto them which are called, both Jews and Greeks, Christ the power of God, and the wisdom of God' (1 Cor 1:24). This means that the Lord Jesus Christ is God's way of salvation. And the way in which he desires to be glorified by men is that they should recognize that he is the way in which God is bringing men to a knowledge of himself, reconciling them unto himself, and preparing for himself this special people. So anybody who recognizes that is glorifying the Lord Jesus Christ, and this includes, too, recognizing the love that made him do it all, the love that brought him into this world and made him suffer the contradiction of sinners against himself, and, above all, the love that took him freely and readily to the cross that he might die for us and purchase our pardon and forgiveness and make us one with God.

All that, but especially our recognition of the meaning of the cross, is a part of the way in which we glorify the Lord. This is why so many of our hymns deal with it: 'In the cross of Christ I glory'. 'God forbid that I should glory, save in the cross of our Lord Jesus Christ,' says Paul in Galatians 6:14, and the hymn echoes it. Or, again,

> When I survey the wondrous cross,
> On which the Prince of Glory died,
> My richest gain I count but loss,
> And pour contempt on all my pride.
>
> *Isaac Watts*

And I pour contempt on everything else that I have ever gloried in. The cross is the only thing in which we should glory; I recognize what is happening there and I know that the Son of God has come down to earth and has come down to that cross, in order that I might be forgiven and that I might be made a child of God. In believing in him in this way I glorify him, and it is my desire that I should do so.

Or, again, we glorify him by asserting that he is everything to us. He has chosen to save mankind, says Paul again, in 1 Corinthians 1, and our only response to that must be 'He that glorieth, let him glory in the Lord' (1 Cor 1:31). The Christian, by definition, is a man who says, 'I am nothing, I am what I am entirely by the grace of God.' He is a man who is always flying to Christ, and one who disclaims anything in and of himself. He has come to an end of his self-reliance, the world has been crucified to him and he has been crucified to the world; he glories in the cross and in Christ alone.

But obviously this implies that we glorify the Lord Jesus Christ by telling other people about him, by pointing them to his glory and by trying to bring them also to glorify him and to glory in his cross. Now that is where verse 18 is so important: 'As thou hast sent me into the world, even so have I also sent them into the world.' And he has sent us into the world, that we might tell the world about him. Acts chapter 4 brings this out very clearly, and it is equally striking in chapter 3. We read the story of Peter and John going up to the Temple, and there seated at the Beautiful Gate of the Temple is the lame beggar. Then we are told that Peter and John fastened their eyes upon him and said: 'Look on us,' and when he looked at them Peter said, 'Silver and gold have I none; but such as I have give I thee: In the name of Jesus Christ of Nazareth rise up and walk.' And the man, we are told, went with them into the Temple, walking, and leaping, and praising God. Here the crowd gathered, full of curiosity, and were on the point of worshipping the apostles, but Peter turned to them and said, 'Why marvel ye at this? or why look ye so earnestly on us, as though by our own power or holiness we have made this man to walk?' Why look on us? It is not us, but, 'The God of our fathers hath glorified his Son Jesus ... And his name through faith in his name hath made this man strong, whom ye see and know: yea, the faith which is by him hath given him this perfect soundness in the presence of you all' (vv 12–13, 16). Peter pointed them to Christ and preached Christ to them.

And the apostles did exactly the same thing when they were brought before the Council – you will find the record in the fourth chapter of Acts. They just looked at those religious leaders and said it was nothing that they had done, 'for there is none other name under heaven given among men, whereby we must be saved' (v. 12). They pointed to him, they preached the name of Jesus, and then they continued and said, 'We cannot but speak the things which we have seen and heard.' They were always proclaiming Christ, telling people that he is the Son of God, the anointed of God, the Saviour of the world, the one to whom everyone must go if they desire salvation. And thus, of course, the whole time, they were glorifying him, they were holding him up as it were, they were flashing this light on to him, and saying, There he is, look at him, believe in him. They were pointing the whole world to Jesus Christ.

Now that is what we are called upon to do; we are meant to talk to people about the Lord Jesus Christ and to tell them he is the Son of God and that he has come into this world in order to save men and women. We are meant to tell them in the midst of all these exciting discussions about politics and these various other things, that ultimately there is no hope for the individual, or for society, apart from this blessed person. We are meant to tell men exactly why the world is as it is; we are meant to tell them about sin in the human heart and that nobody and nothing can deal with it save the Son of God. That is how we glorify him, by talking about him. We are very ready to talk about our doctors, and to praise the man who cured us when so many failed; we talk about some business which is better than others, or about films and plays and actors and actresses, and a thousand and one other things. We are always glorifying people, the world is full of it, and the Christian is meant to be praising and glorifying the Lord Jesus Christ. Speaking to his Father here in John 17, he says, 'I have glorified thee' but the world laughs at me, the world ridicules me, especially my dying upon the cross. My whole reputation is in the hands of these people. Father, he says, look upon them, keep them, I am glorified in them, they are my representatives in the world. If they do not speak about me there, who will? If they do not praise me, who can? I am glorified only in them.

And that obviously leads to the next point, which is that we glorify him by being what we are. Or, to put it another way, we glorify him in that we are living proofs and examples of the truth of what he has said about us. I think that this is tremendously important. I rather like to think of the Christian in this way, and I apply this test to myself. Unless I am giving the impression that I am what I am only because of the Lord Jesus Christ, to that extent I am failing as a Christian. I mean that as a Christian, I am to be the kind of person of whom people say, 'What is it about this man? We cannot explain him.' And they will never be able to explain him until they discover that the secret of this man is that Christ is in him.

I wonder whether this is how people think of us. I wonder whether we can be adequately explained in terms of temperament – that we are undoubtedly the sort of people who would always be interested in religion. If so, we are not glorifying Christ because you can be religious without being a Christian at all; you can be interested in religion and in God and still not be a Christian. Religion can be explained quite easily apart from Christ, and, by definition, the Christian is the man who can only be explained in terms of Christ.

Or can we be explained in terms of our training? People say, 'Oh yes, it is their tradition, they have a sense of loyalty to it, and to the Christian church. There is no difficulty about explaining what they do, they have been brought up to it.' Well, if they can explain us like that, we are not Christian, in this sense because Christ is not being glorified in us.

Or can they explain us in terms of self-government? 'He is rather striking,' they say. 'He has his own moral code, and we expect him to do the things he does, and to refrain from doing others.' Now, if I can be explained like that or in any one of those ways, I say that to that extent I am not glorifying Christ.

No, we glorify Christ in this way. People meeting with us say, 'What is it about them? Our explanations and our categories are of no value, there is something else, there is something mysterious, there is another thing.' That is what they should be saying. The Lord Jesus Christ when he was here in this world, by being what he was, glorified God. People were baffled by him. They saw his miracles and the effect was almost invariably that they glorified God. They said, 'We have never seen things in this way before.' By doing what he did, he glorified God. And you and I are to be exactly like that. We are to be such people that the moment people meet us they think about Christ. We are told a very significant thing in the fourth chapter of the Acts of the Apostles. The Council that was trying the apostles could not understand them. They observed that they were ignorant men and yet the fact was that they had performed a miracle and were speaking in a manner which could not be accounted for. And then we are told that they took note of the fact that they had been with Jesus – it seemed to be the only explanation. And that is the test of a Christian; he cannot be explained apart from Jesus Christ, and thereby he glorifies him.

But we must go beyond this. We glorify him by saying what he has done to us, and by what he has made of us. We are the manifestation of his power. We glorify him by showing that we have been separated from the world. 'I pray for them: I pray not for the world,' says our Lord, and the mere fact that you and I have been separated, set apart from the world, is in and of itself a proof of the power of Christ, the Son of God. There is nothing that can really bring a man out of the world and its mentality but the power of Christ; but he does, he separates us and he makes us different. The man, therefore, who is different is the man who is glorifying Christ. Now I know perfectly well that when I say that, I am saying something that the modern Christian, speaking generally, does not like. The modern Christian has for some time been going out of his way to be as much like the world as he can. His great idea is that he can affect the mannerisms of the particular society to which he belongs, and incidentally be a Christian. But, though he thinks that he is bearing a marvellous testimony, it is a little difficult to find out whether or not he is a Christian.

Now the New Testament always emphasizes the exact opposite. It teaches that the Christian is a man who strikes you at once as being different. He has something about him that nobody else has; he has got something of Christ himself about him, with none of this modern self-assertion and confidence and pride which so often pass for personality. No, the Christian belongs to the meek and lowly Jesus; he belongs to one, who, though he was the prince of glory, had no place, on this earth, where he could lay his head. He was the one of whom it is said, 'A bruised reed shall he not break, and the smoking flax shall he not quench' (Is 42:3). The Christian has been separated and taken out of the world with its mentality and outlook. He stands by the side of Christ, and there is something of the radiance and glory of his Master and Lord and Saviour about him.

But the Father has not only separated us in general, he has made us spiritually alive. Whereas those who are not Christians are not interested in spiritual things, the Christian is. The world is not interested in the affairs of the soul at all and tries to avoid considering them. The world is spiritually dead, dead in trespasses and sins and it regards spiritual things as utterly boring. It wants to enjoy the world, it is out for the glittering prizes that the world has to offer. But the Christian has been made spiritually alive. He is very concerned about the affairs of the soul, they are the things that come first in his life and in all his thinking. How then has this happened? It is the power of Christ that has come upon him: 'You hath he quickened, who were dead in trespasses and sins' (Eph 2:1). We have been quickened together with Christ and raised up with him and he has given us a new life and a new understanding, a new outlook upon everything. And thus, by manifesting in our lives the power of Christ, we are glorifying him – if I may use such a term – we are adding lustre to his name for all who know us and come into contact with us. And we are what we are because the power of Christ has taken hold of us. We are different, we are changed, we have become new men, and the extent to which we give that impression is the extent to which we are glorifying Christ.

You will see that obviously I have not exhausted this subject. The questions with which we need to confront ourselves and by which we must examine and test ourselves are these. Is he being glorified in me? Am I representing my Father? Am I testifying in various ways about him? Not that I become a busybody just buttonholing people in a mechanical manner and asking them, 'Are you saved?' No, but testifying for him by singing his praises and by doing it with the wisdom of a serpent and yet being as gentle as a dove, and, yes, always pointing to him. And I glorify him especially by being what I am, an enigma and a problem to all who do not know Christ, because my life can, more and more, be described in this way: 'I live; yet not I, but Christ liveth in me' (Gal 2:20), or 'By the grace of God I am what I am' (1 Cor 15:10). Oh the privilege of this position, the responsibility of this position and the high calling to which Christ has called us, that he himself should be glorified in us.

8

Manifesting the Work of Christ

I am glorified in them (v. 10).

In our last study we saw that there is nothing that so urges us to a life of holiness and devotion to God as the realization that the Lord Jesus Christ is glorified amongst men in us and through us. We know that the world is antagonistic and that it is not interested in him; and the world is judging him and is estimating him by what it sees in us. So often we have met people who are not Christians and who never go near a place of worship, and the reason they immediately give for this is – 'Look at So and So!' It is because of something they have seen in a church member or someone who calls himself or herself a Christian, and they have been judging the Lord Jesus Christ by what they have seen in this person. Now that is just a negative way of putting what our Lord here puts positively: 'I am glorified in them', because, thank God, the other side can also be presented. There are people who were once not Christians, and who were, indeed, antagonistic to Christianity, who are in the Christian church today because they were arrested by something that they saw in a Christian person.

I heard recently about a candidate who offered herself to a certain missionary society, and her story was that she had not only been a Communist herself, but she had also been the Secretary of the Communist Society in her university. And the thing that arrested that girl and started the whole process of her conversion was, not a sermon, not an address, not a book on apologetics, nor an intellectual argument, but the simple observation of the daily life and walk of a fellow student. Intellectually that other student was not fit to be put into the same category as this Communist, but what she beheld in that girl's life and walk so arrested and so condemned her, and she was so charmed by it, that eventually she became a Christian herself – 'I am glorified in them.' So this is obviously one of the most important things we can ever consider together. We are called to this, this is our peculiar function as Christian people.

What, then, are we called to do? Perhaps we can sum it up like this: we are meant to be a living proof of the fact that the Lord Jesus Christ has finished the work which his Father sent him to do. As he has already reminded us in his prayer, the Father sent him into the world to do a certain task: 'I have glorified thee on the earth: I have finished the work which thou gavest me to do,' he says, and I look to them – to the Christians – to manifest this.

The world, as we have seen, does not believe in him nor in his message. The main object of the devil – the antagonist of God and his Christ – is always to ridicule both the Christian message and the Lord himself. The devil is boldly, actively engaged in the world all the time and it is astonishing to know the way in which the devil is increasingly opposing the Lord Jesus Christ and his work. The world, in its whole outlook and life, with its suggestions, its innuendoes and its ridicule, is always trying to prove that he is not the Son of God. The devil has achieved nothing but evil, and because of that there is nothing in the world now to manifest the truth but the testimony and the witness and the life of Christian people. It is by us and by us alone that he is glorified in this world.

We have begun to consider how we do this and now I want to come to the details. We glorify the Lord Jesus Christ by showing what he really has done to us, what he has made of us, and, in particular, what he came into the world to do. So, why did he come into the world? If you simply read the gospels you will find that they answer the question immediately: 'The Son of man is come to seek and to save that which was lost' (Lk 19:10). 'The Son of man came not to be ministered unto, but to minister, and to give his life a ransom for many' (Mt 20:28). 'I am come that they might have life, and that they might have it more abundantly' (Jn 10:10). 'I am the light of the world: he that followeth me shall not walk in darkness, but shall have the light of life' (Jn 8:12). 'I am not come to call the righteous but sinners to repentance' (Mt 9:13). Those are his statements, and there are many others, and the questions, therefore, which we all have to put to ourselves are these: are we demonstrating these things? Are we today, in our lives, by being what we are, proving that the Son of God has succeeded in his mission? Are we living epis-tles, read of all men, commending him, testifying to him and the power of his grace? That, the New Testament tells us, is what is meant by being a Christian. The Christian is not merely a man who holds certain high ideals and views with regard to various questions and problems – so many think that. No, a Christian is specifically a man who is a living proof that the Son of God succeeded in his mission in this life: 'I am glorified in them.'

We must, therefore, think this through, and in order to help us in this, let us remind ourselves of some other statements which are made with respect to him. The apostle Paul, in writ-ing to the Corinthians, describes him as 'the power of God, and the wisdom of God' in this matter of salvation: 'Unto the Jews a stumblingblock, and unto the Greeks foolishness; but unto them which are called ... Christ the power of God, and the wis-dom of God' (1 Cor 1:23-24). Again, he says that, to the saved, the Lord Jesus Christ has been made wisdom, and righteous-ness, and sanctification, and redemption (v.30); he is the all and in all. Those are the descriptions that are given of him, and so we glorify him by proving that all those statements are nothing but the literal truth. And thereby we establish the fact that we are Christian. In other words, do we individually as Christians prove that Christ and his gospel are indeed the power of God unto salvation? As we have seen, if we can be explained in terms of temperament, or tradition, or backbone, or solely in terms of will-power and our own moral striving and effort – if we can be explained in any way apart from Christ, then, as I understand a text like this, we are just not Christian. A Christian is someone who is all along glorifying Christ, Christ is the only explanation of what he or she is.

How, then, do we prove that he is indeed the wisdom and the power of God? We do so, he has repeated so often in his prayer, by showing that we have been separated from the world and that we are spiritually alive. For the world is not spiritually alive, it is dead, dead in its trespasses and sins, not interested in spiritual things and bored by them. The world regards the Bible as the most boring book under the heavens, and prayer it just cannot understand. To listen to addresses or sermons is the height of tedium, says the world – why? It is because it has not a spiritual faculty. There is a complete deadness and absence of something vital, there is no life. But Christ quickens us to life and power, and thereby he proves that he is the power of God unto salvation.

Another way in which it is often put in the Scriptures is that we have been translated from the power of darkness into the kingdom of God's dear Son. We are all born as the children of wrath and into the kingdom of the devil; we are dupes of Satan and under his dominion. But when a man becomes a Christian, a certain power lays hold upon him and it takes him and transfers him to another kingdom. It is a power; it is not a theory, or a philosophy, it is not a mere point of view. No, says Paul, 'I am not ashamed of the gospel of Christ: for it is the power of God unto salvation' (Rom 1:16) – it translates us, moves us from one position to another. In other words, the Christian is a man to whom something has happened. The power of God has laid hold upon him. That is the first thing that must be true about him, and, therefore, if we would know for certain whether we are Christian or not, and whether we are glorifying Christ or not, that is obviously the first test – are we a living proof and example that the tremendous power of the Son of God has literally taken hold of us and transferred us into the kingdom of God's dear Son? Are we manifesting this power? Have we life and is this dynamic of God and of his Son evident and manifest in us?

But let us look at this in a little more detail. Christ, 'of God is made unto us wisdom, and righteousness, and sanctification, and redemption'. Now that, says Paul in 1 Corinthians 1:31, is God's way of solving the problem of man and the world. The Greek philosophers had done their best, but no, the world by its wisdom knew not God, and they did not succeed. *This* is God's way of doing it, says Paul: Christ and him crucified is God's wisdom. Christ is made unto us redemption and it is a complete redemption – wisdom, righteousness, sanctification and finally redemption – and the Christian glorifies Christ by proving that this is true. One reason for the coming of the Lord Jesus Christ into the world was that mankind was ignorant of God, there was an estrangement between man and God. And the world today still does not know God, and by its wisdom cannot find him. So, in a sense, the first task of the Lord was to bring us to this knowledge of God. As he has already been saying in his prayer, he has come to give 'eternal life to as many as thou hast given him. And this is life eternal, that they might know thee the only true God, and Jesus Christ, whom thou hast sent'.

We are dealing with practical things here, so I simply have to ask a series of questions. Do you *know* God? Is he real to you or is he just a philosophy? Is he but a category of thought, or merely a kind of concept that you play with in working out your system of belief? Or is he the almighty God, real to you – do you really know him? I, says Christ to his Father, am glorified in them. I have come into the world in order to make you known to them and they are the people who prove that I have succeeded, for they know me.

So the first way by which I, in practice, glorify the Lord Jesus Christ is that I can testify that I know God. I do not, therefore, go down on my knees with the poet and say,

I thank whatever gods may be
For my unconquerable soul
W.E. Henley

Not at all! I go on my knees and I pray to one whom I know as my Father, and I know him as my Father because Christ came, and I glorify him in that way. I prove that he has indeed established this righteousness.

But obviously that is not enough. Before I can come to that knowledge, he must have reconciled me to the Father. There is an estrangement between God and man, and that is because of sin: 'Your iniquities have separated between you and your God, and your sins have hid his face from you ...' says the prophet Isaiah (59:2) and the Lord Jesus Christ came into the world to deal with this problem of sin, to remove it, and to get rid of the barrier. He came to make peace between God and man, and no peace is possible between us until the barrier of sin has been removed. He came, as we have seen, to 'give his life a ransom for many' (Mt 20:28), so that our sins might be dealt with and be forgiven, that they might be put away once and for ever.

So a Christian is a person who glorifies the Lord Jesus Christ by knowing that his sins are forgiven, and by showing that he is one who has found peace with God. Surely Christ is glorified most of all when a man who is born in sin, who has been a sinner and has, perhaps, committed terrible sins, can nevertheless say, 'I rejoice now in the knowledge that all my sins are forgiven.' He is not glorifying himself by saying that, but Christ. He cannot himself get rid of his sins, he cannot generate peace, he cannot quieten his own conscience, he cannot say he loves God. No, it is Christ and Christ alone who does it all, and the man who says that he knows his sins are forgiven is glorifying the Lord Jesus Christ. But the man who is doubtful whether he is forgiven or not is not glorifying Christ, neither is the man who says, 'I hope my sins are forgiven', nor yet the man who says, 'I am living as good a life as I can in order to atone for my past.' The man who glorifies Christ is the man who can say, 'Therefore being justified by faith, we have peace with God ... and rejoice in hope of the glory of God' (Rom 5:1–2).

Do you *know* that your sins are forgiven? Have you got assurance of salvation? Are you certain of it? For to the extent that you are, you glorify Christ, and to the extent that you are uncertain, you are not glorifying him. What proves that he has done the work he was sent to do is that we have the knowledge of sins forgiven and that we rejoice in it. He came very specially to do this and therefore we glorify him by proving that he really has done it. It sounds a simple question yet it is the profoundest question a man can ever face, so let me ask it again. Are you certain of God? Do you *know* God? Are you happy about your relationship to him? My dear friends, the Son of God not only came from heaven to earth, he went deliberately to the cross and suffered all the ignominy and shame of that cross in order that you and I might be certain, certain without any doubt at all, of our relationship to God as his children.

But let me hasten from righteousness to sanctification. 'He is made unto us wisdom, righteousness, sanctification ...' and sanctification is that which shows and proves that Christ is in us, and that he is working in us and that he is producing a certain effect within us. He said in the previous chapters of John's gospel that he would pray to the Father and 'he shall give you another Comforter, that he may abide with you for ever; even the Spirit of truth; whom the world cannot receive, because it seeth him not, neither knoweth him: but ye know him; for he dwelleth with you, and shall be in you' (Jn 14:16–17). Don't be brokenhearted because I am going, he says. 'It is expedient for you that I go away: for if I go not away, the Comforter will not come unto you; but if I depart, I will send him unto you' (Jn 16:7). He himself is going to come, through the Holy Spirit. He is going to take up his abode in us, he, and the Father also, are going to dwell in us, and he says that he has come to make that possible. So we glorify him by proving that he has done that, and, to put it negatively again, the extent to which we do not prove that, is the extent to which we are not glorifying him.

How, then, does this work out in practice? We can show it in several ways. We prove it by not living in sin. I am not saying that we are sinless and that we are perfect. No, what I am saying is that the Christian does not live in sin, or dwell in it, he does not 'abide in sin'. That is the great theme of the first epistle of

John, a letter which, as Christians, we can never read too frequently. John says that the Christian does not continue in sin, he does not abide in it, because he has been taken out of it. He may fail sometimes, but he does not continue in sin as he did before. Not only that, he has an increasing awareness of sin in himself, and of the subtlety and the whole meaning of it, and he comes to feel, therefore, an increasing hatred of sin. That is always the effect of the working of the Holy Spirit in us and, too, it is the typical effect of the indwelling Christ, of the residence of Christ in a man's life. He becomes more and more sensitive to sin, and increasingly conscious of it, and so he comes to hate it more and more. The more sensitive we become to sin, the more we glorify Christ. The more we become aware of the blackness of our own heart, and the wretchedness of our old, fallen nature, again, the more we glorify him. The man of the world is not aware of these things. If you talk to him about the old nature and the new, he will regard it as something strange, because Christ is not in him. But the moment Christ comes in there is a conflict: 'The flesh lusteth against the Spirit, and the Spirit against the flesh: and these are contrary the one to the other' (Gal 5:17) – all that is indicative of the presence of Christ and therefore it glorifies him.

But let me come to the more positive statement: it also means that there is now a power within us to resist temptation and sin and to conquer them. Christ conquered the devil. He defeated and routed him, and if he dwells in us, we should defeat him too. 'Resist the devil, and he will flee from you,' writes James (Jas 4:7), and we find Peter saying the same thing: 'Be sober, be vigilant; because your adversary the devil, as a roaring lion, walketh about, seeking whom he may devour' (1 Pet 5:8) – and what do we do about him? – 'Whom resist stedfast in the faith...' (v.9), and thereby you conquer him. Do we conquer temptation and sin? We glorify Christ if we do, but if we do not we are not glorifying him, for if we are still being mastered and defeated by these things; the suggestion is that he has not done what he claimed to do.

But let us go on. We manifest his glory by showing the

world an increasing delight in spiritual things. Has the Bible become more and more interesting to you? Do you enjoy it increasingly? Do you like studying it, not in a mechanical sense, but in a spiritual sense? What about prayer, fellowship and communion with God? He came to earth and he went to the cross in order that we might know this only true God, and Jesus Christ whom he sent. He himself spent much time in praying to his Father, so is prayer an increasing delight to us? The more we pray and enjoy it, the more we glorify Christ because we are a living proof of the fact that he succeeded in doing what he came to do. Fellowship with others? 'We know that we have passed from death unto life, because we love the brethren' (1 Jn 3:14). Do we delight in God's people and the things that they talk about, these things of the soul and of the spirit, rather than in others who have no interest in these things? That is another wonderful way of glorifying Christ.

Furthermore, our Lord says in Matthew 5:6, 'Blessed are they which do hunger and thirst after righteousness.' Can we say that we have an increasing hunger and thirst after righteousness, that we desire more and more to be holy, to 'know him, and the power of his resurrection, and the fellowship of his sufferings, being made conformable unto his death' (Phil 3:10)? Do we know something of this spirit that was in Paul and which made him feel like that, and urged him to press forward to that glorious perfection that is in Christ himself? Yes, that sums it all up – a desire to be like him.

Let me also suggest another great question for our consideration. I suppose that, supremely, we glorify Christ by proving that he has given to us the gift of the Holy Spirit. If you read the gospels and the Acts of the Apostles, you will find it constantly reiterated that he came into the world in order that the promise of the Father might be given to us. And the promise of the Father is the coming of the Holy Spirit. Our Lord goes in order that he may send the gift of the Spirit – it is a marvellous thing. So we glorify Christ by showing that we have received the Holy Spirit, that the gift has come to us. And according to the apostle Paul in Galatians 5:22–23, we do that by manifesting the fruit of the Spirit in our ordinary, daily life.

What, then, is the fruit of the Spirit? First of all, Paul tells us, it is *love*. The Christian whose nature is increasingly one of love shows that he has received the Spirit, and he thereby glorifies the Lord Jesus Christ. I am glorified in them, he says, when they show a loving nature and a loving character. Then there is *joy*. I only touch upon joy here because I shall be coming back to it, but the more joyful we are as Christians, the more we glorify Christ. His was a life of joy in spite of all that he endured, and the more joy there is in our lives, the more we glorify him – 'Rejoice in the Lord alway: and again I say, rejoice' (Phil 4:4).

Next comes *peace*, a peace within, a tranquillity, a steadiness of life. A peacemaker is one who radiates peace wherever he is, he is not a busybody, or a person who upsets everything and causes division. Then after love, joy and peace, there is *longsuffering*, being able to bear with people, not irritable, not easily put out, not angular, not offensive, however sorely tried. And then, *gentleness*. It is a very difficult thing in this modern world to be gentle, but, my friends, the more gentle you and I are, and the more gentle we become, the more the Lord Jesus Christ is glorified in us. And the same is true of *goodness*, essential goodness, a good character, and *faith* – here meaning faithfulness. Then comes one of the most remarkable of all – *meekness*. I do not think that the modern world knows anything at all about meekness; we are all of us given to advertising or propaganda. Of course we do it for the sake of getting on, but if we want to glorify Christ and to advertise him, the high road to that is to be meek ourselves. Then lastly there is *temperance*, which is self-control, discipline in our thought, in our actions, in everything.

We could spend much time with everyone of these, but I am trying here to give you a composite picture. The extent to which this marvellous fruit of the Spirit is manifest in our lives is the measure and the extent to which Christ is being glorified in us, because the fruit of the Spirit is nothing but a description of the life and the character of the Lord Jesus Christ himself.

That is the sort of person he was, and he tells us that he came into the world in order to make us like himself. So the more we resemble him, the more we glorify him, and the more we prove that he really has succeeded in doing what he came to do.

But, further, we glorify him in the most remarkable way by our attitude to this world, and to life in this world. Here again we must be like him. The most difficult thing of all, perhaps, in this life is not to be conquered by the world, not to be mastered or governed by it. Most people are defeated by it. They are slaves to the circle in which they move, and to the way in which they are expected to live. But he did not conform. He lived his own life separate from the world; he overcame the world and the Christian is meant to do the same. 'This is the victory that overcometh the world, even our faith' (1 Jn 5:4). So if you and I show in our lives that we have seen through this world with all its tinsel and all its vain and empty pomp and show, if we prove that we are living above it and mastering it, then we are glorifying him and we are like him. And the extent to which we are certain of the blessed hope that is set before us is again the extent to which we glorify him.

It means, therefore, that we are able to endure trials and persecution for his name's sake, in the way he did himself. I suppose the people above all others in the long history of the church who have glorified Christ the most, have been the martyrs and the confessors, the men who went to the stake without hesitation, glorifying him, while the world stood and looked on, amazed and astounded. These men were prepared to do it for him – 'There must be something in it,' said the onlooking world, and thereby the martyrs and the confessors glorified Christ. Are we ready to be persecuted? Not by being sent to the stake or even thrown into prison perhaps, but by just observing that when we enter a room people look at one another with a smirk on their faces, or a cruel taunt on their lips? Are we ready to endure it for Christ's sake? The world may know nothing about us, our names may never appear in the newspapers, but if we just take that and endure it, as he did, for his name's sake, he is glorified in us.

And I suppose the last way of all in which we glorify him is by the way in which we die. The old fathers always used to observe very closely the way in which Christian people died. It was, they thought, a marvellous test, and you never read the old biographies without noticing a great emphasis on that. If when we are lying on our death bed we hear the trumpet sounding, if we see him awaiting us, if we see something of the glory that is before us and if we can thank him for everything and just surrender ourselves and our spirits into his blessed hands – Oh what a testimony to him, what a way of glorifying him! He has taken the sting out of death for the Christian. To die is gain, says Paul, it is to be with Christ, which is far better.

There, then, are some of the ways in which we can glorify our blessed Lord and Saviour. There is something glorious in these words, but there is also something pathetic about them. 'I am glorified in them.' Look at the sort of people those disciples were! And yet he was glorified in them and he has been glorified in the countless millions of unknown Christian people throughout the centuries. And to us too in this dark, evil, ugly age is given the privilege of glorifying him today.

May I suggest a practical rule for you as I close. I know of no better way of starting my day than by saying to myself every morning: 'I am one of the people in the world today through whom Christ is to be glorified. I am not here for myself, or for anything I want to do, the main thing for me this day is that Christ should be glorified in me.' Start your day by saying that to yourself, and when you are praying to God remind yourself of what you are and what he expects. Remind yourself of it several times during the day, recollect now and again, take a second just to say to yourself, 'I am the one through whom Christ is to be glorified and praised.' And then the last thing at night before you go to sleep ask yourself this question: has Christ been glorified in my life today? Have I manifested the fruit of the Spirit? Have I been showing love, joy, peace, longsuffering, gentleness, goodness, meekness, faith and temperance? – Or have I lost my temper, have I been irritable, have I upset people?

Have I been a storm centre or have I taken with me the peace of Christ and of God? Have I, by being what I have been this day, made people look towards him with a longing to know him and to be like him?

'I am glorified in them.'

9

True Joy

And now I come to thee; and these things I speak in the world, that they might have my joy fulfilled in themselves (v. 13).

We have been considering together the ways in which, as Christians, we manifest our Lord's glory, and we have reminded ourselves of our tremendous responsibility as we realize that we, and we alone, are the people through whom the Lord Jesus Christ is glorified in this world of time.

Now that was the second reason for our Lord's prayer – the first reason, you remember, was because of who and what we are – and here we come to the third reason, which he puts quite plainly in verse 13. He says, in effect, 'I am praying all these things audibly in their presence because I am anxious that they might have my joy fulfilled in themselves.' He is anxious that this joy that he himself had experienced should also be fully experienced by these his followers. There is, therefore, a very definite logical sequence in the arrangement of these matters. In dealing earlier with the ways in which the Lord Jesus Christ is glorified in us, we spoke of the fruit of the Spirit, which is love, joy, peace, and so on. At that point, in dealing briefly with joy, I said that I would not go into it in detail, because we would be returning to it, and this is where we must do that. And what we see here is that one of the ways in which we, as Christians, can glorify Christ in this life and world, is by being filled with this spirit of joy and of rejoicing. This is a fruit of the Spirit which our Lord singles out in particular in this prayer to the Father on behalf of his followers. And so we glorify him in a very special way by being partakers of this his own joy.

Obviously, therefore, this is an important subject. Our Lord would not have singled it out like this and given it a special place and emphasis unless it was something of vital concern. So clearly we must start our consideration of it by reminding ourselves again of what a wonderful display this is of our Lord's care and solicitude for his own people. How anxious he is that their welfare should be catered for! He is going to leave them, he is going back to the Father, but he does not lose interest in them for that reason. In a sense he is still more interested in them, and though he is going to face the shame and the agony of the cross, what is uppermost in his mind is the condition and future of these disciples of his, whom he is leaving behind.

But there is more than that – indeed it is something which is of even more vital concern. All that we have been saying is something to rejoice in, but there is a bigger, deeper lesson here. This whole subject of joy is one which is prominent in the New Testament, and, therefore, it must be of primary importance to Christian people. We can see in John 16 how our Lord constantly referred to it, and if you go through the four gospels and look for it, you will find that he was always emphasizing it. And if you read the epistles you will find the subject of joy there, in perhaps a still more striking manner, for some of them are almost exclusively devoted to it. It is a great theme, for instance, of the epistle to the Philippians. Paul's concern there is that Christian people should experience this joy – 'Rejoice in the Lord alway: and again I say, Rejoice' (4:4). It was his burning desire for all Christian people. And then, what, after all, is the purpose of the book of Revelation except that God's people should be taught how truly to be filled with joy and to rejoice? John himself in his first epistle very specifically says, 'These things write I unto you that your joy might be full' (1:14). He was an old man realizing that he was at the end of his journey and thinking of the Christian people he was leaving behind in this difficult world. So he wrote his letter to them in order that their joy might be full. It is, I say, one of the outstanding themes of the entire New Testament, and so it behoves us to be very clear in our minds about it.

There are certain principles that seem to me to stand out very clearly. The first is that we are not only saved for eternity. The gospel of Jesus Christ, of course, is primarily something that does safeguard our eternal destiny. Its fundamental purpose is to reconcile us to God and to see that we are saved in that final and eternal sense. It puts us right once and for all and into a right standing in the presence of God. It reconciles us to God, and establishes definitely in our experience that we are his children. It takes from us the fear of death, of the grave, and of judgement, and it assures us that our eternity and our eternal destiny is safe and secure. But – and this is what is emphasized in this particular verse – we are not only saved for eternity. It is a very false and incomplete view of Christian salvation that postpones its blessings to the realm that lies beyond this present life and beyond the grave.

This sounds so obvious that it is almost foolish to emphasize it, and yet if you go into the history of the church you will find that very often, and sometimes for a very long period, Christian people, by the subtlety of Satan, have been entirely robbed of this particular aspect. This has very often been a result of our reaction – a healthy and right reaction – against worldliness. Christian people have realized that because they are not of the world they should separate themselves from everything that belongs to it. They interpret that as meaning that while they are in this life they are – to use that line of Milton's – 'To scorn delights, and live laborious days'. So they have thought of the Christian as someone who is melancholic, someone who is never going to experience any happiness or joy in a sinful world like this, but who really does look forward to a great joy of unmixed bliss in the land that lies beyond the present and the seen. Thus they seem to rob themselves entirely of any benefits or blessings from salvation in this present life. Now that is tragically and pathetically wrong. The blessings of Christianity are to be enjoyed in this world as well as in the world to come.

There are different aspects, of course, of salvation, but we must never so emphasize the future as to derogate from the present, neither must we in turn emphasize the present and detract from the future. There are blessings to be enjoyed here and now and our Lord emphasized that very clearly in this verse.

But then I draw a second deduction, which is that one of the particular blessings which the Christian is meant to enjoy in the present life is this experience of joy. Our Lord says that he prays in order that his joy might be 'fulfilled in themselves'. We see that in John 16 when he exhorts us to pray: 'Hitherto have ye asked nothing in my name: ask, and ye shall receive, that your joy may be full' (v. 24). The Christian is meant to be a joyful person, one who is meant to experience the joy of salvation. There is no question about that; it is something which is taught everywhere in the New Testament, and so it is our duty as Christians to have this joy, and to be filled with it. And we must give ourselves neither rest nor peace until we have it.

But there are many obstacles to that, and many things which hinder the Christian from having it. There are certain people, I know, who so react against the false and carnal sort of joy, that they rob themselves of the true joy. But the opposite of carnal and fleshly joy is not to be miserable. It is to have the true joy, the joy of the Lord Jesus Christ himself. And in the light of all these exhortations from him and from the apostles we must start by realizing that it is our duty to possess and to experience this joy of which our Lord speaks. We have no right not to have it. Indeed, I put it as my third principle that it is clearly dis-honouring to the Lord Jesus Christ, and to the work he has done, not to have this joy. The teaching seems to be that he came into this world in order that we might have it. Take, for instance, the words at the end of chapter 16: 'These things I have spoken unto you, that in me ye might have peace' (v.33). That verse couples peace and joy together: 'In the world ye shall have tribulation: but be of good cheer; I have overcome the world.' And because he has overcome the world, we are meant to have this joy and to experience it; we are meant to be Christian people who rejoice.

This links very naturally with the previous subject of glorifying him – a miserable Christian does not and obviously cannot glorify the Lord Jesus Christ. Everybody else is miserable, the world makes people so. But if the Lord Jesus Christ has done what he claims to have done, and has come to suffer all that he suffered in this world, to the end that his people might be made different, they are obviously to be a joyful people. He has done all that in order to make it possible for us, and so our failure to be joyful in our lives is to detract from his glory and to cast queries upon his wonderful work. It thus behoves us as Christian people to realize that it is our duty to be joyful. This is often put to us in the New Testament as an injunction. We are commanded to rejoice and if you are commanded to do something, it means that you *must* do it. Now that, obviously, is going to raise a question in our minds as to the nature of this joy. People say that it is no use going to a miserable man and telling him to cheer up. But there is a sense in which you can do that – not directly, but indirectly – and it will result in joy. This is what we must consider together. 'Rejoice in the Lord alway: and again I say, Rejoice' – that is what we are meant to do, and we are meant to be joyful, not only for our own sakes, but still more for his.

So that leads us to the vital question – what is this joy, and what do we know about it? We will content ourselves, for the moment, with just looking at what our Lord himself tells us in this particular verse. The first thing is that it is *his* joy. 'These things I speak in the world, that they might have *my* joy fulfilled in themselves.' Now this is most important because it means that it is not the kind of joy that some people sometimes seem to think it is. It is the kind of joy that he himself possessed and therefore we can say of necessity that it was not carnal or fleshly, it was never boisterous.

I emphasize those negatives because it is always essential to point out that in a matter like this there are two extremes that must always be avoided. I have already mentioned one of them, that of being so anxious to avoid the carnal as to become almost melancholic, but we must also avoid this other extreme. There are certain people – and they have been very much in evidence

I should think for the last fifty years or so – who, having realized quite rightly that a Christian is meant to have joy, have been so anxious to manifest the fact that though they are Christian they are still joyful, that they assume a liveliness which is certainly not the joy of the Lord Jesus Christ. They are a kind of boisterous Christian, but our Lord was never boisterous. Our Lord's joy was a holy joy. Yes – let us not hesitate to say it – it was a serious joy. He was a man of sorrows and acquainted with grief and yet joyful.

The same thing is obviously true of the apostle Paul. He says of himself that he knows this joy and rejoices, and yet he also says that 'in this tabernacle do we groan, being burdened' (2 Cor 5:4). You just cannot think of Paul as a kind of 'hail fellow well met' man, it is inconceivable. Yet no man had a greater joy. He talked in the terms of our Lord himself, and that is the joy that you and I should have. It is not a kind of joy that you put on as a cloak, nor is it a kind of mask that you put on to impress people with how happy and joyful you are. To start with, that does not mislead anybody except the truly superficial, but in any case it is false. True joy is not something that is assumed, it is, rather, an experience down in the depths of one's being. It is not, therefore, something you try to produce, but something that you are, which manifests itself in your life because you are what you are. There is nothing, it seems to me, that is so irritating as the kind of person who is obviously trying to give the impression that he is happy and joyful because he is a Christian, there is nothing that tends to make some of us more miserable; but that is a wrong sort of joy. The first principle, then, is that it is a particular type of joy. It is his joy, and it is the very antithesis of the carnal and fleshly, which is assumed and affected and acted.

Secondly, it is exactly the joy that our Lord himself knew. You cannot go through the gospels and look at the portrayal of our Lord which is contained therein, without seeing this remarkable theme running right through. In spite of all he had to endure and suffer, he spoke constantly of this joy. There is no more striking illustration of this than that which we find at the end of chapter 16. The disciples, at long last, thought that they had seen and understood, but he turned to them and said – and if I could paint I should like to paint the expression of his face when he said it – 'Do ye now believe? Behold, the hour cometh, yea, is now come, that ye shall be scattered, every man to his own, and shall leave me alone' – then – 'and yet I am not alone, because the Father is with me' (Jn 16:31–32). That is joy, that is the joy which he possessed, it was always a part of his life and experience. And that is the joy which we are meant to have, a joy that can face the cross, yes, and the weakness and the apparent desertion, of those whom we trusted, and on whom we relied – 'Who for the joy that was set before him endured the cross, despising the shame...' (Heb 12:2).

Or, again, you can look at it as the joy that comes entirely and exclusively from him. He is its source, so it is a joy that is impossible apart from him, because it derives and emanates from him. It is a joy that he gives to his own people. Put in another way, it is a part of this wonderful fruit that the Holy Spirit produces in us, so in no sense is it self-generated. We do not produce it, it is his joy which is thus realized by us and manifested through us – that is our first principle.

The second thing he tells us about it is that it is a joy that is entirely above and independent of the world and of circumstances and it is in no way produced by them. That, as we have just seen, is the thing that stands out so marvellously in the life of the Lord himself and that is what strikes you as you read through the gospels. He was in the world yet he was not of it, he was independent of it. He walked through the middle of the storm quite unaffected by it, for he had peace within. It is said that in the middle of a hurricane, or a tornado, there is always a central spot which is quite peaceful, and our Lord was always there. Whatever might be happening around and about him, he had this central point of peace and joy. Again, we see this clearly in the great verse in Hebrews 12: 'Who for the joy that was set before him endured the cross, despising the shame.' He went through it all, for there was that about him which made him quite impervious to these things and they could not get at him. It was a kind of garrison, or, as Paul puts it in connection with peace, 'The peace of God, which passeth all understanding, shall keep [garrison] your hearts and minds' (Phil 4:7), shall surround them, or shall so protect them that nothing can penetrate.

Our Lord was like that; he was kept by this marvellous joy so that nothing could touch or affect him. After all, there is very little value in a joy which does not make us capable of that. If our joy is dependent upon what is happening to us and the world around us, or on what is happening to us physically, then we are not different from the world. The world knows what it is to have a kind of joy when everything goes well, but the tragedy about worldly joy is that it is entirely dependent upon circumstances. We all know that perfectly well in our own experience, and we see it so constantly in others. I know of nothing which is quite so sad in this world as to see a life that has seemed so happy suddenly shattered because of something that happens, such as the death of a loved one, or some disappointment or accident. The joy which is thus dependent upon circumstances outside ourselves or our own condition is not his joy. The glory of this joy of which he speaks is that it is absolutely independent of circumstances. He could face the cross and rejoice, and his prayer to the Father is that this joy might be fulfilled in us.

We must remember, too, the context of this verse. He goes on to say in verses 14–16, 'I have given them thy word; and the world hath hated them, because they are not of the world, even as I am not of the world. I pray not that thou shouldest take them out of the world, but that thou shouldest keep them from the evil. They are not of the world, even as I am not of the world.' That is the promise. He was going to leave them all. They had been dependent on him – for three years they had been hanging on his every word, and the result was that when he began to tell them he was going away, sorrow filled their hearts. And so he started off – we read at the beginning of the fourteenth chapter – by saying, 'Let not your heart be troubled: ye believe in God, believe also in me ...' He tried to comfort them. He said, in effect, 'You are depending too much on my physical presence. I am going to leave you.' But not only that, he was going to leave them in a world full of hate, in a world that hated them, in a world that would be antagonistic to them, in a world that would try to kill them and exterminate them, as a body. He was going to leave them in such a world, and yet his prayer was, 'That they might have my joy fulfilled in them.' In other words, his prayer was that though the world, the flesh, the devil and all hell would be let loose against them and would be violently opposed to them, yet they – like himself, for the joy that was set before them, the joy that they had already experienced – might be more than conquerors. That is the great New Testament theme. Read Romans 8, verses 35–37, where Paul, after he had given his tremendous list of all the things that were happening to them, could write, 'Nay, in all these things we are more than conquerors through him that loved us.' That is the true joy. It is a joy, therefore, that is entirely above circumstances and accident and chance; it is independent of them all even as his was.

And the next principle is the discovery of what it is that makes this joy possible. I can imagine someone saying, 'I would give the whole world if I could have this joy. I recognize that you are right when you say it is the New Testament teaching, and that it is my duty to be like that, but how does one get it?'

Fortunately our Lord answers the question here. He says, 'These things I speak in the world; [in order] that they might have my joy fulfilled in themselves', and that leads us to see exactly how we can obtain this joy. One part of this joy is our certain knowledge that he is praying for us. He not only prayed for the disciples, he prayed audibly, in order that they might hear and know, and what he did there he will do for us now. Therefore the great thing is to know that the Lord Jesus Christ is interceding on our behalf, he is still praying.

And that, in turn, leads us to realize his love towards us. I suppose there is nothing that so tends to rob us of our joy as our realization that we do not love him as we ought, because when we realize this, we become unhappy and miserable. I will tell you the best antidote to that: when you realize your love is weak and faint and poor and unworthy, stop thinking about your love, and realize that in spite of its poverty, he loves you. He has said, 'As the Father hath loved me, so have I loved you' (Jn

15:9). If I did not believe that, then I would be of all men most wretched and miserable, for the whole essence of the Christian salvation is to know that in spite of what I have been and what I am, he loves me. Start with that, and I think he will begin to make you love him, but if you are always looking at your own love and trying to increase that, you will be miserable. Think of his love to you; he has given evidence of it, so accept the evidence and act upon it.

But it also makes us know the Father's love. Our Lord has said it here, in verse 6: 'thine they were' – he reminds us that we belong to God, that we are God's people, the special object of his concern. Or let me put it still more specifically in this way. What are 'these things' to which our Lord refers? They are this great doctrine that he has been enunciating, which is that God has his people, that before the foundation of the world God had his people, his marked people, and that he gave them to Christ – we have already dealt with this in detail: 'I have manifested thy name unto the men which thou gavest me out of the world: thine they were, and thou gavest them me' (v.6). To know the Lord's joy is to realize that, and to realize, furthermore, that the Lord Jesus Christ came into the world for us, that he came in order to prepare us for God, and to deliver us from the guilt of our sin. He has done it all. He has borne the guilt and the punishment and the law is satisfied. It has nothing against us any more, for, 'There is therefore now no condemnation to them which are in Christ Jesus' (Rom 8.1). As the hymn puts it, 'The terrors of law and of God, With me can have nothing to do' (Augustus Montague Toplady). I know that, and he has reminded me of it, so how can I fail to be joyful if I believe what he says?

Then what more can we say about these things? Well, he has given me his own nature. He has made me a child of God. He gives me the blessed assurance that, 'If, when we were enemies, we were reconciled to God by the death of his Son, much more, being reconciled, we shall be saved by his life' (Rom 5:10). He has shown us so plainly and clearly that our salvation depends entirely upon him, and not upon ourselves at all. He has told us that no man shall be able to pluck us out of his hands, that we are indeed safe and secure, and that nothing and no one shall be able to separate us from the love of God which is in Christ Jesus our Lord. It is people who believe things like that, who know what this joy is. Go back and read the history of the church, read the lives of the saints, and you will find that the people who have been the most joyful have always been the people who have been most assured and certain of their salvation.

And then another source of joy is that we can realize, as he did, the joy that is set before us. Whatever this world may be doing to us, if we know of this inheritance that is prepared for us we cannot but be happy. 'Let not your heart be troubled: ye believe in God, believe also in me. In my Father's house are many mansions: if it were not so, I would have told you. I go to prepare a place for you. And if I go and prepare a place for you, I will come again, and receive you unto myself; that where I am, there ye may be also' (Jn 14:1–3). If you believe that, your heart cannot but rejoice. So he speaks 'these things' in the world that we may hear them, and this is the source of joy.

And all that leads in turn to fellowship with the Father, to a life lived with God. John has put that perfectly, once and for ever, in 1 John 1:3–4, 'That which we have seen and heard declare we unto you, that ye also may have fellowship with us: and truly our fellowship is with the Father, and with his Son Jesus Christ. And these things write we unto you, that your joy may be full.' That is the ultimate source of joy, that, realizing the truth as it is in Christ, we are brought into fellowship with the Father. And so, as we walk with him in fellowship we must be joyful. Anything less is impossible, and as our Lord experienced it, so shall we experience it.

So let me end this study with a few practical suggestions. How, then, in practice do we have this joy? The first thing is to avoid concentrating on our own feelings. There are many Christian people who spend the whole of their lives looking at their own feelings and always taking their own spiritual pulse, their own spiritual temperature. Of course, they never find it satisfactory, and because of that they are miserable and unhappy, moaning and groaning. Now that is wrong. First and foremost we must avoid concentrating on our own feelings. We must learn to concentrate positively on 'these things'. In other words, the secret of joy is the practice of meditation – that is the way to have this joy of the Lord. We must meditate upon him, upon what he is, what he has done, his love to us and upon God's care for us who are his people.

This is what I meant earlier when I said we could only produce this joy indirectly. It is not something I assume in order to give the impression that I am a wonderfully happy man, and then go back to being bored and miserable in my own home. No, it is not that, it is something that results from meditation and contemplation upon 'these things', these precious, wonderful things. And I have no hesitation in saying that there is such a marked absence of true Christian joy in the church today because there is so little meditation. Do not misunderstand me. We all constantly exhort one another to have our 'quiet time', which generally means reading Scripture and prayer. It is perfectly right, but if you stop at that, you will probably not have this joy – having read and having prayed, then meditate. Think on these things, set your affection on them, hold yourself before them and bring them to your mind many times during the day. The sum of joy is simple meditation, contemplation, on these things, making time to dwell upon them, putting other things out of the way and spending your time with them. For the more we know 'these things' and dwell with them and live with them, and seek the face of God, the greater will be our joy.

And obviously – this almost goes without saying – we must avoid everything that tends to break our fellowship with God. The moment that is broken we become miserable. We cannot help it; whether we want to or not, our conscience will see to that. It will accuse us, and condemn anything that breaks our fellowship with God and his Son. The joy of the world always drives out the other joy, as does any dependence on the world, so we must avoid sin in every shape and form. Let us stop looking to the world, even at its best, for true joy, and for true happiness. But above all, we must look at 'these things' that he speaks of, these truths that he unfolded. Let us meditate upon them, contemplate them, dwell upon them, revel in them and I will guarantee that as we do so, either in our own personal meditation or in reading books about them, we will find ourselves experiencing a joy such as we have never known before. It is inevitable, it follows as the night the day.

'These things speak I in the world, that they might have my joy fulfilled in themselves.' What a wonderful thing that it is possible for us to live in this world, in a measure, even as the blessed Son of God lived, and that as we do so he is glorified in us.

10

Kept and Guarded but …

And now I am no more in the world, but these are in the world, and I come to thee. Holy Father, keep through thine own name those whom thou hast given me, that they may be one, as we are. While I was with them in the world, I kept them in thy name: those that thou gavest me I have kept, and none of them is lost, but the son of perdition; that the scripture might be fulfilled…. I pray not that thou shouldest take them out of the world, but that thou shouldest keep them from the evil (vv. 11–12, 15).

We have been considering our Lord's main reasons for praying for his disciples, and now we come to his petitions on their behalf, and the first petition is the one which is recorded in verses 11, 12 and 15. It is his great petition that God may keep them and especially that he may keep them in his name. Now this first petition follows very naturally from all that we have been considering hitherto. His desire is that they may be kept continuously in the future, in the condition in which he kept them while he was with them. And he prays that in the light of who they are and what they are, and because of what they are meant to do and the circumstances in which they are placed.

We cannot begin to consider this in detail without again reminding ourselves, with grateful and thankful hearts, of this further expression of our Lord's wonderful concern for his people. We can be quite sure that if we but realized his concern for us, most of our problems would immediately be solved. It is because we forget this and because we fail to realize his love for us, that we tend to become anxious and worried and troubled. It does seem to me, increasingly, that a truly happy and joyful Christian life first begins with just this realization that his concern for us and about us is altogether greater than any concern we may have for ourselves and our well-being, and for our witness and our testimony for him.

Our Lord's great prayer is that God may keep them and keep them in rather a special way. Now there is no doubt but that in this particular instance the translation in the Revised Version is altogether better, and more accurate, than that of the Authorized. The right translation of these verses is undoubtedly as follows: 'Holy Father, keep them in thy name which thou hast given me ... While I was with them, I kept them in thy name which thou hast given me: and I guarded them, and not one of them perished, but the son of perdition ...' (vv 11–12, RV). In other words, the prayer is that he may keep them in his name.[1] The Authorized Version is somewhat misleading here because it says, 'Holy Father, keep through thine own name those whom thou hast given me', when it should really be: '... in thy name which thou hast given me'. We have already seen that God had given him the people, and that has been repeated several times; what our Lord is referring to here is the fact that this particular name of God has been given to him. And he says the same thing in the twelfth verse: '... I kept them in thy name which thou hast given me.' So that, clearly, the petition is that God would keep these, his people, in that name which God had given to him.

In a sense, we have already seen that, in verse 6, where he says, 'I have manifested thy name unto the men which thou gavest me out of the world.' This is the mystic secret, if I may

---

[1] The New International Version has, 'Holy Father, protect them by the power of your name – the name you gave me – so that they may be one as we are one. While I was with them, I protected them and kept them safe by that name you gave me.' (Ed.)

so put it, which the Christian possesses, and it is something which nobody else understands. The Father, when he sent his Son into this world, sent him to declare his name, God's name, and the name, as we have seen, is the peculiar revelation of the person and character of God. This is a name which is only given to those who believe in the Lord Jesus Christ, but the moment we believe, we know God in terms of this, as yet unrevealed to us, secret name. We find this very frequently in the Scriptures. For instance, we are told in Revelation 3 that a name is given to the saints, to God's people, which nobody else knows. It means that the Christian has an understanding of God, and a knowledge of God, which nobody else has. And our Lord's prayer is that these Christians may be kept in that knowledge and in that understanding. It is all summed up by the name – that they may continue to know and to understand through their relationship to God, what God is to them and what they are to God. That is the meaning of this prayer, that they may be kept in the name which God has given them, the name of God himself which the Lord has come to reveal, the special revelation of God which is to be found only in and through our blessed Lord and Saviour Jesus Christ. And that, therefore, is his petition for Christian people now, that we may ever be kept in the full realization of our relationship to God.

But before we can come to consider that in its detail and in its context, we must here, of necessity, notice first of all the claim which our Lord couples with the petition. Not only does he present this petition to his Father, he also adds this: 'While I was with them in the world, I kept them in thy name, which thou hast given me, and none of them is lost but the son of perdition that the Scripture might be fulfilled.'

Obviously we have to deal with this and to define it, not merely because we must do so out of intellectual honesty, nor because we must not omit anything when we are working in detail like this through a passage of Scripture. No, we must look at this because it does contain very high and important and serious doctrine.

First of all, then, let us look at our Lord's claims. He claims two things, 'While I was with them in the world,' he says, 'I *kept* them in thy name which thou hast given me: and I *guarded* them' (RV). Again we must notice the superiority of the Revised Version here, because it brings out the difference between the two words which our Lord uses. 'Keeping' is a more comprehensive word than 'guarding', and the idea behind the word can perhaps best be illustrated by a shepherd's care for his sheep. It is the business of the shepherd to 'keep' the sheep. That means that he always keeps his eye on them. He watches them, supervising them the whole time and taking care of them in the fields so that none stray away or get lost. When they have to be moved he sees to it that they are not driven too quickly, and he always makes sure that they are fed at the right time. Constant care, that is the meaning of the word 'keep'. Now the word 'guard' is a lesser term. To guard means simply to protect against attacks, so you see this covers a more restricted area than the other. Guarding means just that one thing – there are enemies around, and it is the business of the shepherd to protect the flock against them.

But we should thank God for both these terms. They tell us that our Lord does not merely guard us, he also keeps us. He is not only concerned about the attacks on us by the world, and by the evil one, but more than that, he is constantly keeping us, watching over us. He is concerned about our welfare and our well-being positively as well as negatively. He not only prevents attacks, he sees to it that we are always in the right position and in the right place and given the right things. He has this great concern, this oversight. The apostle Peter says, 'Ye were as sheep going astray; but are now returned unto *the Shepherd and Bishop of your souls*' (1 Pet 2:25) – that is what our Lord is to us, the one who looks after all our interests in every way. In these verses his claim is that he has kept them and guarded them, but now he says he is going to leave them, and so he prays to God to keep them and to guard them as he had done.

How, then, and when did our Lord keep and guard them? The gospels, of course, are full of answers to that question, I merely note them. In the first place he had done so by teaching them – in a sense that was the purpose of his teaching, to instruct them in their relationship to God, and in the nature of the Christian life. That is why he preached the Sermon on the Mount, and gave them the Beatitudes, so that they might know the kind of people they were meant to be. All his teaching is designed to do this. He taught them about the world, and its subtlety, about sin, about the flesh and about the devil, for it was only as they were forewarned, that they could be forearmed. So his teaching was a very vital part of his keeping of them.

But not only that. It is remarkable as you go through the gospels to notice the amount of time he spent in warning his followers. There is nothing further removed from the gospels than many of the false cults which say, 'You believe this and all will be well with you.' The gospel does not do that. Our Lord had solemn warnings for these people, and he constantly prepared them for difficulties and dangers. In a sense, they were far too elated; he was almost alarmed at their lack of understanding, and so he warned them. On one occasion they had been out preaching and they had come back so jubilant because, they said, 'Even the devils are subject unto us.' But he said to them, '… in this rejoice not, that the spirits are subject unto you; but rather rejoice, because your names are written in heaven' (Lk 10:17, 20). He knew the things they were going to find, so he warned them, and that is another way of keeping them.

He also keeps them by rebuking them at times, by chastising them. In their lack of understanding they tended to do things which were bad for them and bad for the kingdom, so our Lord rebuked them. 'Whom the Lord loveth he chasteneth' (Heb 12:6) and that is the business of chastening: to keep us, to keep us from straying and from wandering, to keep us from things that are harmful to us. And so in his love he keeps us by rebuking us and by chastening us. But above all, our Lord kept them and guarded them by actual manifestations of his power. He frequently stood between them and the attacks and assaults of the world and the flesh and the devil. That becomes clear quite often. Take, for instance, his words to Peter: 'Simon, Simon, behold, Satan hath desired to have you, that he may sift you as wheat: but I have prayed for thee, that thy faith fail not' (Lk 22:31–32). He knew that these onslaughts were coming, he anticipated them, and in this way he kept them and guarded them.

Now we must surely raise the question as to why our Lord makes this claim at this point. The answer, clearly, is that it is another statement of his to the effect that he has glorified his Father in everything and that he has failed in nothing. You remember we had it at the very beginning of the prayer. 'Father,' he says, 'the hour is come; glorify thy Son, that thy Son also may glorify thee.' That was his purpose, he was always concerned to glorify the Father. In verse 2 he says, 'As thou hast given him power over all flesh, that he should give eternal life to as many as thou hast given him' – and then, in verse 4 – 'I have glorified thee on the earth.' And one of the ways in which he had glorified the Father was that he had kept these men whom the Father had given him. He had not failed in any single respect or detail.

Here again is something which calls for a word of comment. Read the four gospels again and keep this particular point in your mind. Look at the disciples, look at their frailty, their proneness to sinfulness. There was nothing exceptional about them. They were not learned in any way, but just ordinary men in this extraordinary position. Yet our Lord could claim, and claim rightly and truly, that he had kept them, though they were what they were, and in spite of all the temptations to which they had been exposed. He had kept them in these extraordinary circumstances because his strength was sufficient. They were ignorant, they did not understand him at times and they were bewildered and baffled. Yet in spite of all that we may say about them – the impulsiveness of a Peter or the scepticism of a Thomas – our Lord, by his amazing way of dealing with them, had kept and guarded them. And here, at the end, he is able to say to the Father, I have kept, I have guarded these people whom thou hast given me.

Ah yes, but there is, however, one statement which we have to face – '... and,' says our Lord, 'none of them is lost, but the son of perdition; that the scripture might be fulfilled.' Now this is something which is truly remarkable. Here, I would remind you again, is our Lord just under the shadow of the cross, praying to the Father, and in this prayer he mentions the case of Judas. Why does he do that? As we seek to answer that question, I think that once more I can show you that this is a very important doctrine for us. First of all, we must notice here that he says *but* – 'but the son of perdition' – and not *except*. These two words always confuse the exegesis of this verse. Our Lord is saying here that though Judas is one of the twelve, he is not one of those who has been given to the Son by the Father. Judas is not a kind of exception among the apostles, he is in a category apart. He does not really belong to the same group, he is an odd man out: he is in the group but has never been of it. If our Lord had said, 'I have kept them all except Judas', the implication would have been that he had failed to keep one of them. But when he says, 'I have kept them all *but* the son of perdition', he is simply saying, Now of these men who have been accompanying me I have kept those whom thou hast given me, but there is one other who has been in the company, the son of perdition, and that is Judas.

Let me say why it is important for us to put it in that form. We are constantly told in the Scriptures themselves that Judas was not really one of the true company. Judas was never born again, and never became a Christian even though he belonged to the company of the twelve. Let me remind you of John 6:68–70. When Peter makes his great confession: 'Lord, to whom shall we go? thou hast the words of eternal life. And we believe and are sure that thou art that Christ, the Son of the living God,' our Lord turns to them and says, 'Have not I chosen you twelve, and one of you is a devil?' And in verse 71 we read: 'He spake of Judas Iscariot ... for he it was that should betray him, being one of the twelve.'

So, then, let us return to our question – why does our Lord mention that at this point in his most tender prayer? The first answer is one which I have already given – he is praying in an audible manner, and the disciples are listening to the prayer. He speaks thus of Judas audibly, in order that he may again claim in their presence that he has glorified the Father. It is an absolute claim. He has kept and guarded those whom the Father has given him: Judas has not been given to him in that way.

Another obvious reason is that he is anxious that these disciples should know beforehand what is going to happen and what Judas is going to do, lest they be offended when it actually takes place. Here again is an indication of our Lord's lovingkindness and his care for his own. Indeed it is a perfect example of how he keeps them. He knows that Judas is going to betray him but the others do not. Our Lord spoke of it earlier, but they did not understand. He now states it again before them, so that they might know for certain that it is going to happen, and will not be surprised or dumbfounded at the subtlety of it.

There is a further reason, too. He is anxious to reveal to them his own deity and to assert that he is the Son of God. He is also anxious that they should realize his foreknowledge. He knows exactly what Judas is going to do; he prophesied it earlier, as we saw, in the sixth chapter. He repeated it in the thirteenth and now here it is once more. He knows everything. He knows the end from the beginning, and here he has declared once more that he is indeed the Son of God. And also, clearly, he says this in order that he might pay this testimony to Scripture – 'that the scripture may be fulfilled'. The treachery of Judas is prophesied in the Scriptures in Psalms 41 and 109. Psalm 109 in particular gives a detailed description of Judas, and so, as our Lord says here, the scripture has said it all. He says, in effect, 'It is not only I, but the scripture, too. The prophets have seen it coming, and the son of perdition is going to fulfil the prophecy that was already made long ago.'

That, then, is but the mechanics of this matter, so now let us apply this great and spiritual message. It seems to me that here we have, in a terrible picture, the exact difference between belonging to the world and belonging to the Lord Jesus Christ. 'I pray for them: I pray not for the world.' The difference between them and the world is the difference between the eleven and Judas Iscariot. He was not praying for Judas, and he does not pray for anybody who belongs to the Judas position. So this is the essential difference between being a Christian and not being a Christian, it is all depicted in the alarming picture in this most holy prayer.

Here, then, I suggest, is something by which we ought to examine ourselves, because the lesson at this point is that it is possible for one to belong to the innermost circle and yet to be lost – that is the terrible and terrifying lesson which we must take to ourselves. Mere membership of the church means nothing in and of itself. Judas was one of the twelve and yet he was lost. He was one of those who was sent out with the others and he was one of those who had listened to the most intimate teaching. He was right in the inner circle and yet he was the son of perdition. That is why Scripture constantly exhorts us to examine ourselves. A mechanical position does not guarantee that there is life. There are obviously certain things which characterize this condition of Judas, and we must consider them. The mere fact that I am interested in Christian things does not prove I am a Christian. Why did Judas come among the twelve? For three years he had been with the others and there he was following our Lord and listening to his intimate teaching. There must have been something that attracted him. So we have to realize that we may be attracted to the church, and to the gospel and to Christ himself, and yet not be truly Christian, but sons of perdition.

What are the characteristics of such people? Here are some that seem to be indicated in Scripture. First of all, Judas was dominated by Satan. 'One of you is a devil,' says our Lord in John 6:70, by which he means that this man is entirely, as it were, possessed by the devil, dominated and controlled by him. Then another thing that is very obvious is that he was blinded so that he could not see the truth. As the apostle Paul tells us, 'But if our gospel be hid, it is hid to them that are lost: in whom the god of this world hath blinded the minds of them which believe not, lest the light of the glorious gospel of Christ, who is the image of God, should shine unto them' (2 Cor 4:3–4). Here is a man sitting day by day and listening to the truth from the very Son of God, and yet he never sees it, because he is blinded to it. He hears the words but he does not hear the message. He could probably recite certain words, but he does not know their meaning – he is blind to the truth.

You notice, also, the essential baseness of his character and nature. We are told in John 12:6 '... he was a thief, and had the bag, and bare what was put therein' – he was dishonest. He was in charge of their communal bag and stole from it.[2]   People often have mercenary reasons for belonging to the church; they join for their own selfish ends. Judas was a hypocrite and he pretended to be something he was not. He was treacherous. He was always selfish and self-seeking and the whole tragedy of Judas is that he brought his own interests into the presence of the Son of God himself. It was his avarice that seems to have taken him there. He came to Christ because of certain things he wanted, not because of what Christ had to give, and that is the essential difference between a man who is not a Christian and the true Christian. People have their own personal reasons for being interested in religion. There are certain things they want and they think that religion can provide them – that is the Judas attitude. The true Christian is one who goes empty-handed, as it were, with an open mind and heart and just listens and receives. Judas never did that. He always had his own point of view, his own interests, and it was to further them that he kept with the disciples. He never really opened himself to receive the message because he was selfish and self-centred.

And there is another great lesson here. Does it not show us the final and complete fallacy and fatuity of thinking anybody can ever be saved or become a Christian merely by teaching or instruction? So many people think that. They say, 'We do not believe in the rebirth, what is needed is good teaching'. But they say that in spite of the case of Judas. Here is a man who for three years received divine instruction through the lips of the blessed Son of God himself, and yet he is 'a son of perdition'. By mere

---

[2] The NIV translates this: '... he was a thief; as keeper of the money bag, he used to help himself to what was put into it.' (Ed.)

teaching and instruction no man can ever be made a Christian. Or take the people who think that the way to make people Christian is to give them a good example, to put them in the right environment and surround them with the right influence. Is that not the kind of thing that is still being taught? Yet here is a man who had spent three years, not only with the apostles, but in the very innermost presence of the Son of God himself, and yet he is the son of perdition. No, example and influence and environment are not enough. The Christian is not merely a man who is trying to imitate the Lord Jesus Christ, for it cannot be done. In Judas we see a man who has every advantage yet he is lost.

Let me therefore sum it all up in these words. If there is one thing in the Scriptures that proves, more conclusively than anything else, the absolute necessity of the rebirth, it is the case of Judas Iscariot. What differentiates the Christian from the non-Christian is not that the Christian lives a better life than he did before, nor that he knows more of the Scriptures, and all these other good things. Judas knew all that and he probably lived a good outward moral life during the three years he was among the disciples. No, what makes a man a Christian is that he is born again, he has received the divine nature, he has indeed become indwelt by the Spirit of the living God. It is this that gives the understanding, and everything that Judas did not have. It was because Judas was never renewed and given the new life that he remained the son of perdition. And here I want to utter a solemn, terrible word. The end of the non-Christian, even though he may be highly religious, is perdition, which means perishing. Though Judas was in the company of the apostles all along, he really belonged to the world, and the fate of the world is to perish. Whatever its appearance may be, its end is destruction, with no hope whatsoever; because it has not truly believed in the name of the only begotten Son of God, it perishes.

This is an unpleasant subject and yet we have to face it, because, in the very centre of this most wonderful prayer, our

Lord had to mention it as a solemn warning. He was not praying for Judas, he was praying for those who were God's people,
those who belong to God.

My dear friends, are we *certain* that we belong to God? Do
we know that we have received the divine life? Are we born
again, and are we sure of it? I warn you in the name of my blessed Saviour, in the light of this teaching, do not rely upon anything but the certain knowledge that you have received life from
God. Interest in religion is not enough, interest in Christ is not
enough, interest in morality is not enough, membership of the
church is not enough – none of these things is enough. Judas
seemed to have had them all. The one thing about which we
must be absolutely certain is that we are the children of God. If
you are, praise him and give yourself anew to him. If you are not
certain, then I beseech you, learn the lesson of Judas. Go to the
Lord Jesus Christ and tell him that you are uncertain, that you
do not know, that you are even doubtful whether you have new
life. Tell him the truth about yourself. Cast yourself utterly at
his feet and ask him in mercy to look upon you and by his Spirit
give you this new life and the blessed assurance that you are born
again, that you are indeed his child and his heir, a joint-heir with
Christ, and that you truly belong to him.

11

The World and the Devil

And now I am no more in the world, but these are in the world, and I come to thee. Holy Father, keep through thine own name those whom thou hast given me, that they may be one, as we are. While I was with them in the world, I kept them in thy name: those that thou gavest me I have kept, and none of them is lost, but the son of perdition; that the scripture might be fulfilled. And now come I to thee; and these things I speak in the world, that they might have my joy fulfilled in themselves. I have given them thy word; and the world hath hated them, because they are not of the world, even as I am not of the world. I pray not that thou shouldest take them out of the world, but that thou shouldest keep them from the evil (vv. 11–15).

We continue now with our study of our Lord's great plea that God should keep the disciples in his name, the name which he had given to Christ to reveal to them. 'While I was with them in the world,' he says, 'I kept them in thy name', and his prayer is that God will continue to keep them in the name. You notice the urgency of the plea which emphasizes the need of our being kept. We cannot read this prayer without noticing that it was obviously a great burden on our Lord's mind. He was going to leave them in the world, and he was concerned about them, so concerned that though he was going to face the shame and agony and terrible trial of the cross, he really was not thinking about himself, but about them, and about their future. We see this clearly not only in this chapter but also repeatedly in all his teaching at the end of his life. He was, in a sense, almost alarmed about them and thus he offered his urgent plea.

Now this is something which is characteristic of the whole of the New Testament teaching about the Christian and his life in this world. We find in Acts 20 that the apostle Paul had precisely the same concern about the people in the church at Ephesus. He was hurrying up to Jerusalem; he knew that bonds awaited him, and he was quite certain that he was never going to see these people again. So he sent an urgent message to the elders of the church at Ephesus to meet him on the seashore, and there he addressed them. He, again, felt this burden – I know, he said, that you will never see my face again. I cannot come to you any more and teach you as I should like to do, and therefore I want to warn you against certain things. And he proceeded to do that. He told them about the 'grievous wolves' that were ready to attack them, and he added that they would find that even among themselves there were those who were going to rise up and make havoc of the life of the church. The apostle was burdened for these people as he was leaving them, and the last thing he did before he said farewell was to kneel down on the seashore and pray for them. He committed them to God, exactly as our Lord here was committing his disciples and other followers into the hands of his Father. You can find other illustrations of the same concern.

The message for us, therefore, is that the life of the Christian in this world is a life of conflict. The New Testament always, everywhere, gives the impression that all who are Christians are in the midst of a tremendous spiritual battle. Think, for instance, of that great exhortation in Ephesians 6 where Paul exhorts the Christians to 'put on the whole armour of God' in order that they may be able to stand in the evil day. 'For,' he says, 'we wrestle not against flesh and blood, but against principalities, against powers, against the rulers of the darkness of this world, against spiritual wickedness in high places,' or in the heavenlies. Now that is typical and interesting teaching. You cannot read the New Testament without being aware of this kind of tension. The world is the scene of the great battle that is going on between these rival, spiritual forces, and the Christian is involved in all this, of course, because he belongs to the Lord Jesus Christ. The very fact that we belong to Christ means that we immediately become the special targets of the enemies of Christ, those other spiritual forces to whom Paul refers. They are antagonistic to God and his Christ, and, therefore, the moment we belong to God the enemy begins to attack us, not because he is interested in us, but because his one overriding ambition is to mar and destroy God's perfect work. Our Lord knew this and so did Paul and all the apostles. Peter, for instance, puts it like this, 'Be sober, be vigilant; because your adversary the devil, as a roaring lion, walketh about, seeking whom he may devour ...' (1 Pet 5:8). That is the picture, and it is because of this that the need for protection arises.

I wonder whether we are conscious of our position and our condition as Christians? I wonder whether we are conscious of our need to be kept, or whether we are aware of the tremendous spiritual conflict in which we are involved? I ask these questions because I think I know many church members who patently are not aware of this conflict at all and who feel that it is something strange and odd. So I do not hesitate to asssert that one of the most interesting ways of measuring our spiritual understanding and insight is to discover the degree to which we are aware of the fight and the conflict and the position with which we are confronted as Christians in this present evil world. To the extent that we are not aware of it and so not aware of the need for protection, to that extent, I would say, we are simply proclaiming that we are tiros in these matters, and that we are but babes in Christ. The babe never realizes the dangers, everything seems easy and simple and plain, but the more we grow, and the older we get, the more we begin to realize the subtleties and the dangers that confront us. It is exactly the same in the spiritual life and it is the saints, of all people, who have realized most acutely that they are confronted by a mighty, spiritual antagonist. Read the lives of the saints and you will find that they are always aware of this – which is why they spent so much time in prayer. It is the man who realizes his own weakness and the power of the devil, who realizes his need for protection.

Now our Lord here establishes this once and for ever. His great burden under the very shadow of the cross was the condition of these people. He was leaving them and he saw the forces that were marshalling themselves and making ready to swoop upon them and attack them. He saw exactly what was going to take place, and so he pleaded with God to keep them, and to keep them in his name.

And not only that. Our Lord goes on to particularize these forces that are arrayed against us, and they can be summed up under two headings. First of all there is the world itself. In every single one of these verses from verse 11 to verse 15 the world is mentioned, and this is because the disciples are in the world. Indeed the problem arises because that is where he must leave them. Now this does not mean, of course, the physical world, but the world in a spiritual sense, the sense in which the New Testament always uses this expression. It is the mind, the outlook and the whole organization of this present world and scene. 'Love not the world, neither the things that are in the world,' says the apostle John. The Scripture describes the powers and the forces that are opposed to God as 'the world'; it is the realm in which Satan is king, the atmosphere in which the prince of the power of the air rules and reigns. It is the territory of 'the god of this world', everything in life that does not recognize God and submit itself to him.

Now the world manifests itself and its antagonism to the Christian in many ways. Our Lord singles one out here by saying, 'I have given them thy word; and the world hath hated them, because they are not of the world, even as I am not of the world.' He said that many times. He tells his disciples in John 15 that the world will hate them because it hated him and because they are like him and because they belong to him. Our Lord does not argue about this. The world, he says, *will hate you*, and here, in pleading for these people with the Father, he makes the same statement; the world which has hated them will go on hating. This is surely an extraordinary thing. The world hates the Christian. So here again we come across a valuable differentiating point. There are so many things that simulate Christianity in this modern world – indeed there always have been – that it is sometimes very difficult to differentiate between Christianity and a kind of pseudo-Christianity. But this, I think, is one of the best tests. The world never hates the imitation, or the spurious, or the false Christianity, but it always hates the true thing. The world never hates morality, it never hates the merely moral man (which is an interesting point), but it hates the true Christian. You would have thought that if the world hated the one, it would hate the other, but no, the world, in a sense, likes the moral man. It never hates him because it realizes that he is acting in his own strength, and in that way he is paying a compliment to fallen human nature. But the world hated the Son of God himself, and it hates the true saint.

The world hates the true Christian because Christ himself and the true Christian condemn the natural man in a way that nobody else does. Christ and the saint condemn the natural man at his very best, and that is why the world hates him. It is only in Christ and the true Christian that the doctrine of sin is really perceived. The very fact that the Son of God came into this world at all is proof positive that man can never save himself. If man could save himself by his own exertions, the Son of God would never have come. The very fact that he has come proclaims that man at his best and highest will never be good enough. Now the world hates the thought of this because the ultimate trouble with man in sin is his pride, and that is why so often the most moral people have been the ones who have hated the Christ of God most of all. The poor sinner in his rags and filth never hates Christ as much as the good moral man does, the man who only believes in 'uplift' and ideals. He is the man who hates Christ because Christ condemns him. He feels he is better than that other man in the gutter and that he has no need of Christ. Scripture says that 'all have sinned', and he cannot stand the condemnation.

And of course our Lord condemns him in the same way by the cross. The cross proclaims that all are lost and that all are equally under the wrath of God, and the world hates that. Men are so ready to praise the example and the teaching of Christ, but they ridicule his blood, for it is the blood that condemns and what a man cannot endure is the sense of condemnation, the sense of inadequacy, and the sense of failure. Thus it comes to pass that our Lord and his followers are hated by the world. The world says, 'I do not object to religion, but why go so far? Why this separating of yourself from others? I really am not as bad as that after all I confess I am not 100% but ...' and Christ condemns that. He says, 'You are a sinner', and the world hates him for that and it hates his followers. Our Lord's words were of course very soon verified. The spite of the Jews was turned upon the first Christians, and the enmity of the world has continued up to this present time. That is a terrifying thing to say but it is true.

Does the world hate us? I wonder whether it hates us as it hated our Lord? If it does not it is simply because we are very poor Christians. I trust nobody will misunderstand me, I am not saying that a man must try to make himself angular or difficult. Our Lord did not break the bruised reed, or quench the smoking flax. No, it did not hate him because he made himself odd and difficult, it was his sheer purity and holiness, and his teaching that caused the hatred. And it is as true today as it has always been that the nearer we approximate to our Lord the more we experience the hatred of the world. It shows it of course in many ways. It shows it in persecution, which can be open, but which can also be subtle and concealed. It is in an open form in many countries of the world today, and there are people in concentration camps and prisons because the world hates them. But in a different way, there is as much persecution in this country as there is in those other countries. It is the subtle form with which we are all familiar and the man who is a true follower of Christ will inevitably be subjected to it. 'Yea,' says Paul to Timothy, 'and all that will live godly in Christ Jesus shall suffer persecution' (2 Tim 3:12). Let us all examine ourselves.

That is the first thing. The world is opposed and it shows its opposition by means of hatred. But it also has another way of showing it. This is what I would call the Demas way – 'Demas hath forsaken me, having loved this present world' (2 Tim 4:10). The world does not care very much how it attacks his followers. If by throwing them into prison it can wrest them from Christ, it will do so, but if that does not work it will try some other method. 'Demas hath forsaken me' – the love of ease, love of the things of the world, its wealth, its position, its so-called pomp and show, the lust of the flesh, the lust of the eye and the pride of life – how many good men have been ruined by that. Prosperity can be very dangerous to the soul and the world is prepared to use that. If direct opposition will not work, it will pamper us, it will dangle these things before us and thus it will try to wean us from Christ. So it is not surprising that he prayed the Father to keep us in his name.

Then another way in which the world does the same thing is by what may be described as the Barnabas method. We are told in Acts 15 that a dispute had taken place between Barnabas and Paul. Barnabas wanted to take his relative John Mark on their missionary journey but Paul said that he would not have him. Paul felt that John Mark had let them down and deserted them when they had taken him on their previous journey and that he was not, therefore, the man to accompany them. Here we have worldly relationships such as family relationships interfering in God's work. It is always something which to me seems very subtle and pathetic at the same time. You read of men who have been called by God to do a particular work. Their call has been quite clear and unmistakable, but then when these men get old you notice the way they tend to appoint their own sons to carry on the work and how often it leads to disaster. The point is, of course, that the God who called the father, does not of necessity call the son. Indeed I have seen this kind of thing so often that I become very uneasy when I see it taking place. It is the Barnabas method – 'John Mark must come, he is my relative.' In other words, it is the tendency not to judge things in a spiritual way, but to be influenced by these other considerations.

Indeed, this can show itself in still another way, the way which James emphasizes when he says, 'Pure religion and undefiled before God and the Father is this, To visit the fatherless and widows in their affliction, and to keep himself unspotted from the world' (Jas 1:27). It may seem a strange bringing together of two statements, but it is essential that the two should be taken together. It is a right and a good thing to visit the fatherless and the widows, says James, but be very careful that you do not become spotted with the world as you do so. Have we not all, alas, known numbers of men called of God to be prophets and to preach the gospel who have ended as nice, but powerless men, whose congregations have been ruined. They have visited the fatherless and the widows in their affliction, but they have not been careful to keep themselves unspotted from the world. They have been affable and friendly and kind, but they have lost something. It was the world that did it, it came between the man and his calling, between this man and God and his Christ.

There, then, are some of the ways in which the world does this, but our Lord does not stop at mentioning the world. He specifically mentions the evil one – 'I pray not that thou shouldest take them out of the world, but that thou shouldest keep them from the evil' – or 'the evil one' (v. 15). Both renderings, of course, are perfectly true: we pray to be kept from the evil one and the other evil things which belong to the evil one and are prompted by him. In other words, we must see that it is not only the world that is against us, it is also the 'god of this world' behind the world, the devil himself. Our Lord has taught us to pray this in the prayer he taught his disciples: 'Lead us not into temptation, but deliver us from evil' – or the evil one. As I have already reminded you, Peter tells us that this adversary of ours is roaming about like a roaring lion, 'seeking whom he may devour' – he is the devil who is opposed to God's people.

How then does he attack them? Well, sometimes he makes a direct attack on the self, on the person, and there are a great variety of ways in which he does this. I suppose that the commonest way of all is through our pride; he fills us with a sense of elation and self-glorification. Let me give you a perfect illustration of that from Luke 10. Our Lord had sent his disciples out to preach the gospel and to cast out devils and they came back to him full of elation because they said that even the devils were subject to them. Our Lord immediately saw the danger and said to them, 'In this rejoice not, that the spirits are subject unto you; but rather rejoice because your names are written in heaven.' You see, he saw the danger of their heads being turned – as we put it – of their being consumed with self-satisfaction at their success, reporting the results, letting everybody know, and being puffed up with pride. And, of course, this pride leads in turn to self-reliance. We think we are so wonderful and do the work so well that we do not need the Holy Spirit and the power of God. We can do it, so we trust to our organization and all our carnal means and methods, and the devil encourages us in this. He drives us forward in a false, carnal or excessive zeal.

Another way he has, and it is one of his favourite methods, is to make us rush ahead of God. He makes us impatient; we cannot wait for God's time. We are going to do this thing, and we will arrange, we will organize, we will go ahead of God – and the devil is satisfied and well-pleased. Appearing as an angel of light, he encourages us to rely upon ourselves and our own ideas and methods, and thus God's blessing is withheld.

But he is subtle, and sometimes he takes us in, not by puffing us up with pride, nor by encouraging us, but by doing the exact opposite. He fills us with discouragement and doubt or he encourages us in a sense of false modesty. I have seen the devil ruin many a prayer meeting like that. There is a pause in the meeting and if you asked every person who was present why they did not take part, they would say, 'I did not like to push myself forward, I was giving somebody else a chance.' And the prayer meeting is ruined through false, unhealthy pseudo-modesty. He makes us condemn ourselves; he makes us look at some sin which we committed many years ago and he makes us look back at it and feel that we cannot be forgiven. So the result is that we are constantly looking at our failures, and while we are doing that, we are not working for God. We feel that we are altogether unworthy of him; we doubt ourselves and our salvation and we spend the whole of our time examining ourselves.

My dear friends, from the devil's standpoint there is not the slightest difference between being puffed up with pride in yourself or spending the whole of your time condemning yourself. Either way the devil is very well-pleased. Any concentration upon self in any shape or form is always of the devil. Another result, of course, is that while we are looking at ourselves and thinking of ourselves, we are forgetting this name in which our Lord asked his Father to keep us, the name that tells us that all our sins are forgiven and that the blood of Christ still cleanses from all sin and unrighteousness. If that is true, I have no right to look back to that sin; I must turn to the name, and if I feel weak I must remember that God is the almighty Jehovah who has promised not to leave me nor forsake me. So we must not allow the devil to hinder the work of God with a direct attack in one or other of these ways.

Again, he can do it by creating within us a spirit of fear. We read how the devil dealt with Peter and all the disciples immediately after this prayer was offered. Peter, to save his skin, denied his Lord just at the time when his Lord was actually on trial and needed support and help and comfort. Peter denied him and they all forsook him and fled because of a fear of consequences and the desire to avoid pain or persecution. The devil will always encourage that kind of thing and that is why our Lord spoke so often about it. Read Matthew 10 and you will find a long sermon on that very theme – 'Fear not them which kill the body, but are not able to kill the soul: but rather fear him which is able to destroy both soul and body in hell.' Fear takes various forms. For instance we say, 'If I do this, what is going to happen to me, professionally, or in business? Will I get my promotion? Will I be regarded as an odd man out? What is going to happen to my family?' Fear – it is always of the devil and that is why our Lord prayed that we might be kept in the name of God.

Then the devil's second great line of attack is an attack upon the truth, and the Bible is full of warnings about this. The devil attacks the truth by introducing false teaching. That is why, as we read in Acts 20, Paul said what he did to the elders of the Ephesian church. He could see what would happen in Ephesus after his departure. He knew of wolves that were waiting to come in with their false teaching, those men amongst their own number who were out to destroy; the devil was at the back of all that. Read the first epistle of John: it is full of warnings about this – the anti-Christs who had already arisen and were causing havoc in the church. Read in 2 Peter 2 about the people, these 'false teachers', who will insinuate themselves amongst the believers. Read the epistle of Jude with his great exhortation on this theme and all his warnings of the activity of the devil within the life of the church. Is it surprising, then, that our Lord prayed so urgently that his Father would keep his people in his name? He knew that all this was going to come – the devil with his false teaching.

But it is not always bald, false teaching. It is sometimes more subtle, coming in the form of compromise. Of course, if you stand up in a pulpit and say, 'Jesus of Nazareth was only a man, he was not the Son of God', most people would recognize it as not being the true doctrine. But if the preacher does not actually *say* anything wrong, I am afraid that there are often many Christian people who can be entirely taken in by him. It is a subtle compromise which makes a man preach the gospel without any offence in it. He talks about the death of Christ in a way that leads you to pity Christ, and to think that the preacher's picture of the cross is beautiful. But that is because there is no offence of the cross in his preaching, the devil is subtle in this. There are often men who start with a true doctrine but who end with compromise. The offence is taken out of their preaching and out of their gospel. And the same is true of the individual, the Christian member of the church. Oh, very well, we say, for the sake of unity we will not stress that as we used to. For the sake of not offending anybody we will leave out these things and use the things that are generally accepted – compromise. Oh in that way the devil has made havoc of the Christian church during the last hundred years.

And then another way in which he does this is one which I have already mentioned in another connection. He makes us resort to worldly wisdom and worldly methods in order to gain success, and we forget the name. I have no doubt that this came as a real temptation to Paul as he stood outside the city of Corinth. I am sure that he had a fight upon that road. The devil would turn to him and say, 'These people like philosophy, and rhetoric. You know all that stuff – give it to them, and they will like you, and you will have a great church.' But Paul tells the Corinthians in his first letter to them, 'I determined not to know any thing among you, save Jesus Christ, and him crucified.' He would not resort to any such methods. He kept himself to the simplicity that is in Christ, and the purity of the message and the purity of presenting the message. And this is something which he constantly repeats.

But lastly, I would remind you that the devil attacks the truth by means of encouraging schisms and divisions in the church. I am not going to stay with this matter now, because we have to come back to it when we deal with the great plea for unity. Let me just put it like this here. The cause of schism is that men and women have put something other than the truth into the position of truth. They put in the supreme position things that belong to the circumference, and the moment you do that there will be schism. Was that not the trouble with the church at Corinth? Paul deals with this in a very remarkable way in his first letter to the Corinthians. The Corinthians had been putting personality in the position of principle, saying, 'I am of Paul', or 'I am of Apollos' (1 Cor 1:12). Instead of Christ and his gospel, they put a particular preacher in the centre and therefore there was division. Again, take spiritual gifts – they were talking and arguing about which was the superior gift of the Spirit, and because some put miracles etc. in the centre, there was schism, and Paul condemns it in chapter 12, for it is dividing the body of Christ, and the devil encourages that. If he can lead us astray by putting any particular thing in the central position of our faith – a denomination or a man, a cause or a particular aspect of truth – rather than Christ himself, he will always encourage us to do so, and thereby he attacks us and divides us, and he wounds the body.

All these things, as we have seen, are simply meant to draw us away from God and his Christ; they are simply methods by which the devil tries to spoil the work of God. He did it at creation, at the beginning, he has done it ever since and he is trying to do it with the church today. God made everything and saw that it was good, and the devil came in and spoilt it all. It is no new thing; the devil is out with all his might and main to mar and to wreck and to ruin the work of Christ, and our one and greatest comfort is that our blessed Lord not only knows that, but has committed the church to his Father and has prayed and is praying the Father to keep us, to keep us in his own name, that we may be saved from the world and the flesh and the devil. Let us meditate about these things, let us realize the danger, let us realize the subtlety. Let us never allow Satan to gain the advantage over us. Let us be aware of his devices so that we may withstand him, steadfast in the faith, and thus, by the power of God in Christ through the Holy Spirit, be made more than conquerors.

12

God's Perfect Will

I pray not that thou shouldest take them out of the world, but that thou shouldest keep them from the evil (v. 15).

As we start on this final study, let me remind you of our analysis of this second section of our Lord's great high priestly prayer which he prays as he is under the very shadow of the cross. Our Lord, having prayed for himself, proceeds to pray for those he is leaving behind in this world of time, and we find he gives various reasons for praying for them. And so we have this wonderful description of the Christian, found especially in verses 6, 7 and 8 but also running right through the entire paragraph. Then we come to the petitions which he offers for them. The first petition is that God should keep them – 'Holy Father, keep through thine own name those whom thou hast given me' – though they are in the world – 'that they may be one, as we are.' He says that while he was with them he kept them all but the son of perdition – Judas – that the Scriptures might be fulfilled. And now he commits them to his Father and prays God urgently to keep them.

Our Lord asks his Father to keep them because of the world which, he says, hates them: 'I have given them thy word; and the world hath hated them, because they are not of the world, even as I am not of the world.' The world is opposed to the Christian and we have considered the various ways in which it manifests this opposition and hatred. If there is one thing, surely, that is emphasized constantly in the Scriptures, in the Old Testament and the New, it is that the Christian is a stranger and a pilgrim in this world. He is different. He does not belong to the world; he is in it but not of it. His mentality and outlook, his whole central position, are entirely different from that of the world, and it is a fact that the world hates him because of that. As our Saviour has already told these men: 'The servant is not greater than his Lord' (Jn 13:16); 'If they have called the master of the house Beelzebub, how much more shall they call them of his household?'; 'Ye shall be hated of all men for my name's sake' (Mt 10:25, 22). That is why, of course, there is a great conflict going on in this world between unseen spiritual forces, a great and mighty conflict between God and all who belong to him, and the devil and all who belong to him. And the world is controlled by the devil; he is the god of this world; he rules in the midst of men and women who belong to the world. He is 'the spirit that now worketh in the children of disobedience,' says the apostle Paul in Ephesians 2:2. The devil hates God and the Lord Jesus Christ with all his might and being and power, and he hates all who belong to him, and the result is that all who are controlled by the devil are of necessity antagonistic to those who belong to God.

There is no question at all about this. The life of our Lord proves it, the lives and experience of the apostles prove it, and the lives of the saints throughout the centuries prove it. To the extent to which a man is godly and living the life God would have him live, to that extent he will experience malignity and opposition in the world. So our Lord prays to God to keep them against all that. And he likewise prays that God should keep them from the evil one and from evil in all its forms, however it is manifested under the power of the devil. Our Lord's prayer is that God should keep us from the evil, keep us, as it were, out of the clutches of the evil one. As we saw, the devil comes to us and attacks us in various ways, filling us with pride and elation, or depressing us with despair and he works and plays upon us between these two extremes. He knows us all. He is well aware of our every mood and state and condition, he can even affect our physical frame and body and by such things can depress us and hold us down. There is no end to the ways in which the devil in all his subtlety and power is able to attack the children of God, and so our Lord prays that we may be kept.

But we must now go on to consider how it is that God keeps us. In what ways does our Lord ask his Father to do this? The first answer to that question is here in verse 15, and strangely enough we find that it is a negative answer. Now it may surprise us that our Lord should specifically have uttered this negative thought and petition. He says, I do *not* ask you to take them out of the world, that is not my request. And people are often perplexed at this. Indeed it is often the cause of much questioning and misunderstanding.

I suppose that ultimately the sin of which we are all most frequently guilty is the sin of asking certain questions which we would never ask if we were truly mature Christians. Because of our frailty and unbelief we say that there are certain things we do not and cannot understand. Here, surely, is one such question and it is one of the most common of all. Why is it that when we become Christians God does not immediately take us out of the world, especially in view of the state of the world in which we live? But consider what we are told here. If ever anyone experienced the malignity of the world our Lord did, but we see him specifically praying that the disciples should not be taken out of it, even though he knew exactly the kind of world it was. He saw it and knew it, and saw through it, in a way no one else has ever done. He knew its persecution and its scorn and its derision and all its opposition. He knew all about that, for he had experienced it, and yet, though he knew that and though he knew the weakness and the frailty of these men, he did not ask God to take them out of the world. He left them in the world knowing all about what was going to meet them and to confront them. Now that often puzzles many people. They wonder why it is that we are not immediately taken to heaven and to glory when we become Christians – and of course this is one of the questions which we ask far too often.

Another question that is asked is: why is it that when we

become Christians we are not immediately made perfect and sinless? We argue that God has power to do this. We know that God the Holy Spirit can do this, for we know that ultimately we shall be presented faultless and blameless in the presence of God. Therefore, we argue, if God has this power, and if God can completely and entirely sanctify us from all sin, why does he not do it immediately? Why, when we are born again, are we not completely delivered at once from the old man and nature and everything that belongs to sin and its polluting effect? Why are we not immediately made entirely sanctified and holy? You have often asked that question – it is one of those questions which fall into this self-same category. Why are we not entirely taken out of the world? Why are we left in this struggle and in this life?

Or take another question. Since the Lord Jesus Christ dealt with sin upon the cross and in his resurrection, why are we not automatically delivered from all the consequences of sin? As it has been dealt with finally and conquered once and for ever, why is it that its evil consequences are not removed? I refer to things such as sickness and illness and disease which are undoubtedly the consequences of sin and of the fall. Why were they not all immediately taken away? Why do we still inherit these things – the frailties, the weaknesses, the infections and all these diseases to which we are still subject in this world of time? Since sin was dealt with in the matter of guilt and so on, why was not all this removed? You notice I am putting it in question form. There are people who teach that this has been done, but that is an error and a heresy, Scripture itself makes that perfectly clear. I put it in the form of questions, and the people who ask these questions often go on to the error and the heresy.

There is also the fact of death – that is a consequence of sin. If man had not sinned death would not have entered into the world. But God has dealt with sin, so why are we still subject to death? Why does it not come to pass that people who become Christians no longer see death – why do they have to go through that? Why was death not taken right away, once and for ever, as a consequence of Calvary and the resurrection?

Or again, to ask still another of these questions: why should there have been this terrible long interval between Christ's first and second coming? If it is God's plan and purpose that Christ should come back to rid the world of all evil and sin, and conquer death, why this long interval? Nearly 2,000 years have gone and still we have this evil world and we are still confronted by all these terrible things. We believe that he is coming, but why did he not come at once? That is the kind of question we ask, and that leads us right back to a prior question, namely, why was there such a long interval between the fall of man and the first coming of Christ? That is a great question which we often put like this: we believe that even before God made the world and created man, it was his purpose to save the world. Why, then, did he allow 4,000 years to pass between the fall of man and the coming of Christ? Why all this long degraded history with its record of apparent failure and frustration? Why all the long story of the years? Why didn't he send Christ at once? These are the questions we ask and they all arise out of these words which we are considering here: 'I pray not that thou shouldest take them out of the world ...' Why not? Why should we be left in it to suffer and endure? Why is the second coming so long delayed when the whole world will be turned again into a state of paradise?

These are the questions and it is vital, therefore, that we should answer them. Now I am tempted to say that in reality there is only one answer, and that if we were what we ought to be as Christian people, this answer would be enough. The one fundamental, final answer is that it is God's way, it is the way which God has determined and the way that God has planned. And all that I shall say now is really going to lead up to that – that is the beginning and that is the end, and the position of faith is one in which man is content with God's way though he does not understand it. In other words, I really am suggesting that we should never ask these questions at all. It is impudence and impertinence on the part of feeble man to do so. We should never ask such questions because our attitude of faith should be that what God did and what God does is always right and that there is no need for us to ask the reason why. It is for us to believe and accept and above all to submit to it.

However, I believe that Scripture entitles us to give supplementary answers and it is here that we see the mercy and the condescension of God. He does not merely leave us with the words, 'That is my will and you must accept it.' He stoops to our weakness and gives us glimpses into his great and inscrutable reasons. He enables us, while still here on earth and still in our imperfection, to have some kind of inkling of what we shall see perfectly when we arrive in glory. So let us proceed to consider some of these subsidiary or supplementary answers to the question as to why God does these things in this way.

Now it is always good to start with a fact, so let me begin by saying that the great fact here is that God acts as he does because it is his will. I wonder if you have ever noticed that there are three recorded requests in Holy Scripture about which we are told that God did not grant the request? These were from three remarkable and saintly men and the interesting thing is that it was the same petition each time, it was a prayer to the effect that they should die and that they should be taken out of the world.

The first was Moses. Moses had been chosen as God's leader among the people and here he was struggling with this recalcitrant mob. He had gone up to meet God on the mountain and in his absence the people had made a golden calf and were worshipping it. Moses became frantic and said to God, in effect, 'Will you grant me my petition? If not, take me out of this life because I would sooner be dead.' His prayer was not granted.

The second was that mighty man Elijah, one of the most outstanding characters in Scripture, the man who greatly appeals to everybody because he could stand alone and defy a king and a collection of eight hundred and fifty false prophets. But in 1 Kings 19 you will see this self-same man sitting under a juniper tree thoroughly miserable and unhappy. The man who defied the whole world yesterday is today running away from a woman. He does not understand things and his prayer to God is that he should be taken out of it all. He wants to die but God does not grant him his request.

The third case is the prophet Jonah. Poor Jonah! He knew exactly the state of affairs in Nineveh. It was a terrible, sinful city and Jonah wanted it to be blotted out. God sent him to preach repentance to that city but to his amazement God said he would withhold his judgement – and Jonah did not like it. He felt that God was against him and he wanted to die. But he was not taken out of the world and he did not die. So here are three notable saints of God each of whom prayed the same prayer but God did not grant their request.

We are thus confronted by this great fact and, though we have to say that ultimately we do not know the complete reason, we do recognize that in the wisdom of God this is not his way of dealing with his people. 'I pray not that thou shouldest take them out of the world' – but, why not? Well, I think that we can feel after certain answers to that question. Why is our Lord thus concerned that God should not take the disciples out of the world? A part of the answer is that if they were removed like that, who would be left to preach the gospel to the world? Indeed, our Lord says that quite specifically – 'As thou hast sent me into the world, even so have I also sent them into the world.' God sent the Son into the world to preach the truth and to present the gospel and to make a way of salvation and now, as he is going out of the world, he is sending them into it and leaving the message with them. They are going to be the preachers, in their lives as well as with their words – they are going to represent him. As we have seen, he says, 'I am glorified in them.' Therefore they cannot ask to be taken out of the world because they are being sent there to perform this specific task.

It is so tragic to notice how often we forget that, and it is because we forget that as Christians we are God's and Christ's representatives in this world that we sometimes ask to be taken out of it. But we have a great and mighty and noble task to perform. We are the salt of the earth, we are the light of the world shining brightly amidst the gloom and despair and holding forth the word of life – if only we always realized that this is our calling and our business! If I may put it like this it may help us to understand. What if our Lord himself, when he was in this world, had turned to God and said, 'Why do you send me? I do not want to stay here, it is such a terrible, sinful, evil, dark world, let me come back to you, take me out of it'? But he never did – no, he had come deliberately to do the work, to perform the task. He knew why he had come, so he says here to the disciples, 'I did the work and you are to do the same.' That is sufficient reason in and of itself for not desiring to be taken out of the world.

Then the second reason I deduce is that there is no doubt at all but that we are left in this world because it is part of the process of our being perfected. We need to be perfected, a gradual work has to be done in all of us even after we are born again and regenerated, and God, I believe, leaves us in this world in order that we may be so perfected and prepared for him. We all need to be humbled, to be brought down to the dust. It is obviously very clear that the fact that a man is a Christian does not mean that he is entirely delivered from pride and conceit, self-centredness and self-interest; you sometimes see these things in a rampant form even among Christian people. We must be delivered from all that, and if the positive truth of the gospel does not deliver us from it, then God has another way of doing it, and he humbles us by such things as disappointment, failure, weakness, or illness.

I believe that the apostle Paul is referring to this in 2 Corinthians 12. He had had a great struggle over it. There was a danger that he might be exalted and lifted up because of the revelations that had been given to him, and God had had to deal with him by giving him what he calls 'a thorn in the flesh', which humbled him and kept him down. Paul admits it, and it is true of every one of us. We live in this world and we sometimes think that no temptation is ever going to affect us. We have risen above it – we are above and beyond these things! We are even insulted at the word that says, 'Wherefore let him that thinketh he standeth take heed lest he fall.' So, for our humbling and our good, God leaves us to ourselves. Then the devil takes advantage and we fall, down to the very dust, and it is there that God says to us, 'whom the Lord loveth he chasteneth' (Heb 12:6).

He also tries us, tries our faith to see what we are made of, as it were, and it is all part of our development. We start as children and as babes. At first everything seems to be so easy in the Christian life, but a time comes when we realize that it is not. There are many Christian people who look back with longing to the days of their conversion, but they are absolutely wrong in doing so. It is a terrible thing for us to say, 'Where is the blessedness I knew when first I saw the Lord?' We should never say that, and Cowper was a deeply depressed man when he wrote those words. But we, too, tend to say it because we rather like a life of ease; we are like spoilt children, but, thank God, our heavenly Father does not deal with us like that. Times come when we are confronted by problems and difficulties. I have heard of and known men in the ministry who, when they start, are given texts and sermons as gifts from God, but they very often find that as they go on they have to struggle much more than they did at the beginning. They have become men, and are no longer children, and it is right that they should know the difficulties. Mr Spurgeon said he found he had to work much harder in the ministry, making and preparing his sermons, when he was older than he did when he was the famous boy preacher at the age of seventeen or eighteen. It is right, it is part of this process. In other words, God has to show us ourselves, he has to reveal to us our own limitations; the babe in Christ may be happy, but he is very ignorant and he has a lot to learn. Thus, you see, a part of the process of our being made fit for heaven and glory is carried out through our being left in the world and not taken out of it.

But let me give you some other reasons which are more important. We have looked at reasons taken from our side, but there are many reasons from God's side. It is only as we are left in this world in this way that God's marvels and glories are really displayed in us and through us. I suppose that in the last analysis there is nothing that so displays the wonder of God's power than the way in which he can keep people like us as his own in this world. Have you ever thought of it like that? Have you considered the power that is necessary to keep a Christian as a Christian in this world of time, surrounded by suggestions and temptations and everything that is calculated to get him down? I would say that it is a miracle. It is a manifestation of the supernatural power of God that a Christian ever arrives in heaven at all. God leaves us in this world and shows that he has the power and the might to keep us and to hold us and to perfect that which he has commenced in us. It is a display of God's power which nothing else produces.

It also shows us his long-suffering and patience. Can you read the Old Testament without being impressed by these facets of his character? I like the verse that puts it like this – 'And about the time of forty years suffered he their manners in the wilderness' (Acts 13:18). And what a bad set of manners they were! Oh how they ill-treated God and ignored his patience, and it is equally true of us. Though we are Christians, what poor Christians we are! But how patient God is with us and how amazing his long-suffering as he listens to our questions and tolerates us. And so, while leaving us in this world, he shows the fulness and the many-sidedness of his salvation and its completeness. In Ephesians 3:10 Paul talks of the 'manifold wisdom of God', and what a perfect description that is – many-sided, variegated. You do not know what you want, but you will always find that Christ comes to you and meets you just where you are. And thus it comes to pass that as we live in this world with its trials and troubles and perplexities and problems, we come to know God in a way that we could never know him were it not that we have to go through these things. Do you not find that he is ever surprising you; that you are always making some new discovery, arriving at some fresh knowledge of his grace, because of some peculiar circumstance in which you have been placed? You have had some new experience and God has met you there in a way he has never met you before, and so you have come to know him better. He leaves us here in the world, therefore, partly to display to us the riches of his grace and the manifold character of his loving kindness and his mercy.

Those are some of the reasons, but I want to end on a practical note, and so we will consider the practical application of all this by drawing certain deductions from this great doctrine that we are considering together. The first must be that all attempts at delivering ourselves or removing ourselves from this world must be wrong. I am not here speaking about suicide (about which we would all agree) but about monasticism. Men try to deliver themselves out of this world and all its problems and trials, not only by committing suicide, but also by segregating themselves from the world and becoming anchorites and monks and hermits. The whole idea of monasticism, it seems to me, is a blank contradiction of this prayer of our Lord. It is an attempt to avoid all these truths that we have been considering together, so it must be wrong. It is unscriptural.

Moreover it seems to me that it is a complete denial of James 1:27 – 'To visit the fatherless and widows ... and to keep himself unspotted from the world.' In other words, these people want to keep themselves unspotted from the world by going into a cell or a monastery and by having a wall around them and keeping right away from the world. Not at all! We keep ourselves unspotted from the world while we are sweeping floors or going about the ordinary walks of life. Though we are in the world, we still keep ourselves unspotted from it; that is God's way, not by monasticism.

Another thing of which monasticism is obviously guilty is that it tends to externalize sin, regarding it as something that exists in the physical organization of life. It fails to realize that it is something that is within, in the realm of the spirit and the inner man. I think that many monks have discovered that even though they have left the world, the world is inside them and the world is with them in the monastery. A further fallacy, of course, is to regard what they call 'the religious life' as a vocation; you become a monk and you 'take up' the religious life as it were. Now I defy anybody to show me that teaching anywhere in Scripture. Rather, it is a blank contradiction of what the Bible teaches, because we are meant to live in the world: 'I pray not that thou shouldest take them out of the world, but that thou shouldest keep them from the evil.' The monastic view is a complete fallacy in that respect.

And the final fallacy is that it means that they are trusting to their own efforts. They believe that by going out of the world and giving themselves to nothing but prayer and fasting and good works, they find God. But you never can. They are trusting to their own life and power instead of trusting to the power of God to keep them in the world. In other words, monasticism is eventually a lack of faith in God's power. It is as good as saying that the power of God is not enough, you have to segregate yourself. If you stay in the world you become an ordinary Christian; if you want to become an extraordinary Christian, you must become a 'saint' and enter into this 'vocation'. The teaching of Scripture is that the power of God is such that he can keep a man unspotted even in 'a hell on earth'. He can keep him in the midst of it all; and not to believe that, and to think that you have to do it in other ways, is to have a lack of faith in God's power. So we must never seek to remove ourselves from the world.

My second deduction is that God's way is not to take us out of the difficulties and the trials, nor to avoid them. His way is to enable us, and to strengthen us, so that we can go through them with heads erect and undefeated, more than conquerors in them and over them. And that is a wonderful thing.

My next deduction is that we must never grumble at our lot, nor ask these doubting questions. We must rather believe that there is always a purpose in these trials, if we can but see it; we must believe that God has laid this thing upon us and that he has left us in this situation in order that we may show forth his glory. The disciples were left in the world to do that, and you and I can be certain that whatever we may be passing through at this moment is a part of God's plan and purpose for us to show forth his glory. The world may not recognize you, it may ignore and dismiss you, and others may get all that they want from the world. Do not worry about it, Christ knew something similar. The saints have experienced the same thing: 'Woe unto you, when all men shall speak well of you!' (Lk 6:26). Yes, 'And all that will live godly in Christ Jesus shall suffer persecution' (2 Tim 3:12). All is well, you are fulfilling the glory of God as you go through that trial. Paul came to see that about the thorn in the flesh. 'All right,' he says, in effect, 'I asked you three times to remove it but you are leaving it. I see now that your glory is going to be shown through me. Very well, I will glory in this infirmity. I will stop asking you to take it away. It is really when I am weak that your power is made manifest in me and through me.' So we must never grumble. We must gladly accept what he allows, and remember that we are fulfilling the glory of God.

I can put that still more strongly. We must never desire peace and ease in this world. As the hymn says:

> Shrink not Christian, will ye yield,
> Will ye quit the painful field,
> Will ye flee in danger's hour,
> Know ye not your Captain's power?
> *H.K. White*
> *F.S. Colquhoun*

Oh we must never 'quit the painful field' or 'flee in danger's hour'. We must never change our position or go out of the situation simply because it is difficult. It is in the difficult situations that God manifests his power. Now it may be God's will for you to change your position. That is all right as long as it is *God's* will for you; but never take the decision yourself simply because things are difficult. Never hand in your resignation because things are going against you. Never come out of anything simply because it is problematical. Stay there until God moves you. He leaves his people in the world; he does not take them out of it.

And that leads me to my last point, which is that in the midst of all these situations and problems we must always look to him and to his power; we must always look to the ultimate that is destined. We know we are going on to glory – 'We have a building of God, an house not made with hands, eternal in the heavens' (2 Cor 5:1). So, whatever may be happening here, keep your eye on that, hold on to it. You know that he has a purpose in leaving you where you are, but you know, too, that you are going on. Keep your eye on him and on that for which you are destined. And if you do that, you will be able to put into practice my last exhortation – let us therefore live every moment of our lives to the full. Never let us waste a second of God's time in asking these foolish, unnecessary questions, in grumbling or in complaining. Having settled this great question in principle, once and for ever, let us never ask it again, but let us take every moment and live it to the maximum. Let us manifest the praises of Christ and of God every split second of our lives, redeeming the time, and clutching at the opportunities.

Look at it like this. Instead of saying, 'Why does God leave me in this world? Why is he leaving me here for another five, ten, or twenty years?' Rather say this: I have another five, ten, twenty years to manifest his praises, to tell his sinful world about him and I am going to take every opportunity I can to do that. Time is passing, it is short, there is so much to be done and so little time in which to do it. So I will live my life to the full and to the maximum, thanking him that he has counted me worthy to fulfil my station in life as his servant, thanking him that Christ has ever sent me, as God the Father sent him, to do these things in the world. I see myself, therefore, as an imitator of Christ, as a re-enactor of the life of Christ.

Yes, let me rise to the height to which the apostle Paul rose in Colossians 1. He said that the afflictions of Christ were being brought up to the full in his body. Paul was making up that which remained of the sufferings of Christ and he regarded that as the greatest privilege that he was allowed in this life and world. He meant by that, that Christ had left him here as his representative, to be a kind of Christ-man, to be living the Christ-like life to the glory of God the Father.

'I pray not that thou shouldest take them out of the world.' Can you say 'Amen' to that? Let us seek to do that and let us thank him that he has sufficient confidence in us and in the power of his Father to leave us even in a world like this, knowing that he can keep us. And in the meantime let us ask him to enable us to serve him and to tell forth his praise and his glory in the world. Amen.

PART THREE

SANCTIFIED
through the TRUTH

1

The Special People of God

Sanctify them through thy truth: thy word is truth. As thou hast sent me into the world, even so have I also sent them into the world. And for their sakes I sanctify myself, that they also might be sanctified through the truth (Jn 17 vv. 17–19).

In order that we may understand that petition offered on behalf of his followers by our Lord on the eve of his death, let me very briefly remind you of the context. Our Lord is about to go to his death on the cross, about to go out of this world back to heaven and to the glory that he had shared with his Father from all eternity, so he prays for these men whom he is leaving behind him in the world and he gives various reasons for praying for them. He reminds his Father of who they are and what they are; then he comes to his particular petitions for them and his first petition is that God should keep them. He says that he has kept them himself while he has been with them and that none of them is lost 'but the son of perdition; that the scripture might be fulfilled'. Now, however, he is going back to God, and his great prayer is that God should keep them from the polluting influence of the world, and especially from the evil – that is, the evil one. When we considered this great first petition,[1] we noticed that our Lord was very careful to put it in a negative form, as we find in the fifteenth verse: 'I pray not that thou shouldest take them out of the world, but that thou shouldest keep them from the evil.' We considered the various reasons that are given here, and in the Scripture everywhere, why we should never pray to be taken out of the world and why it is for our good and for the glory of God and the extension of his kingdom, that we, his people, should be in this world, and should remain here and use our lives to the full while we are left here.

Now here in this seventeenth verse we come to the second petition: 'Sanctify them through thy truth: thy word is truth.' But though I call this the 'second' petition, it is, of course, intimately connected with, and is, in a sense, a continuation of the first. His great desire is that his people should be kept by God, yes, but not by being taken out of the difficulties and problems. How then are they to be kept? And the answer is that they are to be kept by being *sanctified;* not by being taken out of the world, not by the false solution of monasticism— by a desire to quit life somehow or other—that is not God's way of keeping his people. His method is to ask his Father to sanctify them in the way that is illustrated and emphasised here.

We must, therefore, consider this. What does our Lord mean when he prays, 'Sanctify them through thy truth'—or 'in thy truth'—'thy word is truth'? What is 'to sanctify'? We need to be very careful at this point in our definition of the term, because we must interpret it bearing in mind that the same word is used in the nineteenth verse: 'And for their sakes I sanctify myself, that they also might be sanctified through the truth.' In verse 19 our Lord uses exactly the same word about himself as he uses with regard to his followers here. So we must start by arriving at a true definition of what is meant by 'sanctify'.

Now it is generally agreed that there are two main senses in which this word is used throughout the Bible. The first sense of 'sanctify'—and we must always put this one first because it is the one most emphasised in Scripture—is *to set apart for God, and for God's service.* So you will find that this term 'to sanctify' is not only used of men; it is used even of a mountain, the holy mount on which the Law was given to Moses. Mount Sinai was sanctified, it was set apart for a special function and purpose, in order that God might use it to give his revelation of the Law. The word is used, too, of buildings, and of vessels, instruments and utensils, and various things that were used in the Tabernacle and the Temple. Anything that is devoted to, or set aside for God and for his service is sanctified. So, you see, there is a double aspect to this primary meaning of the word. It means, first, a separation from everything that contaminates and perverts, and the second, positive, aspect is that something or someone is devoted wholly to God and to his use.

Now it is quite obvious that the latter aspect is the only conceivable meaning to this term in verse 19. When our Lord says 'and for their sakes I sanctify myself', he means just that, and nothing else. He cannot be referring to inward purification, because he was already perfect. The word means exactly the same thing in John 10:36 where we read, 'Say ye of him, whom the Father hath sanctified, and sent into the world, Thou blasphemest; because I said, I am the Son of God?' When our Lord tells the people that God the Father had sanctified him, and sent him into the world, he means that the Father had set him apart, it is that sense of the word 'sanctify'.

You will find that this primary meaning of the word sanctify is often applied to Christian people. Read, for instance, 1 Corinthians 6:11, where Paul tells the Corinthians that there was a time when some of them were guilty of terrible sin— drinking, adultery, etc. 'But,' he says, 'ye are washed, but ye are sanctified, but ye are justified in the name of the Lord Jesus, and by the Spirit of our God.' You notice he says they are sanctified before he says they are justified. Now with our superficial and glib ideas about sanctification, we always say, 'Justification first and sanctification afterwards.' But Paul puts sanctification first, which means that they have been set apart by God, and taken out of the world. That is the primary meaning of sanctification and in that sense it comes before justification.

Or take 1 Peter 1:2: 'Elect according to the foreknowledge of God the Father, through sanctification of the Spirit, unto obedience and sprinkling of the blood of Jesus Christ'—sanctification comes before the believing, and the sprinkling with the blood and the justification. So in its primary meaning this word is a description of our position. It means that as Christians we are separated from the world. Our Lord has already said that in verse 16—let me emphasise again the importance of watching every single statement in this prayer and noticing the perfect cohesion of it all—'they are not of the world'. Now he says, 'Sanctify them through thy truth.' They have been set apart, he says in effect; set them still more apart: it means this separation from the world. God said to the children of Israel, 'Thou art an holy people unto the Lord thy God: the Lord thy God hath chosen thee to be a special people unto himself' (Deut 7:6). And that is applied in 1 Peter 2:9 to the Christian church: 'Ye are,' it is said again, 'a peculiar people', a special possession for the Lord. It does not mean that the nation of Israel was sinless, but it does mean that they had been set apart as God's peculiar, special people; and the same is true of the church and of all Christian people. We are a holy nation, set apart for God and for his service and for his purpose. That is the primary meaning.

But there is a second meaning and this is equally clear from the Scriptures. This is that we are not only regarded as holy, we are *made holy* and, obviously, we are made holy because that is how we are regarded. God sets us apart as his peculiar people, and because of this we must be a holy people: 'Ye shall be holy: for I the Lord your God am holy,' says God (Lev 19:2). So that we are to be holy because we are holy, and that is the great New Testament appeal for sanctification. So this second meaning is that God does a work within us, a work of purifying, of cleansing, and of purging, and this work is designed to fit us for the title which has been put upon us. We have been adopted, taken out of the world and set apart, and we are now being conformed increasingly to the image, the pattern, of the Lord Jesus Christ; so that we may in truth be the people of God: in reality as well as in name. So this is obviously a progressive work. The first is something that is done once and for all, and it is because we are set apart that we are justified. God has looked upon his people from all eternity and has set them apart—we dealt with that at great length in verses

6, 7 and 8.[1] He sanctified them before the foundation of the world, and it is because of that, that they are justified, and, again, because of that, they are sanctified in this second sense.

So the question is, which of these two meanings is to be attached to the word in the seventeenth verse? It seems to me that there is only one adequate answer to that: obviously both meanings are involved. Let me put it like this: as his followers we are separated from the world—'They are not of the world, even as I am not of the world'—they are separated for God's special service, to represent him in the world. For he says in verse 18, 'As thou hast sent me into the world, even so have I also sent them into the world.' He has already said that he is to be glorified in us and through us; we have been set apart for this special task of glorifying Christ, of bearing the message to an unbelieving world; and because we have been set apart for that, we must be fitted to do it. We must be kept from the evil, and from the tarnishing effect of the world. We must be fit to represent the Father, to proclaim his message and to glorify his dear Son. In other words, this petition is that we should become more and more the special people of God. Our very task and calling demands that we must be a holy people since we cannot represent a holy God unless we ourselves are holy.

Therefore, we are obviously here face to face with the great New Testament doctrine of sanctification. Now I shall not use this as an occasion for giving a full-orbed description and account of that doctrine—although in a sense I shall be doing so, because I shall be dealing with fundamental principles—but at this point we shall deal with the subject solely in terms of what we are told about it in these three verses.

So then, let me give you the divisions as I understand them. We shall not deal with them all in this study, but let me give you the complete outline. Our Lord here deals with three great matters with regard to this subject of our sanctification. First: *Why* does our Lord pray for our sanctification? And a complete answer is given here to that question. The first answer is

---

[1] Volume 2, *Safe in the World* (Crossway Books, 1988)

that he does so because that is the way in which we are to be kept from the world and from the evil. He also prays for it because of the task which has been allotted to us (v.18), and thirdly, he prays for it because the whole object of his going to the death of the cross is that we might be sanctified—'And for their sakes I sanctify myself, that they also might be sanctified ... ' (v.19).

The second great matter which is dealt with here is the *method of sanctification*: 'Sanctify them,' he says, 'through thy truth'—in thy truth—'thy word is truth.' The way in which God sanctifies us is obviously vitally important, and our Lord deals with it here; we are to be sanctified in the truth.

And the third subject with which he deals is the question of *what it is that ultimately makes our sanctification possible*: and again he gives the answer in verse 19: 'for their sakes I sanctify myself.' Without that we never could be sanctified, it would be quite impossible. So the whole basis of sanctification is ultimately our Lord's action and work on our behalf, supremely upon the cross.

So let us then start our consideration of this great matter by dealing with that first question, though we shall not deal with the whole of it in this study. The first question is, Why does our Lord pray thus for the sanctification of his followers, indeed, as he says in verse 20, of all his people, you and me and all Christian people at all times? As we saw, his answer is that he does so in order that we may be kept from the world and its polluting, tarnishing effect; and above all that we may be kept from the evil one. 'I pray not that thou shouldest take them out of the world, but that thou shouldest keep them from the evil.' And this is God's way of doing that.

Now we come here to the vital subject of the relationship of the Christian to the evil which is in this world. It is a subject which is very often misunderstood, and this has constantly been so throughout the long history of the church; indeed, I suggest to you that it is very frequently misunderstood at the present time. So let me, therefore, put it in what I regard as the most definite form. What is the relationship of the church, and of the Christian, to general morality? What is their relationship to measures which are designed to produce and to preserve the overall moral condition of society? What is to be the relationship of the church and the Christian to councils dealing with moral issues, to temperance societies and organisations designed to defend the observance of the Sabbath and things of that kind? There are large numbers of such organisations in the world at this present time. In the light of what we are told here about the relationship of the Christian and the church to the world, and to the polluting effect of evil, it seems to me that we must think about this question, and I would like to put the following consideration to you.

Let me put it first of all in the form of a blunt assertion which I shall proceed to justify. My reply with regard to the relationship of the church and the individual Christian to such matters and organisations is that the Christian's interest in such things is not direct but indirect. Let me put it in this way: all these matters are a part of the function of the state and not of the church as church, nor of the Christian as Christian—of the Christian as a citizen of the state, certainly, but not of the Christian qua Christian.

Let me then show you the value of these things. The functions of the state are of necessity good because the state has been appointed by God; let us never forget that. It is therefore a good thing to point out things which are wrong. Some organisations quote from statistics and show the harmful effect of certain practices; temperance societies, for instance, prove the evil effects of alcohol. Again, some societies are concerned to show that if a man works seven days a week, his work will be less effective than if he works only six. It is a good thing to give the body physical rest and they use that as an argument for Sunday observance. These things are perfectly all right and we should be glad of them and pay due attention to them. Teaching about morality, in and of itself, is right. It is good to warn people against the consequences and the dangers of wrong actions, and it is right that the law of the land should be enforced. It is wrong to break the law, and it should be the business of all citizens to see that the law of the land and of the statute book is enforced.

I want to go further: it is right that the state should enforce God's law, because the state derives its own being from God. Christian people, let us never forget this. The state is not a human contrivance, it is not man who has conceived the idea of the state and of law, it is God who ordained it. God has ordained the bounds and the habitation of every nation; God has called magistrates and the powers that be, and put them into being. I can say, therefore, that as God has organised the state, indeed all the states in the world, it is the business of all to see to it that the state does its work properly. And one of the duties of the state is, therefore, to see that God's name is honoured and glorified, and that God's day is kept.

And my next step is, obviously, that if all that is right, it is therefore the business of the Christian, as a citizen of the state, to see that all that is done. It is not right to say that because a man is a Christian he should have nothing to do with politics or to say that legislation is thoroughly unscriptural. 'Ah,' says someone, 'politics is a dirty game.' But that is the very reason why Christians should speak out, for if God has decreed that the state is the way in which the world should be governed, Christian people should be concerned to see that it is done in the right and true way. One often wonders whether what is so frequently said about national and local politics is not true simply because so many Christian men and women find politics difficult and unpleasant, and are guilty of avoiding it all. It is the business of the citizen to see that the state functions in the best way and one of the functions of the state is to remind men of God, and to see that the rulers are God-fearing people.

But you will see at once that the purpose of all this is simply to set a limit to sin and to the results of sin and wrongdoing. All that I have been describing can do nothing more than control sin and keep it within bounds. I think it is obvious that it is an entirely negative work. All these enactments and all the councils and committees concerned with morality, and the Lord's Day Observance Society, and all these movements, can never make anybody a Christian. It is a very great sin to confuse law and grace. These movements are really only concerned with law, and it is their function to keep people under the law until they come under grace. And that is the right thing to do. People say that you cannot, by an act of Parliament, make a man worship God, but you can prevent him from desecrating God's Day, so you can and should keep him under the law until he comes under grace.

It is because of this, then, that I go on to say that really these laws and regulations and various other things have nothing to do with the Christian as such, and that is why I said earlier on that these things are not primarily the business of the church. That is also why I, as a minister of Christ and as a minister of the church, never speak on temperance platforms. I have never spoken for any one of these organisations designed to observe the Sabbath, nor have I ever spoken on a morality platform. My reason is that it is the business of the church to preach the gospel and to show what I would call, with Paul, 'a more excellent way'. That is why the church must always be very careful to ensure that nothing she does or says should ever detract from or compromise her message and her gospel. The church derives her power entirely and solely from God and in no sense from the state, or from the law. If there is one thing about which we should be more jealous than anything else it is that within the church we recognise no law, no leader, no ultimate king save the Lord Jesus Christ. He is the sole head of the church—no state, no man, no monarch, no one else, but the Lord himself.

The church, in other words, must never hide herself behind the law of the land and she must never try to enforce her message by using the law of the land, for that is to compromise her gospel. It is to make the unbeliever out in the world say, 'Ah these people are trying to force this upon us, they are using the law in order to get it done.' No, at all costs the church must keep her message pure and clean, and she must take her stand upon the purity of the gospel and upon that alone. Indeed I do not hesitate to go so far as to say that the church, claiming as she does that the gospel is the power of God unto salvation, must be prepared to say that her gospel will work in spite of the world, whatever its state, whatever its condition; that even if hell be let loose on the face of the earth, her gospel is still powerful.

'But wait a minute,' says someone, 'don't you think that you ought to see that these other things may help you to preach the gospel? It is an easier thing to preach the gospel to good people than to bad.' As a preacher of the gospel I must reject that. I would query, as a matter of fact, whether it is easier to preach the gospel to good people than to flagrant sinners. I think that historically the opposite is probably true. But apart from historical facts like that, I must stand on the basis that the gates of hell shall not prevail against the church; that as the power of the church is the power of the Holy Spirit, it matters not what the world may be like, for this gospel is the power of God unto salvation, and in order to get right down into the dregs and do its own work, it needs no help from the state. It does not need to hide itself behind the law, because it can stand on its own feet and trust in the power of the living God.

But to look at it a little more particularly, let me put it like this. The Christian, is not sanctified in those ways at all, but in a much more positive way: the gospel way. In sanctification the Christian relies upon the work of God in his soul. 'Sanctify them,' says our Lord, in effect, to his Father. 'It is your work, it is something that, ultimately, you alone can do.' We rely upon God's work, and, of course, this work of God in the soul is regeneration; it is the making of a new man, the creating of a new being, the giving of a new life. So the gospel way of attacking this problem is not negative, like that of the state, but positive.

Let me elaborate that a little by putting it in the form of a few propositions. The gospel and the church are not so much interested in less sin, as in more and positive holiness. All the other movements I have been describing are interested in avoiding sin, but the Christian life is about sanctification. Though a man may refrain from all worldly pleasures, and may never drink, though he may never, even, do any of the things which are wrong in and of themselves, yet, if he does not see himself as a vile, hopeless sinner who is saved only by the shed blood of the Lord Jesus Christ, he is as lost and damned as the most profligate sinner in the world. The church and the Christian should not be interested only, or even primarily, in the general social effects of salvation, but in the fact that men and women should be brought nearer to God, and should live for his glory. When the church gives the world the impression that she is interested in revival only in order to heal certain moral sores, she is denying her own message. I am not primarily interested in revival in order that the streets of our cities may be cleansed; I am interested in it because I believe that for any man not to glorify God is an insult to God. I know that such a man is held bound, and my desire for him is that he may come to know God and glorify him in his daily life. The church is not interested primarily in the social consequences of irreligion. As I read my history, I see that it was because our fathers and grandfathers made that very error, towards the end of the Victorian era, that Christendom is in its present position. They became so interested in social conditions that they forgot this primary truth. They thought that if everybody was kept in order by certain Acts of Parliament, all would be well. But that is morality, and not Christianity.

So let me come to my next proposition. The church, and the Christian, and the gospel, are not so much concerned about removing the occasions for sin, as in removing from man the desire to sin. 'I pray not that thou shouldest take them out of the world, but that thou shouldest keep them from the evil ... Sanctify them ... ' Our Lord is saying, in effect, 'I am not so concerned that you should take the occasion for sin away but that you should take out of man the desire to take advantage of the occasion.' You see the difference? The gospel of Jesus Christ does not so much take the Christian out of the world, as take the world out of the Christian. That is the point. 'Sanctify them': whatever the world is like around and about them, if the world is not in them, the world outside them will not be able to affect them. That is the glory of the gospel; it makes a man free in the midst of hell.

Or again let me put it like this: the gospel is not so much concerned about changing the conditions as about changing the man. Oh the tragedy of the folly and the foolishness that has been spoken about this! They say, 'But surely you must clear up the slums before these people can become Christians?' My friends, one of the most glorious things I have ever seen is a man who has become a Christian in the slums, and then, though remaining in the same place, has transformed his home and house there. You need not change the man's conditions before you change the man—thank God, the gospel can change the man in spite of the conditions.

Do not misunderstand me. I started by saying that it is the business of the state to change the conditions. I am now talking of the function of the church *qua* church, and I would finally put it in this way: our main concern should be not so much to limit the power of evil, as to increase the power of godliness within us. Let me give an illustrataion at this point. The gospel is not primarily concerned to remove the sores of infection, or to put us out of the danger of infection; what the gospel does is to build up our resistance to infection to such a point that it renders us immune to it. The church is not concerned with trying to destroy the infection. Until our Lord returns again the infection will be there; until Satan is cast into the lake burning with fire, the infection will continue. You cannot stop it. It will be there in spite of all your councils and committees. The Christian is not primarily concerned about that. The business of the Christian and the church and the gospel is to see that you and I take so much of the pure milk of the word and the strong meat of the word that our resistance is built up to such an extent that we can, as it were, stay in a house of infectious disease, and be absolutely immune. The germs are there, yes, but we are filled with these anti-bodies that destroy them the moment they attack us.

'Sanctify them'—that is sanctification, and its whole approach is not negative, but entirely positive. Sanctification means that we become like the Lord Jesus Christ. He was so immune that he could sit with publicans and sinners and not be contaminated by them. People could not understand it, the

Pharisees could not understand it. 'This man is a friend of publicans and sinners,' they said. But because of his resistance, our
Lord could sit there without danger at all; and what our Lord
prays is that we may be made like him. He says, 'As thou hast
sent me into the world, even so have I also sent them into the
world.' 'Sanctify them.' Make them like me, render them so
immune from the assaults of temptation that whenever an
attack comes they will always be guarded against it. 'I pray not
that thou shouldest take them out of the world, but that thou
shouldest keep them from the evil', and that is the ultimate way
in which we are kept. We are to be sanctified and holy; we are to
become like him, charged with his power and filled with his
holiness and righteousness, knowing God and walking with
him in the light. And as long as we do that, the world will hold
no dangers for us. Though in it, we shall not be of it; we shall be
walking through it in the light with God.

2

Sanctification and Evangelism

Sanctify them through thy truth: thy word is truth. As thou hast sent me into the world, even so have I also sent them into the world. And for their sakes I sanctify myself, that they also might be sanctified through the truth (vv. 17, 18, 19).

We come now to consider the second great reason which our Lord deduces for praying thus for the sanctification of his people. It is that *our sanctification is absolutely essential to true evangelism.* You notice how he puts it: 'Sanctify them through thy truth: thy word is truth.' Why? Well, 'As thou hast sent me into the world even so have I sent them into the world'—and that is his second reason. Now we must remind ourselves that this question of evangelism is one that applies to us all. I would again point out that in verse 20 our Lord says, 'Neither pray I for these alone'—lest we might think that he was only praying for the apostles – 'but for them also which shall believe on me through their word.' In other words, he includes all Christian people everywhere, always, and at all times and in all places.

It is, therefore, a fundamental teaching of the Scriptures that as Christians we are all saved, not only that we may be safe, but also in order that God may use us in the salvation of others. That is something which is very clear throughout Scripture; it is God's way of evangelising, his way of saving men. He could have adopted other means, but this is the one that he has ordained and chosen, namely, that the work of salvation should be carried on through human instrumentality. This is something that applies to us all; it is not the prerogative or the special work only of those who are called upon to preach. No, it is the task of all the members of the Christian church.

Our Lord has already been saying that in different ways; he has been praying for his followers and has given this as one of his reasons for doing so. He says, 'All mine are thine, and thine are mine, and I am glorified in them' (v. 10). It is through Christian people that the Lord Jesus is glorified; that is why he is so concerned about these people. Let us remember that the world knows nothing about him apart from us; it gets to know him through us, and judges him by what it sees in us. Indeed, he puts it still more specifically by saying that even as God had sent him into the world to manifest the glory of God, now he sends his people into the world in exactly the same way, so that he may thus be magnified and glorified through them. So then we must recognise that the plain and clear teaching of Scripture is that every single Christian person is an evangelist.

I think that this is perhaps the thing of all things that needs to be emphasised at this present time. Christianity spread at the beginning, as we see in Acts and in early church history, mainly as the result of the influence of Christian individuals. Their method, above all, was that of cellular infiltration. The comparison is often made that Christianity spread at the beginning in exactly the same way as Communism is spreading in the modern world; not by holding great mass meetings, but by one person influencing the next person; two people working at a bench and one talking to the other almost unobserved. It is as quiet as the spread of leaven in flour; that is the kind of way it happens. It happened like that in the first century, and it has also happened like that in all periods of true revival and reawakening; the influence of one person upon another. And it seems to me that this is the only hope for the world at the present time, that we shall find again that the Christian message spreads through the influence, the speaking, and the activity of the individual Christian. Our Lord does not argue about this, he just states it: his teaching is that this question of our sanctification is absolutely essential in order that we may truly and properly do that work of evangelism.

We cannot but notice the striking and almost alarming contrast between our Lord's ideas and the modern idea of how this work is to be done. In all the churches and denominations there is a great deal of talk about evangelism; we see it in the newspapers; it is spoken of everywhere. Here are we, facing this question of evangelism, and here is our Lord facing the identical question with regard to his followers: but notice the striking contrast in the approach. As we consider this problem of how the world is to be evangelised, we immediately think in terms of organisations and methods; that, we say, is what is needed. The problem is difficult, so we must now begin to sit down and plan, and set up a number of committees and organisations. Then we must consider how this message can be made attractive. The modern man always tends to think psychologically, so he has to be approached in a particular manner. We must study him, so perhaps it is a good thing to send ministers to work in factories in order that they may know the outlook of the people they intend to evangelise. It is a question of salesmanship and so we study our methods very carefully in order that we may become highly efficient and effective. We want to know what people like, especially the young people. Do they like a certain amount of entertainment? Then they must have it, if it is going to attract them. Then we must get into training, teaching members of the church how to evangelise, we must give them courses of instruction.

There is, therefore, tremendous activity in the Christian church at the present time over this question of evangelism. Our newspapers sometimes comment on it; our religious papers are full of it and all the interest is upon organisation. That, I think you will agree with me, is the attitude of the church today, speaking generally, to the problem of evangelism and evangelisation. But you notice our Lord's method – what a striking contrast! There is the great world, here is a handful of Christian people. They are going to be sent to evangelise that world – how are they to do it? What is the first thing to consider? You notice what our Lord puts first: it is none of the things I have been mentioning. Rather, it is sanctification: sanctify them, for the work needs to be done in them before it can ever be done in the world. Our Lord starts with his own people, and the supreme thing in the matter of evangelism, according to him, is that his followers should be truly sanctified. I do not know what you feel, but there is nothing that appals me so much in the present situation, as the almost incredible way in which Christian people seem to ignore entirely the teaching of the Scriptures with regard to methods of evangelism: the Scriptures might very well never have been written. In the Scriptures, from beginning to end, the method is always the one that is emphasised here. The concentration of the Scripture is upon the messenger, not on his external methods, but on his character and his being, and on his relationship to God.

There are endless illustrations of this. I just select one or two at random. Take the case of Gideon. A mighty enemy army was facing the Children of Israel, and at first Gideon collected an army of 32,000 people. Then God began to reduce them until in the end there were only 300. God in effect said to Gideon, 'I am not going to do this through that great army of 32,000, but in my way.' So he just reduced the 32,000 to 300 and then he sent them out, not with great armaments, but with pitchers with lamps inside them, along with trumpets to blow; and with that ridiculous equipment they conquered the army of the enemy. That is God's way. God has always done his greatest things through remnants. If there is one doctrine that runs through the Scriptures more prominently than any other it is the doctrine of 'the remnant'. How often God has done everything with just one man. You remember the story in 1 Samuel 14 of Jonathan and his armour bearer? They did not spend their time arguing about the condition of the enemy: one man, with his armour bearer, trusting in the living God, could conquer an entire army! It is the great message of Scripture. It is the thing you find constantly in the Prophets. Jeremiah had to stand practically alone in his age and generation. Amos had to do the same thing – that is God's way.

And when you come to the New Testament, what do you find? You find one man, John the Baptist, living in the wilderness, an odd man, and it is through that man that God started this mighty work. Then you go on and read the account of the beginning of the Christian church as we find it in Acts. Judged by our modern ideas and modern methods the thing seems utterly ludicrous. Who were these first disciples, these apostles, these first preachers? Ignorant men, unlearned, untutored, untrained, yet the Lord called them and committed his message and work to such people. He sent them out into that ancient world, and out of this handful, in the hand of God, these mighty things were done. And why? Because they were sanctified, because they were filled with the Holy Spirit. That is what is emphasised here and everywhere; 'not with wisdom of words,' writes Paul to the Corinthians, not with human understanding, but '... in demonstration of the Spirit and of power'; that is the thing that works.

The apostle Paul says of himself—and he tells us that the Corinthians were also saying of him – that his presence was weak, that he had no personality at all, and that he was not a good speaker (1 Cor 2:3; 2 Cor 10:10). Yet it was through a man like that that the gospel first came to Europe and led to those mighty results. It was because the man was sanctified; he was filled with the Spirit of God and God could use him and bring the enemy strongholds crashing down to the ground. Sanctify them, says our Lord, as they face this task of evangelism.

I could very easily go on to illustrate the same thing in the long history of the Christian church. If you read the story of the church throughout the ages, you will find that it has always been like this. Do you realise that the Protestant Reformation came originally from one man, Martin Luther? One man in God's hand can do everything. As an American put it in the last century, 'One with God is a majority'; no matter how many are on the other side. You find that this is the teaching of the Scriptures and this is the teaching throughout the history of the world.

Take one of the most striking examples in modern history,

the great evangelical awakening of 200 years ago. The moral condition of this country was as bad then as it is today. But what happened? What made the change? Well it began with just a handful of men who met together in Oxford to form what they called 'The Holy Club'. These men did not meet together to plan and organise, but to get to know God, to become more holy. Their one desire was to know God better and to be more like him, to be sanctified. So they formed 'The Holy Club' and it was hurled at them as an epithet of abuse—'Methodists'! But that is God's way and it is the only way; it must be the way. God has always done his work like this by separating people, separating them unto himself. That is the meaning of sanctification, God dealing with them and so turning them into instruments that he can use to carry out his work.

This must of necessity be the only way, and here are some of the reasons for this. Our Lord says here that this is the only way of preserving any true unity in the church. The church is only really experiencing unity when she is truly spiritual; this unity is the unity of the Spirit and the bond of peace, not a mechanical unity. The Bible is not interested in external unity. The essential unity that the Bible seeks is that of the Spirit. It is this pure relationship between the various parts of the body that really matters. So it is vital that we should be sanctified, in order that we should have true unity of spirit.

But there is another obvious reason why this is God's way. Evangelism is done through the individual Christian because the man of the world observes the individual Christian. We live in an age when the world tells us—and we must accept its statement—that it is not interested in preaching. But there is one thing the world is always interested in, and that is life and living; and the world today is outside the church for this reason: 'It is all very well for those men to preach, but what happens in practice?' That is what the man of the world says and we must listen to him in this respect. He says, 'I see no point in being a Christian. What have Christian people got that I have not got? Are they more moral? Are they kinder and more loving? Are they less spiteful? Are they less snobbish? What does Christianity do to people who claim to be Christian?' And those are perfectly fair questions. Therefore, the first great step in evangelising is that we should start with ourselves and become sanctified.

Let us imagine that as the result of some great meetings we collect a crowd of people. What are they going to find when they come into the church? Are they going to find something that substantiates the message? If our lives contradict our message there is no point in our preaching or speaking. No, as Peter puts it, in 1 Peter 2:11–12, 'Dearly beloved, I beseech you as strangers and pilgrims, abstain from fleshly lusts which war against the soul. Having your conversation honest among the Gentiles: that, whereas they speak against you as evildoers, they may by your good works, which they shall behold, glorify God in the day of visitation.' You know, he says, that these people are not Christians, and that they are saying all kinds of things against you. Now prove by your life and by your work that they are wrong, and attract them.

Again we know very well that this is something which is not only true in theory but also in practice. When the man of the world sees that you and I have got something that he obviously has not got, when he finds us calm and quiet when we are taken ill; when he finds we can smile in the face of death; when he finds about us a poise, a balance, an equanimity and a loving, gentle quality; when he finds we are immune to the 'slings and arrows of outrageous fortune', he will begin to take notice. He will say, 'That man has got something,' and he will begin to enquire as to what it is. And he will want it. For the modern man, though he may be putting up a bold front, is really unhappy within himself. He wants this 'something'. He does not know what it is, but when he sees it, he is ready to listen. Mere talk, mere preaching alone, is not going to influence him; we must demonstrate these things in our daily life and living.

Let me illustrate this from one actual case. I remember once in a church which I knew very well, I was being entertained by a lady who seemed to be one of the leading lights in the church, and to my astonishment I found that her husband never went near the place at all. I subsequently discovered that the probable reason was that the lady, while very active and busy in church work, was failing lamentably in certain practical aspects – she did not always pay her grocer's bill, for example. Yes, she was a great church worker but she was negligent in matters like that. Subsequently this lady, who had only been a nominal Christian, really became a true Christian. And what happened next? Only six weeks after his wife's conversion, and without anyone asking or pleading with him, the husband began to attend that place of worship. He now came because he saw that something had happened to his wife. There was no need for anyone to say anything: he saw the genuine thing, he saw the change in her, and then he began to wonder what had happened and so he came to see for himself. That is sanctification. If Christians are to evangelise the world, they themselves must be right, there must be no contradiction between the message and the life. This is vital, and we know perfectly well that failure here is probably the major reason why so many people adopt a kind of cynicism about the Christian faith and message at the present time. All our elaborate efforts to get people to come to church are going to be useless if, when they come, they find the message contradicted within the church herself.

But, I suppose, the ultimate reason why our sanctification is vital for evangelism is that God can only use people who are sanctified: the vessel must be clean and it must be 'fit and meet for the Master's use'. Let us face the facts: there is nothing that is really going to touch the world as it is today except a mighty revival of the Spirit of God. You may think that I am being pessimistic, but I do not hesitate to prophesy that all efforts and all organisations, whether we invoke the aid of the press or not, will come to nothing. I have watched so many campaigns, and the situation of the church has gone steadily down in spite of them all, and that will continue. Nothing but the operation of the Spirit of God can possibly deal with the situation, nothing else at all; and the Spirit of God works through clean vessels and clean channels. He will not work in any other way. It is so plain and clear, and if only men and women would put all the energy that they are ready to put into organisations, into seeking God and living in his presence and becoming truly sanctified, then revival would come at once. But we are willing to do anything rather than this; the thing that God puts first is the thing we never mention – sanctification.

So I suggest that if we are concerned about the present state of affairs we must all ask ourselves this question: If my life is not influencing others and bringing them to Christ, why is it not? My friends, you do not need a course of instruction in how to evangelise people – such a thing, were it not tragic, would indeed be ludicrous! Do you think that that was done 200 years ago? Do you think the early Christians attended special coaching classes? Of course they did not! What happened was that they became true Christians and inevitably they were evangelists. When a man has the Holy Spirit within him he does not need instruction, he does it! It has always been like that and we are no different. We are not a special category of Christian. The Christian is the same in every age and generation and the world is always the same. No, we do not need to organise the thing; we need to start with ourselves and to be in such a relationship with God that he can use us. There should be a kind of radiance about us, and something emanating from us, which, when people meet us, makes them say, 'What is it in this man or woman? What is this peculiar, strange thing?' When people are sanctified, they will act as evangelists.

We have seen then that sanctification is necessary to keep us from the evil one, and that it is necessary for evangelism. Now let me say a word about the third great reason which our Lord gives for praying for the sanctification of his people. This is that our sanctification is God's ultimate purpose for us: 'For their sakes I sanctify myself, that [in order that] they also might be sanctified through the truth.' This again is something you find running right through the Scriptures: 'This is the will of God, even your sanctification' (1 Thess 4:3). You notice how explicitly our Lord puts it in his prayer. He says, I am going to the death of the cross, I am going to face that last agony in order that they may be sanctified in truth. 'Who gave himself for us,' says Paul to Titus, 'that he might redeem us from all iniquity, and purify unto himself a peculiar people, zealous of good works' (Tit 2:14). That is why he died on the cross. As the hymn puts it, 'He died that we might be forgiven.' Yes, thank God. But it did not stop there. 'He died to make us good.' And that is what we tend to forget. This is the object of it all, the whole object of the entire work of the Lord Jesus Christ. He came into this world in order that we might be sanctified.

But we have certain dangers to face at this point. May I put it to you like this. The first danger I recognise is that of isolating doctrines, of separating them from one another in a false manner. You know what I mean. It is the danger of separating justification and sanctification in the wrong way. Of course we have to realise intellectually the difference between justification and sanctification, but we must never separate them in practice, and say that I have one without the other. That is absolutely false. According to the Scriptures a man cannot be justified without being sanctified at the same time. Paul puts it like this in Romans 8:30: 'Moreover whom he did predestinate, them he also called: and whom he called, them he also justified: and whom he justified, them he also glorified.' He goes right to the end. Now the danger is that we tend to isolate these things from one another and we tend to say a man can come to Christ and receive his justification, but that he may not come to Christ and receive sanctification until a number of years later. That is utterly impossible, according to the Scriptures, because everything is a part of one plan, and when God starts this movement it goes on inevitably to the end. The moment a man is justified, the process of sanctification has already begun. It is all in Christ. He is 'made unto us wisdom, and righteousness, and sanctification, and redemption' (1 Cor 1:30). He is everything, and you cannot divide Christ. If you have Christ at all you have the whole Christ. But there is a tendency among us to divide these things in a false manner, and to fail to realise that our Lord died upon the cross not only that we might be forgiven, but that we might be made good.

I am talking about the danger of seeking the experience of forgiveness only, without realising that at the same time we should desire to be holy and to be sanctified. I think that this is very serious. There are so many today who seem to believe that a man can come to Christ for forgiveness, for happiness, for help, for encouragement, for guidance and for a thousand and one things, and yet the whole time they say that he may not receive the blessing of sanctification. That, they say, may come later and men are exhorted to come to Christ for one particular blessing, and sanctification is never mentioned at all. Now this, again, is entirely contrary to the teaching of Scripture. How a man can possibly come to Christ without being concerned about sanctification, I cannot understand. How you can read these descriptions of him in the Gospels, without seeing his holiness and what he had come to do, is indeed beyond my comprehension.

In other words, the real danger is that of a false evangelism that does not include in its preaching the message of sanctification. There is a type of evangelical person who divides these things up to this extent. They say, 'Yes, Sunday mornings you edify the saints; Sunday evenings you give to evangelism with gospel preaching, and, of course,' they say, 'that service means nothing to the believer, it is for the unbeliever.' But that is not true evangelism. That is not the evangelism which I find in the New Testament. It is a false evangelism, and it carries with it a false modern view of an evangelist as a man who is not much of a teacher; he may not know much, but he is good at attracting people. Is that the New Testament picture of an evangelist? Is that the picture of the evangelist in the church throughout the centuries? Is that your idea of men like George Whitefield or John Wesley? The whole thing becomes entirely ludicrous! It is there I think that we go wrong, right at the beginning. It is our whole idea of evangelism that is wrong. We seem to think that the one business of evangelism is to give man a sense of forgiveness and a sense of happiness and joy and peace. But here our Lord reminds us that there is only one ultimate object in evangelism and that is to reconcile men to God. It is the whole end of everything that the Lord Jesus Christ came to do. He came to reconcile men and women to God: not to give us particular advice about how to put ourselves in a right relationship to God. 'God was in Christ, reconciling the world unto himself' (2 Cor 5:19), and therefore the message of evangelism must of necessity include the message of holiness.

So what is evangelism? I am not sure but that the first message of evangelism is that we must tell men about holiness. That is the truth which we must preach to men, the truth about this holy God before whom they will have to stand. The business of evangelism is to tell them that there is one way in which they can stand in the presence of God and that is by being made holy. It is not enough for them to have a sense of forgiveness; the question is, Are they fit to stand in the presence of God? Without holiness they cannot: 'holiness, without which no man shall see the Lord' (Heb 12:14). So an evangelism that does not include that as an integral part of its message is not biblical evangelism. The whole problem with us is that we have all become so subjective, so influenced by modern thought, that we always start with ourselves instead of starting with God. I am unhappy; I want happiness. I want this or that, so I will go to this or that religious meeting in order that I may have what I want; and I get it and stop at that. But, my dear friends, the place to start is right at the other end. It is with *God*. God is, and we are all in his hands and we all have to face him. The first question that we should put to every man is not, 'How do you feel, are you happy or miserable?' No, it is, 'How are you going to stand in the presence of God?' And if we start with that question, it is inevitable that this matter of sanctification is bound to come in. If I stand and face men and ask them how they are going to meet God, I cannot do it flippantly; I cannot do it lightly and glibly. There must be a holy seriousness about the matter. One is appalled when one thinks what is going to happen to the godless and the unbeliever. We must start with God, and if you and I claim to be Christians, the claim we are really making is that we are God's people, his representatives, and that we are going to tell people about God and are going to bring people to him.

Surely it is clear that we can only do so as we ourselves are God-fearing, as we are godly, as we are like the Lord Jesus

Christ himself. He came to this world to be the 'first born among many brethren', and we are formed and fashioned after his image. A Christian, by definition, is one who is to be like Christ. Therefore our Lord prays, 'Sanctify them,' make them like me, so that you can use them to glorify yourself among men and women in the world. So the beginning of everything is a right concept of holiness, the holiness of God, for without that we shall avail nothing.

3

'For Their Sakes'

*And for their sakes I sanctify myself, that they also might be
sanctified through the truth (v. 19).*

We have been dealing with the reasons which our Lord adduces
for praying for the sanctification of his followers. One is that
this is God's way of dealing with his people, and the second
reason, which we considered in our last study, is the vital
importance of this from the standpoint of evangelism. We went
further and saw that this is in reality the end and object, the
ultimate, in the whole matter of salvation. We saw therefore
that to consider salvation apart from sanctification is false.

But now we come to another aspect of this subject, which is
the basis of sanctification; indeed to the only way in which our
sanctification is at all possible, to the very foundation of it. We
find it here, in one of the most glorious statements which can be
found anywhere in the Scriptures: '... for their sakes I sanctify
myself.' I know that I often say about various phrases like this
in Scripture, that it is incomparable and that there is nothing like
it; and of course every time one says that, it is perfectly true,
because so many of these statements, containing as they do the
very essence of the gospel, are indeed incomparable. Furthermore, the Holy Spirit applies these statements to us from time
to time so that, as any particular one is applied to us, it does seem
to us at that moment to be all we need, and then at another time
the same is true of another statement. So there is no contradiction

in saying that both of them, and all of them, are equally incomparable. Here, then, is surely one of the greatest and most glorious statements in the whole range of Scripture. It is like a gem with many facets; it does not matter from which angle you look at it, it shines still more brightly and wonderfully. It is at the same time, surely, one of the most vital statements that we can ever consider together. So let me hold this glittering jewel before you, praying that nothing in our study will in any way detract from its brightness and glory. The whole of the Christian gospel is in this one phrase: 'For their sakes I sanctify myself.'

Now the first thing that must engage our attention is obviously the meaning of Christ's sanctification of himself. Clearly, as we pointed out earlier when we began to consider this doctrine, he cannot mean that he will do anything to increase his own holiness. That is impossible. He was perfect from the beginning, without blemish, without sin and without fault, so that when he says that he is going to sanctify himself he cannot mean that he is going to make himself more holy than he was before. What it means, obviously, is that he is using the term in the primary sense of sanctification, namely dedication, consecration, a setting apart for the special work of God, and for God's purpose in him and through him. It means an entire offering of oneself to God for his glory and for his purpose.

Then, in order to grasp the full meaning of this statement, the next word we must look at is 'myself' – 'I sanctify myself,' our Lord says. And by that he clearly means himself as he is in his total personality, everything that he is, as God and man, all his powers, all his knowledge, all his perfection, all his ability, everything. There is no word more inclusive than this word 'myself'. It means my total self, all that I am, in and of myself, all my relationships, all my privileges, all my abilities and all my possessions. I sanctify myself in the full totality of my being and my personality. So what our Lord is really saying at this point is that all that he is and has, he is now giving entirely and utterly to God 'for their sakes' – they being the Christians then in existence; and for our sakes, too, those who are going to come into existence; all those people he has been talking so much about in this prayer, the people who had been given to him by God, and for whom he has come into the world, and for whom he is now doing everything: 'for their sakes I am giving my total self to you'.

This is, ultimately, the very acme of Christian doctrine and it is astonishing to notice how we tend to forget it. I suppose it is one of those truths we forget because we think we know it, and we tend to take it for granted. We are inclined to stop at certain particulars in the work and actions of our Lord, not realising that the greatest thing of all, the staggering fact, is that the Lord Jesus Christ, the Son of God, has devoted himself entirely to our redemption. He has given himself up in the totality of his personality to this one specific object. Now that, it seems to me, was the thing that was done in the Eternal Council between God the Father, God the Son and God the Holy Spirit, before the world was ever created. All the history of mankind was known, everything was clear and open, the whole course of man, his life and his history. Before the foundation of the world, the Fall, the sin and shame were all foreseen, and what our Lord is really doing here is repeating, reminding God, as it were, that in the Eternal Council he had turned to the Father and said, 'Here am I, send me.' I put myself entirely in your hands, at your disposal, you can use me as you like for the redemption of this people. He sanctified himself, he devoted himself, to this task. He leaves everything else and he excludes everything else.

We are familiar with that idea on a lower and lesser level. We know, for instance, that when a man joins the army to fight for his country he has to give up certain other things. He gives up his business, or profession, for the time being. He has to give up his home and family life. The man is now devoting and consecrating himself to the service of his country, in order to defend it. He is a man who is giving himself exclusively to this one task and it means giving up something else. And the Scripture teaches that that is precisely what the Lord Jesus Christ has done for us and for our redemption. When he says here, 'I sanctify myself,' he is going to do something, and it is very important that we should be quite clear what he means.

There is a sense in which he has already done this; as we have seen, a great promise was made before the foundation of the world in the Eternal Council. But then it was put into practice at the Incarnation; the very birth of our Lord into this world was a part of the sanctifying of himself to this one task of man's salvation. Even at that particular point it involved his laying aside the signs and marks of his eternal glory and Godhead. He did not lay aside his Godhead, that was something he could not do. (That was the false doctrine about 'self-emptying' which came in about sixty or seventy years ago.) No, he did not empty himself of his Godhead, but he certainly did empty himself of some of the prerogatives of his Godhead.

That is the great statement made by Paul in Philippians 2:5–8: 'Who, being in the form of God, thought it not robbery to be equal with God', which means that he did not regard his equality with God as a prize to be held on to, or to be clutched at. He is devoting himself to this peculiar task, so for the purpose of this task he lays aside the marks and the signs of his glory; as the hymn puts it, 'Mild he lays his glory by'. Now that is a part of this sanctification of himself. He laid aside the signs of his glory and he submitted to being born as a babe in weakness and in utter helplessness.

So, then, he had offered himself to the Father and he said, I am going to make myself responsible for the salvation of these people and I care not what it may cost. I give myself entirely to this task. He left the courts of heaven, and took upon himself human nature, which meant that he became man as well as God. He was fashioned in the likeness of man and came into the world as a man among men – that, too, is a part of the sanctification of himself, of setting himself apart for this task. He then lived that extraordinary life for thirty years, apparently nothing but man, working as a carpenter, sharing the life of ordinary people. He so humbled himself that he became liable to temptation by Satan. God cannot be tempted, we read, but here is God in the flesh being tempted by the devil; and all this is part of his setting himself apart. Before he could save mankind, he had to endure this, and so he was tempted in all points like as we are, yet without sin.

It was also a part of his preparation for his high priesthood. You remember that argument in Hebrews 4:15, 'For we have not an high priest which cannot be touched with the feeling of our infirmities.' Because of what he endured and suffered, he was being made perfect as 'the Captain of their salvation' (Heb 2:10) – because he endured temptation by the devil and the contradiction of sinners against himself, and lived an ordinary life in this world.

But now he turns to the Father and he says that he is going to do something even further and deeper than that. What I have been describing is tremendous and staggering, but now there is something glorious! He is now giving himself to God to be made the actual sin-bearer, the offering for sin. He has come down from heaven, he has identified himself with us. He submitted himself to baptism though he never committed a sin, identifying himself with us sinners. He has endured all that I have described, yes, but if man is to be sanctified, if man is to be made so that he can dwell with God and dwell with him to all eternity, something further has to be done. So he gives himself to that something further. He hands himself passively to the Father and he says, I am ready now to be made sin for them. I am here offering myself for their sins; lay their sins upon me, make me their sin-offering. He handed himself over – that is what is meant by sanctification. He made a further devotion of himself, the last act of consecration.

Let me put it in the language of Scripture. He has submitted himself to be made a curse for us: 'Cursed is everyone that hangeth upon a tree' (Gal 2:3, quoting Deut 21:23). To be crucified was to be cursed, it was a fearful disgrace, and here he says to his Father, in effect, 'As this is the only way whereby they can be sanctified, I give myself and I make myself a curse. Let their sin really come upon me that they may be sanctified. I hand myself over to this.' It is simply saying what he said in another way, in the Garden of Gethsemane, 'Father, if it be possible, let this cup pass from me: nevertheless not my will but thine be done'; if there is no other way, I will take the cup and drink it to the dregs. He is setting himself apart into the hands of God for this end and object.

He is now submitting himself, therefore, to the most terrible thing that he ever contemplated, namely that he should be separated from his Father. He had come out of the eternal bosom. He was in God from the beginning, he is co-equal, and co-eternal with God; but here he realises, and he faces it, that in order to save and to sanctify these people he has to undergo this separation from God and to be made a curse. It means the breaking of the contact, and he submits himself even to that. He is prepared to endure even the loss of the face of God on the cross that we might be sanctified. He separates himself to this.

For that is what he endured on the cross; our Lord died of a broken heart. Christ's heart was literally broken, which is why they found blood and water when they thrust the spear into his side. He did not die merely as a result of physical crucifixion, that was not the thing that killed him. His heart was broken. The authorities, you remember, were somewhat surprised when they found him dead already. Usually crucifixion is such a slow death that men had to be killed when they were crucified: the thieves had their legs broken (Jn 19:32–33). But he died quickly, because he bore the punishment of our sin. He endured your hell and mine. This was no mere appearance, but something that was done. He endured our suffering, he consecrated himself to that. He says, Here I am, pour out the vials of your wrath because of the sin of these people upon me. I hand myself over that you may do it. 'For their sakes I sanctify myself, that they also might be sanctified through the truth.'

And then he sets himself apart for death, for burial, for entering into Hades. He descends into Hades (however we may interpret that) in its fullness and entirety. But it does not even stop at that. I think that Scripture teaching shows very clearly that our Lord's setting himself apart for this great end and object goes even beyond death and the grave; it is a part of his resurrection. For when the Lord Jesus Christ rose again from the dead, he rose not merely in and of himself, but also as the representative of his people. Even now his life in heaven is not a life he lives for himself – I say it with reverence – it is primarily a life that he is living for us, his people. He is our Advocate, our High Priest, our representative in the presence of the Father. The Lord Jesus Christ at this moment is peculiarly engaged in the work of the kingdom of which you and I are citizens. He shall reign 'till his enemies be made his footstool' (Heb 10:13).

Oh what high doctrine we are handling here! The Lord Jesus Christ in heaven at this moment, is not the same as he was when he left heaven, to come to earth. When he did that he left it as God, God the Son, but when he returned to heaven he was God and Man. He has taken human nature with him. He is God and Man for ever and for ever; the head of the church, the representative of his people. And the astounding teaching seems to be that he has set himself apart even in the Godhead to this particular work for his people and for his church; that is the thing to which he devotes himself entirely.

So the doctrine can be put like this: he who was co-equal and co-eternal with the Father has come within the bounds of time and has lived a human life here on earth. He has set himself exclusively to this one task: 'From the highest throne of Heaven to the Cross of deepest woe, all to ransom guilty captives ...' That is it; it is all there in these wonderful and magnificent words of our passage. I wonder whether we grasp this, whether we realise what it truly means that this second blessed person in the holy eternal Trinity, brought himself out, as it were, and exclusively gave himself to this one, peculiar task. All that has happened to him, and all that he has done and all that he is doing is designed to this end and object. 'For their sakes I sanctify myself.' That is what it meant to him, and that is what it involved for him.

From all this I deduce, therefore, that clearly it was all absolutely necessary before you and I could be sanctified.

Every part and every step of it was essential. You and I can only be sanctified because the Incarnation is a fact; we can only be sanctified because the suffering and death, the resurrection and the risen life of our Lord were all facts. We must not leave out any one step; we are not only sanctified by the risen Lord, his death was equally essential, and so too was the Incarnation. One of the most subtle errors at the present time is to say that our sanctification is only in the risen, living, Christ, without the death being mentioned at all. It is a denial of vital, essential, New Testament teaching – every step, every movement, every action was a part of this sanctification of himself, and without this we cannot be sanctified.

That, then, leads us to the practical application: how does all this lead to our sanctification? 'For their sakes I sanctify myself, that they also might be sanctified through the truth.' How does it work? Well, as I understand this New Testament doctrine, we can put it like this. Everything is in the Lord Jesus Christ. Everything that we enjoy, everything that we ever shall be, is because of our relationship to him. We are in him, and he is in us. We are parts of him, and we are sharers, therefore, of all that he is. All that he has done, he has done for us as our representative. Therefore all that belongs to him belongs also to us, and by his sanctification of himself he has made our sanctification possible.

It works out in this way. Before you and I could ever be sanctified, the barrier of sin between us and God had of necessity to be removed. Sanctification ultimately means being like God, sharing the life of God, being in the right relationship with God and having perfect communion with him. Sanctification does not just mean being rid of certain sins. No, sanctification is positive. God says, 'Ye shall therefore be holy, for I am holy' (Lev 11:45). But before that is possible it is quite clear that the barrier and obstacle between us and God must be removed. That is why the cross of Calvary is absolutely essential to sanctification, and people who say that we can be sanctified by knowing the living Christ, without talking about the Atonement, have clearly not understood the problem of sin. Sin must be taken out of the way. The first question is the guilt of our sin, and it is only by the death of our Lord upon the cross, by his making himself our sin-bearer, and becoming the sin-offering, that the guilt of sin can thus be taken out of the world. So he tells us here that he is offering himself in order that that may be done. It is the very foundation of sanctification. Justification is the basis of sanctification in this second sense of the word.[1] And that is the error of the Roman Catholic Church when they fail to emphasise the doctrine of justification by faith only; men and women try to sanctify themselves by going into monasteries and so on, and of course it cannot be done, for without justification there can be no sanctification. Sin must be removed, and our Lord has removed it.

Then the next thing that happens is that in him we are reconciled to God. Sin has been taken out of the way, the guilt has been removed, and now God, in a marvellous manner, puts us into Christ; he incorporates and engrafts us into him. As you read the New Testament, keep your eye on that phrase 'in Christ'. Paul talks about certain men and says that they were 'in Christ before me' (Rom 16:7). He had been put into Christ, like a branch being grafted into a tree. We are members of the body of Christ, adopted as God's children, taken into God's family – that is the New Testament language – and if Christ had not set himself apart for us, that would never have been done. He is 'the first born among many brethren', the beginning of a new humanity. He is starting a new race of man, and we who are put into him become the beneficiaries of everything that is true of him. We are received by him, and thus we receive new life from him. We receive a new nature, we become partakers of the divine nature, and we become such that the very Holy Spirit that was given to him without measure can be given to us also. We can be enabled to live life in this world in the way that he

---

[1] See chapter 1 for a discussion of the two meanings of sanctification. (Ed.)

lived it. That is what we are taught. We receive the gift of the Holy Spirit himself. He enters into us and dwells in us, and he begins to form Christ in us. We are made according to the image and pattern of Christ – we are created anew in Christ Jesus.

Now all that could never have been if our Lord had not set himself apart for the birth, the death, the entering into Hades, the resurrection, the seating of himself at the right hand of God, and the sending forth of the Holy Spirit. He has done all this in order thatthat might happen to us, and thus it is that the Holy Spirit works within us, both to will and to do according to God's good pleasure. Let me remind you of Paul's argument in Philippians 2:12–13, 'Work out your own salvation with fear and trembling. For it is God which worketh in you' – he does it through the Spirit – 'both to will and to do of his good pleasure.' The moment the Holy Spirit enters into us, then he begins to work in us. Sometimes when we are quite unconscious of it, he creates desires in us and works upon the will – 'to will and to do'. He empowers us, and he does so because Christ has sent him for that purpose. Thus he links us more and more to Christ, forming Christ in us all the time. Ever increasingly we are enabled to receive of his fullness and 'grace for grace'; power, life – every need can be satisfied. The fullness of the Godhead is included, for all the treasures of wisdom and grace are in Christ and if I am put into Christ then I can receive all that; his life will flow into mine, as the branch takes from the vine. The New Testament is full of this teaching but all I am emphasising here is that if he had not sanctified himself, none of this would be possible, and that is why he had to do it. This is our sanctification, and what he says here again is that he has done it all in order that we might be sanctified in truth.

I cannot leave this wonderful statement without just saying a final, brief word about the amazing thing that led him to do all this. It is all here! 'For their sakes I sanctify myself.' If only we could see this. This is the thing that leads to sanctification. We shall be considering this further, but this is the truth that we need to know; we need to realise something of what this means. 'For their sakes,' he says, he is going to do all that I have been describing to you. Who then are they? Who are these people for whom he does it? Enemies of God and therefore enemies of Christ, self-willed creatures, people who listen to Satan rather than to God, people who deliberately believe the lies against God, people who have set themselves up, and put their own wills and desires against the will of God, people who delight in evil, who are full of malice, envy, lust and passion; you and I as we were in sin and in evil, as the result of the Fall.

For *their* sakes! Recognise it, guilty sinners as we are! It is for us that he has done all this – for them, yes, I sanctify myself, says the eternal Son of God, the holy and pure one, the blameless and spotless, the one whose supreme joy was to do the will of his Father. Can you imagine a greater contrast than that: the contrast between 'them' and 'I'? And yet he says, 'I sanctify myself,' which not only means, as I have described to you, the totality of his personality, but also that he did it voluntarily and willingly. There was nothing in us to recommend this; there was no motive that could arise from anything in us. Man in sin is so damned and hopeless that he does not want to be saved, or even ask to be. No request ever went out from man to God for salvation, it has come entirely from God. Here am I, says our Lord, Send me. There was no compulsion from the Father's side, the Son desired to do this. He gave himself freely and willingly and voluntarily.

I do not suppose it is seen more clearly anywhere than it is there in the Garden of Gethsemane. 'If it be possible, let this cup pass from me.' But if it is not possible, if there is not another way, then I will do it. I will go through with it, though I know what it is going to mean.

The agony of it was so great in anticipation that it made him sweat drops of blood, but he willingly went to the shame and agony and all the suffering, the mocking, the spitting, the jeering and the laughter, the crown of thorns. Yes, he willingly went and endured it all for *your* sake, for *my* sake, not simply that we might have our sins forgiven, but that we might be sanctified.

4

God's Work through the Truth

Sanctify them through thy truth: thy word is truth (v. 17).

Now we come to what I have described in our analysis of this subject as the *method of sanctification*. Our Lord puts it like this: 'Sanctify them through thy truth [or, in thy truth]: thy word is truth.' This is his method of sanctification. We are thus bound to ask this question: How can we become truly holy, how can we become sanctified in truth? Our Lord says, 'For their sakes I sanctify myself, that they also may be sanctified through the truth.' This is not a spurious sanctification, it is real. So, to put it another way, How can we become truly and entirely devoted to God and to his service? How, indeed, can we become like our Lord? He was fully devoted to his Father. He gave himself, he consecrated himself utterly. He was entirely at the disposal of his Father and that is why the Father could use him to bring to pass this great salvation that we enjoy. How, then, can we become as he was? This is obviously a crucial question for all Christian people. I do not hesitate to make the assertion that unless a person is concerned about this question, he or she is not a Christian at all. For it is an essential part of the definition of a Christian that he should be concerned about this matter of becoming wholly and truly devoted to God.

It is not surprising, therefore, that in the long history of the church there have been many different views with regard to the method of sanctification. It is, in a sense, the whole story of the church. A book called, *The Vision of God* by K. E. Kirk gives a very good historical survey of this doctrine. It is a massive book, and one of the most rewarding that I have read on this particular subject. What Kirk does there is to trace historically the two main schools of thought with regard to this question of how one can become holy.

In the one school are the people who believe in the monastic idea that the only way to become holy is to clear right out of the world and to give yourself to nothing but the cultivation of your soul and the development of holiness. Then those in the other school believe that all this can be done in the world as one follows one's ordinary profession and calling among men and women – what might be called the evangelical conception of the method of holiness. Kirk's book is well worth reading, but when all is said, there is still much confusion about this matter and a great deal of perplexity and disagreement.

It is quite a popular thing today to say that it does not matter what you believe about the method of obtaining sanctification as long as it gives you an experience that makes you happy and seems to promote your holiness. There are many who take this view. 'Why be bothered?' they say. 'Why not let one man become a monk if he likes and another man go on with his work in the world? Why not let one man believe that holiness is to be received as an experience and another man believe that it is something which a man has to work out for himself? What does it matter? Why bother about this as long as each man is happy in his own particular way?'

Now it seems to me that such a statement must of necessity be wrong, because if you adopt that line of argument then you have nothing whatever to say to the cults. For whatever we may think about them, if our only test is that of experience, then the cults really do seem able to offer what is required. Yet we would not for a moment grant that they are right, or that the experience they claim is true, because the cults say that they do not believe the truth.

In other words, there must be an objective test for what we believe. Experience is not a test; a man may become very happy and live a much better life than he did before, though he believes something that is not true. Things which are not true in and of themselves may at first appear to do us good because, of course, the devil can turn himself into an angel of light: it is pathetic to notice the way in which people forget that teaching. We must never base our doctrines upon experience, but upon the truth. That is the main reason for not accepting this attitude of letting any man believe what he likes. The Scripture tells us to prove the truth. 'Evil communications corrupt good manners,' writes Paul, to the people in the church at Corinth. You must not say, he tells them in 1 Corinthians 15, that it is irrelevant whether a man believes in the resurrection or not. It does matter, and if men hold a wrong view, eventually it will lead to something wrong in their behaviour. Our duty, therefore, as Christian people is to discover, as far as we can, the teaching of the Scriptures. Obviously we do not do that in a controversial spirit, since controversy for its own sake is always the work of the devil. Remember, however, that the opposite to that is not to say, 'Believe anything you like as long as it helps you.' Rather it is to 'search the Scriptures'. So it is our duty to discover, if we can, what we are told in Scripture about this important and vital matter of the method of sanctification and we do so now in terms of our Lord's teaching at this point in the seventeenth chapter of John.

The first principle, I think we would all agree, is that *this is primarily and essentially God's work in us.* Now the very way in which our Lord puts it, his petition itself, I think, proves that. He is praying to God the Father and he is asking him to do something, and he says, 'Sanctify them'; I plead with you to sanctify these people through the truth. Sanctification, therefore, is essentially and primarily something that God does to us and in us and for us. So it follows that we must never think of sanctification as something which you and I decide to go in for. We must realise that it is always the work of God. We have seen already that the ultimate object of God in the whole process of salvation is our sanctification. That is the end he has in view, the thing which is being brought to pass, and that is the basic principle to which we must always hold. Whatever particular views we may hold about details, we must never forget that, apart from you and me altogether, it is something God does to us. So the main emphasis must never be put upon our deciding to go in for sanctification.

Therefore I would put it like this: sanctification is something that starts within us from the first beginning of the work of grace in us for salvation. There is surely nothing which is more fatal than to separate justification and sanctification completely, and to tell a man that he can be justified without being sanctified, or that you receive your justification at one point, and, perhaps a long time later, you receive your sanctification. The very definition of justification means that that is quite impossible. No man can be justified without his realising that he is a sinner, that he is guilty before God, and that he is exposed to God's wrath and punishment. He desires to get rid of the sin which has put him in that position, to repent and turn from sin and the world, to be put right with God. And the moment a man has realised and said all that, he is giving evidence of sanctification, because sanctification is the process of delivering us from sin in its every aspect. So our justification is proof of the commencement of the process of sanctification, because any dislike of sin, any realisation of what sin cost the Lord Jesus Christ, any movement away from it, however small, is evidence of sanctification. So it does seem to me to be utterly unscriptural to divide these two things and put them into separate compartments, and to say that a man can have one without the other.

Now the way to get out of that difficulty and to avoid that dangerous error, is to realise that the whole work of salvation is God's work, and that every step and movement in God's work of salvation is to bring us to this sanctified, holy position. It is all the work of God from beginning to end. That is why St Paul in Philippians 2:12–13 says, '... work out your own salvation with fear and trembling. For it is God which worketh in you both to will and to do of his good pleasure.' Indeed, he has already said the same thing earlier in the same epistle when he says: 'Being confident of this very thing, that he which hath begun a good work in you will perform it until the day of Jesus Christ' (Phil 1:6).

That is the only true biblical conception of salvation; it is God working in us. God is at work the moment a man even begins to become conscious of sin within himself. God has begun a good work and he is going on with it, and it is all ultimately a part of this matter of sanctification. Therefore we must never think of it in terms of something we decide to 'go in for' or 'take up'. We must realise that God is leading us on in this matter of sanctification, and this can never be over-emphasised. The New Testament makes it so plain that the whole of the work of salvation is God's work in us. A good way of looking at it is like this: we would all agree that in the matter of our justification God has done a lot of work in us even when we did not realise it. Look back across your experience. What was it that ever made you go to that place of worship where you were converted? Do you not see, as you look back, that God was working in you without your realising it? He was bringing certain forces to bear upon you. He brought you face to face with certain people. It seemed accidental at the time – you did not know why you were acting as you did. But the answer is that God was bringing it to pass. No man would come to that point of repentance and belief and faith in Christ were it not that God had been dealing with him, even if the man himself were quite unconscious of it. Now it is exactly the same with regard to this matter of sanctification. He is working in us and upon us, he is doing things to us, and the end and the object of all this is that we may become holy and truly sanctified.

I do not know what you feel, but to me this is my final comfort and consolation in this world. My only hope of arriving in glory lies in the fact that the whole of my salvation is God's work. I therefore know that if I am a child of God, God will complete the work that he started in me. I can never face God and stand in his glorious presence unless I am faultless and blameless. But the practical question is, How am I going to get to that position? I repeat, my only hope and comfort is that, in the last analysis, it does not depend upon me but upon God himself. If I am a child of God and if he has put his hand upon me, then I know for certain that he is going to bring me to that.

And, let me emphasise this very solemnly, Scripture teaches us that God is so determined to bring us to that position, that if we are not prepared to be led by him, he has other methods of bringing us to it. The teaching of the Hebrews 12:6 is: 'Whom the Lord loveth he chasteneth, and scourgeth every son whom he receiveth.' If you are not being chastened, says the author, 'then are ye bastards, and not sons.' It is a terrifying thought and yet it is very comforting. If you are God's child, then God is going to perfect you. If you will not listen to positive teaching, he will chastise you, he will lay his hands upon you. Perhaps your health will suffer or the health of a dear one; there may be an accident, a calamity, a death – the Bible is full of such teaching. God's children are not allowed finally to go astray. He brings them back, if not by one way, then by another. My sanctification is in his hands and thank God it is, for if it were left to me it would be altogether hopeless.

That is another way of presenting Paul's argument in Romans 8: 'Whom he called, them he also justified: and whom he justified, them he also glorified' (v. 30). If God has started this work in us, he is certainly going to finish it and that is our only hope and consolation. Therefore we can say, as Paul does, that we are 'persuaded, that neither death, nor life, nor angels, nor principalities, nor powers, nor things present, nor things to come, nor height, nor depth, nor any other creature, shall be able to separate us from the love of God, which is in Christ Jesus our Lord' (vv. 38–39). So my comfort and consolation is not that I am anxious to be holy and sigh for sanctification, no, my comfort and consolation is that God has set me aside for sanctification, has chosen me unto sanctification, and because he has done so, he is going to do the work.

Or, I can put it like this: my only hope of seeing God and of entering glory is that the Lord Jesus Christ has prayed to God to sanctify me – not that I decide to surrender myself, or to do this, that and the other, but that Christ himself is asking the Father to sanctify me. That is my assurance, that is my comfort. I know that Christ's prayer for his own is always infallibly answered, and it is because I know that I am in God's hands and that God is dealing with me, that I know that ultimately I shall be fit to stand in his holy presence. That then is the first great principle. It is God's work in us, and he does it through Christ who has consecrated and sanctified himself, and has suffered my punishment, and has risen for my justification, and has sent the Spirit in order that I may be sanctified.

So then we must now go on to consider how God does this work of sanctification in us. 'Father sanctify them'; I plead with you to sanctify them. Yes, but how does God do this? The answer is in the rest of the statement: 'Sanctify them through [or in] thy truth.' And then our Lord analyses and emphasises it: 'Thy word is truth.' So the second principle is that *God's way of sanctifying us is through the medium of truth, through his word, which is truth.* God's method of sanctification is that he brings us into a certain relationship to his truth and to his word. He brings us into the realm of the truth, into a knowledge of the truth, so that it is the truth of God working in us that produces our sanctification.

Now that seems to me to be the essence of the method, and again, of course, this is of vital importance. It is at this point that disagreement tends to come in. How does God do this work in us? Let me suggest certain negatives to you, which I regard as of great importance. The first is that God does this work of sanctification in us but not in the sense that he does it all for us so that all we have to do is to keep on looking to him. I am sure that you are familiar with this teaching. People say that if God is the one who produces your sanctification, then, obviously, you do nothing. The greatest hindrance to the work of God, they say, is that you repeatedly try to do something for yourself, whereas all you have to do is to surrender yourself to him, and look to him, and as you do so, he will do the work for you. Then the illustration of the branch and the vine is used to support this view.

But that seems to me to be an entire contradiction of what our Lord says in his prayer at this point. He prays that God may sanctify us in, or through, the truth. It is a great body of truth that we are going to consider, and that does not mean that we do nothing. Surely the whole illustration of the branch and the vine is sadly misunderstood at that point. The branch in the vine is full of life, and full of its own activity. Of course, it must be in communication with the parent trunk, with the tree itself, but it must not be thought of as a kind of tube through which the sap flows and which contributes nothing of itself. The picture is of an active, living relationship in which the branch has its own function in the work which it carries out, though always in fundamental relationship to the trunk. And that, surely, is the teaching of Scripture. Go back once more to that great statement in Philippians 2:13 '... it is God that worketh in you,' says Paul, 'both to will and to do ...' Yes, but because of that, this is what he says: 'work out your own salvation with fear and trembling.' He exhorts them to work it out because it is God who is working in them. God gives the power whereby we are enabled to work for ourselves; that is the method. So though sanctification is fundamentally the work of God, it does not mean that I do nothing at all but look to him. No, he works in me in order that I may work.

Furthermore, Scripture does not teach that this process of sanctification is a very simple one. Someone once said, 'It is all so perfectly simple, and Christian people give themselves such a lot of trouble because they will make these complications. It is as simple as lifting up a blind and letting the sunlight come into the room. All you have to do, therefore, is to surrender to Christ, and look to him and it all happens to you, and the work of sanctification goes on.'

But Scripture, surely, is full of exhortation. It tells us to rend our hearts (Joel 2:13) and to 'be dead unto sin' (Rom 6:11). It says, 'mortify your members which are upon the earth' (Col 3:5) and mortify the flesh. It tells us to 'stand fast in the faith' (1 Cor 16:13) and to have faith in God. It tells us to 'flee these things' (1 Tim 6:11) – certain carnal, sinful practices – to run away from them, not just to lift up the blind and let the sunlight in, but flee! Take to our feet, do something, get away from it! It tells us to put off one thing and to put on another. Paul exhorts the Corinthians like this: 'Let us cleanse ourselves from all filthiness of the flesh and spirit' (2 Cor 7:1). And notice, too, the series of commandments and instructions and exhortations, which we find in the fourth and fifth chapters of Paul's letter to the Ephesians. Now these passages do not teach that you and I just surrender ourselves, and do nothing but look to God in faith. Not at all! We are exhorted to do these things and to work out our own salvation along those various lines.

Furthermore, it is surely right to ask what the point and purpose is of all the arguments of the New Testament epistles, if you and I have to do nothing but just surrender and maintain what is called 'the faith position'. Why all these theological arguments at the beginning of every epistle? Why are these early Christians reminded of their status, and of this great doctrine? For this reason: the New Testament authors always go on to say, Therefore, in the light of all this truth, apply it! Put it into practice! Every one of the New Testament epistles is divided into two sections – doctrine and the application of the doctrine. Paul, for example, puts it so perfectly in Romans 6:1, 'What shall we say *then*? Shall we continue in sin …?' and he goes on to apply the great truths of the earlier chapters. So we must look at it like this: God works in us fundamentally by producing in us a new nature, and disposition. He creates within us new desires and longings after holiness and sanctification and the godly life. Indeed he creates within us the will and the power to live such a life, but he does it all through the word. Nor does he leave us, as it were, doing nothing. He acts upon us so as to produce in us a mighty activity of our own.

Perhaps I can put it best with another negative. God does not do this work in us directly, but indirectly, through the truth. This is a vital principle. So many people think that because we say that this is fundamentally God's work then it is, as it were, something that God does immediately and directly upon our souls and we just have to accept what he does, we just have to 'let go and let God' do these things to us. But that is a false understanding of the teaching of Scripture especially at this point. In our Lord's own words, he does not do the work immediately but mediately through his word, which is the truth. And so he does not teach us to surrender ourselves and every sin to him, and then trust him to deliver us out of those sins, or to take those sins out of us. Some teach that all we have to do, having told God that we want to be delivered, is to believe he has done it, and then we shall eventually find that it has happened. But I do not understand the teaching of Scripture in that way. I do not know of a single scripture – and I speak advisedly – which tells me to take my sin, the particular thing that gets me down, to God in prayer and ask him to deliver me from it and then trust in faith that he will.

Now that teaching is also often put like this: you must say to a man who is constantly defeated by a particular sin, 'I think your only hope is to take it to Christ and Christ will take it from you.' But what does Scripture say in Ephesians 4:28 to the man who finds himself constantly guilty of stealing, to a man who sees something he likes and takes it? What am I to tell such a man? Am I to say, 'Take that sin to Christ and ask him to deliver you?' No, what the apostle Paul tells him is this: 'Let him that stole, steal no more.' Just that. Stop doing it. And if it is fornication or adultery or lustful thoughts, again: Stop doing it, says Paul. He does not say, 'Go and pray to Christ to deliver you.' No. You stop doing that, he says, as becomes children of God. My friends, we have become unscriptural. If you want further evidence, lest somebody thinks it is only the teaching of Paul, let me come to the teaching of the apostle Peter, which is exactly the same; it is the whole teaching of Scripture, which we seem to have forgotten. We read in 1 Peter 1:14 and 15, 'As obedient children, not fashioning yourselves according to the former lusts in your ignorance: but as he which hath called you is holy so be ye holy in all manner of conversation.' It is something that *you* have to do. You must turn your back on these things because you are a child of God. Peter puts it still more strongly, in a sense, in 1 Peter 4:1–4: 'Forasmuch then as Christ has suffered for us in the flesh, arm yourselves likewise with the same mind: for he that hath suffered in the flesh hath ceased from sin; that he no longer should live the rest of his time in the flesh to the lusts of men, but to the will of God' – then listen to the argument – 'For the time past of our life may suffice us to have wrought the will of the Gentiles, when we walked in lasciviousness, lusts, excess of wine, revellings, banquetings, and abominable idolatries: wherein they think it strange that ye run not with them to the same excess of riot, speaking evil of you.'

You must not do it, says Peter. He does not say Surrender it to Christ and ask him to deliver you from it; what he says is, Realise who you are and stop doing it. That is the teaching of Scripture: it tells us that if we really are what we claim to be, then we must stop sinning and we must purify ourselves. It reminds us that God has saved us in Christ, and has put the Holy Spirit into us, and that we already have the power within us, in the Holy Spirit. What we must learn to do is not to grieve the Spirit, but to yield to his promptings and to the strength and power that he gives us. It is we who are exhorted to do these things; God does not do this work in us directly but indirectly.

Not only that, surely we must agree that if the other teaching is right and all I have to do with the sin that gets me down is to take it to Christ, then why should I not do it with all sins? This would mean that I become perfect and sinless – it is the teaching of sinless perfection. The people who hold that teaching would claim that they do not believe in sinless perfection, yet that is the logical conclusion of their teaching. No, that is not biblical doctrine. Rather, the Bible teaches that God does this work in us indirectly through the truth, by the word, by the teaching, by the enlightening, by the understanding, all of which is worked in us by the power of the Holy Spirit. And thus when we come to consider together the various Scriptures and their teaching with regard to this all-important matter, I think we shall see that the argument of the Bible everywhere is perfectly consistent with itself. God does this work in us by reminding us of who we are. He does it by warnings, and by making us realise the truth concerning himself; and the final argument is that 'every man that hath this hope in him purifieth himself, even as he is pure' (1 Jn 3:3).

We have not finished with this yet. There are other propositions I must put to you; there are other negatives that I must of necessity emphasise before we come to look positively at the great and glorious and transcendant truth which God uses in order to sanctify his people.

5

Sanctification – a Continuous Process

Sanctify them through thy truth: thy word is truth (v. 17).

We are still considering, let me remind you, the doctrine of sanctification, which is inevitably brought to our attention by this particular petition here in our Lord's last great high priestly prayer. Our Lord, you remember, is offering certain petitions for those men he is leaving in the world and for all who are going to believe on their word. The first petition is that they may be kept from the evil one, and then follows this petition that God should sanctify them, and sanctify them in and through the truth. We have seen that he prays that because this is the grand end and object of salvation, not merely that we may be forgiven but that we may be sanctified, that we may become entirely devoted to God and fit to spend eternity in his glorious presence. And we have looked together at the way in which our Lord tells us that he sanctifies himself because he must ultimately face death on the cross and all its shame and suffering in order that we might thus be sanctified.

Then we came on to consider the method of sanctification and we began our consideration of that in the last study. It was not a complete consideration, there were many things which we did not deal with, and now as we continue with it I would ask you to be patient and realise that it is a great and vast subject which cannot be dealt with in one short study. Incidentally, may I comment in passing that if a man can present his doctrine of sanctification in one brief study, then I suggest that there is something wrong with his doctrine. Perhaps the main criticism of many a popular teaching about sanctification is that it can be so presented in a few minutes. For that, as we shall see, is something very different from the teaching of the New Testament itself.

So, then, in looking at this doctrine of sanctification we have seen that certain great principles must at once be laid down in the light of this particular verse only. We have seen that it is God's work and that the way in which he does it is in the truth, or through the truth, and in pointing out that particular aspect we have laid down certain negatives. The first was that this does not mean that God does everything for us and that we have nothing to do. We are exhorted to do things, and we are told that God is working in us in order that we may work them out.

The second negative was that God does not do this work directly but indirectly. He does it in and through the truth. This is a principle, of course, that not only applies to this subject of sanctification but to many others also. There is a good deal of interest in faith healing in these days and sometimes some of these friends seem to fail to realise that there again God works indirectly as well as directly. The use of means does not mean absence of faith; these things are not opposites. God does not always heal us directly—indeed the common practice is for God to heal us indirectly through the use of men, physicians and surgeons, medicaments and operations and various other means. It is a great fallacy to think that God must always work directly or he is not working at all. The normal procedure is the indirect method and I am suggesting that that is so in this matter of sanctification. He does it through the truth.

And now we must continue with some additional negatives. I should be very happy if it were unnecessary to introduce these negatives, but after all teaching is not only meant to be positive. We are not only to present the truth we are also to warn people against error, and that is why the negatives are so essential.

That being so, the next negative I would suggest is that sanctification must never be thought of as an experience but always as a state and condition, as the work which God does in us, by the Holy Spirit; or, to use the language of Scripture, it is the process whereby we are being 'conformed to the image of his Son'. That is how Paul describes it in Romans 8:29 and that is the right way to conceive of our salvation, that we are being conformed increasingly to the image, to the pattern, of the Son of God. That is the whole object of salvation, to make us more and more like him. Therefore, it is, of necessity, a matter of our condition and not an experience which we may enjoy for a while and then lose. Read again Ephesians 2:10 where Paul says 'for we are his workmanship' – by which he means that we are something that is being made by him, an object which is being fashioned and formed by God, something which he is bringing into being. We are, Paul continues, 'created in Christ Jesus unto good works which God hath before ordained that we should walk in them'. That again makes it quite clear that it is a condition, and not merely an experiential position in which you find yourself from time to time, so that when you lose the experience you revert to where you were at the beginning.

Or, to put it in the language of the apostle Peter, it is a condition in which we are growing 'in grace, and in the knowledge of our Lord and Saviour Jesus Christ' (2 Pet 3:18). We are growing, developing, advancing! The Scripture talks about babes in Christ, and then about young men and old men. All these pictures are suggestive of growth and development, and that, too, implies a condition and state, and not merely an experience. It is, therefore, a very grievous fallacy to think that sanctification is simply an experience in which one is at that moment conscious of elevated and good thoughts and is free of all evil ones.

However, let us be clear about the relationship of this condition to experience. Since it is a condition of sanctification, and of growth in grace, and development in holiness, it obviously involves experience. And we know that in this process, by the grace of God, we do have experiences which are most helpful for our sanctification. An unusual experience of the nearness of God or of the love of God obviously makes us want to hate sin more, and to strive more after holiness; it makes us hunger and thirst after righteousness to a greater degree than before. Experiences are wonderful things, but what I am concerned to emphasise is that they are not sanctification itself. The experience promotes my sanctification and encourages it, and I think that is where the fallacy probably arises, because it is true to say that when we do have these blessed experiences we are aware of being in a better frame than we were before. As a result, people have tended to identify them with sanctification itself, and they are therefore tempted to say that when they are not enjoying that experience then somehow they seem to have lost their sanctification. But they have not, for whatever their experience may be, the work of God in the soul goes on, and thank God that that is so. It is progressive, so while we thank God for subjective experiences and realise their great value and importance in the work of sanctification, we must never rely upon them.

That, then, leads to another negative, which is that we must not therefore think of sanctification as something which is to be received. You may often have heard it put in that form. We are told that as we receive our justification, so also we receive our sanctification; it is presented to us as something which we can accept. But again it seems to me that if we realise that sanctification means the work of God in us, separating us from sin unto himself, then obviously it is something which cannot be received in that way. As we saw earlier, the work of sanctification is something that starts in us from the very first moment of belief. From the moment I realise what sin is and begin to hate it and long to be delivered from it, from that moment, the process of sanctification is going steadily forward. It is progressive, and not complete in this life and world. And, therefore, because of this and because it advances in this way, it is obviously something which I cannot receive in one act.

There is great confusion at this point. People seem to think of sanctification as if it were similar to justification. A man is justified once and for all. It is one concrete experience, a matter of my standing and status. But sanctification, by definition, is this progressive, increasing work that goes on in our souls, bringing us more and more into the image of Jesus Christ. How can that be received as one experience? Surely it is quite impossible!

We can put it like this. If sanctification were a gift that we received from God, then, as we have seen earlier, I think it follows of necessity that we must be believers in a complete sinless perfection. Every gift that God gives is perfect and entire. God never gives a partial gift and if he gives sanctification to a man as a gift, it is complete and perfect. So if I receive sanctification, I must then and there be made perfectly whole and sinless. Then, of course, the question arises, how can I ever sin again? What is there in me that would ever make me responsive to sin? No, it is quite clear that sanctification is not a gift that one can receive as one can receive the gift of justification. It is rather this continuous, steadily advancing work that God does in us, in order that we may work it out with fear and trembling. And again we are reminded of all those exhortations in the New Testament Scriptures to keep free from sinful lusts – 'Let him that stole, steal no more' and so on. All these exhortations make it quite clear that sanctification is not a gift to be received but is a process which God is working out in us.

Let me put it in another way: in the light of all these things we must not think of sanctification as something which happens suddenly. This again is a point which must be emphasised. People seem to think (and here they are logical though they are wrong) that if it is a gift to be received, then obviously it must be something that happens suddenly; you receive a gift, it happens suddenly, and you take possession of the thing offered you. But surely this is quite incompatible with the New Testament teaching on this matter. It is, rather, characteristic of the cults, of a man-made idea of sanctification. We always like to do things suddenly, and to have anything we want, at once. So you find that those teachings always offer a kind of short cut, and that is their appeal to the carnal mind, because we are always so impatient, always in such a desperate hurry. But this very verse which we are now considering makes it quite impossible for sanctification to be something that happens suddenly. 'Sanctify them,' says our Lord, 'in thy truth.'

Our Lord has already said the same thing in John 8:31–32. He said to certain men who appeared to believe: 'If ye continue in my word, then are ye my disciples indeed; and ye shall know the truth, and the truth shall make you free.' It is always the truth, therefore, and that is something which is progressive. We do not grasp the whole of the truth at once, we go through these stages, from babes to full matured age, from being a child to being an old man, as it were, in terms of faith. We see the same thing again in Philippians 2:12, that verse which I am quoting so frequently, 'Work out your own salvation with fear and trembling' – it is something you keep doing – 'not as in my presence only,' says Paul, 'but now much more in my absence.' The exhortation in all these writings is to continue steadfast, to progress and to go on with the work. That is the great appeal that runs right through the New Testament. You have started, do not stop, keep on with it. And surely that is why this process is not something which we must regard as happening suddenly, and it is astonishing that anybody should ever have had such a false idea about it.

Yet people seem to me to be trying to defend this doctrine of suddenly becoming sanctified because they somehow feel it is dishonouring to God not to believe in it. But there, I think, the fallacy emerges. It is the fallacy to which I have already referred, that of thinking that God must always work directly and yet, as I have already shown you, in the matter of physical healing, for example, God's normal way of working is to do it indirectly. All healing comes from God; no healing is possible apart from him and we should always realise that, whether we use means, or whether we stake our dependence upon God alone. You can use the best means in the world, but if it is not God's will that you be healed you will not be, because all healing comes from God.

But it is not only a matter of healing. Look at God's method in nature, for instance; it is always this same indirect method. God's ordained way is that the farmer should plough the earth, then sow the seed, and then roll it over and wait until the harvest comes several months later. Now it would be equally apposite to ask why God does it like that. Why does he not make the crop and the fruit come the very next day after the farmer has put the seed into the ground? He could do it if he wanted to, for with God all things are possible. Why does God make man wait all these months from the time of sowing to the time of harvest? But that is exactly what God does. He has chosen that it shall happen in that way, and as he does this in the growth of things in nature, and in the whole of life, our physical frames and everything else, that also seems to be his method of sanctification. Indeed, as you look at the experience of the saints throughout the centuries that is the thing to which you find them all testifying.

Take another illustration. Why has God allowed Satan to continue in being? Why do we still have to look forward to the day when Satan shall finally be put down and thrown in to the lake of fire and destroyed? Satan was really defeated by the Lord Jesus Christ upon the cross, but that was nearly 2,000 years ago. Some might well ask, Why did God not immediately destroy Satan? But that is God's way. It has pleased him that Satan should be allowed to continue in being, to trouble and to try and to torment God's own people. Or again we might ask, Why did God not destroy death at once? By rising from the dead the Lord Jesus Christ has really conquered death, and yet it is still true to say that the last enemy that shall be conquered and destroyed is death. Christian people are still subject to it and have to die. So why did God not instantly take it right away from us? But he has not done so; death remains as a fact. It has pleased God, I say it once more, to leave us subject to physical death, and thus we go on in this life and in this world. And in the same way you might ask why God does not give every Christian, immediately he becomes a Christian, perfect health, and deliver him from all the things to which the human physical frame is subject in this life and world. He does not do so because his method all along the line is to work this work in a gradual, progressive and increasing manner.

I sometimes think that here again the confusion has arisen because people fail to differentiate between the sudden realisation of certain aspects of truth, and sanctification itself. And I think, too, that the false teaching often arises in this way. You are told the story of a man who undoubtedly has been converted but he has gone on living a kind of humdrum Christian life for a number of years; then suddenly he hears of a teaching which he had never heard of or realised before, and suddenly, from having seen this wonderful thing, his whole life has been changed. He seems to have had a second conversion, some mighty blessing has descended upon him and he is never the same again after that second experience. Ah, they say, what happened to him at that point was that whereas before he was only justified, he has now become sanctified in addition, and it happened suddenly.

Now let us analyse an experience like that. What really happened? Well I think we must all now agree that if that man was truly converted before the second experience, if he really had seen himself as a sinner, if he had come to see that his only hope of salvation is that Christ had died for him and his sins, and if he was trusting to that in order that he might be delivered from sin and the wrath of God, that man's sanctification was already proceeding. As we have seen, you cannot be saved without the process of sanctification already starting. It is impossible to think of justification in isolation. So that the first fallacy is the view that the man was only justified.

Then what of this next experience? Well, clearly what has happened here is that though the man had received and had believed vital Christian truth, his realisation of it was incomplete, and what undoubtedly happened to this man was that he came to the realisation of other aspects of truth that he had not hitherto understood. In grasping this, perhaps the possibility came to him of a more sanctified condition, of a further advance and growth in grace and knowledge. He came to that realisation suddenly and therefore he, as it were, made a great spurt forward in his sanctification. But what really happened to that man was not that he was receiving sanctification for the first time, but that there was a visible development and advance in the process of sanctification in him.

This, again, is a phenomenon with which we are familiar in

many other realms. It happens to us with regard to secular knowledge. How often have you been struggling with a problem for a very long time and then suddenly you see it, and it is solved? That does not mean that all the struggling that had gone before was useless. Take any one of these great inventions, or take the advance in the realm of science, or the application of science to life, and you will invariably find that there has been a great background of work leading up to the final discovery. It would seem suddenly to have sprung from nowhere to absolute knowledge but only because we have not understood all that has really happened. In spiritual things we realise certain things perhaps suddenly or perhaps gradually; the realisation may be sudden, but that is not the sanctification. Rather, the realisation of some truth leads to the application of that truth and the application of that truth may cause a sudden jump forward, a sudden advance in this process of sanctification.

These sudden realisations of truth are therefore most valuable and helpful. Let me use a simple, homely illustration. Have you not often noticed in the spring that when the farmer has sown the seed, but the weather has been bad, nothing seems to happen – perhaps you can barely see that the seed has germinated and it is only just beginning to show above the ground. Then you get a shower and, following the shower, a burst of warm sunshine. You go out and look at that same field the next morning and you are astonished. Everything seems to have happened in the night. It looks as if all was due to the shower and the sunshine. Suddenly there seems to have been growth and you say to yourself, 'There was nothing yesterday, but look at it now.' But what has really happened? Again, of course, the truth is that the process has been going on for weeks. The shower and the sudden burst of sunshine have made it all leap forward, but the leaping forward is not the beginning of the process, it is but the advancing of it. As you go on you may find that phenomenon repeated many times: another shower, another burst of sunshine, another leap. But the process is one, and continuous; it is progressive and always developing.

And surely it is exactly like that in this whole question of sanctification. I am sure that any Christian looking back across life can testify to the same thing. You can see certain landmarks, certain special periods, certain times when things seemed unusually clear and you seemed to make an advance. Then there seemed to be times when things remained dormant and nothing happened, until, again, something happened. That is the process of sanctification. It is not sudden. The experience and the realisation may be, but the thing itself is progressive.

This brings me to my last negative, which is that we must never think of sanctification as something which happens without a struggle and fight. Here again, of course, we realise that there is a teaching which would emphasise that sanctification is effortless. But I think it follows from the teaching that we have been laying down, that that cannot be the case. Once more, the view that we are delivered from all struggling and strain and fighting is characteristic of the cults and false human teaching. That is why they always tend to appeal to us, because they offer us something easy. But as you look at the teaching of Scripture, I suggest that you do not find anything like that, and I am not only referring to the fight that is outside us, but also to the enemy that is still within us. The Scripture tells us that the remnants of the old man are still here – you do not get rid of him – and as long as that is the case, there will be a fight and a struggle. Scriptural teaching about the flesh involves the necessity of a struggle: 'The flesh lusteth against the Spirit, and the Spirit against the flesh' (Gal 5:17).

'Ah yes,' says someone, 'but that is before you receive the blessing of sanctification.' Wait a minute! Let us be quite honest. Do you know anybody who would tell you that he or she has been entirely delivered from the flesh? Is there no struggle within you? How easy it is to put a theoretical position – is it true in practice? The flesh is allowed to remain just as death is allowed. God does not deliver us from this. He puts in the new man, who can overcome the flesh and the old man, and the old nature, but the remnants of the old nature and the flesh are still there and that means struggle, that means fight. That is why we are exhorted not to grieve the Holy Spirit, not to quench the

Holy Spirit; that is why we are exhorted to mortify our members that are on the earth; that is why we are told to mortify the flesh and the deeds of the body. We are told to watch, to purify ourselves and to cleanse ourselves, and we are told to fight the good fight of faith. All these exhortations arise, of necessity, because of this struggle that is in life.

We must not, however, forget what I have laid down as my first principle, which is that we are not left to engage in this struggle alone. The work of God has been started in us. If you are a Christian at all, the Holy Spirit is in you, and the Holy Spirit gives you the power to fight. But you have to do the fighting, you have to put off the old man and put on the new – that is scriptural teaching and it involves a struggle. But it is not a hopeless fight, because I am certain of the ultimate victory.

As we saw in our last study, if this is not true, then I simply cannot understand a single New Testament epistle, and I do not see why the New Testament was ever written. But these letters were written because these men, whom God appointed as pastors and teachers, knew that the Christians needed to be exhorted continually to go on with the fight and the struggle, for if they did not they were defeated. Therefore we, too, must fight, we must struggle and we must work out our own salvation, not with light-hearted joviality, but with fear and trembling, because it is God that worketh in us, both to will and to do of his good pleasure.

So that brings us to the end of the negatives, all of which have been necessary, not because of the biblical teaching, but because of other false teachings. But having thus dealt with the negatives, we are now free to continue with a consideration of the positive teaching of the Scriptures, which is, 'Sanctify them through thy truth.' We shall look at this blessed, wonderful, large, comprehensive truth of God, this full-orbed gospel that does not separate justification from sanctification, but says that it is all a work of God. We shall consider a great truth that cannot be divided up into separate movements, a movement for evangelism, a movement for sanctification, a movement about the Second Coming, a movement about this and that. No, for the truth is one and it must not be atomised in this way; it is unscriptural and dangerous to do so. We are looking at this great truth in all its wondrous fullness, we see how each aspect of it fits into the whole, and we see the hand of God in it all. We see how he starts the work in the babe, and continues it until eventually we shall all arrive complete and perfect, even into 'the measure of the stature of the fullness of Christ' himself.

May God give us grace to do so and may we all realise that this is not a theoretical matter, but that this is the thing for which Christ died, the thing for which he sanctified himself, namely, that we may be sanctified and might be made meet and fit to dwell face to face with God in glory and to enjoy him for ever and ever.

6

One All-inclusive Truth

Sanctify them through thy truth: thy word is truth (v. 17).

In our last two studies, we have been looking at God's method of
sanctifying us. We laid down the negatives and warned about
certain dangers, and so now we are in a position to approach the
truth positively. The great statement, as we have seen, is that *the
work of sanctification in us is done by God through the medium
of the truth*. If we say that our sanctification takes place by God
bringing us into the realm of the truth, in order that the truth may
act upon us, then the vital question for us is, therefore, What is
this truth which God uses in order to promote our sanctification?

Here again there is more than one view. There are those –
and this is the teaching which I think needs to be coun-
teracted first of all – who seem to regard the truth to which
our Lord refers here as just being some wonderful, special
teaching which they go on repeating. But that, surely, is
quite a false understanding of what our Lord means by the
truth. Indeed, our Lord here, at once realising the danger, it
seems to me, safeguards us against it by defining the truth:
'Sanctify them through thy truth, thy word is truth.' What,
then, is this word? The answer can be found in this chapter
in verses 6, 7, 8, which we have already considered.[1] It is not
some peculiar teaching about sanctification which a man goes

---

[1] In Volume 2, *Safe in the World* (Crossway Books, 1988)

on to after justification. No, it is the holy word. Our Lord says, 'I have manifested thy name unto the men which thou gavest me out of the world: thine they were, and thou gavest them me; and they have kept thy word. Now they have known that all things whatsoever thou hast given me are of thee. For I have given unto them the words which thou gavest me; and they have received them, and have known surely that I came out from thee, and they have believed that thou didst send me.' 'Thy word is truth,' he says here in verse 17 – and that is the truth.

So our Lord is teaching us that God sanctifies us through the truth, by means of the truth and in the truth. He is referring partly to his own teaching – the truth by which we are sanctified is not only what we read in Romans, chapters 6, 7 and 8, it is all the teaching of the Gospels, this word which God had given to the Son, and which the Son taught his followers. It is not just one section of the truth, it is the whole of the truth. Everything he teaches in the Sermon on the Mount, and everything he teaches elsewhere, all that is what God uses in order to bring about our sanctification.

But, of course, it does not only include that. In John 14, 15 and 16 our Lord has just told these disciples that the Holy Spirit, when he comes and is given to them in fullness, will teach them and lead them into all truth; it is still the same idea. Our Lord describes him as the Spirit of truth: not simply as the true Spirit as against the false spirits, but in a very special way as the Spirit through whom the truth of God comes to men and women and is mediated to them. Our Lord says, 'I have yet many things to say unto you, but ye cannot bear them now. Howbeit when he, the Spirit of truth, is come, he will guide you into all truth' (John 16:12 – 13). And, of course, when the Holy Spirit came he did enlighten these apostles, and we have their teaching recorded for us in these various New Testament epistles. So we see that the truth that God uses in order to bring about our sanctification is all the truth we have in the Gospels, together with all the truth that we have in the New Testament epistles. All the demonstration and doctrine, all the exhortation and appeals, the whole of the New Testament, is the truth which he has used in order to bring about our sanctification. So that is our basic definition; the truth about sanctification, and the truth which leads to it, is not some isolated department on its own to which you go, having been somewhere else first. The whole of the truth about the person of our Lord is this word of God which leads to our sanctification.

Because of this, then, we must now consider this truth, because without it sanctification is not possible. We saw in our negatives that sanctification does not take place as the result of God acting directly upon us. No, he does it through showing this particular truth. So if we are anxious that we should grow in grace and in the knowledge of the Lord and that we should conform more and more to the image of God's dear Son; if it is our supreme ambition to know him and to be devoted to him, then the first thing we must do is to pay attention to this truth.

Now it is a truth which is divided up in the Scriptures into many aspects, but before we come to look at them in detail, or in terms of these different facets, it is important that we should begin by looking at it as a whole. To do this, therefore, we must stand back and look at the great New Testament message which promotes sanctification, and realise that there are certain major principles with respect to it. Most people get into trouble in the Christian life, and in almost every profession, because they rush to details before they grasp the principles. In order truly to understand any science or any branch of knowledge, we must start with great fundamental principles, and it is only as we have them firmly in our minds that we can go on to details, because if we have not grasped the principles, the details will not help us. Most heresies have arisen because men have fastened on details in that way.

So, then, here are some of these principles which I would put for your consideration, and which seem to stand out on the surface of this New Testament truth, this word of God. The first is that we again see the importance of not regarding sanctification primarily from the standpoint of an experience. Sanctification is primarily the application of the truth to ourselves, it is not first and foremost having or receiving an experience. Rather, what happens in sanctification is that God takes this truth, this word of his, and by the Holy Spirit brings it to us, opens our understanding of it and enables us to apprehend it. So that after we have received the truth and apprehended it, we then proceed to apply it to ourselves. And the whole time God is enabling us to do that.

I emphasise this first great principle because I would not hesitate to assert that perhaps the main trouble which most of us have in this matter of sanctification is that we tend to be waiting for some experience instead of taking the truth, applying our minds to it, and then applying it entirely to our lives. We seem to think that what happens is that somehow we are put into a sanctified position and that once we get there, everything is going to be all right. But it never seems to happen – we are still waiting for some experience. That is not the New Testament teaching at all. What the New Testament says is that we must realise the truth about God, the truth about ourselves, the truth about what Christ has done for us and about our standing and status.

That is why Paul offered that prayer for the church at Ephesus. What you need, he says, is that 'the eyes of your understanding' may be enlightened (Eph 1:18), because if you only knew the truth, then your position would be changed. So we must not wait for the experience and say that then everything will be all right. No, the way to come to an experience is rather in dependence upon the Holy Spirit who is at work within us, to approach the truth, to study, to understand and to grasp it and then to apply it to ourselves. Now that is surely the argument of all the New Testament epistles. Why were they ever written? Why was not just a brief note sent to all those Christian people saying, 'All you have to do is to wait for an experience of sanctification'? No, these people had received the Holy Spirit, so what they were constantly being told was that they must grasp the truth that had been given to them, live by it, and apply it to themselves. That will become clearer as we come on to certain other things.

I would put my second principle like this: our main and basic need in sanctification is not power but light and knowledge and instruction. Now I put it in that form deliberately. I think it is true to say that we all tend to feel that our basic need is the need of power – we want power in our lives; we feel that we know what is right, and we want to do it, but we somehow lack the power to do it, and we long to be charged with this power, which will enable us to live aright. 'Sanctify them,' says our Lord in his petition, but it is 'sanctify them *in thy truth,* thy word is truth.' Fill them with knowledge, he says, give them the understanding, apply the truth to them.

There is no question at all but that the devil encourages us to think that our need in sanctification is power, because the devil's object is to keep us in ignorance. He first of all keeps the whole world in ignorance about its condition and its relationship to God. He blinds the eyes and the minds of them that believe not, he blinds their minds to the truth about God and about themselves and about righteousness and about judgement. He tries to keep us out of the entire realm of the Christian faith, but if in spite of his efforts we become Christians, he still continues with his work and he now tries to blind us to the real truth about ourselves as it is in Christ Jesus.

I suggest that as long as we are in this life, there is a sense in which even Christian people will always have to fight the battle of justification by faith only. As Paul pointed out to the Galatians, the danger is that having started in the Spirit we continue in the flesh, and we are all constantly faced with this danger. It is always the work of the devil, and he does it in a particular way in connection with this whole question of sanctification. We think that what we need is power, so that we have nothing to do but wait till the power comes, whereas the teaching is that what we need is to know this truth, the truth about ourselves in our relationship to God – 'The eyes of your understanding being enlightened that ye may know what is the hope of his calling, and what the riches of the glory of his inheritance in the saints and what is the exceeding greatness of his power to us-ward who believe' (Eph 1:18–19).

For as Christian people the power is already in us. You cannot be a Christian without having received the Holy Spirit. 'No man can say that Jesus is the Lord, but by the Holy Ghost' (1 Cor 12:3). We are not Christians unless we have received the Holy Spirit, it is a part of our regeneration and rebirth; the gift of the Spirit is the possession of every truly converted Christian believer. Therefore, the power to live the Christian life is already there. So what we really need is to know the truth about ourselves as Christians; we need to know that we are children of God, that our sins have been forgiven, that we are reconciled to God, and that we need have no worry about that. We need to see ourselves 'seated in the heavenly places in Christ Jesus'. We need to know that the very hairs of our head are all num-bered, that we are thus special people in the sight of God and we need to know about the blessed hope that is awaiting us. That is the teaching of the New Testament. For our real trouble is that we tend to have our own ideas as to what a Christian is, instead of accepting the New Testament definition.

I am most anxious to emphasise this, because there is nothing which is so blessed and so releasing as to be taken out of that sub-jectivity that is always looking at itself, and, rather, to see one's self as one truly is in the purpose of God, as it is outlined in the New Testament. The trouble is that we tend to go to the word with these prejudices of ours, and we do not really take in what we are reading; we do not allow it to speak to us. We fail to realise that this description of the New Testament man should be a description of *us*, not only of the first Christians, nor of some ideal person, but a description of every one of us if we are Christians. Thus the vital thing is to realise what we are and if we realise that, then we should begin to realise 'the power that worketh in us' (Eph 3:20).

So my third proposition is that most of our troubles in this matter are ultimately in the realm of the will. Now I want to put this carefully. Here again I say that we tend to fool ourselves and to think that our wills are all right, but that what we need is the power to carry out the will. Once more we are deluded by the devil at that point. People often tend to put it like this: 'You know, I have tried and tried for years to get rid of this thing out of my life, and I pray to God about it.' We need to pause between the two parts of that statement, because it generally happens in this way. They first of all try to get rid of their problem themselves. Then they go to somebody who seems to be an expert in these matters, and he says, 'Ah yes, but of course that is exactly where you have gone wrong. You have been trying to do it yourself, and you never will. You must give up trying and you must pray about it – stop your own efforts and just pray to God about it, and ask him to take it from you, and it will go.' Then they tell you that they have prayed about it, and they have gone to meetings, and heard other people say that their sins have suddenly been taken away, but they themselves are still burdened, and they do not know what to do next. They feel that they are failures and they are desperate.

It seems to me that there is only one real trouble with such people and it is entirely in the realm of the will. Otherwise they are either saying that God does not want to deliver them, or that he cannot deliver them. That is their position. They have tried the proposed remedy, they have tried to surrender themselves utterly and they have asked God to take this burden from them, but they say that they still have it.

But that is where the trouble arises, and I feel that there is only one thing to do at this point, and that is to be brutal, and to say to these friends, 'The real trouble with you is that you have a divided will. You are saying, in effect, either that God does not want to take this thing away, or that he cannot. But the trouble is that you do not really want to get rid of it; you are fond of it. You are not hungering and thirsting after righteousness, you are really unhappy in your mind. You know it is wrong but you like it – that is the trouble. It is as we read in John 3:19 "Men loved darkness rather than light."'

The only thing to do with such people is to bring them face to face with truth, and to confront them with the fact that if they claim to be Christians, they are really saying a number of things about themselves. If they claim to believe in God, and in the Holy Spirit, how can they go on with this particular thing, whatever it may be? You have to convince their wills about this matter, you have to put their will right.

Then the fourth proposition is this: the will, as I understand this New Testament teaching, is never to be coerced or forced into a decision. Now that must be said, even in the light of what we have just been suggesting. I still say the sort of people I have been describing, you have to be brutal and show them that their trouble is in the realm of the will, but it is very important that you do not force the will, or get them to do so. You must show them the truth, in order tha their wills may be persuaded by the truth. Let me put this practically. So often you find that what happens with such people is that pressure is put upon them – 'You must decide it here and now,' they are urged; their will is forced, and then they are told they have promised and that they must never go back on their word.

But people who have done that often find themselves later on in the position that the only thing that really holds them there is their own decision or their own view. Now that may be quite a good thing in a practical sense – it is certainly extremely good psychology, – but it is utterly bad New Testament teaching, if indeed it is New Testament teaching at all. This is because you and I must be held to the New Testament position not by our pledges, but by the truth. We must realise, therefore, that the will is to be persuaded by the truth, and that that is how God works. He never forces our will, but rather presents the truth to us in such a way that we want it – 'Every man that hath this hope in him purifieth himself, even as he is pure' (1 Jn 3:3). So what the New Testament does is hold the blessed hope before us, and then, having seen it for ourselves, we say, 'If I am going there, I cannot behave like this here and now; I am jeopardising my own liberty.' The truth has come to us, and as we see the truth we want to be delivered from sin, and to belong to God.

Let me put it quite plainly. I cannot see, from New Testament teaching, that there is the slightest justification for ever calling upon people in a meeting to decide to go in for sanctification and for bringing pressure upon them to do so by forcing them to a decision. If that procedure is wrong in evangelism, it is equally wrong in this matter of sanctification. A man's will must never be approached directly, because the will must always be approached through the truth. The truth should be presented to the will in such a way that the will desires it, needs and accepts it. This it does freely and without any sense of constraint, and puts into practice what it has willed. Therefore, if you are ever confronted by a man who tells you that he is defeated, and that he is a slave to, or a victim of, something, the thing to do is to remind him of the whole nature of the truth. You do not spend your time discussing the particular problem. Rather, you say, 'Are you a child of God?' You address him in terms of the truth, and so the will, the whole time, is being influenced by the truth which is being presented.

Let me put that in the form of another proposition. According to this truth, this word of God in the New Testament, sanctification is not just a matter of being delivered from particular sins. So often you will find that that is what is taught. People seem to think that if only they could get rid of this one sin, they would be sanctified; and it becomes still worse when the entire doctrine is focussed upon deliverance from one particular sin. No, sanctification is a matter of being rightly related to God, and becoming entirely devoted to him. Sanctification means becoming positively holy. It does not just mean I am not guilty of certain sins, because the moment you begin to think of it negatively like that, you are satisfied that you are sanctified; but you may be as far from sanctification, if not further, than the man who is guilty of one or other of those sins, because now you are now guilty of smugness! Sanctification means being devoted to God, not only separated from the world but separated unto God and sharing his life – it is positive holiness.

I proceed, then, to my next principle, the sixth, which is that the New Testament method of dealing with particular sins is never to concentrate upon the particular sin as such, but to bring it into the light and the context of the whole Christian position. I cannot emphasise that principle too strongly. Speaking out of pastoral experience, I have found in practice, that that particular principle is probably the most important of all. May I give you one illustration. I remember a lady once, some twenty years ago, coming to tell me of a crippling problem in her Christian spiritual life. She told me that she had a terrible horror and dread of thunderstorms. Apparently she had once been in a bad thunderstorm, and it had looked as if she might be killed. Ever since then the fear of thunder and lightning had gripped her, and it had come to such a pass that if she was going to a place of worship and happened to see a large cloud, she would begin to say to herself, 'A thunderstorm is coming! So there would be a terrible conflict within her and it usually ended in her turning back and going home. It seemed to her that the one problem of her life was this fear and dread of thunderstorms. She told me she had struggled with this problem and done her best to get rid of it. She had been to consult many Christian people about it and they all told her to pray about it, and to ask God to deliver her from it. She had been praying for this for twenty-two years, but it was worse rather than better, and she went on to tell me how she longed to be delivered from this one thing which was marring her Christian life.

Now it seemed to me that the one thing to say to that woman was this – and it came as a shock to her – 'Stop praying about this particular fear, for while you are praying, you are reminding yourself of it. You must stop thinking about yourself in terms of fear. Never think about thunderstorms; turn your back upon that altogether. What you must do is to think about yourself as a disciple of the Lord Jesus Christ and as one who belongs to him. You are known as a Christian, therefore you are claiming certain things. You must concentrate upon positive Christianity, not upon a negative fear of one sin.' And after much instruction she saw it and the fear of thunderstorms was forgotten. It did not happen suddenly, but as she concentrated on the Christian life, the fear just went.

Often people come and talk about one particular sin. They have been concentrating upon that one sin as though the whole Christian life is in just that one sin. But I adopt the word of Paul in Romans: 'The kingdom of God is not meat and drink' (Rom 14:17). There were people in the church who seemed to say that

Christianity was one particular thing: What should you eat and drink? Which day should you observe? But that is not the Christian life! So when a man comes and talks to me about one thing, I talk to him about peace and joy in the Holy Spirit, all these positive elements, and I tell him, 'You must be stretching out after them, and if you do so you will be delivered from the one sin.' That is the New Testament method; it brings the truth to us and gives us this glorious picture of the new man in Christ Jesus.

The next principle is that sanctification must never be thought of as an end in itself but rather as a means to an end. Here again is a very important principle. Our eyes should not be only upon the cultivation of a holy life and freedom from sins. I go further: it should not even be our ambition to be holy men and women. I remember a man saying to me, 'You know, my greatest ambition is to be a holy man.' I said to him, 'Yes, that is the trouble with you!' The goal, I say, is not even to be holy men, nor to attain holiness, but rather to live in fellowship with God. Our goal is the knowledge and the love of God and of his Son Jesus Christ. The goal is not that I should be sanctified, but that I should be walking with him in fellowship and communion, in the light of the knowledge that I am going to spend my eternity with him.

This is the main problem during every season of Lent.[1] The Catholic conception of holiness and mysticism, it seems to me, goes wrong at this very point, for it always concentrate upon the holy condition of the believer. If you read any manual on the holy or devoted life ever written by a Catholic or a mystic, you will usually find that you are exposing yourself to that particular danger. They concentrate attention upon the experimental condition, upon the experience, and then, of course, they take you through the different stages – the stage of torment, the stage of the dark night of the soul – until you ultimately arrive at the stage of holy contemplation.

I remember a man once, an old minister of the gospel, telling

[1] This sermon was preached during Lent in 1953.

me that he was struggling, and in a sense really living in order
to pass through the experience of the dark night of the soul,
because he felt that he had never gone through it. Poor man!
It was all subjective; he was simply concerned to be a holy
man. But that is where the error comes in. Is it not exactly the
same with this observance of Lent? To observe Lent for a certain number of weeks during the year is just to concentrate
upon your experience. It is to look at yourself and try to make
yourself better, to pull yourself up to a higher level. And, incidentally, what I am saying is not only true of the Catholic
form of sanctification and holiness, you will find it coming
out in evangelical piety too. The man who is anxious to think
of himself as pious, falls into the same error.

But the whole biblical emphasis is not upon that at all, for
the New Testament truth, the word of God, always puts it in
terms of our personal relationship to the Father and to his Son,
Jesus Christ, through the Holy Spirit. In other words, let us
forget about our state and condition. Instead, the one question
I need to ask myself is this: 'Do I know God? Is Jesus Christ
real to me?' Not, 'Am I now no longer full of the sin of which
I used to be guilty?' Not, 'Am I observing certain rules and
regulations?' It is not, 'Do I spend so much time in reading
and prayer?' No, rather, it is this: 'Am I having fellowship
with him?' If you do not know this living experience of God,
all your negative righteousness is of no value to you.

And that brings me to my last principle which arises out of
all that I have been saying, and it is this: the truth about which
our Lord speaks is a great truth, a large and comprehensive
truth. You can read certain books and listen to certain addresses and you get the impression that the truth which leads to
sanctification is really a very simple truth, just one little message – all you have to do is to surrender and wait and keep
looking. But this truth about which our Lord speaks is the
whole Christian truth! It includes all the epistles, all the Sermon on the Mount and the teaching of the Gospels. It is the
whole Bible; it is everything that tells us anything about God.

We hear complaints sometimes that certain types of teaching about sanctification seem to be running to seed, that they seem to be lacking body. It is not surprising, since if you nail the truth down, you cannot get any other result. No, the truth which is concerned about sanctification is not only found in Romans, 6, 7 and 8 – though you are sometimes given the impression that it is there, and nowhere else – it is everywhere. It is all the truth, it is this vast body of doctrine; it is the whole Christian message. That is why I would reiterate that an evangelistic meeting should include sanctification, if it is truly evangelistic. If a Christian can sit back and feel that the message has nothing to say to him, then there has been something wrong with the evangelistic message, for it is one which tells about the holiness of God, and immediately the process of sanctification is going on as it describes the heinousness of sin and as it tells about Christ dying on the cross. Indeed, I can never look at the cross without that truth prompting my sanctification. It is tragic to think that we have divided these things into departments, and separated them from one another. No message whatsoever about the cross is isolated from sanctification; sanctification is involved in every iota of the truth, in all the knowledge of God and our relationship to him, whether it tells about the Eternal Council before the creation of the world, whether it tells about being foreordained and elected, or whether it tells about principalities and powers and a blessed hope. It is all the truth that works upon me by the Holy Spirit, and leads to and promotes my sanctification. 'Sanctify them through thy truth, thy word is truth': every word of God is a word used in our sanctification. 'O the depth of the riches both of the wisdom and knowledge of God!' That is it! We are facing this never ebbing sea, this ocean of God's eternal truth, and to be sanctified means an increasing apprehension of it and an increasing application of it in our daily life.

7

The Truth about God

Sanctify them through the truth: thy word is truth (v. 17).

We have been emphasising the point that the truth, this word of God which is the truth that sanctifies, is large and great and comprehensive, and that it is wrong to regard it just as one section of biblical teaching, and to say that you have now come to the truth of sanctification, as if that is divorced from every other aspect of truth. Our emphasis is that it is the whole of the truth, every aspect of the truth, that ultimately is used of God by the Holy Spirit in our sanctification.

But obviously, though we hold to that, it is yet a truth which we can sub-divide in an intellectual manner, under certain main headings; Scripture itself does that, and it is right that we should do so also. God condescends to our weakness, and he knows that it is easier for us to receive truth, and to remember it, and to retain it, if it is presented to us under certain groupings or headings. And so it has always been the custom in the church to divide up this one great comprehensive truth, the word of God which sanctifies, under various headings. But again I emphasise that they are nothing but headings; they are not distinct truths which can be isolated and separated from other truths. They are simple sub-divisions in the one all-inclusive comprehensive truth. And it seems to me that we are not presenting the doctrine of sanctification truly unless we at least glance at some of these main headings of the truth which sanctifies.

Clearly we cannot go into any one of them exhaustively at this point. The object is rather that we may make sure that certain key principles are emphasised; and as we come to do this, we shall see that there can be no doubt or question at all as to which comes first. I wonder what your answer would be if I put that question: What should be the first heading when you come to consider in detail the truth which sanctifies? What is the first thing you want to emphasise? This is very important, and surely the heading which, without a doubt, should occupy the first position is the truth about God himself.

I wonder whether we would all have started with that? I want to emphasise it because I think we must all plead guilty to the fact that there is a tendency and a danger among us (I am referring now to Christian people, who think from the evangelical standpoint with regard to truth) – though I say it with fear and trembling – to take God for granted. I mean by that, to assume God, to imagine that because we are Christians, and evangelical Christians in particular, then we do not need to consider constantly the truth about God himself. 'That is a truth,' we say, 'that the unconverted need, of course, because they do not think of God; God is not in all their thoughts or in their mind; they are living a godless life.' We know that we need to preach the truth about God himself to the unconverted, but we think that people who are Christians are obviously believers in God, and that therefore there is no need to preach to them and to present constantly the doctrine about God himself.

I wonder what the result would be if we made a careful examination of large numbers of addresses and sermons on this question of sanctification? I wonder how often we would find that the doctrine concerning God himself has been preached on such occasions? I think we would find the answer illuminating. The tendency, the danger is, as we have seen, that we start with the idea that sanctification is just one department only of salvation. We forget that the first beginning of sanctification is the doctrine of God himself.

Let me illustrate this, remembering always that it is a matter which we must approach carefully. Is it not true to say that among certain Christian people there is a tendency to pray to the Lord Jesus Christ rather than to God the Father? Do not misunderstand me. I am not saying that it is wrong to pray to the three persons of the blessed Trinity separately, for there is evidence in the Scriptures that that is the right thing to do. You will find, incidentally, a much greater tendency to do that in the hymns. There is much more individual prayer to the three persons separately in our hymn-books than there is in the Scriptures. Yet surely no one can dispute the point that in the Scripture itself prayer is generally addressed to God in the name of Christ, through and by the Holy Spirit. We cannot come to God except by the blood of Jesus. We ask everything in Christ's name and for Christ's sake. But the prayer is ultimately addressed to God the Father. I am simply indicating that there is an increasing tendency for people to pray to the Lord Jesus Christ and it is entirely due to the same reason, it is just another indication of the way in which, because our doctrine is not based four-square upon the teaching of the Scripture itself, we have departmentalised it and somehow or other (it is a terrible thing to say) we tend to forget God. I am emphasising, therefore, the fact that the Bible itself always starts with God in every respect. God is at the beginning, and he continues right through. It is a book about God. It is all about him, and everything in it is designed simply to bring us to him. Thus, not to remind ourselves that the doctrine concerning God is central, and always covers and overrules everything else, is, it seems to me, to fall into very grievous error, for if we are wrong at this point it is certain we shall be wrong everywhere else.

Indeed, is it not the case that in this matter of sanctification our tendency is always to start with ourselves, instead of starting with God? I have got this sin that is worrying me and always getting me down, this sin that defeats me, and my tendency is to say, 'What can be done about this sin, this problem of mine? How can I get rid of this thing? How can I get peace?' I start with myself and my problem, and as certainly as I do that when I am considering this doctrine of sanctification, I am sure, in some shape or form, to end by regarding God as merely an agency who is there to help me to solve my problem. And this is a totally unscriptural approach to the almighty ever blessed God.

There was a book, written in the 1930s by a distinguished American preacher, who, incidentally, was a Roman Catholic, with the startling title, *Religion without God*. The contents of the book were equally startling, because they were so terribly true. In many ways religion may be our greatest danger. We can worship religion, and we can be very religious without God. I mean by that, that we can be very punctilious in the observance of days and times and seasons. We can fast, we can deny ourselves things, and the whole time we are just centring upon ourselves and thinking about how we are going to improve ourselves and make ourselves better. We are trying to get certain lessons for ourselves, and the whole thing may be really self-centred. We may be highly religious, but there may be no place for God; or even if he does come in, he is simply there as someone who may be of help to us. We are at the centre of our religion; our religion really is a religion without God. And that is, I suppose, the last, and the ultimate, sin.

However, if we pay attention to these truths about which our Lord speaks we find that kind of position or attitude is a complete impossibility, because the first truth of sanctification, according to the Scriptures, is the truth of God himself. A very convenient way, I find, of realising that and of getting it fixed in my mind, is to look at it as follows. The condition, or the state, of sanctification (let me remind you once more that it is a condition and a state and not merely an experience) is, of course, the antithesis of the condition and the state of sin. Sanctification is that which separates us from sin unto God, whereas sin, ultimately, is to forget God. The essence of sin does not reside in the particular thing that I do, but rather in refusing to glorify God as he should be glorified. And all these sinful actions of ours are the manifestations of that central disease which is forgetfulness of God.

That is why sin is sometimes defined very rightly as self-centredness. It is selfishness. Sin really means that instead of living unto, and for God, and in the way that God desires of us, we are living for ourselves, in our own way, forgetful of him, and after the manner and the fashion of this world. So clearly, therefore, sanctification must of necessity start with this – my relationship to God. The first thing is not my getting rid of this particular sin that is in my life. No! The first thing must be God and my relationship to him. That is why the Bible always, everywhere, starts with God, and that is why we say once more that sanctification is really that condition or state in which a man lives his life continually under God and for God, and for his glory.

In other words, the main characteristic of people who are sanctified is that God is in the centre of their lives. That is the first thing we may say about them. Before we get them to say what they do or do not do with regard to a particular action, we must be clear about the central, primary, most vital thing, which is how the truth sanctifies us. It starts by holding us face to face with God and it tells us the truth about him. The Bible is primarily a revelation of God. It is not primarily interested in man, but in God. It is designed to bring man to a knowledge of God, and so it tells us about him.

And here again we must be careful to take the whole truth, because with our subjectivity we tend to be interested in God only from the standpoint of what we want, so that there is always a tendency to think of God only as a Saviour. But the Bible tells us much more about God than that. It gives us a revelation of the whole truth about God. We cannot take in the whole revelation, but the whole is good. So it tells us about God as Creator as well as God as Saviour. It tells us about his greatness, his majesty, his might and his dominion. It tells us something about the attributes of God. My friends, I am sure that as I bring these things before you, you will agree with me when I repeat once more, startling and surprising though it sounds at first, that the main difficulty with every one of us is that we forget God, and fail to realise who God is. It is because of this subjectivity of ours that we fail to realise, even when we are engaged in prayer, what we are doing and whom we are approaching. We are so concerned about our desires and our petitions that we fail to worship God, and to come to him in the way that the Scriptures everywhere tell us to approach him.

Consider the message of Hebrews 9 and 10. The great theme there is just this question of how to approach God. You go to the Old Testament and you see all that ritual and ceremonial – was it meaningless? Why were all these details given about the building of the Tabernacle and of the Temple? Why were the priests told to present certain offerings and sacrifices? Is this all meaningless? No! The answer is that it is all designed to teach man how to approach God, how to worship him. The shekinah glory was something real and absolute, and people could not rush into the Holiest of all whenever they liked. Only one man went in, the High Priest alone, and then only once a year, and then always with an offering of blood. The whole of the Old Testament, in a sense, is just this great teaching about how we are to approach God.

'Ah yes,' says someone, 'but wait a minute, that is the Old Testament. Do you not realise that Christ having come, everything is entirely different?' It is different in this way, that we are no longer dependent upon the Levitical ceremonial, and that in our Lord, we have the 'great High Priest'. But let us never forget that the New Testament, in the full light of the revelation of the Lord Jesus Christ, still goes on emphasising the importance of realising what we do when we approach God. The fact that I do not go into the 'Holiest of all' in the elaborate way in which the ancients went, but that I go in Christ, does not mean that I therefore need any less reverence! Let us approach God with reverence, and with godly fear, for 'our God is a consuming fire' (Heb 12:29).

The Scripture therefore promotes our sanctification, our holiness, by reminding us about all this; that the God whom we approach and whom we worship is the Creator of the universe, the sustainer of everything. There is no end to his might and his majesty, to his dominion and his power. The Scripture emphasises God's holiness in a very special way. No one ever emphasised that more than the Lord Jesus Christ himself – you never hear him pray, 'dear Lord', or 'dear Father' but rather, 'holy Father'! That is the prayer of the one who was without sin at all, and who was absolutely perfect. When he approaches God, he addresses him as 'holy Father'! This is the truth that sanctifies, the truth that reminds us that God is in heaven and that we are on the earth; the truth that puts us into the right position and setting before God.

The greatest need of all of us is the need to be humble; our greatest lack is humility. It is our whole approach to God that is wrong, and the first great truth that we need to be taught is this truth that overrides everything else in the word of God. It is the truth about God's holiness, about God's eternal judgements and about his absolute righteousness. It is the truth that God is the Judge eternal. 'Ah but,' you say, 'I am a Christian and I am surely not concerned about judgement.' The Bible does not tell you that. The whole epistle to the Hebrews is a warning that we must meet God as Judge, and as Judge eternal. He is the one who shook the earth and who has now shaken the heavens. He is the judge of all men, and we must all appear before him.

That is a part of the truth of sanctification; it is not something that need only be preached in an evangelistic meeting. It is of the very essence of sanctification, and is its first principle. Our God is a consuming fire! John puts it this way, in teaching sanctification in his epistle. The first thing he lays down concerning sanctification is this: 'God is light, and in him is no darkness at all' (1 Jn 1:5); so I suggest to you that we have no right to go on to consider any other aspects whatsoever of the truth of sanctification until we have realised that truth. And then John, having started with this emphasis concerning the truth about God, especially stresses in following verses that salvation is God's plan.

Here again let me put this negatively. Are we not sometimes prone to think that salvation really is something that arises from man; that God is just waiting passively for us to go to him, and that when we do go and ask him for certain things, he will be graciously pleased to give them to us? Our tendency is to think of salvation only from our side. But the Bible puts it solely on the other side. Salvation and heaven are the plan of God. They are the scheme of God. They come from God and originate with him.

The Bible tells us that God's great purpose in salvation is to separate unto himself a 'peculiar people, zealous of good works' (Tit 2:14). Everything that has been done in this great design of salvation – every aspect, every movement, every vision of it – is all designed for that end. I have always found that nothing has helped me with this whole question of sanctification so much as the realisation that I am simply someone who, as a Christian, has been taken into this scheme and plan of God. For instead of thinking primarily of myself and of my problems and of my needs and of my desires, I have awakened to the glorious, stupendous, thrilling fact that the great God who has planned this scheme of salvation has looked upon me, and has brought me into that scheme. So I do not start thinking of myself as myself; I see myself in God's plan and in God's purpose.

You will notice that I am repeating this because it seems to me that not to realise this is the root cause of most troubles. Kierkegaard, the great Danish theologian, who lived in the last century, coined a phrase which has been very popular in our own days. He said that 'religion is subjectivity'. He lived in a country where you had orthodox Lutheranism which had been dead and petrified for a long time. The teaching was perfectly orthodox, they never said anything that was wrong, but it was lifeless. Kierkegaard saw that such orthodoxy was of no value. He said that merely to hold a number of correct intellectual notions and subscribe to a number of correct propositions was not religion. 'That is not what I find in the Bible,' he wrote. 'That is not what I find in the lives of the saints. They had something vital, something living, something had happened to them.' So he said that 'religion is subjectivity'.

He was, of course, over-emphasising. He wanted to shock the people out of their dead orthodoxy. He was right in this, but in the end he went too far. It is always the danger when we try to correct an error. The danger, if we are not careful, is always that we start by speaking out in a striking manner that will shock people out of one error and end by going into another error, which is the exact opposite of the one we are correcting. If Kierkegaard had said that in religion there must always be a subjective element, he would have been right, but when he says that 'religion is subjectivity' he is wrong.

So it would be equally wrong for me to maintain that 'religion is objectivity', and I am not saying that. But what I am saying is that as you tend to need particular emphases at different times and in different epochs, I have no hesitation at all in saying that the emphasis that is needed at the present time is objective, because we are all so subjective in our approach, and we forget God. The truth is that we must start with the objective fact and truth of God, and then think of it as ours in relation to that – our object and our objective. It must be both. It is neither one nor the other; it is both one and the other. It is the objective eternal truth outside myself, God's plan of salvation; and also it is the fact that I myself am brought into that, so that I am aware of God dealing with me, and of things happening to me.

But my emphasis here is that we must start with God and the fact of God, and not simply with our own subjective moods, our own states and feelings and our own personal needs and problems. That then is the truth in general. But there are certain particular emphases that I want also to mention. What is holiness? Well, I do not know a better definition than this: 'Thou shalt love the Lord thy God with all thy heart, and with all thy soul, and with all thy mind, and with all thy strength' (Mk 12:30). *That* is holiness.

For holiness is not simply to have certain problems solved in your life, because you may get certain sins taken from your life and still be far removed from holiness. Essential holiness is a condition in which a man loves God with his heart and his soul and his mind and his strength, and the greater the degree or the proportion of each part of the personality that is engaged in this love, the greater the sanctification. Thus, to be sanctified does not just mean that you are not committing certain sins while you are enjoying that particular experience. No, that is a negative view; that is a corollary.

The essence of sanctification is that I love the God in whom I believe, and who has been revealed to me, with the whole of my being. Indeed I do not hesitate to assert that if I think of sanctification in any lesser terms that that, I am being unscriptural. This is scriptural holiness. This is the holiness, the sanctification, that is produced and promoted by the truth of God, because it is the truth concerning God. Then it follows from that – I think directly – that a man who does thus love God with all his heart and soul and mind and strength does so because he is called upon to do so and is commanded to do so. To such a man the main thing in life is to glorify God and to show forth his praises.

This is the argument of the apostle Peter when he reminds the people to whom he is writing that at one time before they became Christians they were not a people. 'Which in time past,' he says, in 1 Peter 1:10, 'were not a people but are now the people of God.' You who are called out of darkness into light are a 'peculiar people'. Why? What is the object of it all? 'That ye should shew forth the praises of him who hath called you out of darkness into his marvellous light' (1 Pet 2:9). 'Praises' there means 'excellencies' or 'virtues'; it means the glorious, marvellous attributes of God. And so, sanctification is that condition in which we praise God just by being what we are. Of course, it includes not doing certain things, but it is not only that. It is much more. By being what we are in all the totality of our personalities and in the whole of our lives, we reveal and manifest the virtues and the excellencies of God. God, of course, calls us to do that. The whole of the biblical teaching about our sonship of God in Christ, is the same argument. 'Be ye holy,' says God, 'for I am holy.' My reason for being holy must not be that I stop committing that sin so that I shall not suffer remorse and have the need of repentance, and that I shall not be miserable and unhappy. Not at all! I am to be holy because God is holy.

Is that not the teaching right through the Bible, in the Old as well as in the New Testament? Why did God give the children of Israel the Ten Commandments? Why did he tell them in detail what to do and what not to do? The reason he always gave was: You are my people; you are unlike all the other nations. I have adopted you; I have taken you; I have created you. You are my people. I want you to live as my people. I want everybody to know that you are my people. Let your life be such that everybody will know that you are God's people. 'Be ye holy for I am holy.' It is exactly the same in the New Testament. 'Let your light so shine before men [or, among men] that they may see your good works and glorify your Father which is in heaven' (Mt 5:16). 'That is the way you must live,' says our Lord in effect in the Sermon on the Mount, 'that is how I am living. I live in such a way that people see me glorifying my Father.' And when he performed his miracles, people praised and glorified God.

And you and I must live like that. That is sanctification, and it is, of course, impossible unless we understand the truth about God. We must realise that our whole life is meant to be lived to the glory of God. The whole purpose of salvation is to make us such that we shall glorify him, and therefore the test of sanctification is not the giving up of my sins, nor my happiness, nor whether I have sacrificed so much in my life; rather, it is whether I am indeed concerned to live only and entirely to the glory of God.

One further point that we must make is that the essence of the Christian life is that we have fellowship and communion with God. Our Lord has already said in John 17, 'This is life eternal, that they might know thee the only true God, and Jesus Christ whom thou hast sent.' As Christians, then, our first and great claim is that we 'know' God, that we 'know' the Lord Jesus Christ. The privilege that we enjoy as Christian people is that we are in fellowship with God, we are in union with him.

Therefore, say the Scriptures, realise who he is and what he is. The apostle John works out the argument for us in his first epistle. The Christian life, he says, is essentially one of walking with God in this life. Therefore, 'If we say that we have fellowship with him, and walk in darkness, we lie, and do not the truth' (1 Jn 1:6). He goes further in the second chapter and says, 'He that saith, I know him, and keepeth not his commandments, is a liar, and the truth is not in him' (2:14).

John's basic definition of sanctification is clear. He teaches that it is the knowledge of God which leads to a life that corresponds with that knowledge. In other words, we are interested in the commandments. How often, I wonder, have you heard the Ten Commandments preached in sanctification and holiness meetings? But we must keep them; it is a part of the preaching, and of the truth, it is the word that sanctifies. It is the truth about God, because to be sanctified is to be walking in his fellowship, realising what we are doing, and living to his glory. So it is still the truth about God which is applied in our lives, and the result of all this is that we begin to understand what the apostle Paul means when he says, 'Work out your own salvation with fear and trembling' (Phil 2:12).

'Oh,' you say, 'but I thought the truth about sanctification was that it is that which delivers me from fear and trembling, that which makes me happy, and which takes the struggle out of my life.' But we must 'work out', and 'with fear and trembling' because sanctification means essentially that we are in this relationship with God, and that we realise what it means. It is not a craven fear – it is the reverence and the godly fear spoken about by the author of the epistle to the Hebrews (12:28–29). It is the fear of wounding or of offending or of hurting such holiness and such love. It is the fear of marring God's purpose and plan, his scheme and his perfect work that is going on in me, for he works in me both to will and to do.

Let me summarise it all by putting it like this. I notice that the Bible itself always describes sanctification in terms of 'godliness' and 'holiness' and 'righteousness'. I do not see that the

characteristic biblical description of the sanctified life is 'victorious living' or 'the life of victory' or 'overcoming'. We are
familiar with these terms, are we not? They have come in, in
recent years. But the Bible describes sanctification in terms of
godliness, god-likeness; that is its biblical term – holiness,
which is a description of God himself.

We tend to describe sanctification as the 'victorious life'
because we think of it in terms of getting rid of particular sins.
'How am I to get victory over this sin? How am I to get victory
in my life?' Again, you see, I am starting with myself – I want
victory. But the Bible describes it in terms of my relationship
to God. How often do you hear the term 'holiness' used today?
How often do you hear men described as 'god-fearing' men?
Those were the biblical terms; until comparatively recently
those were the great evangelical terms. But the whole outlook
has changed. We have become subjective, and I would suggest
to you that, to that extent, we have become unscriptural.

Of course, if we are godly we shall have our victories; but if
you describe sanctification only in terms of 'victories' you have
got the negative view. If you describe it in terms of 'holiness'
and 'godliness' and 'god-likeness' and 'righteousness', then
your view will always be positive. And though you may not be
guilty of certain sins, you will still see yourself as a sinner; you
will still be dissatisfied, but you will press on; you will still
strive; you will still reckon yourself dead to sin; you will still go
on reaching after holiness, hungering and thirsting after righteousness. Whereas if you only look at it in terms of victory, the
great danger is to be self-satisfied and content, to be smug, and
to lead a superficial, incomplete and inadequate Christian life.

The first message, the first aspect of truth, the truth which
sanctifies, is God – the holy, righteous, eternal, ever-blessed
God, who, in Jesus Christ, has become my Father, and with
whom I can walk while I am left in this life, and with whom I
shall spend my eternity. Let us ever approach him with reverence and godly fear. Let us remember that godlikeness is the
end we strive for.

8

The Truth about Sin

Sanctify them through thy truth: thy word is truth (v. 17).

Thus far we have seen that the specific plan and purpose of everything that God has been graciously pleased to do in and through his only begotten Son, is to bring us to a knowledge of himself. Our Lord has stated that very plainly in this great chapter that we are considering together: 'This is life eternal, that they might know thee the only true God, and Jesus Christ, whom thou hast sent.' And whatever we may have experienced, whatever may have happened to us, if we have not this knowledge of God, then it is doubtful whether we are in a position of salvation at all; and there is certainly no value to any moral or ethical qualities that may belong to us unless they derive centrally from this knowledge. So we have seen that we must start with the doctrine of God.

And now we come to the second great section of the truth, which is, of course, the one that follows by a kind of inevitability and logical necessity from the doctrine of God, namely, the doctrine of sin. We must now consider what the word has to tell us about sin and about ourselves in a state and a condition of sin. If, as I say, salvation ultimately means to know God, then the great problem for us is to know what it is that separates us from God. The biblical answer to that is not that it is a lack of natural capacity, nor is it a philosophical inability. No, the one thing that comes between any one of us and God is sin, and that is the great doctrine which you find running right through the Bible.

Here again is an aspect of the truth which for some reason we tend to neglect. I feel that we can say about this doctrine of sin what I once heard a man say about the observance of the Lord's Day. He said he had come to the conclusion that the Lord's Day, like the Lord himself, was in danger of dying between two thieves, the two thieves being Saturday night and Monday morning! He said that increasingly Saturday night was extended and extended, and blended into Sunday, and then people started their Monday morning quite early on Sunday evening. Sunday becomes just a few hours during the morning, and then we think, 'Well, that is enough now, we have been to church once.' Thus our Lord's Day has been lost between two thieves.

I feel that it is equally true to say something like that about this biblical doctrine of sin, and it seems to me to be happening in this way. When we are dealing with the unconverted, we tend to say: 'Ah, you need not worry about sin now, that will come later. All you need to do is to come to Christ, to give yourself to Christ. Do not worry your head about sin – of course you cannot understand that now. Do not worry either whether or not you have got a sense of sin or deep conviction, or whether you know these things. All you need to do is to come to Christ, to give yourself to Christ, and then you will be happy.'

Then when we are dealing with those who have so come, our tendency, again, is to say to them, 'Of course, you must not look at yourself, you must look to Christ. You must not be for ever analysing yourself. That is wrong, that is what you did before you were converted. You were thinking in terms of yourself and of what you had got to do. The only thing you must do is to keep looking to Christ and away from yourself.' We imagine, therefore, that all that is needed by Christians is a certain amount of comfort and encouragement, of preaching about the love of God and about his general providence and perhaps a certain amount of moral and ethical exhortation. And so, you see, the doctrine of sin is, as it were, crowded out. We fail to emphasise it both before and after conversion, and the result is that we hear very little about it.

Now whether you agree with my explanation or not, I think we must all agree with the fact that the doctrine of sin has been sadly neglected. We know that instinctively. We none of us like it, and thus it comes to pass that this doctrine is so little emphasised. And yet when you come to the Bible you find it everywhere, and for this reason, it should of necessity be central. Why should anybody come to Christ? What do people do when they come to him? What do they mean when they say they believe on him? How can that possibly happen apart from some understanding of sin? You cannot give yourself, or your heart to Christ, you cannot surrender, you cannot use the term, 'Take him as your Saviour', unless you know what he is to save you from.

So it is surely utterly unscriptural to indulge in any sort of evangelism which neglects the doctrine of sin. There is no real meaning or content to the term 'Saviour' or 'salvation' apart from the doctrine of sin, which has this tremendous emphasis throughout the Bible. Our fathers – perhaps I should say our grandfathers, and those who preceded them, they of the older evangelicalism – always laid great emphasis on what they called our 'law work'. They emphasised the importance of a thorough-going preliminary law work before you came to the gospel and its redemption, and they were distrustful of those who claimed salvation except in those terms. And as you read their lives you will find they have a great deal to say about 'the plague of their own hearts'. If you read of saintly men like Robert Murray McCheyne, and men of that generation, and those who preceded them, the men of the eighteenth century, you will find that that was their terminology. But it is a language which has somehow or other dropped out, and I think it has done so in the way I have indicated.

But after all, whatever they may have said and thought, the fact which confronts us is that this is something which is found in the Bible everywhere, in the Old Testament and the New, one cannot ignore it, and it is for that reason that we must

consider it. I suggest that it is absolutely vital to a true understanding of sanctification that we should know something
about the biblical doctrine of sin. It is only as we realise the truth
about ourselves and our condition, it is only as we come to
realise our ultimate need, that we apply to Christ, who alone can
supply it. In other words, there is nothing in our experience that
so drives us to Christ as the realisation of our need and our
helplessness.

> Foul, I to the fountain fly;
> Wash me, Saviour, or I die.

It is because I am foul that I fly to the fountain, and if I do not
realise my need of being washed I will not go there.

> Naked, come to Thee for dress;
> Helpless, look to Thee for grace.
>
> *Augustus Toplady*

These things of necessity go together. 'They that be whole need
not a physician, but they that are sick' (Mt 9:12). You do not go
to your doctor if you feel perfectly well. You never make an
application for any kind of healing or redemption or salvation
unless you are conscious of your need. And that, of course, is the
whole trouble with the world today – it does not realise this
need; that is why it does not believe in the Lord Jesus Christ.

But the same thing is true in principle of the Christian. It is
those who realise their condition and their need most deeply
who are the ones who apply most constantly to the Lord himself. This is the universal testimony of the saints. It does not
matter where they lived, or to what century they belonged.
You read the life of any saint of God, anyone who so stood out
in saintliness that somebody felt it right and good and fitting
that a biography should be written of him or her, and you will
find that invariably this has been a characteristic of such a person. If you read their lives and their diaries, you will find that
they bemoaned the fact that they were aware of indwelling sin,

this 'plague of their own heart' as they called it, this thing in them that so often vitiated their testimony and hampered what they really desired to do and to be for the Lord. It is invariably those who have testified to the most high and glorious experiences, who at the same time testify to this other thing. Indeed the life of the Christian seems to be some sort of an ellipse which runs between these two focal points. At one and the same time you always find in the saint a hearty detestation of, and misery about, self, and yet a rejoicing and a joy in the Lord; and the one of necessity determines the other.

But let us be a little more particular. This is the truth which the word of God teaches us. It teaches us about God, then about sin, and that is the way in which it sanctifies us. There are several ways in which the word of God presents this particular aspect of the truth. I am not going to deal with it exhaustively, but let me give you some of the more obvious and general divisions.

The first way in which the Scriptures do this is, of course, through the teaching of the law – the law of God. There is much about the law of God in the Bible. It was originally given to man in the Garden of Eden, and the Scriptures tell us that there is a law written in the heart of every person born into this world. In Romans 2 Paul teaches that even the heathen, who have never heard the Scripture about the law of God, have it written in their hearts. It is also in the Bible, in a very special way, in terms of the Law which was given through Moses to the Children of Israel. You find the account given in the book of Exodus, there are constant references to it in the Psalms, and the subject also runs right through the Proverbs. These passages are in a sense doing nothing but applying this Law that was given, reminding the nation of it. It is everywhere in the Old Testament, and, indeed, it is true to say that we just cannot understand the Old Testament and its religion unless we are clear about the place and the function of the law of God in it.

Then you come to the New Testament and there again you will find constant arguments concerning the law. But what is their purpose, if we do not really understand what the law is? Now the law is given primarily in order to bring out these two points: the holiness of God and the sinfulness of man in the light of that holiness. It is interesting to observe in this connection the way in which the Jews completely misunderstood that. Their real trouble, as Paul is never tired of arguing, was that they had entirely misinterpreted the meaning of the law. They thought its purpose was to save them; that God had given them the law and said to them in effect, 'Now you keep that, and you will be saved. You save yourselves by keeping the law.' They had conveniently misinterpreted it; then they carried out that misinterpretation and said that they had kept the law and were righteous before God. That was the very essence of their error.

The purpose and the function of the law was really, as Paul argues in Romans 7, to show the exceeding sinfulness of sin, 'Was then that which is good made death unto me? God forbid. But sin, that it might appear sin, working death in me by that which is good; that sin by the commandment might become exceeding sinful' (v.13). The law was not given in order to save man or that man might save himself by it. It was given for one purpose only, namely, that sin might be defined, that it might, as it were, have attention focused upon it. Mankind did not realise its sinfulness, so God gave the law, not that they might save themselves by keeping it, but that their very sinfulness could be brought out. The law is 'our school-master to bring us unto Christ' (Gal 3:24), that is its only function, to show us our helplessness, and our need of grace and of a free salvation. 'Therefore by the deeds of the law there shall no flesh be justified in his sight: for by the law is the knowledge of sin' (Rom 3:20).

Those, then, are some of the scriptural statements, and all this great teaching about the law is simply to bring out in us a sense of sin. Therefore it follows of necessity that if we have never really studied this biblical doctrine, if we have never applied it to ourselves, if we are not doing so constantly, then we are not as aware of our own sinfulness as we should be. That is what the Fathers meant by a 'thorough-going law work'. It is only as I truly face the law of God that I begin to see what I am.

We see this, too, in the Sermon on the Mount. In its essence this Sermon is an explanation and an exposition of God's law.

It is our Lord showing us the real spiritual content of the law, demonstrating the law's spiritual nature, denouncing the false interpretation of the Pharisees, and really bringing us to see what it is telling us. And he does so, surely, with the object of bringing us to realise our sinfulness. The aim of the Sermon on the Mount is to disabuse us of all ideas about human self-righteousness. It is an exposure of the Pharisees and Scribes and of all who tended to follow them. In a sense, its whole purpose is to bring us into a condition in which we shall be 'poor in spirit', in which we shall 'mourn', in which we shall 'hunger and thirst after righteousness'. That is its obvious appeal. It is to bring us into the position and the state of those who are described by the Beatitudes.

Again, we find the same teaching in the epistles. That is the meaning of these discussions and arguments about the law, and of terms such as the 'old man', and the 'new man', and 'flesh' and the 'law of sin and death' and so on. You find this constantly in the epistles, particularly, perhaps, you find it in their exhortations. These are made in order that the people should examine themselves and 'prove' themselves, to make certain that they are in the faith; to 'test the spirits'; to avoid the false and to hold fast to that which is true. All that is part of the teaching concerning sin.

That, therefore, in general, is the way in which you find this doctrine about sin presented in the Scriptures. And that leads me to ask my second question. What in particular is the teaching about sin? Now obviously I am dealing with it here solely from the standpoint of the Christian. I should be emphasising certain other things if I were presenting it to the unbeliever, but I am particularly concerned now about the biblical teaching concerning sin with regard to God's people. And here there are certain principles which stand out very clearly.

The first is the vital and essential difference between sin and sins. The main trouble with a false doctrine of sin is that it tends to make us think of sin only in terms of actions. There have been many schools of false teaching about holiness, which have been wrong entirely because they have defined sin in that way, and, therefore, have taught that as long as we are not guilty of voluntary, wilful sin, we are perfect, we are entire and fully sanctified.

But the Bible draws a very sharp distinction between particular actions and a sinful state and condition, and its emphasis is not so much upon what we do, as upon what we are, upon the condition we are in, which leads us to do these things. That is a broad principle which it lays down everywhere.

So, to put it the other way round, the biblical emphasis is on being rather than doing. It is a positive state. True Christians are not so much people who do certain things, as people who *are* something, and because of what they are, then they do those things. Another way the Bible puts this important principle is in its teachings that sin, primarily, is a wrong attitude towards God, and a wrong relationship with him. Again you see that it defines sin not merely in terms of the moral, ethical character of the action. On the contrary, it goes further back and shows that in its essence sin is a wrong relationship with God and a wrong attitude towards him. Therefore sin, defined comprehensively, is anything or everything that prevents our living only to God, for him, and for his glory.

Those who say that sin ultimately means self are, of course, perfectly right. They are right as far as they go, but they do not go far enough. Sin is self, self-centredness and selfishness. But the real trouble about selfishness is not so much that I am self-centred, as that I am not God-centred. You see, you can have philosophical, and moral and ethical teachings which will denounce selfishness. All the idealistic systems, all the programmes for Utopia, are always very careful to denounce self-centredness. Obviously you cannot have a well-ordered society if everybody is out for himself or herself. There must be give and take. You agree that you must consider the other person, and that you must put in certain limits on your freedom in order that the other person may enjoy freedom. So you can denounce self as such, and still be far removed from the biblical doctrine of sin. Self in all its forms is sinful, says the Bible, because it puts self where God ought to be.

Now if you start with that definition of sin you see how comprehensive it becomes! Take that Pharisee, for instance, who thanked God that he was not like other people. Up to a point he was quite honest and truthful in what he said. He was not guilty of certain things, and he did other things. Yes. But he stopped at that. If he had realised that the essence of sin is to fail to be in the right relationship to God, or to have the right attitude towards God, he would have realised his sinfulness. There are many Christian people who are very careful not to commit certain external sins, but they are not quite so careful about pride and self-satisfaction, and about smugness and glibness; they are not so careful about rivalry and jealousy in their own Christian organisations. No, they have forgotten all that. Self is in the ascendant, at times even in their work, instead of God. But because they think of sin only in terms of actions, and have forgotten that it is primarily relationship to God, they are not aware of their sinfulness. However, that is the very essence of sin – failing to live entirely and wholly to God's glory. And it matters not how good we may be, nor how much better we may be than other people. If we are not loving the Lord our God with all our heart, and all our soul, and all our mind, and all our strength, then we are sinners. 'All have sinned, and come short of the glory of God' (Rom 3:23). That is the biblical teaching.

Then the other great principle is that sin is something which is deep down in our natures; it is not something on the surface. It is not a lack of culture, or of knowledge, or of instruction. Nor is it like a little speck on the surface of an otherwise perfect apple. No, it is at the centre, at the very core. It is not merely something in the stream, but at the fountain out of which the stream comes. It is something which is central to a man's being.

This, again, is emphasised everywhere in the Scripture. Paul refers to it as a principle. It is the whole meaning of the term 'the flesh', which does not mean the physical body, but that principle in a man's life that tends to control him. Indeed the Bible says that sin is so deep in man that nothing can possibly rid him of it, or deliver him from it, except a rebirth. Teaching is not enough, neither are exhortation, nor example. Even the example of Christ is not enough; in a sense it damns more than anything else. There is only one hope, says the Scripture: you must be 'born again'. You must be made and created anew. Sin is so deep down in man himself that he needs a new nature. Sin indeed is as deep a problem as this – that nothing but the Incarnation and all that our Lord did, can possibly deal with it. And so we must realise that though we are Christians and have received a new nature, the problem is still there because of the remnants of old nature. We have not finished with it.

There, I suggest, are the three main controlling principles. But we must still divide that up just a little further. If that is the truth about sin, we must ask the question, How, then, does it show itself? So we turn to the teaching of the Bible. First and foremost, sin is what is always described as 'missing the mark', not being at the place where you ought to be. You are shooting and you just miss the mark; or you are travelling and you do not arrive at the exact destination. That is the very essence of the biblical understanding of sin. It is an absence of righteousness and of holiness. Every sinner is not what he ought to be, and not what he was when he came out of the hands of God. We are not reflecting the glory of God as we were meant to do. We are not as we were when man was made in God's image. The image has been marred. Something has gone.

You see the importance of regarding sin in that way. The man who realises that that is a primary part of the definition of sin, is a man who realises that he is still a sinner. But if you are simply looking at drunkards and prostitutes, or at particular actions, of course you think that you are all right. You are not conscious of sin, so you are not humble and you do not 'mourn'. You are self-satisfied and contented; you are looking down at other people. But once you realise that we are meant to be holy and righteous, and that we are not that, then you realise at once that you are a sinner.

But sin is not only this negative condition of not being righteous and holy, it is also a positive transgression of the law. Consider John's argument about that in 1 John 3, '... for sin is the transgression of the law' (v. 4). Sin is disobedience to God's commandments, and the Bible emphasises this quite as much as the negative. Our trouble is not only that we are not what we ought to be, but that we deliberately do things that we should not do. It is a breaking of the law, a transgression, a cutting across what God has indicated as being his holy will.

Yes, but it is something even worse than that. It is what is described as 'concupiscence'. We find this word in Romans 7 and it is something that we must always preach. 'But sin, taking occasion by the commandment, wrought in me all manner of concupiscence. For without the law sin was dead' (v.8). This is the biblical way of describing desire – evil desire. The trouble is not simply that we break the law and do things that are wrong, the trouble is also that we ever want to do so; that it ever gives us pleasure to do these things; that there ever is an inclination in us to do them; that there is something in us which makes such disobedience appeal to us – that is an element in concupiscence.

But it is even worse than that. Concupiscence is as terrible and as foul a thing as this, that even the law of God inflames us. Look at Paul's argument in Romans 7. He says,

For when we were in the flesh, the motions of sins, which were by the law, did work in our members to bring forth fruit unto death. But now we are delivered from the law, that being dead wherein we were held; that we should serve in newness of spirit, and not in the oldness of the letter. What shall we say then? Is the law sin? God forbid. Nay, I had not known sin, but by the law: for I had not known lust, except the law had said, Thou shalt not covet. But sin, taking occasion by the commandment, wrought in me all manner of concupiscence. For without the law sin was dead. For I was alive without the law once: but when the commandment came, sin revived, and I died. And the commandment, which was ordained to life, I found to be unto death. For sin, taking occasion by the commandment, deceived me, and by it slew me. Wherefore the law is holy, and the commandment holy, and just, and good. Was then that which is good made death unto me? God forbid. But sin, that it might appear sin, working death in me by that which is good; that sin by the commandment might become exceeding sinful' (vv. 5–13).

Paul's argument is as follows. There is this terrible thing called concupiscence in man, and it works in this way. You tell a man, a child, indeed anybody, not to do a thing. Now, it is a good thing to tell people not to do what is wrong, and to do what is good. Yes, says Paul, but this is what I have found, and we have all found the same thing, that the very commandment which tells me not to do that evil thing, by drawing my attention to it, inflames my desire to do it. So that the very law leads me to sin. It is not because the law is not right and good and just and holy. God forbid, he says, that anybody should say that. The problem is this evil thing in me called concupiscence, which will even turn good into evil. To the pure all things are pure. To those who are not pure there is nothing good.

That is why as a Christian I have never believed in morality teaching. Nor have I ever agreed with those who argue, 'Tell people of the evil effects of that sin, and it will keep them from it,' because it will not. It will inflame their desire for that very thing that you are telling them not to do. And that is why people quite often delude and defile themselves by reading books about such things. They say that what they want to do is to see the evil of the thing. What is actually happening is that they are enjoying it. They are sinning in their minds and in their imaginations. That is what is meant by concupiscence; this passion, this flame, this fire, that can even misuse the law of God, and turn it into a kind of bellows that makes the flame worse. Tell a man not to and it may drive him to do it – indeed, you are introducing him to it. So it is a dangerous thing for fallen man to think like that and to imagine that moral instruction about sex and such things is going to control the moral problem. It is having exactly the opposite effect; and to believe in that kind of teaching is to misunderstand the essential biblical teaching about sin. No, our fathers were right. They did not tell their children about sex and morality, and there was less immorality than there is now. It is a dangerous thing to talk about these things; it is like pouring petrol on the fire. Concupiscence – that is the great argument of the seventh chapter of the epistle to the Romans.

Finally, I must put it in these words. Sin shows itself, says Paul, as a kind of law in my life and in my members. You will notice he talks about the 'law in his members' – 'For I delight in the law of God after the inward man: but I see another law in my members, warring against the law of my mind, and bringing me into captivity to the law of sin which is in my members' (Rom 7:22–23). That is sin, with its terrible power. It is a great principle. It is a law, says Paul, and it works in this way: even though we may know that the law of God is right and good and just and holy, and though we believe in it and even want to keep it, we find that we are doing something else. Why? Because there is another law in our members, this thing called the flesh.

Paul therefore comes to the conclusion that '...in me (that is, in my flesh) dwelleth no good thing' (Rom 7:18). As I have said, Paul does not mean the physical body, but this principle of sin, this law of sin, this law in the members. They are all synonymous terms. It is this thing that governs man, so that though I want to do the right thing, and subscribe to it and love it, I nevertheless find myself doing the other thing. That, as I see it, is the biblical teaching in its essence with regard to sin – and we know it is true.

But how often do we think about this? How often do we meditate upon it? How often do we search ourselves and examine ourselves to see how guilty we are? Are we dismissing these things lightly, pushing them away, not really facing them? The Scripture exhorts us to face them: that is why it puts the law before us everywhere. We need to be kept down. We need to be humbled. We need to be convicted of sin.

And it is only as we are, that we shall realise the need of sanctification. It is only as we are, that we shall apply to Christ and seek his face and seek God. It is only as we are, that we shall thank God that the whole of salvation, from beginning to end, is God's work and not ours. It will deliver us out of this superficial dealing with the problem in terms of actions. It will enable us to see our true condition as sold under sin, and covered by the law of sin and death. Then we will know that we are doomed and condemned and hopeless, and needing that mighty operation of the Spirit of God which, blessed be his name, gives us new life and new birth, and then proceeds by the application of this blessed word in us and upon us, to perfect us until eventually, because it is his work and his power, we shall stand before him faultless and blameless, and with exceeding joy.

God grant that we may understand the biblical teaching – the word of God's teaching about sin – that it may drive us to Christ.

9

New Creatures

Sanctify them through thy truth: thy word is truth (v. 17).

We continue now in our consideration of God's way of sanctifying his people, and of the fact that the great emphasis here is that God sanctifies us not so much directly as indirectly, through and by means of the truth. He brings us into the realm of the truth in order that the truth may work upon us, and produce the desired effects and results in us. And therefore we see that the whole of the biblical message – and in a very special way the message of the New Testament – is designed to bring about this final purpose of our sanctification. For that reason we have been at pains to emphasise the unity of the truth and every part of the truth which leads to sanctification. The truth about sanctification is not some special department or one aspect of the teaching of the Bible. Every revelation of God, and everything that brings us to a realisation of our position in God's sight, leads to and produces our sanctification. So that it has been necessary for us to look at the truth as a whole, and we are now in the process of reminding ourselves that this great comprehensive truth has different aspects, or different emphases. And in accordance with the biblical message, we are looking at these different aspects of the truth which lead to our sanctification.

We started with the great truth about God himself. There is nothing more calculated to make a man holy and to sanctify him truly as the realisation that he is in the presence of God. There is no better definition of a true Christian than that he is a godly man, one who walks in the fear of the Lord. That is invariably the biblical description of God's people; clearly, it is the point at which we must start, because it is the centre and the soul of all truth. But then that, in turn, leads us, of course, to consider what the Bible has to tell us about sin. Why do we not all know God? Why are we not walking with him, and enjoying fellowship with him? The answer is sin. And the more we realise the exceeding sinfulness of sin, the more we shall hate it, abominate it, and turn our backs on it, and give ourselves unreservedly to God and to the life which he would have us live.

Then that obviously leads to the next emphasis. Having shown us our utter sinfulness and our complete helplessness, lest we give way to final despair, the Bible presents us with the wonderful truth about what the love of God has done in Christ for us and for our salvation. The great argument of Christ, finally, is that it is our sin which made that necessary, and that Christ died, not only that we might be forgiven, but that we might be delivered from sin.

> Love so amazing, so divine,
> Demands my soul, my life, my all.
>
> *Isaac Watts*

'Know ye not ... ye are not your own? For ye are bought with a price' (1 Cor 6:19–20). '... he died for all, that they which live should not henceforth live unto themselves but unto him which died for them, and rose again' (2 Cor 5:15). If our understanding of the death of Christ upon the cross does not make us hate sin and forsake it, and hate the world and forsake the world, and give ourselves unreservedly to Christ, we are in the most dangerous condition possible. To imagine that Christ died on the cross simply to allow us to continue living a sinful and worldly life in safety, comes, it seems to me, very near a terrible form of blasphemy. There is no more dangerous condition for a soul to be in, than to think: 'Well, because I have believed in Christ and because I think that Christ died for me, it does not matter very much now what I do.' The whole of this message is an utter denial of that, and a solemn warning to us not to make merchandise of the cross of Christ, or to trample under our feet the blood of our redemption. So you see that every aspect of the truth drives us to holiness, and all the teaching urges us to sanctification.[1]

But now we come to another aspect of the truth, one which, again, is vital for our understanding of this subject. It warns us that we must be clear about our actual position as Christians as the result of the work of the Lord Jesus Christ on our behalf. Here again we have one of the major themes of the Bible and one of its major emphases with regard to this particular question of sanctification: the Christian's standing as the result of the work of the Lord Jesus Christ. It is a great theme which is expounded in many places in the New Testament, though I suppose the classic passage is Romans 6. However, it is not only in the sixth chapter of Romans; everything that leads up to this chapter is part of the argument, and it goes on in to the seventh. But in the sixth chapter this theme is presented to us in a particularly concentrated form.

You will notice that the apostle takes up at once the whole question of the relationship between the meaning of the death of Christ upon the cross and our conduct. He imagines the people in Rome misunderstanding this teaching, as others had so often been liable to do. He imagines that they may say to themselves: 'Well, shall we continue in sin that grace may abound? Is this a teaching which says that now that we have believed in Christ we are no longer under the law but under grace, and that, therefore, it does not much matter what we do, indeed, that the more we sin the greater will be the grace? Is that the position?'

---

[1] Unfortunately, at this point one sermon is missing from the John 17 manuscripts. However, Dr Lloyd-Jones often gave a detailed resumé of the sermon of the week before, and we have left this in full, in order to show, however briefly, what the subject was of the missing manuscript, and how it connects with the sermons before and after. (Ed.)

Paul's answer is given with horror – 'God forbid!' God forbid that anybody should argue like that. 'How shall we, that are dead to sin, live any longer therein?' (6:2). The thing is unthinkable. It is a complete misunderstanding of the truth! So he works it out, and the important thing to grasp here is that all along he relates his doctrine to the practice of the Christian. You cannot separate these two things. For the extent to which there is a separation between what we believe, and what we are, and what we do, is the extent to which we have really not understood the doctrine; because there are certain things that are absolutely indivisible. That is why the New Testament is so full of tests which Christians must apply to themselves. There is the danger of our deluding ourselves and falsely imagining that we are Christians. The whole first epistle of John just deals with that one thing – the tests of the Christian life – the way in which we must examine ourselves. It is no use, said the Lord Jesus Christ, pleading, 'Lord, Lord' if you do not do and keep my commandments. 'Many will say to me in that day, Lord, Lord, have we not prophesied in thy name ...?' (Mt 7:22). Have we not done this and that? And he will answer, 'I never knew you: depart from me ...' (v. 23). They thought they believed in him. They said, 'Lord, Lord,' but he never knew them. So we must examine ourselves very carefully, and we do so by always keeping a firm grasp, at one and the same time, upon our doctrine and our practice and our conduct. Life and belief are indivisible; they must go together.

Now that is how the apostle Paul conducts this great argument in Romans 6, and I want to examine it with you in a very special manner here. The great principle, it seems to me, with which we must start is that an assurance of our salvation, of our standing before God, and of the forgiveness of our sins, is an absolute necessity in this matter of sanctification. Let me put it to you like this. I would not hesitate to say that a lack of assurance is perhaps one of the greatest hindrances of all in the Christian life, because while you have not got assurance you are troubled and worried, and that tends to lead to depression. It tends to turn us in upon ourselves, and to promote morbidity and introspection; and in that condition we obviously become a ready prey for the devil, who is ever at hand to discourage us and to suggest to us that we are not Christians at all.

The point I am making is that a condition of spiritual depression is not only bad in and of itself, it is possibly the greatest hindrance of all to the process of sanctification. This is true of us in every respect, is it not? 'The joy of the Lord,' says Nehemiah, 'is your strength' (8:10). And how true that is! I do not care what work you are doing, if you are not happy you will not do it well. If you are preoccupied with yourself, or if you have some worry or something on your mind and your spirit, it will affect all the work you do. You can never work well while there is a kind of division within you. The man who really works well is the man who is carefree and is working with joy.

A great deal of attention is being paid to this whole matter at the present time. It is one of the major problems of our so-called civilisation. Mankind is unhappy, hence all this interest in psychology. It is just being realised that if people are not happy they will not work well. All that is equally true in the spiritual life, and there is no question at all but that a doubt or uncertainty about my real standing before God, a doubt as to whether I am a Christian or not, constitutes a great hindrance to sanctification. In other words, people who are struggling to make themselves Christian can never be sanctified.

I do not hesitate for a moment to speak as strongly as that. Someone may be very pious, but there is all the difference in the world between piety and sanctification. The man who is truly sanctified is pious, but you can be pious without being sanctified. By this I mean that there are people whose whole vocation in life is to be religious. You are familiar with that, perhaps, in a highly organised form in Roman Catholicism. These people enter upon the devout life and make a distinction between the 'religious' and the 'laity'. Now we disagree with that entirely, and I am simply using it to show that these people are trying, by their efforts and exertions, to make themselves Christian.

But the New Testament teaching is that while you are trying to make yourself a Christian you will never be one, and if you are not a Christian you cannot be sanctified. The only people whom God does sanctify are his own people, those who are Christian. That is why I maintain that an assurance of one's standing before God is an essential preliminary to this process of sanctification.

So we must start with this, and the question therefore arises as to how we can arrive at this assurance. And here we must start with the great biblical doctrine of justification. 'Ah,' says someone, 'there you are. You are bringing up those old terms again. These legal terms of the apostle Paul are out of date. "Justification" – I am not interested in theology and in justification!' Well, my friend, all I say to you is that if you are not interested in justification, I can assure you that you are ignorant with regard to sanctification. Justification is an utter, absolute necessity. There is no assurance apart from being clear about the doctrine of justification. Why does Scripture tell us so much about it? Why does it expound it as it does? Is it simply to expound doctrine? Of course not! All these letters were written with a very practical object and intent. They were written to help people, to encourage and strengthen them, and to show them how to live the Christian life in ordinary affairs. And therefore this doctrine of justification is an absolute essential, for without it we shall never really assume a true Christian position and begin to enjoy its great blessings.

What, then, is the teaching? Well, the great argument of Romans is that we are 'justified freely by his grace' (Rom 3:24). This means that God declares and pronounces that you and I who believe in the Lord Jesus Christ are guiltless. Here we are – we are sinners. We have sinned, as the whole world has sinned. 'There is none righteous, no, not one.' We are not only born in sin, we have committed deliberate acts of sin. The greatest sin of all, of course, is not to live our lives entirely for God, not to glorify him as he meant us to do, and not to fulfil the purpose for which he created us. We have all sinned before God. We have broken his laws and his commandments; we are all guilty sinners deserving nothing but punishment and retribution.

But this is the amazing message, and this is what is meant by justification – that God tells us that, as the result of the work of the Lord Jesus Christ, because of his life, his death and his resurrection, if we believe on him and trust ourselves solely and entirely to him, God pardons and forgives our sins. Not only that, he declares that we are free from guilt: more than that, justification includes this. He not only declares that we are pardoned and forgiven and that we are guiltless, he also declares that we are positively righteous. He imputes to us, that is, he puts to our account, the righteousness of the Lord Jesus Christ himself, who was entirely without sin, who never failed his Father in any way, and who never broke a Commandment or transgressed any law. God gives to us – puts upon us – the righteousness of the Lord Jesus Christ himself, and then looks upon us and pronounces that we are righteous in his holy sight. That is the biblical doctrine of justification.

Now you will notice the way in which I am putting this; I am emphasising this pronouncement of God, and I do that very deliberately because the doctrine of justification is what you may call a forensic or a legal statement. It is the pronouncement or the promulgation of a sentence. The picture we should have in our minds is that of a Judge seated upon the bench and there we are standing in the dock, charged by the law, by Satan, and by our own consciences, but without a plea and without an excuse. And there stands the Lord Jesus Christ proclaiming that he lived and has died for us, and that he has paid the penalty on our behalf. Then God the Judge eternal pronounces that he accepts that and that therefore from henceforth he regards us as guiltless. Our sins are all blotted out as a thick cloud. He casts them into the sea of his own forgetfulness, and throws them behind his back – they are gone, and gone for ever.

Not only that, he says that he regards us in the light of this righteousness of his Son, so he pronounces us free from guilt and clothed with the righteousness of the Lord Jesus Christ. The Bible uses many analogies to bring out this idea; here is one of them. It is as if we were standing with our clothes torn almost to rags, covered and bespattered with the mud, the mire, and the filth of this world. Suddenly all that is taken from us, and we are clothed with a most gorgeous, glorious and perfect cloak, spotless in its whiteness and in its purity; the transformation is entire and the picture is altogether changed. It has all been done for us freely and for nothing.

Indeed we can put the doctrine of justification like this: if we believe on the Lord Jesus Christ and belong to him, God regards us as if we had never sinned at all. It is nothing less than that! It is actually that God in all his holiness and in the light of the law and everything else, looks down upon us, and then, having thus covered us by his Son, sees us in Christ and regards us as if we had never sinned at all. If we believe anything less than that, we are not believing the New Testament doctrine of justification by faith only: that we are justified freely by the grace of God. That is the doctrine, and I would emphasise that it is the essential preliminary to this process of sanctification which God then works in us and brings to pass in us by means of his wonderful truth. That is the argument you must derive from the work of Christ upon the cross and from the Resurrection.

But clearly that is only the essential starting-point. It is a point which we must always bear in mind, but we do not stop at that. We must go on to say that not only are we thus declared to be righteous in a forensic or a legal manner, but that we are actually in union with Christ and joined to him. You cannot have read the New Testament even cursorily without noticing this constantly repeated phrase – 'in Christ' – 'in Christ Jesus'. The apostles go on repeating it and it is one of the most significant and glorious statements in the entire realm and range of truth. It means that we are joined to the Lord Jesus Christ; we have become a part of him. We are in him. We belong to him. We are members of his body.

And the teaching is that God regards us as such; and this, of course, means that now, in this relationship, we are sharers in, and partakers of, everything that is true of the Lord Jesus Christ himself. In other words, our standing before God is not only a legal one – it is a legal one, and we must start with that – but we go beyond the legal standing to this vital fact that our position is in Christ.

Now we must watch the apostle working that out in Romans 6. The first thing that is true of us, he says, is that we have died with Christ and have been buried with him. 'Shall we continue in sin, that grace may abound? God forbid!' Why? Because 'How shall we, that are dead to sin, live any longer therein?' (vv. 1–2).

'But,' one might ask, 'what do you mean by saying that I am dead to sin? I am in the flesh and I am still the same person, and I am still in the same world. What do you mean by saying that I am dead to sin? I am still being tempted, I still sometimes fall. How do you mean I am dead to sin?' But, read on. 'Know ye not,' says Paul, 'that so many of us as were baptized into Jesus Christ, were baptized into his death? Therefore we are buried with him by baptism into death: that like as Christ was raised up from the dead … even so we also should walk in newness of life. For if we have been planted together in the likeness of his death' – if that is true – 'we shall be also in the likeness of his resurrection' (vv. 3–5).

Paul goes on repeating that truth and working it out. But are we clear about this? Do we realise that as Christians we must make these assertions about ourselves? As we saw, the first assertion which I must make is that because I am joined to the Lord Jesus Christ and am part of him, everything that is true of him is true of me, and therefore the first thing which is at once true of me is that everything that happened to him in his death has happened to me also. That is the argument – I am in Christ.

It is important that we do not take this chapter on its own, but along with the previous chapter. There the great statement has been that we were all in Adam. And so we sinned in

Adam. Everything that Adam did has been imputed to us and has become true of us. In exactly the same way, everything that is true of Christ is true of us because it is all imputed to us. And this is the first thing: the Lord Jesus Christ was made of a woman, made under the law. He lived his life in this world under the law of God. The law made its demands upon him, and if he had broken any of it, he would have suffered the consequences. But he kept it perfectly. Not only that; he died under the law. He took the sins of men, who had been condemned by the law, upon himself, and for them he died, under the law and to the law.

So henceforward the law has nothing to say to him, or to do with him. He has died to the law once, and what Paul says is that that is equally true of me. He says that as a Christian, as one who is in Christ, I have finished with the law, it has nothing to do with me and I am dead to it. Paul goes on to work that out in Romans 7 in his figure of the married relationship. He says that the Christian was once like a married woman who was bound to her husband while he was alive. But when the husband died she was no longer bound to him and she was free to marry again. He says that that was exactly our position; we were once married to the law, but that is finished with, and we are therefore married to another, even to Christ. That is why we all, as Christians, should be able to sing the words of Augustus Toplady's hymn:

> The terrors of law and of God
> With me can have nothing to do;
> My Saviour's obedience and blood
> Hide all my transgressions from view.

'There is therefore now no condemnation to them which are in Christ Jesus' (Rom 8:1) – none. From the standpoint of salvation, we are dead to the law; we are finished with it.

Not only that, Paul says, we are equally dead to the dominion of Satan. He works that out here – 'Sin shall not have dominion over you' (Rom 6:14). You are not any longer under the dominion of sin. We have been translated out of the kingdom of darkness into the kingdom of God's dear Son. We are taken out of the whole realm over which Satan rules; we are dead to that.

This again is a very vital aspect of the truth in its practical application. 'The whole world,' says the apostle John, in his first epistle, 'lieth in wickedness' – but we do not; 'and that wicked one toucheth us not' (1 Jn 5:19, 18). He cannot touch us. We do not belong to the kingdom of Satan; we belong to the kingdom of the Lord Jesus Christ. Satan is governing and ruling and controlling and dominating the lives of all who do not belong to Christ. Whether they know it or not, it is an absolute fact. He is just gripping them and controlling them utterly and absolutely. They cannot move without him. But a Christian is one who has been taken out of that and put into this other kingdom. He has finished with the dominion of Satan.

'Ah yes,' you may say, 'but we still sin, and Satan can still get us down.' Yes, but not because you are in his dominion, but rather because you are foolish enough, having been taken out of his dominion, still to listen to him. He has no authority over you, no power at all, and if you yield to him it is entirely due to your own folly. We are dead to Satan as well as dead to the law, and we are equally dead to sin. 'How shall we,' Paul asks, 'that are dead to sin, live any longer therein?' Here he means dead to the dominion of sin, and he puts that in a positive form by saying, 'Sin shall not have dominion over you.' You may fall to temptation, but that does not mean that it has dominion over you. Your life is no longer controlled by the sinful outlook. You are not living in the realm of sin. You are not 'continuing in sin' as John puts it in 1 John 3. We are dead to all that.

Yes, but we must go even further: the Christian is one who is even dead to his old self, to his old nature, to that condition which he inherited from Adam. We are all born with this Adamic nature, governed by passion and lust and desire and controlled by the way of the world. I need not keep you about this: we are all perfectly familiar with it. The tragedy with men and women who boast about their freedom because they are not Christians, is that they are utter and absolute slaves to the way of the world. Look at the poor creatures as you see them depicted so constantly in the newspapers, all doing the same thing, rushing about like sheep. They never think; they are simply carried away by what is being done. That is the serfdom of this old Adamic nature. If we are Christians we are no longer like that; we are dead to it all. We are dead to that old self, to that old life. We have been given a new nature. We have finished with the old self once and for all. We are now in Christ. We have a new life and a new outlook. 'Old things are passed away; behold, all things are become new' (2 Cor 5:17).

So let me put it very plainly in this way: there is no point in our saying that we believe that Christ has died for us, and that we believe our sins are forgiven, unless we can also say that for us old things are passed away and that all things are become new; that our outlook towards the world and its method of living is entirely changed. It is not that we are sinless, nor that we are perfect, but that we have finished with that way of life. We have seen it for what it is, and we are new creatures for whom everything has become new.

But I can imagine somebody saying, 'Don't you think that this is rather a dangerous doctrine? Don't you think it is dangerous to tell people that they are dead to sin, dead to the law, dead to Satan, and that God regards them as if they had never sinned at all? Won't the effect of that make such people say, "All right, in view of that, it does not matter what I do"?' But Paul says that what happens is the exact opposite, and that must be so because to be saved and to be truly Christian means that we are in Christ, and if we are in Christ, we are dead to sin, dead to Satan, dead to the world, dead to our old selves: we are like our Lord.

Let me put that positively. We have not only died with Christ, we have also risen with him: 'Therefore we are buried with him by baptism into death: that like as Christ was raised up from the dead by the glory of the Father, even so we also should walk in newness of life' (Rom 6:4). So you do not say at a meeting, 'Yes, I believe in Christ, I accept forgiveness,' and then go back and live exactly as you lived before. Not at all! We live in 'newness of life'. We have been raised with Christ. Notice Paul's logical way of putting this – he says, '... reckon ye also yourselves to be dead indeed unto sin, but alive unto God through Jesus Christ our Lord' (v. 11). For before we were not alive unto God, but were dead in trespasses and sins. Oh yes, we prayed when we were in trouble, we perhaps said our prayers once a day, but we were not alive unto God.

But when we become alive to God, it means that he is at the centre of our lives; God is a living reality to us. God is not just a term, not just some mechanical agency to dispense blessings to us. God is a person, whom we now know. 'This is life eternal,' as our Lord has already reminded us, 'that they might know thee the only true God, and Jesus Christ, whom thou hast sent.' We are alive unto God. He is real; he is living; we have fellowship with him. And when we pray we do not just utter some thoughts, and hope they will do us good, we know that we are speaking to God, that we are in his presence and that he speaks to us. It is a living fellowship.

More than that, in Christ we are not only alive to God, we have become children of God. He is the Son of God, and all who are in him are therefore God's children. We receive his life; the very life of God himself has entered into us and into our souls, and thus we are living a new type of life altogether – a living life in the presence of the living God.

John's dictum is that the Christian is one who goes through this world realising that he is 'walking with God'. It is a great walk, a companionship. You journey through life, through the darkness of this world, in the light of the presence of God. That is what it means to be a Christian; hating sin and evil and everything that tends to separate us from God. If you should for a moment turn away and fall, then you go back to him and confess your sin, and we know that 'he is faithful and just

to forgive us our sins, and to cleanse us from all unrighteousness' (1 Jn 5:9). Yes, but that does not just lead us to sin again:
no, we have learned to hate that, and we hate ourselves for
having looked at it, instead of always looking to him. We do
not want what is wrong, but rather to be alive unto God in a
living, loving fellowship, walking with him through this life
and all its temptations and all its sin and shame; dead to sin
with him; buried with him; risen and alive with him; in him;
partaking of his life; a child of God.

And the last thing which is emphasised is that we have not
only died with Christ, but that even at this moment we are
seated with him in the heavenly places. We are far away,
above all principality, might and dominion, and every power
that can be named, because being in Christ means that what is
true of him, is true of us. That is what you are, says the New
Testament.

As we consider this, I think we see that it is obviously the
profoundest doctrine we can ever contemplate. Is there anything that is more encouraging, more uplifting, than to know
that all this is true of us? That is what Paul is telling these
Romans; that is what the other New Testament writers are
constantly stressing. We must cease to think of ourselves
only in terms of the forgiveness of sins. We must never isolate that, and leave it on its own. The Christian is one; his life
is a whole and indivisible. As truth is one, he is one, and he is
one with Christ; and if he is a Christian at all, all these things
must be true of him. It is because these things are true, that
God forgives us, and regards us as justified. That is the truth
about us – the whole, wonderful truth – that I am dead even
to the law of God. There is now no condemnation. I am dead
to sin, dead to Satan; right outside their territory, outside
their dominion altogether. I am alive to God, his child, a partaker of the divine nature, and in a living fellowship and communion with God. That is the doctrine, that is the argument.

But see the deduction: if all that is true, how can we continue in sin? Why do we even want to? The very fact that we
want to should make us wonder whether we are Christians at

all. It is impossible if this is true of us and if we realise this. Therefore Paul brings out his great deductions at the end: 'But God be thanked, that ye were the servants of sin, but ye have obeyed from the heart that form of doctrine which was delivered you. Being then made free from sin, ye became the servants [the bond-slaves] of righteousness' (Rom 6:17–18). As you wanted to do one thing, you now want to do this other. As you were a slave to that, you are now a slave to this.

Then he says, 'I speak after the manner of men because of the infirmity of your flesh ...' (v. 19). He is going to use an illustration and he apologises for doing so. He says, You force me to do it because you are so slow to understand: '... for as ye have yielded your members servants to uncleanness, and to iniquity unto iniquity; even so now yield your members servants to righteousness unto holiness.'

In other words, he says, because of this entire change in your position, take your very faculties and powers, your enthusiasm, your joy, your happiness, take all the thrills that you used to get in that old life and turn them into this new direction. Let me put it as simply as the apostle does, and even more simply, almost in a childish manner. If you want to know whether you are a true Christian according to Romans 6, you can put it like this: Do you get the same thrill out of your Christian life as you used to get out of that old life? Does a prayer meeting thrill you now as much as a cinema used to? That is his argument. Your 'members' that used to be given as 'servants to uncleanness and to iniquity unto inquity', must now be 'servants to righteousness unto holiness'.

Let me use the modern jargon – you got a great kick out of that old life did you not? Are you getting a kick out of your Christian life? Do you find it exciting? Do you find it thrilling? Do you find it wonderful? Do you find yourself at times almost beside yourself with joy? Is it bubbling over from within? As you used to speak, going home in the underground or in the bus, after you had seen a play or something like that, and you were so animated and excited, do you ever speak like that about the word of God and about fellowship with the saints, and about praying to God, and the contemplation of eternity? That is the argument – you were that, you are now this. As that was true, so this must now be true. And as we understand something of all this, and begin to apply it and to practise it, God's marvellous process of sanctification will be going on in us.

I have reminded you every time, from the very beginning, that sanctification means being separated unto God. It means being prepared for heaven and the vision of God and glory eternal. There is not much time to be lost, my friends. We are here today and gone tomorrow. The end of all things may be at hand – I do not know. But I do know this, that if I really believe I am going to him to spend my eternity with him, then the sooner I leave these other things the better. They keep me from him. They are unlike him, and if I do not know what it is to enjoy God here in this life and in this world, then it seems to me that heaven will be the most boring place imaginable for me: my heaven will become hell. The truth is, of course, that in that case I shall never get there, because I have never belonged to him. Let us examine ourselves to make sure that we really believe in Christ and his work on our behalf. It leads to all this – we have died with him, we have risen with him. We are alive to God, children of God. We are new creatures. Oh, beloved Christians, let the whole world know that this is true of us!

10

Christ in Us

Sanctify them through thy truth: thy word is truth (v. 17).

We saw in our last study how nothing so promotes sanctification as the realisation that we are in Christ; the realisation that we are declared righteous by God, that we are justified, and that God looks upon us now as in Christ. So here we are, then, people in Christ facing a new life, the kind of life that he lived, and we realise now that we are called to live in that way. John puts it in his first epistle like this: 'As he is, so are we in this world' (1 Jn 4:17). We are to follow in his steps who did no wrong: '... neither was guile found in his mouth: who, when he was reviled, reviled not again; when he suffered, he threatened not; but committed himself to him that judgeth righteously' (1 Pet 2:22–23). That is what is meant by being sanctified – we are to be like him. Sanctification is not so much an experience, as to be like him; to be separated from the world and sin; to be separated unto God. This is the whole process of the teaching; being in Christ, we are called to live even as he lived in this world.

But then, I imagine someone saying at this point, 'How can this be done? Who are we that we should even attempt to live such a life?' And that brings us to the next aspect of the truth that we must consider, for we are told very plainly in the Scriptures that we are not left to ourselves. God does not call us to an impossible life, and command us to live it, and then leave us to ourselves to do so somehow, anyhow. That is an entirely false understanding of the scriptural teaching, for here we come to this next great emphasis, which is that the Christian is one who is regenerated. All the ethical teaching of the Scriptures is based upon that supposition. All the appeals made in the epistles for conduct and behaviour – and we must never be tired of pointing this out – are always made to Christian people.

It is a fatal thing to expect Christian conduct from people who are not Christians. The Bible never asks that. The Bible knows that the natural man, the man born with human nature as it has been since the fall of Adam, cannot possibly live such a life. The whole point of the giving of the Ten Commandments under the moral law is, in a sense, just to prove that. As Paul argues in the epistle to the Romans, the law was added 'that sin by the commandment might become exceeding sinful' (Rom 7:13). God did not give the law to the Children of Israel in the hope that possibly they might keep it and thereby save themselves. That was impossible. It could not be done. The 'carnal mind is enmity against God, for it is not subject to the law of God, neither indeed can be' (Rom 8:7). So the law was given in order, to use a modern phrase, to pinpoint sin, to bring home to us our sinfulness; to establish our guilt; to show us our utter helplessness.

Furthermore, if it is impossible for man, as he is by nature, to keep the moral law as given by God to man through Moses, how much more impossible is it for any man, in his own strength or power, to live the kind of life that the Lord Jesus Christ lived, or to live the Sermon on the Mount. It is utterly and absolutely impossible. On the contrary, let me say it again, all the ethical and moral appeals in the New Testament are always based on the assumption that the people to whom they are addressed are Christians; that they are regenerated; that they have undergone what is called a 'new birth'.

This is great and vital teaching. We could very easily occupy ourselves for some time with this, but I do not propose to do that now. I am simply indicating here the big principles which we can work out for ourselves, and at this point I am concerned only with the doctrine of regeneration or rebirth as it has this very practical bearing upon the process of sanctification. My argument is that it is only as we know ourselves to be new men and women in Christ Jesus, that we really can be sanctified. Now that is the kind of terminology which you find so freely in the New Testament. We are told that we have become 'partakers of the divine nature', so that, as we confront this great task of following Christ, of living in the world the kind of life that he lived when he himself was here, we have no excuse. We must not say, 'Oh, but who am I? I am so weak and so frail!' The Scripture comes at once and says, 'But you are born again; you are a new creature. You have been created anew. You are a partaker of the divine nature. You are not simply a natural man, there is a new man in you.' And it is in the light of this that it presses its great teaching about sanctification.

Without going into this in detail, let me summarise it by putting it in this way. The teaching in the Scripture is that there is a new principle of life in us and that God, by the work of the Holy Spirit, has implanted this new principle in us. It is not something substantial – no new substance has been injected into us. There is, however, very definitely, a new principle at work in us which leads to a new disposition, and its effect is that we are now made capable of doing things that we were not capable of doing before.

It starts, of course, by giving us an entirely new view of everything: '... if any man be in Christ, he is a new creature: old things are passed away; behold, all things are become new' (2 Cor 5:17). Or take it as our Lord put it to Nicodemus in the famous interview in John 3. Nicodemus was trying to understand, and he was obviously about to put a whole series of questions which might help him to grasp what our Lord was saying. But Christ stops him and says, 'Verily, verily, I say unto thee. Except a man be born again, he cannot see the kingdom of God ... Except a man be born of water and of the Spirit, he cannot enter into the kingdom of God. That which is born of the flesh is flesh; and that which is born of the Spirit is spirit' (Jn 3:3, 5, 6).

Our Lord is saying, Nicodemus, you must not try to understand. You need this new principle, this new life, this new power, this something must happen to you which is compara-ble to the effect of the wind – '... thou hearest the sound thereof, but canst not tell whence it cometh, and whither it goeth: so is every one that is born of the Spirit' (v. 8). It is a supernatural operation of the Spirit of God upon the soul of man, and a man finds himself different. He is a new creature, a new creation, and he has a new outlook, and a new attitude towards everything.

So it is obvious, surely, that this is a most potent influence in the matter of our sanctification, for when a man is born again he has an entirely new view of God. The trouble with the natural man is that his view of God is wrong. He is 'at enmity against God'; an enemy and an alien in his mind, says Paul. He is outside the 'commonwealth' of Israel, 'without God in the world' (Eph 2:12). That is the difficulty with the man who is not in Christ, he is a God hater. Even when he claims that he believes in God, he really hates him. He does not know God and his ideas concerning him are all wrong. What the devil did to man was to insinuate a false view of God which has persisted ever since. But when we are given this new nature and when the new principle comes in, we have the right view of God for the first time; and obviously we can never be sanctified until this happens to us.

Then we also have a new view of God's law. The law of God is no longer grievous to the Christian. '... his commandments,' says John, 'are not grievous' (1 Jn 5:3). Christians love God's law. They know that it is right and true. It does not go against the grain for them because now their whole attitude is changed. This is an essential part of their sanctification. Formerly they looked at the law and saw that it was against them. They wished that it was not there. But now they love it; they delight in it; they want it; they want to be conformed to it. The whole position is changed.

And in the same way they have an entirely different view of sin. Those who are born again hate sin. They bemoan the fact that there is any sinful principle still left in them. They know something about the experience of Romans 7. Have you been there? Have you been in Romans 7? Have you ever known what it is to hate the sin that is in you – this principle, this law in your members? Have you ever felt desperate about yourself? Have you ever cried out, 'Oh wretched man that I am! who shall deliver me from the body of this death?' People who are born again inevitably know something about that experience. They cannot help it; they must know it. Sin has become abhorrent to them – hateful – because it is unlike God. It is the greatest enemy of their souls.

In the same way, of course, the Christian's whole view of Christ is changed. Only the one who has been born again truly knows the Lord Jesus Christ. The princes of this world do not known him; it was they who crucified him, says Paul. And they did so because they did not know the Lord of Glory: if they had known him they would never have done it. It is only the Holy Spirit who can enable a person truly to understand and to know the Lord Jesus Christ. That is why we should never be surprised that very able, intelligent people do not believe the gospel. They cannot. 'The natural man receiveth not the things of the Spirit of God ... neither can he know them, because they are spiritu-ally discerned' (1 Cor 2:14). We need the 'mind of Christ', and in the regeneration, we have the mind of Christ.

And thus, the New Testament tells us, the Christian is entirely new and entirely changed, and he hungers and thirsts after righteousness. Now at the very minimum, regeneration means that, and you cannot be a Christian without that having happened to you. That is what makes us Christian – that God has worked this mighty operation upon us, and has implanted in us this new principle of life. As that other principle came in at the Fall, so this new principle now comes in, and it changes our entire outlook. But I must leave it at that and go on to what is, in a sense, another aspect of the same great truth.

We were emphasising earlier the fact that, as Christians, we are in Christ. I am anxious to emphasise now that it is equally true that Christ is in us. There are two sides to this. We have seen that we are united to Christ, and that therefore all he has done we have done. But it is also true to say that he is in us. You notice if you read John 14, 15 and 16 – the introduction, if you like, to this great prayer – that our Lord keeps on saying, 'I in you, and you in me.' 'The Father in me, and I in the Father.' That is his language. We are in him and he is in us, and this emphasis, this aspect of the truth, is as vital in the matter of our sanctification as is the other truth which emphasises that we are in him.

There is great teaching about this everywhere in the Scriptures. I again commend to you those three chapters in John; but you will find it richly in all the New Testament epistles, and in particular, perhaps, in the epistles of the apostle Paul. Let me just quote to you at random some of the leading statements. In Romans 8:10 he puts it like this: 'And if Christ be in you, the body is dead because of sin; but the Spirit is life because of righteousness.' But you notice the statement – 'if Christ be in you'. Paul's argument is that if he is not in you, you are not a Christian: but if you are a Christian, then he is in you.

Or take 2 Corinthians 13:5: 'Know ye not your own selves, how that Jesus Christ is in you, except ye be reprobates?' What a tremendous statement! Then of course, there is the great statement in Galatians 2:20: 'I live, yet not I, but Christ liveth in me: and the life which I now live in the flesh I live by the faith of the Son of God, who loved me and gave himself for me.' Again in Ephesians 3:17 Paul prays for the Ephesians: 'That Christ may dwell in your hearts by faith.' Then listen to him in that great triumphant statement in Colossians 1:27: 'To whom,' he says, 'God would make known what is the riches of the glory of this mystery among the Gentiles; which is Christ in you, the hope of glory.' And again in the same epistle, in 3:4, he says, 'When Christ, who is our life, shall appear, then shall ye also appear with him in glory.' He is our life now, and he is going to appear.

I have simply taken some of these great statements at random, but you notice that they all unite in saying that if we are Christians, the simple truth is that Christ is in us. Not only am I united to Christ indissolubly and am a sharer, therefore, of all that is true of him, but Christ is in me. He turned to those disciples, who were crestfallen and heartbroken when he told them that he was about to leave them, and said, Do not worry, do not let sorrow fill your hearts. 'Let not your heart be troubled: ye believe in God, believe also in me' (Jn 14:1). He said, Do you know, it is a good thing for you that I am going. As it is now, I am with you, but I am outside you. My going will mean that I shall not only be with you but that I shall be *in* you: I am going to take up my abode in you. The Father and I will take up our abode in you through the Holy Spirit. We are going to send the Holy Spirit, and in him we will come and reside – take up our residence, dwell – within you. 'It is expedient for you that I go away: for if I go not away, the Comforter will not come unto you; but if I depart, I will send him unto you' (Jn 16:7). That is the argument.

Christian people, is it not obvious to us all that we are living very, very much below the position which we are meant to be in? Do you realise that Christ is in you, that Christ is in your heart by faith? What is the thing we preach? asks Paul, writing to the Colossians, who, remember, were Gentiles. He says, This is the mystery, this is the marvellous mystic message, the astounding thing that has been committed to me and to the other preachers of the gospel – 'Christ in you, the hope of glory' (Col 1:27). What hope have I of glory? It is that Christ is in me; Christ dwelling in our hearts by faith.

I wonder whether we can appropriate the language of the apostle Paul, and whether we can say, honestly and truly, 'I live, yet not I but Christ liveth in me'? My friends, the Lord Jesus Christ came into the world and endured all he did, and went to that agony and the shame of the cross, in order that you and I might be able to say that. You notice that I am dealing with this doctrine only from the standpoint of sanctification. It is a doctrine that can be worked out on many other lines, but we are concerned in particular about the truth that sanctifies – 'Sanctify them in [or through] thy truth: thy word is truth' – and here is an aspect of it. 'How can I live a sanctified holy life?' you ask. The answer is, Christ is in you, living his life in you. Let nobody try to say that this is a truth about certain special Christians: it is true of all Christians. The apostle Paul not only says this about himself, he presses this upon all others. His prayer for the Ephesians is that they may be 'strengthened with might by his Spirit in the inner man' and that 'Christ may dwell in their hearts by faith', and so on.

Therefore, as we look at this great truth it seems to me that one of the first things we must lay hold of is the solemn and simple fact that if we are believers at all in the Lord Jesus Christ, we are in him and he is also in us. This means that as you wake up in the morning and consider the kind of life you are expected to live, as you realise the sinfulness of the world in which you walk, as you know something of the attacks of the devil, the principalities and powers, the rulers of the darkness of this world, the spiritual wickedness in the high places which are set against you, you must put up, against all that, your shield of faith, by which you say, 'Yes, that is all true, but Christ is in me. I am not alone, because he dwells in me.' And you live by that faith, and you go on and you conquer and you prevail.

Now, let me divide that up a little by showing how this works. And I suggest that the first thing we must do is to realise this truth. Notice how our Lord has put it in John 6:53: 'Except ye eat the flesh of the Son of man, and drink his blood, ye have no life in you.' But then he goes on to say, 'Whoso eateth my flesh, and drinketh my blood, hath eternal life; and I will raise him up at the last day. For my flesh is meat indeed, and my blood is drink indeed' (vv. 54–55). Then he repeats it all – 'He that eateth my flesh, and drinketh my blood, dwelleth in me, and I in him. As the living Father hath sent me, and I live by the Father: so he that eateth me, even he shall live by me. This is that bread which came down from heaven ... he that eateth of this bread shall live for ever' (vv. 56–58).

The argument is perfectly plain and simple. What you and I need in order to be able to live this sanctified, holy Christian life, is spiritual life, energy and power. Where can I get these things? Our Lord tells us that there is only one way: we must 'eat his flesh and drink his blood'. Is that a reference to taking communion regularly? Not at all! 'The words that I speak unto you,' he says in verse 63, 'they are spirit and they are life.' No, he means that we realise that he is in us, and that, as it were, as we partake of our food and drink, so we shall partake of him spiritually. He is speaking in a spiritual sense, not of something material. No grace can be infused by baptism, or be received in bread or wine, it comes by a spiritual partaking of him. The people asked materially, 'How can we eat of his flesh?'

You do not understand, he says, you will always materialise everything; you are carnal in your outlook. My words, 'they are spirit and they are life', understand them spiritually.

In verse 57 of the same chapter it is made very clear. He says, 'As the living Father hath sent me and I live by the Father: so he that eateth me, even he shall live by me.' How did he take of the living Father? Did he eat bread and drink wine? No, of course not: he partook of his Father spiritually, and we are to partake of him in exactly the same way.

To do so means meditating upon him; thinking about him; realising these truths; masticating them, as it were; dwelling upon them; taking them into ourselves; saying by faith, 'Yes, I believe the word, Christ is in me, and I am going to partake of him.' But not only that. We must not only live by him in the sense I have just been describing; we must go to him constantly and take of his fullness. John puts it in the prologue of this Gospel when he says, 'And of his fulness have all we received, and grace for grace' (Jn 1:16). What he means is, I am living by him, I go to him for everything. In him are treasures for ever more, the treasures of grace and of wisdom and of goodness. God has put all this in Christ, and all I must do is to go to Christ and I receive it.

Now this is a very practical matter. We find our Lord constantly saying it throughout this Gospel of John. For example, in chapter 7:37, he cries: 'If any man thirst, let him come unto me, and drink.' And remember that 'come' here has the sense of 'keep on coming', so what he says is: 'If any man thirst, let him keep on coming unto me to drink.' Let us be very practical here; it is as simple as this. If you find yourself at some time, at any point in your life in this world, tired, weary, not only physically, but mentally, and perhaps still more, spiritually, what do you do about it? Well, he tells you to go to him! He is in you, dwelling in you. Go to him as you would go to a fountain or a tap to draw water – go to Christ. Tell him about your thirst and your weakness, your lethargy and your helplessness, and ask him to give you life-giving water, to give you this heavenly bread: to give you himself. He is pledged to do that, but we only know it for ourselves as we realise that he is in us, and as we turn to him and go to him.

He puts it like this, in effect, when he turns to the disciples who are troubled about his leaving them, and says, 'You are so unhappy because of a weakness in your thinking. You say, "Whenever we have been in trouble we have just gone straight to him and asked him a question, and he has always been able to answer it. He has given us power to cast out devils, and to speak to people, but if he is going away, what shall we do?"' His answer is this: 'It is going to be better, because, though I am going away, I am coming back and I am going to be *in* you: I will always be in you. You simply turn to me and I will give you all you need.' So we must draw 'of his fulness'. Indeed, I am not going too far when I put it like this: the New Testament tells us that there is no excuse for failure in the Christian. If we fail it is because we are not taking of his fullness and the promised grace upon grace.

Let me repeat that in another way: we must realise his strength and his power. He has already been emphasising that in the fifteenth chapter. He has compared us, in our relationship to him, to branches in the vine, and he has said categorically that 'without me ye can do nothing', nothing at all (Jn 15:5). A branch can do nothing except in its relationship to the trunk, the parent tree and we are exactly like that. But what power there is in the tree! Take Paul's prayer for the people at Ephesus, in Ephesians 1. Paul prays that the 'eyes of your understanding [may be] enlightened that ye may know ...', and he goes on to request three main things. I am emphasising the third here, and it is this: 'What is the exceeding greatness of his power to us-ward who believe, according to the working of his mighty power, which he wrought in Christ, when he raised him from the dead' (v. 19). *That* is the power that is working in us as Christians; that is the power that is working in us now. The power that raised Christ from the dead is now working in us mightily in our sanctification. Or consider again the apostle Paul's great doxology at the end of Ephesians 3: 'Now unto him that is able to do exceeding abundantly above all that we can ask or think, according to the power that worketh in us.' This is not in the apostles only, but in *all* Christians. That is the power – 'exceeding abundantly above all that we can ask or think'. Or hear him as he writes to the Colossians. He says that he is preaching the gospel, 'Whereunto I also labour, striving according to his working, which worketh in me mightily' (Col 1:29); the power of God in Christ through the Holy Spirit.

That, then, is the way in which we become sanctified and live the sanctified life. We must stop talking about our weakness: we must take more of his power! We must realise that Christ is in us with all this power: that the power that enabled him to resist the temptations of the devil is the power that is in us.

Lastly, I would put it like this – and sometimes I think it is the most effective argument of all. The truth about Christ dwelling in me promotes my sanctification by giving me an entirely new view of sin. I find so often, when people come to discuss with me this problem of sin, that all along they are tending to think of sin in terms of this or that particular sin that gets them down. This doctrine we are looking at gives us a new view of it, it makes you look at it like this: What is sin? Well, sin is not so much something that I do or that I should not do: sin is that which separates me from God. He is in me, dwelling in me, and my life is meant to be a life of communion and of fellowship with him. Sin is allowing myself, even for a single moment, to turn away from him.

Imagine yourself having audience with the Queen or somebody whom you regard as great in this world. What would she say if, instead of looking at her and listening to what she was saying, you were looking at someone else or gazing out of the window, patently thinking about something else? She would feel insulted, and rightly so. Nothing is more insulting than not looking at the person talking to you and not listening to what is being said. The New Testament tells me that Christ is in me,

and I am meant to live a life of constant fellowship and communion with him. Sin is to look away from him; to be interested
in anything that the world can give rather than in him. Oh, if it
is something foul it is ten times worse; but the best that the
world has got to give me is an insult to him, if I put it before him.

There are endless statements of this; Paul puts it in terms of
the Holy Spirit, 'Know ye not that your body is the temple of
the Holy Ghost which is in you?' (1 Cor 6:19). The argument
is about fornication and adultery. Paul does not give a moral lec-
ture on immorality; he says in effect, 'What is wrong about that,
is that you are joining your body, which is a temple of the Holy
Spirit, to another, and you have no right to do it. The way to
overcome that sin is not to pray so much that you may be delivered from it; it is to realise that your body is the temple of the
Holy Spirit, and that you have no right to use it in that way.'
Another way he puts it is this, and it is very tender: 'Grieve not
the Holy Spirit of God' (Eph 4:30). He is tender, he is sensitive,
he is holy; do not grieve him.

And if you and I would only think of our lives like that, it
would very soon begin to promote our sanctification. May I
again commend to you that simple morning rule. When you
wake up, the first thing you should do (and I too need to do the
same) is say to yourself, 'I am a child of God. Christ is in me.
That old self is gone: I died with Christ. "I live; yet not I, but
Christ liveth in me." Everything I do today, everything I think
and say, must be in the light of this knowledge.' Keep him, my
dear friends, in the very front of your mind and heart. Eat his
flesh and drink his blood. Be constantly living on him and dwelling on him. The world will do its utmost to prevent you. 'This
is the victory that overcometh the world, even our faith' (1 Jn
5:4). That means that we should realise constantly that he is in
us, dwelling in our hearts by faith, and that all that we do is done
as in his presence and under his holy eye. We are in Christ.

Yes, but Christ is also in us, and as we realise it we shall cast
away depression and fear of the devil. We shall realise that we
are not only living like him, but living with him, for him, and
living by means of his power which worketh in us mightily.

What a wondrous truth is this truth by which God produces
our sanctification!

11

The Doctrine of the Resurrection

Sanctify them through thy truth: thy word is truth (v. 17).
Be not deceived: evil communications corrupt good manners
(1 Cor 15:33).

As we continue with our consideration of this great verse –
'Father, sanctify them through thy truth [or in thy truth], thy
word is truth' – I should like to link with it the statement out of
the mighty fifteenth chapter of the first epistle to the Corinthians: 'Be not deceived: evil communications corrupt good manners' (1 Cor 15:33). In other words, I want to consider with you
the relevance of the doctrine of the Resurrection to the whole
question of our sanctification, and I propose to do so by considering the essential message of this particular chapter. Every
aspect of Christian truth, every aspect of the gospel, should
influence us and thereby promote our sanctification. We have
already looked at a number of doctrines that do this, and now
we are to consider how the particular doctrine or emphasis on
the truth of the fact of the Resurrection has a vital bearing upon
our growth in grace and our sanctification.

Now 1 Corinthians 15 is generally regarded as the great chapter on the Resurrection, and so of course it is. But there is always
the danger, it seems to me, that unless we are very careful and
consider it in its context we will not entirely understand its point
and purport. The context is always important and it is exception-
ally so in connection with this particular chapter, because it is not

merely a general statement of the doctrine of the Resurrection. It is that, but it is not primarily that. It was not even written for that purpose. The apostle did not sit down and say, 'Well now, it would be a good thing for me to write to the people at Corinth an account of this doctrine, and of this vital fact of the Resurrection.' There was no need for he had already done that on his first visit to Corinth with his great message.

He tells us here what he did preach to them: 'For I delivered unto you first of all that which I also received, how that Christ died for our sins according to the scriptures; and that he was buried, and that he rose again the third day, according to the scriptures: and that he was seen of Cephas, then of the twelve …' and so on. He had already preached the facts and the interpretation and the significance and the meaning of the facts. So at this point, he was not just setting out to write an account, or make a statement of the doctrine of the Resurrection.

Neither must we regard this great chapter, as I am afraid so many tend to do, merely as a very appropriate chapter to read at a funeral. We all probably know this chapter very well for that reason. It is the custom to do this, and I am sure there are large numbers of people who instinctively think of it only in terms of a funeral – as something which is meant to give comfort and solace to the relatives of the one who is being buried. That is the context into which we tend to put it, but, as I want to show you, all that is entirely wrong. This chapter, indeed the whole epistle, was written with a very practical end in view.

The first letter to the Corinthians was not written primarily as a sort of theological treatise. There is a great deal of theology in it, as I am going to show you, but when the apostle wrote it, he was not setting out merely to write a series of statements on doctrine. Nor was it meant to be some sort of compendium of doctrine of all the letters he ever wrote. In many ways it is the most practical of his letters. It is one of those great omnibus epistles in which Paul takes up a number of questions, most of which had been sent to him by the members of the church at Corinth, or else had arisen out of certain things he had heard about some of the Christians there. If he ever sat down to write a very practical, pastoral letter, the apostle Paul did so when he wrote this one.

Paul had become very concerned about the life of the members of the church at Corinth, and, in particular, he was concerned about their behaviour. In other words, he was concerned about their sanctification. Things were happening there which were quite wrong. For instance, there was the abuse of the Communion Service, with some people eating too much and drinking too much. There was also trouble about the weaker brother, about meats offered to idols, and about the whole question of sects and divisions and schism. Now the apostle was concerned about these matters, not only from a primary theological standpoint, but particularly because of their effect upon the daily life of the church, and the life of its members.

And in exactly the same way he was concerned for them over this question of Resurrection, because certain people had been teaching them a false doctrine about it. They had been saying that it was not a fact and that there was not to be a general resurrection at all, but that resurrection was some kind of spiritual continuation of life. They were evacuating the whole idea of the Resurrection of our Lord of its true meaning and significance, and the apostle was very concerned about this. And why? Because 'evil communications corrupt good manners'. You cannot believe a wrong thing and still live a right life, says Paul. Your conduct is determined by what you believe, so evil communications, evil teachings, evil beliefs, are going to corrupt your conduct. He could see quite clearly that if this false teaching concerning the Resurrection really got a grip on these people at Corinth, then their whole life and conduct, their morality and behaviour were going to deteriorate. He declares that there is nothing, therefore, which is more vital and more urgent than that they should be right about this particular matter.

Let me translate all this into modern terms. According to the apostle Paul here, there is nothing which is quite so dangerous as to say that it does not matter very much what a man believes so long as he somehow believes in Christ; that you must not particularise over these things, and insist upon believing this or that, in detail, about these great matters. According to the apostle, that is about the most dangerous statement a person can ever make. To Paul this is so vital that he writes this powerful chapter about it.

It is important for this reason: the people who had been teaching this false doctrine regarded themselves as Christians. If they had gone to the church at Corinth and said that Christianity was all wrong and that they did not believe in Christ at all, nobody would have listened to them. But they did not do that. They purported to be Christians; they said they were preaching Christ. Yes, but they had denied his literal physical resurrection, and they still called themselves Christians. And the members of the church at Corinth who had been listening to this false teaching, and who were ready to accept it, were also members of the church, and regarded themselves as Christians. They never imagined for a moment that by believing this false doctrine they were ceasing to be Christian; they even thought it was an improvement upon the doctrine that Paul had taught them.

We begin, therefore, to see the significance of all this. There are many in the church today who would have us believe that so long as a man says, 'I am a Christian, I believe in Christ,' all is well and you do not ask him any questions at all. That is not the position of the apostle Paul. He says, in effect, 'It is not a matter of indifference as to whether Christ really did rise in the body on the morning of the third day or not. To me,' he says, 'it is not a matter of indifference as to whether Christ merely goes on living in a spiritual sense and never really came out of the grave and appeared and showed himself to his disciples and to certain chosen witnesses, and then ascended in their presence. To me it is absolutely vital, and there must be no uncertainty about this at all.'

So it is not a matter of indifference; it is not enough just to say that though Christ was crucified on the cross, he still goes on living and can still influence us in this world in a spiritual sense. The gospel of the New Testament, the message of the Christian church from the beginning, is one which is based on the literal physical resurrection of the Son of God from the grave. It is based on the empty tomb, on the literal historical fact of Christ risen in the body from the dead.

And this is vital, as the apostle here emphasises, from the practical standpoint. Its importance emerges as we see the effect of wrong doctrine upon our daily life and living. Do you notice his argument? He says, Why baptise for the dead, '… if the dead rise not at all? … And why stand we in jeopardy ever hour?' (vv. 29–30). If I am risking my life and my reputation on this matter, as I am, says Paul, I am a fool if this fact of the resurrection is not a fact. 'I protest by your rejoicing which I have in Christ Jesus our Lord, I die daily' (v. 31). He was dying daily for the gospel, but he says, this is all wrong if that other doctrine is right. 'If after the manner of men I have fought with beasts at Ephesus, what advantageth it me, if the dead rise not? let us eat and drink; for tomorrow we die' (v.32). So let there be no mistake about all this, says the apostle. What a man believes does matter; what a man believes in detail does count.

And it is as true in the church today as it was when Paul penned those words. What a man believes is ultimately going to determine his life. A man who is loose in doctrine eventually becomes loose also in his life and in his behaviour. And I do not hesitate to say that the church of God on earth is as she is today primarily because of the looseness of belief in doctrine which entered in the last century, and has continued to the present time. You cannot separate these things; doctrine and conduct are indissolubly linked. That is why the apostle writes the chapter and fights as he does for the truth of this particular doctrine.

Let us, therefore, see why all this is true and how it works out. Why must we believe in the New Testament doctrine of the literal physical Resurrection? I will give you a number of answers to that question. The first is that it is the one thing, above everything else, which really proves that Jesus of Nazareth is the eternal Son of God. I do not want to concentrate on this now, as we are more concerned with the practical aspects of the letter. But let us be clear about this. He was 'declared to be the Son of God with power, according to the spirit of holiness, by the resurrection from the dead' (Rom 1:4). It was the Resurrection that finally convinced the disciples, who hitherto had been uncertain and doubtful and sceptical. They were crestfallen and dejected because of the death on the cross. It was when they knew that he had risen, that they knew he was the Son of God. The Resurrection is the final ultimate truth of the unique deity of the Lord Jesus Christ. It is the ultimate certainty of the fact that he is indeed the only begotten Son of God.

And that, of course, leads to this: it substantiates his claim that he had been sent into the world by the Father to do a particular work. He kept on saying that; it is the great theme of John 17. He had been sent into the world by the Father to do a given work, and here, by the Resurrection, he proves that he has done the work, and completed it. Paul says in Romans: 'Who was delivered for our offences, and was raised again for our justification' (Rom 4:25). If the Lord Jesus Christ had not literally risen physically from the grave, we could never be certain that he had ever really finished the work. And what was the work? It was to satisfy the demands of the law. The law of God demands that the punishment for sin shall be death, and if he has died for our sins, we must not only be certain that he has died, but that he has finished dying, and that there is no longer death. He has answered the ultimate demands of the law, and in the same way he has answered all the ultimate demands of God. The argument of the New Testament is that when God raised his Son from the dead, he was proclaiming to the whole world, I am satisfied in him: I am satisfied in the work he has done. He has done everything. He has fulfilled every demand. Here he is risen – therefore I am satisfied with him.

Not only that. The Resurrection proved that he has conquered every enemy that was opposed to him, to God, and to us. He has not only satisfied the law and conquered death and the grave, he has vanquished the devil and all his forces, and hell and all the principalities and powers of evil. He has triumphed over them all, and he proves it in the Resurrection. The devil cannot hold him; death and hell cannot hold him. He has mastered them all; he has emerged on the other side. He is the Son of God, and he has completed the work which the Father had sent him to do.

And all this, of course, is of vital importance to us. It is only in the light of the Resurrection that I finally have an assurance of my sins forgiven. It is only in the light of the Resurrection that I ultimately know that I stand in the presence of God absolved from guilt and shame and every condemnation. I can now say with Paul, 'There is therefore now no condemnation to them which are in Christ Jesus' (Rom 8:1) because I look at the fact of the Resurrection. It is there that I know it.

You notice how Paul argues in 1 Corinthians 15:17 when he says, 'If Christ be not raised, your faith is vain; ye are yet in your sins.' If it is not a fact that Christ literally rose from the grave, then you are still guilty before God. Your punishment has not been borne, your sins have not been dealt with, you are yet in your sins. It matters that much: without the Resurrection you have no standing at all. You are still uncertain as to whether you are forgiven and whether you are a child of God. And when one day you come to your death-bed you will not know, you will be uncertain as to where you are going and what is going to happen to you. 'Who was delivered for our offences, and was raised again for our justification' (Rom 4:25). It is there in the Resurrection that I stand before God free and absolved and without a fear and know that I am indeed a child of God. So you see the importance of holding on to this doctrine and why we must insist upon the details of doctrine, and not be content with some vague general belief in the Lord Jesus Christ?

'But wait a minute,' I can imagine someone saying. 'Yes I believe all that, but my problem is, how am I to live in this world? You announce that great doctrine to me, but I am still confronted by the world, the flesh and the devil, and how am I going to meet that? My problem is, how to be sanctified, how to become holy; how to advance in grace and in the knowledge of God, and to follow Christ as I want to do?' Well, the answer to it all is given here in 1 Corinthians 15:19 – 'If in this life only we have hope in Christ, we are of all men most miserable', together with the other verses I have already quoted to you – verses 13, 32, 33. All these have a very practical effect upon our lives in this world.

Let me summarise all this. If we are concerned about our life in this world, and the fight against the world, the flesh and the devil, the first thing we must do, says the apostle, is to take an overall look at this great doctrine of the Resurrection of our Lord. The important thing always is not to be content only with considering your own particular sins. We have been emphasising that a good deal in considering this matter of sanctification, and we have seen that most people are defeated because they start with their own particular sin – the thing that gets them down. And, of course, they cannot get away from it: they are held captive by it. No, says Paul, the way to deal even with that particular problem is to turn your back upon it for the moment, and to look at the whole general situation and see yourself as a part of it, in this world.

The Lord Jesus Christ, according to this teaching, came into the world because of this problem of sin and evil: that is the whole meaning of the Incarnation. He came in order to fight the kingdom of darkness, the kingdom of sin, and of Satan. That was the whole purpose of his coming. Not only did he come to do that, he has succeeded in doing it. He was tempted of the devil, and he repulsed him every time: he mastered him. He defeated and conquered the devil and all his powers and all the forces of Hades. And he has finally done so in his death and in his glorious resurrection.

'Yes, that is all very well,' says our questioner, 'but after all, when I look around me I do not seem to see that. I see sin and temptation flagrant, rampant. I see men intent upon evil. I see wars and hear of rumours of wars. It is all very well for you to say that Christ has conquered all these powers, but I do not see that in this world. How is all you are saying really going to help me?'

The answer is here in verses 23-25. 'But every man in his own order: Christ the first fruits; afterward they that are Christ's at his coming. Then cometh the end, when he shall have delivered up the kingdom to God, even the Father; when he shall have put down all rule and all authority and power. For he must reign, till he hath put all enemies under his feet.'

Now this means that the Lord Jesus Christ is still continuing the fight. When he was on earth in his own person he defeated the enemy at every point, and he finally routed and defeated him on the cross and in the Resurrection. Yes, but now having ascended up into heaven, he has led captivity captive, and is seated on the right hand of God's throne and authority and power. And what is he doing there? Well, according to this teaching, he is reigning there. This world has not got out of hand. It is still God's world, and Christ is still ruling and reigning over it. All authority is in his hands. He has been able to open the Book of history and the Book of destiny. He alone was strong enough to break the seals and to open the Book. So what we are taught by the Resurrection is that Christ is still there bringing his own purpose to pass.

We do not understand it all; we do not understand why he did not immediately bring it all to an end, but he has chosen not to do so. He has chosen to save a certain number of people; the fullness of the Gentiles and the fullness of Israel have got to come in. But this is the thing that is certain: as certainly as Christ rose triumphant over the grave, he is reigning at this moment, and he will reign until the time comes for him to return. The Lord Jesus Christ is going to come back into this world, and finally take the devil and all his forces, and cast them into a lake burning with fire. Evil and sin and wrong, and everything that is opposed to God, are going to be destroyed completely, and Christ will hand back a perfect kingdom to his Father. It is absolutely certain: he must reign, he will reign, until all his enemies have been put beneath his feet.

Now we must start with that. Our tendency is to be frightened by the devil and by temptation and the power and the forces of evil. 'Ah,' we say, 'how can a man, a weak man, fight against all that?' I say, look away from yourself for a moment; look at what is coming. He is reigning; he rules, and he is finally going to rout his enemies, and end it all. That is the general picture.

But let me show you the argument in a slightly more personal manner. How do I apply all that to my own case? I do so in this way. In a spiritual sense I am already risen with Christ: we have seen that in our previous studies. I am in Christ and Christ is in me. I am to reckon myself to be dead indeed to sin, and alive unto God. I have died with Christ; I have been buried with him; and I have risen with him. As a new man, I am in Christ, and as a new man in Christ I have risen; I have finished with death. I have got to die physically, but I have finished with the con- demnation of death, and the terror and the sting of death have been taken out, as far as I am concerned. I am risen with him already spiritually.

But here I want to emphasise this other aspect. I am already risen with him spiritually, but I am yet going to rise with him in a physical and in a literal sense. 'For as in Adam all die, even so in Christ shall all be made alive. But every man in his own order: Christ the firstfruits, afterward they that are Christ's at his coming ...' (vv. 22–23), and then all the others. The resurrec- tion of Christ, and the fact of the resurrection of Christ, is a cer- tain, absolute announcement and proclamation that you and I and all people likewise rise from the grave in the body. The apostle explains how it all happens in the later portion of this great chapter – read it for yourselves, it is all there. 'We shall all be changed' (v. 51). It will not be flesh and blood. There will be a change in 'the twinkling of an eye'. But we are all going to rise as the Lord Jesus Christ rose from the grave on that third morn- ing. There will be some people left on earth when the Lord comes and they will be changed; it comes to the same thing.

But what does all this mean? Let me tell you what the Scrip- ture says, and you will see its significance in the matter of our sanctification, and in the matter of our daily living. What I do know is that we shall all appear before the Judgement Throne of Christ, and give an account of the deeds done in the body, whether good or bad. And let me remind you, Christian people, that that is true of you and of me. Every one of us who is a Christian will have to appear before that Throne and give an account. But you see now the significance of the doctrine of the Resurrection: 'Evil communications corrupt good manners.' A man who realises every day of his life that he has got to stand before Christ and give an account, is a man who is very soon going to pay attention to the way he is living.

We shall all appear before him, and not only that, we read in 1 John 3:2 that, 'We shall see him as he is.' What a tremendous thought that is! Here on earth we have spent our time reading about him, thinking and meditating concerning him, but then we shall see him as he is. 'Now we see through a glass darkly, but then face to face' (1 Cor 13:12). Do you realise that? It is the Resurrection which tells you that – his resurrection, your resurrection. Furthermore, the next phrase in 1 John 3:2 tells us that we shall be like him. Paul says here in 1 Corinthians 15:53 that we shall be incorruptible – 'This corruptible must put on incorruption' – and in Philippians 3:21 he tells us that the Lord will return and that he 'shall change our vile body [the body of our humiliation] that it may be fashioned like unto his glorious body, according to the working whereby he is able even to subdue all things unto himself.' My very body shall be changed; I shall be incorruptible; I shall be glorified; I shall be like him even in my body. What a staggering thought!

And then beyond all that, these Scriptures tell us that we shall spend our eternity in his glorious presence. We shall be with him, with God, with Christ, with the Holy Spirit, with the spirits of just men made perfect, with holy angels. Because we shall rise we shall go on and spend our eternity in that indescribable glory. That is what the Scripture tells us is the significance and the meaning of this doctrine of the Resurrection.

What, then, do I conclude from all this? What are the deductions that we must inevitably draw from all this if we really believe it? Well the first, surely, is that if that is true, then we must have nothing to do with this condemned world. If I really believe that this world is evil and that it belongs to Satan, I must believe the apostle when he says that Christ must reign until he has put all his enemies under his feet. 'Then cometh the end, when he shall have delivered up the kingdom to God, even the Father; when he shall have put down all rule and authority and power' (1 Cor 15:24). The New Testament message is that the world is controlled by the devil and by hell. Worldliness is evil – the lust of the flesh and the lust of the eye and the pride of life. It is all evil; it is all under condemnation. It is going to be destroyed, utterly and completely. If we believe all this, can we still desire that? Do we still want it? Do we regard the gospel that tells us to turn our backs upon it all as narrow? What interest can we possibly have in it?

My dear friends, we are inconsistent, we are false, if we say one thing and do the other. We are contradicting our own doctrine. If we really believe this message, how can we desire the world, and how can we enjoy it? It is to be destroyed, and if we belong to it we shall be destroyed with it. 'Evil communications corrupt good manners.' Those who really believe this doctrine that we have been looking at together will not want to compromise with that world which is under condemnation, and with evil and sin. I do not understand it when I see people who call themselves Christian attaching great significance to worldly position and worldly pomp and power, to things that belong to the realm of the condemned, to the realm of evil. There is nothing of that in the New Testament. We are all one before Christ, every one of us. Whatever we may happen to be by birth or position, we are all sinners, we are all under judgement, we are all condemned by the law. We have nothing to do with those worldly things, and if we believe this doctrine we must turn our backs upon them all, whatever may be the consequences. That is the first inevitable deduction.

The next thing I deduce is that it is our business and our duty always to keep our eyes on the ultimate. Half our troubles are due to the fact that we fail to do so. We are always looking at this sin of ours, this thing that gets us down today. But we must look at the ultimate. We must keep our eyes on the eternal. 'For our light affliction, which is but for a moment, worketh for us a far more exceeding and eternal weight of glory; while' – and only while – 'we look not at the things which are seen, but at the things which are not seen ...' (2 Cor 4:17–18). Does that sin get you down? Have you been praying to be delivered from it and yet are still committing it? Well, let me give you a piece of advice. Stop praying about it; rather, remind yourself that you are going to die, and that after death you will rise from the dead, and that you will stand before the Judgement seat of Christ, that you are going to look into his face – into his eyes – and that you are going to 'see him as he is'. And then if you can still go on doing that particular thing, I do not understand it. That is how the New Testament tells you to face your particular sin: just put it into the light of this ultimate doctrine. Realise that you call yourself a Christian, and all that that means, and what it is going to mean. Put everything into the light of that.

My third deduction is that having looked thus at the ultimate, we must never be discouraged. Oh, I am going further still – we have no right to be discouraged. It is a sin to be discouraged. A discouraged Christian is a contradiction in terms; he is denying his Lord. We must not be discouraged, because we are not left to ourselves. He is there seated at God's right hand. He is reigning, and he has said, 'All power is given unto me in heaven and in earth' (Mt 28:18). Do you not know, says Paul, writing to the Ephesians, the power that works in you? It is 'his mighty power, which he wrought in Christ, when he raised him from the dead' (Eph 1:19–20). You have no right to be discouraged. He, unseen, is still with us, bringing his purposes to pass, forming his kingdom, gathering out his elect, working it all to that ultimate end. We are not left to ourselves.

Then there is this great word with which Paul ends 1 Corinthians 15 – 'Therefore my beloved, be ye stedfast, unmoveable, always abounding in the work of the Lord, forasmuch as ye know that your labour is not in vain in the Lord.' It cannot be, in the light of this ultimate fact. It does not matter very much what men may say of you; it is what the Lord thinks that matters. Men may laugh at you, they may deride you; they may dismiss you, they may forget all about you, and of course, if you are thinking in terms of time, that is very serious. If you are only thinking of this world, then the greater the praise you get from men the better for you. Our Lord said about people like that: 'Verily I say unto you, They have their reward' (Mt 6:2). It is the only reward they are going to get – the praise of men in this passing, temporary world. But if you know that you are a child of God and that you are going to stand before him and see him face to face, the only thing that is going to count with you is what he thinks, not what anybody else thinks. Do not be discouraged.

Then I draw this fourth deduction: that the world cannot separate me from him and from his love. 'For I am persuaded, that neither death, nor life, nor angels, nor principalities, nor powers, nor things present, nor things to come, nor height, nor depth, nor any other creature, shall be able to separate us from the love of God, which is in Christ Jesus our Lord' (Rom 8:39). I have despaired of myself a thousand times, and my only hope at such times is that though I cannot see anything in myself, he has loved me and has died for me, and will never let me go. I am certain of it.

But I also draw this deduction: if all this is true – and it is – then I have no time to lose or to spare. I shall see him as he is. I shall be like him. I shall stand before that Judgement Throne of his. Have I got time to waste in these days and in this world? The days and the weeks, the months and the years are slipping through my fingers. I will be dead before I know where I am. I have not a moment to waste. If I believe I am going there, it is about time that I began to prepare. If you knew you were going to have an audience at Buckingham Palace in a week, you would be getting ready, would you not? You would be preparing your clothing, and your appearance, and rightly so. If, therefore, you are going to face the King of kings and the Lord of lords and have an audience with him, have you a second to spare? 'Every man that hath this hope in him, purifieth himself, even as he is pure' (1 Jn 3:3). If you do not want to feel ashamed of yourself, and feel that you are a cad when you stand and look into his blessed holy face, and see the marks of the nails, and the wound in his side, which he suffered for you, then prepare for the sight of him, prepare yourself to meet him.

Then, above and beyond everything else, let us dwell upon the glory of it all. Here we are still in this sinful world, and there are so many discouragements, and people may misunderstand us, and things seem to go against us. My friends, do not look at them. 'While we look not at the things which are seen, but at the things which are not seen: for the things which are seen are temporal; but the things which are not seen are eternal' (2 Cor 4:18). Oh, that the Holy Spirit might open our eyes! If we could but see something of them: 'The things which God hath prepared for them that love him' (1 Cor 2:9). The vision of God! To be with Christ! The ineffable purity and holiness of it all: the joy and the singing and the glory! No sighing, no sorrow, no tears, all that left behind: perfect, unmixed, unalloyed glory and happiness and joy and peace. The Resurrection tells us that if we belong to Christ we are going on to that.

So, then, this is the last conclusion, 'Awake to righteousness, and sin not' (1 Cor 15:34). The trouble, says Paul, is that 'some have not the knowledge of God: I speak this to your shame.' The real trouble with a man who is living a life of sin, and who is not sanctified, is that he lacks the knowledge of doctrine. That is his trouble: he does not know these things. And if you and I are not more determined than ever to 'awake to righteousness' and to forsake sin, then the only explanation is that we do not believe the doctrine of the Resurrection. And if we do not, we are yet in our sins and are destined for hell, and may God have mercy on us.

But then to crown it all, in the last verse of this chapter 15 Paul uses the word 'Therefore'. That is the argument, you see the logic – you cannot get away from it. It is not just beautiful language. You have heard people revelling in a beautiful service, and saying, 'How marvellous, how beautiful, how perfect – the balance and the cadence and the lilt of the words!' But that is not what the apostle wants you to feel. He wants you to say this, 'Therefore' – 'Therefore, my beloved brethren, be ye stedfast, unmoveable.' Let them say what they like about you: stand on your doctrine like a man, unmoveable. It is the doctrine of God; it is eternal. Stand steadfast, unmoveable, 'always abounding in the work of the Lord'. In your personal life and living, in your life in the church and for him, in your personal witness and testimony, in the whole of your life – 'abounding!' 'Forasmuch as

ye know that your labour is not in vain in the Lord.' The doctrine of the Resurrection. What a stimulus to our sanctification!

Let nothing come between us and all this mighty truth that
we have been considering together. This is vital. This is life.
This is everything.

> Love so amazing, so divine
> Demands my soul, my life, my all.
>
> *Isaac Watts*

PART FOUR

GROWING IN *the* SPIRIT

1

'Take Time to be Holy'

Sanctify them through thy truth: thy word is truth (John 17:17).

These words are an extraordinary and most comprehensive petition offered by our Lord and Saviour Jesus Christ on behalf of his immediate followers and disciples, and, indeed, on behalf of all his followers and disciples in all ages and in all places. We have been expounding verse 17 in detail, because it is one of the crucial petitions in this high-priestly prayer which our Lord offered and which is recorded in John chapter 17.[1] He is concerned about these people not only because of themselves, but because he is leaving them in the world to do certain work. He reminds his Father that as his Father has sent him into the world, so he is sending them into the world; it is for this reason that he prays that they may be kept from the Evil One, and, further, and positively, that they may be sanctified. We have looked in particular at the method of sanctification as it is here taught by our Lord, and as it is taught everywhere in the Scriptures. 'Sanctify them,' he says, 'through thy truth.' Bring them into the realm of the truth; keep them there so that the Truth shall work upon them and influence them and produce their sanctification.

Furthermore, we have been at pains to emphasise that this process of sanctification depends finally and essentially upon

---

[1] See Vol. 3, *Sanctified Through the Truth* (Crossway Books, 1989).

our understanding of what this truth is. Our Lord says, 'Thy word is truth,' so the way to be sanctified is to look at this word and to receive it. And we have seen that it is a great word and a great truth which can be divided into certain central propositions. The whole word itself is something which promotes our sanctification, but there are certain aspects, certain emphases, which are of particular importance and significance, and we have looked at six of them. These, I would suggest to you, are the six main aspects of this great truth of our salvation. First is the truth about God himself: we must ever start there, everything in connection with our salvation concerns our relationship to God. To be saved is not primarily to be happy, it is not primarily to have an experience; the essence of salvation is that we are in the right relationship to God. From the beginning, the great promise of God with regard to salvation is this: 'I will be your God, and ye shall be my people' (eg Lev 26:7), so if we find that our tendency is to view salvation in any way except directly in terms of our knowledge of God and our relationship to him, it is a false tendency. We must ever be careful to avoid that subtle temptation and we must never be tired of reminding ourselves of the danger of being too subjective.

We might, I know, immediately add that there is an equal danger of being too objective, but let us remember that both are true, and perhaps the greater danger is that of being too subjective. We are living in a difficult world. The times are cruel; we are all tired as the result of wars and the uncertainty that has followed this last world war, and the craving at the present time is for some release and quiet. We require that subjectively and that is quite a good thing, but we must be very careful lest we put it in the first position and fail to realise that the thing which, after all, marks and differentiates the Christian is that he is someone who is in a given relationship to God. The great doctrine of God, the being and character of God, must override everything else. The whole purpose of the Bible is to reveal God to us and to bring us into communion with him, which is the life eternal. Why? So that I should be happy? No! '...that they might know thee the only true God, and Jesus Christ, whom thou hast sent'

(Jn 17:3). That leads to untold happiness and the greatest bliss imaginable, but there are times when it leads to trembling and to fear and drives us to Christ.

Having looked at that, we then went on to look at the doctrine of sin, so that we might see man as he really is in the sight of God; and all this promotes our sanctification. From that, we looked at what God has done for us in our sin, the doctrine of the sending of his Son into the world, and especially his death upon the cross, that amazing action whereby we are purchased and reconciled, redeemed and rescued – all that is absolutely vital to the doctrine of sanctification. And our emphasis there was that we must never regard the cross as something that belongs to the initial stages of our Christian life; we must never get the impression that we have passed by the cross. No, we do not go on from the cross to sanctification, but we find our sanctification in the cross. It is by the precious blood of Christ that we have been purchased, we are not our own – that is sanctification.

Then, having laid down the great fundamental proposition of our fall, we went on to see how Scripture, particularly in this matter of sanctification, introduces us to the great doctrine of our identification with Christ and of the fact that we are in Christ. And from there we considered the truth that always should be taken with that: that Christ is also in us. We are in him and he in us – how astounding that is! Then we considered the relevance of the doctrine concerning the Resurrection to this question of our sanctification. The argument, according to 1 Corinthians 15, is not that the doctrine of the Resurrection is only a comfort to those who are dying or bereaved, it is not something that we should rejoice in on one Sunday in the year only – rushing to church on that Sunday, then neglecting to go again until the next Easter Sunday comes along. No, says the Apostle, in the light of this doctrine, 'Therefore,' and the 'therefore' leads to concentration upon daily life and living: '...be ye stedfast, unmoveable, always abounding in the work of the Lord' (1 Cor 15:58); 'evil communications corrupt good manners' (1 Cor 15:33). So we must 'awake to righteousness and sin not' (v. 34); and we must go on to labour and to realise that our labour is not in vain in the Lord. Those, then, are the great fundamental doctrines, and our sanctification is ever, always, the result of our realisation of them.

So having laid this down, we now come to a more practical aspect of this whole matter. 'Sanctify them,' says our Lord, 'through [or in] thy truth.' But before that can happen, we have to learn that this great, vital truth, at which we have been looking, is something that must of necessity be constantly applied by us, and that the application of the truth is quite as important as the truth itself. There is no value whatsoever in having an intellectual awareness of the truth unless we proceed to apply it, and there are many who fail at that point. So I want now to come to this truth and to its application, and if you read Romans 6 you will see that this is precisely what the apostle Paul does. In the previous chapters he has been laying down his great doctrine of justification by faith only. He has been demonstrating it from the Scriptures, making it perfectly plain and clear. So he has stated the doctrine, but, wise teacher as he is, he knows that men and women in a state of sin and under the influence and at the suggestion of the devil, are liable to fail to apply it at all, or to apply it in the wrong way.

Now the Christians in Rome, having heard the doctrines of justification by faith only, of their union with Christ, and incorporation into him – as you were once in Adam, Paul has just taught them in chapter 5, so you are now in Christ; and as the result of Adam's transgression came upon you, so everything that Christ has done has happened to you – having heard this, they might come to a wrong conclusion. Paul realises that some might say, 'Very well, then, if that is so, it does not matter what we do.' They might even say, 'The more we sin the greater will grace abound, or the more we sin the more grace will show itself, therefore let us continue in sin.' And, immediately, he rejects this with abhorrence and alarm, and proceeds to work out this great argument in Romans 6, the essence of which is that, in a final sense, you must not divide justification and sanctification. For the man who realises truly what it is to be justified, is one who realises the absolute necessity of sanctification.

Let me put that in a slightly different form. I want to suggest to you that it is not enough, even, to be aware of this great doctrine; but before our sanctification can proceed, these doctrines must be applied. There are many ways in which we can apply them. One way is to consider together what it means to walk and live by faith. William Romaine, a great evangelical clergy-man who lived in London some two hundred years ago, published a book which he called *The Life and Walk and Triumph of Faith*. This title correctly indicates that the whole of the Christian life is a life of faith. We walk by faith not by sight – all the great doctrines are held by faith and as Christians we must view our life in this world as a walk, as a great progression in this life of faith.

But people encounter many difficulties with regard to this life, and I want to mention two of them in particular. Further-more, I shall deal with them purely on a practical level because any preacher who is not practical is not a true preacher of the gospel. The first danger is that of imagining that because we have believed, because we are Christians, these truths are going to apply themselves automatically in our lives. That is a great fallacy. Faith is not passive, it is very active. We must, it is true, always be aware of the danger of relying upon our own activity, but the opposite of that is not just to do nothing! Faith is active. The first step in the life of faith is the constant application of the truth which we have believed, the bringing to bear upon our daily lives of these great doctrines which we have been studying. That is the first thing. In other words, we must not wait for some great experience. Rather, if we want the great experience, the thing to do is to apply what we believe. Then we shall receive it.

The second difficulty which people encounter with regard to the sanctified Christian life is this: they expect to feel something special happening to them. We must learn that sanctification is not so much a matter of feeling and sensibility, as the application of the truth which we have believed. This is almost a constant problem. We all seem instinctively to desire to have the feeling before we believe, and there are large numbers of people who spend years in waiting and pleading for some particular sensation, some experience. The argument is: 'If only I knew these things, if only I were absolutely certain, if only I could experience what I read has happened to others, then I would live the "sanctified life".' So they wait for an experience which never seems to come, and the result is that their lives are bound in shallows and miseries. And there again is this same fallacy, for the Christian life is a walk of faith, it is a life of faith. The feelings may come and they may go, but the walk of faith must always continue. The Bible does not say anywhere that whosoever *feeleth* certain things shall be saved, but whosoever *believeth*, and we must grasp that. We must not be waiting for these sensations and feelings, but, having looked at these great doctrines, we must proceed to walk in them, to live by them, and to apply them to our daily life.

What does this actually mean in practice? Let me try to summarise like this. First and foremost, of course, we must familiarise ourselves with the doctrine. That almost goes without saying. If we are not aware of these doctrines we cannot live by them. We must believe them and we must accept them. There is no Christian life at all apart from that. We must accept these doctrines because they are revealed in the word of God, the same word of truth of which our Lord speaks. So we start there; but that is not enough. The point I want to emphasise in particular here is that we must constantly remind ourselves of them. I can best put it in the words of Romans 6:11: 'Likewise reckon ye also yourselves to be dead indeed unto sin, but alive unto God through Jesus Christ our Lord.' That is what we must do, and the life of faith, the walk of faith, the life of sanctification, is, in reality, just that – reckoning ourselves to be dead indeed unto sin but alive unto God in and through Jesus Christ our Lord.

How, then, do I remind myself in this way? Let us be perfectly simple and practical. The most essential step is constantly to read the Scriptures. If you look at any saint who has ever adorned the life of the Christian church, you will find that they

have always done that. They have always been men and women
who have spent a great deal of their time in reading the Bible,
studying it and familiarising themselves with it.

Once again I want to issue a very important warning. There
are many ways of reading the Bible, and I mean reading it in a
very particular way. I have known people who seem to read
their Bible like this: they say, 'Yes, I am now a Christian. I
believe in the Lord Jesus Christ and have surrendered myself to
him. I have had this experience.' So now they seem to be living
on that experience and they believe that henceforth they have
nothing to do but look to him.

'Well then,' you say, 'do you not read your Bible?'

'O yes,' they reply, 'I read my Bible.'

But they seem to read the Bible as a good bit of discipline, as
the sort of thing a Christian is expected to do. That is not the
way of reading the Bible that I mean here. I am advocating that
I should read my Bible daily not because I believe it is a good
thing for me to read the word every day, not because I think it
is going to do some general good, not because it is a good thing
to be familiar with the word of God – no – I must learn to read
the word of God in order to look for the doctrines that are in it.
I must search for doctrines which I can apply to myself, I must
be looking for particular teachings. My reading of the Bible
must not be general, but very specific.

It is possible to be very familiar with the letter of the Scriptures and yet not to know its doctrines; indeed, there are many
who are familiar with the words of the Scriptures who are not
familiar with the word of God. You can know your Bible in a
mechanical sense without ever having come face to face with its
doctrines. And my whole understanding of John 17:17 leads me
to say that all that is useless. In other words, if I do not read my
Bible in such a way as to come to a deeper knowledge of the
greatness and holiness of God, there is something wrong in my
reading, and the same is true if my reading of the Bible does not
humble me, or bend me to my knees. In other words, my
attitude towards Scripture reading must not be, 'I have a certain
amount of time before I go to work,' or, 'I read my daily portion

if I can' – that is not the way to read the Scriptures. We must be very careful not to become slaves to the daily portion. We must be searching for the doctrines not merely that we may know the contents of particular books of the Bible, but also that its spiritual message may come out to us. We must see it and know it, and we must daily remind ourselves of it.

Every day I must remind myself of God and his character, and of my position as a human being, an inheritor of original sin in Adam, the remnants of which – the pollution of sin – still remain. Day by day, then, I must remind myself of the law and of God's condemnation of sin; I must ever look at the cross, and meditate upon it every day, bringing it constantly before me. You see what I am saying? We all know from experience how easy it is to take these things for granted, and so much for granted that we never stop to think about them at all. Christians are people who live daily in the light of these things; and they must go to the Scriptures more and more frequently in order that they may remind themselves of these things which are so absolutely vital to their sanctification.

Then you must not only read the Scriptures, you must also meditate upon them. There is a line of a hymn which says, 'Take time to be holy.' I am not sure but that it is not something which we all ought to have pasted upon the walls of our homes in this foolish, ridiculous, hectic age in which we are living. We are all involved in this mad rush which is so meaningless. We allow the world to govern us and our time. We say we have no time to do these things I have been talking about – people are not reading the Bible as they used to, because they are doing something else. The hours of work are shorter than they have ever been, so why do we have less time? It is because we are reading other things, for if we spend our time reading journals and magazines, obviously we have no time to read our Bibles, nor do we have time to meditate. Indeed, the art of meditation has practically disappeared out of life; people do not think. As the poet tramp said:

What is this life if, full of care,
We have no time to stand and stare?
        W H Davies

We do not look at things, we do not consider them as we ought, and above all, we fail to meditate upon these spiritual things.

So we must turn them over in our minds – and we have to make ourselves do this; we need discipline. We must confront these things. How easy it is to find that our day has gone before we think it has started – time slips between our fingers and it is gone. The days hurry along and the weeks and the months. We are all hurrying towards the end of our life in this world, and we have not done all that much. We must take hold of ourselves firmly and be drastic with ourselves. We must insist upon these things and make ourselves confront them day by day.

I suggest that this means that we must cultivate the lost art of talking to ourselves. Do not misunderstand me. I do not mean talking to ourselves audibly. But more and more I find that the very essence of the truly spiritual life is that people talk to themselves about these things. It is my business as a preacher not only to preach to others, but to myself also, and the real value of my preaching to others is the extent to which I preach to myself before I preach to them. As I understand this term 'reckon yourself to be dead unto sin', it means that I talk to myself, and I say, 'Do you know who and what you are?' I preach to myself as I get up in the morning and I say, 'You are a creature in this world of time who has been placed in it by Almighty God. You are not merely an animal evolved out of some primitive slime, you are a man made in the image and likeness of God, there is that dignity about you – remember it!'

How easy it is to take a false value of ourselves from the newspapers, or from the way of the world. If we unconsciously tend to do that, our life will not be truly sanctified. So talk to yourself about yourself, and talk to God about yourself. Talk to yourself about sin; examine yourself; view the day that is ahead of you and at night review the day that has gone. Have you ever tried to do that seriously? Have you gone over the day and the things you have done during the day, even the good things you have done? When you examine them, my friends, you may find that you have done even the good things in a very bad way. You have to know yourself, you have to know what you are doing and you talk to yourself about yourself, and then you talk to yourself about the cross, because if you do not talk to yourself about the cross you may go for months and years without knowing anything about it. Remind yourself of what happened there, that the Son of God died and rose again, and say, 'If he rose, I rose with him.' Say that to yourself daily! Remind yourself daily of who and what you are. Talk to yourself, too, about the fleeting character of your life here and about the glory that is coming.

Oh, I do commend this to you. God knows I do so as a man who is a failure himself at doing what he is advocating, but I do it, and I want to do it more and more, and I can assure you that there is nothing so blessed and so rewarding. Have you ever conceived of yourself and thought about yourself in the glory? Have you ever thought of what it is going to be to look into his blessed face and to see him as he is? Remind yourself of these things, reckon yourself to be dead unto sin but alive unto God. Say to yourself that you are only a stranger in this world, a sojourner, a traveller. Tell yourself, 'Heaven is my home, I am a citizen of heaven, I belong there. I daily, nightly, pitch my moving tent a day's march nearer home.' That is what it means to 'reckon yourself dead unto sin'. It is not only that I know the doctrines of justification and sanctification, and something of the doctrine of God. Yes, but what matters is whether I am applying them. Am I living in the light of these things? That is the life and walk of faith. Faith means that this is the truth about me and therefore I live like this.

That, then, is the great emphasis, and from that I must go on to draw certain deductions. First, I must work out this great argument in the same way as the Apostle does in Romans 6. If all this is true, then I am in a very definite and given relationship to God – I am in Christ. This means that I am dead to sin and I am alive unto God. I sometimes think that if we only realised that, we would not need to worry about anything else. It means that God is my Father and I can go immediately into his presence and speak to him in Christ. If only we realised that, there would be no need for us to exhort one another to prayer and to a life of prayer, it would follow inevitably. If only we knew God's love to us; if only we realised that God is indeed our Father; if only we realised that he is interested in us, in everything we are and in all we do to the very smallest, minutest details of our life – even to the numbering of the very hairs of our head – if only we realised all these things, what a difference it would make!

But our problem is that we get up in the morning and there are things to be done. Then we read a hurried word of Scripture and off we go. We might as well not have done it, I am afraid. Rather, we must 'take time to be holy', we must take time to realise what we are doing. If only, when we are on our knees, we could realise what the real truth is at that moment, that the eternal, everlasting God is listening to us, is stooping towards us, waiting to hear what we have to say, waiting, not for our hurried petitions, nor to hear us, like fretful children, asking for this, that and the other; but rather waiting to hear us thanking him, praising his name, loving and adoring him, giving ourselves to him and telling him we want to live day by day to his honour and glory. If only we took time to think like that! For that is real prayer; that is the life of the saint; that is the life of faith and we must take time to remind ourselves of these things – to 'reckon' as Paul tells us.

You may wake up in the morning feeling dry and hard in spirit and absolutely lifeless in a spiritual sense. The reason may be partly physical or any number of other things, and you may feel utterly opposed to real prayer. But it does not matter what you feel. You must say to yourself, 'I reckon myself to be dead to sin and alive to God; I know that this is true and therefore I am going to talk to my Father.' In the natural sense we do not wait to feel like doing things before we do them – at least, I hope we do not. I trust that as husbands and wives and parents and children we do the things that we must do, however we feel.

The same applies to our relationship with God. Reckon yourselves, act on this great truth which you say you believe, and go
into his presence, asking him first and foremost to forgive you
for your dryness and for your lack of a lively sense of the Spirit.
Confess it, acknowledge it, and ask him to give you liberty and
to manifest himself to you. That is the life of faith, and you have
to do it. Do not wait until you are moved; move yourself and
then you will find that the Spirit will be present.

And, secondly, in the same way we are to realise that our life
should consist of walking in the light with him, and that, of
necessity, will lead us to a dedication of ourselves and of our
faculties to him: 'Neither yield ye your members as instruments
of unrighteousness unto sin: but yield yourselves unto God as
those that are alive from the dead, and your members as instruments of righteousness unto God' (Rom 6:13). You go to him
and say: 'Here I am, my body, my mind, my spirit, every
power and faculty which I have. You have given them to me.
I have not generated them, they are gifts from you. I am giving
myself to you from this day, use these gifts, take possession of
them, every faculty I have, let them be used, that you may be
glorified.' You are reckoned to be dead to that selfish life and
you are living to God and righteousness.

And, finally, you draw the deduction that sin is something
which is quite unthinkable. Listen to this: 'What fruit had ye
then in those things whereof ye are now ashamed? for the end
of those things is death' (Rom 6:21). When we are Christians we
have an entirely new view of sin. But it is only as we remind
ourselves of these truths, and apply them to ourselves, and talk
to ourselves about them that these deductions become evident,
and at the same time inevitable.

So let me sum it all up again in that little phrase: 'Take time
to be holy.' It does take time. Read the lives of the greatest saints
this world has ever seen and you will find that they spent hours
every day in reading their Bibles. John Wesley said that he had
a very poor opinion of Christians who did not spend at least four
hours every day in prayer. The great saints agonised and strove
in prayer. Some of them prayed so much that when they got up

from their knees there was a pool of sweat on the ground. Others wore out their chairs or tables, or the oilcloth on the floor (you can see where Henry Martyn did that in Cambridge); that is the life of faith. These people took time to be holy. They did not say, 'It is quite simple, all you have to do is accept it.' They trusted finally, as we must inevitably do, to the action and the power of God. But trusting to that, they studied the word of God and loved it, they laboured, they agonised in prayer, they meditated, and thus they grew in grace and in the knowledge of God, and were sanctified and holy persons for whom we still continue to thank God. 'Take time to be holy' – 'If ye know these things, happy are ye if ye do them' (Jn 13:17).

2

'Mortify, therefore ...'

Sanctify them through thy truth: thy word is truth (John 17:17).

In the last chapter we saw how we need constantly to remind ourselves that the great doctrines of the truth apply to us and we ended by saying that this led to certain inevitable deductions. Now that is what the apostle Paul is always concerned about in all his epistles. For instance, in Romans 6, where he is writing about a very practical question – 'Shall we continue in sin, that grace may abound?' – Paul is really concerned about ordinary daily life and living, and his argument is that people who realise the truth about themselves in Christ will of necessity have a new view of sin. Sin will become something hateful to them, something abhorrent, something which is quite incompatible with their Christian position and their Christian relationships. They will come to regard it as something which is quite profitless. 'What fruit had ye then,' Paul asks, 'in those things whereof ye are now ashamed? for the end of those things is death' (Rom 6:21). That is the argument which you find running through the Bible everywhere, and sin is, therefore, something which the Christian must renounce completely.

So now we come again to the practical application even of that, because there is always the danger that we shall be content with a theoretical understanding, and the Scripture does not allow us to stop at that. We are sanctified by the truth, and through the truth in this way. Therefore, this truth does not merely lay down general principles for us, but it shows our life, and emphasises the all-importance of applying the truth. So if someone comes to us and says, 'I accept all that, but what do I do in practice?' the Scriptures give us our answer, and show us how we are indeed to realise these things in our ordinary daily life.

I wonder whether it has struck us, as it should have done, what a tremendous space is given in the New Testament, in the Gospels and in the epistles, to this ethical teaching, to these very practical matters of daily life and living? It is indeed astonishing to notice this, and especially to notice the detailed character of the teaching. The New Testament never leaves us with generalities; it is never satisfied with laying down principles only. The Bible knows us so well, if I may put it that way. The men who wrote the Gospels under the leading of the Spirit understood both themselves and us so well that they knew that it is never enough merely to state the truth; it has to be applied. Of course, we do not like the application, because when truth is applied it begins to hurt. We like to listen to great pictures of the truth which never become personal; but whether we like it or not, the Scriptures do apply it. They come down, as I shall show you, to the smallest details of life and of living, so that we cannot sit back and just look at this great display of truth which we have here and say, 'That is marvellous,' and then go out and do something which contradicts it all. No, on the contrary, Scripture says everywhere, in the words of our Lord, 'If ye know these things, happy are ye if ye do them' (Jn 13:17). And they are there in order that we may do them and put them into practice. Now I do not know what your impression is, but I sometimes think that this aspect of truth – this detailed application – has been strangely neglected among us; and I wonder whether this has not been partly due to the fact that the tendency of much holiness teaching has been to talk about nothing but surrender. It is said that all you have to do is to surrender yourself, and to be willing to surrender yourself; as if, having done that, you have done everything. But the Scriptures do not teach that. Rather, they bring us down to details and insist upon ourapplying the truth. Certainly, we surrender ourselves, but we are to surrender ourselves in actual detail and practice all along the line. I think that the results of our failure to remember this detailed ethical teaching, of the epistles in particular, are obvious among us, very often in a failure in things which are quite elemental; and we are not truly evangelical until we are evangelical in our conduct as well as in our belief.

Let us therefore consider how this practical application of the truth, and of the doctrine, is worked out in the Scriptures themselves, and as we do so, let us hold in our minds the order in which the Bible puts it. 'Sanctify them through thy truth' – yes, first and foremost we must be quite clear about the way of salvation, about our position in Christ, and Christ in us. We must start with this great basic doctrine, for if we do not do that, we shall go entirely astray. To start with the principles of daily life and living before considering the doctrines is a complete error, that is to be outside Christ altogether. Indeed, that is the whole error of Roman Catholic teaching, which tends to give the impression that you become a Christian by following a certain ethical practice. But that is to reverse the scriptural order. No, we must start with the great truth, we must see our position, and it is only after we have seen our position in Christ that we begin to say, 'So, then, how do I live it out?' You will find that every New Testament epistle starts with doctrine and then goes on to apply it. Having laid down the doctrine, it says, 'Therefore,' and so we too must put these things in the order in which we are given them. Then, having laid down our doctrine, we come to the application with regard to our conduct.

What, then, is the teaching? Well I think it can be conveniently divided in the way that Scripture commonly does it, in a two-fold manner: it tells us to 'put off the old man' and to 'put on the new man'. You notice the practical way in which it talks. 'Put off the old man' – because of what is true of you, because you are a new man, because you are in Christ and Christ is in you, put off the old man and put on the new.

'I see that,' says someone, 'but what do you mean by putting off the old man? I want to know what that means in daily practice.'

The first answer to that question is that it is another way of saying the words that we have already considered together: 'Reckon ye also yourselves to be dead indeed unto sin, but alive unto God.' When you 'put off the old man', you reckon yourselves to be dead unto sin. When you 'put on the new man', you reckon yourselves to be alive unto God in Jesus Christ and through him.

'Very well, but,' again someone may ask, 'what do you mean by saying I should reckon myself to be dead unto sin?' And so here we come to the details. Reckoning myself to be dead unto sin means, first of all, that there are certain things that I must stop doing. Whatever view we may hold of sanctification and holiness, I can very easily demonstrate to you that the Scriptures come to us and just tell us quite simply and plainly that we must stop doing certain things. For instance, Paul says to Timothy, 'Flee also youthful lusts' (2 Tim 2:22); he does not tell him to spend his time praying about them, he tells him to flee from them!

Let me give you some other examples: 'Let him that stole steal no more' (Eph 4:28); and then we have many examples in the epistle to Titus, where Paul says that the aged women are not to be false accusers and not given to much wine, but teachers of good things; the young women are 'to be discreet, chaste, keepers at home' – not to gad about, as it were, but to realise that they are meant to spend most of their time at home doing the things which they should be doing as wives. Servants, likewise, are not to be guilty of purloining, they are not to answer back (Tit 2:3-10). It is all very detailed. And it does not matter where you turn in the epistles, you will find exactly the same kind of exhortation. You will find that as Christians we are told not to be guilty of foolish talking and jesting, but rather to 'walk in love, as Christ also hath loved us, and hath given himself for us as an offering and a sacrifice to God' (Eph 5:2). Paul says in Ephesians 5:3-4 – and he is writing to Christians, remember – 'But fornication, and all uncleanness or covetousness, let it not be once named among you, as becometh saints. Neither filthiness, nor foolish talking nor jesting, which are not convenient: but rather giving of thanks.' We are just not to do such things. We are not to wait for a special experience of sanctification, we are not to spend the whole of our time in praying; we are just not to do them. We are not to get drunk, we are not to speak evil of one another, and we are not to be guilty of all the other things which the Apostle lists in Ephesians 5.

Surely nothing can be plainer than that. It is the truth which sanctifies, which tells us simply and plainly that we are not to do such things because they are sinful. And we are exhorted as Christian people to break ourselves of such conduct. It may be that we have developed a habit of doing some of these things. We are all guilty of a number of sins of the flesh and of the spirit, and the Scripture says you must break that habit because you are a Christian; you must not do it. Paul speaks in this way to the members of the churches to whom he writes, and he urges a pastor like Titus constantly to remind the people of this: '... these things I will that thou affirm constantly, that they which have believed in God might be careful to maintain good works' (Tit 2:8). He tells them, and Timothy too, that they must cease from these sinful, unworthy habits and practices. It is very difficult to know how to put this plainly, because people often come to me and talk about the great struggle that they are having, and as I listen to them I feel that their real need is just to read the New Testament epistles.

But Paul does not stop at that; that is to do with our actions, the first step in the building. But he goes beyond that and says that we are also to avoid certain things in general. This is an essential part of New Testament teaching at this point. There are certain things that are just not compatible with the Christian life. Now when I say 'things', I do not now mean individual actions, but certain patterns of behaviour which are not compatible with the Christian life and position; the New Testament tells us that we are to avoid all such as a principle and in general.

Let me explain. The apostle John says, 'Love not the world, neither the things that are in the world' (Jn 2:15). The world stands for a certain type and pattern of behaviour, and as Chris-

tians (as we have already seen in our great fundamental principles) we no longer belong to the world. We are dead to the
world through our union with Christ. When he died, we died,
so we glory in the cross of our Lord Jesus Christ 'by whom the
world is crucified unto me, and I unto the world' (Gal 6:14). So
it is a perfectly fair argument that we are not to love the world,
nor the things of the world. Of course, we must remember
what worldliness means. We agree that it does not mean some
two or three sins which we have long since given up; it is an
outlook and mentality, it is 'the lust of the flesh, and the lust of
the eyes, and the pride of life' (Jn 2:16). People can be guilty of
these things who never darken the door of a theatre or a cinema.
This astounding pride which is based upon the flesh, upon what
is natural and human – that is the essence of the pride of life and
we are not to be guilty of that. Rather, we are to finish with it,
however it may manifest itself, and it has many ways of doing
so: pride of appearance, pride in clothing or pride in ancestry
and all such things. We no longer belong to them, and we must
not conform to their pattern in any way whatsoever – love not
the world.

Peter puts it like this: '... the time past of our life may suffice
us to have wrought the will of the Gentiles' (1 Pet 4:13) – there
is a kind of life which is the opposite to that of the Christian.
'You want to continue with that sort of thing,' says Peter in
effect, 'but surely you must see that you have already spent
enough time out of your life on all that; leave it alone, you do
not belong to it.' Or again, as Paul says, 'Ye have not so learned
Christ' (Eph 4:20). Read the epistles for yourselves; read Paul
again in Ephesians 4: 'This I say therefore, and testify in the
Lord, that ye henceforth walk not as other Gentiles walk, in the
vanity of their mind' (v. 17). You are no longer to go on doing
that, says Paul, you are to be 'renewed in the spirit of your
mind' (v. 23): 'Wherefore putting away lying, speak every man
truth with his neighbour: for we are members one of another.
Be ye angry, and sin not: let not the sun go down upon your
wrath: neither give place to the devil. Let him that stole steal no
more: but rather let him labour, working with his hands the

thing which is good, that he may have to give to him that needeth. Let no corrupt communication proceed out of your mouth, but that which is good to the use of edifying, that it may minister grace unto the hearers' (vv. 25-29).

Now this is the pattern of behaviour to which we are to pay attention, because the truth of God which sanctifies tells us that we no longer belong to the old realm. Or again, the Apostle puts it quite explicitly in 2 Corinthians 6:17 where he says, 'Come out from among them and be ye separate.' Come out from among these people who are not Christian, in your conduct, in your attitude towards life, in the things you enjoy and in the things you read. It may seem narrow, and I agree that it is. But the Christian way of life is narrow, it is the narrowness of the Son of God himself who walked through this world without becoming contaminated by it. We are to separate ourselves from the way which is characteristically worldly. Again, Paul puts this in the form of a great principle – I am simply taking certain characteristic statements at random in order to show you the principles – when he says, 'Make not provision for the flesh' (Rom 13:14). I wonder whether we grasp the meaning of that? Never do anything which you know perfectly well is going to be the means of temptation to you. If you know that certain things, which may not be bad in and of themselves, generally get you down and you are a worse person afterwards than you were before, do not do them; never, as it were, provide yourself with the occasion to sin.

It is amazing how often we do that. I suggest that every time you take up a newspaper you should bear in mind that particular exhortation: 'Make not provision for the flesh.' You see a heading in the newspaper, something in you wants to read it, but something else within you says, 'No!' You know if you read that, it will not do you any good. If you do not read it, you will not lack anything. If you do not know the latest details about the latest sensational murder, it cannot affect your life in any way. If in fact you did not see a newspaper at all, it would not make any real difference. But you are sitting with your newspaper before you and something within you lusts to read it, and if you read it, you know you will not be quite as chaste and pure at the end as you were at the beginning. So by reading that, you have made provision for the flesh and we are told we are not to do so. There are certain things we must not do because we know of their effects. 'Make not provision for the flesh' is the great principle, and because of it we must recognise that certain things are incompatible with our Christian life, and we must just finish with them.

May I enforce all this by telling you a very simple anecdote within my own experience? I do so because I think it not only illustrates my point, but it just shows what the Spirit of God does when he is given free play in a man's life. I refer to a man whom I saw converted to Christ and to the gospel out of, I think I can say without any fear of exaggeration, the most degraded condition in which I have ever seen a man. He lived such a life of sin that he could not read or write. He lived a life of drunkenness and debauchery, but there was one odd thing about this man – in a sense it was laughable and yet it shows what sin can do – he took a particular pride in his moustache. He cultivated this moustache and was very proud of its length. People who knew him assured me that many a time in a state of semi-drunkenness he had fought with men because they had said something about it. Now we may laugh at that, but I could show you things in the life of some polite people which are equally ridiculous.

But this man was converted. Some six weeks after his conversion he came to a mid-week meeting and I noticed to my amazement that he had completely shaved off the moustache. I immediately came to the conclusion that some busybody – perhaps a member of the church – had told him to do so. There was certainly, from my standpoint and from the Christian standpoint, something very ridiculous about this wonderful moustache, and I feared at once that somebody had taken it upon himself to speak to this good man, this lovable character, and had told him to do something about it. So I asked him to remain behind as I wanted to speak to him.

When we were alone, I asked him, 'Who told you to shave

off your moustache?'

'Nobody,' he replied.

But I pressed him because I was curious to know who had made him do it. But he repeated that nobody had told him to shave off his moustache, and I had to believe him.

'All right,' I said, 'if nobody has told you, why have you got rid of it?'

'I will tell you,' he said. 'I got up this morning and after I had washed, I was brushing my hair and I happened to notice myself in the mirror, and I said, as I looked at myself, "That moustache doesn't belong to a Christian!"'

So he had shaved it off. That is it! That is how the truth sanctifies. The man realised that this sort of thing belonged to his old life, and had nothing to do with the new life, though it was the thing of which he was so proud, and for which he had fought and suffered – and he just got rid of it. It is a simple story, but to me it is a very profound one. In the same way, you and I must realise that there are certain things which are not compatible with the life of someone who is in Christ and in whom Christ dwells, and we are bound to have nothing to do with them.

The third step in putting off the old man or reckoning ourselves to be dead unto sin is what has generally been given the scriptural term of 'mortification'; the apostle Paul, for example, says, 'Mortify therefore your members which are upon the earth' (Col 3:5). Now let us hold firmly to the development of the argument. You stop doing certain things and then you go beyond that to the topmost rung of the ladder, and you 'mortify your members'. Let me give you some of the scriptural terms. The apostle James says, 'Cleanse your hands, ye sinners; and purify your hearts, ye double-minded. Be afflicted, and mourn, and weep ...' (Jas 4:8–9). Now certain types of holiness teaching tell us that we are not to mourn and weep, but all we have to do is surrender ourselves and be completely happy. But James exhorts us to grieve because of our sinfulness.

Or again, Paul writes to the Corinthians, 'Having therefore these promises, dearly beloved ...' – and the promises are the

doctrines we have already been considering – 'let us cleanse ourselves from all filthiness of the flesh and spirit, perfecting holiness in the fear of God' (2 Cor 7:1). I am told that I must cleanse
myself. When Paul tells me that I must mortify my members
which are on the earth, he gives a list of what he means by that,
and tells me how I am to do it. Then in Romans 8:13 he says, 'If
ye through the Spirit do mortify the deeds of the body, ye shall
live.' Again, take his great statement in 1 Corinthians 9:27
where, referring to himself as a preacher, he says, 'I keep under
my body.'

Now all this is just the scriptural way of putting before us the
doctrine of the mortification of the flesh. Yes, I know about the
dangers. I know we are all beginning to think of camel hair
shirts and of anchorites and hermits living on a lonely island far
away from everybody. That, however, is false asceticism,
which the Scripture never teaches. But because we dislike false
asceticism, we must not deny the scriptural doctrine of mortification of the flesh, which is something we are all expected to
do. This means that we must realise that as a result of sin and the
Fall, the very powers and qualities which God has put in us by
nature tend to become our enemies; and though we are Christians, the remnants of the old man are still here and we are not
perfect. The flesh remains and because of that we are always to
be watching the body. 'I keep under my body,' says the Apostle
in 1 Corinthians 9:27, for he realised that if he did not, he would
go astray.

There is great teaching on that in the New Testament. You
will find, for example, that one of the most solemn warnings
that our Lord gave to his people was when he warned them of
such things as gluttony – excess of eating and drinking. We can
indulge the body, not only by committing acts of immorality,
but in other respects such as food and drink and sleep, and a
general spirit of lethargy, and I must not sin in these things
either. I am sure we all know ourselves well enough to understand that the body reacts upon the spirit and the spirit upon the
body, and if my body, due to any excess in any respect, is
lethargic and dull, if I have not had enough sleep and am over-

tired, or if I have slept too much, or done too much – and we are all guilty of these things – then I find it very difficult to read my Bible intelligently. We must not let the body dictate. It is always anxious to do so, and if we listened to the body, we should always be guilty of some excess or other. The Apostle said he kept it under – the original Greek says he pummelled it, or made it black and blue – and he did all this in order to keep it down, because if he did not, he would suffer spiritually.

And so, here we are, confronted by this great teaching about the mortification of the flesh. In other words, we are not only to refrain from certain actions because we know they are sinful, but must also realise that we must actively carry out these scriptural commands in order to keep down the motions of sin which are yet within us, for if we do not, they will get the ascendancy. The thing I am anxious to impress upon you is that all that I am putting before you is a part of the truth by which we are sanctified – 'Sanctify them through thy truth.'

Let me finally deal briefly with the other aspect. There is another side – 'Put on the new man ...' 'Reckon yourselves to be alive unto God through Jesus Christ.' This is another way of saying, you must think all this out in practice; you must remind yourself of who you are; 'Work out your own salvation with fear and trembling ...' Why? '... For it is God which worketh in you ...' (Phil 2:12-13). Those were our first great principles. Because God is 'working in you both to will and to do', you 'work it out with fear and trembling'. Because you are who you are and what you are, '... follow after righteousness, godliness, faith, love, patience, meekness. Fight the good fight of faith, and lay hold of eternal life' (1 Tim 6:11-12). You and I are exhorted to do these things – to follow after, to lay hold upon them. '... giving all diligence,' says Peter, 'add to your faith' – furnish it with – 'virtue; and to virtue knowledge; and to knowledge temperance; and to temperance patience; and to patience godliness; and to godliness brotherly kindness; and to brotherly kindness charity' (2 Pet 1:5-7). And as you read on in 2 Peter chapter 1, you will find he tells us that the man who does not do these things is blind and cannot see afar off; he does not realise that he has been purged from his own sins; but the man who does these things is making his calling and election sure. We must 'put on the new man' and do all these things. A further great illustration of this is in the epistle to Titus, where the Apostle tells Titus that he must exhort these people to be 'careful to maintain good works' (Tit 3:8).

We must leave it at that now, though we shall have to return to it again, but I was anxious that we should see the two sides and that we should work them out in detail – put off, put on; reckon yourselves to be dead, reckon yourselves to be alive.

All this is addressed to us, and it is something which we are called upon to do. It is as we thus obey these exhortations and the things of the Spirit, that we find ourselves becoming sanctified. Do not forget the order in which I put this truth to you. We must always start by saying that sanctification is God's work in us. It is a prayer to God – 'Sanctify them through thy truth' – it is God who does it, but he does it by giving us the truth, and by giving us the Holy Spirit who enables us to understand the truth and apply it. The work of the Spirit is to bring us into this relationship to the truth by opening our eyes to it, by giving us a desire to practise it and by enabling us to do so; but he sanctifies us through the truth. Let us never forget these details. Let us never argue about certain things or wait to have some big experience before we stop doing all these wrong things. No, we are told immediately: Stop doing it, avoid all that type of behaviour. Remember and realise the danger and therefore constantly mortify the flesh and keep under the body. May God in his infinite grace and kindness enable us to receive such teaching and practise it day by day.

3

Spiritually Well Dressed

Sanctify them through thy truth: thy word is truth (John 17:17).

As we continue with this great petition which our Lord offered
for his immediate followers, and for his followers at all times,
it is good for us to remind ourselves again that the ultimate end
and object of our salvation is that we should be able to stand in
the presence of God. That is the only right way of considering
our salvation. Salvation is not just a question of being forgiven;
that is essential, of course, and the first essential, but it is only
the negative aspect. The wonderful thing about our salvation is
that we are promised that we shall finally stand faultless and
blameless, without spot and without rebuke, in the presence of
God. That is the blessed hope that is set before us, and therefore
Scripture argues in so many places that '... every man that hath
this hope in him purifieth himself, even as he is pure' (1 Jn 3:3).

So as I understand this New Testament teaching, holiness is
not something about which we should make appeals to people.
It is our business to set scriptural doctrine before them, and the
man who really believes what he claims to believe is a man who
must be urgently concerned about this question of his sanctification. If this doctrine of sanctification is unimportant to anyone,
then such a person is just confessing that he or she is not a Christian. If we really believe that we are going on to stand in the presence of God and of Christ, there is no time to be lost, and the
most urgent problem before us is, therefore, to learn how this

sanctification of ours takes place; and that has been our immediate theme. We have seen that God sanctifies us through the truth, through the great doctrines, and we have shown from Scripture how these must be applied in our lives.

In our last study we were considering the negative aspect of this application, and now we come to the positive. Having put off that which was characteristic of the old man, and having reckoned ourselves to be dead unto sin, we are now reckoning ourselves, regarding ourselves, as Christians, to be alive unto God – we are looking at positive holiness, the positive living of the godly life. Now it seems to me that one of the most convenient ways of considering this positive emphasis and this aspect of the doctrine is to study the message of Colossians 3 which is a perfect statement of this truth, although, of course, parallel statements are to be found elsewhere, in Ephesians, for instance. Indeed, you find this teaching in every single New Testament epistle, for all the epistles are concerned about holiness; they are written to Christians and their one object is to get these people to know who they are and to live accordingly.

Let us look, then, at Colossians 3 in order that we may see how the Apostle develops his argument. To me there is nothing more fascinating than to observe the way in which Paul states this great truth in different ways. It is ever the one message, but he puts it in different forms. Here in Colossians he starts with his doctrine: 'If ye then be risen with Christ ...' Well, how do you know that that is true of you? That is where the doctrine comes in; the fact is that you are in Christ, that you are united to him, and therefore everything that has happened to Christ has happened to you. You have died with him, you have been crucified, you are buried with him, yes, but you have also risen with him, and so, 'If ye then be risen with Christ, seek those things which are above, where Christ sitteth on the right hand of God.' 'Set your affection,' says Paul, 'on things above, not on things on the earth.' Why? 'For ye are dead, and your life is hid with Christ in God. When Christ, who is our life, shall appear, then shall ye also appear with him in glory.'

What a marvellous summary of those great items of doctrine

which we have considered one by one! I have had to mention
them again because you will always find that the Apostle never
deals with any detailed, or any small problem without putting
it into the context of the truth and of the doctrine, and that is one
of the most important things we can ever remember. That is, as
I have often pointed out, the whole tragedy of the Roman
Catholic conception of holiness, for, with all its detailed information, it so often loses the connection. The sanctified life
becomes an end in and of itself. But that is never scriptural. It
is because of certain things that we do other things. We do not
do them in order to be Christian, we do them *because* we are
Christian. 'If ye be risen with Christ ...' and so on – it is the same
idea as 'reckoning ourselves'. 'Set your affection on things
above' – think on these things which are above, and seek them.

We should start every day of our lives, let me emphasise this
again, by saying to ourselves, 'I am a child of God, I died with
Christ, I am dead unto sin, I am risen with Christ, I am in this
new realm.' *Therefore*, 'Set your affections', seek these things,
which must ever be first and foremost and uppermost in our
minds, and in our whole outlook. Remember, too, that this is
an exhortation, it is a command, and I must do it. I do not just
wait until a feeling possesses me and makes me do it. No, I have
to seek these things, and set my affections on things above. I
must be doing it myself. Then, having said that, as we saw earlier, Paul brings in his negative – 'Mortify therefore your members that are on the earth.'

But now we are interested in the positive side to all this,
which begins at verse 12. Again I pause to make the point clear,
that I have no right to start here unless I have previously grasped
the doctrine of the eleven verses that go before it. But having
done that, I now come on to the message of verse 12, and here
again there are certain words which we must stress, because,
once more, they emphasise our activity. To grow in grace, and
to become ever increasingly sanctified, calls upon us to do certain things. It is not just a question of surrender and looking to
the Lord. No, I am commanded to do certain things, and here
they are. The characteristic terms come out once more, so let me

note them before we come to look at them in detail. I have to 'put on', and I have to 'let' certain things – 'let the peace of God rule in your hearts'. I am told, indeed, to be 'thankful' and told that everything I do must be done 'in the name of the Lord': '... whatsoever ye do in word or deed, do all in the name of the Lord Jesus, giving thanks unto God and the Father by him' (3:17).

I think, therefore, that the principle which we have already laid down is once more illustrated here very abundantly, namely, that you and I are told to put these things into practice; God's commands are positive, as well as negative. We can divide this positive teaching into two main sections. First of all, Paul gives certain general principles in connection with this godly, holy, sanctified life, and then he goes on to his detailed application. It is the method of division that the Apostle always employs: realise your character, develop it and then work it out in detail. He does not start with the details, but with the character and disposition. What is it, then, this disposition that the Christian has always to be bearing in mind and always to be developing and nurturing?

The first exhortation is in verse 12: 'Put on therefore as the elect of God', and the picture, clearly, is of putting on certain items of clothing. It is, of course, an illustration and we must be careful not to press the illustration too far. It does not mean, obviously, that the Christian just puts on a certain kind of behaviour while he himself is something apart from that which he puts on. No, when Paul says 'put on', he means not only *look* like this but *be* like this. It is a good illustration, and the Apostle is very fond of it. Take, for instance, how he uses the same picture in writing to the Philippians, to whom he says, 'Only let your conversation be as becometh the gospel of Christ' (Phil 1:27). He is thinking in terms of clothing, and he says, in effect, 'Now think of yourself putting on certain apparel, let it be becoming, let it be consistent with your complexion and figure. There must be no clashing of colour and style, everything must harmonise and go together.' Then in his exhortation to Titus, the Apostle talks about 'adorning the doctrine' (Tit 2:10). In other words, you can think of the doctrine as a man's suit, or clothing, and our conduct and mien as a kind of adornment which adds the finishing touches.

Now that is the idea which Paul has here in Colossians 3:12, but, again, as a wise teacher he knows that it is not enough just to make a general statement. He goes on to particulars: 'Put on therefore, as the elect of God, holy and beloved, bowels of mercies, kindness ...' – these things need no explanation, I know. What I want to emphasise is that you and I are *told* to be kind; the teaching of sanctification is not one that tells you just to wait and hope that something is going to happen to you, a great experience which will make you kind. Not at all! If you want the big experience, be kind. You will get it by being kind. Nobody can be kind for us, it is something we must do ourselves. Then the next characteristic which Paul refers to is humbleness of mind, which means humility, and this, too, is something we must develop in ourselves. None of us are humble-minded by nature. We are all aggressive and assertive. Some show it in different ways from others, but it is true of all of us, and if we are to be truly humble, it will mean watching and controlling ourselves: humility is something that you and I are to 'put on'.

Then there is meekness. It would be good to consider all these words one by one slowly, but I am trying to give a composite picture here. However, for your own interest, work out the difference between humility and meekness and you will see that it is very significant. Next we have longsuffering – being patient with one another. It is very difficult, as we all know, to be patient with certain people, it is not easy to be longsuffering, and yet if we are to be sanctified, we must take ourselves in hand and develop this part of the Christian character. If you claim to be born with an impatient temperament, then you must control it. You are given strength and power to do this, but it is you who have to do it.

We must put all these things into practice. It is something which you and I must do day by day, hour by hour, and minute by minute. We start well in the morning, then something happens and at that moment we must watch and remember and develop this character; and the more we develop it, the more we are unlikely to fail in detail at odd moments.

Then in verse 13 Paul says, '... forgiving one another, if any man have a quarrel against any: even as Christ forgave you, so also do ye.' This again is something we just have to do. A person has wronged us. Very well, we do not turn our backs and pass that person without looking at him or her – not at all! We must face this matter and reason with ourselves about it in terms of the gospel. We must say to ourselves, 'God forgave me in Christ, he even sent Christ to the cross in order that I might be forgiven, though I repeatedly insulted him and deliberately sinned against him. If God has done that for me, I must forgive this person, come what may.' We make ourselves do it. That is the New Testament teaching on sanctification.

And then another most interesting way of applying the truth is given in verse 14: 'Above all these things put on charity [love] which is the bond of perfectness.' This is an interesting picture. 'Above all these things' really means over or upon all these things. You notice what Paul is doing. We have, as it were, been putting on item after item of clothing, and having done that, we hold them all in position by putting on this garment of perfectness which is love. All these different items must be held together by this wonderful cloak, which binds everything together in perfect harmony, and presents a complete and perfect and unified picture.

Now that is the first great exhortation. We are to put on all this, and you see how it illustrates perfectly those words to which I have already referred, that line in the hymn which tells us to 'Take time to be holy.' Take time to dress yourself spiritually, do not dress in a hurry every morning. And notice, too, that the tense is present. We do not just put these things on once, and think that we are dressed for the rest of our lives. On the contrary, we are to keep on doing it. How true that is in our own experience! Take time to dress spiritually in the morning, and then throughout the day check that everything is in position, look regularly at yourself in the mirror, as it were. Take time to be holy.

Paul's next general exhortation is in verse 15. He says, 'Let the peace of God rule in your hearts, to the which also ye are called in one body; and be ye thankful.' That is again a wonderful thing. Another way of translating it would be, 'Let the peace of God act as an umpire in your hearts ...' It is the peace that Christ gave to his disciples just before he died: 'Peace I leave with you, my peace I give unto you' (Jn 14:27). Well, says the Apostle, see that it rules among you. If you feel you are hurt, take it to the umpire. Do not decide for yourself, or say, 'This is my right.' Let the peace of God act as an umpire – the peace of Christ both in your own heart, and also among you. You are called into one body, so let nothing disrupt the peace of Christ. Then, as you learn to take difficulties to the umpire, you will be growing in sanctification.

The last exhortation in that verse is, 'Be ye thankful.' We tend to think of thankfulness as a feeling, but the Apostle commands us to be thankful, whether we feel like it or not. We must, he says, keep on becoming thankful – that is another way of translating it. 'But if it is not a feeling,' says someone, 'what is it?' Again, a well known hymn puts it perfectly, when it says:

> Count your blessings, name them one by one
> And it will surprise you what the Lord hath done.

But suppose you wake up in the morning and do not feel at all thankful. In fact, suppose you feel the reverse, so that though the Apostle says, 'Be ye thankful,' you answer, 'I cannot honestly say I feel that way.' How, then, can you make yourself thankful? You do it by just waiting for a moment and considering. You count your blessings; you just go back over your life and list the things that have happened to you. Why are you a Christian at all? Why are you forgiven at all? What has your story been? Have goodness and mercy followed you? Go back over it all. Yes, count your blessings, name them one by one, and if you do this, it will surprise you what the Lord has done. If you take the trouble, you will find yourself thankful.

And the next word for us is. 'Let the word of Christ dwell in you richly in all wisdom; teaching and admonishing one another in psalms and hymns and spiritual songs, singing with grace in your hearts to the Lord.' Again, notice the command. The word of Christ, the word that Christ himself taught, *must* dwell in us richly. 'But how do I let it dwell in me richly?' you ask. We do that by reading it, by meditating upon it, and by talking to other people about it. We must soak ourselves in it, for we can never read it too much. The more we read it, the more it will be in us. And as we are keeping and controlling all this, as we are letting it dwell in us, we shall have a marvellous life, we shall enjoy ourselves all together; and at the same time we shall be demonstrating to the world God's handiwork in us as Christian people.

And then, lastly, Paul sums it all up by saying, 'And whatsoever ye do in word or deed, do all in the name of the Lord Jesus, giving thanks to God and the Father by him.' Do it all, in other words, in the spirit of Christ himself. Not only are we to do these things, but the way in which we do them is so important: 'Do all in the name of the Lord Jesus.' Do it in the way he did it. Again, I could illustrate almost endlessly. You remember how Paul, in taking up the collection of the church at Corinth, tells us how to put our contribution on the plate? We must be wholehearted givers, we must give happily, not grudgingly with a sort of hesitancy – no! God loves the cheerful giver (2 Cor 9:7). So we must do all things like this. As he gave himself, let us do these things; let us put on these articles of clothing with cheerfulness in the spirit of Christ. Let us not regard them as a kind of straightjacket, but as the most beautiful robe the world has ever seen – we must do it as Christ did it.

There, then, are the general principles. But we must look briefly at the details, which Paul now goes on to apply from verse 18. Scripture never stops at general principles, it always goes on to the details, and Paul does that here. For example, 'Wives, submit yourselves unto your own husbands, as it is fit in the Lord.' As he puts it in Ephesians 5:23: 'The husband is the head of the wife, even as Christ is the head of the church' – that is Christian doctrine – is it being remembered and observed today? I must point out again that there are evangelical people who seem to me constantly to ignore the plain teaching of the word of God, because it does not tally with modern ideas. But that is the teaching of the Scriptures. But then, you notice, Paul says to husbands, '... love your wives, and be not bitter against them.' You can see that in every one of these exhortations the Apostle seems to put his finger directly on the thing which is most dangerous – it is clear both in the case of the wife, and of the husband. The peculiar temptation of the husband is to be bitter against his wife, to look down upon her, perhaps to despise her in certain ways, to regard her as someone who is meant to serve him. He is the head, he is put into that position, but he must not lord it over his wife in any spirit of bitterness.

Then we come to the children: 'Children, obey your parents in all things: for this is well pleasing unto the Lord' (v. 20). How this doctrine is needed today. Even among Christian people discipline seems to have vanished. But then you notice that there follows a wonderful and glorious appeal: 'Fathers, provoke not your children to anger lest they be discouraged.' Compare our age with the Victorian age. The bitterness or the lack of discipline among children is obvious today, but this exhortation to the fathers does not seem to be needed so much in these days as it was by the typical Victorian father. But in a sense it is always needed. We must always observe this appeal, because if the children are to obey their parents, the parents are not to be unreasonable with the children, they are not to provoke them lest they be discouraged. Parents are not merely to say, 'Because I say so – therefore you have to do it.' No, give reasons to your children as far as you can, let your command be made reasonably. Do not discourage them, says the Apostle.

And then he comes to the servants: 'Servants, obey in all things your masters ... not with eyeservice, as menpleasers; but in singleness of heart, fearing God.' Be careful you do this in the right way; and again, 'Whatsoever ye do, do it heartily as unto the Lord and not unto men' (v. 23). That applies to the husband, to the wife, to the children, to the parents, to the masters and to the servants. We must not just say, 'I suppose as a Christian I ought to' – that is not the way to do it. Do it gladly and heartily *because* you are a Christian. Rejoice that you are given such a high standard, and that you are privileged to do so. But then Paul goes on still further in the fourth chapter and says, 'Masters, give unto your servants that which is just and equal; knowing that ye also have a Master in heaven.' We still need to be reminded of that. There are people who would say that the church is as she is today because so often our fathers and our forefathers forgot this detailed injunction. They might be in church on a Sunday morning but some poor slave was staying at home to cook the dinner. No, this is the Christian injunction and the injunction was not only to the servants, it was also to the masters. It is universal: we are all Christians together.

And then Paul talks about prayer, and about the way in which we are to speak. Our speech must be with grace, seasoned with salt, because there are others watching us who are interested in our conduct and our behaviour.

You see, therefore, how the Apostle has not only taken us through the principles, but has also applied them in detail. I would again emphasise this all-important general point that covers everything – it is you and I who are called upon to do these things. This is God's way of sanctification; this is the way we put on the new man, and the way in which we reckon ourselves to be alive unto God. I must examine myself; it is not merely what I feel in church services, but how I have been living. How am I behaving as a husband or father? How am I behaving as a master? How am I behaving in all these relationships in life? Have I lost my temper? Have I become irritable? How have I behaved as a Christian? Some of the greatest saints throughout the ages, men like John Fletcher of Madeley, asked themselves such questions at the end of every day, and we, too, must examine our lives in detail. We have no right not to do so; we must implement these detailed exhortations. We must take these things one by one, and it is only as we do so that we become sanctified through the truth, in the truth, by the truth. Here is the truth, the word of God himself, and it is as this word comes to me in the power of the Spirit, and as I give obedience to it and apply it, and put it into practice, that I shall find that I

am being given strength to obey. So, 'work out your own salvation' – it is you who must do it – 'in fear and trembling. For
it is God which worketh in you both to will and to do ...' (Phil
2:13). And it happens like this. As I read this word, God creates
within me a desire to be like that. He makes me long to be like
that, and as I am desiring it, I try to put it into practice, and I find
that he gives me strength: 'both to will and to do...' So you need
not wait for power; as you do these things you will be given it.
God gives the power to people who want to be like this. As you
are making your effort you will find this strength, for he
empowers you by the Holy Spirit.

So there it is. We have hurried through it in order that we may
have a composite picture and see the method, and now we go
out to live this kind of life in detail. You and I are to be such that
as we walk up and down the streets of life, people will be struck
and attracted. You have seen them turn and look at a well-dres-
sed person. Well, it is something like that. They should be
struck by us, and look at us, and think, 'What is this person? I
have never seen anybody quite like this before! What perfection!
What balance! How everything fits together! How graceful!'
That is the kind of people we can be and the kind of people that
we must be. And when we become such people, believe me, the
revival we are longing for will start, and the people outside, in
their misery and wretchedness, will come in and will want to
know about it.

O may God enlighten us and give us understanding concerning this plain, simple, direct teaching, and above all enable us to
put it into practice. Then, when the day comes for us to stand
before him, let us be ready, always 'well dressed', always clean,
always ready to be ushered into his glorious presence.

4

The Work of the Holy Spirit

But the Comforter, which is the Holy Ghost, whom the Father will send in my name, he shall teach you all things and bring all things to your remembrance, whatsoever I have said unto you (John 14:26).

This verse introduces us at once to the essential teaching in the New Testament concerning the work and Person of the Holy Spirit, and we must consider it in the context of John 17:17, where our Lord prays, 'Sanctify them through thy truth: thy word is truth.' We have been engaged in a consideration of this whole question of our sanctification; and of the various aspects of the truth from which our sanctification is produced and is promoted. And, of course, in considering this great comprehensive truth, we come, of necessity, to the truth concerning the Holy Spirit, his Person and his work. This is an essential part of the message of salvation and it is, therefore, an integral part of the doctrine concerning our sanctification. There is no doubt at all but that that is why our Lord specifically introduces this particular teaching at this particular point. From chapter 14 right into chapter 17 of John's Gospel you will find our Lord's most explicit teaching concerning the Person and the work of the Holy Spirit, and it is not surprising that he should have done so at that precise juncture.

Here he is, about to leave them. He has already told them that he is about to go from them; he has said to Peter, 'Whither I go,

thou canst not follow me now; but thou shalt follow me afterwards' (Jn 13:36); and the effect of that is that the disciples' hearts
are troubled. That is why our Lord begins this wonderful passage by saying to them, 'Let not your heart be troubled: ye
believe in God, believe also in me' (Jn 14:1), and that in turn
leads on to this doctrine of the Holy Spirit. 'If you love me,' he
says in verses 15 to 18, 'keep my commandments. And I will
pray the Father, and he shall give you another Comforter, that
he may abide with you for ever; even the Spirit of truth; whom
the world cannot receive, because it seeth him not, neither
knoweth him: but ye know him; for he dwelleth with you, and
shall be in you. I will not leave you comfortless: I will come to
you.'

Our Lord then elaborates this great teaching on the work of
the Holy Spirit and we can summarise it like this. Our Lord tells
these men that they must not grieve because of his departure.
Indeed, he actually says in chapter 16:7 that it is expedient for
them – that it is a good thing for them – that he should be going
away, because, he says, 'If I go not away, the Comforter will
not come unto you; but if I depart, I will send him unto you.'
And that is good because the Comforter is going to take his
place, as our Teacher, as our Leader, as our Strengthener, and
as the one who stands by us and with us, to help us. He will be
our Advocate in that sense, and therefore, clearly, the business
of the Holy Spirit is to continue, and, indeed, to increase the
work which the Lord himself had begun to do while he was here
in the days of his flesh. He says in this same context, 'I have yet
many things to say unto you, but ye cannot bear them now.
Howbeit when he, the Spirit of truth, is come, he will guide you
into all truth ...' (Jn 16:12–13).

In other words, while our Lord was yet with them they could
not fully understand the significance of his Person, neither could
they understand the purpose of his death, and they stumbled at
it. But afterwards, after the death and the Resurrection, when
the Holy Spirit came, he would explain and apply these things
to them and enable them to reap their wonderful benefits. And
so our Lord tells them here about this other Comforter whom

he is going to send to them, and we, at the moment, are particularly interested in this from the standpoint of our sanctification. So we will look at the place and the work of the Holy Spirit in our sanctification.

Clearly this is a vital subject for us, and we cannot be too careful in our handling of it. We have seen from the very beginning how our Lord has prayed that God should bring about our sanctification: 'Sanctify them through thy truth,' he prays. Sanctification, basically and ultimately, is the work of God; the whole of our salvation is the work of God, but sanctification is so in particular. It is something that God does to us and in us, and we have seen that he does it by means of the truth. But the doctrine of the Holy Spirit reminds us in particular that it is God's work, and therefore it behoves us to discover how it is done. God does this work in us and upon us through the Holy Spirit, but the question is: how does the Holy Spirit do this? Now I need scarcely remind you that there is a great deal of confusion with regard to this subject. There are devout people in the church who hold different opinions as to the way in which the Holy Spirit works. The doctrine of the Holy Spirit, not surprisingly, has often been used by our adversary the devil to lead people astray, so that we cannot be too careful about this matter.

Therefore it seems to me that we must start with the great basic fact that we must always be careful to draw a sharp distinction between the gifts of the Spirit, and what we may call the graces of the Spirit. The Holy Spirit, it is clearly shown in the New Testament, does two main works. First of all there is what is more or less an external work of witness. Peter, we are told in Acts 5:32, says to the authorities, 'And we are his witnesses of these things; and so is also the Holy Ghost, whom God hath given to them that obey him.' It is quite clear that what happened on the Day of Pentecost in Jerusalem – the events which are recorded in Acts 2 – has reference mainly to this external work of the Spirit. There the Holy Spirit descended upon the church in that particular form, 'cloven tongues like as of fire', and gave them an ability to speak in different tongues in order that this external witness might be borne, and of course we are given references to the same thing elsewhere in the Scriptures.

Therefore, in that connection the work of the Holy Spirit was to draw attention to these men who constituted the Christian church. They were given power and authority, and also different abilities, and by means of these things, as the record shows, they arrested attention. People said, 'What is this? What has happened to these men? They are obviously Galileans, yet we hear them all speaking in our own tongues? What is this phenomenon?' Some even said, 'These men are drunk!' It was obvious that there was something very strange about them, and that attracted attention. As a result the Apostle Peter had liberty to preach the gospel and to present the great facts of salvation. Indeed, as you go through Acts, you will find a similar work done; the Spirit comes in this external form and gives men these abilities in order that they may act as witnesses.

But there is another work of the Spirit, and that is his work specifically in connection with our sanctification: the work that he does within us, the work that he does down in the very depths and recesses of our personalities. Often people do not keep these two things separate; there is confusion between the external and the internal work of the Spirit. People often imagine that the work of the Spirit in sanctification is manifested and demonstrated in terms of gifts, rather than in terms of that which is done deep down in the soul; and it is at that point, I think you will agree, that most of the confusion tends to occur. Therefore, let us start with this great, fundamental distinction. There are gifts of the Spirit and they vary from case to case as Paul teaches us in 1 Corinthians 12, but all that is something different from the work that the Spirit does within us. You remember how Paul, having enumerated these various wonderful gifts, says, 'Yet shew I unto you a more excellent way' (1 Cor 12:31), and the more excellent way is the way that leads to this work of the Spirit within us, producing the fruits of the Spirit and the graces of the Spirit – Paul's great disquisition upon the subject of love. If we hold that in our minds as our basic distinction, it will save us from many troubles.

Having said that, let me still ask the same question – how does the Holy Spirit perform this work of salvation within us, and, especially how does he do this work of our sanctification? Here again I feel it is important for us to start with two negatives – the first is that *we must never regard the doctrine of the Holy Spirit in isolation.* By this I mean that we must always realise that the work of salvation is one. There are various aspects of it, and we must distinguish between them, but there is all the difference in the world between distinguishing them as aspects of salvation, and separating these various aspects into differing entities and parts in and of themselves.

Let us look at it like this. We have been at pains to remind one another that we must never separate justification by faith from sanctification. You can distinguish between them but you must never separate them. What I mean by separating is this: there are people, as we have seen, who will tell you that you can be justified without being sanctified, and then they say that as you have received your justification by faith, you now go on to receive your sanctification by faith. That is patently false teaching because it is pressing the distinction into something that separates. You cannot be justified without the process of sanctification already having been started. From the moment that a man is justified by faith in Christ, his sanctification has commenced; and it is for this reason that you cannot divide the Lord Jesus Christ, who himself is made unto us wisdom, and righteousness – or justification – and sanctification and redemption (1 Cor 1:30). You cannot receive parts of the Lord Jesus Christ; you receive him as a whole, so that Christ who is your justification is already your sanctification. And we must be careful that we do not fall into exactly the same error with regard to this question of the work of the Holy Spirit in our sanctification.

Again, people tend to do it like this: they say, 'O yes, of course, you need to be introduced first to the teaching about the Lord Jesus Christ, and then, if you have received that teaching, you go on to the teaching about the Holy Spirit.' Indeed there are some who would even regard those who make this distinction as unusually spiritual Christians because they do that. They say, 'We are not still interested in the doctrine of the Lord Jesus

Christ; that happened when we were converted.' They have now left that behind them and have gone on further and are now always teaching about the Holy Spirit. But that is very false, unscriptural teaching. The whole work of salvation is the work of the blessed triune God, and the three Persons of the blessed Holy Trinity are always engaged in this work.

If you want to draw a distinction, it is that the eternal Father planned and originated the work; God the Son, the second Person, has actually come into the world and has carried out the work, and it is the special function of the Holy Spirit to apply that work to us. But, obviously, you cannot isolate these three and separate them. You distinguish between them in your mind and thinking, and it is right that you should do so – indeed we must do so. But we must obviously never speak of having now gone on from the doctrine of Christ to the doctrine of the Holy Spirit, because that is a sheer impossibility. You cannot separate the three Persons in the blessed Trinity, they are eternally one. They have divided up the work in this way among themselves as a kind of function, but always, everywhere, we are concerned about them all, and concerned about them all at exactly the same point.

So we must always be careful not to isolate this great doctrine of the Holy Spirit. It must be held together with all the other doctrines. We can look at it in particular but never in the sense of putting it into a compartment by itself and inviting people to go on from there to something else. As we cannot divide the Trinity, so we cannot divide in this fundamental sense the work of the Trinity. The doctrine of the Holy Spirit must be held together with the full doctrine since this is an aspect of the great, wonderful, central doctrine.

My second negative is that *we must not isolate the activity of the Holy Spirit*. You will know that in the history of the church there have been people who have isolated the work of the Holy Spirit from everything else. I speak with considerable admiration of the great George Fox, the founder of the 'Friends' and I can say truthfully that I have never read anything about or by George Fox, without feeling my heart warmed and without feeling that I have derived a blessing. Yet there is no question at all but that at certain points he introduced a teaching which is directly contrary to that of the Scriptures, namely, when he isolated the activity of the Spirit, and put his emphasis upon what he called the 'inner light'.

Now I am in considerable sympathy with him, for he did it, of course, as a reaction. George Fox could see that there were many people who were highly orthodox, who knew their Scriptures from cover to cover, who could recite them and reason about them and argue about them and preach about them – people who knew their doctrine, but it was very clear to George Fox that it was all head knowledge, it was purely intellectual. Indeed when you looked at these people in the context of the New Testament, you could see that they were lacking in life and in spiritual power and spirituality. They were often living worldly lives, indeed, they seemed to be living their life in compartments. To George Fox, these people were formalists who regarded their houses as preaching houses. He did not hesitate to go in and upset their meetings, and he preached in the power of the Spirit. But in reaction to all that dead formality, he went to the other extreme, and said that nothing mattered except that they should listen to the 'inner light' and be guided by it – they should listen to the Spirit within them.

Now George Fox himself had a strong belief in orthodox doctrine, but he taught it in such a way as really to deny it, and the result was that many of his followers have taken up the position of saying that all you have to do is to listen to this Power within you. He taught that the Holy Spirit is in every man and all you have to do is be obedient to this Spirit within you and obey the 'inner light'. He said you do not need anything else, you do not need any external teaching. Those who hold this view tend to contrast the inner light with the teaching of the word of God; they isolate the work and the activity of the Holy Spirit. And of course this is the danger to which we are all subject. Our error is that we tend to isolate, not only the doctrine concerning the Spirit, but even the activity of the Spirit as well.

How, then, do we avoid falling into this error? I suggest to you that we avoid it in the following way. There are two main tests which we must always apply to anything that we feel is the work of the Spirit, or anything that may be represented to us as being the work of the Spirit. The first test is to ask whether we are being directed to the word of God. The New Testament teaches that in the work of sanctification the Holy Spirit works in connection with the word. He does act upon us directly, but almost invariably he does so in connection with the word, the Scripture. This is a very fundamental point. If you read the scriptural teaching concerning the Holy Spirit and his work, if indeed you read in general about the work of sanctification, you will always find that the work of the Spirit and the word go together and that the terms are used interchangeably. Sometimes we are told that we are sanctified by the word; at other times that we are sanctified by the Spirit. Sometimes we are told we are born again and regenerated by the Spirit; at other times we are told we are regenerated by the word. Both James and Peter teach that our regeneration is the result of the word; at other times the emphasis is upon the Spirit. Thus what is clearly meant is that the Spirit does this work in and through us, and upon us, by means of the word – by using the word.

You notice, too, that our Lord describes the Holy Spirit as the Spirit of truth. He is the Spirit who brings and will lead us in to all truth. He is not only the true Spirit, but he is also the Spirit who particularly reveals the truth. That is his greatest function. Our Lord says in John 14:26, 'The Comforter, which is the Holy Ghost, whom the Father will send in my name, he shall teach you all things, and bring all things to your remembrance, whatsoever I have said unto you.' What we have to discover is: how does the Holy Spirit fulfil his great task of revealing the truth? There is no doubt at all about this. The apostle Paul in 1 Corinthians 2:12, a most important verse, says, 'Now we have received, not the spirit of the world, but the spirit which is of God; that we might know the things that are freely given us of God.' That is the difference, says Paul, between the Christian and the non-Christian. The non-Christian does not understand these things of God, he does not understand this question of salvation. The average person of the world today is not interested in salvation at all, nor in his relationship to God. This is because he has not the Spirit, but the Spirit is given that we might know the things that are freely given to us by God.

And what are these things? What are the 'wonderful works of God' referred to in Acts 2:11? How may I know about them; how may I understand them? The answer is that I cannot know anything about them until I come to this book. It is here that I discover them; it is here and here alone that I know what God has done. I may have certain experiences, but the question is, have they anything to do with these wonderful works of God? It is only in the word that I discover what God has done, and it is only here that I can discover what these things are that are freely given to us of God. It is the Spirit who has done it and he has done it by taking hold of certain men and doing two things to them.

He has, first of all, given them a revelation of the truth. He has given information concerning the facts – which is what revelation means. But he has not stopped merely at revelation, he has also inspired them, which means that he has so controlled them that in giving their accounts of these facts, they have been kept free from error. It is the double work. Revelation means a knowledge of the facts of salvation; inspiration means the work of controlling men and guiding them in recording these facts so that they are free from error. And that is what we have in the Scriptures. Prophecy, says Peter in 2 Peter 1:20–21 is not the result of any private interpretation; prophecy did not come in past times because certain men had what they called 'insight' into the events and facts. Not at all! Prophecy is not man putting down on paper what he thinks is happening in the world or what is going to happen; it has not come by any private excogitation in that way. Rather, as Peter puts it, 'Holy men of God spake as they were moved by the Holy Ghost' (2 Pet 1:21). Holy men spoke from God, as they were controlled, carried along, driven and guided by the Holy Spirit. So we see, then, that it is the Holy Spirit himself who has given us the word.

Obviously, therefore, when the Holy Spirit works in us he

does so through his own word. He does his work of sanctification in us by leading us to contemplate the truth that he has recorded in this word. So we become sanctified and are dealt with by the Holy Spirit, not by contemplating beautiful thoughts, not by some sort of science of the mind, cogitating on the beautiful and the prophetic, turning our minds away from that which is hurtful to the beautiful, and training our minds to it – that is not the work of the Holy Spirit. Rather, the Holy Spirit always directs us to the truth, the truth that he himself has given, that he himself has inspired men to write. Therefore, whatever you and I may feel, if it is not directly related to this truth, it is not the work of the Holy Spirit.

There I think we see very clearly the difference between the Christian message and that of any of the popular cults that are in the world today. These cults do undoubtedly influence people and make them feel much better. This is very good psychology, because it is a good psychological rule always to look on the bright side of things and to think beautiful thoughts – it would be nonsense to deny that. But though you may be doing that and may be feeling better physically, and better in every respect as the result of cultivating beautiful thoughts, it need have no connection whatsoever with the Christian faith and the Christian message. Indeed, it may even be the greatest hindrance to that message. The Christian message and the Christian way of salvation is directly connected with this truth from beginning to end. Beautiful thoughts may do you good, but the question is: are those thoughts centred on the wonderful works of God? Is your happiness based upon what God has done, upon the activity of this mighty God, and the things that are freely given us of God? The Spirit always directs to the word.

But my second point is even more important: the Spirit not only always directs us to the word, he always directs us, in particular, to what is, after all, the special message of this Word – the Person of our blessed Lord and Saviour Jesus Christ. 'But I thought,' says someone, 'that you were preaching exclusively about the Holy Spirit, at this point.' But I cannot do that, because our Lord himself told us that when the Holy Spirit came he would not speak of himself. This means not only that he will not speak from himself, but also that he will not speak about himself or about what he is going to do. Our Lord tell us, 'he shall testify of me' (Jn 15:26), and 'he shall glorify me' (Jn 16:14). The special work of the Holy Spirit is never to direct attention to himself, but always to direct it to the Lord Jesus Christ.

Peter, again, said: 'The God of our fathers raised up Jesus, whom ye slew and hanged on a tree. Him hath God exalted with his right hand to be a Prince, and a Saviour, for to give repentance to Israel, and forgiveness of sins. And we [the apostles] are his witnesses of these things; and so is also the Holy Ghost, whom God hath given to them that obey him' (Acts 5:30–32). 'We,' says Peter, in effect, 'were witnesses of the Lord Jesus Christ. We spent three years with him; we are telling you about him, what he did and said. We saw him nailed to a tree, and die upon the tree; we saw them take down his body and put it in a grave. We saw the stone rolled away, yes, and we were together in a room when he came into it, even though the doors were shut; and he appeared to us on other occasions too. We are witnesses of these things and so also is the Holy Spirit.' The Holy Spirit is a witness to these things, even as the apostles were. You will find that the author of the epistle to the Hebrews says exactly the same thing. He talks about the gospel which, he says, 'At the first began to be spoken by the Lord, and was confirmed unto us by them that heard him; God also bearing them witness both with signs and wonders, and with divers miracles, and gifts of the Holy Ghost' (Heb 2:3-4).

Indeed, the apostle John is most specific on this point, writing, in 1 John 4:2: 'Every spirit that confesseth that Jesus Christ is come in the flesh is of God.' This, therefore, is the vital test which we must always apply: the Holy Spirit always points to and glorifies the Lord Jesus Christ. Therefore when we come to test ourselves and ask ourselves, 'Have I received the Spirit, is the Spirit working in me?' the question I ask myself is not, 'What feelings do I have?' There are many agencies that will give me wonderful feelings, the cults, for instance, or poetry can give wonderful feelings, so can a sunset and so can drugs. Feelings are not the test. The Holy Spirit does give feelings, thank God, but the question I ask is this: 'If I have a feeling of joy and happiness, is it because of the Lord Jesus Christ, or is it not?' If I cannot directly relate my happiness, my joy, my peace, my all, to my blessed Lord, it is probably the spirit of anti-Christ and it has nothing to do with God at all. For the Holy Spirit always glorifies the Lord Jesus Christ.

The same applies to gifts. There are many agencies that can give men wonderful gifts, but unless these gifts are directly related to the Lord himself, they are not of God. I will go even further and say without any hesitation that you may have experiences of conquered sins and wonderful deliverances from things that have got you down for years, but I still assert solidly that it is not sanctification unless it is directly related to the Lord Jesus Christ. For I would remind you again that there are many cults that can deliver you from various sins. There are many things in this world that have enabled people to give up particular sins. You can read their stories, and you will find that the Lord Jesus Christ is not mentioned at all. So I assert that if the Lord Jesus Christ is not at the centre, if the glory is not given to him, it is not the work of the Holy Spirit, for the Holy Spirit always glorifies him. He always puts him in the centre, and brings us into relationship with him.

Thus, the Holy Spirit came in order to reveal Christ to us. His primary work is to make Christ real to us, to show us what Christ has done for us, to remind us of his teaching, to give us a longing and a love for Christ, to enable us to live as Christ lived, to conform us to his image – it is all centred on the Lord Jesus Christ. That is why I say with such emphasis that I must never isolate the doctrine of the Holy Spirit. Whatever I may think I have, whatever experience I think I may have, if I have the Holy Spirit, he will make me centre it all upon the Lord Jesus Christ, for he always leads to him. The other spirits do not, they say 'Glorify me.'

If you want to know whether you have the Holy Spirit and whether he is in you and dealing with you, that is the only safe and valid test. Feelings come and go, gifts come and go, you can become devout and careful in your life without him, but the hallmark of the work of the Holy Spirit is that he presents the Lord Jesus Christ to us, and brings us to an ever-increasing intimacy with him, and an enjoyment of his glorious presence. The Spirit sanctifies us by bringing us to the word, the word that brings us to a knowledge of him.

5

Different in Everything[1]

Submit yourselves to every ordinance of man for the Lord's sake: whether it be to the king, as supreme; or unto governors, as unto them that are sent by him for the punishment of evildoers, and for the praise of them that do well. For so is the will of God, that with well doing ye may put to silence the ignorance of foolish men: as free, and not using your liberty for a cloke of maliciousness, but as the servants of God. Honour all men. Love the brotherhood. Fear God. Honour the king (1 Peter 2:13-17).

So far, our studies in this seventeenth chapter of John have convinced us that the fundamental thing about the Christian is that he is one who is sanctified, sanctified by God; and to be sanctified means to be separated from the world and from sin and separated unto God. That is the scriptural teaching everywhere about the Christian, and we are reminded of that very forcibly in 1 Peter 2:13-17, and indeed, in the whole chapter, which we shall be looking at together. The Christian is a new creation: in the world but not of it; he is a man still, and yet he is not as he was. His fundamental postulate is, 'I live; yet not I, but Christ liveth in me' (Gal 2:20) – that is the essential meaning of sanctification – so that the Christian is different in every respect from the non-Christian. And there is nothing more

---

[1] This sermon was preached in 1953, on the Sunday before the Queen's coronation.

important, as I understand the New Testament teaching, and especially the teaching of the apostles, than that we should always be conscious of this, and that our entire lives may be governed by that realisation.

Now when I say that the Christian is one who is different in *every* respect, I use my words advisedly – '... if any man be in Christ, he is a new creation: old things are passed away; behold all things are become new' (2 Cor 5:17). And that word 'all' is as inclusive and as comprehensive as a word can be; everything is new and everything is different if we are truly Christian. And we all of us betray whether we are Christian or not, by everything we do and say, and by what we are. Our Lord taught on one occasion, you remember, that we shall all be judged by every idle word that we have uttered, and 'idle' means not premeditated, our casual words, our casual actions (see Matthew 12:36). The fact is that we are all along betraying what we are by our reaction to things, by our conduct and by our behaviour, and it is very interesting indeed to observe this. Our spirituality, ultimately, should be estimated and measured by the consistency of the whole of our life and living. There are people who, as it were, have to put on their Christianity for the time being, but if you see them in their casual moments, in their ordinary daily lives, you might perhaps not even suspect that they are Christians at all – they are living in compartments. But the more spiritual, the more sanctified we become, the more are we characterised by a wholeness and consistency, and it shows itself in all we do, and in our reaction to everything.

In the same way, and this has a particularly powerful emphasis in the New Testament, our thinking is governed by a new principle. Our whole outlook is new, we do not see things as we used to see them, nor do we see them as the natural man sees them. We were once governed by the world and its outlook, but that is no longer true of us. Notice how Peter puts that in verse 10: 'Which in time past were not a people, but are now the people of God: which had not obtained mercy, but now have obtained mercy.' In other words, as the result of regeneration, as the result of the operation of the Spirit of God upon them, and as a result of the fact that they are now partakers of the divine nature and have been born from above and of the Spirit, Christians must of necessity see things in an entirely new way. Their whole perspective is different, everything takes on a new colour. In particular, of course, we can put it like this: Christians are those whose outlook on all matters is to be controlled and governed entirely by the teaching of the Scriptures. They do not revert to the world in any respect at all. They must not merely say, 'I do not take the worldly view about certain practices,' the scriptural teaching is that they must not take the worldly view about *anything*. Not only do they not take the worldly view about things that are bad, they do not take the worldly view about things that are good either. Their outlook upon life is a totality, and it is entirely determined by the teaching of the Bible; they are men and women of one Book, and their whole outlook conforms to this.

Now this is clearly a very important principle, and it applies not only to the individual but also to the church and to the message and preaching of the church. These, too, are to be determined and controlled by nothing but the word of God. Our forefathers had to fight for this. As a result, today the state does not govern the preaching of the church and it must never be allowed to do so. There is no power on earth or among men which can be allowed to determine the message of the Christian church. The message of the preacher should be God-given and Spirit-inspired, and he must be controlled entirely and exclusively by the word as it comes to him and is brought to him by the Holy Spirit of God. We, therefore, are not controlled and governed by times and seasons or by circumstances. The tragedy of the Christian church has been that for so long she has indulged in what is called 'topical preaching', messages determined by the things that are happening around and about her, rather than the message which comes from God – the burden of the Lord; our preaching must always be out of the word, from the word, Spirit-inspired and Spirit-led.

So, then, we turn to the word, and the word speaks and takes hold of us, and we find that it teaches very plainly and clearly that our sanctification is something that applies to the whole of our lives and to every facet and aspect of our activities as human beings in this world. This is the glory of the Scriptures; no human relationship, no eventuality can possibly meet us, but that we find instruction concerning it somewhere in the word. And the word gives us very particular and definite instruction and teaching with regard to our relationship to the state, our relationship to the world in which we are bound to live and the country to which we are bound to belong; the word of God does not leave us without guidance.

This is something that many people seem never to have realised. They regard the Bible as if it had but the one theme of personal salvation: that is an utter travesty of the truth. The great primary and central theme is, of necessity, personal salvation, but the Bible does not stop at that. It gives teaching and instruction for this personal, saved life, as it is lived in this world, in its relationship, as we see in 1 Peter 2, with kings, with authorities and powers, with masters and servants – every conceivable relationship in life. It is an essential part of our sanctification to realise that we are to be governed by the word and its teaching in every relationship, and there is no exception whatsoever.

Therefore, I want to call your attention in particular, at this point, to the way in which our sanctification is shown, and is encouraged and developed, with respect to this whole matter of our relationship to the country to which we belong, the state under which we happen to be living. There are two main principles here. The first is that we must realise clearly that the church, the gospel, has only one message to the world and for the world. We must always start there. The Scriptures speak directly to individuals, not to nations or states; I cannot see that there is any message at all in the New Testament for nations as such. There is of course, in that respect, a difference between the Old Testament and the New; the church in the Old Testament was a particular nation, a particular state. But that is no longer the case, because, as Peter writes in this chapter, there is now a new nation: 'But ye are a chosen generation, a royal priesthood, an holy nation' (1 Pet 2:9). The words in Exodus 19 that were spoken to the children of Israel only are here spoken by the apostle Peter under divine inspiration and applied to this new nation, the church. In Matthew 22:43 our Lord himself said that the kingdom should be taken from the Jews and given to another nation, and this other nation is clearly the Christian church, which consists of men and women called out of every nation under heaven. Consequently, we have this new situation, that the New Testament does not address its remarks and its teaching to nations and to states, but primarily to individuals. It is a personal message calling men and women out of different nations into a new nation, this new kingdom in the Lord Jesus Christ.

If that is so, then there are certain deductions which we must draw quite inevitably, one of which is that there can be no scriptural authority for calling this nation, or any other country at the present time, to an 'act of rededication'; such a thing seems to me to be quite inconceivable and meaningless and indeed anti-scriptural. As the New Testament speaks not to nations, but to individuals, it has no 'call to rededication' to a nation as such, because as I want to try to show you, that is something of which the nation is incapable.

In the same way, therefore, I would argue that we cannot be party to any call to people, 'whatever their religion', to pray God's blessing upon our country. For, as I understand the New Testament and its teaching, that again is a non-Christian statement. The church does not call upon all people 'whatever their religion' to pray for God's blessing upon our country, and for this good reason: that as Christians we say there is only one faith. We do not recognise any other religion, indeed, we say that all other religions are false: 'There is none other name under heaven given among men, whereby we must be saved' (Acts 4:12), save that of the Lord Jesus Christ. So we send our missionaries to every country, whether Hindu, or Moslem or Confucian, because we say and believe that those religions are not true – there is only 'one mediator between God and men, the man Christ Jesus' (1 Tim 2:5). We assert that these people are worshipping God in a false manner and we send our missionaries to teach and train and enlighten them. We know that there is only one way to God in the Lord Jesus Christ, for, 'No man hath seen God at any time; the only begotten Son, which is in the bosom of the Father, he hath declared him' (Jn 1:18); and again, 'I am the way, the truth and the life; no man cometh unto the Father, but by me' (Jn 14:6) – so, as Christians, if we believe these things, we clearly and obviously cannot appeal to people of 'any religion whatsoever' to pray God's blessing upon us as a nation and as a people. It is tremendously important that our thinking should be governed by the Scriptures lest we contradict ourselves; lest, on the one hand, we send missionaries to convert people to the Christian faith, but then, at the same time, treat them as if they were on an equality with us in the matter of our approach to God.

Then we move on from that to the following proposition. The gospel of Jesus Christ, the Christian church, has but one message to the world, which is to warn men and women of the wrath to come, to proclaim to them that they are moving in the direction of the Day of Judgement, and to call upon them to realise that they have immortal souls for which they will have to answer in the presence of God. The church calls them, therefore, to repentance and to faith in the Lord Jesus Christ. Surely, as Christians we must take this position: if a man is not a Christian he is fundamentally wrong. He may be a good man, a moral man, he may be a good citizen in general. But we are not primarily interested in him as such, we are interested in him as a soul, and we know that no man can truly be the citizen he should be until he is a Christian; he is failing at some point or other. The message is that we become good and noble and true citizens to the extent that we are loyal and obedient servants to our Lord and Saviour Jesus Christ. Men and women who are not Christians in this nation today cannot rededicate themselves to God. They must repent, they must come before God on bended knee and recognise that they have sinned against him and that they have forgotten him. They must be born again. I cannot call them to any act of rededication or reconsecration because they must go down before they can rise; they must repent before they can be received; they must believe on the Lord Jesus Christ as their only Saviour, Redeemer and Lord. The Christian message does not vary because of circumstances; and that is the unchanging message of the Christian church to the world and to men and women in this nation who are not Christians.

But that is only the beginning. Having said that the church has only one message for the world, I now go on to ask, what, then, is the relationship of the Christian to the state and to these other things? We have seen the position of the non-Christian, but what is that of the Christian? And here it seems to me that the teaching of this verse in 1 Peter, as indeed the teaching of the entire Scriptures, can be summarised under a number of very definite propositions. The first is that we must start with our basic position as Christians. Peter says, 'Dearly beloved, I beseech you as strangers and pilgrims ...' (1 Pet 2:11) – that is the basic position. Our relationship to the world is determined and governed by that definition. As Christians we are but strangers and pilgrims, travellers and sojourners in this world of time.

Or again, the apostle Paul puts it still more specifically in Philippians 3:20 where he says, 'Our conversation [our citizenship] is in heaven,' or, if you prefer it, 'we are a colony of heaven'. That is our fatherland, the state to which we belong: our citizenship is in heaven. And you notice how the apostle rejoices in the fact that he, who was once such a zealous, narrow-minded Jew, can now say: 'there is neither Jew nor Greek' (Gal 3:28), and, indeed, still more specifically, 'where there is neither Greek nor Jew, circumcision nor uncircumcision, Barbarian, Scythian, bond nor free: but Christ is all and in all' (Col 3:11). Then in Ephesians 2 he rejoices in the fact that the middle wall of partition which hitherto had divided the Jews from the Gentiles has been broken down. It was once there in the Temple itself but it has now been demolished.

How, then, do we interpret these statements (and they are but a selection from a number of similar statements which I might have put to you)? It seems to me that we must put it like this:

as Christians, our first and highest loyalty must always, inevitably, be to God and his Christ; that must come even before our loyalty to country and to king or queen. Our loyalty to God and Christ comes before our loyalty to any nationality; we are primarily the people of God, we are his special possession. He has taken hold of us and brought us out of these various natural relationships into this special, personal relationship to himself. Therefore in all my thinking I must start with that – that is the thing which is to control me and govern me, and I must never think or do anything which violates that preliminary, fundamental postulate.

Then, of course, that position works itself out in this way. We have been delivered – as G K Chesterton put it – 'that we might be delivered from pride and from blind prejudice'. I do not want to elaborate all this now, because I am anxious to give you a number of headings. But I think we must all know that the great cause of warfare and turmoil, and difficult and troublesome times, is pride, whether between individuals or between nations. Indeed, there can be little doubt but that the most prolific cause of war, in both the ancient and the modern world is a narrow nationalism. The tragedy is, of course, that we all recognise that in others, but are not always so ready to see it in ourselves. I am sure that in general all of us are prepared to denounce narrow nationalism, but how difficult it is to 'see ourselves as others see us'. Yet the New Testament, bringing us fundamentally into our relationship to God, makes it impossible for any Christian to say 'my country right or wrong'. Christians cannot say that because to do so would be to deny their own faith. They have been delivered from every natural pride, indeed, they regard all such things as their greatest enemy, the biggest obstacle to their true growth in grace, and to their sanctification. They are anxious, therefore, that they may be delivered from hatred, from despising others, and from glorying in the flesh in any shape or form – they see that all these things are antagonistic to the Spirit of Christ and of God.

Christians are those who see themselves as sinners. Our Lord starts off the Sermon on the Mount by saying, 'Blessed are the poor in spirit' (Matt 5:3) – and those who are poor in spirit are people who do not take any pride in themselves, in what they are or what they have done. They are not always beating the big drum about their own achievements and their greatness and superiority to others – they are the very antithesis of that. Christians see themselves as sinners with nothing to boast of, they know that what they need above everything else is the new nature, the rebirth; they thank God for it, and they give their primary, fundamental loyalty to God. And because they rejoice above everything else in the fact that they are now citizens of the heavenly kingdom, they have been emancipated from that tendency to pride, self-satisfaction and conceit, from hatred and from despising of others. They are totally unlike the Pharisee in our Lord's story, for the Pharisee thanked God that he was not like other people, because he had done this and that, while the other man had done nothing. And what Christians think about themselves as individuals, applies also to the way they regard their nation. Their thinking is consistent and it is worked out in the whole of life and in every relationship.

Then I go one step further. Because Christians glory in the Lord, because this is their fundamental loyalty, they feel the bond of unity, fellowship and brotherhood with those who belong to Christ in any nation whatsoever. They feel this deeply and in a more real sense than they feel any natural ties or bonds. Now this is strong doctrine, but our Lord put it like this: 'He that loveth father or mother more than me is not worthy of me: and he that loveth son or daughter more than me is not worthy of me' (Matt 10:37). Indeed, in one Gospel it says that we must *hate* father and mother for his sake – that is how our Lord puts it about the individual. We are to feel a relationship to him and a bond to him closer and dearer and more intimate and valuable than even the dearest earthly tie. If that, then, is to be true of us with regard to our closest and our dearest, how much more is it to be true of us in our relationship to those who are bound to us by general ties of nationality and country? Christians, therefore – and this is a test of the Christian – should feel more closely bound to a Christian from any country under the sun than they do to anyone who is not a Christian in their own country. Their loyalty to Christ comes before loyalty to country; their relationship to Christ and to all who are in Christ is bigger and more vital than the other relationship which belongs only to nature and to the flesh. These are some of the implications of this doctrine, and you see why I emphasised at the beginning that a Christian is a man whose outlook is governed everywhere by the teaching of Scripture.

'But,' someone may say, 'what about the apostle Paul in Romans 9, 10 and 11? Does he not there glory as a Jew, and does he not seem to put nationality into the first position?' The answer is, of course, that when the Apostle writes as he does about the Jews, he is referring to them as God's own people, not as Jews qua Jews, and not in any nationalistic sense. He writes as he does about them because they were God's chosen people, who were meant to be witnesses of God and of the coming Messiah, but who had failed to recognise him. Thus Paul's interest in them is a spiritual interest and not a mere national or natural one.

All these things show that our fundamental position, our basic loyalty, is to God and to the Lord Jesus Christ. But let me add that this does not mean that all these other relationships are abolished. This is a most important point – the balance of Scripture is most wonderful. Why did the apostle Peter write these words in the verses we are considering? Why do you think the apostle Paul does the same thing? There can be no doubt as to the answer. The early Christians, listening to the high doctrine which I have been expounding, were led into error by the devil, and were saying that because we are Christians we have nothing to do with these lands and nations to which we belong. Indeed, some of them, who were slaves, were saying that because they had become Christians they had no loyalty any longer to their masters, but could do as they pleased.

'Certainly not!' says the Scripture; that is an entirely false deduction. We are not to assume that all these other relationships have been abrogated, for they have not. We teach, on the basis of Scripture, that all the fundamental ordinances of God still stand. In other words, it is God who has divided the nations and placed their boundaries and brought them into being. It is he who has appointed legislators and decreed that there should be kings and governments and authorities and powers – these are all ordained of God. It is the scriptural teaching that there shall be magistrates. Even though the magistrates may not be Christians, while I am a Christian, I must nevertheless obey them, and the laws of the land, because Scripture tells me to do so. We are to conform to all these things. Peter even tells these servants to be subject to their masters, not only to the good and gentle but also to the 'froward' or harsh (2:18).

Some of the first Christians were obviously arguing about these things. Some had been brought up under paganism. They were married people, but now that they had become Christians, some of the married men tended to leave their wives because they were unconverted. But the teaching of Scripture is that a man is not bound to leave his wife because he is a Christian and she is not. In other words, these natural human relationships are not abolished, instead, the teaching is, clearly, that we must look upon them in a new way. We do not become anarchists because we are Christians. We do not say that we refuse to recognise any law or authority or power at all – that is as wrong as to remain in the other natural position, which we have already criticised and dealt with. The apostle Paul uses a phrase which seems to me to sum up the true Christian position perfectly – we are to 'use this world as not abusing it' (1 Cor 7:31). In other words, all our conduct is to be controlled by this new point of view, and if we are only governed by this, we shall never go astray.

Take, then, our relationship to the Queen and to the government and to the various authorities in this country, how are we to carry it out? Well, this is how Scripture puts it – 'Submit yourselves to every ordinance of man *for the Lord's sake*: whether it be to the king, as supreme; or unto governors, as unto them that are sent by him for the punishment of evildoers, and for the praise of them that do well' (1 Pet 2:13–14). It is, in other words, for the Lord's sake that we do these things; we do not do it simply because it is our country or our Queen or our government. Everything we do, we do for the Lord's sake, and you will find the same teaching with respect to our duties to masters and servants and so on. Our reason for submitting ourselves to human ordinances is entirely different from that of the non-Christian; he does it with his worldly, carnal, fleshly motive, whereas we do everything for the Lord's sake. We obey the Queen, we submit to the government, in order that we may tell forth his praise who has called us out of darkness into his most marvellous light. We do all these things as an opportunity of showing what God has done to us and for us in the Lord Jesus Christ. This is something that governs us everywhere.

But I must go on to add that if we should ever reach a point at which any authority that is above us should ask us to disobey God, then we must refuse, because our primary and fundamental loyalty is to God and not to any human authority. Let me quote the words of the apostle Peter in Acts 4:19: 'Whether it be right in the sight of God to hearken unto you more than unto God, judge ye ...' The authorities were trying to prohibit him and his fellow apostles from preaching the Lord Jesus Christ and that is his reply. In Acts 5:29 he puts it like this: 'We ought to obey God rather than men.' And our forefathers have had occasion in times past to utter the same words. Thank God, we have no occasion to utter them in our country at this present time, but our gospel is for all times and should a time ever come in our country when we have to face the choice of obeying God or obeying the most august human authority, we, as Christian people, must always obey God, whatever the cost. So let us at this moment give honour to those men and women in other lands and countries who are doing this very thing at this very hour. Let us not forget the doctrine. We live in this way because of our fundamental postulate that now we look at nothing as the world looks at it. Rather, we look at everything through spiritual eyes, because we are controlled by the fact that our ultimate loyalty is to God and to the Lord Jesus Christ.

Therefore, finally, we can put it like this: we obey all these ordinances of man for the Lord's sake. Let us remember that we do everything in the fear of the Lord. The Christian should never do anything in a worldly spirit. He should not honour the Queen in a worldly spirit; he should not do anything as the world does it, for he does everything in the fear of God, as one in whom the Holy Spirit dwells. His conception of citizenship and of loyalty is determined not by the mind and outlook and spirit of the world, but by the Spirit that is of God.

So the Christian, you see, is a unique person. He is not merely a new man, but also a new creation. He both thinks in a different way, and does everything in a different way. May God grant that in all we think, and in all we do, we may always make it evident that we are these 'peculiar', special, spiritual people. 'Dearly beloved, I beseech you as strangers and pilgrims' – it is we alone who realise that that is the truth. The world never stops to think about that, but we know that we are sojourners and pilgrims in this world. So, 'abstain from fleshly lusts' – in every form – 'which war against the soul; having your conversation honest among the Gentiles: that, whereas they speak against you as evildoers, they may by your good works, which they shall behold, glorify God in the day of visitation' (vv. 11-12). The Christian is always different and he is different in everything.

6

The Yearning of the Holy Spirit

Sanctify them through thy truth: thy word is truth (John 17:17).

As we continue with our study of the work of the Holy Spirit in our sanctification, let me remind you that we have seen clearly that we must never isolate this doctrine and regard it as something separate and distinct. The Holy Spirit has been sent and is among us to glorify the Lord Jesus Christ, and we must never think of sanctification and holiness apart from him. We saw, secondly, how the Holy Spirit guided the 'holy men of God' as they wrote the Scriptures, and kept them from error; and then we considered together how he works in us through the word.

Let us proceed, then, from that point, but let me remind you that we are not here considering the whole doctrine of the Holy Spirit. We know something of the work of the Spirit in creation, and in many other respects, but we are now concerned in particular with the work of the Holy Spirit in sanctification, and are confining our attention to that.

So we come once more to the question of how the Holy Spirit carries out this work in us. I need scarcely remind you that it is a subject which has often been misunderstood and has often led to disagreement. It has provoked much discussion and has produced many errors and heresies in the Christian church, and still tends to do so. It is, indeed, as has often been pointed out, a very remarkable thing that this truth, which of all others was meant to demonstrate unity, has perhaps caused more division than any other particular aspect of the truth. It was the Holy Spirit who produced that great and amazing unity on the Day of Pentecost. On that day, men of different nations were all made one by this power, and yet, since then, because of the misunderstanding of the doctrine, it has often led not only to disagreement, but even to schism. We must therefore approach it with caution, and be very careful to allow the Scriptures to speak to us.

I would suggest to you that an important principle stands out very clearly in scriptural teaching with regard to this subject. This is that the Holy Spirit dwells within all Christians. Now this is a most important point. There are people who would have you believe that you can be a Christian without receiving the Holy Spirit. But that is thoroughly unscriptural. I would affirm once more that it is impossible for us to be Christians at all without having the Holy Spirit in us. Let me give you some of the Scriptures which assert this. In 1 Corinthians 12:3 we read, 'No man can say that Jesus is the Lord, but by the Holy Ghost.' No man can *really* say; it does not just mean that you say it with your lips, because obviously a blasphemer and unbeliever could utter these words – but if when he says it a man really means it, then that man can say 'Jesus is Lord' only by the Holy Spirit. But the Apostle is still more explicit in Romans 8:9: 'If any man have not the Spirit of Christ, he is none of his.' Now there we have a categorical statement to the effect that if a man does not have the Holy Spirit of Christ within him, he is not a Christian at all, and does not belong to Christ. So it is surely the height of folly, and a complete error, to suggest that one can be a Christian and then later receive the Holy Spirit – we cannot be Christians at all apart from the Holy Spirit, and his work in us and upon us.

But let me give you some more passages, for this is a vital subject. In 1 Corinthians 12:13 the Apostle teaches, 'For by one Spirit are we all baptised into one body.' Christians are members of the body of Christ; 'Ye,' he says in 1 Corinthians 12:27, addressing the church, addressing Christians, 'Ye are the body of Christ, and members in particular.' Thus, to be a Christian means to be a part of the body of Christ, and how does this happen to us? The answer is: 'By one Spirit are we all baptised into one body.' In other words, the point we are emphasising is that by definition, we cannot be Christian at all except the Holy Spirit should thus have put us into this one body of Christ.

Then again, in 1 Corinthians 6:19 the Apostle Paul says: 'What? know ye not that your body is the temple of the Holy Ghost which is in you, which ye have of God, and ye are not your own?' He is writing there to the members of the church at Corinth, not to some of them, but to all of them, and he is writing about a most unpleasant and unsavoury subject. He is particularly warning them against the sin of fornication, of which some of them had been guilty, and his argument is: This is impossible, you must not do this. Do you not know that your body is the temple of the Holy Spirit, and for this reason you cannot be joined in that way to a harlot? He reminds these members of the church at Corinth, many of whom were guilty of such extraordinary sins and weaknesses, that even their bodies are the temples of the Holy Spirit which God has given them and that, therefore, the Holy Spirit is in them. Our Lord had promised this particularly. He had promised his disciples that if they believed in him, he would give them the Holy Spirit.

But let me give you one more quotation, which again is very striking, and this time it is found in James 4:5. In the Authorised Version it reads like this: 'The Spirit that dwelleth in us lusteth to envy', but I think it is generally agreed that that is not the best translation at that point. It ought to be put like this: 'The Spirit which he made to dwell in us yearneth over us even unto jealous envy.' The point I am emphasising at this moment is 'the Spirit that he made to dwell in us' – again, a statement that the Holy Spirit is resident in all Christian people.

I could give you other quotations, but let those be sufficient. The point I am anxious to establish, and you will appreciate what an important one it is, is that we must lay down the basic position that it is impossible to be a Christian at all unless the Holy Spirit is in us; for to be a Christian means that the Holy Spirit has taken up his abode in us. Or take the way John puts it. He says in chapter 2:17 of his first epistle that all Christians have received the anointing of the Holy Spirit. John's epistle is to all Christians, and their understanding is dependent upon the fact that they have received the anointing, they have received this gift which the Lord Jesus Christ promised that he himself would give to all who believe in him.

So, then, if that proposition is true, we can proceed to ask our vital question: how does the Holy Spirit do this work of sanctification within us? Now here we find two remarkable, scriptural, statements. I have already quoted one of them, James 4:5, and I want to put this very plainly. The Authorised Version, you remember, says, 'The Spirit that dwelleth in us lusteth to envy,' but I have suggested that a better translation is, 'The Spirit which he made to dwell in us yearneth over us even unto a jealous envy.' Then I want to take with that verse a statement made in Galatians 5:17 where we read that 'the flesh lusteth against the Spirit, and the Spirit against the flesh.'

Now there, it seems to me, is the basic position with regard to the work of the Holy Spirit in our sanctification. We are told that the Holy Spirit, who has been given to us by the Lord Jesus Christ, has been given in order that he may produce our sanctification. It is thus that God sanctifies us. In the first place, we are told that the Holy Spirit within us is yearning for our sanctification with a jealous envy. Look at it like this. The Holy Spirit comes into us, but by nature, and as a result of sin and the Fall, we are fleshly, we are all creatures of lust, and not only lust of the flesh but also of the mind. That is the teaching of the apostle Paul in Ephesians 2:3; we were all, he says, subject to these lusts and we all know this very well from experience. We are governed by passions; there are lusts and there are desires within us, and of course the world and the flesh and the devil play an equal part. There are these promptings, these desires, these evil powers within us striving for mastery over us.

Then into all that comes the Holy Spirit of God, and the Holy Spirit is a Person. He is not a mere power, nor just an influence, but a Person. Our Lord, you remember, told the disciples just as he was leaving them, 'Let not your heart be troubled ...' I am going to leave you but, 'I will pray the Father, and he shall give you another Comforter' (Jn 14:1, 16), another Person and he will do certain things for you and to you.

So these two statements tell us that as the flesh is there lusting within us and drawing us away from God, and into sin and evil, so the Holy Spirit is yearning for us, desiring the mastery over us, desiring to control us, desiring us for God and for Christ. He yearns over us, he desires us – the word that is really used is 'lusteth' – even to a jealous envy. In other words, the Spirit of God, and of Christ, and the Holy Spirit, the three Persons in the blessed Holy Trinity, desire us. The Holy Spirit sees these evil influences in us and he hates them, and is yearning to deliver us from them and to set us on the other side. The Holy Spirit is opposed to everything that represents the world and the flesh and the devil. He is against everything in us that is opposed to God, and his work within us is to deliver us from these evil things and to emancipate us from them in order to make us what God intends us to be, and to accomplish what the Lord Jesus Christ has died for.

There, then, is the great truth, and to me it is one of the most comforting, consoling and wonderful truths that a Christian can ever discover; that as a Christian I no longer just live to myself, I have the Holy Spirit dwelling within me, lusting, striving, yearning, that there is this blessed conflict. Indeed, unless we know something about this conflict we obviously are not Christians at all, for it is there in every Christian. Once we were only the flesh, now we are spirit and flesh and these two are opposed to one another. There is the flesh dragging us, drawing us down, and the Spirit drawing us up. There is a fight going on within, because the Holy Spirit has come into us to reside within us, and God does this work of sanctification within us, through this energy and activity, through this longing of the Spirit within us.

So now, if that is the great general principle of the Holy Spirit's work in us, how does he do it in particular? We can divide his method up very simply. The first thing he does is to call our attention to the truth, all of the truth which we have been considering, the amazing truth about the being and the character and the nature of God, and, too, the truth about sin. We can never know the truth about God, and about sin, until we find it in this word of God. It is the Spirit who gave the word and it is he who leads us to it, to this great word about the Lord Jesus Christ, his Person and his work – it is the Spirit that leads us to that. By nature I am not interested in those things. By nature I like to read the newspaper, all the detailed reports of the Law Courts, and about what the world is doing with all its gaiety and pleasure. I do not want to read this word, but the Spirit leads me to it. His work is to glorify Christ, to reveal him and all the other great and rich doctrines that we have been studying – it is the Spirit who calls my attention to the word, and who goes on drawing my attention to it for every detail of my life.

It is the Spirit, also, who shows me my position as a Christian: this extraordinary doctrine of my being placed in Christ, of my relationship to Christ as a branch in the vine, I in Christ and Christ in me. No man could think of that or discover it, and no man has ever done so. It is the Spirit who leads on to these things, and it is extraordinary, as we examine our experience, to see how he does that. Has this not often surprised you? Here we are, we have had an open Bible before us all our lives, with all these rich truths and doctrines; and yet must we not all admit, as we look back across our lives to having this kind of experience. One day we read a passage, and suddenly we were led to see some great truth, but then we seemed to stop there, we did not do anything about it. Years passed by, and then one day that truth dawned upon us again and we were called to see it and to act upon it. It is always the work of the Spirit: he presents the truth to us. Sometimes we brush it aside and show that we are not interested in it, but he keeps on bringing it back – not only directly by the word but by a book, maybe, that someone brings to our notice. It is all the work of the Spirit. He puts the truth before us, he presents it and shows us these great possibilities that are there for us.

Furthermore, we must not stay even with that. The Holy Spirit not only puts the truth before us and leads us to it, it is he alone who enables us to understand the truth. Now that is the great theme of 1 Corinthians 2, a vital passage in this connection. The Apostle writes there that 'The natural man receiveth not the things of the Spirit of God: for they are foolishness unto him: neither can he know them, because they are spiritually discerned' (1 Cor 2:14). He comes to us: 'We have received, not the spirit that is of the world, but the spirit which is of God' – why? – 'that we might know the things that are freely given to us of God' (v. 12), and we will never know these things apart from the anointing of the Holy Spirit. You can talk to the natural man at his highest and his best, you can talk to the world's greatest intellect and greatest philosopher, you can ask him to read the New Testament, and as a natural man he will know nothing about it. He will understand nothing at all about this amazing doctrine of what is possible to the Christian, for he cannot do so until he receives the Holy Spirit.

Then you may go to him and tell him about this wonderful truth – about the Christian being in Christ and Christ in the Christian – but to him it will be idle nonsense, mere rubbish, a fairy tale. He cannot receive it because he has not the gift of the Holy Spirit. We can only know these things that are given to us of God, and by God, as we have the Holy Spirit within us; these things are foolishness to the natural man, because his way of life consists only of amassing knowledge of truth and philosophy and then proceeding to apply it. That may be his idea, but it is not that of Scripture. The scriptural idea is to be baptised into Christ like the branch in the vine, and the love of Christ comes into us and fills us and does these wonderful things in us and through us. To the natural man that is foolishness, but we have the mind of Christ.

So we see that the Holy Spirit works in two ways. He leads me to the word, and then he does something to me which enables me to receive it. Thus it is that he goes on working within us, yearning with this jealous envy that we may be sanctified, and as I am led by him, I begin to understand this truth and to realise it. We see in Ephesians 3 that the apostle Paul was praying for the Ephesians that they might be 'filled with all the fulness of God' (v. 19), and as I realise that I am meant to be filled in that way, I begin to desire this and to hunger and thirst after it – but I would never have done so if the Holy Spirit had not been working within me. He leads me to the truth and then I desire it, and begin to long for it. Then I seek for it, and I hunger and thirst after righteousness. That is the method of the Spirit, and that is something of his procedure.

Let me remind you again of those well-known words in Philippians 2:12-13. The apostle Paul says, you remember, 'Work out your own salvation with fear and trembling. For it is God which worketh in you both to will and to do of his good pleasure.' That is a great statement. Let me give it to you again in a still better translation: God is one who through his Spirit is constantly supplying you with the impulse, giving you both the power to resolve, and the will and the strength to perform, from his good pleasure. He does it all. We must work it out with 'fear and trembling'; we do not remain passive but we work only because he is working in us the desire to work it out, and he gives us the power to do so.

And, finally, I would like to put it in this way – have you noticed the remarkable prayer of the Apostle in Ephesians 3, beginning at verse 14? Read it once more: 'For this ... cause I bow my knees unto the Father of our Lord Jesus Christ, of whom the whole family in heaven and earth is named, that he would grant you, according to the riches of his glory, to be strengthened with might by his Spirit in the inner man; that Christ may dwell in your hearts by faith; that ye, being rooted and grounded in love, may be able to comprehend with all saints what is the breadth, and length, and depth, and height; and to know the love of Christ which passeth knowledge, that ye might be filled with all the fulness of God.'

What does that mean? Let me put it simply like this. The real need, of course, of every Christian is that Christ may dwell in our hearts by faith; that is the extraordinary thing which he again promises. He has said to the disciples: It is good for you that I go away, but if I go away I will send him unto you.

This is why the Comforter comes. The astounding thing that

the Scripture offers me is that the Lord Jesus Christ should come and dwell in me here on earth. How can he do this? Knowing myself as I am, and what I am, as the result of sin and the Fall, I say it is impossible, and it is impossible apart from the work of the Holy Spirit, who strengthens me with his own power in the inner man, in order that Christ may dwell in my heart by faith. What a wonderful picture this is! The work of the Holy Spirit in men is to prepare a home for the Lord Jesus Christ. He is the servant who is sent along to prepare the palace for the King, to put it in order, to make everything fit and meet, to get rid of all that is unworthy. That is his purpose. The supreme height of sanctification and of holiness is that Christ dwells in us, living his life in us and through us. 'I live; yet not I, but Christ liveth in me' (Gal 2:20) – that is the height of Christian achievement.

And this is how it becomes possible. We need to be strengthened by might, by the Holy Spirit, in the inner man, in order that Christ may dwell in our hearts by faith, so that Christ may take up his abode with us as a permanent guest – not come and go, but abide – settle down. Here in Ephesians 3:17 the Apostle is repeating Jesus' own word, and it is the Holy Spirit that makes that possible.

So we end as we began, by pointing out that all this must be thought of in terms of Persons. We must not think of our sanctification in terms of gifts or experience or anything like that. It is really being made fit and ready to receive the Lord Jesus Christ as the permanent guest in our hearts and in our inner man; and it is the Holy Spirit who does that work. He covets us for Christ, he yearns over us, and longs for us, 'he yearneth over us even unto jealous envy' that we may be Christ's and not the world's. And what he desires above everything else is that he may so deal with us and so work in us that we shall be ready to receive this heavenly guest himself, and he does that in the ways that I have been describing to you. He leads us to the truth, he enables us to receive it, giving us a longing and a hunger for it. He also gives us the power to do that. He undertakes for us and so he prepares us to receive the Lord Jesus Christ. That, then, is the work of the Holy Spirit, that is what he is yearning for and longing for us. Therefore, surely it comes to this: our greatest concern should be to conform to that and to allow the Spirit to do all his work in us.

7

Be Filled with the Spirit

Sanctify them through thy truth: thy word is truth (John 17:17).

In our continuing study of the work of the Holy Spirit in our sanctification I should like us at this point particularly to consider Ephesians 5:18. We finished our last study by emphasising the supreme importance of allowing the Holy Spirit to have his way with us, and we saw that the Scriptures are constantly exhorting us to do that. What we have in this particular verse is a very strong and graphic instance of that very teaching: 'Be not drunk with wine, wherein is excess; but be filled with the Spirit.' Now there are some preliminary remarks which we must make before we come to a detailed examination of this verse, and the first is to draw your attention to the setting. Here is a great statement which comes in that part of the epistle which is devoted to practicalities. The Apostle has dealt with the doctrine, and has now come to its application. He is dealing with details of conduct and behaviour and it is in the midst of such details that he introduces this sentence. In other words, he introduces this idea of being filled with the Spirit, not as some great doctrine standing apart on its own, but when he is dealing with ordinary life and living. Again, it rather suggests, does it not, that we must be very careful not to isolate this doctrine and put it in a compartment on its own. It is as we are living our ordinary lives that we realise this doctrine, this truth.

We notice also here the scriptural way of dealing with sins.

This verse comes in the midst of exhortations about what to drink and what not to drink, what to speak about, what is to interest and amuse us; exhortations about the duties of husbands towards their wives and wives towards their husbands – that is the context. Therefore we deduce that the scriptural way of dealing with all these problems is not so much to concentrate on the problems themselves, as to approach the whole of life in this positive way. We have been at pains to point out many times in the course of these studies on the question of sanctification that, surely, in the light of the Scriptures, any teaching must be wrong which concentrates primarily upon sins. Any holiness teaching or any doctrine of sanctification which begins by saying, 'Now about getting rid of that particular sin of yours,' is in itself starting in the wrong way. The scriptural method is positive; the way to deal with these things is to be filled with the Spirit.

There are many analogies which make it clear what I mean by that. For instance, there are two ways of facing the problem of physical disease or lack of health. You can deal with the infection, or whatever it is, directly, but the still better way, and the way which is increasingly used, is to concentrate on the positive concept of health. For far too long even medical science has been thinking in terms of diseases, but the better idea is to think in terms of health. Public health is rightly receiving more attention than it has ever done, for we should all be interested in being well, rather than in avoiding diseases. Now that is exactly what the Scripture does, because if you are, as Scripture enjoins, filled with the Spirit, then you will not be able to do these things, nor will you want to. The scriptural way of dealing with them is to clarify our thinking about these various sins, and it says: Can you not see that those things are incompatible with this great truth? The Apostle does exactly the same thing in his letter to the Galatians when he says, 'Walk in the Spirit, and ye shall not fulfil the lusts of the flesh' (Gal 5:16). If you want to avoid the pestilences and diseases that arise out of the swamps down in the valleys, the best thing to do is to walk to the top of the mountain. That is the way to look at it – the positive approach – being filled with the Spirit.

What, therefore, in detail and in practice, is the meaning of this exhortation, 'Be filled with the Spirit'? Very fortunately for us, the Apostle leads us into an understanding of his own exhortation by giving us an illustration: 'Be not drunk with wine wherein is excess, but be filled with the Spirit.' If we want to know what it means to be filled with the Spirit, let us make use of his own analogy. Here we would observe that this is not the only time that this analogy is used of the Spirit. On the Day of Pentecost, when the Holy Spirit descended upon the believers, the people in Jerusalem looked at them and said, 'These men are full of new wine' (Acts 2:13). The disciples behaved in a strange and unusual manner and the people jumped to the conclusion that they were drunk. But it was an explanation that was immediately dismissed by Peter. 'These,' he said, 'are not drunken, as ye suppose,' and then he went on to explain what had happened.

There is even, I think, the same suggestion in Luke 1:15 where the angel spoke to Zacharias about John the Baptist. There is at any rate an implied contrast between wine and strong drink on the one hand, and the Holy Spirit on the other, when Zacharias is told that his child who is to be born shall not partake of wine and strong drink, but shall be filled with the Holy Spirit. Thus it is obviously a helpful comparison.

What, then, does this suggest to us? Well, to be drunk with wine means that we are under its influence or control. To be drunk with wine means that our faculties, our mind, our feelings, our wills and our actions are all under another influence. This thing that the man has been drinking is now, as it were, controlling him; at least, that is the way in which we normally think of it. That is the illustration that Scripture itself uses in order to help us understand what it means to be filled with the Spirit.

But let me give you some other analogies which will suggest the same thing. For instance, we often speak about being 'full of life'. Or we say of certain people that at the moment they are really full of something. Someone maybe is proposing to take

a holiday in the summer in some foreign land, and we say he is
absolutely full of the idea. We mean by this that he is obviously
possessed by it; every time you meet him he talks about it – he
is full of it. Or we talk, in the same way, of being full of ideas,
full of interests or even full of a person; the idea is that we are
controlled by this interest or by this person, or whatever it may
happen to be; we are full of it, it is the thing that absorbs and controls us.

Now the words that were used by the Apostle really do convey all that. The exact definition of the words would be something like this: anything that wholly takes possession of the
mind, is said to 'fill the mind'; or, to put it another way: to be
filled with anything means that it takes possession of us. That
is what the Apostle tells us should be our relationship to the
Holy Spirit. To be filled with the Spirit means to be controlled
by him in that sense: we are filled with him and he controls our
thoughts and minds, our emotions, our feelings, our desires,
our words, our actions, our everything; it follows of necessity.

As you read the Scriptures and the examples and illustrations
which it gives of this very thing, you see that that is exactly what
is implied. We are told, for instance, of our Lord himself after
his baptism, and after the Holy Spirit had descended upon him,
that he, 'being full of the Holy Ghost returned from Jordan, and
was led by the Spirit into the wilderness, being forty days tempted of the devil' (Lk 4:1-2). He returned from the Jordan filled
with the Spirit, controlled and dominated by the Spirit for the
work that lay ahead of him. There are, of course, many other
examples of this. Take, for instance, what we are told of
Stephen: we read that he was full of faith and of the Holy Spirit.
We are told the same thing about Barnabas, that he was a good
man and full of the Holy Spirit and of faith. There are also
instances of Peter and Paul and other apostles, where we are told
that 'filled with the Spirit' they did certain things.

The whole idea must be thought of in that way, and perhaps
it is important that one should put it negatively at this point. Far
too often, it seems to me, we tend to think of being filled with
the Spirit in mechanical terms. The idea seems to be conjured up

in our minds of an empty vessel and of something being poured into it. I think if you examine yourself and your thoughts, you will find that instinctively you tend to think of being filled with the Spirit in that way. We regard the Spirit as a kind of power that is poured into us; we are some kind of empty vessel and when we become empty, this Spirit, this power, this influence is poured into us until we are full. But clearly that must be wrong, because the Holy Spirit is not an influence, nor a power. We must not think of him in terms of electricity or of steam, for the Holy Spirit is a Person; he is described everywhere in the Scriptures in a personal manner. So when we think of being filled with the Spirit what we really mean is that the blessed Person of the Holy Spirit is controlling us, dominating and influencing us. That is why in my analogy I talked about being full of a certain person. We see that in everyday psychology. When a man becomes interested in some special person he is absolutely full of that person. It does not mean that the person is poured into him, but it does mean that the person is controlling his thoughts, his desires, and his activities, dominating the whole of his life and especially his thoughts. He is thus under the influence of and is being mastered by that person. I think you will find it is a very great advantage to have that conception clear in your mind, because most of the excesses and errors into which people have fallen with regard to this doctrine of being filled with the Spirit are almost invariably due to the fact that they think of the Spirit as some force or power that can be injected or transfused into us, instead of thinking of him in terms of this relationship to the Person who has been given to us and who dwells with us. This will become clearer as we proceed.

Let me, therefore, put a second proposition. What exactly are the results of this filling of the Spirit? For as we look at that, we shall find it will clarify our ideas. How do we know whether we are really filled with the Spirit or not? Once more, we can do nothing better than follow the examples which are provided for us in the text: 'Be not drunk with wine, wherein is excess; but be filled with the Spirit.' We are clearly confronted here by a similarity and contrast and we must pay careful attention to both. There is, as we have seen, something comparable between the influence of wine and strong drink upon a person and the effect of being filled with the Spirit. The analogy would never have been used, it would never have entered the mind of the crowd on the Day of Pentecost at Jerusalem, unless that were so. There are certain respects in which the similarity is very striking.

So that leads us to ask the question: what is the effect of wine or strong drink upon a person? Here again I must say something for the sake of accuracy and carefulness. When the Scriptures use an analogy and an illustration like this, they are obviously not speaking in a strict scientific sense. Rather, they are using the description in the way in which these things are commonly regarded. I emphasise all this because unless I safeguard myself at this point it could be said that my view of the effect of alcohol upon the body is not scientific.

But having said that by way of a preface, my first observation is that the effect of alcohol upon a man is to stimulate him. Now I am well aware of the fact that pharmacologically that is not true. Pharmacologically, alcohol is not a stimulant but a depressant; there is no question about that at all. But if you look at a man who takes alcohol you get the impression that it is stimulating him, and people take it in excess because they think it is a stimulant – in a very odd way alcohol does seem to stimulate a person. The immediate effects of alcohol are, secondly, an enhancement of all the faculties; thirdly, joy; fourthly, fellowship. Now you see how, in interpreting the Scriptures we do expose ourselves to misunderstanding from small pedantic minds; it sounds as if I am advocating alcohol because of its effect.[1] In fact, I am simply pointing out to you that alcohol, whether we like it or not, does lead to those effects and it is for these reasons that people partake of it. The man who is nervous drinks, and he is a foolish man for doing so, but he does it because it does help him for the time being – it seems to

---

[1] Dr Lloyd-Jones did not himself drink alcohol.

enhance his faculties.

Furthermore, people drink when they want to be happy. They find life with its cares and problems very trying and depressing, so they take alcohol and it makes them feel happy. There is no question about it – they do, for a time, feel happy, but they fail to realise the terrible risk they are running of still more depression. They take it because it promotes an immediate sense of joy and fellowship; it is one of the most pathetic things of life at the present time that men and women are so unhappy and self-centred that the vast majority seem to find it impossible to have fellowship with others without the help of drink. They have to drink and drug themselves before they get on with one another! Drink, they say, makes them convivial, they are not convivial without it, and thereby they are attesting to the fact that one of the effects of alcohol is to give this sense of good fellowship.

Those, then, are in general the effects of wine or alcohol, and Scripture states this many times. The psalmist spoke about wine which 'maketh glad the heart of man' (Ps 104:15). So now we must take all this and apply it in terms of the work of the Holy Spirit upon us, when he is controlling us. Quite clearly, you cannot read the book of the Acts or the New Testament epistles without seeing that on the surface the analogy is very close. Here are some of the effects upon these disciples and apostles of being filled with the Spirit. First and foremost, they had a clearer understanding of truth. Look at it in the Gospels. There is the greatest teacher the world has ever known. He speaks the word to them, but they stumble at it, and cannot understand it. They do not know what it is all about. But then they are filled with the Spirit and they understand the Scriptures. Listen to Peter preaching on the Day of Pentecost; he expounded the Scriptures and he had a clear understanding of them. It was the Holy Spirit who enabled him to do it. His faculties had been enhanced, and he saw things clearly – the Holy Spirit always does that. Then the disciples also had great joy in the Scriptures, and, furthermore, they clearly had power to explain and preach the word of God and to deliver it. All this was the effect of the Holy Spirit, and as a result of that one sermon by Peter on the Day of Pentecost three thousand souls were converted. It was not Peter, but the Holy Spirit. The word went to the conscience of the hearers, it disturbed them and they were converted. They cried out, 'Men and brethren, what shall we do?' (Acts 2:37) – that is the power that the Holy Spirit gives to a man when he fills him. The man is above himself – you cannot explain him in terms of himself.

But did you notice, too, the boldness that it gave them? Alcohol seems to do that also, which is why it is wrong for a man who has been drinking to drive a car. He seems to have a daring and a boldness. This, again, is all wrong pharmacologically, but we are looking at it generally, and we can understand it, because a man under the influence of alcohol loses his nervousness. And we see the parallel in the New Testament. In Acts we see Peter, who a few days before had denied his Lord three times because he was afraid, now standing before a huge crowd in Jerusalem, and even when confronted by the Sanhedrin saying boldly, 'Whether it be right in the sight of God to hearken unto you more than unto God, judge ye. For we cannot but speak the things which we have seen and heard' (Acts 4:19-20). He had boldness in witness and in testimony, and was ready to suffer anything for the sake of his blessed Lord. Indeed, all the disciples had a boldness which they had never known before, desiring to witness and then witnessing. And then there was the remarkable joy that came into their lives, a joy that nothing could hinder or control. You see the closeness of the analogy? These men were rendered immune to circumstances. They were quite impervious to the things that were said of them, and done to them. There is that glorious example of Paul and Silas in the prison at Philippi, praying and singing praises to God, even though their feet were held fast in the stocks and their poor backs were sore from being scourged and lashed by the jailers. Later, Paul wrote to the Philippian converts, 'Rejoice in the Lord alway' (Phil 4:4). And this they did, even when they were thrown to the lions in the arena; they thanked God they had been counted worthy to suffer shame for his name's sake. It was a joy which was irrepressible, that nothing could quench, and it was all the result of being filled with the Spirit.

Then there was the fruit of the Spirit in their lives: love, joy, peace, longsuffering, meekness, and so on: as you look at these men and women and read about them, you can see those characteristics exemplified in their lives. For when people are filled with the Spirit they do show these things – they cannot help it. The Spirit is controlling them is the Spirit of love; they become like Christ himself, who was filled with the Spirit.

And then another great characteristic was a wonderful sense of thankfulness to the Lord, and a love of the Lord. Having received the enlightenment of the Spirit, they loved the Lord and were grateful to him. They could not do too much for him. The first thing Paul said to the Lord when he saw him on the road to Damascus was, ' Lord, what wilt thou have me to do?' because he knew this sense of thankfulness and of gratitude.

And the last thing I would note is their sense of true fellowship together, their love for one another, and the way in which they felt they belonged to one another. There was no stiffness among them. They did not stand on ceremony, neither did they hold themselves at a distance from one another lest they give themselves away. There was freedom and they mixed with one another, they sang together, they prayed together and they enjoyed one another's fellowship and society. There was no distinction of class or order, nor of wealth or poverty; in all these things they all became one. This amazing unity was present because they had come to see that they were all sinners; they were all equally failures in the sight of God, and all other distinctions were irrelevant and unimportant. They were all filled with the same Spirit; Jew and Gentile no longer existed since they were, now, all one in Christ, having access by one Spirit unto the Father.

Those, then, are some of the results of being filled with the Spirit, and you see how similar they are to the effects of alcohol, and the closeness of the analogy . But let me hurry to point out the contrast between the two. It is that the way of alcohol leads ultimately to an excess, which you can translate by the word riot, or lack of control, and finally to a moral wreckage. Paul's injunction is, 'Be not drunk with wine, wherein is excess' – this disorder and confusion – but, rather, 'be filled with the Spirit.' 'At first,' says the Apostle in effect, 'they seem alike, and yet how different they are!' When it is the work of the Holy Spirit, all these things that I have just been enumerating are under perfect control.

The Scripture is full of this. Did you notice how Paul immediately illustrates what he means by this difference? 'Be not drunk with wine, wherein is excess; but be filled with the Spirit ...' Then, still the same sentence, 'speaking to yourselves in psalms and hymns and spiritual songs, singing and making melody in your heart to the Lord; giving thanks always for all things unto God and the Father in the name of our Lord Jesus Christ.' That is the happiness produced by the Spirit. It is a holy happiness which expresses itself in that way. But then he goes on in verse 21 to put it like this: 'Submitting yourselves one to another in the fear of God' – there is no lack of control there. Wine produces lack of control, and some people's conception of being filled with the Spirit obviously suggests the same thing, but here there is control: submitting yourselves one to another in the fear of the Lord. You realise you are in the presence of God. Certainly, you are filled with joy, you are filled with the Spirit, but everything you do is in the fear of the Lord. Your joy is immense, and some people think that that means riot and confusion. Not at all! We are still in the presence of God, whom we must always approach with reverence and godly fear.

Let me give you some other examples and demonstrations of this truth. The classic passage on this subject is 1 Corinthians 14. It is there that Paul shows us clearly that to be filled with the Spirit means control. Take, for example, verse 14, where he is talking of speaking with tongues: 'For if I pray in an unknown tongue, my spirit prayeth, but my understanding is unfruitful'; and then in verse 15 he says, 'What is it then? I will pray with the spirit, and I will pray with the understanding also: I will sing with the spirit, and I will sing with the understanding also.' Verses 18 and 19 add: 'I thank my God, I speak with tongues more than ye all: yet in the church I had rather speak five words with my understanding, that by my voice I might teach others also, than ten thousand words in an unknown tongue.' He preferred to speak five words with his understanding than ten thousand words in an unknown tongue, in order that he might teach others also.

Then there is the famous exhortation, 'in understanding be men' (1 Cor 14:20), not children but adults, grown up, so that you have a true understanding. Next, Paul says quite categorically in verse 32, 'The spirits of the prophets are subject to the prophets.' I once met a man who could not control himself, he could not restrain himself from calling out in meetings. He was ruining services by his interjections, and of course he thought he was filled with the Spirit, and was appreciating truth. On my speaking and appealing to him he said, 'I cannot help it, I am filled with the Spirit. I am a prophet.' But then I pointed out to him that the Scripture says that the spirits of the prophets are subject to the prophets. Paul says that you must only speak one at a time, and if you see somebody else is giving a message you sit down, and, again, you do not speak in tongues unless there is someone to interpret. The Scriptures teach order. Indeed, Paul sums it up in verse 33 by saying, 'For God is not the author of confusion, but of peace, as in all churches of the saints.' He is always the author of peace and not of confusion.

Finally, he says in verse 40, 'Let all things be done decently and in order.' He is talking about public services and he visualises a stranger coming in and wanting to know what it is all about. The stranger will think you are all mad, says Paul, unless there is control and discipline. Certainly, be filled with the Spirit, but that does not mean you have lost control of yourselves. Rather, it means having a good understanding, this amazing control of the Spirit. As Paul again puts it in 2 Timothy 1:7, 'For God hath not given us the spirit of fear, but of power, and of love, and of a sound mind.' The Spirit is the Spirit of power and love and, at the same time, of control and discipline.

There, then, is what is meant in the Scriptures by being filled with the Spirit. I have tried to put the two sides, the positive and the negative. I have no doubt at all but that for many of us it is hardly necessary that I should emphasise the similarities and the contrasts, for there is not much danger of our giving way to excess and riot! Indeed, I fear our tendency is the exact opposite. Are we filled with the Spirit? Have we got this clear understanding? Do we know anything about this joy? Do we know anything about a holy boldness? Do we *really* know the fellowship? That is the question! These are always the results of being filled with the Spirit. Is there a deep sense of thankfulness to God and Christ in our hearts? These are the manifestations of the Spirit, and the proofs of our being filled with the Spirit.

Let us examine ourselves, my friends. Merely to be decent and controlled, does not mean being filled with the Spirit – all these aspects of the Spirit have to be taken together, for there is a kind of polarity about them. The Christian is the man who seems to be always walking on a knife edge: there is ever the danger of excess, yet he does not give way to it, because he is controlled. It is this perfect balance. He is controlled by the Holy Spirit. It was the Spirit who brought order into chaos in the world at the beginning and he has always been the Spirit of order, but the two things must go together. There is a difference between order and lack of life; there is no disorder among the dead. But the truth before us is the order of the living. It is control of power, fear of God and a sound mind.

So I trust that we shall start examining ourselves and asking if there is something about us that at first might lead men to think that perhaps we are under the influence of wine. Is there something exalted and free; is there a sense of power; is there a sense of knowledge; is there a sense of almost being possessed; is there something about us that makes people feel we are not ordinary people? That is always true of those who are filled with the Spirit. They do not have to drag themselves wearily to God's house, nor do they have to force themselves to try to be Christian, and to behave as such. No, they are controlled by the Holy Spirit.

Those are the characteristics, the manifestations, and the results of being filled with the Spirit. Oh that we were all such people! Oh that the first reaction of anybody meeting us, the first thing they sensed, was something unusual, some strange power, some strange peace and joy and equanimity, the fruit of the Spirit, something suggesting the Lord Jesus Christ himself! 'Be not drunk with wine, wherein is excess; but be filled with the Spirit.'

8

Controlled by the Spirit

And be not drunk with wine, wherein is excess; but be filled with the Spirit (Ephesians 5:18).

We have been considering together Paul's injunction to us to be filled with the Spirit, and so obviously the great question for us to consider is how this can be true of us. How are we to become the kind of person delineated in the New Testament – rejoicing in Christ Jesus, filled with love and joy and peace and all these other manifestations of the gracious work of the Spirit? In order to consider that, we come back again to this verse in Ephesians, and there are a number of preliminary points to which I must call your attention. In the first place, we notice that this is a command: 'Be not drunk with wine, wherein is excess; but *be filled* with the Spirit,' and then, secondly, we see that it is a continuous command. It really means *'go on* being filled' with the Spirit. Paul does not tell us to be filled with the Spirit once, and from then on to live on this great gift we have received. Rather, the command is that we should be constantly filled with the Spirit, it is a continuous performance. And the last general point I would make in this connection is that the verb is in the passive – it says, 'go on *being* filled'. It does not say, 'go on filling yourselves with the Spirit', because that is patently something we cannot do. Now that is important. It is a reminder again that the Holy Spirit is a Person; so that we cannot, as it were, fill ourselves with the Holy Spirit whenever we like. But what we can do is allow the

Holy Spirit to fill us – we can go on being filled with him; it is a command, a continuous command, and in the passive.

Now there is a good deal of confusion in people's minds with respect to the way in which we can reconcile these two – the command and the passive element. There are two main schools of thought with regard to this, as there generally are with regard to all these matters. They both take their case to different extremes, whereas scriptural teaching combines the two. As I have just said, it seems to me that the only way of holding these two ideas comfortably in our minds at one and the same time is to take a firm hold of the fact that the Holy Spirit is a Person. We must therefore, as we have seen, cease to think in terms of some power, like electricity, or some liquid being poured into us, like some kind of force or energy. Rather, because the Holy Spirit is a Person, then the essence of being filled with the Spirit is that our lives should be consciously controlled by him.

What exactly, therefore, does this involve? 'That,' someone may say, 'is what I desire above everything else, but how does it happen? What do I have to do?' Let us start again with the negative: there is no teaching in the Scriptures that tells us that what we have to do is wait or agonise in prayer for this to happen to us. Nor must we allow ourselves to go into a state of complete passivity, neither in the form known as 'tarrying' nor in any other form. There are some people who do not teach the tarrying, but who do teach complete passivity. They would say that if we want to be filled with the Spirit we must just cease from action altogether and even from thinking; and that the whole art in this matter is the art of abandonment, of resignation, an attempt, as it were, to annihilate our very personalities and to surrender ourselves in that complete sense.

But here, again, I suggest that that is a teaching which cannot be substantiated from the New Testament. If that teaching were true, then we would find that all Christians were identical and there would be no manifestations of individuality and personality whatsoever in any teacher or preacher. That, however, is clearly not the case; the apostle Paul retained his essential personality, so did the apostle Peter. People have fallen into the same error with regard to the inspiration of the Scriptures, but here again, personality remains, and the styles of writing of the apostle Peter and the apostle John are entirely different, although the message is the same and it is all perfectly controlled by the Holy Spirit. Thus, it is surely obvious that to be filled with the Spirit does not mean a kind of mechanical passivity, with a man's personality going out of action – it is something much more wonderful than that. It means, rather, that though the man's personality is still there it is entirely controlled by the Holy Spirit – that is the principle.

Perhaps the best way I can put this to you is to put it in terms of the supreme example of it, and that is none other than the Lord Jesus Christ himself. I wonder whether we have grasped this as we should? It is indeed one of the most astounding things in the Scriptures – it is certainly the essence of understanding the Incarnation and all that followed. We are told two things about the Lord Jesus Christ which on the surface seem to be quite incompatible. Firstly, we are told that he is very God of very God. While he lived here on earth, he was still the eternal Son of God, not in any way shorn of any of the powers that were his in heaven. He did not divest himself of his godhead; he was still God in the fullest sense conceivable. Yet we are told about him that he was baptised with the Holy Spirit, that the Holy Spirit descended upon him, and John tells us that 'God giveth not the Spirit by measure unto him' (Jn 3:34). We are also told that he was filled with the Spirit and led of the Spirit. Indeed, he himself says things like this – he, the very eternal Son of God, co-equal, co-eternal with God but undiminished in his power, he says, 'As my Father hath taught me, I speak these things' (Jn 8:28). He says that all his words and all his works are given to him by his Father. He is told what to say, and he is told what to do. He says, 'I seek not mine own will, but the will of the Father which hath sent me' (Jn 5:30).

How do we understand all this? How do we reconcile these statements with one another? Surely the answer must be that the Lord Jesus Christ, the eternal Son of God, having taken unto himself human nature and having appeared, therefore, in 'the likeness of sinful flesh' as a man, deliberately took upon himself the form of a servant, and subjected himself and his own personality to the leading and the guidance of the Spirit. He did not do away with his personality, nor even with his gifts, but he chose, for the sake of our salvation, to humble himself in that way. He did not exercise his own will, nor did he depend upon his own power, in order to achieve our redemption, but lived life as a man. So, while all these powers and faculties and propensities were there, he did not exercise them, but was dependent and subservient to the Father and the Holy Spirit. Thus we find ourselves confronted by the whole marvel and miracle of the Incarnation and his life here upon earth – that he, who had created all things and by whom all things consist, seemed to be entirely dependent, weak and helpless. The explanation is that he willed all this, quite deliberately. He submitted himself to this control and leading.

When you and I are exhorted and commanded to be filled with the Spirit it means exactly the same thing. We are to do, in turn, what the Son of God did when he was here on earth. We are to realise that the Holy Spirit is within us, and we are to realise what his desire is with respect to us. We put that earlier in terms of James 4:5, 'that the spirit' that God has caused to dwell within us 'lusteth to envy' for our sanctification – the 'flesh lusteth against the Spirit, and the Spirit against the flesh' (Gal 5:17). His supreme desire is that we may be sanctified and holy, that we may really be separated from the world, and unto God. We must realise that and submit to him, allowing him to do his work within us. We must know something of his great power within us, that he is working within us 'both to will and to do of his good pleasure'. Therefore, that is obviously the essential principle in this matter. We must submit ourselves to his control in all things, and that is the essence of this command to be filled with the Spirit.

But I know that having said that I am still leaving large numbers of people in difficulty with regard to how exactly these two things can be put together. How can I, living my life in the flesh, manifest the personality which God has given me, and yet at the same time be subservient to the power of the Holy Spirit and be led and controlled by him? What exactly is our relationship to the Spirit? At this point people generally use illustrations and there is no doubt that a picture or analogy can be of value. Yet I think we must always be very careful with illustrations. If I venture to put one to you now, in order to make this point clear, I realise that I am doing something that is attended by considerable risk; for no one illustration can convey the whole truth, though different illustrations may perhaps represent different aspects of the matter. There are two illustrations that are very frequently used which seem to me to be quite wrong and utterly misleading. The first illustration which is used is this. Imagine a man in the sea or in a pool of water. 'Now,' it is said, 'the body of that man has a tendency to sink and will probably do so, for that is the natural thing to do – to go down. But,' they continue, 'if that man puts a lifebelt on he will no longer sink, because the lifebelt holds him up.' So, according to that illustration, our Lord, through the Holy Spirit, is, as it were, a kind of lifebelt that keeps us from sinking. That, therefore, is the way not to sin and to be sanctified and to live the holy life: you abide in Christ, you put on the lifebelt and the lifebelt will hold you up. But the difficulty with that illustration, it seems to me, is that it suggests utter passivity: all you do is don your lifebelt; indeed, they go so far as to say that the moment you are out of the lifebelt, down you go.

Then another illustration used by the same people is the famous illustration about the poker. The poker is black and cold and rigid, but if you take it and put it into a fire it will become hot and you will be able to bend it. While it remains in the fire it is red hot, but the moment you take it out it becomes cold and black and rigid again. So the only thing you have to do is to see that the poker is kept in the fire, because while it is there, the fire will do all these things to it and for it. Once again, I suggest that that is a representation of pure passivity and for this reason those two illustrations have never commended themselves to me. So I would venture to put to you some other pictures. I remind you again that I am well aware of the defects of all illustrations, but

I am trying to take spiritual teaching a little further and it seems to me that a figure like this surely does help at this point.

Imagine a man starting up a business – it does not matter what sort, take a grocer's, if you like. There is the man, working in that business, weighing up his pounds of sugar and doing the things that have to be done. He is, of course, doing his best, working as hard as he can, because the harder he works the more business he gets, and his bank balance is going to show the result. However, for various reasons this man decides to sell this one-man owned business to a company, to a chain store. But a part of the agreement is that he should stay on in the same shop as manager. The position now is that that man, in the self-same shop, should be doing exactly what he did before. He should be equally careful, equally zealous, equally polite, equally anxious to attract business, equally careful in his weighing. Yet there is this obvious difference – he is no longer doing it for himself, and at the back of it all he is being controlled by another power who can step in at any time and suggest various things to him. Beforehand, he decided everything, now he is subservient to another authority, to which he submits. He does all he can, he is not passive, he is going on as he was before and yet he is being controlled. The control of the business, its ultimate prosperity, success and profit are not in his hands. As a result, at one and the same time, the man's individuality and personality are preserved absolutely and yet he is being controlled by this company, by this higher power.

That is one illustration, and yet it seems to me that there is a difficulty about it which I must correct by giving you another. It does not represent the power that works *within* us. It deals with the question of control, and of the relationship of wills, but it does not show that over and above the Holy Spirit is within us, working within us both to will and to do. This is the ultimate guarantee of our being sanctified and living the holy life.

So I must take a second illustration, which is perhaps a little more difficult and involved. Yet it is very helpful to me personally, and so I want to suggest it to you. Let us try to look at this in terms of a man who is subject to seasickness, sailing on a boat.

Now this man's desire is to avoid being seasick. There is one method that is advocated for dealing with this which, from the standpoint of physiology, is very sound, and which has the advantage of being successful in practice, and it is this. The man is told first and foremost to stand as far forward as he can upon the ship. Then he is told that at all costs he must not look at the waves, nor at the side of the ship nor immediately in front of him. Even though everything within him wants to do this, it is the one thing he must not do; instead, he must look at the horizon in the far distance. Not only must he avert his gaze from the waves, he must also look at the horizon, and, furthermore, he must deliberately try not to balance himself, he must relax completely.

Now the reason why the man is told to do this is that there is a mechanism in our bodies, in what is called the inner ear, which is especially put there by God to keep us in a balanced condition; a wonderful little mechanism called the semi-circular canals. This mechanism is most intricate, but as long as we can relax, it will work. We must avoid doing anything that makes us think about it, in order to give these semi-circular canals a chance to do the work which they have been put into our body to do. We must also avoid the things that makes us feel sick, but though we may keep all these rules about diet, yet if we still keep looking at the waves we will probably be ill. So we keep all those rules, we avoid looking at the waves, and trying to balance ourselves, and holding ourselves rigid. We let these semi-circular canals in our body do their work, and if we do this we will find that we will not suffer from seasickness.

There, it seems to me, we have a very helpful analogy. You have perhaps been told by sailors and others that for the first few days at sea they are generally seasick but, they say, it passes and they are all right again. What happens is that unconsciously they get into the way of doing all the things which I have been describing to you. We talk about 'the rolling gait' of the typical sailor; it is because he has got into the habit of rolling backwards and forwards with the ship. He is allowing the mechanism of the body to maintain his balance. Now for all its imperfections,

I suggest to you that this illustration again points to something that is being taught by the Scriptures. The Holy Spirit is in us. He is there to do this work, so we must let him do it. But it is not a complete passivity on our part because there is a great deal which we have to do. Even though the Holy Spirit is in us, if we keep looking at the world and its enticements and attractions, we will go down. So what we must do is realise God's provision for us in this respect and co-operate with him. We must work with the Spirit, and as long as we are working with the Spirit, and carrying out these instructions, we shall not be fulfilling the lusts of the flesh.

Those, then, are two pictures which I have offered for your consideration in order to illustrate certain things which are stated so clearly in the Scriptures. Listen, for instance, to the apostle Paul. When dealing with this subject he almost seems to be contradicting himself, but there is no contradiction if you remember the principle – 'I can do all things through Christ which strengtheneth me' (Phil 4:13). You see the apparent contradiction? There was once an old-style preacher, who kept on saying over and over again, 'I can do all things ...' Then he put a question to the Apostle and said, 'Paul, do you mean to say you can do this and that?'

'Yes,' said Paul, 'I can do it.'

So the preacher came to the conclusion that Paul was a great egoist who was always boasting, and he was very doubtful whether Paul really could do all the things of which he boasted. But Paul kept on saying, 'I can do all things' – and then he went on to say, 'I can do all things *through Christ which strengtheneth me.*'

'I beg your pardon,' said the old preacher, 'I did not realise there were two of you!'

That is so characteristic of the Scriptures. I can indeed do all things. I am the one who does them, but in a sense I am only doing them because of this higher control. I can do all things through Christ who strengthens me, by means of the power which he is giving me through his Holy Spirit. I cannot do them alone, but I do them because of the way in which he enables me to do them. I am not passive, but active, as we see also in Galatians 2:20. Notice how Paul goes on, each thing seeming to contradict the one before, but there is no contradiction at all. What Paul is saying, in effect, is this: 'I am no longer living for myself; I am now submitting myself to and am controlled by the Holy Spirit. I am doing this deliberately, I am subjecting myself.' How zealous he was! He worked harder than any other preacher, 'more than them all', as he constantly says, and yet he is not boasting because it is all being done after, and according to, the life of the Spirit.

But perhaps the final example of this is the one which we find running through the Old Testament. The whole trouble with the children of Israel was that they failed to realise this particular principle which we are considering together. That is what God keeps on saying to them: 'Why do you not listen to me? You do not realise who you are and what you are! They constantly failed to realise that they were God's people. They forgot that if they would but realise that, if they would only keep in the right relationship to him, they would have nothing to worry about at all. Look at the amazing way in which God routed their enemies. He had promised to do that and he used the children of Israel to accomplish it, but they kept on forgetting, and kept comparing themselves with the other nations. 'We must have a king,' they said, 'because the other nations have one.' They could not trust God, so they had a human, earthly king. And then they saw other nations making alliances in order to defend their territories, and they said that they must do the same; so they made alliances with the Syrians and others. Then they said that others were using horses, so they must use them too. All along, their trouble was due to the fact that they did not realise who they were, what God's promises were and the power of his might.

'Let me be your rear-guard,' says God in effect. 'Let me be your horsemen and your horses and your chariots. I can be, I will be – trust me, co-operate with me. Do all that you are doing by my power and by my strength. Let me work in you and through you.'

It was because they constantly failed to realise that teaching that they went so frequently and so sadly astray.

So there we have what, it seems to me, is the essential principle in this great matter – this relationship between myself and the Spirit, my will and his will; how at one and the same time I can say that I do something and yet that he does it. Think of it supremely in terms of our Lord himself and the way he lived his life as a man here in this world, dependent upon the Father for words, for works, for everything. And you and I are to realise that God has put his Spirit within us. We must listen to him and be attracted to him and be controlled by him and work with him as he enables us. Again, we must turn to Paul's great statement in Philippians: 'Work out your own salvation with fear and trembling. For it is God which worketh in you both to will and to do of his good pleasure.'

There is the principle, and having laid that down, we are now in a position to proceed to the practical instructions that are given. If all this is true in essence, this is what I must remember: I must never grieve the Spirit, and, positively, I must walk in the Spirit.

9

The Temple of the Holy Spirit

Walk in the Spirit, and ye shall not fulfil the lust of the flesh (Galatians 5:16).

And grieve not the holy Spirit of God (Ephesians 4:30).

We are in the process of considering what is meant by the command, 'Be filled with the Spirit.' Having seen that it means to be controlled by the Person of the Spirit, who is at work in all Christians, we tried, in chapter 8, to rid our minds of the confusion which so often exists in the matter of how we reconcile our wills with the will of the Spirit. We saw that we can easily slip into a false passivity and fail to give due weight to the various exhortations of the Bible. Now clearly the Scriptures do not tell us that we have nothing to do, indeed they address many negative injunctions to us. The Apostle tells the Ephesians, for instance, that they are not to steal any longer, that no corrupt communication is to proceed out of their mouth, that they are to cleanse themselves from all filthiness of the flesh and of the mind, and that they are to avoid fornication and all uncleanness or covetousness, or foolish talking and jesting. All these things we are told to refrain from; but at the same time the Scriptures teach that we are to work out our own salvation with fear and trembling because God works in us, and we illustrated this by a number of analogies.

So, having considered this in general, let us now round off

this matter by coming down to a more practical aspect; because it is not enough merely to grasp the principles, we must know something of what this means in detail – how am I to be filled with the Spirit? We have already got rid of the idea of just being filled in the sense that a vessel is filled by liquid being poured into it. As we saw, it is not merely receiving a force, or a power, or energy, but rather a question of being controlled and led by this Person, the Holy Spirit. That is the key to the understanding of the practical aspect of this matter, and I suggested, at the end of the last study, that we must bear in mind the two main things which are taught in the Scriptures themselves. The first is that there are certain things which we must avoid. Now the Bible is very careful to call our attention to this. Three different terms are used in this connection. First, we are told that when Stephen preached to the people, he said, 'You do always resist the Holy Ghost ...' (Acts 7:51). Then you find in 1 Thessalonians 5:19 the injunction: 'Quench not the Spirit'; and, thirdly, in Ephesians 4:30 Paul says, 'Grieve not the holy Spirit of God.'

Those are the three great negative injunctions with regard to this matter, but it seems to me that for practical purposes the only one we need to concern ourselves with is the third. The first about 'resisting' the Spirit was addressed to unbelievers, and I think that it is a term that is always more applicable to an unbeliever than it is to a believer. The one who resists the operation of the Spirit is the unbeliever, and I would say that a believer cannot resist the Holy Spirit in that sense. Then the second term about 'quenching' the Spirit has reference not so much to the individual and his not being filled with the Spirit, but rather to the conduct of public services. If you read the context in 1 Thessalonians 5, you will find that it has reference to what Christian people do to other Christians. Its whole context concerns prophecy and manifesting the various gifts of the Spirit, and the Christians in Thessalonica are exhorted not to quench the Spirit in his operations and manifestations in a public service in the church of God. So, strictly speaking, I think it is wrong to appropriate that term about quenching the Spirit to this whole matter of Christians individually being filled with the

Spirit, although, of course, there is a sense in which it does come in.

But the third injunction really includes everything. So that if we are thinking of being filled with the Spirit, the negative term that we must bear in mind is that we are exhorted not to grieve him. Now Paul puts that statement right in the midst of a great ethical exhortation to the Ephesians: 'Let no corrupt communication proceed out of your mouth, but that which is good to the use of edifying, that it may minister grace unto the hearers. And grieve not the holy Spirit of God, whereby ye are sealed unto the day of redemption.' Then immediately – 'Let all bitterness and wrath, and anger, and clamour, and evil speaking, be put away from you, with all malice: and be ye kind one to another, tenderhearted, forgiving one another, even as God for Christ's sake hath forgiven you.'

What, then, does this mean in practice? How are we to avoid grieving the Spirit? Now the very terms, it seems to me, suggest the answer. Take the very word 'grieve', for instance, a word which at once conveys to us the sensitive character of the Spirit. He is compared to a dove and he came more than once in the semblance of a dove, suggesting again his gentle, sensitive character. The Holy Spirit, if one may speak with reverence, never forces himself upon us. He is a Person and one who has those particular characteristics. If, therefore, we are anxious to be filled with the Spirit – which means being controlled and directed by him – then obviously the first thing which we must bear in mind is that in view of his character we must be careful not to grieve or offend him in any way. Still more, we must remember what his object is and what his desires are. We must never lose sight of the fact that the Holy Spirit is primarily concerned about our sanctification. He is in us, and, as James reminds us, he is 'lusting even unto envy' for our sanctification. He wants to draw us from the world and to separate us unto God. He is working in us to do that. Therefore, if we want him to have his way, we must be very careful not to grieve him.

How, then, do we grieve him? I am coming right down to the practical aspects of this question because every single item is of extreme importance. This will not be an exhaustive list, but here are some of the most important aspects of the matter. We grieve the Spirit, first of all, by forgetting him altogether and entirely ignoring his existence. Here we are confronted by the extraordinary fact that through Christ God has given us the gift of the Spirit. When our Lord had finished his work on earth, when he had gone through death and had borne our sins, when he had vanquished death and the grave, and had ascended to heaven and there taken his seat at the right hand of God, in view of all that he had done, God gave him the gift of the Spirit to give to his people and he has given us that gift. Yet we are so often entirely oblivious of that fact. We do not realise it, we do not stop to consider it. We fail to realise as we should the fact that the Holy Spirit is within us.

Now some of those members of the church at Corinth, to whom we have already referred, those people who had believed that Christ had died for them, clearly did not realise that they were guilty of sins; and Paul says to them, 'Know ye not that your bodies are the temples of the Holy Spirit which is in you?' (1 Cor 6:19). You are grieving him, acting and behaving as if this were not a fact, says Paul, and that is why you are in trouble. There is nothing more insulting to a person than to forget or ignore him. To pretend that you have not seen people is the supreme way of insulting them. You are walking along the street and you do not want to see someone, so you just pass him or her by – you cannot insult anybody more than by behaving like that. And yet, my friends, is not that the way we all of us tend to treat the Holy Spirit? To forget him for a moment is to grieve and insult him, and we are called upon to avoid doing this above everything else. The thing is unthinkable, and yet how frequently we behave in that way. Whatever you and I may do, the Holy Spirit is within us and he knows it all. He who is the guest within us is with us in every action and every thought, and nothing is more terrible than to forget and ignore him entirely.

Next, we ignore the Spirit by neglecting his word. The Bible, the word of God, is the work of the Holy Spirit – we have agreed about that. It is his book, written not merely by men, but by men who were inspired and moved, borne and carried along, by the Holy Spirit: 'Holy men spake as they were moved by the Holy Ghost' (2 Pet 1:21). The Bible is the special work of the Holy Spirit. He is really the author of the book, and he has given it to us in order that we may learn what to avoid and what to do: so that we may be sanctified – 'Sanctify them through thy truth: thy word is truth.' Thus, if there is one thing of which we can always be absolutely certain, it is that the Holy Spirit is always guiding us to this book. It is his way of leading and directing us. He does not only lead us directly, but indirectly also, and particularly through this word. Obviously, therefore, we are grieving the Spirit if we do not study the Bible as he means us to, if we are not regular in our reading of it, or if we do not grow in our knowledge of it. Now there are many people in that position. You will often find it in discussions. You talk about a certain subject and ask how a certain problem can be solved, and you find that there are large numbers of people who regard themselves as entirely scriptural and yet say that they pray to the Spirit to guide them. But that should be quite unnecessary, because if they went to the Bible, they would find the answer to their question! It is not honouring him to ignore the word and to go directly to him, because he has already given us the answer there. The Bible is the word of the Spirit and he works in it and through it. Indeed, there are some who would say he only guides us in that way, but that, I think, is going too far. However, I would go so far as to say that his normal way of working is to guide and direct us through the word.

Once more I would commend to you a study of this matter as it is to be found in the history of the Puritans of the seventeenth century; such a study is most instructive. The great division that took place within the Puritan movement, with the Quakers on the one side, and men like Dr John Owen on the other, was on this very subject. The tendency of the Quaker was to say that he did not need the word but that the Spirit did everything for him in the 'inner light', by operating directly upon his mind. So they tended to depreciate the word, which is clearly wrong. But we must not go as far as the Puritans went and say it is the *only* way. The true balance is to realise that this is the *normal* way. Thank God that that is so, because if we are without the word because of circumstances, the Spirit can deal with us directly and he does so.

The next way we should avoid grieving the Spirit is that we must never be in any doubt or unbelief concerning the purposes and the desires of the Holy Spirit within us; and still less must we ever doubt his ability to help us. I take it that we all know what I mean by that. It is one thing to believe these things theoretically, it is quite another to believe them in actual practice. Do we really rely upon the power of the Spirit within us, or do we doubt it? Do we still harbour a certain amount of unbelief? Are we all perfectly certain that God has given us his Spirit, in order that his great purpose of sanctification in us may be brought to pass? Are we quite sure that the power of the Spirit is really sufficient and that it matters not at all what the problem is, nor how powerful the enemy, for the Spirit that is in us is greater than that which is in them? The apostle John says to his young followers, You need not be afraid. I know all about the world, the flesh and the devil. I know its subtlety, but I assure you, 'Greater is he that is in you, than he that is in the world' (1 Jn 4:4). The power that is in us is greater, and let us never forget it. We must be grieving the Holy Spirit terribly when we doubt his sufficiency. Furthermore – I am going to say something now that can be misunderstood, but it is the teaching of the Scriptures – as Christians, we must not be afraid of ourselves. That does not mean we are self-confident; because self-confidence is not a fruit of the Spirit. But we are told not to be frightened of the devil in the sense of being afraid of temptations. Rather, we are told to resist him in the faith. I must have this element of confidence in the ability and the power of the Holy Spirit within me.

But that leads me on to another terrible way of grieving the Spirit, and I can sum it up in one word: 'self'. I suppose this is the way in which we grieve him most of all – when we elevate self in the place of the Spirit. I cannot think of a better way of illustrating this than to go back again to what I have reminded you concerning our Lord in his earthly life. Paul puts it in that great sentence: 'Let this mind be in you, which was also in Christ Jesus' (Phil 2:5). What sort of a mind was that? We are told that he was one who 'made himself of no reputation' (v. 7). In other words, he did not think of himself, but submitted himself. He always submitted to the will of his Father, to the will of the Spirit, and you and I are to do the same. Self-will in a Christian means grieving the Spirit. He wants us to submit our wills to his, to co-operate with him and to be led by him. Not that we become passive machines but, rather, we put our wills into his, and, having submitted ourselves, we then exercise our wills because they now conform to his. My illustration of the man in business applies here again. He is working as hard as he can, yes, but for a new management, not for himself. So any manifestation of self is grieving to the Spirit. If I want my way, my rights, my will, if I am sensitive about myself and my reputation, I must be grieving the Spirit, for all manifestations of self are grieving to him.

Then I go on to the next point, which is sin in all forms. It does not matter what form it takes – thoughts, imaginations, desires, lusts, passions and all wrong actions – sin is always grieving to the Spirit. We can sum this up by saying that anything which is not Christian, or which is opposed to the fruit of the Spirit, is a grief to the Spirit. Paul has put it so clearly in Galatians 5, in his contrast between the works of the flesh, and the fruit of the Spirit. Anything, in any shape or form, that belongs to the category of the works of the flesh is grieving to the Spirit – 'the flesh lusteth against the Spirit, and the Spirit against the flesh'(Gal 5:17). He is sensitive, tender and gentle, and if you and I could only begin to think of sins in terms of grieving the Spirit, I am sure we would sin much less than we do. As I have often said, the mistake we all make is to think of a particular sin as 'a sin', whereas we should be thinking of it as something that is incompatible with the Spirit within us. It is not so much a matter of doing wrong, as of hurting a Person, and once we begin to think of it in that way, we are 75% on the way to victory over it.

The next thing I would emphasise is that any hesitation about doing the will of the Spirit is obviously very grieving to him. You know what I mean. The Spirit enlightens our conscience, so that when we are tempted we know exactly that any hesitation about doing the will of the Spirit is a source of grief to him. Or, to take it positively, if he has indicated through his word, or in some other way, that you and I are to do something, and we do not want to do it because it hurts our pride or our flesh or our self-esteem, and we hesitate because we want to do something else instead, can anything be more grieving than that? Can anything be more insulting than to question what is clearly the will of the Spirit? We grieve him by so doing.

But let us now consider two final points, to which I attach very great significance. Surely, to be more interested in the power of the Spirit, or in the experiences and gifts which are given by the Spirit than in the Spirit himself, is to grieve and to insult him? I do not think that that needs any elaboration, since obvious illustrations come to the mind. You can never insult people more than by giving them the impression that you are not really interested in them but merely in what they can do for you. Is there anything more hurtful than to feel that we, as people, are not wanted for ourselves, but only for what we can provide? Yet we can very easily drop into that condition with regard to the Holy Spirit. If we desire experiences and gifts and manifestations rather than the Spirit himself, we are insulting him. Oh, how often we are guilty of that! We are anxious for power in preaching, power in our lives, anxious to be able to show certain spectacular things in our experience, but in the meantime the Spirit himself is forgotten, and so we are guilty, oftentimes, of grieving the sensitive, holy, delicate Spirit of God.

But, lastly, I will put it like this: what is the supreme ambition of the Holy Spirit? There can be no doubt of that, we have it so clearly in the Scriptures. The supreme desire and object and ambition of the Holy Spirit is to reveal, to manifest and to glorify, the Lord Jesus Christ. 'He shall not speak of himself ... he shall glorify me,' says Christ (1 Jn 16:13–14), and he has come in order to do that. His supreme work, as we have seen, is to make the Lord Jesus Christ real to us. Therefore, my friends, if we are interested in anything other than a more intimate knowledge of the Lord Jesus Christ, we are grieving the Spirit. The supreme ambition and object of the Christian should be to know Christ, and how often we forget that, because we are interested in these other things. The peculiar temptation of any preacher is to want power in his preaching, and yet his supreme ambition should not be to become a powerful preacher, but to know the Lord Jesus Christ so intimately that, like the nineteenth-century American missionary George Bowen, he should be able to stand before a congregation of people, and say that the Lord Jesus Christ is more real to him spiritually 'than you people who are sitting on those seats in front of me'. That is it! Of course we need gifts, and power, and victory, of course we need power in preaching, but all those things are means to an end. The supreme desire should be 'that I may know him and the power of his resurrection, and the fellowship of his sufferings' (Phil 3:10). What we need to know about each other is not what gifts we have, nor what experiences we get, but how well we know the Lord Jesus Christ. How real is he to us? How intimate are we with him? How deep is our personal consciousness of his presence? That is the supreme test of the fullness of the Spirit.

We now turn from the negative aspect, which I have emphasised because it is so important on the practical level. Let me give you some headings on the positive side. For if I do all that to avoid grieving the Spirit, what do I do positively? Again, the directions are simple: I must walk in the Spirit, I must be led by the Spirit. That is how Paul puts it to us in Galatians 5:16: 'Walk in the Spirit, and ye shall not fulfil the lust of the flesh'; and again he says in verse 25: 'If we live in the Spirit, let us also walk in the Spirit.' The other term is 'being led by the Spirit' which means exactly the same thing. How, then, am I to walk in the Spirit? And the answer to that really does come down to two things. If I want to be filled with the Spirit I need not go to tarrying meetings and agonise and fast. No – what I have to do is to realise that he is within me. I must not grieve him, and I must walk in the Spirit and be led by him.

Now, obviously, this means avoiding everything which we have already been considering together, but I do not want to leave it negatively, I want to put it positively as well. Walking in the Spirit means, first of all, that once again I must always remember that the Holy Spirit is a Person, and I must always recognise the fact that this Person is within me. I have ventured in earlier studies to put a simple rule for life to you in this way: it is a very good thing for Christians, the moment they wake up in the morning, to say to themselves, 'I am a child of God'; but I will give you another way of saying that: 'If the Holy Spirit is within me, my body is the temple of the Holy Spirit; I have this gracious guest within me. Wherever I am today, and whatever I may be doing, the Holy Spirit will be with me. I am not alone, I do not live an isolated life. There is nothing that I can do or that can happen to me but that the Holy Spirit is a sharer in it.' If we but walked with that realisation uppermost in our minds, it would transform everything. That is why we must not commit these sins, says Paul, because of the fact that we have this 'gracious, willing guest' within us. Let us concentrate on this, let us take time to do this, especially first thing in the morning, before the world, the flesh and the devil get in. We have to do this because it will not be done for us. We have seen that we must 'take time to be holy', and that is the first thing we must do: remind ourselves that he is within us and that he is a holy Person.

Then the next thing is that we must deliberately desire to be controlled by him. You say to yourself, 'Well, I know from past experience how easy it is to be controlled by my flesh, and by the world. Therefore I desire that this day I am going to be controlled by the Spirit.' For if you do not do that, you will find that before you have gone many minutes into the day, the flesh will be controlling you. You will become irritable with yourself or with somebody else, and the Holy Spirit is being grieved. So we have deliberately to submit ourselves to him and his control. The moment you read that newspaper the world will take control of you unless you are already being controlled by the Holy

Spirit. If your life and flesh determine what you read in the newspaper, it is quite certain that you will go down and you will suffer for it, but if the Spirit is really controlling you, you will not read much of it, nor will you waste much of your time with it, because it is something outside and it has nothing to do with the spiritual life.

The next thing, therefore, is to trust him and to rely upon his work and power within us. This, again, is a deliberate action of our wills. It is not enough to believe in theory that the Holy Spirit is going to use and control me, I have to rely upon that fact, and in all I do and say I must be conscious of the fact that the Holy Spirit is empowering me. If I have submitted myself to him, he will enable me. He it is who enhances my will and power and I must remind myself of that.

I can give you a simple illustration to prove what I mean. Any man who preaches the gospel must start by saying to himself, 'I can never convert anybody, no man can convert another. If men and women are spiritually dead in trespasses and sins, I cannot convert them by preaching, by eloquence, by argument, by logic, or by demonstration. I cannot do it, it is the Spirit alone who can do this.' But yet, at the same time, of course, we know that the Spirit uses all the things I have just mentioned. The Spirit can use eloquence, as he did in the case of the great George Whitefield, the greatest orator this country has ever known. He used his oratory, yes, but Whitefield did not rely upon his oratory; Whitefield relied upon the Spirit, and the moment he did so the Spirit used his oratory. In the same way, the Spirit used the logic of John Wesley, but he could only use John Wesley's logic after Wesley had submitted himself to him and we, too, must do that with the whole of our life.

The next obvious thing to do is to spend much time with the Scriptures. You cannot be reading the word truly without walking in the Spirit. Then I would put prayer, which really means seeking fellowship with God and with the Lord Jesus Christ. To be led of the Spirit, to walk in the Spirit, means that we spend our time seeking that fellowship. 'This is life eternal, that they might know thee the only true God, and Jesus Christ whom thou hast sent' (Jn 17:3). And if you read the lives of all the men throughout the centuries who have been filled with the Spirit, you will find that they spent a great deal of their time in prayer. The Spirit obviously leads us to God and to Christ. He wants us to have this fellowship and communion. He himself, as it were, has this aspect of communion with the blessed eternal Trinity and he brings us into the fellowship and into the communion.

Then I would enforce all this by saying that we must constantly remind ourselves of these things. The trouble with us, as I have already said, is that we do not talk enough to ourselves. We do not preach enough to ourselves; we all ought to be preachers preaching to that congregation that consists of self. Indeed, half the battle is to talk to ourselves about these things. Address yourself, as the psalmist did. He turns to himself and says, 'Why art thou cast down, O my soul? and why art thou disquieted within me? hope thou in God' (Ps 42:11). He is preaching to himself, and we must do the same. We must take time during the day, indeed many times, to recollect these things, to detach ourselves from business affairs and to say, 'Now I am still this person in whom the Holy Spirit resides and I am using my body and mind in the realisation that it is all the temple of the Holy Spirit.'

So let us remind ourselves, let us refresh our memory, and meditate upon all these things, and, above everything else, let us ever keep ourselves in a sensitive condition. You know what I mean by that. You know what it is to feel yourself becoming hard and insensitive. The moment we discover that, we must be drastic. We must keep ourselves sensitive to the movements and the promptings and the guiding of the Holy Spirit. It will mean repentance, it will mean going back to God and confessing our sin, it will mean humbling ourselves – it does not matter what it may mean, but we must keep ourselves in this sensitive spiritual condition so that we may be conscious of his slightest movement, and we are encouraged to do all this by this great assurance of the Apostle: 'Walk in the Spirit, and ye shall not fulfil the lusts of the flesh.'

Thank God it is a positive gospel! The way to avoid sin is to be walking in the Spirit. The way to avoid going down in life and to live on the high level is to walk in the Spirit, to be led by the Spirit, to meditate upon these things, to be controlled entirely by him. Are we filled with the Spirit? Are we manifesting the fruit of the Spirit? Do we know the joy and the happiness and the peace that the Holy Spirit alone can give? Are we attractive Christians? Do we give people the impression that the most marvellous thing in the world is to be a Christian and to have the Spirit of God within us? This is the thing to which we are called and the way to do that is positively to avoid grieving the Spirit, and to walk in him, to dwell in him as he dwells in us, and to be led by him in all things. 'Be not drunk with wine, wherein is excess; but be filled with the Spirit.'

10

The Wiles of the Devil

Finally, my brethren, be srong in the Lord, and in the power of his might. Put on the whole armour of God, that ye may be able to stand against the wiles of the devil (Ephesians 6:10–11).

We have been looking, during several studies, at the various aspects of this great truth, the whole truth of the Bible, and have been trying to discover how it is used by the Holy Spirit to produce our sanctification. I do not claim that we have dealt with it in an exhaustive manner, we obviously have not, but I have been trying to take out and to select the greater, larger and more obvious principles. We come, now, to an essential aspect of this question of our sanctification through the truth, for no consideration of this doctrine would be adequate without including the teaching which we find stated so perfectly in Ephesians 6, starting especially at verse 10: 'Finally, my brethren, be strong in the Lord, and in the power of his might. Put on the whole armour of God, that ye may be able to stand against the wiles of the devil.'

Now we have seen that God has many ways of promoting our sanctification, which are all taught and enumerated in the word. We saw very clearly at one point that God can use circumstances, that at times he chastises us through them, all with the desire and object of increasing our sanctification. In exactly the same way, it is perfectly clear from the teaching of the Scriptures that God uses even the activity of the devil and his powers to promote our sanctification, which is why we must of necessity look at it. Here is the teaching, which is so plain and clear, that we 'wrestle not [only or merely] against flesh and blood, but against principalities, against powers, against the rulers of the darkness of this world, against spiritual wickedness in high places [in the heavenlies]' (v. 12).

But before we come to analyse this in detail, I feel constrained to ask why it is that this aspect of the truth is so little stressed in our day and generation? It is one of those aspects of truth that is neglected and almost forgotten. Furthermore, I am not here referring to those who are outside the church, nor to those who hold so-called liberal views of the Bible and its teaching, I am referring to those who regard themselves as evangelical Christians. Why is it that we have neglected this? I am constrained to ask that question because you cannot read the Bible without finding teaching about the devil everywhere. Indeed, I would not hesitate to go so far as to say that without this, one cannot understand the Bible at all. It is no use just saying that you believe in sanctification and in a positive act of salvation. We need to know what we are to be delivered *from* and we do not begin to understand that until we really see and grasp this aspect of the teaching. The Bible is not only an outline of the way of salvation; it contains the only teaching that we have concerning the cause of our fall and of our trouble. The Bible shows us that the activity of the devil and his hosts is the whole cause of man's troubles: and yet we so frequently neglect this teaching. When we look at the world in the light of this teaching we see that the activity of the devil is a major factor in the whole life of mankind.

But, to put the argument at its strongest, is it not something we see so clearly in the earthly life of our Lord himself? Our Lord, while he was here in this world, was struggling and fighting against these powers. The biblical view of life in this world is that it is a mighty, spiritual conflict, and even the Son of God himself when he was here in the flesh was involved in this. We all think of his temptation in the wilderness, and we are reminded also of how the devil came back to him in the Garden of Gethsemane and upon the cross itself. There was a mighty battle going on, a tremendous spiritual conflict. We can feel the tension as we read the accounts. Then, when we come to the lives of the apostles, we find exactly the same thing. The apostle Paul always gives the impression that he knew something about this battle against these powers and forces. We wrestle and struggle against them, he says, for this is the thing with which we are confronted: we are not merely up against man but infinitely more important are these tremendous spiritual powers that are arrayed against us.

In other words, it does seem to me that we cannot really read our New Testament without being conscious of this spiritual tension, this spiritual conflict, that is going on. That is why these men prayed so much, and, perhaps, we pray so little, because somehow or other we have forgotten this spiritual conflict in the midst of which our whole life is set. Indeed, when you read the history of God's people throughout the centuries you will find that they testify to the same thing. We all remember the famous story of Martin Luther. One afternoon in his study he was so conscious of the presence of the devil that he took hold of his inkpot and hurled it at him. I do not think that that speaks to us modern Christians as it should. Are we aware of that? Do we know anything about that when we tend to dismiss Luther as almost being a psychopath? Is it imagination? But it is the testimony of all God's people, especially those who have been concerned about knowing God most intimately, those who have striven after holiness, those who have worked out their salvation with fear and trembling. They all testify to the same thing, to this trouble in the spiritual realm, this conflict, this battle.

So, therefore, we must of necessity face the question as to why we so seldom hear about this, and why it is preached about so infrequently. Why, too, do we speak about it so infrequently in conversation with Christian people and as we give our testimonies to one another? I have little hesitation in answering that question. I feel that the main explanation is a false doctrine of sanctification which makes sanctification appear quite simple and easy. We think that we have only one thing to do, then all will be well, and we will live this easy life ever afterwards. But the result is that we hear nothing about this wrestling 'not against flesh and blood, but against principalities, against powers'. We have been taught a doctrine which gives the impression that any sense of tension or struggle in any respect is wrong and false; that we all ought to be always at ease and perfectly happy. Of course, we all understand the desire to be happy, but whether we should desire ease is another matter. However, the point I am making is that surely that view of sanctification inevitably conflicts with this particular aspect of the truth that we are considering together here.

Furthermore, has it not happened because we have been concentrating upon only one aspect of sanctification and not upon the whole? We have been so concerned about a particular sin which tends to get us down that we have forgotten the principalities and powers. Consequently, we have regarded sanctification as something that gives us deliverance from one particular sin, as a kind of clinic to which we go to be delivered from that sin. We have been so constantly dwelling on that one aspect of sanctification and of the truth, that we have failed to remember these other aspects. We have forgotten the devil, the fight and the conflict, and have thereby tended to forget that we need the whole of the truth before our sanctification can be truly promoted. I do feel, therefore, that this is a vitally important matter. We often hear people talking about the 'lost note' in modern evangelism, and for myself I have no doubt that *this* is the note which has been lost. As a result, we have somehow or other lost this conception of the bigness and the mightiness of this Christian life, the fact that we are engaged in a struggle between the almighty God and this amazing power that is set against him, and that if we are truly Christian we, too, are partakers in the struggle.

So let us look at this. Obviously I cannot in one study hope to deal with it in the way it deserves. I am simply giving you some headings in order to show the big principles. So let us, first of all, look at the struggle. This is, we are told, the conflict 'against principalities, against powers, against the rulers of the darkness of this world, against spiritual wickedness in high places.' We shall not go into detail about the words, because what matters is that we should have some understanding of what they represent. We are concerned about the devil; you know the names that are given to him – Satan, Beelzebub, the prince of the power of the air, the god of this world, the prince of this world, and so on.

And what do these names tell us? Once again, the first thing we must bear in mind is that the devil is a person. I have already emphasised the truth that the Holy Spirit is a Person because we tend to forget that and think of him as an influence; and it is exactly the same with the devil. We tend so much to think of the devil as just some general influence, or perhaps not even that, we merely explain his activity in psychological terms. But according to the Scriptures there is a person called the devil who is the 'god of this world', and the Bible teaches, too, that he was a very high, bright and powerful angelic being, created by God before the world was ever made, before man ever came into existence. But he raised himself against God and rebelled against him. He pitted himself against God. The implication is that it was his ambition, his desire, to be equal with God; he refused to subordinate himself to God or to acknowledge God as supreme. So he rebelled against God and persuaded other angels to agree with him, and there was this mighty fall in the angelic realm.

There is, therefore, a kingdom of Satan, a kingdom of the devil. He is the head of that kingdom and he has power and he has his emissaries. That is what is meant by 'principalities, powers and the rulers of the darkness of this world, the spiritual wickedness in high places.' I shall not go into a detailed consideration of what 'high places' or 'heavenlies' mean; it does not matter as long as we know that there is a kingdom with all these forces and powers, of which the devil is the head, and that his ambition is to destroy the work of God; that he pits himself against the almighty God and all who belong to him, and that he is intent upon the destruction of all that God is and all that God has done.

The next thing that is emphasised is the greatness of the struggle, which is due very largely to the greatness of the devil's power. That is why our neglect of the devil is so serious. It is also why the tendency of Christian people to laugh at the mention of the name of the devil is not only alarming, but is a manifestation of the grossest ignorance. The devil is not a joke. He is, according to the Scriptures, such a mighty power that he did not hesitate to pit himself against the Son of God and even appeared at one point to have triumphed. What is this greatness? Well, he is described as 'a roaring lion ... seeking whom he may devour' (1 Pet 5:8) – that is the devil. Our Lord himself referred to him as 'the strong man armed' whose 'goods are at peace' (Lk 11:22) – such is his power. He is altogether more powerful than man, more powerful than man even in a state of perfection, because he was too much for Adam and Eve. It was he who persuaded, and apparently with great ease, this man in a state of perfection. Indeed, he is even greater in power than the archangel Michael himself, because we read in the epistle of Jude that even the archangel 'durst not bring against him a railing accusation, but said, The Lord rebuke thee' (v. 9).

That is something of the power that is opposed to us; such is the struggle in which we are involved. The moment we belong to God and his Christ we are engaged in this struggle. Before that, we belonged to the kingdom of darkness – we were part of the goods he keeps at peace. We also see something of his power as we read the book of Job. He is one who is able to wander to and fro in the earth (Job 1:7). In Job chapter 1 he has power even over the winds and the very elements. In Hebrews he is described as the one who 'had the power of death' (Heb 2:14). I am saying all these things so that we may have some conception of his power. Paul describes him in Ephesians 2:2 as 'the prince of the power of the air, the spirit that now worketh in the children of disobedience'. Then in 2 Corinthians 4:4 the Apostle does not hesitate to say that if men and women do not believe the gospel of the glorious God, there is only one reason for it, it is that their minds have been blinded by 'the god of this world'.

Such, then, is something of this terrible power of the devil and his emissaries and forces. He is set against God and his work, and God's people and all that they have, and he is intent upon our destruction. He will do anything he can to hinder our sanctification, to bring us again out of the kingdom of God, and back into his own kingdom. That is what he is concerned about, and he rules in the world, and in the flesh, attacking us from the outside in this violent manner. Nothing is so important, therefore, as that we should know something of his power and of his methods, and that is the thing that Paul is concerned about here in Ephesians 6.

And then, in addition to his strength, we must also emphasise his subtlety. The Apostle speaks of the 'wiles of the devil'. I wonder if you have ever stopped to think about them? Paul writes in 2 Corinthians 2:11: 'We are not ignorant of his devices.' I am afraid that one of our greatest troubles is that we *are* ignorant of them. We do not seem to know enough about his subtlety, which is why he so often fools us. Consider these statements: 'As the serpent,' says Paul again, 'beguiled Eve' (2 Cor 11:3) – read Genesis 3 and watch him doing it. He comes as a friend, as one who is interested in us, someone whose supreme concern is our well-being and our success. In short, he *beguiles* us. Why, says Paul, he can transform himself into an angel of light (2 Cor 11:14). He can come, as it were, as an advocate of the gospel, as one who is interested in evangelism. He proposes methods to us that are so much better than the biblical ones!

So if he can do all that, it is not surprising that we may be ignorant of his devices; that is why in 2 Corinthians 2 Paul is emphasising the kind of conflict in which we are engaged. The devil is not someone who comes in an openly evil manner, as someone who is obviously opposed to God. No, rather, he came to our Lord in this way: If you are the Son of God, why do you not feed yourself? If you are the Son of God, why do you not rely on his promises and cast yourself down from this pinnacle and give the glory to the greatness of God? You say you are interested in the kingdoms of this world, I will give you all that if you will bow down and worship me. The devil seems to be concerned about the evangelism of God's kingdom – he comes as an angel of light. So are we aware of his wiles? Are we on guard? Are we watching? That is the exhortation of the Scriptures: 'Watch ye, stand fast in the faith' (1 Cor 16:13). You must watch and pray. We find these exhortations everywhere, because of this spiritual conflict, and yet how infrequently we talk about it, how infrequently we look out for it in our daily lives and in our spiritual activities. The subtlety of it all!

But let us go a step further, let us be more practical and come down to details. In what ways does he manifest this power and this subtlety? This is a great theme, even though at this point we shall only be dealing with it briefly. Here we come to this whole realm where so many seem to find it difficult to differentiate between the psychological, the physical and the spiritual; but let us confine ourselves to the answer to that question given by Paul in Ephesians 6. The only way to deal with him is to put on the whole armour of God. Paul is not content with stating that in general, so he divides it into its component parts in order that we may follow the lines along which the devil comes. There he is opposed to us in all his subtlety and his malignity. He throws these darts at us, these fiery arrows which, when they strike an object, burst into flame.

What are these innuendoes, these things that he is throwing at us as God's people? Well, here are some of them. Firstly, there are doubts – I mean by that, doubts about the faith, about the gospel, uncertainty about it with respect to ourselves, doubts as to whether we are saved. Now I know that large numbers of Christian people today testify that ever since they were converted they have never been tempted to doubt. I wonder whether that fits into this passage? If you read the lives of some of the greatest saints you will find that the devil has tried to persuade them to doubt not only their own salvation, but the gospel itself. We must be careful and examine once more the type of belief and teaching which seems to exclude doubts entirely. In view of the adversary by whom we are confronted does it not savour rather of the psychological than of the spiritual? He insinuates the doubts; it is he who throws the fiery darts.

And then there are all the types and kinds of fear, not only about our own salvation or a wrong fear of God and a fear of death, but sometimes a fear of the physical aspect of death. Then perhaps one of his favourite methods is to produce a state of introspection and morbidity. We all know what is meant by introspection – it is self-examination carried out to a point at which it ceases to be beneficial, so that instead of examining yourself in a spiritual way to see whether you are in the faith or not and looking to Christ, you spend the whole of your time looking into yourself, examining the blackness of your own heart. You become such an expert in your own deficiencies, in the blackness of your own condition and the blackness of your own soul, that you drop down into the depths. That is no longer self-examination, but introspection, and it leads, of course, to this state of morbidity in which you are so aware of your own unworthiness and sinfulness that it becomes a cloud which hides the face of your Saviour. It almost seems to do away with Calvary and you are persuaded that nothing can save you. You are so aware of your sin and your blackness that you tend to allow yourself to see nothing else and it obscures the gospel.

How often we prove, by our conduct and behaviour, the truth of the Bible; we always oscillate between extremes. One is the condition in which we never examine ourselves at all. We say we must always look at Christ and not at ourselves; but the Scripture tells us to look at ourselves. We are so objective and we have forgotten the devil. We are not aware of the spiritual conflict at all, we are perfectly happy all the day long and nothing whatsoever troubles us. Then we go right from that to the other extreme, in which we are down in the depths of introspection and morbidity, which is also always produced by the devil. The devil as an angel of light comes and says, 'The Scriptures tell you to examine yourself, so you must do so.' Then he starts us on the process which we have just seen and he does it to such a degree that the end of it is spiritual depression of which there is a great deal in these days. (I do not think, however, that there is as much as there once was, and I am even prepared to say that

that is a bad thing. I prefer spiritual depression to that superficial glibness which is not even aware of the process, but both are wrong.) It is not that he has made you cease to be a Christian; but he has made you a miserable one, and because of that you are a bad recommendation to the gospel. He fills you with such a concern about yourself that you have no time to think about anybody else. You cannot forget yourself, you are always down in the depths, and it is all the work of these principalities and powers. It is a part of the method of the devil as an angel of light.

But he does not even stop at that. How many of God's greatest saints have testified to the fact that they have been attacked by blasphemous thoughts entering their minds? Where have they come from? They are fiery darts thrown by the devil. Do you know anything about these? Have you been on your knees praying to God, and then found that the most horrible blasphemous thoughts have come to you? They have come from the devil. He not only hurls doubts, he even puts these vile, awful thoughts into your mind. Then there are temptations – he is the merest tyro in this matter who thinks he has once and for all finished with certain temptations; because they may come back to you at any moment, the devil will see to that. And we must realise here the importance of differentiating between temptation and sin. To be tempted does not mean you have committed an act of sin. The devil can subject the greatest saint to some of the grossest temptations to sin even after years of growth in the Christian life. It is the devil who does it, not the man himself. The devil hurls it at him – it is, once more, the fiery darts of the wicked one.

And on top of it all – and I must mention it because it is to be stressed in this passage – what does the Apostle mean in Ephesians 6:13 by 'the evil day'? I think he means that over and above all these things we have been looking at, there are special occasions when the devil seems to be let loose and comes upon us in all the might of his ferocity. Job knew something about that. But let me put it to you in the words of a great hymn written in the eighteenth century by the saintly

John Newton – he says it all perfectly. I do not know that it is in a single modern hymnary belonging to any denomination – such are the times in which we live – and to find it we must go to the Gadsby Hymnbook!

> I asked the Lord that I might grow
> In faith and love and every grace
> Might more of His salvation know
> And seek more earnestly His face,
> 'Twas He who taught me thus to pray,
> And He, I trust, has answered prayer,
> But it has been in such a way,
> As almost drove me to despair.
> I hoped that in some favor'd hour,
> At once He'd answer my request,
> And by His love's constraining power
> Subdue my sins and give me rest.
> Instead of this, He made me feel
> The hidden evils of my heart,
> And let the angry powers of hell
> Assault my soul in every part.
> Yea more, with His own hand He seem'd
> Intent to aggravate my woe
> Cross'd all the fair designs I schemed,
> Blasted my gourd and laid me low.
> Lord, why is this, I trembling cried,
> Wilt Thou pursue Thy worm to death?
> It is in this way, the Lord replied,
> I answer prayer for grace and faith,
> These inward trials I employ,
> From self and pride to set thee free;
> And brake thy schemes of earthly joy,
> That thou may'st seek thy all in Me.

You see what he is saying? John Newton, having been converted from the terrible life he once lived, was now concerned about his sanctification, and he prayed to God that in one stroke he would cleanse his heart and deliver him from all sin, that he might enjoy peace and rest for ever afterwards. He asked the

Lord to sanctify him, but what in fact happened to him was that he was given a view of himself and of the blackness and foulness of his own heart. Then hell was let loose upon him and he could not understand it. So he asked God why he was doing it, and that was the answer – God said that that was his way of sanctifying people. You have to have self crushed out and it is the only way. The 'positive' gospel will not do it and so you have to have hell let loose and you will be crushed to the ground. You will cry to me, says God, and then I will tell you that I have to smash you before I can reveal myself to you. Yes, God sometimes allows the devil to do as he did in the cases of Job and John Newton. Do you know anything of that sort of experience? If you read the lives of the greatest saints, you will find they all knew something about it. They never knew short cuts to sanctification, but they knew something about this. This is God's way. Thus it is clear that God permits this and uses it to produce and promote our sanctification.

Lastly, how do we meet the struggle? How do we stand in such a condition? The answer is given perfectly here in Ephesians. The first thing is to realise that this is so, that this has happened. For if we do not realise that we are involved in this spiritual struggle, it means that we are so duped by Satan that we have not been aware that he is there. We know nothing about him as an angel of light. The second thing, obviously, is that the moment we realise this, we know at once that there is only one strength that is great enough to stand up to this, and that is the strength of the Lord: 'Finally, my brethren, be strong in the Lord and in the power of his might' (v. 10). Nothing else can do it, for the devil is stronger even than the archangel, and who are we?

Therefore we must put on the whole armour of God, and the apostle Paul takes us through the parts. The first is truth. This means that the only way finally to stand in this day is to know the truth, the faith, to have a clear knowledge and understanding of the gospel – and that is why I have been going through it all in these studies. It is only as we have this whole armour that we stand – the whole gospel – sanctification is not one special doctrine, it is the whole doctrine, the holiness of God all the way through everything else. There must be no doubt or uncertainty as to the way of righteousness. We must rely entirely upon the finished work of Christ – justification by faith only. We must be absolutely clear about it because if we are not, the devil will get us. We must realise our utter dependence thus upon God and have a clear knowledge of the fact that we are no longer under the dominion of the devil. We must read Romans 6, we must study it and realise that though the devil attacks us, we are not under his dominion any longer, and how vital this is!

'That wicked one,' says John in 1 John 5:18, 'toucheth him not,' but though he cannot touch us, he can frighten us, he can throw his darts at us. But he will never get us back into his kingdom again; we have been taken out of it and are now under the dominion of the Son of God. Let us make certain of it, so that even when the devil attacks us, we can defy him to the face and say, 'You cannot touch me!' Though he is our adversary, though he comes as a roaring lion, we are to resist him and stand steadfast in the faith. So we must know the faith. If we neglect Christian doctrine, it just means that we are ignorant of the devil. For, ultimately, the way to defeat him and to master and defy him, is to stand in the doctrine, not a superficial Bible study but the great biblical doctrines. The more we know of them, the more we will be able to withstand the devil.

And then, in addition to all that, we need to be 'shod with the preparation of the gospel of peace'. In other words, we need to be quick, we need to be subtle ourselves, because he is subtle. We must answer him and tell him that we can work as quickly as he can. It is a battle of wits. So have these sandals on your feet, says Paul, in order that you can move as quickly as he can. And the gospel enables us to do this. But even after all this is done, we need to remain on the offensive, we must, 'take ... the sword of the Spirit, which is the word of God' and strike at the devil with the word. We must attack him, and when he comes we must strike him – that is the method. There is the essence of it, and we must work it out in detail. Then in verse 18 Paul adds 'watching with all perseverance and supplication for all saints' –

we must always be watching and praying. Watch, stand fast in the faith, quit yourselves like men, be strong: that is it; the same truth is repeated everywhere – watchfulness, waiting for the subtlety. We must learn to discriminate, we must not believe in everything that appears to be good; everything that appears good is not of necessity of God. The devil is subtle, we must differentiate, we must be watchful and we are ever exhorted to do this.

Above all, Paul exhorts us to prayerfulness: living and dwelling in God's presence, drinking in his life and being constantly built up in the faith. And so, in this way, in spite of the power and the malignity and the subtlety of the devil, we shall be able to stand; and even should an evil day come, when hell itself is let loose upon us, though we may not understand, we shall be able to stand in his might and in the power of his love, we shall overcome the enemy. O may the Lord God open our eyes to realise this aspect of our Christian life and warfare, because it is only as we realise something about it that our sanctification will proceed gloriously and we shall see that in every way God himself is sanctifying us.

11

The Unity of the Spirit

*Neither pray I for these alone, but for them also which shall believe
on me through their word; that they all may be one; as thou, Father,
art in me, and I in thee, that they also may be one in us: that the
world may believe that thou hast sent me. And the glory which
thou gavest me I have given them; that they may be one, even as
we are one: I in them, and thou in me, that they may be made perfect in one; and that the world may know that thou hast sent me,
and hast loved them, as thou hast loved me (John 17:20–23).*

We come now to deal with a petition which our Lord has
already offered on behalf of his disciples as it is recorded in the
eleventh verse of this chapter: 'And now I am no more in the
world, but these are in the world, and I come to thee. Holy
Father, keep through thine own name those whom thou hast
given me, that they may be one, as we are.' In our analysis of
this chapter[1] we have pointed out that it can be divided into three
main sections: the first from verses 1 to 5, in which our Lord
prays for himself; the second from verses 6 to 19, where he prays
particularly and more especially for his immediate followers,
the disciples that are around and about him; and then the third
from verse 20 to the end, where he prays not only for them but
for all who throughout the centuries, until the end of time, shall
believe on him.

---

[1] See Volume 1, *Saved in Eternity* (Crossway Books, 1988).

We spent most of our time on that section which runs from verses 6 to 19, and we showed that our Lord gives certain reasons why he prays for his disciples. We then went on to study the petitions that he offered on their behalf. There were three main petitions. The first was that they might be kept from the evil one, from the evil that is in the world, but supremely from the evil one himself: our Lord is going to heaven and he is leaving them in an antagonistic world, and they are opposed by this powerful, subtle enemy, so he prays his Father to keep them from the evil one. Then, as a continuation of that petition, he prays the petition which we have been considering very fully for several chapters: 'Sanctify them through thy truth, thy word is truth.' The way to be kept from the evil one is, of course, to be sanctified; it is God alone who sanctifies, and he does it through the truth, in the way that we have seen.

So now we come to the third and last of these petitions, and it is in this petition that our Lord prays that his people and his followers might be one, even as he and his Father are one. And what we really have in verses 20–23 is an elaboration of that particular petition. He talks to them, as it were, about that petition which he has already offered, and now he repeats it, and repeats it more than once. He elaborates his reasons for doing so, and explains what he means by it. Clearly we are face to face here with a very important principle in connection with our Christian life, and it is essential that we should consider it.

It is a principle which is of particular interest at this present hour, because I suppose that if there is one thing that characterises the life of the church and of Christian people more than anything else in this particular generation, it is the interest in what is called 'ecumenicity'. We are constantly reading about it and conferences and meetings are being held almost without intermission, with respect to it. An interest in it began about 1910, but it has been particularly to the forefront during the last twenty years. What we are generally told can be summarised like this: the greatest scandal in the world is a disunited church, and this scandal must be removed; it must also be removed because it is the greatest hindrance to evangelism. It is the multiplicity of denominations that constitutes one of the greatest hindrances to men and women who are outside the church believing the gospel. If we could only get rid of these denominations and have one great world, or 'super', church, then people would be ready to listen to the gospel and probably to accept it. Further, this movement for church unity – this movement of ecumenicity – is 'the greatest movement and manifestation of the Holy Spirit since the Day of Pentecost'. That is a summary of what many people are saying.

In the light of all this, we obviously must give some consideration to this subject. But our method of doing so is rather different from that which, speaking generally, characterises the life of the church at the present time; for you notice at once, that there are certain things that are characteristic of all this modern interest and talk about ecumenicity. The people concerned are very fond of quoting John 17, it seems to be *the* chapter on which they base everything, but what interests me is that they invariably seem to speak of this chapter as if there were nothing in it at all except this plea for unity. Well, I think that the time we have spent with this chapter is proof positive that that, at any rate, is completely wrong! There is no richer chapter in the whole Bible than John 17 and we have done some thirteen studies on the first five verses only.[1]

How little we hear about the work which the Father had given the Son to do, about the people whom he had given to him, and so on. Instead, the impression is given that John 17 has only one message in it, and that is this great question of unity.

In other words, we see the terrible danger of isolating a text, extracting it from its context, and forgetting the need to have a balanced view of Scripture and to grasp what we may call the wholeness and the unity of the scriptural teaching. Because if you read this chapter thoroughly, and study it as it should be studied, you will see that this whole question of unity is not something that our Lord deals with on its own; it is a part of the entire outlook, and of this whole petition that he offers for his

---

[1] Volume 1, *Saved in Eternity* (Crossway Books, 1988).

followers. It is not a doctrine that is to be found in isolation. And we have said the same thing about the doctrine of sanctification also. For that is our trouble; we constantly regard the truth of God as if it were a number of propositions, instead of realising the truth as a whole, seeing that each particular part belongs to the whole, and that if it is to be grasped truly, and in proportion, it must be taken in its context. We must arrive at our particular point only after we have followed the scriptural method, and the scriptural pattern.

My suggestion, then, as we approach this subject of unity, is that we can only begin to understand it if we are perfectly clear in our minds as to what constitutes a Christian. Our Lord says that in verses 6 to 8 of this chapter, and we spent some time considering the subject. The modern idea seems to be that it does not matter about the definition; if people call themselves Christians, that is all that matters. But our Lord takes care to define who a Christian is, and to show how Christians are utterly different from the world. In the same way, he has also dealt with this vital subject of our sanctification. I cannot see, as I study this chapter, that one can ever say that it does not matter very much what people believe, or how they live or behave, so long as they call themselves Christians. According to our Lord, we use this designation of a Christian wrongly. Christians are those who have been sanctified by the Father – and nobody else – and you see the relevance of this in the modern situation. Surely we must all agree that not all who use the name Christian can, in the light of this chapter, be called Christians; it is not that we sit in judgement on others, but we do face the word of God and seek to be guided by it.

So it seems to me that the most convenient thing to do is to extract the principles which are clearly indicated here by what our Lord says. The first is that we must be clear as to the nature of this unity about which he is speaking. You notice that every time he mentions it, he does so in a particular way: 'Holy Father, keep through thine own name those whom thou hast given me, that they may be one, as we are' (v. 11). Then he goes on in verse 20: 'Neither pray I for these alone, but for them also which shall believe on me through their word; that they all may be one; as thou, Father, art in me, and I in thee, that they also may be one in us; that the world may believe that thou hast sent me' – and again he repeats it – 'And the glory which thou gavest me I have given them; that they may be one, even as we are one.' And then he is not content even with that: 'I in them, and thou in me, that they may be made perfect in one; and that the world may know that thou hast sent me, and hast loved them, as thou hast loved me.'

It is to me almost incomprehensible that people can quote this seventeenth chapter of John on unity, while at the same time they seem to forget and ignore entirely what our Lord is always so careful to repeat and elaborate every time he mentions the subject of unity. Such people are thinking in terms of external unity, a mechanical, organisational unity, while all the time our Lord is teaching what we must describe as an inner and mystical unity. The unity that he is concerned about is the unity of life and the unity of spirit. He makes that very plain by the analogy he draws between Christian unity and the unity in the Godhead, an analogy which he is always careful to keep in the forefront. In other words, if we are to understand the character of this unity about which our Lord is concerned, we must realise that there are certain indications of mystical unity which are very clearly given in the Scriptures. Now let me say at once that this is a very high and difficult subject. I believe that, in the last analysis, it is the most abstruse subject in the entire realm of revelation, because we are, of necessity, considering the Almighty God himself. But our Lord compels us to do this, because he always considers the unity which is to characterise his people as being analogous to this other mystical, eternal unity.

Four types of unity are dealt with in the Scriptures. The first is the unity between the three Persons of the blessed Holy Trinity – 'I in them, and thou in me'; 'My Father and I are One' – that inscrutable eternal unity which exists and subsists between them. Of course, let me repeat, we are dealing with something that patently is entirely beyond human understanding. We say,

'How can three be one and one be three at the same time?' And the answer is that we cannot understand it. The Scripture tells us that the blessed God is three Persons, and yet that the three are one, one eternal substance, three Persons and yet not three Gods but one God. There is only one true and living God, but that one eternal God exists as three separate and distinct Persons, and yet there is this perfect, marvellous, wonderful, mystic unity. That is the kind of unity about which our Lord is speaking.

The second kind of unity of which we read in the Bible is the union of the two natures in the one Person of the Lord Jesus Christ, and that is the great theme of the New Testament. Here is the Lord Jesus Christ, perfect God, perfect Man, truly God, truly Man, and yet he is not two Persons. It is rank heresy to think of him as such because he is one Person, but in that one Person there are these two natures, not at all mixed, not at all fused or intermingled: they are there, but they are quite distinct. Yet they are not separate, because there is a unity between them, and it is a perfect union, the mystical unity of the two natures in the one Person of the Lord Jesus Christ. That is another mystical unity and it is analogous, obviously, to the union that exists between the three Persons of the blessed Holy Trinity.

Now the next unity that our Lord speaks of is the union of his people with himself. He deals with that at great length in chapters 14 to 16 of John's Gospel, but we find it in many other places also, and the apostles deal with it in their epistles: 'Christ in you, the hope of glory' (Col 1:27); 'I live; yet not I, but Christ liveth in me' (Gal 2:20). There it is in particular, but the whole body of Christian people is in Christ. We read in Ephesians 4, about the wonderful body, Christ being the head, and we all members of the body; it is the mystical union which is between Christ and the church which Paul expresses in Ephesians 5 in terms of the illustration of the union between the bridegroom and the bride.

And the last, of course, is the one with which we are dealing here; the union of Christian people among themselves and with one another, and the point I would emphasise is that our Lord always, everywhere, teaches that this is to be thought of in terms analogous to the others which I have already mentioned. When we come to this, we must not forget the others; we must not suddenly become external, mechanical or organisational in our ideas and concepts. The unity which he prays for, for his people, is the unity which is analogous to that of the Father, the Son and the Holy Spirit – this mystical union between the blessed Persons – and to the unity between Christ and the church. Now this can never be emphasised too frequently. It is a spiritual unity, 'the unity of the Spirit', as Paul puts it in Ephesians 4:3, and the same thing that he elaborates in 1 Corinthians 12.

It is the only unity that the New Testament knows, and it is the only unity in which it is at all interested. So we must get right out of the realm of the mechanical and external and organisational, and we must say that whatever this unity is, it is similar to that wonderful union which is between Christ and his followers: '… that they all may be one; as thou, Father, art in me, and I in thee, that they also may be one in us' (v. 21). Then he elaborates it again: 'even as we are one: I in them, and thou in me, that they may be made perfect in one' (vv. 22, 23). There is no gap, there is to be no interval, it is all in a series, and that is the nature of the unity about which he is concerned. The only other point I should like to make about the character of this unity is that our Lord is not praying anywhere in this chapter that this union may come to be; what he prays here is that this union, that is already in existence, may be kept, may be continued, and may be preserved by his Father.

That, then, is the nature of the unity, so we now move on to our second point: what are the conditions of this union? What is it that makes and produces it? Those are vital questions, especially in the light of the modern discussion on unity, and the answer given here is perfectly clear. It is in the twentieth verse: 'Neither pray I for these alone, but for them also which shall believe on me through their word.' What, then, is going to preserve this unity? 'Well,' says our Lord in effect, 'it is the word, which these followers of mine are going to preach after I am gone; and as the result of the preaching of this word people are going to be converted and come into the church.' In verses 16 and 17 he says that it is like this: 'They are not of the world, even as I am not of the world. Sanctify them through thy truth, thy word is truth.' And then he prays not for them alone, but also for all others, 'who shall believe on me through their word'. The same thing, of course, has already been said in verse 11, and we saw, when we considered in detail our Lord's phrase 'through thine own name', that it meant that the Lord Jesus Christ has revealed his Father's name to those people who belong to him, but not to the world.[1] The world does not understand it, but these people do, and what makes us really the people of God is that through the word we have understood the meaning of the name of the Lord.

So we are back again to this same question of the word; indeed, we might argue that the one thing that produces unity is what our Lord tells them in verses 6 to 9: 'I have manifested thy name unto the men which thou gavest me out of the world: thine they were, and thou gavest them me; and they have kept thy word. Now they have known that all things whatsoever thou hast given me are of thee. For I have given unto them the words which thou gavest me; and they have received them, and have known surely that I came out from thee, and they have believed that thou didst send me. I pray for them: I pray not for the world, but for them which thou hast given me, for they are thine.' That is the character of these people: 'I pray for them, I pray not for the world ...' the world does not believe these things.

Now surely this ought to be abundantly clear to us. What makes these people, and what makes the greatest unity of these people, is this word, this message of God which has been given to them, first by the Lord himself, and subsequently by his apostles and disciples – that is the basis of the unity. We can translate that into modern terms and put it like this: what makes the greatest unity is the common faith, what we believe, what

---

[1] See Volume 2, *Safe in the World* (Crossway Books, 1988).

we have received together, and what nobody else has received. That is the unity which our Lord is concerned about in this chapter; it is all entirely dependent upon this particular word, and it is only as men and women are agreed about this word and accept it and subscribe to the same faith and to the same common salvation, that there can be any conceivable unity among them; any other unity is of no value whatsoever.

But he also puts that in a slightly different form. The word, after all, creates the unity by bringing us into a particular relationship to him – that is the message of verse 22: 'And the glory which thou gavest me I have given them; that they may be one, even as we are one.' He says that it is because he has given them this glory that they are one, even as he and the Father are one. He speaks also of this glory which the Father has given to him: 'The glory which thou gavest me I have given them.' What, then, is this glory? Obviously it cannot be the eternal glory of the Son of God, because that is not a glory which has been given him by the Father, it is a glory which he has always shared with the Father from all eternity. It must, therefore, be some kind of glory that the Father gave to the Son while he was here in this life and in this world, and a glory which, in turn, he is able to impart unto his own followers. And what is that? I suggest to you that there is only one adequate answer to that question, and that is this special relationship to God which becomes ours through the work and the operation of the Holy Spirit. While our Lord was here in this world and when he had taken upon himself human nature, when he had decided to live life in this world as a man and in the likeness of sinful flesh, the Father gave him this glory, this union with himself, this intimate relationship, this knowledge of the Father, so that he would always depend upon his Father and be always receiving grace and glory from him. And that is what, he here tells us, he has also given to his followers.

If you want that in detail, go back to chapters 14 to 16 and read there his teaching about the work and the operation of the Holy Spirit. He is going to send them the Spirit, and the effect of that will be that he will dwell in them. They will be in him, he will be in them, and they will not feel that they are orphans because they will have an intimacy with him such as they have never had before; that is the glory which he gives. It is, in other words, as I have shown earlier, our being united to him and his being in us – we in him and he in us – and thus we are able to receive of his grace and of his glory, and grace for grace. Now what I am emphasising is that all this is obviously impossible apart from the word. It is the word that teaches this, it is the word that mediates this to us, so that all who really are to receive this, receive it through and by means of the word, and that, I suggest to you, is the only union and unity which is dealt with in this chapter, the only unity in which our Lord is interested.

Let me put it like this: a mere coalition of organisations or denominations has in reality nothing whatsoever to do with this unity. Indeed, it may even be a danger. The unity that our Lord is concerned about is a unity which is spiritual. It consists of a unity of spirits, and it is a unity, therefore, which is based solidly upon the truth. It is based upon the whole doctrine – regeneration and the rebirth, the receiving of the Holy Spirit – and obviously the doctrine must be dependent ultimately upon the Person of our Lord and upon his work. It is a unity of people who have become spiritual and who have been born again: we are made one with one another, because we first of all are united to Christ and made one with him, and, through him, one with God.

Therefore, to argue that the one thing that matters is some sort of organisational or external unity is not only to fall short of this conception, it is even to do something which is highly dangerous. If a man comes to me and says, 'It does not matter what you believe as long as you call yourself a Christian,' I reply, 'No, that is impossible.' And I must ask that man certain questions and get his answers. What is his view of the Lord Jesus Christ? Is the Lord Jesus Christ just a man to him? There are many people in this world who call themselves Christians, yet who, alas, regard the Lord Jesus Christ as nothing but a man. Well, all I can say to that is that I have no fellowship with such people. I have no unity with them for they take from the very foundation and basis of my faith, and my whole position and standing. What do these people believe about the work of the Lord Jesus Christ? What is their view of his death? Is it just a tragedy; is it just the death of a passive resister; is it the death of someone who was not understood by his contemporaries? Is it a murderous death or is it a substitutionary death? Is it the Son of God dying because that is the only way whereby my sins may be forgiven, and therefore the essential preliminary to my becoming a child of God, and a partaker of the divine nature? If it is essential, and the other man says it is not, how can it be possible for there to be unity between us? And the same is true with all these other cardinal doctrines of the Christian faith.

Now there is no unity unless we stand on this – one Lord, one faith, one baptism. There is only one Lord Jesus Christ, and I must be clear about his Person and about his work. There is only one faith (I do not mean here my faith in him, but the faith about him), the faith that the apostles preached. They preached that Jesus is the Lord, the Son of God, that he died for our sins and that he was made a substitute for us. That is their faith, the word that they preached, and it was as the result of hearing and believing this word that the people became members of the church, and one with others who were in the church before them.

So you see that these things are vital; this is the unity that was to be found in the early church; it is the unity that is found at all times of true reformation and revival; and, thank God, it is the unity that is in existence at the present time, in spite of the multiplicity of denominations and organisations. There is nothing, I sometimes think, in the realm of Christian life and experience, which is quite as wonderful as the demonstration of this unity. Is it not a fact, my friends, that we who are Christians recognise one another the moment we meet? It is the greatest privilege in my life as the minister of a church that as I stand in the vestry to meet the people coming in to see me, often people whom I have never seen in my life before, that I at once recognise them. I know them. I know that they are brothers and sisters of mine. I do not know where they come from – they come from all parts of the world – and yet at once I know them, and I feel that I have known them for years. Why? Because it is the unity of the Spirit.

I can go even further – and let me put it quite simply and bluntly – I have some interesting experiences in that room in this very connection. Some people come in to me and they say, 'I am glad to meet you, I come from India (or Australia, America, or some other country), and I am a good Congregationalist'; or others come and say, 'I am a good Methodist', or 'I am a Baptist', and immediately I feel there is no union. But others come, and they do not tell me whether they are Baptist, or Methodist or Congregationalist, they just come in and say, 'What a wonderful Lord we have! Thank God this is the same gospel here as in my home country, and my home town!' And immediately I am one with them. We are related, we are in the same family, there is a fundamental union of Spirit. I feel that I have known them all my life, and that if I were to meet them again in the future, I would never be more close to them than at that first moment. That is the unity our Lord talks about; it is not an external matter, nor a matter of denomination or organisation.

Let me go further. If you were to abolish all these denominations, you still would not create unity, because these people who come and say they are good Congregationalists, or good Baptists, and so on, would still be the same sort of people, and by doing away with these distinctions you would not change them. If they came to see you, they would still not be able to talk about this wonderful Lord, they still would not be able to exchange spiritual experiences, because they would be essentially the same people. To think of unity in these external terms is to depart from the glory of our Lord's petition, this unity of faith and belief, this unity of spirit, which is the result of believing the truth and of being made one with the Lord Jesus Christ and therefore one with one another.

If that is true, then, let us move on to my third proposition and consider briefly the things that hinder or break the unity. First of all, you can do that in the matter of the faith; there is nothing that so breaks the unity as a deviation from any part of the word of God. We believe the whole word of God, and to leave out certain parts of it immediately breaks the unity. 'Ah,' they say, 'you must not be particular, the thing is for you who call yourselves Christians to pray together.' But is it not rather important that we should all be praying in the same relationship? How can I pray in unity and in fellowship with a man who may tell me he can go direct to God without the Lord Jesus Christ at all? There are many people who say things like that. They do not see that the only way to enter into the holiest of all is by the blood of Jesus, and not only do they not mention the blood, they do not mention Jesus either. They say, 'You can start listening and talking to God just as you are.' But I say that I have only one way of entering into the holy, eternal Presence, and that is by the blood that was shed for me. Without it I cannot approach God, I dare not approach him. So I cannot respond to these sentimental appeals to start praying together because I must know the basis of my prayer and be certain that I really am accepted of God.

But there is another way – the opposite, in a sense, to that last one – which defeats fellowship and unity; it is this: addition to the word and demanding things that are not demanded in the word. That is why I have no fellowship with the Roman Catholics. Up to a point I am with them, but then they put in their plus – I must believe certain things about the Virgin Mary, etc. But I do not believe these things and I say that to do so is to deny the gospel of the glorious liberty of the children of God. Thank God, there are people even among the Roman Catholics with whom I can have fellowship, but they are those who do not hold to the whole Catholic teaching; they believe in the centralities, and they leave out the additions.

But let me go one step further. We can break the unity in this matter of faith by exalting things to the first position which should be in the second or third place. There are certain great doctrines about which there never has been unity in the Christian church and I take it there never will be, but I would not separate from any brother or sister on matters like that. If I am not certain, I am prepared to be charitable; I stand for certainties, not for things that are doubtful or uncertain. 'In things essential, unity; in things doubtful, liberty; in all things, charity.'

In the same way, the unity can be broken because of the way we live and conduct ourselves. A person's self-assertion always upsets fellowship, so if my spirit is wrong I am making fellowship impossible, and, as I have already said, exalting matters that are secondary. Take, for instance, the church at Corinth. The thing that divided the church was their emphasis on personalities: some of Paul, some of Apollos, some of Cephas. They were worshipping men, arguing about which was the best preacher of the three, getting excited, and forgetting the message because of the men. And if we do that, we are upsetting the unity and fellowship, we are bringing in something that causes a barrier – and that is schism.

And yet another way in which we can break up the unity is in boasting of spiritual gifts. If we single out a spiritual gift and say that it is absolutely essential for everyone, we are breaking the fellowship, because if you read 1 Corinthians 12, you will find that the Holy Spirit dispenses these gifts to different people as he wills. But we must all have the Spirit and manifest him in our lives. So in practice we can break the unity by failing to demonstrate the faith. Any member of the church who falls into grievous sin is also breaking the unity; immediately that happens, there is a break, so failure in conduct and behaviour can do it too.

My last word you can work out for yourselves – it is in many ways the glory of it all. What is the function and purpose of the union? Our Lord answers this question: 'That they all may be one; as thou, Father, art in me, and I in thee, that they also may be one in us: that the world may believe that thou hast sent me' (v. 21). But he adds another answer in the twenty-third verse, and this is one of the most glorious things in the realm of Scripture. Have you ever seen that when you have read this chapter? Why is this union of ours so important? It does not say that if we all become one, then the whole world will believe on Christ – that is patently contradicted in Scripture. But what it does say is this, 'That they may be made perfect in one' – not that the world may believe on me, but – 'that the world may know that thou hast sent me', which is a very different thing. To me, it seems almost childish to be told that if only you were to do away with your denominations then the world would suddenly believe in Christ and everybody would be converted. What a pathetic valuation! You could have one great world church, and there would still be unbelievers, as there are now. The world did not believe when the Son of God was here and speaking with his own lips. No, he does not pray for them, he prays that the world may know that God has sent him. In other words, our unity manifests that we are not merely men, but that God has done something to us in Christ, that we are what we are because the Son of God has come into the world and has borne our sins and given us a rebirth, and has sent his Holy Spirit into us – the unity is to manifest that.

And the second thing our unity is to manifest is that God loves us in exactly the same way as he loved Christ. I ask again if we are able to realise that? Do you know that God in heaven at this moment loves you in exactly the same way as he loved his only begotten Son? We know his love for the Son; remember that he loves you in exactly the same way, and you and I are to live in fellowship in order to demonstrate that. Both all together and individually we are to demonstrate that we are the special subjects of God's love. Whatever happens to us, whatever our circumstances, we are to be demonstrators of the love of God. God loved his Son, and though it led him to be persecuted and tempted, though it led him to be scourged, though it led him to be crucified, God still went on loving him, and the Son showed he was still being loved by the way he lived and died. And you and I are to live and die in that way, and the world will look at us and say, 'What are these people? Look at them in their suffering and in their agony. What enables them to be like this?' And the answer is, 'It is the love which God has towards them. They know his love, they are feeding on it and they are being sustained by it.'

That is why we are to be one; we are to demonstrate these things. The early church did it, that is how it impressed the ancient world. Those people, even when they were thrown to the lions in the arena, were still praising Christ and his love. That is the unity our Lord is interested in. That is the unity that shakes the world. It is not a matter of numbers or great organisations, or one mammoth church. This has nothing to do with numbers; it is a unity of the Spirit; just a handful of men living with Christ led to three thousand converts on the Day of Pentecost, and it is always like that. What we need is not a big church, it is a pure church; it is a holy church, it is a truly Christian church. So for myself, I am not interested in any talk or any appeals which put mechanical, external, or organisational unity above the unity of the Spirit, the unity of faith, and the unity which is based on sanctification. *That* is the unity for which our Lord prays; the unity which you and I are meant to exemplify in our individual lives, and in our corporate lives together as members of the church; that we may be one, as God and Christ are one, in that mystic, spiritual, glorious, perfect unity.

12

With Him in the Glory

Father, I will that they also, whom thou hast given me, be with me where I am; that they may behold my glory, which thou hast given me: for thou lovedst me before the foundation of the world (John 17:24).

We come here, in verse 24, to a consideration of the last great petition of our Lord and Saviour Jesus Christ for his followers and disciples. It is actually the last of the petitions which he offered, and, in many ways, the end of the prayer; in the final two verses he again just reminds his Father of the character of these people for whom he is praying: 'O righteous Father, the world hath not known thee: but I have known thee, and these have known that thou hast sent me. And I have declared unto them thy name, and will declare it; that the love wherewith thou hast loved me may be in them, and I in them' (vv. 25 and 26). It is, then, the last of the great petitions, and, at the same time, in a remarkable and extraordinary way, it sums up in itself the entire prayer, so that as we look at it, we shall not only be considering the special new request, we shall also be reminding ourselves of certain things which we have been considering regularly as we have worked our way through this glorious and tremendous chapter.

Now as we come to look at verse 24, we must all surely agree that the main trouble with us (I am speaking of Christian people) is that we will not realise the truth about ourselves. In this Christian life there are many problems and difficulties, but more and more it seems to me that most of our problems, indeed, if not all of them, arise simply from the fact that we fail to realise, and to understand and to appreciate as we ought, what is the real truth about us as Christian people. In the Scriptures we have great words such as these in this verse, these exceeding great and precious promises, and they are all for us. They are meant for us, they were spoken for us; many of them are descriptions of us, and yet how little do we grasp this fact, how little do we seem to realise the truth that is enshrined in them and how slow we are to apply these things to ourselves! I have increasingly come to the conclusion that somehow or other our trouble lies in the fact that we do not read our Scriptures properly; that is, we tend to read them without meditating upon them, without taking a firm grip of them and grasping them for ourselves, and realising that these truths are truths about us. It seems perfectly clear that if only we did that our entire lives would be revolutionised, indeed our whole demeanour would be entirely changed. You cannot read the New Testament without coming to the conclusion that God's people are meant to be full of the spirit of joy and rejoicing. One of our Lord's last words with respect to them was that they might know his joy and peace, that seemed to be his supreme concern, as it is here in this verse. And yet how slow we are to realise these things. We are content to think of ourselves in ways that are far removed from the New Testament description of the Christian, and our experiences are correspondingly far removed from what our Lord has depicted here.

I wonder how many of us can truthfully say that we are rejoicing with 'joy unspeakable and full of glory' (1 Pet 1:8) in the Lord Jesus Christ? We are exhorted to 'rejoice in the Lord alway: and again,' says the great Apostle in Philippians 4:4, 'again I say, Rejoice.' I suppose the final charge which will be brought against us all is the way we have so misinterpreted our blessed Lord by giving the impression that we are living a weary and laborious life, struggling hard against difficulties and obstacles. Indeed, far too often the impression is given that those who are right outside Christianity and the church seem to be very much happier. Now we know that that is merely a matter of appearance, and that in reality such people are not happy at all but profoundly miserable, but by appearance alone you might often gain the impression that they are happier than many of God's people. And the answer to all that is to realise the truth about ourselves, to realise who we are, to realise what we are, to realise everything that the New Testament tells us about ourselves.

In working through this chapter we have been doing that constantly, and now we are going to look at one of the most extraordinary and glorious things of all. Here is our Lord's last petition for his people: 'Father, I will that they also, whom thou hast given me, be with me where I am; that they may behold my glory which thou hast given me: for thou lovedst me before the foundation of the world.' He is about to leave these followers of his; he is going to the cross, to its agony and its shame; he is going to death and to burial, to the Resurrection and to the Ascension, but his concern is about them, and that is what he prays for. So let us look together at this summary of the main teaching of the entire chapter.

First of all, let us look at the One who prays for us. This is the first thing always, the thing we need to grasp before everything else. Here is someone praying to God for us; we people are being prayed for. So who is this who is praying for us? Well, the very terms that he himself uses in this verse tell us who he is. He does not hesitate to address the almighty and eternal God as 'Father', suggesting at once an intimate relationship. In the first verse also he begins by saying, 'Father, the hour is come; glorify thy Son, that thy Son also may glorify Thee.' 'Father': he is indeed none other than the Son of God.

The next word we must look at is the word 'will'. 'Father,' he says, 'I will' – a most astounding word. He does not say, 'I request' or 'I petition' or 'I desire', and it is unfortunate that the Revised Standard Version has translated it as 'desire', for that is not the word, it is much stronger. He says, 'Father, I will,' and we must not reduce that. In other words, here is someone who can come into the presence of the eternal God and say, 'Father, I will, that these may be with me where I am,' at once suggesting, of course, an equality with God; with reverence, he says 'I will' to the almighty Father.

And then, of course, the other phrase that tells us exactly the same thing about him is this phrase 'before the foundation of the world': 'For thou lovedst me before the foundation of the world.' He has said that before, earlier in this prayer: 'And now, O Father,' he says in verse 5, 'glorify thou me with thine own self, with the glory which I had with thee before the world was.' We must not stay with this now, but unless we grasp it, we shall not be able to learn the great lessons of this phrase. He is praying there for us, because, remember, he is not only praying for his immediate followers – 'Neither pray I for these alone, but for them also which shall believe on me through their word' (v. 20). He is praying for Christians in all places and at all times, everywhere; and the One who is praying there for us is none other than the eternal Son of God. That is the whole basis of our standing and our position; we are Christians today because he came from heaven to earth and took upon himself the likeness of sinful flesh and did all that is recorded of him in these Gospels. A Christian, therefore, primarily, by definition, is one who is being prayed for by the eternal Son of God.

Furthermore, at the same time you cannot help noticing at the same time his concern for us. If only we realised that, when besieged and attacked by the devil and sin and temptation! As we face certain difficulties in the Christian life which trouble and perplex us, and, too, the difficulties which we have with ourselves and with other people, our tendency is to feel that we are quite alone and that no one understands. But to all that the answer is that here is the Son of God under the very shadow of the cross, knowing what is before him, and yet his great concern, his primary concern, is for his people. You would have thought he would be spending all his time praying for himself, but if you look at this prayer you will notice that the first five verses only are devoted to himself, the remainder are devoted entirely to this intercession of his on behalf of his followers. There is nothing that is more important for us to grasp than the fact that our Saviour is the eternal Son of God, that he prayed for us on earth and that at this moment he is interceding for us at the right hand of God's glory and power in heaven.

What, then, does he say about us? We have seen the truth about the One who prays, so the second thing we must ask is, what is true of us? Once more we find the answer in this phrase which our Lord has used frequently in this prayer: we are described as 'those whom thou hast given me'. 'Father, I will that they also, whom thou hast given me, be with me where I am.' Christian people are those whom God the Father has given to his Son. You remember how he puts it earlier on where he says in verse 6, 'Thine they were, and thou gavest them me; and they have kept thy word.' I do not know of anything more comforting than this. I, as a Christian, am one of God's chosen people. It is the great doctrine of the Scriptures, you find it everywhere; and our Lord actually repeats it seven times in this last prayer to his Father. These are the people whom God had chosen before the foundation of the world, people belonging to God, and he has given them to his Son, the Lord Jesus Christ. Is there anything more wonderful than this?

Then you note that we are the special object of God's interest and concern. He knew us even before we were born, before he ever made man or created the world, he had these people whom he had chosen, and there he gave them to the Son. As we have seen, there was a great meeting of the Trinity in eternity, and the Father gave these people to the Son and he sent him on this great mission of preparing them for the eternal enjoyment of God.[1] That is what Christianity means, just that; that is why the Son of God ever came into this world. All mankind had sinned and had fallen away from God, and were outside God's life and love. God sent his Son into the world to do certain things for these people whom he had given him, and everything that the Son did in this world he did for these people, he did for us. God sent him for that purpose. As our Lord himself has already pointed out,

---

[1] See Volume 1, *Saved in Eternity* (Crossway Books, 1988).

'... thou hast given him power over all flesh, that he should give eternal life to as many as thou hast given him' (v. 2). So he is able to turn to his Father and say, 'I have glorified thee on the earth: I have finished the work which thou gavest me to do' (v. 4), and now he says he is going back to the Father.

Now if you are a Christian, that is what is true of you. All along you have been the special object of God's interest and concern; he has loved you to the extent that he even sent his Son from heaven to earth for you, even to the death of the cross that you might be truly one of his people, that you might have a new nature, a new life, that you might be fitted for standing before him and enjoying him throughout eternity. 'They whom thou hast given me.' Then you notice that negatively we are contrasted with the world. Our Lord has done this throughout the prayer: 'I pray for them: I pray not for the world, but for them which thou hast given me [out of the world]; for they are thine' (v.9), and now he goes on in verse 25, 'O righteous Father, the world hath not known thee' – so he is not concerned about them at this point – 'but I have known thee, and these have known that thou hast sent me.' 'These' – who are they? They are obviously not of the world, they are separated, taken out of this present evil world, and given to our Lord, as God's chosen and special people.

Now the aspect of this that I would stress at this point is the comfort of it all; the comfort of knowing for certain that we are in this wonderful and blessed relationship to God. Do we meditate upon this truth? Do we think about it, do we rejoice in it as we should rejoice? Let me repeat, we see here the very Son of God just before the end, and this is the thing that is uppermost in his mind; these 'people whom thou hast given me', these people for whom I am going to die, these people I am going to save by giving my life a ransom for them. 'Father,' he says, 'I will' this thing concerning them. But the question is, do we recognise ourselves? Do we know ourselves in these terms? Is it not the case that far too often we think of ourselves as men and women who decide to be righteous, or to be Christian; *we* have taken it up, and *we* are going to do this? But before you and I were ever born we were chosen of God and given to the Lord Jesus Christ. He came into the world because the Father had given you and all other Christians to the Son, in order that he might rescue and redeem them; and he has come and has done that and you are one of his people purchased by his precious blood. Oh the tragedy of failing to realise these things! The tragedy of trusting to ourselves and our own activities so much that we lose sight of the most precious truth of all!

We have considered, then, the One who prays, and the people for whom he prays and so now our third question must be: what does he pray for us? You will remember that in going through this chapter, we have seen certain petitions: he prays that we may be kept from the evil that is in this world, and the Evil One at the back of it all; that we may be kept from the devil and his machinations, that we may be kept from his subtle power and jealousy and everything that he would do to separate us from God. Our Lord prays that we may be kept from that; and then, positively, he prays that we may be sanctified, that we may be made more and more fit for God. And that is the way to look at our lives in this world as Christians. This world is a preparation for the next, we are being prepared for glory – that is sanctification. We are being separated from the world and sin, we have been separated to God and brought more and more into fellowship and communion with him: 'Holy Father, sanctify them through thy truth.' And then he prays that we may maintain the spiritual unity into which he has brought us by the rebirth and the gift of the Holy Spirit. This is not a mechanical external unity but an inner, spiritual, vital, organic unity and he prays that it may be preserved. And having prayed all that, he comes to this last and most glorious prayer of all in which he expresses his will.

In other words, in this prayer our Lord has dealt with our past, he prays for our present, and he also deals with our future. The Christian life is a life that is catered for in its entirety, that is the great glory of it:

> The past shall be forgotten,
> A present joy be given,
> A future grace be promised,
> A glorious crown in heaven.

So says the hymn, and here our Lord is now, looking into the future, looking in through the veil, and giving us a glimpse of what awaits us. You see how in every respect he has catered for us. He has interceded on our behalf while we are still alive in this world, but he does not stop at that, he goes on; and as he wills this for his followers, he incidentally teaches us with respect to our own glorious and wondrous future.

What, then, is the future that awaits us as Christians? Let me remind you again of our tragic failure to realise the truth about ourselves. What is it that awaits us when we come to die? I want to put this message to you by way of contrast at this point. As contrast at this point. As I was preparing this very message I happened to read a passage in a daily newspaper, under the heading 'These great words'. And the 'great words' were these:

I love to consider a place which I have never yet seen, but which I shall reach at last, full of repose, and marking the end of these voyages, and security from the tumble of the sea. This place will be a cove set round with high hills on which there shall be no house or sign of men, and it shall be enfolded by quite deserted land; but the westering sun will shine pleasantly upon it under a warm air. It will be a proper place for sleep. The fairway into that haven shall lie behind a pleasant little beach of shingle, which shall run out aslant into the sea from the steep hillside, and shall be a breakwater made by God. The tide shall run up behind it smoothly, and in a silent way, filling the quiet hollow of the hills, brimming it all up like a cup – a cup of refreshment and of quiet, a cup of ending. Then with what pleasure shall I put my small boat round, just round the point of that shingle beach, noting the shallow water by the eddies, and the deeps by the blue colour of them, where the channel runs from the main into the fairway. Up that fairway shall I go, up into the cove, and the gates of it shall shut behind me, headland against headland, so that I shall not see the open sea any more, though I shall still hear its distant noise. But all around me, save for that distant echo of the surf from the high hills, will be silence; and the evening will be gathering already. Under that falling light, all alone in such a place, I shall let go the anchor chain, and let it rattle for the last time. My anchor will go down into the clear salt water with a run, and when it touches I shall play out four lengths or more, so that she may swing easily and not drag, and then I shall tie up my canvas and fasten all for the night, and get me ready for sleep. And that will be the end of my sailing.

'These great words'! Thank God they are not from the Scriptures. They are what the world calls great words and I suppose they are very beautiful in a literary sense, but I thank God that I am not called to preach literature. I will grant, if you like, the beauty of the language, but I cannot think of anything that produces such a striking contrast to the text we are considering together now. Is that the end? Is that what death means for the Christian, to be alone – no man, or anybody – alone, turning a little boat round the corner of the headland from the mighty ocean into this little eddy and there alone you fall asleep and end the voyage? Oh, how I thank God for the Christian gospel! I cannot imagine anything more terrible than that, that is pessimism, that is despair, this desire to be alone. My friend, if you are a Christian, that is not what awaits you, it is this: 'Father, I will that they also, whom thou hast given me, be with me where I am.' You see the contrast – the Christian desire is *not* to be alone, regarding that as supreme bliss, it is to be where Christ is – '... where I am.'

Where are we going? Are we going into some silent place surrounded by wonderful hills and the shimmer of the light upon the waves? No, that is not the gospel! We are going where Christ is: '... to be with Christ; which is far better' (Phil 1:23). To the Christian death does not mean being alone, it means going on to be with him. That is what he said, you remember, to the thief dying by his side upon the cross: 'Today,' he said. You are not going into some little eddy, and there be alone and put down the anchor, and fall asleep – 'Today shalt thou be with me in paradise' (Lk 23:43) '... to be with Christ; which is far better.'

And you notice that our Lord is very concerned here to impress upon us that not only shall we be with him but that we shall *all* be with him: 'Father, I will that they also, whom thou hast given me, shall be with me where I am' – I believe it actually means the total aggregate of Christians, the whole company of the redeemed, all of us together will be with him; we do not look forward to being alone at last, no longer buffeted by other people, and thinking, 'Thank God, at last I'm alone!' – not a bit of it. That is a travesty of the gospel which merely appeals to the natural mind because of the beauty of its language. What the Christian looks forward to is this:

> Ten thousand times ten thousand
> In sparkling raiment white,
> The armies of the ransomed hosts,
> Throng up the steeps of light,
> 'Tis finished, all is finished,
> Their fight with death and sin,
> Fling open wide the golden gates,
> And let the victors in.
> *Henry Alford (1810–71)*

The very essence of the Christian position is that Christians want everybody to share what they have, and they look forward to heaven and to being with all the ten thousand times ten thousand. That is heaven; not to be alone, thank God, but to be among this ransomed throng of the redeemed, safely gathered in, all who have been with us here on earth sharing Christian fellowship, joining with us in song – the saints who have gone before us, the saints who come after us, we all will be there together. What a wonderful vista, what a vision of glory! That is what he wills, '... that they' – all of them – 'may be with me where I am.'

And what shall we be doing there? Well, this is what he says, 'Father, I will that they also, whom thou hast given me, be with me where I am; that they may behold my glory, which thou hast given me.' It is a great word, this word 'behold'; to behold means to gaze upon as a spectator, but it also means to gaze upon some extraordinary sight, something quite exceptional and unusual. We often have that kind of experience, do we not? Maybe we are out walking and suddenly we turn a corner and see some marvellous sight; we behold, we gaze, we stand and look – it is there, in our Lord's phrase, multiplied by infinity. But this word goes even further than that. It is a continuous word – 'that they may continually behold my glory'; we go on beholding! That is not the whole of heaven, of course, but it is perfectly clear from the Scriptures, and especially from the book of Revelation, that this is one of the main things in heaven: to look at the Lord Jesus Christ, to gaze and gaze upon him, to behold him, yes, and very specially, he says, to behold his glory.

Now this is very important. He says, '... that they may behold my glory, which thou hast given me.' We must understand this clearly. Again, as we saw in our last study, it obviously cannot mean his inherent eternal glory as the Son of God, because that was not given to him. He is from eternity the eternal Son of God, co-equal with his Father in glory and in everything else, so it cannot mean the glory which is inherent in the Son of God, as the Son of God. The glory of which he speaks here must be that glory which was given to him after he returned from earth into heaven with his human nature. You see, he came out of heaven and took on him human nature. He went back into heaven God-Man. He did not leave human nature behind when he went back to heaven, he took it with him, so that one who is truly human is at the right hand of God's authority and power in heaven. He went back as God-Man, and a special glory was given to him as the God-Man and the Saviour of his people.

Paul deals with that in Philippians 2, in his great statement about the Incarnation. You remember how he tells us that our Lord had gone back to heaven, and then he says, 'Wherefore God also hath highly exalted him.' Paul has talked about how our Lord 'made himself of no reputation', as Man, he humbled himself, wherefore, because of this, 'God hath also highly exalted him and given him a name that is above every name that at the name of Jesus every knee should bow of things in heaven, and things in earth ...' That is the glory, this peculiar glory that God has given to his Son because of what he has done for us men and women and for our salvation.

And what our Lord wills here is this: he speaks to his Father and he says in effect, 'Father, I am looking forward to this.' As the author of the epistle to the Hebrews puts it, 'Who for the joy that was set before him ...' (Heb 12:2) he saw it, he knew what was coming. So here he turns to his Father and says, 'Father, I will ...' They have seen me here in the flesh, they have seen me as a man of sorrows and acquainted with grief; they have seen me as one who had 'no place to lay his head'; they will see me with the crown of thorns upon my brow and they are going to look upon me with blood oozing out of my hands and my side. They have seen me in the days of my humiliation and have believed on me, Father, and I would that they should see me thus also, see me in my glory and gaze and gaze upon me as I truly am, and as I shall be. That is what is awaiting you and me.

But let me go on and complete this, for I find in 1 John 3:2 that to see this glory of his also means to share it: 'It doth not yet appear what we shall be: but we know that, when he shall appear, we shall be like him; for we shall see him as he is.' In other words, you cannot look at this glory without its being reflected in you; to look at it means to be like it, to be transformed. Paul says the same thing when he says, 'We look for the Saviour, the Lord Jesus Christ: who shall change our vile body that it may be fashioned like unto his glorious body according to the working whereby he is able even to subdue all things unto himself' (Phil 3:20–21). In other words, we look forward not only to seeing and beholding him and looking at his glory, but also to being changed into the likeness and image of his glory.

And still more wonderful of all is the very fact that our Lord wills this for us, which means that it is going to happen to us for certain. You see, it is at this point that we do not understand ourselves; how can we be what we are as Christians? Do you know that you, a humble child, an ignorant Christian, who may feel you are more of a failure than anything else, buffeted by the devil, tossed here and there, do you know that I can tell you this now – you are destined to experience these things, of which we have been thinking. When you come to die, you will be with Christ; you will see his glory, you will behold it, and will become like him, and enjoy the glory for ever and ever. Paul puts it in this way in Romans 8:29–30: 'For whom he did foreknow, he also did predestinate to be conformed to the image of his Son, that he might be the firstborn among many brethren. Moreover whom he did predestinate, them he also called: and whom he called, them he also justified: and whom he justified, them he also glorified.' In the council of God it has already happened, it is as certain as that. You and I, wherever we are at this moment, are going to look into the face of Jesus Christ in all his glory and be made like him and enjoy him through all eternity. That is his will for us, and because he wills it, it is absolutely certain.

The conclusions we draw from this are quite inevitable, are they not? If we all realised these things, would we go on living as we do? Would we be as concerned as we are about this world and its passing pleasures and its glories, its states and pomp and positions? Would we give the time we do give to such worldly things, and so little to this? If we really realised what we are told here, would we be apologetic, sometimes almost afraid for people to know we are Christians? Would we be like that if we believed this; if we knew it was going to happen? But if we are Christians this is going to happen; it is absolutely certain, it is more certain than anything under the sun today that we shall behold him and his glory and become like him.

Whatever, then, you may be doing, put this at the forefront of your mind; think about it in a way that you have never done before; never let a day pass but that you remind yourself of who and what you are. You are one of God's people – 'thine thy were, and thou gavest them me' – and I have done for them the work that thou gavest me to do, and I am coming back to thee. 'Father, I will that they also whom thou hast given me, be with me where I am, that they may behold my glory, which thou hast given me' – hold that before yourself day by day, start your day with it, remind yourself of it constantly, 'Set your affection on things above, not on things on the earth' (Col 3:2), for 'our light affliction, which is but for a moment, worketh for us a far more exceeding and eternal weight of glory, while we look' – we gaze steadfastly – 'not at the things which are seen, but at the things which are not seen: for the things which are seen are temporal; but the things which are not seen are eternal. For we know that if our earthly house of this tabernacle were dissolved, we have a building of God, an house not made with hands, eternal in the heavens' (2 Cor 4:17—5:1).

So let us always 'nightly pitch our moving tents, a day's march nearer home'. Oh, do not think of the end of your life in this world as sliding out of the ocean into some little eddy where at last you can be alone. Rather, think of it as going to be with him and with all the ransomed saints, to see and meet people again who were pilgrims with you in this world, and to join with them in singing praises unto him who loved you to the extent of dying for you, and rising again to save you. Think of yourself among the ransomed hosts, the ten thousand times ten thousand, singing for ever and ever the praises of the Lamb who once was slain and who has redeemed us. What a heritage! What a promise! What a hope! What a glory! Blessed be the God and Father of our Lord and Saviour Jesus Christ. Amen.

"WHY AM I THE WAY I AM?"

"WHY IS LIFE SO HARD?"

"IS THERE ANY HOPE?"

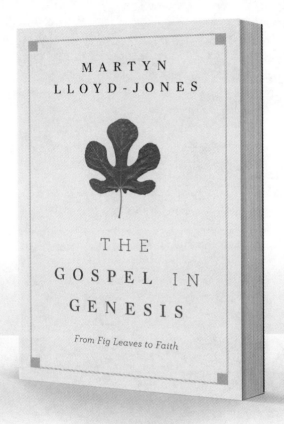

MARTYN
LLOYD-JONES

THE
GOSPEL IN
GENESIS

From Fig Leaves to Faith

In this series of never-before-published sermons, Martyn Lloyd-Jones preaches the gospel of Jesus Christ from the early chapters of Genesis. These 9 sermons feature the eternal perspective, sense of urgency, and unapologetic honesty that characterized his preaching.

In *The Gospel in Genesis*, Lloyd-Jones emboldens Christians to believe firmly the only gospel that offers answers to life's biggest questions.

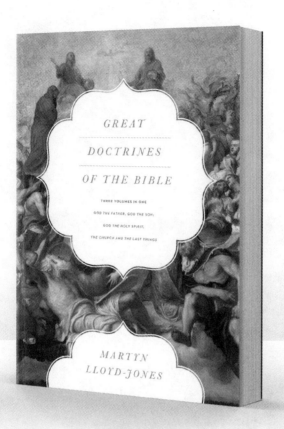

GREAT

DOCTRINES

OF THE BIBLE

THREE VOLUMES IN ONE
GOD THE FATHER, GOD THE SON,
GOD THE HOLY SPIRIT,
THE CHURCH AND THE LAST THINGS

MARTYN
LLOYD-JONES

A *comprehensive* and *accessible* *systematic theology* of the *Christian faith* from *Martyn Lloyd-Jones*

This volume includes the following three books in one:

GOD THE FATHER, GOD THE SON
GOD THE HOLY SPIRIT
THE CHURCH AND THE LAST THINGS

Martyn Lloyd-Jones' Classic Work on Acts 1–8

In this newly revised, three-volume collection of sermons, Lloyd-Jones explains the message of the first eight chapters of Acts with clear language and pastoral warmth. From Peter's bold preaching to the dramatic stoning of Stephen, Lloyd-Jones points readers back to the foundational figures and key events of the Christian faith, emphasizing the basic truths that undergird genuine belief.

"One of the greatest preachers of the 20th century was Martyn Lloyd-Jones."

JOHN PIPER, founder, Desiring God ministries

A Challenge to Reevaluate Our Focus and the Object of Our Affections

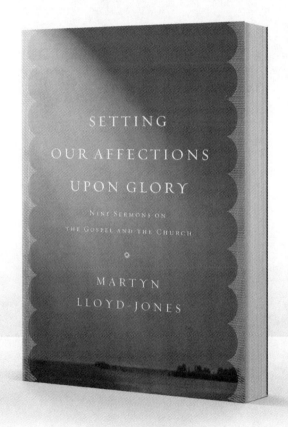

In this compilation of nine never-before published sermons, Lloyd-Jones powerfully exhorts Christians to focus their affections on the God of the Bible, addressing issues such as prayer, the church, and evangelism.